Cultural Anthropology

Cultural Anthropology: Global Forces, Local Lives presents all the key areas of cultural anthropology as well as providing original and nuanced coverage of current and cutting-edge topics. An exceptionally clear and readable introduction, it helps students understand the application of anthropological concepts to the contemporary world and everyday life. Thorough treatment is given throughout the text to issues such as globalization, colonialism, ethnicity, nationalism, neoliberalism, and the state.

Changes for the third edition include a brand new chapter on medical anthropology and an updated range of case studies with a fresh thematic focus on China. The book contains a number of features to support student learning, including:

■ A wealth of color images
■ Definitions of key terms and further reading suggestions in the margins
■ Summaries at the end of every chapter
■ An extensive glossary, bibliography and index.

Further resources are provided via a comprehensive companion website.

Jack David Eller is Associate Professor (Emeritus) of Anthropology at the Community College of Denver, USA. An experienced teacher and author, his other books for Routledge include *Introducing Anthropology of Religion* (second edition, 2014), *Cultural Anthropology: 101* (2015), and *Culture and Diversity in the United States* (2015).

Cultural Anthropology

Global Forces, Local Lives

Third edition

JACK DAVID ELLER

Routledge
Taylor & Francis Group

LONDON AND NEW YORK

Third edition published 2016
by Routledge
2 Park Square, Milton Park, Abingdon, Oxon OX14 4RN

and by Routledge
711 Third Avenue, New York, NY 10017

Routledge is an imprint of the Taylor & Francis Group, an informa business

© 2016 Jack David Eller

First edition published by Routledge 2009
Second edition published by Routledge 2013

British Library Cataloguing in Publication Data
A catalogue record for this book is available from the British Library

Library of Congress Cataloging in Publication Data
A catalog record for this book has been requested

ISBN: 978-1-138-91443-8 (pbk)
ISBN: 978-1-315-69079-7 (ebk)

Typeset in Berkeley
by Keystroke, Station Road, Codsall, Wolverhampton

Contents

Detailed chapter outline

Illustrations

We are indebted to the people and archives below for permission to reproduce photographs. Every effort has been made to trace copyright holders. Any omissions brought to our attention will be remedied in future editions.

IMAGES

Introduction

Are the Chinese happy? China's economic growth has been spectacular and world-altering, but it has also left income inequality, unemployment, population upheaval, and destruction of entire neighborhoods in its wake. No wonder "there are low levels of self-reported happiness" (Yang, 2013: 295) in the country. *Xiangpi ren* (literally "rubber people") has become a popular term for the common syndrome of "numbness, hopelessness, loss of passion in life" (299) experienced by overworked and underpaid Chinese. However, as in many parts of the contemporary world, the official message is that workers' problems are their own doing, a consequence of bad attitude and lack of adaptability rather than of structural abuses. Consistent with global neoliberalism, China has engaged in individualization and "psychologization" of social ills, encouraging citizens to practice happiness as they cultivate their individual "potential"—even if this is *wei xingfu*, "false/fake happiness" (293). One of the key vehicles for spreading the message of (fake) happiness is television, specifically televised "counseling programs" (292) like *The Secrets of My Happiness*, which "celebrates individuals from all walks of life—but especially disadvantaged citizens—by demonstrating how their optimism and happiness helped them realize their potential and achieve success" (293). Not all Chinese viewers are seduced by the rhetoric of happiness, and Jie Yang argues that the government intentionally promotes happiness as a distraction from the social and political injustices of a rapidly changing society

and as an obstacle to collective political action that would threaten the state and its ruling party.

A century ago, during its infancy, cultural anthropology might have been described as the study of "traditional" or "primitive" societies, and some observers may still imagine it as such. However, as it has matured—and as the world that it studies has transformed—it has become a much more relevant and exciting investigation into the cultural processes that construct and conjoin modern societies and the modern global system, of which those traditional or primitive societies have become part. People still live local lives, in their particular places and times, but they are increasingly influenced and interlinked by global forces.

Cultural anthropology is the science of contemporary human behavioral diversity. It puts "culture" or learned and shared ways of thinking, feeling, and acting at the center of analysis, but it maintains a "biocultural" perspective, in which bodies, the surrounding environment, and even physical objects are integral to social life. It takes "change" or dynamism as seriously as "tradition" or the past, and it reveals the lived experiences of people, often obscured or distorted by official accounts and policies. Finally, culture no longer stays within the confines of a specific society—if it ever did—but rather flows and circulates and fuses into infinite new combinations. The case of Chinese happiness exemplifies many of the interests of present-day cultural anthropology—culture change, industrial work, state policies, and popular culture. It is to introduce and celebrate the achievements of cultural anthropology, and to indicate the contributions that it can and will make to our understanding of contemporary and future cultural circumstances, that this book was written.

PHILOSOPHY AND HISTORY OF THE BOOK

I have taught cultural anthropology for over twenty years, yet I was frustrated from the very start of my teaching career with the organization of most courses and texts on the topic. All of them naturally include a discussion of the concept of culture and its major components, like language and gender and personality. All of them present an analysis of the important areas of culture—economics, politics, kinship, and religion. However, typically they offer at most a couple of concluding chapters on "culture change" and "the modern world" as if these matters are tangential, almost anathema, to anthropology and barely within its purview. This is simply not true: Movement is an inherent part of culture, and the modern world is the most critical subject for all of us, since it is the world that we, modern nation-state populations and indigenous peoples alike, inhabit.

So, I found teaching a course with thirteen weeks dedicated to the basics of cultural anthropology and a couple of weeks devoted to "the modern world" to be akin to spending thirteen weeks learning the grammar and vocabulary of a foreign language and only two weeks actually speaking (that is, *applying* or *using*) the language. That is inadequate. If cultural anthropology cannot be applied usefully to contemporary life, then it is fatally flawed. Fortunately, it can be and has been. Of course, in the days before the internet, it was more difficult to provide students with information that was not already integrated into textbooks. It was possible, although costly, to photocopy materials for distribution; often, as a teacher I was compelled to talk about topics for which the students had no readings in hand.

In response, I created my own addendum to formally published books, covering crucial issues like colonialism, nationalism and ethnic conflict, economic development and global poverty, indigenous peoples, and cultural movements. That

addendum evolved into the third section of this book, which was composed first. Subsequently, I realized that I had a worthwhile perspective on the entire discipline of cultural anthropology, one that would allow me to craft a complete textbook embodying the same principles as I had established in the final section. The result is the book you are holding in your hands.

COVERAGE OF THE BOOK

There are many fine and venerable textbooks, and some innovative new ones, on cultural anthropology. The world does not need another one unless it has something new to offer. The student and instructor, and anyone interested in the discipline, will find that this book covers more topics more deeply than rival texts and in so doing immerses the reader in the worldview, the history, the literature, and the controversies of cultural anthropology like no other.

Certainly, the present book includes all of the standard and necessary topics of a cultural anthropology text, as mentioned above. Even these are presented in novel and usefully organized ways. However, it also provides original and nuanced coverage of a number of topics that are customarily given insufficient attention or no attention at all, such as:

- a sophisticated and subtle discussion of cultural relativism
- an integrated analysis of the biological and evolutionary basis of culture
- a meaningful description of the emergence of anthropology out of Western intellectual traditions
- details on culturally relevant genres of language behavior, such as political speech, jokes and riddles, and religious language, based on the notion that language is social action
- a refined discussion and critique of the race concept
- the presentation of gender not only in relation to women, but also to the construction of maleness and of alternate genders across cultures
- the inclusion of consumption as part of the anthropology of economics
- the integration of kinship-based groups into a more general analysis of social group formation
- a contribution to an anthropology of war

- a cutting-edge description of the composite nature of religions, set within the question of social legitimation
- extended discussion of colonialism and post-colonialism
- serious presentations on nationalism, ethnicity, and other forms of identity politics
- major attention to development policies and practices and the role anthropology has played and can play in them
- the recognition and inclusion of indigenous sources and voices
- a balanced analysis of possible futures of culture based on integrative and disintegrative processes
- inclusion of state-of-the-art anthropological concepts including globalization and glocalization, multi-sited ethnography, world anthropologies, microfinancing, diaspora, cultural tourism, popular culture, and multiple modernities

FEATURES OF THE BOOK

The present book offers a number of features, within specific chapters and across the structure of the entire book, which enhance the readability and the utility of the text. Each chapter, for example, includes:

- an opening vignette
- at least three boxed ethnographic case-studies to pursue issues in more depth
- a closing "Contemporary cultural controversy" box to spark analysis and debate
- a brief but meaningful summary
- a list of key terms
- notes in the margins of pages, providing definitions, intra-text references, resources (books, videos, etc.) for further research, and references to the companion website

In addition to chapter-specific features, the overall construction of the book includes:

- colorful and relevant illustrations
- organization into three sections of equal length, with one-third dedicated explicitly to contemporary cultural processes

- extensive intra-textual references, so that readers may find links between subjects discussed in more than one chapter
- three in-depth case-study discussions, entitled "Seeing culture as a whole," distributed evenly through the text (one-third, two-thirds, and end point) to summarize and integrate the preceding chapters
- a glossary
- an unusually thorough bibliography
- a bonus online chapter on the anthropology of art

GUIDE TO MARGINS

The margins contain:

- Definitions of key terms
- Cross-references to other chapters
- Key texts
- Key film resources
- Key websites

The ⊳ icon refers to an audio introduction by the author available on the companion website for each chapter.

The ▤ icon refers to supplementary reading available on the companion website.

The (www) icon refers to further resources curated by the author on the companion website.

The (Q) icon refers to multiple choice and fill-in-the-blank questions available on the companion website.

COMPANION WEBSITE

The book is supported by a rich and dynamic companion website, with resources for student and instructor alike, including three or more supplemental original readings per chapter, providing significant and extensive additional material. See: www.routledge.com/eller.

Features include:

- Bonus chapter on art
- Supplementary readings
- PowerPoint slides

- Study guides
- Audio guides
- Testbank (multiple choice and fill in the blanks)
- Questions for review/discussion
- Glossary flashcards
- Links to useful websites and video material

CHANGES TO THE THIRD EDITION

The third edition is a significant modification and update of the second edition, which itself was a substantial modification of the original text. In addition to the features retained from the second edition, the new edition includes the following expanded or enhanced features:

- new opening vignettes for almost all of the chapters
- new closing "Contemporary cultural controversy" cases for the majority of chapters
- a new topical theme—China—with nine boxed case studies on China, one "Seeing Culture as a Whole" case, and numerous other references across chapters
- new boxed case studies—almost all of them ethnographic—for all of the chapters, evenly distributed across the world's geographic areas and as recent as 2015, featuring examples like anthropology in the global Ebola crisis, important women in early anthropology, Mexican beach vendors, Iranian temporary marriage, international journalists, Pentecostal television, forest conservation, the U.S. automobile industry, and surgical training, to name a few
- extensive revisions to chapters 3 (Origins of Cultural Anthropology), 7 (Economics), 9 (Politics), 12 (Colonialism), 13 (Postcolonial politics), and 14 (Post-colonial economics)
- condensed discussion of pre-modern economic, political, and religious systems to

allow more space for contemporary topics like the corporation, work, and the informal economy; citizenship and policy; and Christianity, Islam, paganism, and cognitive-evolutionary theory of religion, among others (much of the previous materials on pre-modern systems has been retained as supplemental readings on the companion website)

- extended or brand new discussions of enskilment, materiality, consumption, age and youth, friendship, colonialism and governmentality, borderlands and illegality, and the precarity of work under new regimes of accumulation
- two new "Seeing culture as a whole" extended case studies, on Western "transnationals" living in China and on Boko Haram and Islamic violence in Nigeria
- an entire new chapter on medical anthropology
- more supplemental readings on the companion website (at least three per chapter) more tightly integrated with the textbook

My hope is that this textbook, the fruit of two decades of my teaching experience and more than a century of the experiences of cultural anthropologists, will communicate the relevance, urgency, and excitement of cultural anthropology that I feel and that I try to convey to my students. Culture matters, and there is no more pressing task for professional anthropologists and for the educated public than to realize that most if not all of the present problems and challenges facing humanity are cultural at heart—related to how we identify ourselves, how we organize ourselves, and how we interact as members of distinct human communities. Cultural anthropology has made significant contributions to these questions, and it is my heart-felt hope that this book will help future anthropologists and world citizens make even more significant contributions.

1. Argentina
2. Bangladesh
3. Barabaig
4. Bosavi
5. Canada
6. Cashinahua
7. Cherokee
8. Cheyenne
9. China
10. Croatia
11. Democratic Republic of Congo
12. Egypt
13. Ethiopia
14. Georgia
15. Germany
16. Guatemala
17. Haiti
18. Hausa
19. Hawai'ian islands
20. Iceland
21. India
22. Iran
23. Israel
24. Japan
25. Java
26. Kalasha
27. Korea
28. !Kung or Ju/hoansi

29. Liberia
30. Limba
31. Mauritius
32. Melungeons
33. Mexico
34. Mongolia
35. Muinane
36. Na/Mosuo
37. Navajo
38. New Zealand
39. Newar
40. Nigeria
41. Nuer
42. Papua New Guinea
43. Peru
44. Russia
45. Scotland
46. Seminole
47. South Sudan
48. Spain
49. Tahiti
50. Tajikistan
51. Turkey
52. United Kingdom
53. United States
54. Uzbekistan
55. Warlpiri
56. Yir Yoront

MAP 0.1 Major societies mentioned in the text

Understanding anthropology

Why do we gather customs all the world over? Because science is comparative; it has to be, for the reason that one case is never sufficient to serve as the basis for theory; no more is a large number of cases all identical. It is only in variation that we can observe under what conditions certain phenomena appear, and under what conditions they do not appear.

(Hocart, 1936: 580)

In 2001, fifty-two years after Mao Zedong's communist revolution, China unveiled a new national garment, the *tangzhuang*. The occasion was the Asia-Pacific Economic Cooperation (APEC) Summit in Shanghai, a testament to the economic and fashion advances of China since Deng Xiaoping announced a change of course in 1978 from the former Communist Party planned economy to a path of "modernization," essentially (and apparently contradictorily) Communist Party-sponsored capitalism. As customary, the heads of state attending the APEC meeting gathered on the final day of the event wearing "clothes presented by the host country that reflect its culture and tradition" (Zhao, 2013: 70), and the *tangzhuang*, a silk jacket, was chosen over several other proposed designs.

Named after the Tang dynasty (618–907 CE), which is recognized as a high point in Chinese culture and closely associated with Chinese-ness, the coat "looked ambiguously traditional" (71) and was described by a Chinese newspaper as expressing "both traditional Chinese flavor and modern ideals" (69). It was, as Jianhua Zhao puts it, "something new that appeared to be old" (73), a mixture of local and Western elements. The same could be said, of course, about the overall Chinese garment industry, which had grown dramatically in previous decades largely to fulfill Western demand for cheap clothes (such as blue jeans and t-shirts), as well as of the entire Chinese economy and society. China has indeed undergone a rapid modernization influenced by the West, but Zhao argues that "the growth of Chinese textile and apparel industries is not a simple modernization process that spread from the West to China" (39). Rather, China modernized and industrialized in a distinctly Chinese way, combining the old and the new in a unique blend symbolized by the *tangzhuang*. Both the designed coat and China's designed culture have been embraced by its people, although not without concerns about authenticity and not always as the government anticipated. For example, if the government

IMAGE 1.1 *Tangzhuang* in a shop.

**CALENDARS AND
CULTURES**

intended to create a new national dress, it failed because the *tangzhuang* was a short-term craze that, ironically, settled into "a traditional dress for traditional holidays" (82).

Culture shapes everything that humans do, and a particular culture is conventionally attributed to a particular people and a particular place. Further, culture is often classified as "traditional" or "modern." However, neither of these assumptions survives the case of the Chinese *tangzhuang* nor of all the other cases of cultural contact, interaction, and borrowing in the contemporary world.

The twenty-first century (by Western time-reckoning; it is the fifteenth century by the Muslim calendar and the fifty-eighth century by the Hebrew calendar) is a complex era of difference and connectedness. The much-discussed processes of "globalization" have linked human communities without eliminating human diversity; in fact, in some ways they have created new kinds of diversity while injecting some elements of commonality. The local and particular still exists, in a system of global relationships, resulting in what some have called "glocalization" (more on this below). But above all else, the conditions of the contemporary world

virtually guarantee that individuals will encounter and deal with others unlike themselves in various and significant ways. This makes awareness and appreciation of human diversity—and one's own place in that field of diversity—a critical issue. It is for exploring and explaining this diversity that anthropology was conceived.

THE SCIENCE(S) OF ANTHROPOLOGY

Anthropology has been called the science of humanity. That is a vast and noble calling, but a vague one and also not one that immediately distinguishes it from all the other human sciences. Psychology and sociology and history study humans, and even biology and physics can study humans. What makes anthropology different from, and a worthy addition to, these other disciplines?

Anthropology shares one factor with all of the other "social sciences": They all study human beings acting and interacting. However, all of the other social sciences only study *some kinds* of people or *some kinds of things* that people do. Economics studies economic behavior, political science studies political behavior, etc. And above all, they tend to study the political, economic, or other behaviors of certain kinds of people—"modern," urban, industrialized, literate, usually "Western" people. But those are not the only people in the world. There are very many people today, and over the ages there has been a vast majority of people, who are not at all like Western people today. Yet they are people too. Why do they live the way they do? In fact, why do *we* live the way *we* do? In a word, why are there so many ways to be human? Those are the questions that anthropology asks.

Any science, from anthropology to zoology, is distinguished in three ways—its *questions,* its *perspective*, and its *method*. The questions of a science involve what it wants to know, why it was established in the first place, and what part of reality it is intended to examine. The perspective is its particular and unique way of looking at reality, the "angle" from which it approaches its subject, or the attitude it adopts toward it. Its method is the specific data-gathering activities it practices in order to apply its perspective and to answer its questions.

As a unique science, anthropology has its own distinctive questions, ones that no other science of humanity is already asking or has already answered. Some sciences, like psychology, suggest in their very name what their questions will be: psychology, from the Greek *psyche* meaning "mind" and *logos* meaning "word/study," declares its interest in the individual, internal and "mental," aspect of humans and human behavior. Sociology, from the Latin *socius* for "companion/ally/associate," implies the study of humans in groups. The name anthropology does not speak as clearly, and many readers, and many members of the public, may have little notion of what anthropology is or what anthropologists do. Anthropology is a fairly new word for a fairly new science, asking some fairly new questions. Derived from two Greek roots, *anthropos* for "man/human" and *logos*, anthropology was named and conceived as the study of humanity in both the biological and behavioral sense.

Anthropology's uniqueness is thankfully not in its name but in the questions it asks, which include:

■ How many different ways are there to be human? That is, what is the range of human diversity?

■ What are the commonalities across all of these different kinds of humans and human lifeways?
■ Why are humans so diverse? What is the source or explanation of human diversity?
■ How do the various elements of a particular human lifeway fit together?
■ How do human groups and their lifeways interact with each other and change over time?

Given these questions, we can think of anthropology as not just the study of humans but the study of *human diversity*. Further, humans are diverse along two dimensions. The first dimension is the past versus the present; the second dimension is the physical versus the behavioral, our bodies as opposed to the ways we organize ourselves and act. Therefore, the definition of anthropology can be refined or expanded to *the study of the diversity of human bodies and behavior in the past and the present*. We can now see that there are several possible subfields of anthropology, depending on exactly what area of this diversity each focuses on—what specific anthropological questions it seeks to answer. These subdisciplines give anthropology its familiar "four-fields" character.

Physical or biological anthropology

Physical or biological anthropology is the area that specializes in *the diversity of human bodies in the past and present*. It is plain to see that humans differ in their physical appearance: We have different skin colors, different hair colors, different body shapes, different facial forms, etc. What can we hope to learn from it? First and foremost, we learn that *there is more than one way physically to be human*. All of the various human body shapes and facial features are human. Physical anthropologists can also relate those physical traits to the natural environment: Is there a reason why people in some parts of the world, in some climates for instance, have this or that physical characteristic? This is the question of physical adaptation, and it is entirely possible that a group, if it has lived in a particular environment long enough, could develop traits that fit well in that environment. Finally, physical anthropologists can discover things about human migrations, intermarriages, and such phenomena from the distribution of traits like blood type, gene frequency,

Physical anthropology
the study of the diversity of human bodies in the past and present, including physical adaptation, group or "race" characteristics, and human evolution

See Chapter 3

See Chapter 6

Primatology
the study of the physical and behavioral characteristics of the category of species called primates

Archaeology
the study of the diversity of human behavior in the past, based on the traces left behind by past humans or societies

Artifacts
physical objects created by humans, often specifically the "portable" objects like tools, pottery, jewelry, etc. (as opposed to the non-portable ones like buildings and roads, etc.)

Features
in archaeology, the large and non-portable objects or structures created and left by humans, including walls, buildings, roads, canals, and so on

See Chapter 2

Ecofacts
the environmental remains from past human social contexts, including wood, seeds, pollen, animal bones, shells, etc.

and so on. We will return to the question of "race and ethnicity" below.

In addition to the present diversity of human bodies, there is considerable historical diversity as well. The evidence indicates overwhelmingly that humans have not always had the bodies we have today. This evidence is fossils. Anthropologists have found no human bodies quite like ours that are older than a couple of hundred thousand years at most, and even during that time there were other "humans" who looked remarkably different from us. If you saw a Neandertal (who lived between 130,000 and 40,000 years ago) on the street today, you would recognize him or her as human but not exactly "normally" human. As we look further back in time, human-like beings become progressively less human-like while still retaining certain critical human features, like upright walking, a relatively large brain, and a human-like face. How then did we humans come to have the bodies that we have today, and what other forms did our human ancestors take in the past on their way to becoming us? That too is a question for physical anthropology—the question of human evolution. Some scientists even specialize in the physical characteristics of other species that are similar and related to our own, the primates, for which their science is called **primatology**. We will touch on the subject of human evolution later.

Archaeology

One popular image of the anthropologist is a sort of Indiana Jones character, a researcher who digs up pyramids in Egypt or ancient cities in Mexico. In fact, the researchers who conduct this kind of work are archaeologists. From the root *archae* for "beginning," **archaeology** is *the study of the diversity of human behavior in the past*. Archaeologists may do their work in the company of physical anthropologists, who examine the actual anatomical remains of past humans. However, the archaeologists do not focus on the bodies, but on the behaviors of those humans. How can they do that, when the people are all dead and their ways of life have vanished? The answer is that they examine the things those humans left behind. Archaeologists divide this evidence roughly into two categories—artifacts and features. **Artifacts** are the more or less portable objects that people made and used; things like pottery, clothing, jewelry, tools and weapons, and the like are considered artifacts. **Features** are the larger, more or less immovable objects like buildings, walls, monuments, canals, roads, farms, and such. To understand more about the environmental setting of these societies and how the humans made use of them, archaeologists also consider **ecofacts** such as plant (wood, seeds, pits, pollen) and animal (bones, shells) remains.

IMAGE 1.2 Archaeologists study the sites of past societies, such as Teotihuacan near Mexico City.

BOX 1.1   MUMMIES, MATERIALITY, AND MEANING

Despite differences in subject-matter and method that have threatened to divorce archaeology from cultural anthropology, the two kindred subdisciplines emerged from a shared commitment to material objects and their collection and display, and cultural anthropology has come once again to value materiality—the expression of culture in physical objects and the role that objects play in social action and meaning. A quintessential archaeological object is the mummy, which blurs the line between person and thing. However, Christina Riggs makes the surprising assertion that Western emphasis on the personhood of the mummy may betray the ancient Egyptians' own understanding of it as both thing and trans-person. The inclination of nineteenth-century discoverers was to unwrap a mummy to expose the person inside, discarding or destroying its linen wrap. This "scientific" practice failed to grasp that "the wrapping was as important as what was wrapped" (2014: 23), which "offers an entirely different perspective on the ancient Egyptian worldview" (79). Mummification, she contends, was "a fundamental transformation of the human body's own materiality," explicitly intended to "make it less human, more divine" (89). Mummification was not about preserving but about *transforming* the person: A human being looked like a statue in the end (and statues too were ritually wrapped and unwrapped), the linen functioning as the body's "new skin, muscle, and tissue, so that textile and object—or textile and body—became a unity" (140). This new appreciation of the role of linen leads Riggs to explore the cultural processes by which linen was manufactured and used in ancient Egypt, as well as its social and ritual meaning, noting for instance that many temples had in-house linen workshops.

Studying artifacts and features is fascinating, but archaeologists do not study them just to learn about them. They excavate and interpret this evidence to discover the thoughts, the ideas, the feelings, and the social patterns of the people who fashioned them. How did those past people make these things? Why did they make them? How did they use them? What did the objects mean to the makers and users? Archaeologists try to go from the objects themselves to the minds and hearts of the people who lived among those objects long ago. It is a creative, interpretive activity, but the artifacts and features are often the only traces that those people and their ways of lives have bequeathed to us.

Archaeologists do not look exclusively at the ancient past. They can also study the recent past, such as medieval Europe or colonial America. And since modern humans also make and leave remains behind them, archaeologists have found that their methods can be practiced on living societies to learn how contemporary humans exploit and affect their environments. One recent form of this work has been dubbed **garbology**, since it sifts through contemporary trash to discover what kinds of objects humans produce, consume, and discard today.

Linguistic anthropology

Linguistic anthropology focuses on *the diversity of human language in the past and present.* Linguistic anthropologists study the similarities and differences between living languages, looking into their grammar, their vocabulary, and their everyday use. This will not only shed light on each language but also on the possible relationships between languages. Are there, for instance, language "families" that are related historically, by migration or intermixing or other processes? Linguistic anthropologists also investigate changes within a language over time. Anyone who has read Shakespeare or even older English literature knows that English has evolved fairly dramatically over recent centuries. All languages undergo similar processes, and linguistic anthropologists analyze the reasons for and the particular directions of this change. They may also attempt to reconstruct "ancestral" languages—

Linguistic anthropology
the study of the diversity of human language in the past and present, and its relationship to social groups, practices, and values

Garbology
the study of contemporary trash to examine how humans make, consume, and discard material objects in the present

ones that link, say, English to German and both to ancient Greek or Sanskrit—even to the point of reconstructing the very first language.

More essentially, linguistic anthropology attempts to understand language use in relation to social life and social practices. How are values and concepts captured in and expressed by language? How does language structure and communicate social differences, for example of status and rank or age or gender, etc.? Linguistic anthropology has increasingly emphasized the element of "performance" in language, discovering specialized forms for various purposes (for example, speech-making as opposed to story-telling) and the role of language in forming and maintaining social relationships, including power relationships. Language in the anthropological perspective will be the subject of another chapter.

Cultural anthropology

Cultural anthropology
the study of the diversity of human behavior in the present

Cultural anthropology, also sometimes called (yet different from) social anthropology, is *the study of the diversity of human behavior in the present*. The large majority of anthropologists are cultural or social anthropologists, and they have one tremendous advantage over both physical anthropologists and archaeologists: They have living people to talk to. The goal of cultural anthropology is still to learn about the thoughts, feelings, action, and institutions of people, but now we can ask them, "Why did you do that?" or "How did you make that?" or "What does that mean to you?" Cultural anthropology is the activity that many people associate with *National Geographic* magazine, the Discover Channel, or similar media, where strange-looking (to us) people are portrayed doing exotic or unfamiliar or maybe even shocking (to us) things. Of course, observers can appreciate the sheer spectacle of such people and their behavior, but cultural anthropology is more than the observation and collection of behavioral curiosities. It is about making humans unlike oneself seem less "exotic" and more human—in fact, every bit as human as each of us. It is about getting to the heart and mind of people very different in at least some ways from oneself. But it is also about getting to one's own heart and mind, since "we" are one of the diverse kinds of human as surely as "they" are. In so doing, cultural

anthropology penetrates to the very nature of humanity. What separates one kind of human from another yet unites us all? What makes one group's way of life different from another group's and yet similar and related?

Please remember, as the first lesson in cultural anthropology, that while others may appear strange and incomprehensible, even abnormal, to us, we may appear just as strange, incomprehensible, and abnormal to them.

TRADITIONAL ANTHROPOLOGY AND BEYOND

We have now seen the traditional four subfields of anthropology. However, in important ways, anthropology has outgrown this narrow categorization, if it was ever actually constrained by it. For instance, a number of well-developed subdisciplines have emerged under the general heading of cultural anthropology, including, among others:

- Urban anthropology, or the study of humans in urban settings, the effects of urbanization on previously non-urban societies, and the relationships between cities and their surrounding hinterlands (such as labor migration).
- Medical anthropology, or the study of knowledge systems and practices concerning health and medical treatment cross-culturally.
- Forensic anthropology, or the use of (mainly physical) anthropological knowledge and methods to solve crimes (e.g. identify murder victims, determine time and cause of death, etc.).
- Visual anthropology, or the study of the production, presentation, and use of material or "artistic" media such as painting, body art, clothing designs, and so on. It can include not only the arts that other societies make, but the arts that anthropology employs to study them, such as film and photography.
- Ethnomusicology, or the study of musical forms and their relation to culture.
- Ethnobotany, or the study of knowledge and uses of plants in various cultures.
- Development anthropology, or the study of as well as the practical contribution to how "modern" forces affect and change societies.

BOX 1.2   URBAN ANTHROPOLOGY

Most people associate anthropology with tribal societies in remote villages on some island or in some jungle, and much conventional anthropology has indeed been of the "village study" sort. As recently as 1980, Ulf Hannerz could claim that urban anthropology was little more than a decade old. But anthropology, as the study of human diversity, certainly *can* examine the city as a form of social behavior, and it *must* examine it, because cities have been part of human experience for thousands of years and because urbanization has finally brought the majority of humanity into cities. While sociology entered the city ahead of anthropology (and anthropologists duly acknowledge this), Alan and Josephine Smart found in their 2003 review of urban anthropology that the field had "made important contributions to our understanding of migration, housing, social and spatial organization, informal economies, and other topics" (2003: 267). Anthropology's explicit interest in urbanization began in colonial Africa, especially the "copperbelt" of Zambia where new cities arose and formerly non-urban people migrated. Anthropologists noticed new organizations and identities forming, such as mutual aid groups, trade unions, nationalist movements, and "supertribes" or what we would today call ethnic groups. However, critics often accused urban anthropology of perpetuating the village focus by examining communities or enclaves within the city—that is, doing anthropology "in the city" but not "of the city." In more recent years, urban anthropologists have investigated the city as a social system, finding great diversity inside as well as between cities; not all cities are alike, nor are all inhabitants of any particular city alike. They have also studied the links between cities and their non-urban surroundings, as well as between specific cities and the wider and global economic and cultural system.

URBAN ANTHROPOLOGY

This can include attempting to minimize the negative impact of change on traditional societies and even in some cases advocating for the rights and wishes of those societies.

■ Feminist anthropology, originally the study of women's issues and roles across cultures. This subfield has expanded to include gender issues and roles more generally, particularly how gender is defined, practiced, and controlled through language, values, and power.

It is important to understand that anthropology is not and never has been a purely "academic" pursuit, disconnected from the real world. In its pre-modern form it was to be found in the early European colonial encounters with non-Western peoples, providing data and often service in the colonial enterprise, for better or worse. Some of the first anthropologists, like Franz Boas (1858–1942) in his 1928 book, *Anthropology and Modern Life*, were deeply concerned with practical social issues, like racism, nationalism, eugenics, criminology, and education.

And of course, all anthropological findings can be used for real-world policy- and decision-making.

But many anthropologists overtly practice a kind of "applied anthropology" intended to bring the concepts, perspectives, and methods of the science to non-academic initiatives (see discussion of anthropological careers below).

The continuing evolution of cultural anthropology

Who are the subjects of cultural anthropology's curiosity—what we sometimes call the "anthropological gaze"? The conventional impression (virtually the stereotype) of the science is that it is exclusively concerned with small, "traditional," even "primitive" groups. Actually, one of the great early anthropologists, A. R. Radcliffe-Brown, defined anthropology as "the study of what are called primitive or backward peoples" (1965: 2). The equally esteemed E. E. Evans-Pritchard asserted that anthropology was the branch of social science, "which chiefly devotes itself to primitive societies" (1962: 11). However, Evans-Pritchard situated the emphasis on remote exotic peoples within the context of anthropology's greater subject, which

Boas, Franz. 1928. *Anthropology and Modern Life*. New York: W. W. Norton & Company, Inc.

Radcliffe-Brown, A. R. 1965 [1952]. *Structure and Function in Primitive Society*. New York: The Free Press.

See Chapters 3 and 11–15

Evans-Pritchard, E. E. 1962. *Social Anthropology and Other Essays*. New York: The Free Press.

IMAGE 1.3
Anthropologists study the
city as a distinct social
system and way of life.

See Chapters 12–15

"embraces all human cultures and societies, including our own" (4).

If you consider the questions posed by anthropology generally and cultural anthropology specifically, you will immediately realize that there is nothing that limits them to any particular kinds of peoples or cultures. Accordingly, as the human world has changed—especially becoming more interconnected, more fluid, more "modernized"—cultural anthropology has changed too, partly because it can and partly because it must. Cultural anthropology was never really exclusively the study of small, isolated, traditional societies, although it did occupy the "savage slot" (Trouillot, 1991), for tactical reasons (because it is easier to analyze compact and unfamiliar cultures) and for the simple reason that no other science did. But anthropology cannot and does not aspire to remain in that slot, if only because there are no more isolated and "primitive" societies and arguably never were.

See Chapters 11–15

The three main phenomena that have forced a reconceptualization of cultural anthropology are colonialism, postcolonial independence and nationalist and indigenous movements, and

modernization and globalization. Colonialism brought far-flung societies within a single political, economic, and cultural sphere, imposing changes and inequalities. Independence, nationalism, and indigenous movements have transformed the sometimes "passive" objects of anthropological scrutiny into active subjects, actors and producers of culture who speak for themselves. Finally, modernization and globalization have threatened and attempted to integrate cultures into a single world system, which is, Thomas Friedman (2005) notwithstanding, anything but "flat," if only because they are driven from centers of wealth and power and generate uneven outcomes. In the contemporary world, globalization is the most heralded cultural force, regarded as "processes that take place within [groups] but also transcend them, such that attention limited to local processes, identities, and units of analysis yields incomplete understanding of the local" (Kearney, 1995: 548). But the local does not disappear, nor is it bleached of all its distinctive characteristics; rather, in each location and occasion, a distinct combination or manifestation of the local and the global emerges, leading to a result that some observers have wryly called **glocalization**, linking local or small-scale changes to large-scale or global factors. The message is that even within a global context, cultural realities are local, and therefore cultural anthropology's questions, perspectives, and methods still apply.

In response to "glocal" realities, some anthropologists have taken "big picture" approaches to the world, as in Eric Wolf's (1982) *Europe and the People without History* and the various works of Ernest Gellner (e.g. 1988). Others have explored specialized aspects of human behavior, such as war and conflict (e.g. Eller, 1999, 2005; Fujii, 2009; Scheper-Hughes and Bourgois, 2004), globalization (e.g. Eriksen, 2014; Lewellen, 2002), consumption and shopping (e.g. Counihan and Van Esterick, 2007; Howes, 1996; Miller, 1998), environment and conservation (Guneratne, 2010; Igoe, 2004), homelessness (Finkelstein, 2005), natural disasters (Hoffman and Oliver-Smith, 2002), material culture like denim (Miller and Woodward, 2007, 2011) and lycra (O'Connor, 2011), and even psychedelic trance dance (St. John, 2010).

THE "ANTHROPOLOGICAL PERSPECTIVE"

Cultural anthropology is distinct among sciences for the questions it asks, but it also stands out in its approach to or its way of thinking about its subject, that is, its perspective. The **anthropological perspective** has three components. The first is obvious, the second less obvious but fairly uncontroversial, and the third not at all obvious and quite controversial. They are:

1. comparative or cross-cultural study
2. holism
3. cultural relativism

Comparative or cross-cultural study

Cultural anthropology does not look at just one kind of culture, certainly not just the anthropologist's own kind of culture. A **cross-cultural** approach means that anthropologists are curious about human behavior in a wide and inclusive sense, embracing all human ways of being. Anthropologists

are perhaps peculiarly interested in cultures that are *unlike* their own. After all, people already know their own culture pretty well—or think they do. One premise of human sciences is that most people in fact are not as aware of the causes and consequences of their own behavior as they often (or like to) think that they are. This is a reason why sociologist C. Wright Mills (1959) referred to the "sociological imagination": Researchers must learn to see meanings, rules, relationships, institutions, and such phenomena that are "invisible" to or outside the attention of group members even as those phenomena influence human behavior, individually and collectively. Therefore, one reason why cultural anthropology has insisted on a comparative perspective is that it is often easier to see what is unfamiliar than what is familiar; familiar things tend to be taken for granted or overlooked, whereas the unfamiliar demands attention. Anthropology, if anything, serves to question assumptions and to expose the taken-for-granted.

However, even if anthropologists knew their own culture very well, that would not be sufficient. Anthropologists, like all scientists, cannot use a sample of one to draw conclusions about other cases. Whether it is plants, planets, or people, it is not acceptable to assume that they are all alike. In fact, it is wise to assume exactly the opposite. Anybody who is truly interested in knowing and understanding humans needs a bigger sample than one. We cannot know ourselves, no matter how thoroughly, and claim that we know *humanity*. Actually, in almost every way, Western culture in general or American culture in particular is quite atypical and non-representative. But then, there is no "typical" culture. Since no culture pertains to all humans, or even a majority or close to it, every culture is a minority. *Whatever you do or think or feel, in the human world you are in the minority*.

So it should be apparent why cross-cultural or comparative study is a valuable part of anthropology. The first reason is that the diversity is there. There simply *are* other cultures than one's own. But more, by exposing ourselves to the plethora of human cultures, we can make two important discoveries:

■ the commonalities or "universals" that occur across cultures—that is, is there anything that most or all cultures do, that seems to be *necessary* for humans?

Glocalization
a combination of the words "globalization" and "local," suggests the unique local and situated forms and effects of wide-spread and even global processes

Wolf, Eric. 1982. *Europe and the People without History*. Berkeley: University of California Press.

Anthropological perspective
the unique "angle" or point of view of anthropology, consisting of cross-cultural or comparative study, holism, and cultural relativism

Cross-cultural study
the examination of a wide variety of societies when considering any particular cultural question, for purposes of comparison

the full range of variation between cultures—that is, just how different can humans be? How many different kinds of language, personality, economics, religion, etc. are there? Just how many ways are there to be human? In other words, what is *possible* for humans?

I like to think of anthropology, then, as the study of what is possible and what is necessary for humans.

Holism

Holism
the part of the "anthropological perspective" that involves consideration of every part of a culture in relation to every other part and to the whole

Holism refers to "the whole," the entirety. Each particular culture is and must be approached as a whole, not just as a single trait (say, a political system or an economy) or as a disconnected bundle of traits. A whole, cultural or otherwise, is a system containing multiple parts in some kind of structured relationship with each other. The first significance of this fact is that a culture *has parts*, and anthropologists discover these parts and the different forms they can take. If, for instance, kinship is a part of culture, then what different kinds of kinship are there? What are the possibilities of marriage, child-rearing, household residence, descent, and so forth? The second significance is that the parts are interconnected in some way. If an anthropologist wants to study, say, the marriage customs of a particular society, s/he cannot study marriage in isolation; rather, s/he must consider language, politics, religion, gender roles, etc. Potentially—and actually—every part of a culture relates in some way to every other part. The parts might not be as tightly integrated as the parts of a car engine, but they are interrelated. The third significance is that each part has its unique function and each contributes to the function of the whole. Just like an organ in the body or a part in a car, each has its own "job to do" and each contributes to the overall job of the whole. So, wherever we enter a culture to begin to analyze it or whatever we care to focus on, we will find ourselves swept into considering all of its parts and the whole which they constitute.

The holistic perspective has led cultural anthropology into a "case study" approach. In a traditional or classic anthropological description of a specific culture—known as **ethnography**—the writer typically would begin with a discussion of the environment in which the group lives (mountain,

IMAGE 1.4 The author standing in front of the Basaki Temple in Bali, 1988.

desert, jungle, island, etc.) and then proceed to provide details on each aspect of the culture. Sometimes these accounts would center on a particular part of the culture, depending on what was most noteworthy, but all of the parts required analysis. In some instances an entire book was written on one aspect of culture, as in the case of *Nuer Religion* (Evans-Pritchard, 1956), but even then it was a contribution to a body of literature including all facets of that particular society. In other words, any single ethnography prepared by a cultural anthropologist might not cover every single aspect of the culture, but collectively, the research on the culture would. Recently, though, Tim Ingold (2008) has reminded us that anthropology is not the same thing as ethnography, the latter being a specific form of anthropological knowledge and a means to a deeper anthropological end.

Cultural relativism

It is a fact that cultures are different; that is why anthropologists study them. Cultures are different in how they see, interpret, value, and respond to the world, including other human beings in their world. What is done in one culture may not be done in another. What is important or valuable in one culture may not be in another, and what is good or right in one culture may not be in another. For example, in mainstream American culture, polygamy is deemed to be bad, immoral, and illegal (there are of course minority sections of America that practice and value polygamy, such as the sect of "fundamentalist" Mormons). However, in many

See Chapter 2

Ethnography
a written account or description of a particular culture, usually including its environment, economic system, kinship arrangements, political systems, and religious beliefs, and often including some discussion of culture change

cultures—in fact, in most cultures—polygamy has been not only acceptable, but normal or even preferred. Who is right about this?

Actually, that is not the correct question to ask. In fact, it is not even a possible question to ask. But let us say this for now: *Different cultures can and do have different notions of what is good, normal, moral, valuable, legal, etc.* An anthropologist investigating a headhunting society would find men with human heads in their possession, perhaps displayed on their walls or hung from their ceilings. The tendency might be to judge them with the anthropologist's own values and norms: "Those men are all immoral, criminal killers!" An outsider might want to call the authorities and have the "deviants" and "murderers" arrested. The visitor might then be surprised when the authorities ask why s/he is bothering them; in fact, the owners of the heads may be the authorities—the chiefs, the priests, or other leaders. That might be hard to accept, but imagine this: A man from the same headhunting society comes to your society and sees that you do not have heads on display. What would he think? He might conclude you are weak or inconsequential, a person of no courage, fame, or prominence, or that you are just "deviant" from the ideal of headhunting. If the headhunter visited the White House or Ten Downing Street and observed no heads, he might assume that the resident has no political authority, since, in his view, great men collect heads.

Notice that the headhunter got Western people wrong, just as Western people got him and his culture wrong. What do we learn by thinking this way? Not very much, at least not very much about each other. We do learn about ourselves (that we disapprove of headhunting), but we already knew that. Clearly, understanding—let alone judging—others by our standards is not helpful.

If anthropologists want to understand another culture, then *we must understand or judge that culture in terms of its own notions of good, normal, moral, valuable, meaningful, etc.* That is **cultural relativism**. Cultural relativism asserts that an observer cannot apply the standards of one culture to another culture, at least not in an informative way. Rather, a phenomenon in a culture must be understood and evaluated *in relation to, relative to,* that culture. Why? It is always tempting and easy to conclude that different is bad: "They do not do it my way, so

they are wrong." Scientific observers must avoid such arrogance and shortsightedness, which is quite likely to breed misunderstanding. This happens, for instance, in international business. A meeting of Western and non-Western businesspeople might easily end with each side thinking it understands what happened in the meeting. Later, if one side does not respond as the other expected it would, there can be confusion, anger, even real financial loss. What went wrong? Each side interpreted the meeting from its own cultural point of view, not realizing that the other side had a different point of view—until it was too late.

Accordingly, any judgment about norms, morals, values, meanings, laws, and so on is a cultural judgment, made *in relation to* some cultural standard of norms, morals, values, meanings, and laws. Sticking out one's tongue is an insult here, a greeting there. If an anthropologist gets mad or offended when members of a society where tongue-sticking is a greeting stick their tongue out at him or her, those members will be quite surprised and confused by the anthropologist's response. This experience is called **culture shock**—the surprise, confusion, and actual pain that one feels in the presence of the profoundly unfamiliar and unexpected. This is probably the most common experience in the world. So is the reaction: to judge people from other cultures by the standards of one's own culture. This is called **ethnocentrism** (from *ethno* for a way of life or culture and *center* for putting it in the center or pride of place), the attitude or practice of assuming that one's own cultural point of view is the best, the right, or even the only point of view. Of course, ethnocentrism is possible—it is the easy, even the automatic, thing—but it is simply not helpful. One can be ethnocentric from one's own cultural perspective, but others can be ethnocentric from their cultural perspective. Nothing is gained by this except mutual (and probably negative) judgment.

Every judgment, then, of good or bad, moral or immoral, normal or abnormal, valuable or valueless, and so on is made from some cultural point of view—in relation to some standard of good, moral, normal, valuable. And a culture is precisely a set of standards for such judgments. Cultural relativism says that we need to take this fact into account when we confront and interact with other cultures; it must be part of our perspective

See Chapter 8

Culture shock
the surprise, confusion, and pain we feel when we encounter a way of life that is very foreign to our own

Ethnocentrism
the attitude or belief that one's own culture is the best or only one, and that one can understand or judge another culture in terms of one's own

ISLAM IN TEXAS

Cultural relativism
the reaction to the fact of cultural diversity in which one attempts to understand and judge the behavior of another culture in terms of its standards of good, normal, moral, legal, etc. rather than one's own

on cultural difference. However, there are many fallacies and misconceptions that people, both relativists and non-relativists, have about cultural relativism.

1. **Cultural relativism** *does not mean* **that "anything goes" or that judgment is impossible.** Some critics of relativism insist that it means, or leads to, a position of no standards at all, a "do what you want to do," "if it feels good, do it" ethic or antiethic. That is not at all what cultural relativism advocates. It does not say, "Anything goes," but rather, "Here this goes, and there that goes." It is *descriptive*. It does not tell us what moral or value judgments to make, only that diverging moral or value judgments are made. And it certainly does not conclude that value judgments are impossible. Rather, it is a description of exactly how such judgments are made—in relation to some standard of judgment—and investigators should find out what that standard of judgment is. But there is no such thing as a "standardless" judgment, and there does not appear to be a single standard that all cultures share. Instead, there are multiple standards.

2. **Cultural relativism** *does not mean* **that anything a culture does is good, moral, valuable, or normal.** Some critics of relativism claim that taking a relativistic stance toward another culture is essentially condoning it. But to condone means to judge favorably, and relativism is not about judging but about understanding. If we encountered a culture that practiced polygamy or infanticide or "honor killing," cultural relativism would not require us to say, "Those attitudes and behaviors are good or acceptable." What it would require us to do is determine where those attitudes and behaviors come from and what they mean to the people who practice them. One certainly does not have to approve in order to understand. In fact, not only do anthropologists not have to condone these or any other behaviors, they *cannot*, as *condoning, like condemning, is a value judgment*. To say a behavior is good or bad is to judge it, and that means judging by some particular value standard. That would entail abandoning the relativistic perspective and referring to one's own community of values, one's own culture. As an anthropologist it is possible to understand a behavior without judging—in fact, it

is *only* possible to understand without judging—while as a member of one's own culture one can say that s/he does not share or condone that behavior. But you must always remember that your judgment is a product of your culture and may not be shared by all cultures.

3. **Cultural relativism** *does not mean* **that anything a culture believes is true.** Some critics of relativism assert that relativism compels us to accept as valid any belief or "knowledge" that a culture asserts. If, for instance, a culture believes that the earth is flat, then it is flat *for them*, even while it is round for us. This is of course nonsense and has nothing whatsoever to do with cultural relativism. There is a philosophical position known as "epistemological relativism" that does actually hold that all knowledge and truth is relative, but that is not the claim made by cultural relativism and is quite beyond the ability or need of anthropology to address. Let us consider the problem of knowledge by contrasting two different kinds of statements:

Polygamy is good.   Earth is round.

Both take the superficial form of *noun*-is-*adjective*. But the similarity ends there. The latter is a fact-statement, or rather a fact-claim. Is it true or false? More importantly, how do we determine? We make observations and measurements, that is, we check against reality. We find that the earth really is round, not flat, and verify the initial statement. How about the statement on polygamy? Is it true or false that polygamy is good? The answer is—neither. It is culturally relative. That is, in Warlpiri (Australian Aboriginal) or in fundamentalist Mormon culture, polygamy is good. In mainstream American society, polygamy is bad. So "polygamy is good" is not the same kind of statement as "Earth is round." Again, the latter is a fact-claim (either true or false), but the former is a *value-claim*. It is neither true nor false.

Value claims are judgments and therefore must be made by reference to, relative to, some value standard. But what standard? Shall we use mainstream Western standards, or Warlpiri standards, or Japanese standards, or Yanomamo standards, ad infinitum? The answer is that any of those standards is equally usable—and equally used by somebody.

Therefore, a value statement like "polygamy is good" is not and cannot be true or false, because *it is not even a complete statement yet*. Before we can evaluate the statement, we need to know more: good *for what*, good *according to whom*? If one says, "Polygamy is good among the Warlpiri," an anthropologist can respond, "That is true." If one says, "Polygamy is good," the anthropological response is not "True" or "False," but "Please finish your statement." It is not clear yet which cultural value-standard the speaker is applying, so the statement is unfinished and meaningless as formulated.

Since there are multiple potential and actual value standards that can be used to evaluate the claim, the final judgment will be *relative to* whichever standard one ultimately uses. In other words, value statements are culturally relative, whereas fact statements are not. Or, we might say that fact statements are relative to a single standard (reality) that is objective and universally shared. The acceleration of gravity on Earth (thirty-two feet per second per second) is the same for all people in all cultures because they share a single common physical reality. If all people in all cultures shared a single common standard—a single common cultural reality—for evaluating polygamy, then they would all come to the same evaluation, but then there would not be many different cultures for it to be relative to.

4. Cultural relativism *does not mean* that cultures are different in every conceivable way, that there are no cultural universals. Cultural relativism does not rule out the possibility of any commonalities or universals among humans. Relativism does not say that commonalities cannot exist; it merely correctly asserts that we cannot *assume* that they exist. The question of cultural universals is an empirical question: That is, if we find them, then they exist. If we do not find them, then they do not exist. But the lack of *universal meanings or values* is not the same thing as the lack of *meanings or values*. Even if there are not universal ones, there are "local" ones geographically and historically—very many local ones, in fact—and if that is all there is, then that has to be enough.

5. Cultural relativism *does not mean* that "everything is relative," including cultural **relativism itself (cultural relativism is not self-contradictory).** Some things are culturally relative, and some things are not. Cultural relativism is simply an awareness and acknowledgment of differences in human judgment about norms, values, meanings, and so on. It amounts to saying, "Different cultures have different notions of good, normal, moral, valuable." But that statement is not a value statement itself; it is a fact-claim. It is not saying culture is good, or cultural relativism is good, or multiple value standards are good. Perhaps from certain viewpoints, multiple value standards— multiple cultures—are not good at all. They definitely make the human world more complicated and contentious. Still, culture *is*; multiple value standards *exist*. That is a fact. How we respond to it, what sense we make of it, is the important question.

6. **Cultural relativism *does not mean* that cultures cannot be compared.** Cultural relativism does not mean that comparison is impossible, any more than it means that judgment is impossible. What it means is that when any comparison is being made, the terms or criteria of the comparison must be specified. One cannot say culture X is "better than" culture Y without specifying "better at what?" Some cultures certainly are larger than others, and some cultures certainly are better at hunting or making war than others. As long as the standards of comparison are stated (and perhaps it is also explained *why those particular standards* were selected), comparisons can of course be made. In fact, recall that the first part of the anthropological perspective was "comparative" study. We can compare two or more cultures on any variable without making value judgments about them.

In short, cultural relativism is three things simultaneously. It is a fact: Cultures are different in their standards, values, meanings, and judgments. It is a method: If we want to understand a culture accurately, we must understand it in its own terms. And it is a theory: The explanation of *how* individuals and groups make their determinations of judgment and action depends on the awareness of the role of cultural meanings and standards. That is, there is no way for humans to behave or evaluate *other than* relative to some standard of behavior and evaluation.

IMAGE 1.5 Warlpiri (Australian Aboriginal) women preparing ritual objects.

PRACTICING ANTHROPOLOGY

You may be wondering at this point what an anthropologist does and what you could do with a degree or a career in anthropology. Anthropology is a lively, diverse, and growing discipline. According to a survey undertaken by our primary professional organization in the United States, the American Anthropological Association, the number of Bachelor degrees earned in anthropology nearly doubled from 1992–1993 to 2001–2002, from 5,945 to 9,728; the number of Master degrees rose by around fifty percent (1,049 to 1,519), while almost three times as many doctorates were awarded (367 versus 1,025) (Boites, Geller, and Patterson, n.d.). Significantly, more than half (up to sixty percent) of anthropology graduate degrees are earned by women. Another study (Givens, Evans, and Jablonski, 2000) happily discovered that the vast majority of anthropology graduates (eighty-five percent) would choose anthropology again as their major and career if they had it to do over.

The U.S. Bureau of Labor Statistics also recently issued a prediction for the job market in anthropology: During the decade from 2008 to 2018, they projected a growth of twenty-two percent in all social science occupations and a growth rate of twenty-eight percent in anthropology and archaeology.

Careers in anthropology

What exactly do anthropologists do for a living? Many are teachers and scholars (researchers and writers) of anthropology, but not all. Givens et al. (2000) calculated that only a little over half (fifty-nine percent) of all anthropology PhDs worked in academia in 1990, with somewhat more (seventy-one percent) holding academic jobs in 1997. The U.S. Bureau of Labor Statistics data mentioned earlier indicate that only a little more than a third (34.2 percent) of anthropologists and archaeologists in 2008 worked in the conventional area of research and advanced teaching, with almost as many (thirty percent) employed by government. The remaining third performed many tasks, including management and consulting, museum and historical site work, and even architecture and engineering. Indeed, the Society for Applied Anthropology estimates that most anthropologists work outside of colleges and universities, if Master degree-holders are included, and no doubt the number would be greater still for Bachelor degree-holders. Givens et al. conclude: "Presently, there is no discernible ceiling or cap . . . for PhD anthropologists targeting the nonacademic realm of employment." An anthropology major or minor can in fact be a fine preparation for a non-anthropological career, in education, business, law, journalism, and medicine, especially if one expects to be working with diverse populations or in an international setting.

For anthropologists who want to practice anthropology but do not seek academic careers, many opportunities exist in business and government, and anthropologists have made important contributions in both areas. For instance, writing in the bulletin of the National Association for the Practice of Anthropology (NAPA), Shirley Fiske (2008) finds that the federal government is probably the single largest employer of anthropologists in the United States after colleges and universities, especially archaeologists, but also cultural, physical, and linguistic anthropologists. The five main federal agencies that hire people with anthropological skills are the Census Bureau, the National Park Service, the National Marine Fisheries Service, the Centers for Disease Control (CDC), and the U.S. Agency for International Development (USAID). For instance, at the Census Bureau, "anthropologists have played a critical role in identifying the causes of and recommendations for overcoming the traditional undercounts of nontraditional households and populations in U.S. decennial censuses"; the expertise of anthropologists has helped the Bureau "improve its methods and approach to enumerating the national population, develop reliable methodologies for identifying marginalized and difficult-to-enumerate populations . . . and to recruit community-knowledgeable people to help conduct the census" (111–114). There are even anthropologists in the employ of the Department of Defense.

Anthropologists have been equally if not more successful in the world of business and commerce. According to Ann Jordan (2003) in her book titled, *Business Anthropology*, corporations can benefit in at least five ways from hiring anthropologists: They can better understand their own work processes as well as the processes of their users or customers, they can comprehend and manage group behavior in the company, they can navigate organizational change, they can facilitate diversity within the corporation, and they can cope with globalization and international business. As early as 1931, American anthropologist W. Lloyd Warner, who had done research on Australian Aboriginals,

investigated how the workplace environment at the Western Electric Company affected worker productivity. The 1930s and 1940s were a busy period for industrial anthropology, and Warner subsequently became the chairman of the Committee on Human Relations in Industry. In 1941 the aforementioned Society for Applied Anthropology was formed, and in 1946 Warner joined some other experts in creating Social Research Incorporated, an anthropological consulting firm with such clients as Sears, Roebuck and Company.

In the contemporary high-technology and information economy, knowledge about learning, change, and user and customer behavior is more important than ever. Anthropologists have been especially valuable in studying how employees and customers interact with technology, leading to better training methods and better design features. The most famous example is the Xerox Palo Alto Research Center (PARC). PARC was established in 1970 not only to invent new products but to innovate knowledge, learning processes, user experiences, and the Xerox corporation itself, and "some of the most important research at PARC in the past decade has been done by anthropologists" (Brown, 1991: 106). Two key hires for Xerox were anthropologists Lucy Suchman and Jeannette Blomberg, who "studied occupations and work practices throughout the company—clerks in an accounts-payable office who issue checks to suppliers, technical representatives who repair copying machines, designers who develop new products, even novice users of Xerox's copiers" (106–108). One of Suchman's most important discoveries was that official procedures and knowledge often did not reflect how people actually did their jobs; rather, workers and customers possess informal knowledge and skill that they use to accomplish their tasks—and which managers and product designers can use to improve their processes and products. There may have been an anthropologist's hand in the copier or other product that you buy or use every day.

Other companies, from huge corporations like Microsoft and Intel to smaller ones like the Minneapolis marketing agency Olson, do better business by hiring anthropologists. And anthropologists have founded their own businesses, like LTG Associates, Inc., which describes itself as "the oldest and largest anthropologically-based

www. practicinganthropology.org

ANTHROPOLOGISTS AT WAR

BOX 1.3   ANTHROPOLOGY IN A GLOBAL HEALTH CRISIS

In December 2014, in reaction to the escalating Ebola epidemic, the World Health Organization posted a job opening (vacancy notice no. AFRO/14/TA187) for an "Ebola Outbreak—Surge Capacity— Anthropologist." The candidate was expected to "support the EVD [Ebola Virus Disease] Response Teams through the application of ethnographic methodologies in order to understand factors that drive the spread of EVD and apply findings to programme and policies." Specifically, the anthropologist would conduct research "that will help better understand local cultural attitudes, beliefs, and practices related to EVD" and "advise on ways to integrate understanding of cultural and social norms of communities to develop better rapport and trust between government, response staff and communities across various EVD issues" (World Health Organization e-Recruitment site). As remarkable as this charge is, it is hardly the first time that anthropologists have contributed to health-related issues. Cora Du Bois was hired by WHO in 1950; Thomas Csordas participated in the Navajo Healing Project in the 1990s not only to learn about Navajo health conditions, but "to produce knowledge that could be circulated back in the Navajo community in a way that could enhance health care providers' understanding of their Navajo patients" (Csordas, 2000: 466); Jean Schensul founded the Institute for Community Research in 1987 to address public health problems (among other justice and equity issues) in Hartford, Connecticut; and in 1999, Nancy Scheper-Hughes co-founded Organs Watch to document and end illegal organ trafficking.

See Chapter 16

See Chapters 14 and 15

consulting firm in North America," specializing in "the development and conduct of health and human services programs" (ltgassociates.com/pdf/LTG%20 Flyer.pdf).

Beyond the university and the corporation, there are many important and even critical applications of the discipline. NAPA promotes the use of anthropology "to address social issues related to public health, organizational and community development, information technology systems, housing, social justice, law, the media, marketing, environmental management, and the arts." Ervin (2000) mentions a wide variety of ways for putting anthropology into practice, including policy-making in such areas as health, education, social-economic problems, environment and resource management, and technology. Anthropologists can perform functions in needs assessment (determining what problems need to be solved and what inputs will be required), program evaluation (determining the effectiveness of programs), and social impact analysis (determining the effects of programs on people). Some of the specific tasks that anthropologists can perform include training, supervision, administration, consultation, interviewing, grant-writing, and expert-witness testimony.

One particular arena where anthropologists can make and have made a contribution is in advocacy for indigenous peoples, bringing cultural considerations to the attention of governments and corporations. Organizations like Cultural Survival (which publishes a magazine by the same name) in the U.S. or Survival International in the U.K. promote awareness of indigenous issues. The American Anthropological Association maintains a Department of Government Relations, which "works to increase public understanding of anthropology" and to lend an anthropological voice to political discourse. Some of its activities include initiating and responding to governmental policies, working with federal agencies, preparing briefings from the anthropological perspective, serving in advisory positions, and developing testimony to support funding allocations. Participation and advocacy can take many other forms as well, such as working for indigenous groups like Native American communities and societies to help them advance their practical claims (e.g. water or land rights) and cultural interests. When I was doing my fieldwork in Australia, there were anthropologists assisting Aboriginal groups to collect and present their tradition-based land claims in Australian courts; they would conduct the research, brief the lawyers, and sometimes even testify themselves in court. Others were helping them produce and sell their art.

Anthropology in careers

Most students who take an introductory anthropology course will not go on to a career in anthropology. However, most if not all workers and citizens of the future will find anthropology in their careers. Given the diversity and interconnectedness of the human world, even if you are not a professional anthropologist, *you will be an amateur anthropologist whether you know it or not.* Most jobs will require interaction with diverse coworkers, colleagues, customers, or clients, and the skills and perspectives of anthropology will be increasingly valuable, whatever work you do.

In its "Future Work Skills 2020" report, the Institute for the Future (Davies, Fidler, and Gorbis, 2011) identifies six factors that will shape the work and the world of tomorrow—extremely long lifespans, the rise of smart machines, the computational world, the new media, superstructured organizations, and a globally connected world. These circumstances, which are largely already here, demand a set of capabilities beyond merely knowing one's job. The "ten skills for the future workplace" mentioned in the report include:

1. sense-making, "the ability to determine the deeper meaning or significance of what is being expressed" (8)
2. social intelligence, "ability to connect to others in a deep and direct way, to sense and stimulate reactions and desired interactions"
3. novel and adaptive thinking
4. cross-cultural competency, "ability to operate in different cultural settings" (9)
5. computational thinking
6. new media literacy
7. transdisciplinarity, "literacy in and ability to understand concepts across multiple disciplines" (11)
8. design mindset, "ability to represent and develop tasks and work processes for desired outcomes"
9. cognitive load management, "ability to discriminate and filter information for importance, and to understand how to maximize cognitive functioning using a variety of tools and techniques"
10. virtual collaboration

Most of these are precisely the skills on which anthropologists depend and which are conferred through the anthropological perspective.

BOX 1.4 CONTEMPORARY CULTURAL CONTROVERSIES: BITING THE HAND THAT FUNDS YOU

Like any science, anthropology tries to maintain a certain level of neutrality and objectivity in its work. Yet, exposing inconvenient practices and relationships can be a political and economic problem for anthropologists and other social scientists. Scholars living in Michigan find themselves in the "long shadow" of Dow Chemicals, a rich corporation that invests millions of dollars in the state's universities, including $5 million in 1996 for the Dow Institute of Materials Research at Michigan State University (McKenna, 2013: 61–62). Brian McKenna rightly contends that such a corporation is "tailor-made" for anthropological analysis, because it "is perhaps the most animistic entity known to man" (61), that is, we experience corporations as virtual (and legal) living things. The presence of Dow in Michigan "is like having a foreign country in your own backyard" (68), so anthropologists "need not travel to all four corners of the globe in search of the exotic: it is right before their eyes 'at home'" (61). However, because Dow is such a significant donor to universities—which also house three Michigan public television stations—the company not only exerts influence over knowledge in the state but "remains off-limits to critical enquiry" (68). What do you think?

Many careers already urge a kind of "cultural competency" akin to the anthropological perspective. The Center for Effective Collaboration and Practice (http://cecp.air.org) defines **cultural competence** as "the integration and transformation of knowledge about individuals and groups of people into specific standards, policies, practices, and attitudes used in appropriate cultural settings to increase the quality of services; thereby producing better outcomes." More specifically, cultural competence entails valuing diversity, being able to assess one's own culture, being conscious of intercultural interaction, institutionalizing this cross-cultural knowledge, and developing procedures to deliver culturally-appropriate services. A number of professions have formally integrated cultural competence into their standards for job performance, including nursing, pharmacy, health care of all kinds, social work, policing and criminal justice, counseling, and education. The National Association of Social Workers has published guidelines for cultural competence in social work practice, and there is even an organization called the National Center for Cultural Competence (http://nccc.georgetown.edu).

Cultural competence
the skills necessary in the workplace and in life to recognize and value diversity, see one's own cultural influences, understand the dynamics and challenges of intercultural interaction, institutionalize cultural knowledge, and develop practices and policies for delivering culturally appropriate services

SUMMARY

Humans are diverse. Anthropology did not create this diversity but emerged as a response to and an investigation of it. Anthropology is thus the science of human diversity; it takes as its "question" or subject matter the full spectrum of human forms and ways and the explanation of that spectrum. The diversity that anthropology observes takes the form of bodily and behavioral differences, for which specialties within the field have been established:

■ physical anthropology to study diversity of the human body in the past and present
■ archaeology to study diversity of human behavior in the past
■ linguistic anthropology to study diversity of human language in the past and present
■ cultural anthropology to study the diversity of human behavior in the present

In addition to its question, anthropology is distinguished by its perspective, or the approach or attitude it takes toward its subject. This "anthropological perspective" includes:

■ comparative or cross-cultural study, or the description and analysis of the complete range of variation of humans and our ways
■ holism, or the interrelatedness of all of the "parts" of culture and of the culture to its natural environment
■ cultural relativism, or the awareness that we can make (useful) judgments of a culture only in terms of its own standards of good and normal and moral and meaningful and legal

There are many ways to practice anthropology, only one of which is as a teacher, researcher, or writer. Anthropologists outside academics work in business and government, among other occupations. Even academic anthropologists may be involved in consulting, policy-making, and advocacy.

Most people in the modern world are not professional anthropologists (and none were until fairly recently). However, all of us today live "anthropological lives" in the sense that we will experience and deal with human physical and cultural diversity continuously, both locally and globally, both professionally and personally.

MCQS

FILL IN THE BLANKS

Key Terms

anthropological perspective	cultural relativism	garbology
archaeology	culture shock	glocalization
artifacts	ecofacts	holism
cross-cultural study	ethnocentrism	linguistic anthropology
cultural anthropology	ethnography	physical anthropology
cultural competence	features	primatology

2 Understanding and studying culture

"If you *really* want to know what the fishing industry is all about, you must go fishing," the ship's captain told the anthropologist (Pálsson, 1994: 905). A good Icelandic skipper guides his ship and crew to success by "skill," which means his "dexterity and alertness to the tasks at hand"; he certainly uses his technology and gadgets, but these tools are "an extension of his person" (910) as he executes the complex and dangerous work of finding a fishing spot, setting nets, drawing in nets, removing fish, and sailing home. Becoming a skipper "demands several years of training, both formal and informal. A prospective skipper, usually a fisherman's son, began his career as a deck-hand" while still a teenager (915). To earn an official skipper's license, he "has to receive formal training in a specialized institution, the Marine Academy," the two-year classroom program of which entitles him to the title, rights, and duties of "skipper," but "you learn even more by simply taking part, by living the life at sea" (915). Preparation for the contingencies and dangers of the real world depended on the elusive quality of *experience*, which often was not or could not be put into words. Indeed, although they valued "attentiveness," skippers

rarely mentioned how they actually make decisions. One reason is that they are guided more by practical results than by an interest in theoretical advancement. Often they "simply" notice that a particular strategy seems to work, without worrying about why that is the case . . . . What fishermen label as hunches and fishing mood is particularly difficult to verbalize; some important decisions are "out of the blue". . . . Decision-making, then, is based less on detached calculation or "mental" reflection than on practical involvement.

(1994: 919)

The same was true, of course, for his crew, who had to perform elaborate tasks in concert without Marine Academy training. "Such mutual attentiveness, the result of *collective enskilment*, is essential for efficient team-work" (920, emphasis added). The message is "that learning is not a purely cognitive or cerebral process . . . but is rather grounded in the contexts of practice, involvement, and personal engagement" (920).

"Culture" (derived from the Latin root *cultus* for "cultivate") is obviously a central concept in cultural anthropology (but not, significantly, in social anthropology). Culture is typically understood as the shared ways of thinking, behaving, and feeling in a group or society. However, the habit—and it is a deep habit in Western civilization—has been to emphasize "knowledge" in the cognitive or mental sense, in the sense of factual knowledge or propositions that can be put into words. The case of the Icelandic fisherman and other cases below challenge the overly cognitive, propositional, and linguistic nature of culture and of human knowledge in general. Cultural anthropology has come to stress practice or skill—the embodied ability to do things—as a key, perhaps *the* key, aspect of culture, envisioning much of culture as analogous to playing a sport like football or an instrument like the piano or as throwing pots or weaving cloth. This is why Pálsson described the process of becoming a fisherman as "enskilment," the acquisition of skills or bodily competencies that may or may not be expressed or expressible in words. Learning to be a member of a group—a profession, an organization, an entire society—is a sort of apprenticeship, and in order to learn about another society, the anthropologist essentially apprentices him/herself to that group.

DEFINING CULTURE

Part of the methodology of every science is its vocabulary, its set of core terms and concepts. In physics, these include mass, force, velocity, and momentum. Cultural anthropology too has its core terms and concepts, which, according to Evans-Pritchard (1962: 2), include "society," "custom," "structure," "function," and of course, culture. Of these, culture is the most central to cultural anthropology. The problem is that there is no single official definition of culture. There are almost as many definitions of culture as there are cultural anthropologists; in fact, there are fundamentally different approaches to a definition. One approach understands culture as primarily ideas or beliefs, that is, as basically "in people's heads." From this perspective, we cannot really "see" culture, but we can infer it from the behaviors of people. Another approach construes culture as a set of real facts, albeit "social facts," including observable behavior and the products of that behavior, such as the rules,

groups, and institutions that shape people's lives. Culture can even refer to material objects like tools and houses. Ultimately, culture undoubtedly encompasses all three.

So there is no authoritative or universally shared definition of culture. But the oldest and most widely cited anthropological definition of culture was given by E. B. Tylor in his 1871 book called *Primitive Culture*. It is quoted here not because it is perfect or authoritative, but because it captures most of the components of culture and of cultural anthropology.

> Culture or Civilization, taken in its wide ethnographic sense, is that complex whole which includes knowledge, belief, art, morals, law, custom, and any other capabilities and habits acquired by man as a member of society.
>
> (1958: 1)

Culture, then, can be understood as those lifeways, and the social and material products of those ways, that are shared among a group of people not because they are innate or inborn, but because they are observed and experienced in the group. This and Tylor's characterization of culture include several key notions which we may consider the classic qualities of culture:

- learned
- shared
- symbolic
- integrated
- adaptive

Contemporary encounters with culture in the modern globalized context suggest that these standard features do not quite capture its full richness, though. In particular, culture is and always has been characterized by its "mobility (geographical and social), complexity, fragmentation, contradiction, risk, and disembedding" (Coupland, 2007: 29). Therefore, we could and should add that culture, at all times and places but especially and crucially in the present moment, is produced and practiced through situated human action, and it circulates across social and national borders. This means that "a culture" cannot be simply and unproblematically attributed to "a society" nor restricted to some clearly-bounded territory.

See Chapter 3

Tylor, E. B. 1958 [1871]. *Primitive Culture*. New York: Harper Torchbooks.

THE ANTHROPOLOGY OF APPRENTICESHIP

Culture is learned

Culture is not something in our genes or brain or blood or any other aspect of our body. No one is born with a particular language or religion or gender role or political persuasion or occupational skill. Neither is any particular language or religion determined in any way by human biology. The evidence for this is simple: Any human baby, given the experience, can potentially speak any language, believe any religion, or master any skill (for example, throw a spear, play a guitar, program a computer). Culture is not "in" humans in the sense that skin color, eye color, blood type, or height is "in" humans.

So, if culture is not "inside" the individual at birth, where is it? The obvious answer is "outside" the individual. Culture, at the moment of birth, is what is going on around the individual, what the people in his/her social environment are doing. Think of culture as a great, ongoing conversation (which to a large extent it is). When a person is born, the conversation is already in progress. The new member does not create it and is not initially capable of it. Gradually, s/he begins to participate, haltingly and imperfectly. Eventually, the person becomes competent and joins the conversation. Maybe in small or large ways s/he alters the content or direction of the conversation, adding new words or ideas. Then, ultimately, each individual leaves the conversation for good. However, during his/her time, the person "kept it going." Moreover, each individual served as part of the social environment for members born later, who experienced what the individuals in the group did and said and who learned to be competent and full participants in their turn, they too keeping the conversation going—maybe in old channels, maybe in new ones.

Humans, then, are not born with a culture, but acquire one. That is easy to say, but not so simple to grasp. What does it mean to acquire a culture? What process takes place from the learner's point of view—and from the teachers'? Anthropologists most often call it **enculturation**, although it is also known as **socialization**. Basically, enculturation or socialization is the process by which a person masters his/her culture, ordinarily as a child.

While culture is not "in" humans at birth, it is "in" humans by the time they reach maturity. That is, culture "gets in" over time and by some means.

Until recently, many scholars thought that the means was a straight-forward process of observation, imitation, and reward and punishment. However, this account is insufficient. What humans appear to do is observe behavior, surely, and not simply imitate it, but rather somehow actively extract meaning from it, derive the rules or principles by which good language or good behavior is produced. In other words, culture-learners are not passive recipients of culture, but active constructors of their own cultural lessons. Clearly, adults do not model every possible behavior for a child, nor do they explicitly describe every rule and principle; the adults do not have the time, and often they do not know the principles or "grammar" of their own culture. Instead, they provide an environment in which and from which children actively "learn." In other words, to paraphrase Hans Freudenthal (1973), enculturation consists of a **guided reinvention of culture**. New humans must essentially reconstruct culture for themselves from their experiences, with of course the assistance and guidance of fully-competent members of the group, who correct "mistakes."

The case of Victor and other so-called "feral" children suggests that culture is not an option, a superficial extra for a human like a coat that can be

IMAGE 2.1 Feral children.

Guided reinvention of culture

the process by which individuals, ordinarily children, acquire ideas, concepts, and skills actively by observing the behavior of others, extracting meanings and rules, and testing those meanings and rules in social situations; fully competent members "guide" the learning by providing models of behavior and correction for inappropriate behaviors

Enculturation

the process by which a person learns or acquires his/her culture, usually as a child. Also known as *socialization*

Socialization

from an anthropological point of view, a synonym for *enculturation*

See Chapter 5

BOX 2.1   LIVING WITHOUT CULTURE—THE "WILD BOY OF AVEYRON"

What would a human being be like without culture? In 1797 a boy was seen running, naked and on all fours, alone through the French forest. In 1799 he was captured and brought to Paris for observation and training. The boy, eventually named Victor, was described by Pierre-Joseph Bonnaterre, who, like others at the time, knew that he had come across something unique and important. In his report (Lane, 1977: 35–54), Bonnaterre claimed that, while Victor did not in fact walk on all fours, he also did not walk normally and "steadily," but rather rocked "from one side to the other" and that he never seemed to tire, no matter how long he ran. The boy's senses were "more like an animal than a man"; his senses of smell and taste were the most developed, the observer reasoned, because Victor would sniff foods before deciding what to eat or refuse. He seemed indifferent to cold. He had no language at all, making only "cries and inarticulate sounds." "His expressive sounds, rarely emitted unless he is emotional, are rather noisy, especially those of anger and displeasure; when joyful, he laughs heartily; when content, he makes a murmuring sound, a kind of grunting. He does not utter raucous or frightening cries; almost all of them are guttural and depend only slightly on the movement of the tongue." He was an intelligent child: Presented with a mirror, "he looked immediately behind it, thinking to find there the child whose image he perceived." However, he lacked "conventional" knowledge or morality: "While not wicked, he is not good, for he is unaware of both." He showed no glimmer of a religious or spiritual nature. Emotionally, he displayed excitement and agitation and anger, but not love. "He loves no one; he is attached to no one; and if he shows some preference for his caretaker, it is an expression of need and not the sentiment of gratitude: he follows the man because the latter is concerned with satisfying his needs and satiating his appetites."

put on or off at will and without consequence. The American anthropologist Clifford Geertz insisted that culture is *necessary to our humanity*: Humans at birth are "incomplete or unfinished animals who complete or finish ourselves through culture—and not through culture in general but through highly particular forms of it" (1973: 49). Other beings come more or less ready-made with a set of instincts that suffice for them, although often not quite as completely as we think: Predators like lions and birds of prey can and must learn how to hunt, and primates like monkeys and apes can and must learn how to parent. So humankind is not the only species that depends on learning to complete its behavioral possibilities; humans just depend more totally and urgently on this learning.

Culture is shared

Since culture is learned, it clearly cannot be a trait or possession of only one individual. Culture is "outside" the individual before it is "inside," and so its location is within the community that "has" it or "does" it. Such a community we call a **society**, that is, a group of humans who live in relative proximity to each other, are more likely to marry each other than members of different groups, and share a set of ideas and behaviors. Culture, then, becomes the learned and shared ways of thinking, feeling, and behaving of the societal group.

It is not quite so simple, though. Surely, an individual can originate something—a new behavior, a new word, a new style, a new invention, a new religion—that becomes culture; an individual can also be the last person to use some word or style or religion. Surely too, any item of culture need not be *completely* shared within a society to qualify as culture. "Cultural" does not mean "shared by one hundred percent of a society." But if not one hundred percent, what is the quantitative cutoff? Perhaps culture is not exactly a quantitative thing. Ralph Linton (1936: 272–274) suggested that culture resides in a variety of "modes" or "degrees" of shared-ness. Or rather, culture may not be so much shared as *transmitted and distributed*. Some individuals and

Society
a group of humans who live in relative proximity to each other, tend to marry each other more than people outside the group, and share a set of beliefs and behaviors

Geertz, Clifford. 1973. *The Interpretation of Cultures*. New York: Basic Books.

See Chapter 15

FIGURE 2.1 Ralph Linton's modes of cultural distribution

Universals ←—→ Alternatives ←—→ Specialties ←—→ Individual Peculiarities

subgroups in a society may have part of it—possess certain knowledge or skill—while others have other parts. Yet it is still culture if it is acquired through social experience.

Linton used the term "universals" to designate those things that all or the vast majority of a society know or do in roughly the same way; a common language may be an example. "Alternatives" refer to things that some individuals or subgroups know or do in one way but other individuals or subgroups know or do in another way; different religions or cuisines within a society would qualify. Even less widely shared, "specialties" are things that some individuals or subgroups know or do while others do not (playing the guitar, for instance, is learned but is not learned by everyone). Finally, some capabilities and habits are very narrowly distributed; such "individual peculiarities" may be practiced by one person or at most a small number of people. Some members of the group may even judge such practices—and the people who practice them—as "abnormal," yet they are still cultural.

One important angle on cultural knowledge and skill is the existence of "expert knowledge." Priests usually know a lot more about religion than laypeople do, and professional chefs are able to cook more and better than amateurs. Further, Western societies are accustomed to the notion that cultural knowledge and skill is public and available to all. However, not every society holds this view. Knowledge or skill is often exclusive to a subgroup, a particular category of people, or even a single individual; sometimes it is actually secret. In many religions there is the "popular" version of doctrines or rituals and the "esoteric" version for the worthy or the fully initiated. Among Australian Aboriginal societies, knowledge is socially distributed. First of all, there is discrete male knowledge and female knowledge. Some aspects of religion are public and open to all, but some are highly closed, to the point of death for revealing them. The secrets of male ritual practices are not only limited to men, but to adult circumcised men. The secrets of women are likewise limited to fully initiated women. Of course, such knowledge is also stratified by age: Young people will not and cannot possess it all, and they

will achieve greater and greater "sharing" as they mature and prove their ability and worthiness. Finally, even knowledge that one is qualified to "hear," one may not be qualified to "speak" or perform (like painting certain images or doing certain dances). Some knowledge is virtually private property, and no one but the rightful owner may perform it or transmit it. Certainly it must be transmitted if it is to endure, but only the owner may confer rights on others to perform it. Accordingly, no man or woman would be allowed to possess all the knowledge and skill of the society, even if s/he could potentially remember and master it all (see e.g. Bell, 1993; Dussart, 2000; Keen, 1994; Morphy, 1991).

Society then—especially a society of greater size and complexity—will consist of subgroups with their own distinct knowledge, skills, beliefs, values, norms, and such. In traditional Plains Indians societies like the Cheyenne, various named warrior associations had their own traditions and symbols and interests (Hoebel, 1960). In modern Western societies there are many **subcultures** and even **countercultures** that vary from—often deviate from—each other and the "mainstream" culture. Certainly, an anthropologist would not want to study only tattooed and pierced skateboarders to learn about American or Canadian culture, but neither would s/he want to ignore them. They would represent one "tributary" or "rivulet" or "current" in the cultural stream—one that belongs to the culture as much as any and sheds light on it like all the others.

Culture is symbolic

Earlier we likened culture to a conversation. The analogy immediately suggests language; however, not all human communication is linguistic, and not all language is verbal (hearing-impaired people have rich manual languages such as American Sign Language). What is really interesting and important about language in particular, and culture in general, is that it is a set of meanings based on the human capability and need to create and assign meaning.

Subculture

a group or subset within a society that is distinguished by some unique aspects of its behavior (such as clothing styles, linguistic usages, or beliefs and values)

Counterculture

a group or subset within a society that more or less intentionally adopts behaviors, beliefs, or practices that are at odds with or opposed to the mainstream of society

IMAGE 2.2 Culture is composed of symbols, like these Australian Aboriginal artworks.

Humans are beings who can and must "mean." No doubt, other beings also "mean" sometimes. When a cat snarls and hisses, it means something. However, a cat apparently does not have to learn to snarl and hiss, nor do different cats in different places snarl and hiss differently. Their gestures are natural or instinctive. And when a fire gives off smoke, the smoke means that there is fire below, but the fire hardly has an intention to mean. The meaning is natural and objective, directly connected to the event that causes it.

Symbols are things with meaning too. However, unlike the smoke of a fire or the hiss of a cat, the meaning of a symbol is added on, "bestowed upon it by those who use it," and this meaning "is in no instance derived from or determined by properties intrinsic in its physical form" (L. White, 1940: 453). That is, a symbol's meaning is *arbitrary and conventional*, not immediate, natural, or necessary. As a symbol, the sound "dog" represents or means the familiar domesticated animal. However, the symbol does not sound like a dog or look like a dog. There is no obvious or objective connection between the sound and the creature. The proof of this is that different societies use different verbal symbols for the same creature—*chien* in French, *Hund* in German, *perro* in Spanish, *maliki* in Warlpiri, and so on. Any of these symbols equally suffices, as long as users know the symbol and know that others know it. Similarly, a shake of

the head can mean "yes" in one culture and "no" in another—and nothing at all in a third.

Certainly in many cases there is a contingent relationship between the symbol and its meaning. The cross as a symbol for Christianity is not utterly arbitrary, but it is not the necessary or only possible symbol, nor was it the first. Even more importantly, the cross *does not always* mean Christianity: Other societies have used cross-like designs without "meaning" Christianity. Geertz called a symbol a "vehicle for a conception" (1973: 91), but what precise conception is loaded into what precise vehicle depends on the society and even the historical moment of that society. A dramatic example is the swastika, a symbol with very potent meaning for most modern Western people. However, this ancient symbol has not always been associated with Nazism and Hitler; long before National Socialism was imagined, South Asians and some Native Americans used a similar design to convey radically different thoughts.

Culture, thus, is a great meaning system—a "web of significance" in which we are suspended, as Geertz said (5). The symbols of a culture act like a lens, shaping the reality that is refracted through them. No person experiences the natural or social world except through the symbol-lens of culture, which no doubt affects how different peoples perceive and respond to their world.

Symbol

an object, gesture, sound, or image that "stands for" some other idea or concept or object; something that has "meaning," particularly when the meaning is arbitrary and conventional and thus culturally relative

Culture is integrated

Tylor opened his definition of culture by calling it a "complex whole." Any particular culture, that is to say, is not a single item or a homogeneous mass. Neither is it a jumble of loose parts. Rather, a culture is a system composed of many elements in some structural interrelation. Some of the early analogies for culture were highly "organismic," depicting culture as an organism with internal organs and organ systems. Although the metaphor goes a bit too far, it may be useful. Each part or domain of a culture, like each organ in a body, has its own particular function, its own job to do, even as each part contributes to the functioning of the whole. This position is known as **functionalism**. As a model it provides a way to conceptualize culture—internally differentiated, multiply functional, and structured. The specific structure in any particular culture may differ from another, but a structure of some sort is always present. That is, culture is a (loose) system—or better yet, a set of systems, a system of systems. As a research method this gives anthropologists something to look at or for. Researchers can aim to identify the various parts, examine their separate functions or contributions, and relate them to the functioning of the whole.

Cultural anthropology has analyzed cultural systems into four rough areas of functionality. This does not mean necessarily that all cultures have equally articulated and formalized institutions of all four kinds, but it does mean that all cultures have

four kinds of functions that must and will be performed by some means. These areas of functionality or "domains" of culture include economics, kinship, politics, and religion. One way to visualize them and their interconnections is as four circles within the larger circle of culture.

Each domain is analytically distinct, but each is integrated with every other just as the parts of a car or the organs of a body are interrelated. In fact, the domains actually overlap each other, such that sharp lines between them cannot be drawn. No matter where cultural anthropology starts its research and analysis, it will be unavoidably drawn into consideration of all of the other domains. Even more importantly, the addition, removal, or modification of a part can and often will have consequences for the functioning of the other parts and the whole—often unforeseen and undesired consequences.

Culture is an adaptation

Cultures and their societies do not float in space. Every society and its culture exists in a specific physical context, an environment. That environment may be desert or jungle, volcanic island or arctic tundra, but each presents unique practical challenges and opportunities. There may be too little water or too much, certain kinds of plants and animals, harsh and unpredictable or gentle and consistent climates, and so on. Most living species

Functionalism
the method, and eventually the theory, that a cultural trait can be investigated for the contribution it makes to the survival of individual humans, the operation of other cultural items, or the culture as a whole

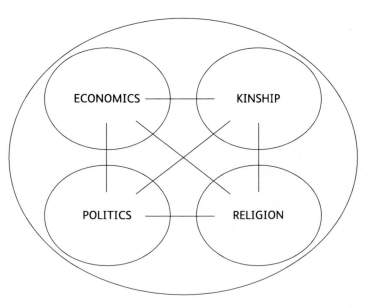

FIGURE 2.2 A model of cultural integration

are highly specialized to live in a particular environment; even our primate cousins tend to need forest habitats to survive. Humans, on the other hand, are the most non-specialized, the most "generalized" of beings (see below). Because humans come with so little genetic or instinctive preprogramming (as Geertz stated), humans can be culturally programmed in nearly infinite ways. More than for any other species, there are many ways to be human.

The adaptive power of human culture is a quantum leap above physical or genetic adaptation. Physical adaptation is slow; cultural adaptation is fast. Physical adaptation is "chance" or random— that is, a species cannot will itself to have thicker fur or a bigger brain. Cultural adaptation is intentional and comparatively "free"—that is, humans can innovate where they perceive a need. Anthropologists must not overestimate the creativity of humans: Most people in most places and times have been much more imitative than inventive. Still, the overall creativity of humans makes it possible and inevitable that there will be many diverse human lifeways. Finally, cultural adaptations and inventions are simple to transmit across group boundaries and require nothing more than social interaction.

So, the diagram of culture above should be set within some environmental context. Perhaps we should draw another larger circle that encloses the circle of culture. Then, we can relate not only the domains of culture to each other, but each of them and the cultural whole to its environmental setting. Again, without major inputs of energy and technology, the environment will be a limiting and shaping factor on how the society works, organizes itself, and even relates to the natural and supernatural world. In a word, culture is how humans get along in and with the external world.

As with so many claims, anthropologists must be cautious about the adaptive quality of culture. For one thing, human societies are not always in harmony with their environments. It is something of a romantic fallacy to assert that pre-modern societies lived in perfect ecological balance, and it is clearly impossible to think that modern industrial ones do. Australian Aboriginal hunters burned the desert flora, and Easter Islanders stripped their homeland bare. For another, when societies migrate, as they often do, they bring with them practices and values that may have been adaptive in the former environment but are less adapted to the new one; over time, they may conform themselves more to the requirements of their new location but not always or quickly enough. Finally, it cannot be said that culture is always advantageous for all of its members. Societies have engaged in activities from war to slavery to human sacrifice to the extermination of twins that were certainly not beneficial to the victims of such behaviors. The perpetrators of these actions may have felt that the actions were justified, even necessary (as in Aztec sacrifice, to keep the sun alive and strong), but that does not mean that the actions were good for all involved. In short, the "freedom" of humans enables us to engage in activities that are not always rational or healthful.

Culture is produced, practiced, and circulated

Too often, social scientists and the public have labored under a static view of culture—static historically as in fixed and unchanging (i.e. "traditional") and static geographically as in tied and limited to one local group or society. Members of a society tended then to seem like passive recipients of a discrete and immutable culture, which we realize from our discussion of the Chinese *tangzhuang* in Chapter 1 to be untrue. Individuals and groups do not so much *have* culture as *do* culture, or as Tim Ingold has advised, it "might be more realistic, then, to say that people *live culturally* rather than they *live in cultures*" (1999: 334)—that is, we might consider treating "culture" as a verb or an adverb instead of a noun.

If we reconceive culture as a verb, a process, then humans—individually and even more so collectively, in groups, organization, corporations, governments, and such—are easily seen as active in producing and reproducing aspects of culture. This is most evident in the realm of arts, which are obviously produced, usually by a single person or small collection of people; however, it is equally relevant to science, technology, language, law, and religion—indeed, all areas of culture. These production processes also link our descriptions of culture to processes of media and culture-making and culture-disseminating technologies (like recording, publishing, broadcasting, etc.), of markets (for the sale and purchase of cultural products), and of power (in terms of who owns or dominates these media, machines, and markets). Anthropologists have examined, for example, the uses of cinema in Peru (Himpele, 2008) and India (Velayutham, 2008), radio among the Ojibwe of Canada (Valentine, 1995), and television in Aboriginal Australia (Deger, 2006; Michaels, 1986), among many others.

The production and reproduction of culture has consequently shifted focus away from traditions and rules to, as already mentioned, the *practice* of culture; that is, culture is presently seen less as a fixed body of knowledge or as a set of coercive rules than as socially-structured action. Geertz was one of the first to suggest that culture is best understood not as abstract ideas or as concrete behaviors but "as a set of control mechanisms—plans, recipes, rules, instructions (what computer engineers call 'programs')—for the governing of behavior" (1973: 44). In this view, human activity and the groups and institutions that emerge from it are not simple enactments of cultural rules, but neither are they random products of free individuals. Rather, according to Pierre Bourdieu (1977), who attempted to formulate a theory of practice, human behavior is an outcome of predispositions, strategies, and skills—acquired capabilities and habits, in Tylor's formulation—which are produced in the individual by culture and enculturation and then reproduced through the culturally-informed and culturally-situated action of the individual.

Cultural anthropology has been strongly influenced by the practice and production perspectives, which are intimately linked. Together they offer to transcend oppositions like individual/culture and action/structure. The other common dualism is local/global, which is transcended by the notions of cultural circulation and glocalization. Indisputably, an item of culture (a work of art, a piece of technology, a clothing style, a word, a song, a religion, etc.) is not contained within the boundaries of a particular society. Culture circulates within a society—between regions, classes, generations, and so on—and between societies. Culture is mobile, along chains of migration and chains of exchange, and this is no recent fact: In pre-contact Australia, societies traded not only materials like stone and objects like axes, but entire religious complexes (sets of rituals, myths, songs, and dances) and kinship systems. In the modern globalized

world, the paths of exchange are only extended and accelerated, so that one finds blue jeans and rock'n'roll music in non-Western societies, and sushi and Buddhism in the U.S. and Europe. Culture flows, blending with or beating against elements already in place, and cultural anthropology has discovered that it must go with the cultural flow.

Culture is in places and things

The contemporary emphasis on production and circulation of culture, together with the recognition of culture as *skill* in addition to knowledge, has contributed to the recognition of the importance of physical objects as part of the cultural process. Humans do not live in an immaterial world of pure ideas; rather, we are embodied persons ourselves and interact with each other's bodies—and with material things—in the course of social action. Accordingly, cultural anthropology has increasingly appreciated the "materiality," the "thingness" or physical presence and qualities of objects (including human bodies, alive or, in the case of mummies, deceased) in society. There are even entire academic journals dedicated to the topic, such as *Journal of Material Culture* and *Material Religion: The Journal of Objects, Art and Belief*.

Material things become important in culture not merely for the ideas or meanings they convey, but for their literal visceral qualities. The very sensuous feel of a substance can suggest cultural ideas and experiences, as Anne Meneley finds in her study of the social role of olive oil in Palestinian culture. Olive oil, like other fats, is distinctive "in its capacity to absorb and its capacity to penetrate" (2014: 19); the oil is then believed to be effective at absorbing and conferring spiritual power, which is only enhanced by its "illuminating" quality when it is burned. Due to other capacities—to lubricate, to cleanse, to seal and preserve, and to strengthen—olive oil is perceived "as itself intimately bound up with the biological and social reproduction of Palestinian households and families and healthful, strong bodies" (23). Olive trees themselves "are often spoken of as kin" (23).

Humans of course make all sorts of objects (artifacts, clothing, tools, houses, statues and icons, and what have you), but once made, these objects have a sort of life of their own, as Arjun Appadurai's

Bourdieu, Pierre. 1977. *Outline of a Theory of Practice*. Cambridge: Cambridge University Press.

See Chapter 11

BOX 2.2   ANIMALS, PERSONS, AND MORAL SUBSTANCES AMONG THE MUINANE

The Muinane of the Colombian Amazon assert that humans are "intrinsically moral" (Londono Sulkin, 2012: 48), tending toward "loving care, a sense of purpose, coolness or calm equanimity, respect, and good humor" (30). Muinane morality is fundamentally about body and more generally about substance; people are "alive, aware, articulate, and capable of competent, moral, and sociable action in part because of 'speeches' and 'breaths' that constituted their bodies and resonated inside them" (31). The moral person or body is built by these multiple speeches and breaths from interaction, including interaction with the physical world. Each plant, animal, and other substance has its own speech and breath. Tobacco is perhaps the most moral of substances, giving humans "proper thoughts/emotions and the capacity to learn, remember, and discern" (96). Both male and female bodies consist of tobacco juice, but only men can trade and share tobacco. Coca is only consumed by adult men and is closely associated with morality in its cultivation, preparation, and consumption. Women's bodies and morality, by contrast, are associated with and composed of manioc, chilies, and cool herbs. The connection between bodies, substances, and morality in Muinane culture can be traced to two ideas. First, different people have different substances—even different tobaccos—that breed different behaviors in them. Second, animals are said to be essentially immoral, ignoring the social and sexual norms of humans. Animal species have their own speeches and breaths, even their own tobaccos, but if an animal speech, breath, tobacco invades a human, immoral behavior results. Thus, "it was not rare for people to claim that a man who misbehaved had a jaguar inside, or that he spoke the speech of a jaguar" (55). In short, the Muinane assert that "hot speeches or breaths ensuing from animals' tobaccos and other substances altered people's sensibilities so much that they did not perceive or act as real people" (50)—that is, as moral people.

Biocultural
the mutual interaction between physical/biological and behavioral/cultural factors, in which physical traits make certain behaviors possible, and behavior feeds back to influence physical traits

Appadurai, Arjun, Ed. 1986. *The Social Life of Things: Commodities in Cultural Perspective*. Cambridge and New York: Cambridge University Press.

THE NEURAL BASIS OF CULTURE

Primate
the term for the classification of mammals, including prosimians, monkeys, apes, and humans, that share a collection of physical characteristics including a distinct tooth pattern, five-fingered hands, a tendency toward erectness of the spine, large eyes and good vision, and a relatively large brain in relation to body weight, among others

(1986) *The Social Life of Things* suggests. In a real way, humans and objects interact or participate together in society, material things often possessing a "career" or "biography" and *personal* qualities of their own. Catherine Allerton (2013) describes how the Manggarai of Indonesia attribute personhood to their houses and to their land: People speak of "what the land wants" and interact with it as an other-than-human person.

THE BIOCULTURAL BASIS OF HUMAN BEHAVIOR

The diversity of human behavior proves that this behavior is not programmed in the human body in any precise way. However, the fact that all humans can and must learn culture, and that no other beings do or can learn culture fully, means that there is something about human beings that makes culture possible and necessary. Culture is founded on biological characteristics, which, while they do not determine behavior in detail, set the general outlines for the kinds of behavior that humans can and must perform. This reciprocal relationship between biology and culture makes humans **biocultural** beings—not merely biological or merely cultural, but both.

The distinctive human physical traits are not uniquely human but are generally shared by the category known as **primates**, which includes apes like the chimpanzee and gorilla, monkeys of various kinds, and the most "primitive" of primates classified as prosimians. Primates are grouped together in the first place on the basis of these common characteristics, such as:

- hands with five fingers and (usually) fingernails instead of claws, with an opposable thumb that makes grasping possible. The fingers have sensitive tactile pads on the tips, and the hands and feet (which are also "grasping" in orangutans) come at the end of very flexible limbs capable of a wide range of motion.

■ teeth that are varied and generalized, with cutting teeth in the front and grinding teeth in the back. There is even a regular pattern of teeth, consisting of two incisors, one canine, two premolars, and two or three molars on each side, top and bottom. The variety of teeth makes a varied and omnivorous diet possible.

■ large brains relative to body weight, with special development of the frontal and back areas. There is also an emphasis of eyes over noses on the face. Vision is acute, while the sense of smell is weaker. The result is a flattened face with large eyes.

Erectness

the tendency to have an upright posture based on a spine that is vertical rather than parallel to the ground

■ a tendency toward spinal **erectness**, with the head on top of rather than in front of the spine. This gives primates a relatively upright posture and a tendency toward **bipedalism**, or walking on two feet.

Bipedalism

the ability and tendency to walk on two feet

■ a relatively long lifespan, with a long period of immaturity or "childhood," during which youths are highly dependent on and very interactive with parents as well as other members of the group.

This constellation of traits allows for freedom or openness of behavior, an adaptability which most other species lack; primates are not highly physically specialized for any single way of life, which means that they—and we—are capable of diverse ways of life. The biocultural approach suggests not only that human physical characteristics make human culture possible, but that *culture is not an "all or nothing" phenomenon.* Humans have a great deal of culture, but other species may have some measure of it too, depending on how human-like their bodies are.

Beings with primate bodies are prone to engage in primate behaviors. The most fundamental primate behavior is social living. Other animals (and even plants) live in groups, but social groups are distinguished by their internal diversity of rules and roles—that is, different parts to play or "kinds of individuals" to be. One particularly clear and important expression of social behavior is

BOX 2.3 PRIMATE CULTURE

In 1949, Japanese scientists began observing a troupe of small monkeys called macaques on the Japanese island of Koshima and providing them with food. In 1953, one young female, whom the researchers named Imo, was seen carrying a sweet potato to a stream where she rubbed it in the fresh water. On subsequent trips to the stream, she waded deeper into the water and held the food with one hand while washing it with the other. Within three months, three other individuals copied the behavior, and after five years, seventy-five percent of the younger members of the group were habitual potato-washers. Only the old males did not adopt the behavior. But sweet potatoes are a big food that allowed them to eat fast and flee. So observers decided to give them small foods like wheat or rice, which the macaques would have to laboriously pick out of the sand. Imo once again outsmarted the scientists, inventing a new behavior by scooping a handful of sand and grains and tossing it in the water, skimming the food off of the surface. This new solution also spread among most members of the group (Kawai, 1965). No other population of macaques had ever been observed engaging in this behavior. What researchers witnessed was the innovation, learning, and sharing of a new behavior as an adaptation to a novel circumstance—the key qualities of culture. Since then, scientists in the field have noted many more "cultural" behaviors, such as tool use and tool making, and even some that appear to be "symbolic." For instance, in 1993 a young male chimpanzee dubbed Kakama moved through the forest in Uganda with his mother, clutching a small log. At first he handled it the way a female handles a baby. He went to considerable trouble to bring the log along as they traveled, eventually stopping to build a nest for it in the branches. Over the course of two hours, Kakama took the log everywhere he went, carrying it on his back or hip. When it fell to the forest floor, he retrieved it. Wrangham and Peterson concluded that they "had just watched a young male chimpanzee invent and then play with a doll" (1996: 254–255).

dominance or hierarchy, in which some individuals have more status or social power than others. This can of course be based on sheer strength, but typically is not. Such factors as age, sex (males are often but not always dominant), family relations, and "alliances" with other individuals can all enhance status and the likelihood of achieving leadership and enjoying its benefits, such as more and better food and mates. Indeed, as Frans de Waal's chimp "ethnography" *Chimpanzee Politics* (1998) suggests, primates engage in distinctly "political" behavior when they are seeking or exercising power. There is even data to support the conclusion that sex roles in some primate societies are learned. Hamadryas baboons, for instance, live in male-dominated harems, while savannah baboons do not. When Hans Kummer (1995) transplanted Hamadryas females into savannah troops, the females initially acted submissive, only to discover that the males did not herd and bite them, and they quickly became as "free" as native female savannah baboons; on the other hand, freedom-loving savannah females placed in Hamadryas troops were bitten and herded by males and eventually "learned their place," although they still remained rebellious and hard to control.

There is reason to believe that primates not only enjoy being social but *need to be* social. The famous primatologist Robert Yerkes went so far as to claim that one primate is no primate at all (Lorenz, 1963: 100). A series of experiments by Harry Harlow (1959) supports this position. He raised baby rhesus monkeys in isolation from other animals. The result was often a "neurotic" monkey who cringed in the corner of his cage and even rocked back and forth the way some disturbed humans do. When introduced to other monkeys, they tended to respond with either fear or aggression, but hardly ever interacted successfully. And if an isolated female became a mother (difficult enough, since mating behavior itself appears to be learned), she usually had little or no idea what to do with the infant; she would either be neglectful or actually aggressive toward it, often ending in its death.

Non-human primates evince a range of other behaviors that are familiar and similar to humans. Among these behaviors are:

Aggression and territoriality. Primates tend to defend a specific territory or "home range" within which they move about but generally remain. Essentially, each local group within the species has its "borders" it patrols and polices. Other local groups of the same species that infiltrate these borders may encounter aggressive resistance. An important aspect of primate aggression is intergroup or intraspecies aggressive behavior (IAB), which is defined as aggressive or violent interactions between two or more spatially separate, distinct, and identifiable groups by individuals acting as members or representatives of such groups. Johan van der Dennen (2002) identified sixty-four species practicing IAB, of which fifty-four were primates. Most such aggression is "ritualized" and not fatal. Individuals will "display" with threatening gestures or sounds and perhaps tussle for a few moments until one realizes he is the loser of the encounter and runs away or displays submissive behavior, which ends the face-off. However, not all aggression concludes so peacefully, and the more human-like the primate, the more human-like the aggression. Jane Goodall, the pioneering primatologist who has observed chimps in the wild since the 1970s, reported what could only be called a war between two groups of chimps that had recently split apart. Over a period of years, the larger group hunted down the smaller splinter group and killed the males and killed or captured the females until the latter group was exterminated. She even calculated that approximately thirty percent of male chimp deaths were due to violence (Goodall, 1986).

Communication and social interaction. While all animals communicate, primate communication is also unique in many regards. For one, primates communicate visually much more than other species, given their evolved vision. When a primate encounters a novel situation, it explores the situation by *looking* rather than smelling. Primates also interact with each other and their world by touch more than most species, employing the sensitive pads on their fingers. One classic primate behavior is grooming by running fingers through each other's hair. This is no doubt both hygienic and pleasurable, but it also has a social component: grooming shows and establishes affiliation, even affection. Friends groom each other, adults groom infants, and males groom females as part of courtship. Grooming behavior indicates or creates social ordering: Lower-ranking individuals tend to

Dominance
the social relationship in which certain individuals have higher prestige or power in the group, allowing them to enjoy more or better resources as well as the deference of lower-ranked members

Hierarchy
see *dominance*

de Waal, Frans. 1998 [1982]. *Chimpanzee Politics: Power and Sex among Apes*, revised edition. Baltimore: Johns Hopkins University Press.

Goodall, Jane. 1986. *The Chimpanzees of Gombe: Patterns of Behavior.* Cambridge, MA: Harvard University Press.

groom more dominant ones, unless the dominant one is seeking allies, in which case dominant ones may groom subordinates to win their favor. Chimps in particular will put their arms around others or pat them on the back to comfort them. They even appear to hold or shake hands and kiss hands, especially as an introduction between strangers. Bonobo or pygmy chimps are famous for their much more sexual touching which has little or nothing to do with reproduction; this touching even takes place within the same sex. Finally, primates communicate orally or with sound. Apes have even been shown experimentally to communicate linguistically (that is, to use language symbols like sign language or meaningful shapes and objects).

Eating and hunting meat. It was believed prior to the 1970s that chimpanzees were primarily vegetarian and that they might occasionally eat a small animal or bird but not deliberately and systematically kill larger animals for meat. However, as Goodall witnessed, they not only eat and relish meat but also hunt for meat. In particular, they hunt monkeys, which are not easy to catch for the larger and more terrestrial chimps. Hunting such prey

PRIMATE MORALITY?

requires cooperation and coordination, foresight and planning. The hunters usually divide the assignment between those who will give chase through the branches and those who will pursue along the ground below. Together they try to steer the prey to a congenial spot for capture. A successful hunt is often followed by sharing or "politicking" with the resultant meat. Hunters may bring meat back to share with females and young, and they may share it with (or steal it from) other males to form or secure alliances. Successful males may occasionally keep all their catch to themselves, but the dietary advantage of such behavior is set against the social disadvantage of the selfish and unfriendly aspect of it.

Tool use and production. For a long time, it was supposed that humans are the only primates that use tools; in fact, the accepted definition of human was based on tool use. A few species here and there appeared to use tool-like objects as well, including otters that bash open mollusks with a stone, but these are not full tools. A tool is a natural object that is not only used, but is made or modified for use to accomplish some task that the body cannot do or cannot do as effectively. So, when we smash a can

IMAGE 2.3 Chimpanzees learn to use twigs or grass stems to "fish" for termites, an example of non-human culture.

of beans with a rock to open it, that is tool-like, but when we sharpen the rock to make a cutting edge for slicing open a dead zebra, we are making a true tool. Goodall was the first to document that chimps use and make simple tools. Chimps like to eat termites, but termites retreat inside their hard hills. Another animal would wait patiently or dig or try to insert a claw or tooth into the hole—that is, use its body—but chimps will search for a good-sized and -shaped branch or stem, trim and fashion it just so, and stick it into the hole, pulling it and the clinging termites out. This kind of "fishing" behavior requires not only mental skills like imagination and foresight, but a dexterous and grasping hand. Since that time, primatologists have watched chimps and a few other primates using stones or sticks to hammer nuts, leaves to scoop water, and chewed leaves to soak up juices from their meat. Even more interestingly, they have noticed regional diversity within a given species of primate; that is, chimps in one location have been seen learning and practicing one set of behaviors, while members of the same species in other locations have their own distinct local cultures. In the laboratory, chimps have shown powerful cognitive abilities in using and combining objects to achieve goals (like stacking boxes to reach bananas hanging from the ceiling or using keys to unlock chests with food inside). There is little doubt that the more we give primates to think about and do, the more they will surprise us with their intelligence and ability.

Finally, just as culture as a general phenomenon or capability is apparently not all-or-nothing,

neither is human culture in particular all-or-nothing. Rather, what we see in the fossil and archaeological record is that as humans developed into their present-day physical form, something like present-day culture gradually but inexorably emerged. For instance, the most ancient well-documented genus of pre-humans is called **Australopithecus**, which includes the famous species Australopithecus afarensis, known popularly as "Lucy." Living three to four million years ago, these pre-humans already had some key human traits like upright bipedal walking and smaller teeth, but also some primitive traits like a small brain (no larger than an ape's). There is no firm evidence that they made or used tools.

Around 2.5 million years ago, a new species, designated **Homo habilis**, commenced the category or genus called **Homo**, which would eventually include modern humans. This species, its descendants, and their key physical and behavioral characteristics are as follows:

Homo habilis. They possessed a larger brain than Australopithecus afarensis, up to half of modern size (600–700 cubic centimeters versus 1200–1400 for moderns). They showed the first firm evidence of stone tool use and manufacture, based on a simple stone chopper, called **Oldowan**, made by hammering one stone with another to produce a cutting edge.

Homo erectus. First appearing around 1.8 million years ago, **Homo erectus** is another advance in

Australopithecus
a genus of the category Hominid, closely related to and earlier than genus Homo

Homo habilis
an extinct human species that lived from over two million years ago until less than two million years ago. They are also known as the first stone tool makers.

Homo
the genus that contains the modern human species (Homo sapiens) as well as several other extinct human species

Oldowan
the earliest known stone tool technology, associated with Homo habilis and named for the location of its discovery, Olduvai Gorge in East Africa

Homo erectus
an extinct human species that lived from approximately 1.8 million years ago until a few hundred thousand years ago or perhaps even more recently

BOX 2.4   THE DISCOVERY OF ARDI

In 2009, a series of papers announced the oldest well-established hominid species (so far). Technically named Ardipithecus ramidus, but more affectionately known as "Ardi," this small female individual lived a million years before Lucy, approximately 4.4 million years ago. According to the principal investigator, Tim White (White et al., 2009), remains of Ardi were first found in 1994, but it took fully fifteen years to complete the analysis and to publish the results. Inhabiting present-day Ethiopia, Ardi had a small brain, no larger than a chimp's, but reduced incisors, a flatter face, and a less-prominent brow. Most significantly, the skeleton indicates bipedal walking: The pelvis is short and broad, like the human pelvis, and the spine is long and curved, also like humans. White and his collaborators conclude that Ardipithecus shows a compelling blend of pre-human and human-like traits and supports the interpretation that humans diverged from a hominid ancestor sometime around six or seven million years ago. Ardi became something of a media sensation, even getting its own PBS special.

brain size, reaching two-thirds or more of modern brain volume (1,000 cc). They were also the first species of fossil humans to migrate out of Africa, eventually reaching most of Eurasia (where they are popularly known as "Peking Man" and "Java man"). They developed a more sophisticated stone tool technology called **Acheulian** in which the entire surface of the stone was chipped to yield a symmetrical "bifacial" tool. They apparently used fire and may have also built rudimentary shelters.

Archaic Homo sapiens. By around 600,000 years ago, the first **Homo sapiens** appeared, although they were not quite our own modern humans. Their brains were equal to or larger than modern, and their bodies were similar enough to be placed in the same species. They lived in many parts of Eurasia, where they had regionally diverse behavior and, in some cases, probably language. The best-known of the archaic Homo sapiens populations is the **Neandertals**, a local group that inhabited Europe and the Middle East starting about 130,000 years ago. They had large bodies and brains, and their behavior was remarkably sophisticated. They made new and better tools, labeled **Mousterian**, which included a variety of implements specialized for particular purposes, with more "finishing" of the

tools. Most notably, there is evidence from various sites of intentional burials, suggesting some symbolic abilities and perhaps some beliefs about death and after death. Some anatomists conclude that they had the anatomy for speech.

Modern Homo sapiens (Anatomically Modern Humans). As long ago as 200,000 years, the first fully modern Homo sapiens appeared, almost certainly in Africa. They migrated to the rest of the world, displacing the Neandertals in Europe by 35–40,000 years ago. Their tools and culture were not initially more advanced than other species, but in the past 30,000 years, their—or our—cultural development has been rapid. Soon they were producing realistic paintings, often on cave walls, as well as carving and jewelry and other "arts." New "composite tools" (made of multiple parts, like an arrow or a spear) distinguished their technology, as well as fast-changing and regionally diverse technologies and cultures. No doubt they had fully functional languages and belief- and meaning-systems comparable to those found in any society today. Students of early modern humans agree that, if one of them could be brought to the present day, he or she would look like and learn to act like a normal modern human.

Acheulian

the stone tool technology associated with Homo erectus, which involves a more complex flaking of bifacial implements

Homo sapiens

the species name for modern humans

Neandertal

the species or subspecies of Homo that first appeared around 130,000 years ago and is associated with the cold climate of Europe. They became extinct in the last 35–40,000 years and are generally not regarded as direct human ancestors, although this interpretation is still somewhat controversial

Mousterian

the stone tool technology associated with Neandertals, first appearing less than 130,000 years ago

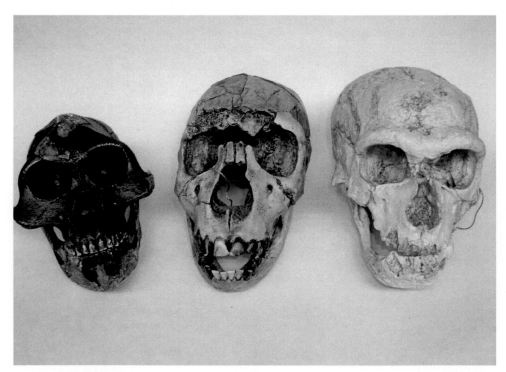

IMAGE 2.4 Hominid fossil skulls (from left to right): Australopithecus afarensis, Homo erectus, Neandertal.

STUDYING CULTURE: METHOD IN CULTURAL ANTHROPOLOGY

Our presentation of anthropology began by introducing its distinct questions, its distinct perspective, and its distinct set of terms and concepts. But in order to answer its questions, to put that perspective into action, and to employ those terms and concepts, cultural anthropology also needs a method. How exactly do cultural anthropologists go about answering their questions, in particular collecting the data they require to solve the problems they have put before themselves? The social sciences have a battery of tried-and-true data-collecting techniques. These include surveys, interviews, questionnaires, experiments, and of course analysis of the data that other social scientists have already collected. Cultural anthropology would be remiss to ignore these techniques. However, none of them, nor all of them in combination, are adequate to accomplish the goals of cultural anthropologists. Imagine, for example, that you wanted to learn about Nuer cattle-herding culture in Africa, or the Japanese tea ceremony. What would you do? You would probably first read every available book, watch every available movie, talk to every available researcher and traveler, that/who might provide some information. One profound limitation of this procedure is that you would not learn anything new; there would be no opportunity for original discovery.

Seeking new knowledge, you might design a survey or a questionnaire to probe the issues you want to understand. There being so few Nuer or Japanese nearby, you would have to send it to them by mail or email. You might find that very few receive mail or email, even fewer read it, and fewer still respond. Besides, they may not speak your language, and they definitely do not know who you are or why you are asking these strange and perhaps personal questions. Even if they did receive it and cared to respond, they might find the questions invasive, or they might be inclined to tell you what they think you want to hear or what makes them look good. It is possible you would not ask the right questions to begin with, and it is highly probable that you would not understand the information you received anyhow.

Or, to make the example even closer to home, imagine that a cultural anthropologist wanted to learn about the life of students at a college. The problems are roughly the same. Students at the college might not respond, or perhaps only the "good" ones will respond (giving a skewed sample). Knowing the researcher plans to publish the results, and that the findings may come back to haunt them, the students might lie or admit only the positive parts of their behavior. And the anthropologist still might not really understand the results that come back. In order to overcome the limitations of these techniques—whether in foreign or familiar contexts—a cultural anthropologist has only one real choice: go and live among the subjects.

Anthropology solves this problem with **fieldwork**. All sciences depend on some manner of fieldwork. Geologists go out and dig rocks. Paleontologists go out and excavate fossils. Marine biologists go out and observe ocean life. What they have in common is *going out*. Accordingly, anthropologists cannot complete their research in a library or classroom; a person can *study cultural anthropology* in the classroom (that is, what anthropologists have done and learned from it) but not *culture*. Culture is where the practitioners of that culture are.

So anthropologists go to the "field." They could take their surveys and questionnaires with them, recruit a sample of volunteers, and administer the tests to them. The researcher could get closer, perhaps get a house near the subjects and sit on the porch and watch them go by, perhaps even invite them to sit on the porch too. The researcher would see where the people are going and what they are doing, but would that necessarily provide any understanding of what is happening?

Cultural anthropologists have discovered that the only way to acquire a serious, deep understanding of the lives of other people is to place themselves as much as possible within those lives. This is known as **participant observation**. Participant observation is the truly unique and original aspect of cultural anthropology. Anthropologists go to live among the peoples they study, but more than that, they go to live *like* the peoples they study. No other social science does quite the same thing, although some have adopted the method on occasion. The first step in successful anthropological fieldwork is learning the local language. This is critical not only because most of the locals probably will not know the anthropologist's language, but because even if they do, their ideas and concepts likely cannot be

Fieldwork
the anthropological method of traveling to the society one wants to study and living there for a prolonged period of time to collect data first-hand

Participant observation
the anthropological field method in which we travel to the society we want to study and spend long periods of time there, not only watching, but joining in their culture as much as possible

Structured interview
a fieldwork method in
which the anthropologist
administers a prepared set
of questions to an
informant/consultant

Unstructured interview
a fieldwork method in
which the anthropologist
conducts a relatively free-
flowing conversation with
an informant/consultant,
either without prepared
questions or unconstrained
by these questions

Genealogy
kinship or "blood" and
"marriage" information
about a society

properly conveyed in another language. A language, like the cultural whole of which it is part, is a lens for seeing the world. Forcing the people to function in the anthropologist's language is forcing them to reshape, perhaps fatally distort, their thinking into something that is familiar to an outsider. There would be something—maybe something crucial— lost in translation. It is much better to learn their words, their concepts, and their realities. There are often no exact equivalents for their words and ideas in English or other foreign languages.

Learning the language is not only a necessary step, but a good method to earn one's way into the society and to spend time with them. An anthropologist will eventually want—and if lucky, be able—to visit with them, travel with them, work with them, even live with them. They are not coming to the anthropologist's world; the anthropologist is going to theirs. The goal is to eat their food, perform their tasks, partake of their rituals. In this way, cultural anthropology is the most intense and personal of the sciences. No other research demands such a commitment of one's life. An astronomer may spend every night for weeks peering through a telescope, but at least s/he goes home, takes a shower, and sleeps in his/her own bed. Anthropologists may not even have showers or beds where they do their studies. Often there is no going home for a long time. A typical fieldwork experience may take a year or more. And usually, a professional anthropologist goes back to the field periodically to see what new things have transpired, what s/he missed before, or simply what one cannot learn in such a "short time." Some anthropologists take their families with them, but most travel alone. Depending on how far away the society is, the anthropologist may not see friends or family during the entire period. The work can also be physically challenging—climate extremes, natural dangers, strange food, exotic diseases, few amenities, few or no facilities in the event of injury, even war. It can be lonely and isolating.

But if all goes well, the anthropologist slowly wins his/her way into the confidence and friendship of the people. S/he may even be adopted into a family, given a kinship name, and assigned local responsibilities. This is not easy to achieve or to perform. Generally the local people do not know the anthropologist when s/he first arrives. It would be like someone coming to your neighborhood,

knocking on your door, and asking to live in your house for a year or two. New people are always strangers first, friends later (if they are lucky). And anthropologists depend on that friendship— sometimes to keep them fed, always to keep them informed. An anthropological fieldworker needs at least a few good informants or consultants, people who will take the time and effort to share their culture. That sounds very scientific, but it is not. Informants or consultants are the people who like and trust the fieldworker well enough to want to take time from their busy lives to talk to the stranger, answer silly questions, and teach their ways. In an essential way, the informant or consultant is a teacher. Likewise, anthropologists in the field are students or apprentices, virtually children. Many local people consider anthropologists to be literally like children—petulant, demanding, prone to error (see e.g. Briggs (1970) for an unusually honest account of the foibles of fieldwork). The analogy is not bad: If anthropologists are like children, then anthropological fieldwork is like enculturation. The fieldworker is learning the culture from the inside.

Once in the field, there is a variety of activities that the researcher can conduct. S/he may still administer surveys and questionnaires. Interviews are a standard technique in the field, either in a **structured** (with the questions prepared in advance) or an **unstructured** (unplanned and free-flowing) format. It is always important to collect genealogical information, not only because anthropologists need to know who is related to whom and how, but because kinship and **genealogy** are so central to the organization of most societies. Commonly, anthropologists will collect oral histories, either biographies of individuals or accounts of the history of the group; a well-told life story can shed light on a society far beyond the experiences of that single individual (see e.g. Shostak (1983) for a classic biography of a hunter-gatherer woman; see also Oakdale and Course (2014) for the value of auto-biography in lowland South America). And a few anthropologists, especially in the early twentieth century, carried formal tests (for instance, psychological and "projective" tests, like the Rorschach "ink blot" test) into the field to measure specific cognitive or perceptual tendencies and to compare these to other traditional and modern societies.

Often enough, even the best-prepared anthropologist will encounter two surprises: (1) the things that s/he came to study are not the really important things and (2) s/he does not even know what the right questions are at first. By jumping into the society and its culture, by taking his/her place in its structure, the researcher gets a better idea "on the ground" of what should really be studied. Most fieldwork diverges from its initial plans when it confronts the reality of the new culture, and this is fine: One cannot know what one will find, or what will be important to consider, before arriving in the field. But if there is one critical fact to remember, it is that anthropological fieldwork is a relationship, and the knowledge an anthropologist brings home is a product of those relationships. S/he will have talked to specific people at specific times in specific contexts, and each anthropologist as an individual adds a certain quality to the experience. Cultural anthropology is science, but it is also a personal encounter between human beings.

The ultimate goal for most anthropologists is what Geertz, following the philosopher Gilbert Ryle, called "thick description" (1973). We do not only want to report the facts from the field, but communicate the quality of life, the systems of meaning and structures of relationships, the "webs of significance," within which real-life people think, feel, and act. This offers one solution to the problem of urban anthropology met in the previous chapter, where it was complained that anthropologists tend to "study in cities" but not to "study cities." Geertz answered that the "locus of study is not the object of study. Anthropologists don't study villages (tribes, towns, neighborhoods . . .); they study *in*

villages" (1973: 22). Or rather, we might now say that anthropologists examine the thick lives of humans wherever and however they interact—even if they do not interact in a "place" at all.

Fieldwork in a globalized world: multi-sited ethnography

The classic image of anthropological fieldwork is the solitary researcher sitting in the forest or desert with an isolated "primitive" tribe. This approach may have been, and may still be, appropriate in certain times and places. However, increasingly this sort of "village anthropology"—or what we might call more technically "the intensively-focused-upon single site" style of observation (Marcus, 1995: 96)—is inappropriate and inadequate in many contexts. Local cultures, or subcultures, classes, ethnic groups, and so on, are affected by and implicated in wider networks of institutions and relations, including "media, markets, states, industries, universities" (97), from the regional to the national to the global level. In a real sense, not all of the culture that influences the people under investigation, and therefore not everything that the anthropologist wants or needs to know, is "in" the local society. Accordingly, "in response to empirical changes in the world and therefore to transformed locations of cultural production" (97), fieldwork methods have also changed.

The most interesting and important shift is toward "multi-sited ethnography," which literally

THE ETHNOGRAPHER'S MAGIC

IMAGE 2.5 A virtual fieldwork site: doing anthropological research in Second Life.

Tom Boellstorff. 2008. *Coming of Age in Second Life: An Anthropologist Explores the Virtually Human.* Princeton University Press.

BOX 2.5   DOING PARTICIPANT OBSERVATION IN VIRTUAL SOCIETIES

People are spending more of their time than ever before online, interacting with each other in cyberspace, in virtual communities and "massively multiplayer worlds." Should anthropology study this? *Can* anthropology study this? In his cleverly named *Coming of Age in Second Life* (playing on the title of a famous book by Margaret Mead, *Coming of Age in Samoa*), Tom Boellstorff proves not only that anthropology can investigate "cybersociality," but that we must investigate it—in fact, that "ethnography has always been a kind of virtual investigation of the human" (2008: 249). His goal is explicitly to "take the methods and theories of anthropology and apply them to a virtual world accessible only through a computer screen" (4). By creating a character or avatar and "living" and even interviewing people within the Second Life world, he illustrates how virtual communities are not mere copies of the real world, nor are they autonomous communities detached from the real world. Rather, they are specific if non-physical "places" or contexts within which people interact. They develop their own language (like "afk" for "away from keyboard"), their own conventions, their own relationships and intimacies, even their own political and economic practices and institutions. He concludes "that virtual worlds are distinct domains of human being, deserving of study in their own right" (238) and that anthropology is up to the challenge.

takes the fieldworker to multiple physical locations in order "to examine the circulation of cultural meanings, objects, and identities in diffuse time-space" (96). For instance, the anthropologist may move from the village to the city to the factory and beyond, even to the national and international levels.

Multi-sited research, Marcus wrote, is premised not on enclosed societies and cultures, but on "chains, paths, threads, conjunctions, or juxtapositions of locations in which the ethnographer establishes some form of literal, physical presence" (105). The fragmented and mobile quality of such work reflects the fragmented and mobile quality of modern global culture. Instead of becoming rooted in one place, the anthropologist travels through a discontinuous sequence of "positions" or "scapes," guided by the imperative to follow the people, the "things" (commodities, money, cultural products like art), the ideas and metaphors and narratives, the lives and life-stories, and the conflicts as they circulate, coalesce, and clash (106–110). In this practice, fieldwork itself, and the reporting on culture, becomes both local and global, truly glocal.

The ethics of fieldwork

Anthropological fieldwork is a social activity in a way that no other science's method is. The fieldworker injects him/herself into the lives of other people—often people who do not know him or her, want him or her there, or particularly want to help him or her. In an earlier era, an anthropologist could often rely on a colonial administrator to order the natives to accept and assist a stranger. Those days are for the most part long gone. In many parts of the world, local peoples have acquired at least some modicum of control over their lives, so outsiders cannot just barge in and expect the locals to do their duty as anthropological subjects and informants. At the very least, they may ask, "What's in it for us?", and at the very most they may say, "Go away!" I was personally told to get the Warlpiri's permission before entering their community or face the prospect of being marched straight out of town.

Participant observation by definition puts researchers skin-to-skin, life-to-life, with "subjects" who are living people. This fact demands a particularly self-conscious code of ethical behavior. At the minimum, this includes, "Do no harm." Increasingly, it includes, "Ask first." At the highest level, it includes, "Make a contribution" (perhaps an opportunity and call for more applied anthropology), and "Consider your own impact on them."

In the contemporary context, fieldwork usually commences with some form of permission from the local society; for such purposes, institutions like community governments or regional associations, like the Aboriginal "Land Councils" in Australia, have been established. By now most well-known traditional societies have been studied repeatedly, and the locals know what anthropologists want and what the arrangement will be like. Some members are warm to the idea, some not. An anthropologist should never expect to make friends with every member of the society, any more than people expect to make friends with every member of their own society. A few friends are worth the world in the field.

In the field, it will be necessary, and desirable, to abide by their rules and norms as much as possible. Local people usually understand that the foreigner is not one of them; the anthropologist is an outsider, a stranger, a child. Sometimes a fieldworker will arrive with the reputation (often nothing to do with that individual personally) of an oppressor, colonizer, or at least of the last bad anthropologist who passed through. On the other hand, s/he may benefit from a previous positive experience with an anthropologist, as I did in one community: The famous Jane Goodall had been there long before, and they assumed that I knew and worked with her. Accordingly, one evening a man walked me around the settlement, introducing me as the "anthropology man" and friend of Ms. Goodall. At any rate, the local people frequently feel that anthropologists come to learn their secrets and publish those secrets for the world to see. They may understand that anthropologists come for their own

career advancement. They know that the fieldworker will stay for a while and leave, maybe never to return again. In ways, they know the outside world better than the outside world knows them.

Having obtained permission somehow (the "somehow" will depend on the circumstances of each field experience), it is obligatory to be as honest as possible about why the anthropologist is there. Professional standards require informed consent. If s/he has come to study religion, the locals should not be told that s/he merely wants to "learn the language" or some other neutral excuse. Some anthropologists have shown their research notes to the local people before leaving or before publishing them, but that is not always possible or politic, especially in the case of sensitive or personal data. But we must always remember that some of them can read English or other world languages and will see what is written about them—in case the writer ever wants to come back again. Also, there is value in showing them these notes and analyses in advance, because they may be able to correct or interpret certain items that have been misunderstood or misinterpreted.

There is no ignoring the fact that much of the world today is a battleground and that many fieldwork settings are tense and dangerous. If an anthropologist wants to do fieldwork among refugees, for example, or in a war zone, or among a "terrorist" or insurrectionist group, life will be more complicated and research will be more sensitive. They may perceive the outsider—rightly

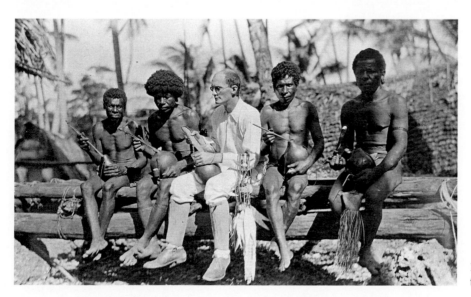

IMAGE 2.6 Bronislaw Malinowski conducting fieldwork with Trobriand Islanders.

See Chapters 14 and 15

or wrongly, intentionally or unintentionally—as a threat, a "security leak," even a spy. I was personally accused (falsely) by a Warlpiri man of being a spy for the CIA on one occasion, but these concerns are real enough. They never know who foreigners are really sent by, what foreigners will do with the information, or who else might see it.

One way that anthropologists have traditionally handled the problem of "cooperation" is by giving gifts, trading, or paying for information. All of these practices have their issues. Giving gifts to some people and not others can hurt feelings and promote jealousy as well as inequalities in the society that may have never existed before. Trading is a good idea but can become expensive and saddle the researcher with lots of stuff that s/he doesn't really want; it can also upset the local economy, as they begin to produce goods for trade rather than consumption. And paying for information can undermine the friendship aspect of fieldwork, although it is sometimes necessary and appropriate. Fieldworkers may even want to hire an informant, translator, or travel companion.

In the contemporary context, one of the best exchanges for information—while also being a great way to learn—is offering some useful service that the local people need. (Ironically, this can also foster dependence and resentment.) For example, many indigenous societies have been involved in land claims or development struggles (for example, over dam projects or mining or similar related issues) for decades, and many anthropologists have helped by researching culture (land tenure, political

See Chapter 11 and beyond

organization, kinship structure, etc.) and organizing this data for presentation to courts, corporations, or governments. Along the way, scholars have learned many valuable things about these and other aspects of the culture by being so intimately involved with real-life practical matters. It has been good for the local people and for scholars. At the same time, it is important that the fieldworker not "go native" and lose him/herself among the locals. This means, among other things, that visitors should probably not get too intimately involved in their daily lives, especially sexually. Like any professional, one must maintain a certain distance from one's clients or subjects. Often this is difficult: One may be inclined to intervene in domestic matters, to introduce one's values, medicines, or other practices. Each situation will be a judgment call, and each person must be his/her own judge. But there are lines that should not be crossed, and a trusty rule of thumb is this: After the anthropologist is gone, the local people still have to live there. We can walk away, but they cannot. Do not leave things worse for them and for the next anthropologist who may visit.

In the end, it is unavoidable that one will have some impact on the society where one lives. These days, the impact may be fairly light, as many major changes have already long since occurred. The introduction of new tools and technologies, new ideas and concepts, new diseases, even the mere awareness that there is a bigger world out there with strange-looking and strange-acting people in it irretrievably changes local peoples. Anthropologists can neither force them to alter their ways of life nor

---

BOX 2.6   CONTEMPORARY CULTURAL CONTROVERSIES: THE VIRTUES OF "DIVERSITY TRAINING"

The concept of culture and the value of diversity are not exclusive to anthropology, nor should they be. In fact, many organizations, including government agencies and corporations, have recognized the importance of diversity, among their own staff and in dealing with their clients and customers. Predictably, an entire industry of "diversity training" has emerged, one purveyor being the Cultural Intelligence Center (www.culturalq.com), which promotes the reasonable notion of "cultural intelligence" or CQ. It offers training, certification (for the cost of $2,100 for Level I and $2,600 for Level II), and assessment tools, along with books and a "Great Courses" video class. It claims BMW, Coca-Cola, Google, IBM, and many other major corporations as clients. However, some observers have been openly critical of diversity training. David Bregman (2012) contends that diversity training not only fails to extinguish prejudice, but actually increases it, since trainees are encouraged to categorize people and to attribute cultural stereotypes to those categories. What do you think?

prevent them from doing so, but anthropologists and all other outsiders can never forget the fact that we ourselves are agents of change. The ethical guidelines that have been adopted by the American Anthropological Association are available on their website.

www.aaanet.org/ committees/ethics/ethics. htm

SUMMARY

The questions and perspectives of anthropology lead almost inevitably to its concepts and methods. Central to cultural anthropology is the idea of culture—that humans are not born knowing and doing all of the things we see them do. Rather, from the experience of human diversity, anthropologists have determined that culture is

- learned
- shared and distributed
- symbolic
- integrated
- an adaptation

In the modern global context, it is increasingly clear and important that culture is also produced, practiced, and circulated. Finally, culture is materialized in objects and places.

While culture is not "in" the body in any particular way, human physical characteristics make cultural behavior possible—that is, human behavior has a two-part biocultural basis. Therefore, culture is potentially not exclusive to humans. Beings with physical traits similar to humans have behavioral traits similar to humans, and as humans gradually acquired their present traits, their behavior became more recognizably cultural.

Anthropology has developed special methods for collecting the information that it needs to answer its questions. The most fundamental method is participant observation, during which researchers may perform a variety of kinds of activities. Everything that anthropologists do includes some degree of interaction with "subjects" who are real human beings, and fieldworkers must conduct that interaction ethically, aware that they are humans too and that their actions will have impacts on the people in that society.

Q
MCQS

Q
FILL IN THE BLANKS

WWW

Key Terms

Acheulian	genealogy	participant observation
Australopithecus	guided reinvention of culture	primate
biocultural	hierarchy	socialization
bipedalism	Homo	society
counterculture	Homo erectus	structured interview
dominance	Homo habilis	subculture
enculturation	Homo sapiens	symbol
erectness	Mousterian	unstructured interview
fieldwork	Neandertal	
functionalism	Oldowan	

3 The origins of cultural anthropology

In 1901 Franz Boas dispatched Berthold Laufer on an anthropological mission to China. At the time, Boas taught anthropology at Columbia University and curated the ethnology (the study of peoples or cultures) and somatology (the study of the body) section of the American Museum of Natural History (AMNH). Also at the time, American anthropology (the American Ethnological Society had been founded in 1842) was understandably focused on Native American societies, so the Laufer expedition was a significant new direction for the field. Even so, based very much in the museum as an institutional site, anthropology "was still a material as much as an ethnographic enterprise" with its eyes set firmly on gathering "collections of the material culture of those whom they encountered, measured, photographed, and recorded" (Kendall, 2014: 8). In particular, Laufer was commissioned "to document Chinese handicraft industries and acquire the tools of production" (20), so as to create a display of Chinese technical and material culture at the AMNH; he also sought to obtain some heads from executed Chinese criminals. Trained in languages and philology, Laufer concentrated too much on texts and art for Boas' taste, and he also complained of "the particular

difficulty of documenting the highly developed and often jealously protected techniques of Chinese handicraft production" (22) in a society that was every bit as complex as any Western country. The expedition was eventually terminated; Laufer faded into obscurity, while Boas is celebrated as a founding father of modern anthropology. Yet in some ways Laufer anticipated twenty-first century anthropology, in which "material culture studies have returned in a new incarnation and 'multi-sited'

IMAGE 3.1 An image of Manchu women, taken during the Laufer Chinese expedition (1901–1904).

ethnographies are considered valuable ways of recording mobile subjects and the things they make and consume" (32).

Although the first recorded appearance of the word "anthropology" in English has been dated to the late sixteenth century, in 1901 the modern discipline was still very much in its infancy. This is not to say that contemporary academic anthropology was invented out of thin air in the past hundred years; quite to the contrary, the discipline has ancient roots in Western scholarship and Western civilization. Yet, anthropology today is significantly different from how it was imagined and practiced just a century ago. In this chapter, we will examine how—and why—anthropology originated and how it has evolved over a very productive and tumultuous one hundred and fifty years.

WHAT MAKES CULTURAL ANTHROPOLOGY POSSIBLE— AND NECESSARY

Clearly the world got along (although not necessarily well) for millennia without anthropology; in other words, the sheer fact of human diversity was not sufficient to spark a systematic professional study of that diversity. As just established, anthropology is a very new science, so despite the eternal reality of human diversity, anthropology must be a very unlikely science. The first of these claims is easy enough to understand and defend. Some social and natural sciences, from history and philosophy to mathematics and physics, were conceived quite early, more than two thousand years ago. Anthropology is among the last of the major social sciences to emerge, and what we recognize as contemporary cultural anthropology assumed its form less than a century ago. Why was this discipline so late to appear on the horizon of human inquiry?

Another way to ask this question is to ponder why the observation of human diversity did not lead to a science of human diversity. The issue is not the observations themselves but the responses to the observations. Human diversity has always been an acknowledged fact, but what humans do with— or about—that fact is another matter entirely. Clearly, anthropology is not the default response. Rather, the default or first response seems to be some combination of:

- indifference toward the Other
- fear and hostility toward the Other
- judgment and condemnation of the Other
- desire or effort to eradicate the Other, either through conquest or "conversion"
- rejection of the Other as less than one's own kind—and sometimes less than completely human

These attitudes are imminent in the record of societies ancient and not so ancient. Other peoples were typically condemned as "savages," "barbarians," "infidels," "primitives," "uncivilized," "evil," and so on. To be different was to be bad, to be wrong. This is definitely not a perspective from which cultural anthropology will grow.

Only thirty years ago, George Marcus and Michael Fischer expressed an insight into what makes a discipline or perspective like anthropology possible, likely, and ultimately necessary. One aspect, but only one and arguably the less motivating one, is an interest in "the capturing of cultural diversity, mainly among tribal and non-Western peoples"; the other is a willingness, indeed an eagerness, to engage in "a cultural critique of ourselves, often underplayed in the past, but having today a renewed potential for development" (1986: 20). In other words, there must be a major transformation about how we think about others *and about ourselves* before anthropology is possible, and the practice of anthropology only accelerates this transformation.

THE PRE-MODERN ROOTS OF ANTHROPOLOGY

The ancient Greeks were enthusiastic travelers and chroniclers, including of course the historian Herodotus, whose encounters with peoples throughout the classical world led him to conclude that "custom is king over all"—in other words, that the values and behaviors of societies are driven less by reason or nature than by tradition and learning. The philosopher Xenophanes made an equally remarkable observation about the difference and the relativity of religion across cultures:

Ethiopians have gods with snub noses and black hair, Thracians have gods with gray eyes and red hair. . . . If oxen or lions had hands which enabled them to draw and paint pictures as men do, they would portray their gods as having bodies like their own; horses would portray them as horses, and oxen as oxen.

(quoted in Wheelwright, 1966: 33)

Many other writers and soldiers, including Julius Caesar, produced reports about the peoples they encountered (such as the Gauls or Germanic tribes), and the philosophical school of Sophism even explained social institutions like religion or politics as products of human convention (*nomo* or *thesei*). Nevertheless, neither Greece nor Rome invented an academic inquiry quite like anthropology.

Medieval Europe, as well as most other religious and cultural traditions, did no better. In fact, during the "dark ages" dominated by Christianity, social life was seen as divinely given, and diversity was discouraged or persecuted (e.g. as heresy): "For the Middle Ages only the 'Christian man'—an expression still familiar from Luther—was really a man in the full sense of the word" (Landmann, 1974: 31). Like their ancient predecessors, Medieval Europeans suffered from two recurring obstacles that blocked the very possibility of something like cultural anthropology: absolute certainty in the truth and goodness of one's own culture (ethnocentrism), and lack of information about other societies, or poor or patently false information about them.

Certainty in one's own truth and goodness, a kind of "one-possibility thinking," is characteristic of most societies, traditional or modern. But if our society is good and true, then all others are by definition bad or false. Why then would you want to know more about those barbarians, those infidels, those blasphemers? Lack of information or possession of poor information is equally problematic. If you do not know much about other societies or cultures, you cannot say much meaningful and useful about them; the natural reaction is to try to assimilate the Other into your own pre-existing knowledge and belief. For example, even the most hard-headed Europeans could not ignore the fact of anomalous archaeological features on their land. Saxo Grammaticus, writing in the twelfth century about the enormous stone edifices of Denmark, opined that

> the country of Denmark was once cultivated and worked by giants. . . . Should any man question that this is accomplished by

superhuman force, let him look up at the tops of certain mountains and say, if he knows how, what man hath carried such immense boulders up to their crests.

(quoted in Slotkin, 1965: 6)

Of the Stone Age artifacts scattered around Europe, Ulisse Aldrovandi said that "they were natural accretions developed by geological processes," while Conrad Gesner guessed "that they were thunderbolts. Stone projectiles were usually called 'elf arrows' or 'thunderbolts' by laymen . . ." (quoted in Slotkin, 1965: 44). In yet other cases, unexplainable but obviously non-Christian phenomena were either ignored or dismissed as demonic. (Similarly, just a decade ago the devoutly Muslim Taliban destroyed the enormous Buddhist statues at Bamiyan rather than allow those idols to corrupt Afghanistan.) Worst of all was the supposed "knowledge" that monstrous races of pseudo-humans stalked the earth, like the Amyctyrae, beings with such large lower lips that they could use them for umbrellas; the Astomi, people with no mouths who survived by smelling food; the Blemmyae, creatures who had no heads but faces in their chests; the Cynocephali, people with dog-heads; and many others. More amazing still, writers described them as if they were real, and maps illustrated where each imaginary monstrous race dwelt—Astomi in east India, Blemmyae in Libya, etc. Such "knowledge" was actually taught in ancient and medieval schools.

The Other in early modern experience and thought

At some point, all of these (mis)conceptions had to change if anthropology was ever to emerge. So the question for us is, what is it that makes a science like anthropology possible? And more than just possible but *necessary*? What kind of society can, and must, enter upon a line of inquiry that will end with the birth of anthropology—and not specifically professional anthropology so much as the anthropological perspective described previously? It must be a society that has lost or at least shaken its own cultural certainty as well as one that has accumulated a body of accurate and useful information about the Other. This will inevitably depend on and follow from a new and sustained kind of encounter

Slotkin, J. S., Ed. 1965. *Readings in Early Anthropology*. London: Methuen & Co. Ltd.

THE EXPERIENCE OF DIVERSITY IN THE ANCIENT WORLD

See Chapter 2

IMAGE 3.2 A Blemmyae, one of the monstrous races of ancient and medieval literature.

with the Other. That is, no one says, "Let's invent anthropology" and then starts to seek out different forms of humans. Instead, one first bumps into different kinds of humans and then, gradually and grudgingly, comes to an anthropological awareness.

Some key factors in this civilizational shift were:

The encounter with other major Eurasian civilizations. An epochal and shattering experience for Western Christians was the Crusades, which brought them into sustained contact with—and ultimately defeat by—Muslims in the Middle East. Since at least the 1300s, European adventurers traveled to and brought reports from distant civilizations like Central Asia and China, the best known of whom was Marco Polo. These travelers could not help but notice that other societies were not only different from but in some inescapable ways superior to their own, often more urban, more literate, richer, more "cultured," and more powerful than anything in Europe. This was inconceivable: Europe supposedly had the "true" religion and culture, foreigners were idolaters, infidels, devil-worshippers, and yet those peoples were ahead of the West in technology, scholarship, and art.

The "voyages of discovery" and the rise of colonization. A new day dawned for European thought with the discovery of new lands and new peoples in places where lands and people were not known or even imagined. Contact with Native Americans and

eventually African, Asian, and Australian peoples opened their eyes to a diversity that was previously undreamed of. But, as exciting (and profitable) as all this discovery was, it presented a psychological and cultural challenge. Who were these people? How did they get all the way out there? In fact, were they people at all? Were they descendants of Adam and Eve, like the Western Christians and supposedly all humans? The question of the humanity of the "Indians" was quite serious. Within decades of Columbus' arrival in America, there was a debate within the Catholic Church about the identity of the natives. The "conservative" position was that the natives did not have souls and therefore were not human; if this were the case, then they could be classified and treated as animals (also believed to have no souls)—chased off, carried away, enslaved, or killed as suited the conquerors. The "liberal" position, championed by Bartolomé de las Casas, was that they did have souls and therefore were human; therefore, they deserved "humane" and "Christian" treatment. They could not be killed or enslaved wantonly, but neither could they be left alone; their human souls required "saving," and they deserved and needed the benefits of the "true" culture and the "true" religion. The Church finally ruled in 1537 that the Indians were humans and ordered that they be dealt with in a humane manner, but this did not stop the ravages and abuses to which they were subjected by administrators, missionaries, soldiers, traders, and settlers. And despite their devastating effect on indigenous peoples, early visitors and

See Chapters 12 and beyond

settlers often produced important documents of native languages, religions, and cultures. One of the best examples is *The Jesuit Relations*, an annual report from the Jesuit missionaries in "New France," or Canada, that preserved a valuable record of Aboriginal Canadian cultures beginning in 1610 (see http://puffin.creighton.edu/jesuit/relations).

The Renaissance and Reformation. Internally, Europe was simultaneously undergoing tectonic changes. The so-called Renaissance of the fifteenth and sixteenth centuries was a "re-birth" of urban life, literacy, long-distance trade, and the widespread exchange of ideas that marks the modern world and marked the ancient Mediterranean world. Specifically it was a rebirth of ancient Greece and Rome culture, as seen through the lens of late-medieval or early-modern Europe, which had always maintained a vague dream of Rome but knew little about it. Ancient texts had long been lost, and the ability to read what remained suffered as well. Of course, the assumption was that, while

BOX 3.1   UTOPIAS—AN EARLY FORM OF ANTHROPOLOGICAL IMAGINATION

IMAGE 3.3 Utopian literature was an important precursor to modern anthropology.

While professional anthropologists travel to other places to observe diversity, humans have also traveled in their minds to "no place"—the literal meaning of *utopia*—to envision alternatives and to criticize their own culture and era. Sometimes, as when kings or churches were very strong, veiled fictional criticism was the only acceptable kind. But as Lewis Mumford wrote, "Nowhere may be an imaginary country, but News from Nowhere is real news" (1962: 24). The first utopia in recorded history was Plato's *Republic*, with a well thought-out political system and culture, including what form of music and poetry citizens should be exposed to. But the early modern era was the great age of utopian literature, often presented as if they were narratives of real voyages. Sir Thomas More's 1516 *Utopia* gave the genre its name; fully titled *On the Best State of a Republic and the New Island of Utopia*, it claimed to refer to a real place called Utopia—and to describe a better society than More's own. Many other writers offered their images of an ideal society, including Johannes Valentinus Andreae's 1619 *Christianopolis*, Francis Bacon's 1624 *New Atlantis*, and Jonathan Swift's 1726 *Travels into Several Remote Nations of the World, in Four Parts, by Lemuel Gulliver*. Again, such writings were often a parody and critique of the author's society, and they were clearly inspired by the actual explorations of the age. The second great era of utopian writing was the nineteenth and twentieth centuries, which produced Samuel Butler's 1872 *Erewhon* (roughly a reversal of the word "nowhere"), Edward Bellamy's socialist and futuristic 1888 *Looking Backward*, and Jules Verne's 1863 *Paris in the Twentieth Century*. More recently, utopias have sometimes given way to dystopias—bad places—like Aldous Huxley's 1932 *Brave New World* or George Orwell's 1948 *1984*. Contemporary science fiction performs many of the same functions as this utopian literature, allowing writers to explore futures just beyond the present horizon and to play with alternatives to or extensions of present-day society.

the Greeks and Romans could not possibly be Christians, they were in some way "pre-Christians" or "proto-Christians." Europeans simply presumed that the ancients were a lot like them. However, the reality was different—and disturbing. Greeks and Romans had their own distinct and non-Christian religions, their own political systems, kinship systems, economies, and so on. The ancients lived in a very different mental and cultural world. But this meant that Europe's own ancestors exhibited otherness. It was one thing to face the Other in a rival civilization or "primitive" tribe; Europeans could disregard or belittle such difference. It was much more troubling to confront the Other in one's own ancestry. Early-modern Europeans found that their own ancestors were Others to them.

Then suddenly, after almost fifteen hundred years of religious unity, the Other was a neighbor.

Certainly there had been previous attempts at reform and even total schisms (like the break between the Roman and Eastern Orthodox churches). Within Western Europe, though, Martin Luther's movement in the 1500s was unique. It caught on, much to the consternation of authorities. Luther claimed (often in the most shocking language) that the Church was wrong about many of its beliefs and was actually anti-Christian. He called the Pope and all Catholics blasphemers and atheists. And he said he could prove it: just go back to the "source," to the Bible itself. To assist, he produced a German translation of the Bible. For decades—including the Thirty Years War (1618–1648)—Catholicism tried to stamp out this heretical division, until a peace was declared, allowing the two "religions" to co-exist. But this peace did not tolerate all religions; other "protestant" sects like Unitarians, Shakers, Quakers, Anabaptists, as well as non-Christian religions like Judaism, were still out of bounds. Even so, the religious monopoly in Europe was broken forever. Never again would the continent be a homogeneous, one-possibility place; instead, two religions or denominations gave way to three, then dozens. Westerners from that day forth would be the Other to each other.

IMAGE 3.4 The Renaissance introduced new interests in ancient culture, visual perspective, and humanism.

All of this turbulent experience was fodder for Western thought. By the mid-1600s political philosophers were speculating on the origins of society and on the history of social and political institutions. Thomas Hobbes lived through the trial and execution of the English king, Charles I, in 1649, spurring him to consider human nature and the development of society. In his famous 1651 *Leviathan*, he characterized native peoples as living "in a state of nature" without society or government, which might sound like a good thing. Hobbes of course never set foot in a "primitive society," and his judgments of them are at best derived from second-hand accounts if not pure fantasy. His assessment was clearly negative: Probably the most quoted phrase in his entire work describes the quality of primitive and allegedly pre-social life as "solitary, poor, nasty, brutish, and short." This was not anthropology, to be sure, but it was a real (if troubled) step in our direction, since it held up other societies as a crucial mirror and model for his and our own.

Almost exactly a century later, Jean Jacques Rousseau, author of the 1762 *The Social Contract*, compared "**savages**" favorably to his own countrymen and institutions, finding in them the very archetype of free and natural humanity. He saw them as living in a "state of nature," independent and equal, enjoying "the peacefulness of their passions, and their ignorance of vice." He contrasted their "natural existence," distinguished by instinct, amorality, appetite, natural liberty, and individual strength, to his own "civil society," with its formal justice, morality, reason, civil liberty, and public will. Of course, Rousseau's image of primitive society is as simplistic and stereotyped as Hobbes'; there is no such thing as "natural man," since all humans are cultured and none live in a state of raw nature, and there is no such thing as "savage society" but rather a staggering variety of traditional cultures—from the happy to the miserable, from the peaceful to the warlike. Rousseau was not doing anthropology any more than Hobbes was—we would never call our subjects "stupid and unimaginative"—but both philosophers and others like them at least took the Other seriously, declaring them a worthy—even a necessary—subject of study and discussion. And especially in Rousseau's view, not only were there things to learn *about* distant societies, there were actually things to learn *from* them.

THE NINETEENTH CENTURY AND THE "SCIENCE OF MAN"

In 1798, the Enlightenment philosopher Immanuel Kant published *Anthropology from a Pragmatic Point of View* in which he defined anthropology as the systematic knowledge of humankind. This knowledge necessarily consisted of two kinds— physiological understanding of humans as biological beings, and pragmatic understanding of humans as free beings who make themselves through their behavioral practices. Although not generally considered a direct ancestor of modern anthropology, Kant captured the essence of the biocultural perspective.

Significantly, as anthropology first coalesced in the nineteenth century, it was the biological side of humanity rather than the cultural side that received the primary attention. Already in 1863 Theodor Waitz, in his *Introduction to Anthropology*, postulated that the discipline aspired to be "the science of man in general; or, in precise terms, the science of the nature of man" (1863: 3), which should "study man by the same method which is applied to the investigation of all other natural objects" (5). Armand de Quatrefages concurred, stating that anthropology should investigate humanity "as a zoologist studying an animal would understand it" (quoted in Topinard, 1890: 2), and Paul Topinard himself was clearer still that anthropology was "the branch of natural history which treats of man and the races of man" (1890: 3).

The nineteenth and early twentieth centuries were accordingly the great era of biology and of "scientific racism," when humans were prodded and measured mainly for their physical and racial characteristics. Decades prior, Linnaeus had boldly placed mankind in the animal kingdom and identified several distinct human "races," and others like Johann Friedrich Blumenbach followed suit. Some of the leaders of the young field, then, were biologists and physicians, like the renowned brain scientist Paul Broca (1824–1880), who, according to Alice Conklin, with his students, "virtually reinvented the field of anthropology, by measuring more carefully and more completely than any before them the cranial cavities of those groups deemed inferior in intelligence (so-called primitives)" (2013: 26). Broca headed the *Société d'Anthropologie* in France as well as founding a

Noble savage
the notion, often associated with Rousseau, that non-Western or "primitive" people are actually happier and more virtuous than Westerners; based on the idea that humans are free and equal in "a state of nature" but that social institutions deprive them of that freedom and equality

See Chapter 6

laboratory and a school for anthropology and publishing *Revue d'Anthropologie* beginning in 1872. Quatrefages was also a scholar of medicine and zoology.

Much of early anthropology's energy was applied to biological or racial questions, but, as Kant had suggested, champions of anthropology like Topinard also recognized that the science of man was really "two distinct sciences": "Anthropology" was viewed as the discipline that "occupies itself with Man and the races of mankind"—that is, the physiological dimension of humanity—while "ethnology" concerned itself "with such peoples and tribes as geography and history hand over to us" and documents their "manners, customs, religion, language, physical characteristics, and origins" (1890: 8–9). Writing years later, E. E. Evans-Pritchard defined ethnology as the project "to classify peoples on the basis of their racial and cultural characteristics and then to explain their distribution at the present time, or in past times, by the movement and mixture of peoples and the diffusion of cultures" (1962: 4). Eventually this dual science would differentiate into physical anthropology and cultural or social anthropology.

The history of institutions

At the same time as some thinkers were pursuing biological or ethnological questions, another set of scholars was investigating the history of institutions like law, marriage, and religion. As noted above, philosophers like Hobbes and Rousseau sought similar knowledge, but largely through rumination instead of research. The nineteenth century, though, saw a florescence of books on pre-modern institutions such as Henry Sumner Maine's 1861 *Ancient Law* and 1883 *Dissertations On Early Law and Custom*; Johann Jakob Bachofen's 1861 *Mother Right*; John Ferguson McLennan's 1865 *Primitive Marriage*; Lewis Henry Morgan's 1871 *Systems of Consanguinity and Affinity of the Human Family*; William Robertson Smith's 1889 *Religion of the Semites: Fundamental Institutions*; James George Frazer's 1890 comparative mythology *The Golden Bough*; and most influentially, Émile Durkheim's 1915 *The Elementary Forms of the Religious Life*.

Much of this work was heavily indebted to evolutionary theory, proposing stages through which specific institutions or society in general passed. According to **cultural evolutionism**, culture developed through a sequence of stages or phases; whether there was a single (unilinear) series of cultures or several independent (multilinear) series was an open question. Either way, cultures had a "history" which could and should be reconstructed. The goal was to arrive at a set of cultural types or stages that would describe the actual process by which cultures evolved from one state to another—something like a timeline with different cultural types attached to certain moments in time.

Different scholars arrived at different solutions to the question of cultural evolution, but all of the solutions shared a few features. For one, they arranged the observable societies "in order" of evolutionary progress. The "simplest" or "most primitive" naturally filled the "lower" and earlier spots; Australian Aboriginals were a common candidate for that honor. The best-remembered evolutionary model of the era belonged to Lewis Henry Morgan, who boiled the stages of cultural history down to three—savagery, barbarism (each subdivided into lower, middle, and upper), and civilization—characterized by certain diagnostic cultural features (e.g., bow and arrow, farming, writing). Progress was judged by technological achievement (the threshold from savagery to barbarism was the invention of pottery, for instance), a standard that was important to Westerners and in which Westerners excelled. And of course, "civilization" was Morgan's own nineteenth-century Euro-American culture.

A related approach to cultural history was called **diffusionism**, the idea that Culture (with a capital "C," as a single great human phenomenon) had originated once or at most a few times and then spread from that center or those centers of origin outward to other locations on the globe. This approach was expressed in the German *Kulturkreis* ("culture circle") school of thought associated with writers like Leo Frobenius (in his 1897 *Der westafrikanische Kulturkreis* [The West African Culture Circle]) and Grafton Elliot Smith and envisioned culture as one or more circles emanating out from their center(s) like ripples on a pond. The greater the proximity between societies in space, the greater the similarity in culture. The center was identified sometimes as Egypt, sometimes elsewhere, but the idea of following the ripples

Cultural evolutionism
the early ethnological or anthropological position or theory that Culture started at some moment in the past and evolved from its "primitive" beginnings through a series of stages to achieve its "higher" or more modern form

Morgan, Lewis Henry. 1877. *Ancient Society, or Researches in the Lines of Human Progress from Savagery through Barbarism to Civilization*. New York: Henry Holt and Company

Diffusionism
the early ethnological or anthropological position or theory that Culture, or specific cultural practices, objects, or institutions, had appeared once or at most a few times and spread out from their original center

Durkheim, Émile. 1965 [1915]. *The Elementary Forms of the Religious Life*. New York: The Free Press.

"backward" in space suggested the possibility of following them backward in time as well—back to the first culture.

The institutionalization of anthropology in the nineteenth century

Anthropology obviously did not appear suddenly out of nowhere in the twentieth century, although sometimes the discipline's mythology makes it sound as if it did. More importantly, the success of a discipline depends on establishing viable, self-perpetuating institutions such as academic departments, professional organizations, and research facilities. One of the earliest was a *Société Ethnologique*

de Paris operating in France, founded in 1839. The horrors of colonialism led to the creation of the international Aborigines' Protection Society in 1837 as an early "human rights" organization, followed by the more scholarly Ethnological Society of London in 1843. The Royal Anthropological Institute of Great Britain and Ireland was established in 1871, the same year as Tylor's *Primitive Culture*, and Tylor went on to write the first textbook in anthropology, simply called *Anthropology*, in 1881. Meanwhile, the Bureau of American Ethnology was founded by John Wesley Powell in 1879 as the premier agency of American anthropology, and the journal *American Anthropologist* made its debut in 1888. In 1902, the American Anthropological Association opened with 175 members, with its stated mission to:

BOX 3.2   THE UNSUNG WOMEN OF EARLY ANTHROPOLOGY

One of the more noteworthy facts of anthropology is that, at a time when women were largely excluded from the academy, women were among the earliest and most illustrious contributors to our field. Many of Boas' first generation of students were women, including Margaret Mead and Ruth Benedict. Others actually predate the supposed founding fathers, Franz Boas and Bronislaw Malinowski. Among the women who deserve to be counted as founding mothers of anthropology are:

Erminnie Platt Smith (1836–1886)—An ethnologist and geologist, Smith was attached to the Bureau of American Ethnology in 1880, through which she studied Iroquois culture and folklore and published *Myths of the Iroquois* in 1883.

Alice Fletcher (1838–1923)—Fletcher conducted fieldwork among the Omaha and Sioux as early as 1879. Affiliated with the Peabody Museum at Harvard University, she wrote *A Study of Omaha Indian Music* in 1893 and an unpublished chronicle called *Life Among the Indians*. She assisted the tribes through the allotment process that divided and distributed their reservation land and became a defender of Indian rights.

Matilda Coxe Stevenson (1849–1915)—After spending thirteen years with her husband James Stevenson sojourning in the Rocky Mountain region, Stevenson became the first president of the Women's Anthropological Society of America in 1885, served on the staff of the Bureau of American Ethnology from 1889, and carried out studies of Taos and Tewa society between 1904 and 1910.

Elsie Clews Parsons (1875–1941)—Parsons worked among the Hopi and Pueblo peoples, earning a Ph.D. from Columbia University in 1899, serving as the president of the American Ethnological Society from 1923 to 1925, publishing her two-volume *Pueblo Indian Religion* in 1939, and becoming president of the American Anthropological Association in 1940.

Other prominent women in the first decades of anthropology included Ruth Bunzel, Ella Deloria, Viola Garfield, Zora Neale Hurston, and Lila O'Neale.

promote the science of anthropology, to stimulate and coordinate the efforts of American anthropologists, to foster local and other societies devoted to anthropology, to serve as a bond among American anthropologists and anthropologic [sic] organizations present and prospective, and to publish and encourage the publication of matter pertaining to anthropology. (http://www.aaanet.org/about)

However, despite these promising advances in organizing the field, through the nineteenth century there were not yet any formal training programs in anthropology nor many professional ethnologists. This fact is well illustrated by considering the "guidebook" for anthropology known as *Notes and Queries*. Originally published in 1874, *Notes and Queries* was essentially a manual for "the man on the spot," who might have been an explorer, trader, missionary, soldier, or government official. Much valuable material was collected by such people. Remarkably, *Notes and Queries* acknowledged this fact and tried to exploit it: As the preface to the first edition suggested, "those who are not anthropologists themselves" are able "to supply the information which is wanted for the scientific study of anthropology at home" (Garson and Read, 1099: vii). *Notes and Queries* then contained a list of questions that "travelers" could ask to ensure that their information was complete and standardized.

Revealingly, the layout of *Notes and Queries* reflected the primacy of the physical over the cultural. The first section was dedicated to "anthropography" or the measurement of the body, covering such topics as measuring instruments, the skeleton, physiological factors like respiration and odor and the senses, and medical questions like diet, pathology, surgery, diseases, and insanity. "Ethnography" received secondary attention and was considered to be less readily accessible and less concrete. Indeed, even in the case of "culture," scholars preferred "hard evidence" over the dubious verbal accounts that natives gave; hence, a favorite tool of research was the newly invented camera (Pinney, 2011), which produced photographs, or what *Notes and Queries* called "facts about which there can be no question" (Garson and Read, 1899: 87).

Because anthropology was not yet professionalized before 1900, it was practiced at many disparate sites by an array of characters. Among the most important and memorable, if problematic, were:

Adventure travelers and travel literature. Travelers as ancient as Herodotus had documented their experiences for scholarly and popular consumption. By the nineteenth century there was a thriving industry of travel writing, with many authors becoming celebrities who conducted lecture tours and gave visual presentations with the new technology of the day. Even before 1800, Joseph Lafitau had published his 1724 *Customs of American Savages Compared with Those of Earliest Times*. As the new century turned, explorer Mungo Park released his 1799 *Travels in the Interior of Africa*. The many further entries into the market of travel literature featured Charles Sturt's 1848 *Narrative of an Expedition into Central Australia*, Richard Burton's 1856 *First Footsteps in East Africa*, James Johnstone's 1896 *My Experiences in Manipur and the Naga Hills,* and Henry Stanley's 1898 *Through South Africa*.

The museum and museum curator. As the case of Berthold Laufer in China shows, much of early anthropology was concentrated on collecting material objects, and a natural home base for anthropology was the natural history or ethnological museum. Museums were also places where European societies could display the spoils of empire and educate and inspire their citizenry. Among the oldest ethnological museums in the world are those in Haarlem, Netherlands (founded 1784), St. Petersburg, Russia (1836), Leiden, Netherlands (1839), and Copenhagen, Denmark (1839). The first anthropological and archaeological museum in the United States was the Peabody Museum of Harvard University (1866). As mentioned, before Franz Boas was a professor of anthropology, he was curator of both cultural and anatomical objects at the American Museum of Natural History in New York City. Museums were key spaces for creating ethnological knowledge— for collecting, labeling, organizing, and displaying objects representing the diverse peoples of the world.

Exhibitions, Fairs, and Zoos. Speaking of the peoples of the world, the nineteenth century was also distinguished by some questionably tasteful

PHOTOGRAPHY IN THE EARLY HISTORY OF ANTHROPOLOGY

practices in collecting and displaying human beings. Among these practices were world fairs, colonial exhibits, circuses, traveling shows, and literally "human zoos." The United States was both a source and destination for the exhibition of native peoples: Buffalo Bill's traveling "Wild West" show featuring Native Americans was a sensation in Europe, while scholar and eugenicist Madison Grant put African pygmy Ota Benga on display in a cage in the Bronx Zoo in 1906. The so-called Great Exhibition of 1851 in London and the 1893 World's Columbian Exposition in Chicago were occasions for gathering and presenting the peoples of the world, as was the 1931 Colonial Exhibition in Paris. For these occasions, individuals or entire families or villages were transported from colonial places to Europe or America for exhibition; sometimes they were provided with props like huts and tools, becoming living tableaux for viewers who would never make the long voyages to their homelands. Sometimes they were displayed nude, so as better to observe their "primitive anatomy" (and no doubt titillate their audiences), their bodies exposed to the Western gaze as in the case of the South African woman Saartje Baartman, nicknamed the "Hottentot Venus." And while gawkers were able to see exotic peoples for the price of a few pennies, serious scholars seized these chances to do their science. By mid-century, "commercial exhibitions began to be routinely advertised as educational opportunities for budding ethnologists" (Qureshi, 2011: 187). Leading scientists in fields from anthropology to anatomy attended such events, recognizing that the humans on display were "usable experimental material," and "the opportunities they provided for research were . . . taken up with enthusiasm" (221).

THE TWENTIETH CENTURY AND THE FOUNDING OF MODERN ANTHROPOLOGY

By the turn of the twentieth century, a few observers were despairing of the ethnological, diffusionist-evolutionist, and amateur approach to anthropology. Although many figures, male and female, would contribute to the establishment of modern professional anthropology, two men were especially influential in putting their stamps on the new science. They are Franz Boas and Bronislaw Malinowski.

Boas (1858–1942) is widely regarded as the father of American cultural anthropology. Although his formal training in Germany in the late 1800s was in physics and geography, there was already a tradition at the time of "human geography" or "cultural geography," which considered the relationship between humans and the natural environment. Best represented by Friedrich Ratzel's *Anthropogeographie*, composed between 1882 and 1891 and read by Boas shortly before his first major fieldwork, cultural geography led Boas' interest in Arctic landscapes, where "population distribution, migratory movements, types of settlement, travel routes, and use of renewable resources among the Inuit were influenced by temporal fluctuations in the natural conditions of the Arctic environment" (Müller-Wille, 2014: 42). Consequently, Boas conducted research on Baffin Island in northern Canada in 1883–1884 and produced one of the earliest ethnographies in his 1888 *The Central Eskimo*.

This experience encouraged Boas to reject the diffusionist and evolutionist—and racist—theories

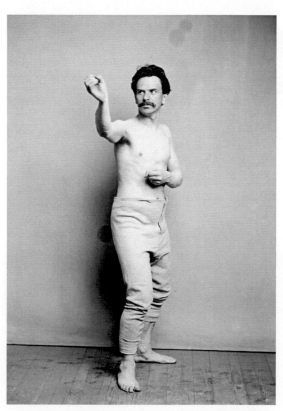

IMAGE 3.5 Franz Boas, one of the founders of modern anthropology, posing for a museum exhibit around 1895.

of the day. Indeed, in one of his first and most important statements about what would become anthropology, "The Limitations of the Comparative Method of Anthropology" (1896), he proposed that there are no "higher" or "lower" cultures and that all such judgments are merely relative to one's own standards of culture. Thus, any "ranking" of cultures is suspect from the outset and probably says more about the student than about the cultures studied. Rather than ordering cultures on the basis of supposed progress or similarity, he recommended actually observing each single culture in maximal detail and each single part of a culture within the context of the whole.

Still, according to the premier historian of anthropology, George Stocking, Boas' interests and methods were not quite what cultural anthropology would eventually become. Stocking argued that Boas depended more on collecting "texts" (often oral accounts of folklore and mythology) than on participant observation (Stocking, 1974: 85) and that in fact much of this material was collected for him by trained assistants in the field like George Hunt (son of a Scottish father and a Tlingit mother) and Henry Tate (a full-blooded member of the Tsimshian people). Also, as others have judged, Stocking found that Boas "directed his study to the past rather than the present" (86), intent to reconstruct and "salvage" traditional culture rather than document how indigenous people were living in the twentieth century.

Nevertheless, Boas was essential to the growth of anthropology in America, where he served first at the American Museum of Natural History and then taught at Columbia University, as well as publishing prolifically, editing journals, and presiding over professional organizations. Over almost forty years he was the teacher and mentor of the first generation of American anthropologists, overseeing forty-seven graduate students—including twenty-one women—among them Alfred Kroeber, Frederica de Laguna, Margaret Mead, and the first generation of American anthropologists.

Bronislaw Malinowski (1884–1942) did his work a generation later than Boas, but had an equally profound impact on the discipline. Originally trained in math and physics in Poland, Malinowski turned to the science of humanity after reading James George Frazer's classic comparative mythology *The Golden Bough* in 1910. He studied under the pioneering psychologist Wilhelm Wundt in Germany as well as important early ethnologists like C. G. Seligman and Edward Westermarck in England before joining an expedition to Papua New Guinea in 1914. By this time, ethnological expeditions were becoming more commonplace: A team from Cambridge University traveled to the Torres Straits in 1898–1899, while another mission went to India in 1901–1902 and still another to Melanesia in 1907–1908. However, most of these visits were extremely short (often only a few days), were conducted by people who were not specially trained in anthropological field methods (since such methods did not really exist yet), and necessarily involved working through interpreters and acculturated local people.

Malinowski practiced a very different kind of research. He spent four years in the field, including more than two years in the Trobriand Islands in 1915–1916 and 1917–1918. Famously, he pitched a tent among the native people, learned their language, and participated in their daily life. In so doing, he helped establish the modern method of participant observation. In 1922 he published his epochal ethnography, *Argonauts of the Western Pacific*, on Trobriand economics and exchange activity, followed by his 1926 *Crime and Custom in Savage Society*, his 1929 *The Sexual Life of Savages in Northwestern Melanesia*, and his 1935 *Coral Gardens and their Magic*.

Based on this intimate contact and knowledge of native peoples, Malinowski determined that there were three general types of cultural data, each requiring its own collection technique. The first was the description and analysis of institutions, which were to be studied by thorough documentation of concrete evidence. More precisely, this meant the creation of charts of activities and customs associated with a particular institution, based on accounts given by the natives as well as on observations by the investigator. This method would yield a literal visible representation of the "mental chart" that members of the society possess. The second type of data, constituting another dimension of cultural reality, was the minutiae of everyday life, which filled out and deepened (if complicated) the analysis of general institutions. As he noted, the emphasis on rules and structures and institutions left an impression of more precision and consistency than is actually seen in real life. So, abstract or generalized

VOLKERPSYCHOLOGIE: A PRECURSOR AND SOURCE OF MODERN ANTHROPOLOGY

Malinowski, Bronislaw. 1984 [1922]. *Argonauts of the Western Pacific*. Long Grove IL: Waveland Press, Inc.

Kuper, Adam. 1983. *Anthropology and Anthropologists: The Modern British School*, revised edition. London and New York: Routledge.

presentations of social structures had to be complemented with particular and personal instantiations or uses of those rules and structures in the details of everyday life, anticipating the distinction between "structure" and "action" that anthropologists like Raymond Firth would elaborate. The third type of data included cultural content like narratives, utterances, folklore, and other conventional sayings and activities.

The other profound influence of Malinowski on the fledgling field of anthropology was his theoretical approach, which was significantly connected to his method. Like Boas, he rejected cultural evolutionism and speculative historical reconstructions. As he wrote:

> I still believe in evolution, I am still interested in origins, in the process of development, only I see more and more clearly that answers to any

evolutionary questions must lead directly to the empirical study of the facts and institutions, the past development of which we wish to reconstruct.

(quoted in Kuper, 1983: 9)

Thus, anthropologists should study the present with all possible attention and clarity before they indulge in speculations about the past—a point on which he openly criticized the Boasians. What a fieldworker sees today is institutions, the individuals acting within them, and standard "narratives" or "scripts" those individuals produce and reproduce in the process. These investigators can hunt for—and perhaps only for—the *function* of institutions and practices today, in the present. Hence, he recommended an approach known as functionalism. Rather than pursue its history (a potentially vain pursuit), the anthropologist can observe its

---

BOX 3.3   A FORGOTTEN HERO OF EARLY ANTHROPOLOGY: W. H. R. RIVERS

No project as grand as anthropology is the product of just one or two men, and we have seen that the work of Boas and Malinowski was made possible by many predecessors, just as their legacy was carried and embellished by many followers. Other contemporaneous scholars made important contributions as well, such as A. C. Haddon, A. M. Hocart, and Baldwin Spencer and Francis Gillen, the latter two of whom collaborated on the highly influential 1899 *The Native Tribes of Central Australia*. However, perhaps no one at the turn of the century was more crucial to anthropology than W. H. R. Rivers. Although trained in medicine and psychology, Rivers was profoundly interested in ethnology and accompanied the 1898–1899 Torres Strait expedition mentioned above. He produced his own ethnography in his 1906 *The Todas* on a native group in India and led the Percy Slade Trust Expedition to the Solomon Islands in 1908 with Hocart, which Edvard Hviding and Cato Berg characterize as "an ethnographic experiment, whereby emerging anthropological theory and method would be brought to bear on, and tested through, encounters with so far undocumented examples of social life" (2014: 3). Simultaneously with Boas and before Malinowski, Rivers called for more "intensive" research than was common in his day,

> in which the worker lives for a year or more among a community of perhaps four or five hundred people and studies every detail of their life and culture; in which he comes to know every member of the community personally; in which he is not content with generalized information, but studies every feature of life and custom in concrete detail and by means of the vernacular language.

> (quoted in Kuper, 1983: 7)

He was also ahead of his time for recognizing the links between cultures, which were especially evident in the Pacific region where people, ideas, and objects traversed long distances in complex cultural chains. Using his medical and psychological background, Rivers went on to diagnose the decline of many indigenous populations as a kind of "shell shock" from the experience of colonialism.

function here and now. What is the function, for example, of marriage, or political systems, or religion?

For Malinowski, the essence of function was to be found in the needs of the individuals who compose a society. Society, he asserted, is ultimately a collection of individual human beings. So, culture functions according to the needs and nature of those individuals, who have two kinds of needs—physical and psychological. Each item of culture, or culture as a whole, must serve to fill one or more of these needs. It is the job of the ethnographer to determine what needs it fills and how.

Like Boas, Malinowski institutionalized British anthropology around himself from his home base at the London School of Economics. There he trained an equally illustrious set of students, such as Raymond Firth, E. E. Evans-Pritchard, Edmund Leach, and Meyer Fortes. However, no one was as important for British social anthropology as Alfred Reginald (A. R.) Radcliffe-Brown. Even before Malinowski, Radcliffe-Brown made his own field trip to the Andaman Islands in 1906–1908, eventuating in his ethnography *The Andaman Islanders: A Study in Social Anthropology*, published in the same year as Malinowski's great study (1922) and under Radcliffe-Brown's original name, A. R. Brown. Radcliffe-Brown helped launch anthropology departments in South Africa (University of Cape Town) and Australia (University of Sydney), but it was also Radcliffe-Brown more than anyone who put the "social" in British social anthropology.

Under the influence of Émile Durkheim's new sociology, Radcliffe-Brown insisted that "social structure" rather than "culture" was the proper subject for anthropology:

> I conceive of social anthropology as the theoretical natural science of human society, that is, the investigation of social phenomena by methods essentially similar to those used in the physical and biological sciences. I am quite willing to call the subject "comparative sociology" if anyone so pleases.
>
> (1965: 189)

Indeed, he denied that culture could be the subject of scientific investigation: "We do not observe a 'culture' since that word denotes, not any concrete reality, but an abstraction, and as it is commonly used a vague abstraction" (190). Social structure, by which he meant actual organized behavior and

the institutions into which it settled, was "just as real as are individual organisms" (190), but culture was nothing more than "a characteristic of a social system. . . . If you study culture, you are always studying the acts of behavior of a specific set of persons who are linked in a social structure" (106).

Thus, Radcliffe-Brown agreed with Malinowski that culture does function, but he disagreed on precisely what that function was. Radcliffe-Brown maintained that individuals are relatively trivial; what is important—and enduring—is society itself, the community, the social whole. In opposition to Malinowski's functionalism, he advocated a "social" or **"structural" functionalism**, the social function of institutions defined by him as "the contribution that they make to the formation and maintenance of a social order" (154). Radcliffe-Brown's focus on institutions versus individuals and on order versus action was hugely influential on the British tradition of social anthropology, which came to emphasize law, kinship systems, and such.

THE ANTHROPOLOGICAL CRISIS OF THE MID-TWENTIETH CENTURY AND BEYOND

Just as approaching maturity often entails a life crisis and a rebellion against received conventions in individuals, so cultural anthropology suffered a disciplinary crisis and rebellion in the mid-twentieth century that was perhaps a sign of maturation and a breakthrough to a deeper level of understanding—and self-understanding. The sources of this crisis and the call to rethink or reinvent anthropology probably included the aging and passing of the founding generation, as happens in all disciplines. However, even more important was the change in the subjects of cultural anthropology themselves, the "primitive peoples" and small traditional societies, which forced a change in the science that purported to study them. Not the least of these changes was the rush of independence movements that ended the centuries-old European project of colonialism and empire. Finally, perhaps a critical point had been reached that compelled anthropology to look at itself in new and sometimes uncomfortable ways—not only at what it was doing, but even at the very tools and concepts it was using to do it.

Structural functionalism the theory that the function of a cultural trait, particularly an institution, is the creation and preservation of social order and social integration

See Chapter 13

Wagner, Roy. 1975. *The Invention of Culture.* Englewood Cliffs, NJ: Prentice-Hall, Inc.

Hobsbawm, Eric and Terence Ranger, Eds. 1983. *The Invention of Tradition.* Cambridge: Cambridge University Press.

Hymes, Dell, Ed. 1972 [1969]. *Reinventing Anthropology.* New York: Random House, Inc.

Leach, Edmund R. 1954. *Political Systems of Highland Burma.* Boston: Beacon Press.

Neo-evolutionism

the mid-twentieth century revival of focus on the historical development of cultures and societies, as in the work of Leslie White and Julian Steward, which generally sought to repair the failings of nineteenth-century evolutionism by proposing specific processes and a "multi-linear" path of change

Structuralism

the theory (associated most closely with Claude Lévi-Strauss) that the significance of an item (word, role, practice, belief) is not so much in the particular item but in its relationship to others; in other words, the "structure" of multiple items and the location of any one in relation to others is most important

One of the first and most important moves in this "new anthropology" was the announcement by Edmund Leach that societies are not always as discrete and traditional as we think they are. In his seminal *Political Systems of Highland Burma* (1954), he described a situation in which societies overlapped each other without clear and permanent boundaries and in which the very politics and culture of the multicultural system fluctuated over time. Given the realities of highland Burmese social relations, he concluded that "ordinary ethnographic conventions . . . are hopelessly inappropriate" (281). In fact, he went so far as to argue that the entire notion of discrete societies was an "academic fiction": "the ethnographer has often only managed to discern the existence of 'a tribe' because he took it as axiomatic that this kind of cultural entity must exist" (291). At almost the same moment, J. S. Furnivall published his study of Burma and Indonesia entitled *Colonial Policy and Practice* (1956), in which he introduced the concept of "plural society" to describe the mixed yet segregated social realities in those locations. Burma and Java were not homogeneous societies at all, but a jumble of "separate racial sections," which "mix but do not combine" (304), linked (and stratified) by sheer economic interests.

One of the other conventions of early anthropology—the peacefulness and stability of traditional societies—was upset by ongoing researches in Africa. Meyer Fortes and E. E. Evans-Pritchard had already discovered that various supposed tribes "appear to be an amalgam of different peoples, each aware of its unique origin and history" (1940: 9) and not always on easy terms with each other. Max Gluckman even more decisively burst the fiction of simple integration of societies in his aptly-named *Custom and Conflict in Africa*, which found that not only are societies not as integrated and harmonious as thought, but that conflict could actually be the social structure of the society: By way of the contours and variations within a society, "men quarrel in terms of certain of their customary allegiances, but are restrained from violence through other conflicting allegiances which are also enjoined on them by custom" (1956: 2). The simple view of primitive order was forever dashed.

These reports from the field heralded an identity crisis within anthropology that was expressed in such subsequent titles as *The Invention of Culture* (Wagner, 1975), *The Invention of Tradition*

(Hobsbawm and Ranger, 1983), *The Invention of Primitive Society* (Kuper, 1988), and first and perhaps most dramatically, *Reinventing Anthropology* (Hymes, 1972). These books and others like them shone the spotlight directly on anthropology itself, clearly identifying anthropology's own culture and how its methods, concepts, and assumptions had influenced its findings and conclusions. Anthropology would subsequently become more self-reflective as it discovered that it was at least in a sense not only science but also literature—that is, a tradition of writing—as in James Clifford and George Marcus (1986) *Writing Culture: The Poetics and Politics of Ethnography.*

Along the way, cultural anthropology split into more schools and theoretical camps than ever, as some practitioners returned to the roots of the discipline to reform them, while others took inspiration from fields and advances outside anthropology. Among these elaborations of anthropology are:

Neo-evolutionism. Leslie White (1949, 1959a, 1959b) and Julian Steward (1950, 1953) are considered the most prominent thinkers to re-introduce a more sophisticated version of cultural evolution. White suggested a principle behind the evolutionary progress of societies, namely the amount and kind of energy it could harness and exploit. As societies developed newer and greater sources of energy (from domesticated animals to electricity and nuclear power), not only their economic, but also their other social characteristics would change in correspondence. Steward contributed the notion of "multilinear" evolution to combat the impression that all societies evolved in the same manner or that all societies were part of some grand Cultural evolution. In this view, each particular culture pursued its own developmental course, and societies at similar points in their evolution (perhaps due to their similar environments) would exhibit similar cultures.

Structuralism. Instead of looking back into the heritage of anthropology, Claude Lévi-Strauss looked across at the developing discipline of linguistics for a new approach to vexing problems like kinship and religion (e.g. the analysis of myth). Drawing on the work of Ferdinand de Saussure in particular, Lévi-Strauss took the notion of culture as a language seriously: Language has "bits" or elements (sounds, words, and so on) in structural relationships with each other (that is, grammar). The grammatical relations between linguistic elements determine their meaning more than the individual elements themselves. Therefore, he proposed that we might approach anthropological problems in the same way. Rather than looking for the "meaning" of some cultural element—totemism, mother-in-law avoidance, a particular theme in a myth—in the thing itself, he proposed that we look for it in the relations between the elements. In other words, if a society has the crocodile for a totem animal, the meaning of that totem is not to be found in the properties of the crocodile, but in the system of relationships between the various totem-animals and, more importantly, the system of relationships between the social groupings associated with those species.

Ethnoscience. Combining two interests of American anthropology in particular—personality or cognition and classification—**ethnoscience**, also known as cognitive anthropology, sought to examine and expose the mental classification systems that shaped local people's experiences and actions. As formulated by Ward Goodenough (1956), Charles Frake (1962), and Stephen A. Tyler (1969) among others, ethnoscience aimed to be more scientific while also pursuing the psychological side of culture, which

had always been a focus in American cultural anthropology. The point was to bring to light the intellectual models of reality that humans have in their heads (often if not usually implicitly) that organize their world in specific ways. Thus, the scientific anthropologist would reconstruct the "folk taxonomy" or the "knowledge structure" of a society, which was the skeleton and structure of its entire meaning and action system.

Symbolic or interpretive anthropology. In some ways moving in the opposite direction and in other ways very comparable, **symbolic anthropology** also sought to get access to the deeper meanings of other societies, but it tended to do this through symbols rather than through taxonomies. Influenced heavily by the philosophies of Susanne Langer (1942) and Ernst Cassirer (1954), who saw all human thought and action as mediated by symbols, the meanings of which could not always be described rationally, anthropologists like Victor Turner (1967, 1981), Clifford Geertz (1973), and Sherry Ortner (1973) attempted to identify the "key symbols" that functioned as lenses through which people perceived their worlds. It was at least in part a reaction against Lévi-Straussian structuralism, which posited a single mental structure for all human beings and stripped away all of the particulars and

Symbolic anthropology
the school of thought (often associated with Clifford Geertz and Victor Turner) that the main goal of anthropology is to elucidate the meanings within which humans live and behave; rather than focusing on institutions and rules, it focuses on symbols and how symbols shape our experience and are manipulated by people in social situations

Ethnoscience
the anthropological theory or approach that investigates the native classification systems of societies to discover the concepts, terms, and categories by which they understand their world

Turner, Victor W. 1967. *The Forest of Symbols: Aspects of Ndembu Ritual*. Ithaca and London: Cornell University Press.

IMAGE 3.6 Claude Lévi-Strauss integrated anthropology, psychology, and linguistics in his work.

context from anthropological analysis. Geertz coined the phrase "thick description" for the practice of trying to penetrate to the deep meanings of people's realities and to present that meaning in all of its richness and complexity. Anthropological analysis and description thus became an interpretive or "hermeneutic" exercise, aiming to "read" a culture and to render its symbols and meanings understandable to us without washing out all of the uniqueness and particularity of the society in question.

Marxist/critical anthropology. In the second half of the twentieth century especially, Marxist or "critical" theory exerted a strong pull on cultural anthropology. In the works of Maurice Bloch (1983), Maurice Godelier (1978), and many others, there was a new concern for issues of economics, class, power, and domination. Working from the Marxian claim that the culture of a society is the culture of the dominant class of that society, they looked for practical and material relationships that shaped the ideologies and institutions of any social group. A key concept was "mode of production," the means and relationships of the production of goods and wealth, which led to and shaped the "relations of production," that is, the actual social relationships between individuals and groups like ownership and property relations, kinship and gender relations, and so on. This perspective emphasized and actively looked for competitive or conflictual relations in society in a way that early anthropology did not and perhaps could not, with its perspective of integration and homogeneity. While it claimed to be scientific and practical, it also tended to be abstract and "theoretical" (even inventing a new word for practice—"praxis") and often openly partisan and critical of existing values and institutions.

Cultural materialism. Advocated especially by Marvin Harris in popular writings like *Cows, Pigs, Wars, and Witches* (1974) and technical books like *The Rise of Anthropological Theory* (1968) and *Cultural Materialism: The Struggle for a Science of Culture* (1979), this perspective extended the ecological views of White and Steward as well as the Marxist view, basing cultural behaviors firmly on "the practical problems of earthly existence" posed by the encounter between "womb and belly" on one hand and the material world of food, climate, and

competition for territory or offspring on the other (Harris, 1979: xv). Like ethnoscience, it aimed at a more scientific anthropology, exposing the "causes" of human action.

Feminist anthropology. A feminist approach to anthropology also appeared in the 1970s as a reaction to male-centered perceptions of the field and its literature ("man the hunter" type approaches and so on). Despite the prominence of women in the anthropological lineage, literature on women and their activities across cultures had been lacking, partly because many cultures have sex-segregated knowledge, which male anthropologists could not access. Michelle Rosaldo and Louise Lamphere (1974) and Rayna Reiter (1975b) were three of the early founders of the movement to explore gender relationships, gender inequalities, and the participation of women in cultures where that participation had been overlooked or minimized. **Feminist anthropology** does not focus exclusively on women but rather on gender diversity and gender issues broadly conceived.

Finally, one of the most exciting and promising new directions is the emergence of a **world anthropologies** perspective, the recognition that, just as there are many diverse cultures in the world, there are many diverse ways to do anthropology. The fact is, as the editors of the recent volume entitled *World Anthropologies* explain, the existence and practices of various local anthropologies, especially in the non-Western world, mean that "the idea of a single or general anthropology is called into question" (Ribeiro and Escobar, 2006: 1). Indeed, anthropology as it has been traditionally known and done has, it turns out, been distinctly Western, and world anthropologies promises to expand anthropology while "provincializing Europe"—not denying or denigrating the Western perspective but showing conclusively that Western thought, and with it anthropological thought as it has so far existed, "are particular and historically located, not universal as is generally assumed" (3–4).

Happily, organizations like the World Council of Anthropological Associations, the World Anthropologies Network, and International Union of Anthropological and Ethnological Sciences, represent anthropologists from Africa, Latin America, Europe, North America, and Asia, to embody and advance just such a global prospect.

Harris, Marvin. 1974. *Cows, Pigs, Wars, and Witches: The Riddles of Culture*. New York: Random House.

Marxist/critical anthropology
the theory, based on the work of Karl Marx, that emphasizes the material and economic forces that underlie society, relying on notions of power and inequality, modes of production, and class relations and conflicts

Rosaldo, Michelle and Louise Lamphere, Eds. 1974. *Women, Culture, and Society*. Stanford: Stanford University Press.

Reiter, Rayna, Ed. 1975. *Toward an Anthropology of Women*. New York: Monthly Review Press.

See Chapter 7

Feminist anthropology
the anthropological theory or approach that focuses on how gender relations are constructed in society and how those relations subsequently shape the society. Also examines how gender concepts have affected the science of anthropology itself the questions it asks and the issues it emphasizes

Cultural materialism
the theory that practical, material, or economic factors can explain some or all cultural phenomena

www.wcaanet.org

www.ram-wan.net/

www.glocol.osaka-u.ac.jp/iuaes/

BOX 3.4   ANTHROPOLOGY IN CHINA

Among the Western ideas introduced to China in the twentieth century was anthropology. A German text on the subject was translated into Chinese in 1903, introducing the fledgling discipline to the country, and naturally the early experience of anthropology focused on race, including a course at Peking University called Human Being and Study of Race soon after 1912, and a 1918 book by Chen Yinghuang of the same university titled *Anthropology* mainly dealing with biological traits and the distribution of races (Liu, 2003: 217). A 1926 essay by Cai Yuanpei titled "Talking about Ethnology" appears to be the first Chinese reference to ethnology, which was understood as describing and comparing cultures instead of dwelling on race. In 1928 Cai founded the Ethnology Research Group and later the Anthropology Research Group, primarily with the mission to conduct fieldwork among ethnic minorities in China. Indeed, in China, ethnology (*minzuxue*) came to mean the study of "nationalities" or ethnic groups (*minzu*), while anthropology (*releixue*) encompassed the study of humanity in general. By the 1930s there were several university departments of anthropology, over thirty academic journals on "anthropology, frontier studies, and minority studies" (218), and more than one hundred books; in 1934 the Chinese Society of Ethnology was founded, and Huang Wenshan, a student of Boas, attempted to construct a Boasian "culturology" in his country. After the Communist revolution in 1949, anthropology and other "bourgeois sciences" were cancelled in mainland China, although it survived in Taiwan. The closest thing to Communist-era anthropology was the Central Institute for Nationalities and the Institute of Nationality Studies, and such programs were largely dedicated to examining ethnic minorities for the purpose of guiding them toward "development," that is, communism and absorption into the Han Chinese mainstream. Anthropology was revived after the death of Mao Zedong in the form of the Chinese Ethnological Society, established in 1980. After 1980, "Chinese anthropologists and ethnologists continued their study on the traditional culture of minority nationalities. At the same time, they also paid great attention to the research on the new situation and new problems that appeared in the minority areas in the course of 'modernization'" (220–221). This movement is part of what became known as the "localization" of anthropology in China, also called *zhongguohua* (Sinicization or Chinese-making) or *bentuhua* (indigenization or nationalization), that is, "the necessity of bringing the social realities and problems of Chinese society into social science work" (Dirlik, 2012: 27) and "bringing in . . . Chinese voices, sentiments, and the social and cultural characteristics of Chinese society" to disrupt the "contemporary hegemony" of American and European social science (21). Although localization is an essential dimension of contemporary Chinese anthropology, Mingxin Liu contends that it began in the 1930s, as Chinese scholars discovered that "it would not work if Chinese anthropologists use western [sic] theories indiscriminately to explain Chinese society"; instead, European and American ideas, questions, and methods—which imagined themselves as universal but were really local to the West— would have to be re-invented by the Chinese for the Chinese.

BOX 3.5   CONTEMPORARY CULTURAL CONTROVERSIES: THE FUTURE OF ANTHROPOLOGY

Anthropology has changed and will continue to change, as the world in which it lives and works changes. Some wonder and even worry about the future of the discipline: What is anthropology today, and what will it be tomorrow? Will it survive at all? Surely the intent of anthropology as Marcus and Fischer saw it is still valid, if not more urgent than ever:

> to offer worthwhile and interesting critiques of our own society; to enlighten us about other human possibilities, engendering awareness that we are merely one pattern among many; to make

World anthropologies
the perspective that anthropology as developed and practiced in the West is not the only form of anthropology, and that other societies may develop and practice other types of anthropology based on their specific experiences and interests

accessible the normally unexamined assumptions by which we operate and through which we encounter members of other cultures.

(1986: ix)

But, perhaps reflecting the world around it, anthropology today is fragmented and fluid: "the current absence of paradigmatic authority is registered by the fact that there are presently many anthropologies" (16) with no single driving or unifying question or theory. Further, other disciplines have adopted or invaded some of anthropology's traditional field, including sociology, ethnic studies, and "cultural studies." The future of anthropology is uncertain but potentially very exciting. What do you think?

SUMMARY

Anthropology is a new science and an unlikely science, and it is new because it is unlikely. If people had thought to do anthropology—that is, the study of human diversity—as easily as they thought to do history or algebra, then they would have done it long before. The two main barriers to an "anthropological perspective" were always, and continue to be certainty in one's own correctness and goodness and lack of information or poor information about others.

Western civilization like all others suffered from these two limitations, although there had always been a somewhat dissatisfied and self-critical tendency in it. However, a series of experiences around the early 1500s forever shattered that certainty while providing a new quantity and quality of experience of the Other. These included encounters with other advanced civilizations, voyages of discovery to new continents, and the Renaissance and Protestant Reformation.

While European societies first struggled with and tried to assimilate these new cultures, they also began to use them for purposes of their own imagination—in particular, to imagine alternatives (whether positive or negative) to their own contemporary social and cultural realities. Hobbes and Rousseau were two of the first to do so, with diametrically opposed results. Even so, the first steps toward viewing other cultures seriously were taken.

Early anthropological thinkers typically came from a historical and "progressivist" direction, interested in the origins of culture (or Culture) and the stepwise "progress" of culture from "primitive" to "modern." Nineteenth-century anthropology, as a "scientific study of man," was also preoccupied with physical and racial description and classification. However, the first modern anthropologists, like Franz Boas and Bronislaw Malinowski, rejected this approach and adopted a more empirical, relativistic, holistic, and humanistic stance. The main thing was to collect good data and use that data to understand cultures as we found them—not as they (allegedly) once were or as we would like them to be. Since those early days, anthropology has altered as its subjects have altered, referring back to its origins, looking for models from other fields, and studying itself with the same tools and the same intensity as it studies other cultures. Anthropology will continue to grow and change for these same reasons. What the anthropology of the future will look like is as hard to predict as—and will depend critically upon—the cultures of the future.

(Q)
MCQS

(Q)
FILL IN THE BLANKS

(WWW)

Key Terms

cultural evolutionism

cultural materialism

diffusionism

ethnoscience

feminist anthropology

Marxist/critical anthropology

neo-evolutionism

noble savage

structural functionalism

structuralism

symbolic anthropology

world anthropologies

Language and social relations

In 2005 Carmel O'Shannessy announced the discovery of a new language in the northern Australian Aboriginal community of Lajamanu. Children and young adults have combined the indigenous Warlpiri language with English and "Kriol" (itself a blend of Warlpiri and English) into what older members of the society call "light Warlpiri." The new language "draws verbs and verbal morphology from Kriol, nouns from Warlpiri and English, and nominal morphology from Warlpiri. It has an innovative auxiliary paradigm, which is derived from Warlpiri and Kriol auxiliaries" (2005: 31). While the linguistic details are complex, she asserts that younger Warlpiri speakers use light Warlpiri for speaking to each other, not—as with most pidgins or creoles (see below)—for speaking to outsiders. In present-day Lajamanu, children learn both standard and light Warlpiri, but they speak light Warlpiri first "as the language of their everyday interactions" (32). One example of light Warlpiri that she offers is "*uuju-ng im habum ngapa*" ("The horse is having water"), composed of two Warlpiri words (*uuju* for "horse" and *ngapa* for "water") and two distinctly non-Warlpiri items (*um*, a third-person singular auxiliary, derived from "him," and *hab-um*, the verb "have" with an *um*

suffix). What is truly remarkable about light Warlpiri is that individuals under thirty years old speak it to each other and to elders, even though the elders themselves do not speak it. Even so, "adults and children think of it as a kind of Warlpiri" (32).

One of the most conspicuous areas of difference between human groups is their languages. Sometimes language difference has been taken as the defining feature of a distinct society, although not always: Two or more societies can speak the same language (e.g. the U.K. and the U.S.), and one society can speak two or more languages (e.g. French, German, Italian, and Romansch in Switzerland). The traits of language—the specific sounds, words, and grammars of each—are easy to observe and clearly fall within the prerogative of anthropology. In fact, language is such a vast subject that anthropology has developed a specialized subdiscipline to investigate it, namely, linguistic anthropology. However, linguistic anthropology is interested in more than sound and grammar. It is also concerned with what kinds of variations and choices exist within a language, how people use those variations and choices to convey social information and to express and maintain social relations, and how the concepts and values in a language

IMAGE 4.1 Linguistic anthropologists began collecting language in the field in the late 1800s.

shape the experience of its speakers. That is, linguistic anthropology finds that language is not merely a communication system but a kind of social action with real (at least as perceived by the society) effects and consequences.

HUMAN LANGUAGE AS A COMMUNICATION SYSTEM

Humans are hardly the only species to communicate. All species, even plants, communicate in various ways, in the sense of transmitting and receiving information, for example by exchanging chemical markers. Bees are famous for their "dance" that communicates the distance and direction to flowers. Humans are not even the only species that communicates "orally." Cats, dogs, and birds, and of course monkeys and apes, make sounds that carry meaning for others of their kind. In the laboratory we have discovered that the primates most closely related to us are the most like us linguistically; they cannot speak, but they can understand speech and can communicate through linguistic media like hand signals, shapes and objects, and buttons and keyboards. That non-human primates have some linguistic ability is no surprise, given their physical and behavioral similarity to us.

Most of what we consider human language is performed in the medium of speech, but not all of

it. People who are completely without speech ability can communicate linguistically, as with American Sign Language. Beyond that, all humans communicate non-verbally all the time, using hand gestures, facial expressions, body postures, and so on. Regardless of the medium, however, language has a set of distinct characteristics, referred to as "design features" (Hockett, 1958; 1977). Among these features are:

- rapid fading—the communication lasts only a brief time (except for writing)
- interchangeability—individuals can be both senders and receivers of messages
- feedback—language users can monitor their own messages and correct errors in them
- semanticity—the elements of language have meaning or reference to the world
- arbitrariness—the connection between a linguistic signal and its meaning is not natural or "given"
- discreteness—language is composed of small, separate, and reusable "bits"
- **displacement**—language can refer to things that are not present in time or space
- productivity—language users can make and understand new messages using old familiar bits
- reflexiveness—language users can employ language to communicate about language

Displacement

the linguistic feature that allows for communication about things that are "not here" in the sense of absent or out of view, past or future, conceptual or even imaginary

- prevarication—language use can be false, deceptive, or meaningless
- learnability—users of one language can learn another language
- cultural transmission—the rules or conventions of language are the property of a social group and are acquired or learned by interacting with that group

Clearly, language is profoundly connected to culture. The same abilities or skills or tendencies that make culture possible also make language possible. In fact, many of the features of language on Hockett's list are also features of culture in general.

Language first of all consists of symbols; it depends on the capacity to engage in symbolism, to think symbolically. Language is a set of acts or gestures—largely but not essentially verbal—that mean something. Many things mean something: When a dog barks, it means something to the dog, to other dogs, and to us. When dark clouds appear on the horizon, it means something (that it might rain, for example). But no one would call the dog barking, or the clouds appearing, symbolic. The difference between such signs and real symbols is that a **symbol** is a *conventional and arbitrary* vehicle for a meaning. There is no necessary or "natural" relationship between a symbol and its meaning. We could use any sound or hand gesture or facial expression or picture to represent any meaning, as long as we all agree to use it and understand its use. There are of course certain words in any language that sound like the thing they mean, such as the word "boom" for an explosion or the child's word "choo-choo" for a train, but these are a special class of words called onomatopoeia and are not typical of human language.

All languages contain a relatively small number of basic units (sounds) that can be combined in various ways to produce a theoretically unlimited number of meanings or utterances. This is what Hockett called the feature of **productivity**: Sounds are arranged into words which are arranged into sentences which are arranged into statements or speech-acts. And while the sounds are finite and conventional, we can produce infinite and original utterances with them. Still more remarkably, humans can talk about things that are "not here" in a variety of senses. For example, humans can talk about things that are not immediately in front of us—behind us or in another room or on the other side of the planet. We can also talk about things that do not exist in the present at all, that is, the past and the future. Humans can talk about things that are blocked from view, invisible, or abstract or general—things like ideas or concepts or relationships, like "justice" or "same/different." We can even talk about things that are purely imaginary or fictional: We can talk about dragons and leprechauns and elves and Hamlet or Harry Potter just as easily and surely as about dogs and cats and clouds. Indeed, in a certain important way, it does not matter whether these things are real or not; if people think they are real and act as if they are real, the words have real social consequences.

The point is that human language ultimately and crucially exploits some profound cognitive or mental abilities. Humans could not produce symbols unless they were cognitively "free" to make meaning. Similarly, our kind of language would be impossible without the human talents of creativity, imagination, and even fantasy. In language, as in culture in general, humans invent their own worlds and live in them. Humans *can* create their own cognitive, "meaningful" world, and they *must* create it.

THE STRUCTURE OF LANGUAGE

Any particular language has a finite set of elements and sets of rules for combining those elements into larger and more complex units. The speaker of the language must learn and master these elements and rules, achieving linguistic **competence**, the ability to make intelligible utterances. To learn a language— and to study the cultural phenomenon of language anthropologically—we must start with the smallest bits and build up higher and more complex linguistic behavior out of these lower-order units. Language thus proceeds from sound to meaning to utterance and finally to practical use.

Phonology

The most basic bits in any human language are its sounds, and **phonology** (from the root *phone* for "sound") is the study of how those sounds are organized and used in language (*phonetics* is usually understood to refer to the processes of the physical

Competence
in language, the mastery of the elements (sounds, semantics, and grammar) of a language to be able to make intelligible utterances

Productivity
the capacity of language to combine meaningless sounds to create new words or to combine words to create new utterances

Phonology
the study of how sounds are used in a language (specifically which sounds occur and the practices for how they combine and interact)

production and sensory reception of sounds). More specifically, phonology is the study of which sounds are used in a language and how those sounds are used to generate words. We are not talking yet about meaning; we are still at the pre-meaningful stage of language.

Humans can make very many different sounds, but no language employs all of them. Any particular language contains some sounds and not others; it uses sounds that other languages do not and uses them in ways that other languages do not. Linguists call the smallest bit of conventionalized sound in a language a **phoneme**. English contains /th/ and /f/ and /sh/ sounds or phonemes that do not occur universally, and some speakers of other languages have difficulty distinguishing or making such sounds. French for example does not contain the /th/ sound, which is often replaced with a /z/ sound, rendering the word "the" as "ze." Japanese speakers struggle with the /r/ and /l/ sounds in English. Other languages employ sounds that are foreign to English. The !Kung or Ju/hoansi in Africa's Kalahari Desert use a set of click sounds in their words that English speakers can make but would never include as parts of English words. (Even the names for their society include sounds that are not part of any possible English word and for which English has no alphabetic symbol, which is why we use punctuation symbols to represent them.) The total number of sounds available in a language can vary widely: Warlpiri (Australian Aboriginal) has only three vowel sounds—"ah," "ee," and "oo"—while Nuer (East African) reportedly has fourteen vowels, each with at least three "lengths," two degrees of "brea-thiness," and three "tones," producing over two hundred possible combinations (Needham, 1972: 18). When a person pronounces the words of one language with the phonology of another, it is known as "speaking with an accent."

The production of speech sounds is of course a physical skill or action, literally bodily movement. For instance, Tagalog, the predominant local language of the Philippines, requires speakers to manipulate their vocal tracts in ways unfamiliar to English speakers:

> The Tagalog /L/ differs from the English /L/ in that in the formation of the former the tongue is relatively straight and flat from the tip to the root, whereas in the corresponding English sound it forms a deep hollow in the middle

with the air coming out of one or more sides of the hollow. When pronouncing any Tagalog word with /L/, with final /L/ particularly, the English speaker must be careful not to lower the middle part of the tongue. The English /L/ is very noticeable and its pronunciation in Tagalog words brands the speaker as definitely non-Tagalog.

> (Philippine Center for Language Study, 1965: 175–176)

This is one reason why speaking a foreign language often feels strange and difficult.

The second issue is how those sounds are used in combination. There are often rules or norms for which sounds may occur together or where in a word a sound may occur. English allows for clusters of consonants, as in the word "straight," with its initial string of three consonants, /s/, /t/, and /r/. Linguists would represent the sound-structure of the word "straight" as CCCVC, abbreviat-ing "consonant" with C and "vowel" with V. Not every language can form such clusters, and some do not do it at all. English also allows many other variations, such as CVC ("sat"), CV ("so"), VC ("is"), VCV ("away"), V ("a"), and even CCCVCCC ("squirts"), some of which are difficult or nearly impossible for other language-speakers to master. Languages like Tahitian and Hawaiian only allow CV or V syllables, that is, every consonant must be followed by a vowel, and a vowel can occur alone.

There are also linguistic norms governing where in a syllable or word a sound can occur. The sound /ng/ (as in "sing" and rendered by linguists as /ŋ/) exists in English but has specific (if implicit) rules for its use: It may come at the end of a word (like "sing") or in the middle of a word (like "singer") but never at the beginning of a word. Any word that started with the sound /ŋ/ would be immediately recognizable as a non-English word. Warlpiri, on the other hand, uses the /ŋ/ phoneme as an initial sound in many words, such as *ngapa* (water), *ngarni* (to eat), *ngaka* (after), and *ngarlarrimi* (to laugh). Most English-speakers, while they can make the sound, cannot pronounce these words easily; the initial /ŋ/ is unnatural. Conversely, the Shoshone (Native American) language contains several consonant sounds (including but not limited to /ch/, /f/, /j/, /k/, /p/, /sh/, /t/, and /z/) that cannot be used as initial sounds.

Phoneme
the smallest bit of contrastive sound in a language, that is, the minimal sound unit that serves to distinguish between word meanings in a language

THE INTERNATIONAL PHONETIC ALPHABET (revised to 2005)

CONSONANTS (PULMONIC)

© 2005 IPA

	Bilabial	Labiodental	Dental	Alveolar	Postalveolar	Retroflex	Palatal	Velar	Uvular	Pharyngeal	Glottal
Plosive	p b			t d		ʈ ɖ	c ɟ	k g	q ɢ		ʔ
Nasal	m	ɱ		n		ɳ	ɲ	ŋ	ɴ		
Trill	ʙ			r					ʀ		
Tap or Flap		ⱱ		ɾ		ɽ					
Fricative	ɸ β	f v	θ ð	s z	ʃ ʒ	ʂ ʐ	ç ʝ	x ɣ	χ ʁ	ħ ʕ	h ɦ
Lateral fricative				ɬ ɮ							
Approximant		ʋ		ɹ		ɻ	j	ɰ			
Lateral approximant				l		ɭ	ʎ	ʟ			

Where symbols appear in pairs, the one to the right represents a voiced consonant. Shaded areas denote articulations judged impossible.

CONSONANTS (NON-PULMONIC)

Clicks		Voiced implosives		Ejectives	
ʘ	Bilabial	ɓ	Bilabial	ʼ	Examples:
ǀ	Dental	ɗ	Dental/alveolar	pʼ	Bilabial
ǃ	(Post)alveolar	ʄ	Palatal	tʼ	Dental/alveolar
ǂ	Palatoalveolar	ɠ	Velar	kʼ	Velar
ǁ	Alveolar lateral	ʛ	Uvular	sʼ	Alveolar fricative

OTHER SYMBOLS

ʍ Voiceless labial-velar fricative
w Voiced labial-velar approximant
ɥ Voiced labial-palatal approximant
ʜ Voiceless epiglottal fricative
ʢ Voiced epiglottal fricative
ʡ Epiglottal plosive

ɕ ʑ Alveolo-palatal fricatives
ɺ Voiced alveolar lateral flap
ɧ Simultaneous ʃ and X

Affricates and double articulations can be represented by two symbols joined by a tie bar if necessary.
k͡p t͡s

VOWELS

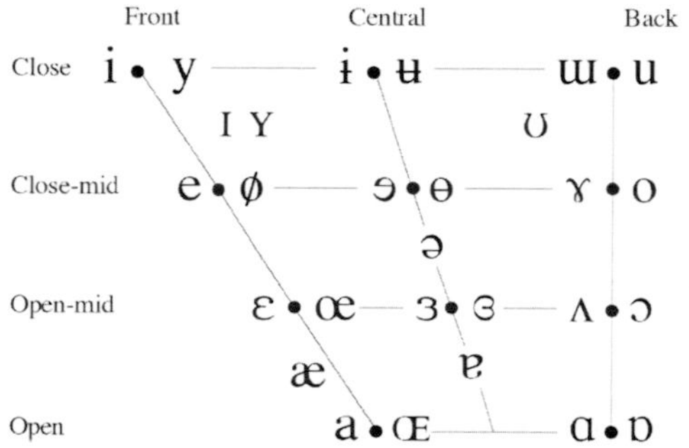

Front — Central — Back

Close: i • y — ɨ • ʉ — ɯ • u
    ɪ ʏ   ʊ
Close-mid: e • ø — ɘ • ɵ — ɤ • o
    ə
Open-mid: ɛ • œ — ɜ • ɞ — ʌ • ɔ
    æ   ɐ
Open: a • ɶ — ɑ • ɒ

Where symbols appear in pairs, the one to the right represents a rounded vowel.

SUPRASEGMENTALS

ˈ	Primary stress
ˌ	Secondary stress
ː	Long
ˑ	Half-long
˘	Extra-short
|	Minor (foot) group
‖	Major (intonation) group
.	Syllable break
‿	Linking (absence of a break)

ˌfoʊnəˈtɪʃən
eː e' ĕ
ɹi.ækt

DIACRITICS

Diacritics may be placed above a symbol with a descender, e.g. ŋ̊

̥	Voiceless	n̥ d̥	̤	Breathy voiced	b̤ a̤	̪	Dental	t̪ d̪
̬	Voiced	s̬ t̬	̰	Creaky voiced	b̰ a̰	̺	Apical	t̺ d̺
ʰ	Aspirated	tʰ dʰ	̼	Linguolabial	t̼ d̼	̻	Laminal	t̻ d̻
̹	More rounded	ɔ̹	ʷ	Labialized	tʷ dʷ	̃	Nasalized	ẽ
̜	Less rounded	ɔ̜	ʲ	Palatalized	tʲ dʲ	ⁿ	Nasal release	dⁿ
̟	Advanced	u̟	ˠ	Velarized	tˠ dˠ	ˡ	Lateral release	dˡ
̠	Retracted	e̠	ˤ	Pharyngealized	tˤ dˤ	̚	No audible release	d̚
̈	Centralized	ë	̴	Velarized or pharyngealized	ɫ			
̽	Mid-centralized	e̽	̝	Raised	e̝	(ɹ̝ = voiced alveolar fricative)		
̩	Syllabic	n̩	̞	Lowered	e̞	(β̞ = voiced bilabial approximant)		
̯	Non-syllabic	e̯	̘	Advanced Tongue Root	e̘			
˞	Rhoticity	ɚ a˞	̙	Retracted Tongue Root	e̙			

TONES AND WORD ACCENTS

LEVEL			CONTOUR		
e̋ or ꜜ	↑	Extra high	ě or ᷄	⟋	Rising
é	˥	High	ê	⟍	Falling
ē	˧	Mid	e᷄	᷄	High rising
è	˩	Low	e᷅	᷅	Low rising
ȅ	ꜜ	Extra low	e᷈	᷈	Rising-falling
↓		Downstep	↗		Global rise
↑		Upstep	↘		Global fall

FIGURE 4.1 International phonetic chart

The location of a sound in a syllable or word may affect its surrounding sounds. Turkish contains eight vowels, classified as "front" or "back" depending on where the tongue is positioned to make them. Then, any particular word can include front vowels or back vowels but not both; of course, suffixes added to words must agree with the vowel-type and thus come in two different forms. In French, on the other hand, rules of *liaison* and *elision* link one syllable or word with another: *ils ont* ("they have") is pronounced "eel zon" ("on" being pronounced nasally, not as in English), somewhat similar to the English tendency to run sounds together ("the mall" sometimes sounds like "them all"). The French *je* ("I") and *ai* ("have") are linked as *j'ai*, while *de* ("of") and *les* ("the"—plural) are combined as *des*.

Morphology or semantics

The practices for the combination of (meaningless) sounds take us to meaning: Upon the foundation of orderly sound, speakers build a set of meanings, depending on the structural relations between these sounds. Therefore, linguists call the study of the "meaningful bits" of language **morphology** (from the root *morph* for "form" or "shape") or **semantics**.

Just as phonemes are the smallest bits of useable sound in a language, **morphemes** are the smallest bits of meaning. Words constitute a class of morphemes called **free morphemes**—that is, morphemes that can stand on their own to convey meaning. "Dog" is a free morpheme, since it is independently meaningful. **Bound morphemes**, however, convey meaning only in conjunction with another morpheme. In English, these usually take the form of prefixes and suffixes. The morpheme *-s* means "plural," just as the morpheme *un-* means "not," when attached to a free morpheme in the right orientation. For instance, if an English speaker simply says "-s," no one knows what it means. But if the speaker binds the sound to "dog" and says "dogs," other speakers understand perfectly. In the wrong order ("sdog" or "happyun"), they would find the words erroneous, unclear, or nonsensical.

Not all languages function the same way morphologically. In English there is only one semantic plural form, which means "two or more" (although there are two phonetic forms, /s/ and /z/,

depending on what sound precedes it, e.g. dog/z/ but cat/s/). However, Warlpiri has two plural forms, neither of which use /s/. To say "two dogs" in Warlpiri, the suffix *-jarra* is attached to the word for dog, *maliki*; this means exactly two dogs. To say "three or more dogs," the suffix *-patu* is used. German tends to use *-en* as the suffix to indicate plural (*Frau* for "woman" becomes *Frauen* for "women"). Languages with "gender" like French and Spanish and German add another wrinkle: For instance, French words tend to attach an *-e* at the end of feminine words, which is not pronounced but changes the pronunciation of the syllable before it. Thus, *chien* (male dog) becomes *chienne* (female dog), changing the nasal *-ien* of the first word into a more familiar /n/ sound for English speakers.

Many languages apply stress or emphasis to certain parts of words, which can alter their semantic meaning. English is a stress-language, with every word given its unique emphasis pattern, producing a kind of "rhythm" in speech which can be exploited in poetry (known technically as meter). There is no consistent rule on how English stress operates, but one frequent pattern is emphasizing the final vowel (by stressing or "lengthening") in verbs but other vowels in nouns or adjectives; thus "to elaborate" or "to articulate" stresses the final /a/ sound, while "elaborate" or "articulate" as adjectives shorten it. Old Irish, by comparison, always stresses the first syllable of nouns and adjectives, with stress on the second syllable for some adverbs. In Tagalog, sound stress has more serious morphological consequences, changing the word's meaning completely: For instance, *gabi* with emphasis on the second syllable refers to a particular starchy root but with emphasis on the second syllable means "night."

Other languages do not use stress or emphasis but rather tone to convey meaning, that is, the meaning of the word depends on the pitch or change of pitch in which it is spoken. Instead of rhythm, this gives the language a melodic quality. While rare in Western languages, this practice is common in Eastern and African ones; in fact, more than half of the world's languages incorporate tone in some way (Crystal, 1987: 172). Some like Zulu use only two tones (high and low), others like Yoruba use three (high, middle, and low), and Cantonese Chinese uses six (middle, low, high-then-falling, low-then-falling, high-then-rising, and low-then-rising). Thus a single "syllable" like *si*

Morphology

the area of language dealing with how meaningful bits (usually but not exclusively words) are created and manipulated by the combination of language sounds

Semantics

the study of meaning in language. See *morphology*

Morpheme

the smallest bit of meaningful sound in a language, usually a word but also a prefix or suffix or other meaning-conveying sound that can be used in conjunction with a word

Free morpheme

a morpheme that has meaning in its own right, that can stand alone as a meaningful sound (for the most part, a word)

Bound morpheme

a morpheme that has meaning but only when used in conjunction with a word (such as the suffix -s to indicate plural)

in Cantonese can mean "poem," "to try," "matter," "time," "to cause," and "city" depending on how it is intoned. The Tai-Kadai language family of Southeast Asia and southern China reportedly contains eleven different tones.

Semantic characteristics extend—and differ—far beyond the simple construction of words. If words were merely names for things, then the morphology of language would be relatively trivial. However, words vary across languages in their **semantic range**, that is, the "area" of meaning that they cover, the variety of things to which they refer, or the constellation of meanings that they embrace. For comparison, the English word "to be" covers a wide range of meanings, which are divided in Spanish between two words, *ser* and *estar*. While there is no easy way to distinguish the two Spanish words, roughly *ser* refers to intrinsic qualities (what something "really" is), and *estar* refers to conditional qualities (what something currently or situationally is). Old Irish provides three forms of "to be," depending on whether the state of being is inherent and intrinsic, a temporary condition, or a regular condition. Warlpiri, in contrast, has no word for "to be." Obviously, in translating from English to Spanish or Old Irish, you must choose the *correct* "to be." Semantic range becomes an even more complex problem when we realize that words in one language often have no precise equivalent in another; this problem is especially acute when talking about religion, since many languages and cultures have no such word or concept as "god" or "sin" or "hell," etc. More often than we realize, the semantic range of a word is highly or purely cultural, as with words such as "weed" or "drug" or "game" or even "food."

Grammar or syntax

Grammar or **syntax** refers to the rules for combining words (and other morphemes) into meaningful and intelligible utterances, like sentences. Obviously, being able to say "dog" or "dogs" is necessary, but it would not be very useful if that was all a speaker could say. Hopefully speakers can use the words in more sophisticated and informative utterances to convey complete ideas or statements.

There are some basic grammatical rules in each language that organize the structure of normal

"good" speech. In English, the most fundamental rule or variable in sentences is word order. That is, English speakers make and understand sentences based on the sequence of the words: In a regular declarative sentence, they know to put—and expect to hear—the "subject" word first, then the "verb" word, then the "object" word (notated as SVO). Of course, things can get much more complicated, with dependent clauses and participial phrases and such, but this is the skeleton of a basic sentence. So, the sentence "The man hit the dog" has a specific meaning. The sentence "The dog hit the man," with exactly the same words in a different sequence, has a clear but different meaning. And any other sequence—like "The the hit man dog"—yields no meaning at all.

Up to seventy-five percent of the world's languages follow a SVO or SOV pattern (Crystal, 1987: 98). However, other orders exist. Standard Turkish sentences place the subject first and the verb last. Old Irish typically took the VSO order. Tagalog can give the predicate before the topic (according to the Philippine Center for Language Study (1965: 13), concepts of "subject," "verb," and "object" do not quite apply to Tagalog grammar, since a verb can be a subject) or in reverse order with the addition of the morpheme *ay*. Thus "The dress is beautiful" can be said as *Maganda ang damit* ("beautiful" + "is" + "dress") or as *Ang damit ay maganda* ("is" + "dress" + *ay* + "beautiful").

Some languages do not depend on word order at all or do not have to provide every grammatical element for a sentence. The order of words in a Warlpiri sentence does not determine its meaning. For instance, to communicate that a man hit a dog, in Warlpiri one would use the words *wati* (man), *pakarnu* (hit—past tense), and *maliki* (dog), but to make the appropriate sentence one cannot simply say *wati pakarnu maliki*. The subject-word in a Warlpiri sentence is identified not by its location in the sentence but by a bound morpheme that indicates "subject," in this case the suffix *-ngki*. The correct utterance thus is *wati-ngki pakarnu maliki*. In any order the meaning is the same. To change the meaning so that the dog is doing the hitting, the suffix must go on *maliki*, the correct suffix being not *-ngki* but *-rli* (based on the number of syllables and the terminal syllable of the word). Now the sentence is *maliki-rli pakarnu wati*, which can be arranged in any order. Latin is similar in using

Semantic range
the set of meanings conveyed by a particular word, that is, the "range" of its referents or the variety of phenomena or conceptions that it names

See Chapter 10

Grammar
see *syntax*

Syntax
the rules in a language for how words are combined to make intelligible utterances of speech acts (for example, sentences). Also known as *grammar*

suffixes to indicate a word's role in a sentence, rather than the order of words.

Some languages do not even require that all of the elements of a "good" English sentence be included. The Spanish equivalent of the English "I love you" can take the form OV, without a "subject": *Te amo* ("you"-object + "love"). If an English speaker said "You love," the meaning would be ambiguous, since "you" can be a subject pronoun or an object pronoun, but Spanish clarifies the grammar through the verb and its conjugation (*amo* is "love"-first person, as opposed to *amas*, "love"-second person). While this might seem confusing to English speakers, English does something similar in imperative sentences, like "Go to the store!" in which the subject is not spoken but understood ("you-understood"). Meanwhile, Arabic does not use or include a verb for "to be" in the present tense, so an Arabic sentence may lack a verb; for instance, "The teacher is a man" can be stated in Arabic as *al-mudarris rajulun*, literally "the teacher man." (Interestingly, Arabic does use a "to be" verb, *kaana*, in the past tense.) Old Irish, finally, has no personal pronouns at all; while pronouns are optional in Spanish, Old Irish cannot include one and conveys all "person" information (see below) through verb endings.

Syntax and grammar can of course be much more intricate than these simple matters, and grammatical principles found in English may be absent in other languages and vice versa. For instance, English contains articles ("a" and "the"), but Turkish and Warlpiri do not. At the same time, many languages, including French, Spanish, and German, contain the concept of "gender," in which every noun is assigned one of two (or in the case of German, three—masculine, feminine, and neuter) genders. So, *chat* ("cat") in French is masculine, and *television* is feminine. Then, articles and adjectives must agree with the noun in gender and in number: *le chat, la television, les chats, les televisions, le grand chat, la grande television*.

In English, nouns and pronouns are distinguished by "case," that is, their role in a sentence (basically, subject and object). In other languages the situation is considerably elaborated. For instance, German has four cases ("nominative" or roughly subject, "accusative" or roughly direct object, "dative" or roughly indirect object, and "genitive" or roughly possessive), each of which

requires a modification of articles; added to three genders and two numbers (singular and plural), many people find German declensions maddeningly difficult. In Russian, nouns have cases—six of them, depending on the noun's function in the sentence (as subject, direct object, possessive/quantity/negation, indirect object, location, or means [i.e., by or with])—and must be conjugated with the proper suffix (also considering gender, of which there are three). Swahili, an East African language, possesses as many as eighteen noun cases, differentiating between persons, abstract nouns, mass nouns, location and movement, and even the shapes of objects.

Last for our purposes are "person" and "tense." "Person" is the grammatical category that identifies the speaker and the audience of an utterance; in English this includes the first (I/we), second (you/you all), and third person (he/she/it/they), divided into singular and plural. Verbs are conjugated somewhat differently for each person (although not as differently as in Spanish). Warlpiri contains more person-forms than English, including a second- and third-person inclusive and exclusive (that is, "we-but-not-you" and "we-all," and "they-but-not-you" and "they-all"), each taking a different verb ending. "Tense" is, generally speaking, the time-element in speech—present, past, and future—although this can be joined with "aspect"—that is, the relation of the action to other facts or events (e.g. completed in the past, ongoing in the present, simultaneous with some other actions, etc.). Not all languages can be fit neatly into the tense and aspect categories of English. For example, Shoshone verbs can take progressive (ongoing over time), continuative (happening over and over), customary-habitual, resultative (resulting from some previous action), future, completive (finished in the past but having effects in the present), and expective (expected to occur) tenses and aspects, each with different suffixes and other rules of use (Gould and Loether, 2002).

Pragmatics or sociolinguistics

Our speech choices have social meanings and social consequences. There might be a grammatical way to say something that is not an *appropriate* way to say it. This is a crucial point: Language does much more than exchange factual information. It may actually be, in the end, that most of what language conveys is not facts but other kinds of social information.

Pragmatics (from the root *pragma* for "practical" or "practice") or **sociolinguistics** (literally, "society" + "language") refers to the rules or conventions for using language appropriately in social situations—that is, for saying the right thing to the right person in the right circumstances. The point is that *a language is a "code" not only for factual information, but for social information as well.* The kinds of social information encoded, and how, will depend upon the society and the distinctions it makes between different kinds of people and situations. There is no society in which all individuals are exactly equal in status or in which all situations are exactly the same in meaning and value. Minimally, some people are "higher" than others, and some situations are "more important" than others. Different speech forms will be appropriate in regard to these different people and conditions.

One good example of the social use of language is the area of **honorifics**, or language forms specialized to indicate the relative social status or relationship of the speakers. In French, there are two forms of the subject pronoun "you"—the singular or familiar *tu* form (for friends and equals) and the plural or formal *vous* form (for strangers and superiors). Using the *tu* form to your superiors would either indicate closeness, disrespect, or error, just as using the *vous* form to your spouse or friends would seem overly formal or distant. English lacks such basic vocabulary distinctions, but there are ways to convey respect, from "polite" terms of address like "sir" and "ma'am" to more specialized ones like "your honor" and "your majesty," as well as semantic additions like "please" and "may." We might even use a respectful syntax, like a question rather than a command, and a deferential tone of voice.

Other languages can go much further. For instance, thirteen different forms of the first person pronoun ("I") exist in Thai, depending on whom one is addressing. *Phom* would be appropriate between equals, while *kraphom* would be polite when talking to someone of higher rank (say, a monk or a government official), and the most formal, *klaawkramom*, would be correct for addressing

a member of the royal family. Japanese also has an extensive set of linguistic choices, expressed most simply in the distinction between *tatemae* (polite forms for strangers or people outside your in-group) and *honne* (familiar forms for close friends and family). The idea "Sakai drew a map for Suzuki" can take the following forms for the following reasons (Foley, 1997: 319–321):

1. *Sakai ga Suziki no tame ni chinzu o kai-ta* (used if the two people mentioned, Sakai and Suzuki, are familiar or inferior to the speaker)
2. *Sakai san ga Suzuki san ni chizu o kai-ta/kai-mash-ta* (used if Sakai and Suzuki are equal to the speaker)
3. *Sakai san ga Suzuki san ni chizu o o-kaki-ni nat-ta/nari-mashi-ta* (used if Sakai is considerably higher in status than the speaker)
4. *Sakai san ga Suzuki san ni chizu o o-kaki shi-ta/shi-mashi-ta* (used if Suzuki is considerably higher in status than Sakai)
5. *Sakai san ga Suzuki san ni chizu o kai-te kudasai-ta/kudasai-mashi-ta* (used if Suzuki is considerably lower in status than Sakai but the speaker wants to show his solidarity or familiarity with Suzuki)

And so on. Clearly, learning Japanese involves much more than simply learning the Japanese translations for English words. Indeed, it would be difficult to render the Japanese connotations of these sentences into everyday English at all.

The style variations in a language can be understood as codes for the important social distinctions made by the society. These may include such social factors as age, gender, power, office, education, interpersonal relationship, class, title, race, geographical region, and many others. No doubt if a non-native speaker said any of the five Japanese sentences above, all Japanese speakers would understand the factual content of the utterance: Somebody drew a map for somebody. However, all but the correct form would "feel wrong" to the native speakers and perhaps evoke negative reactions.

The sociolinguistic practices of a language say a lot about the society that speaks the language. In the U.S. in particular, there are not many honorific forms because there is no use for them. Americans do not make the same social distinctions, or attach

Pragmatics
the rules or practices regarding how language is used in particular social situations to convey particular social information, such as the relative status or power of the speakers

Sociolinguistics
see *pragmatics*

Honorifics
specialized forms of speech (terms, titles, tones, grammar, etc.) that convey respect or deference

the same importance to them, that, say, the Japanese do. It is probably fair to say that Americans, as a people with an egalitarian ideology, deliberately and consciously avoid making many social distinctions in their speech. For example, the fact that students usually speak in a comparatively informal style to teachers indicates that the social distance between students and teachers is not great. Americans would even address their president with the informal "you" because they have no other semantic choice (although they might express respect in other ways, including polite forms, tone of voice, and body language).

MAKING SOCIETY THROUGH LANGUAGE: LANGUAGE AND THE CONSTRUCTION OF SOCIAL REALITY

The previous discussion of speech styles and social status barely scratches the surface of the complex and intimate relationship between language and society. Language is much more than a set of words for things. It also fundamentally expresses and constructs social relationships, including political and religious as well as gender and age and other status relations, not just in terms of what different individuals and groups talk about, but how they talk. We should think of language and its skillful manipulation as a social resource that both is produced by and produces interpersonal and intergroup bonds and fractures.

Language as performance

One of the best ways to introduce the social efficacy of language is in terms of what J. L. Austin called **performatives**. In *How to Do Things with Words* (1962), Austin distinguished between speech acts that describe the world and ones that *change* the world in some way. For example, there is a big difference between a declarative sentence ("You are getting married") or an imperative sentence ("Get married!") and a performative sentence ("I now pronounce you man and wife"). In such utterances, the saying of it makes it so—the words are more than words, but a real social act that accomplishes some social effect. Put another way, speaking in such cases is not just saying something, but doing something.

There are many kinds of linguistic performatives in any society. When a judge says, "Case dismissed" or a king says, "I knight thee," a social

Performatives
linguistics utterances that do not merely describe but actually accomplish a transformation in the social world

Austin, J. L. 1962. *How To Do Things with Words.* Oxford: Clarendon.

IMAGE 4.2 The courtroom is a typical site for the use of linguistic performatives.

effect has been achieved. Notice that only certain kinds of people can perform certain linguistic acts; issuing performative statements is part of the role they occupy. Ordinary citizens cannot dismiss court cases or bestow knighthoods (in fact, no one in the United States can bestow knighthoods). Furthermore, the social context must be correct: A priest cannot walk down the street marrying people by saying, "I pronounce you man and wife." In extreme situations, the proper people must be present, the proper rituals must be observed, perhaps even the proper clothing must be worn. The speech act is part of a much more comprehensive social setting or ritual.

Austin distinguished a variety of kinds of performatives, including "verdictives" in which a "ruling" of some sort is made, "exercitives" in which power is exercised such as to appoint or advise or warn, "commissives" in which a commitment is made, such as a promise or agreement (e.g. an oath), and "behabitives" that express a socially recognized behavior, like as an apology or a congratulation. Performatives also allow for the possibility of deception or failure; that is, I can say, "I promise to do so and so" and never intend to do it, and I can attempt to apologize and fail, either because the recipient sees through my false sentiment or because I do not execute the verbal behavior correctly. Then they might say, "No, give a *real* apology!" or "Apology not accepted."

Performatives have what Austin called "illocutionary force" in that they do not convey meaning so much as bring about a social outcome—actually making someone a knight or a married person. Other kinds of utterances can have "perlocutionary force" in that they can have an effect on the audience and lead them to have certain feelings or take certain actions. Persuading is a key perlocutionary effect; others include frightening and upsetting. Perlocutionary acts do not directly change the social world, but they change people's attitudes, who may put those changes into action.

Language and political power

One thing that gets a leader elected in a democracy is the ability to give a good speech; sometimes it is the main thing. Pericles in ancient Athens and Marc Anthony in Shakespeare's *Julius Caesar* swayed the crowd with skillful oration. Language is central to obtaining, exercising, and challenging power in many societies.

Michelle Rosaldo described the Ilongot of the Philippines as a society that took linguistic abilities very seriously; for them, "true verbal art has social

---

BOX 4.1   HOW TO DO THINGS WITH WORDS THE LIMBA WAY

The Limba people of northern Sierra Leone had their own set of performative utterances, suited to their agricultural economy and their chiefly politics. Three of the most important Limba performatives were "I accept/agree/approve" (*yaŋ yergkei*), "I announce (formally)" (*yay teŋ dantheke*), and "I plead/entreat/apologize/pray/acknowledge a fault" (*yaŋ theteke*). "All these terms are central to Limba day-to-day transactions and in particular to formal negotiations. They are used in making contracts, in the various stages of transactions, and in formal law cases" (Finnegan, 1969: 537). For example, in social disputes, the chief or elders would strive to make the parties "speak well between them, the one to apologize (*theteke*), the other to 'accept'" (538). Acceptance was also the final stage in marriage negotiations. Announcing was part of many situations, from visits and ceremonies to interacting with the chief: A visitor to a village was expected to "announce" his/her arrival to the chief "and in so doing accepts the chief's authority" (540). Pleading constituted a request for aid or forgiveness. In addition, Finnegan noted that thanking, greeting, and saying goodbye were crucial sociolinguistic performances. "Making these utterances is, for the Limba, essentially to perform an act of commitment—to acknowledge indebtedness or dependence as well as, on occasion, a particular transaction" (542). Such words were "part of the duty expected of any important man: he must speak well to people" (546).

IMAGE 4.3 Masterful use of political speaking is a path to power in many societies, as for American President Barack Obama.

REGISTERING POWER: THE MAGICAL POWER OF WRITING IN ECUADOR

Folklore

the "traditional," usually oral, literature of a society, consisting of various genres such as myth, legend, folk tale, song, proverb, and many others

force" (Rosaldo, 1984: 140). Oratory or *purung* was a highly prized and formally structured speech form in which "art and politics are combined" (138). It was contrasted to ordinary forms such as gossip or *berita*, myths or *tadek* or *tudtud*, and tales, where the content was more important than the style; in *purung* the most important thing was how things were said rather than what was said.

One of the characteristics of good Ilongot *purung*, as in many societies, was a certain amount of indirectness and wit (*beira* or elaboration, *'amba'an* or witty flourish, *'asasap* or "crooked" speaking). This was possible because the community already shared knowledge and memories of past actions and events, and it was important to prevent emotions from becoming too enflamed. In practice, *purung* was delivered in the form of verbal exchanges, in which the speakers claimed that they were "giving" or even "feeding" each other words. The target of a speech would repeat the words of the speaker, insisting that they "will not 'hide' their hopes, that in their hearts are no ill thoughts, that in their breath they know that they are kinsmen" (143). The ultimate purpose of these performances was to restore the kin bonds of the two speakers or sides, but this was accomplished "through deception, pretense, wit, and the display of unity and strength by 'sides' that are, initially, opposed" (143). As in this and most such instances, a kind of verbal negotiation not only of interests but of statuses was taking place, and neither side could afford to totally dominate or humiliate the other.

From the holistic perspective of anthropology, it is clear that the style and substance of political speaking would be related to the general quality of

politics and to the hierarchies or lack thereof in the society. Wana society on the island of Sulawesi in Indonesia was acephalous (i.e. without a head or leader) and mostly egalitarian, in which no enduring political roles or groups existed. When Wana men met for the purpose of public speaking, they practiced *kiyori*, an extremely stylized poetic form broken into stanzas with rigid principles about syllabification, emphasis, and rhyme. They might also use specialized terminology, especially as part of religious or legal occasions. It was ordinarily addressed to one man by one man, and the listener might repeat the speech several times as if memorizing it. Sometimes the receiver of the *kiyori* would answer with his own, setting off an exchange of lines. The intentions of speaking *kiyori* varied from establishment of alliances to advice to strong criticism. One of the key features of *kiyori*, however, was the use of ambiguous or conventional references, like aphorisms and metaphors. In fact, it was "an expressive form well suited for speaking in oblique and clever ways" (Atkinson, 1984: 57), and skillful speakers took full advantage of the potential for ambiguity.

Oral literature and specialized language styles

There are many other areas where language and social relationships intersect, including gender, to which we will return in the next chapter. However, one more that calls for our attention at this point is "cultural knowledge" and the specialized language styles that communicate it. Anthropologists and others often refer to this body of knowledge and the genres in which it occurs as **folklore**, a society's primarily oral and traditional knowledge which is told or performed in specific appropriate ways. To get some idea of the range of linguistic activities that can be regarded as folklore, consider Alan Dundes' list:

> Folklore includes myths, legends, folktales, jokes, proverbs, riddles, chants, charms, blessings, curses, oaths, insults, retorts, taunts, teases, toasts, tongue-twisters, and greeting and leave-taking formulas. . . . It also includes folk costume, folk dance, folk drama, folk instrumental music . . ., folksongs . . ., folk speech . . .,

folk similies . . . , folk metaphors . . . , and names. Folk poetry ranges from oral epics to autograph-book verse, epitaphs, latrinalia (writings on the walls of public bathrooms), limericks, ball-bouncing rhymes, jump-rope rhymes, finger and toe rhymes, dandling rhymes (to bounce children on the knee), counting-out rhymes . . . , and nursery rhymes. The list of folklore forms also contains games; gestures; symbols; prayers (e.g., graces); practical jokes; folk etymologies; food recipes; quilt and embroidery designs; house, barn, and fence types; street vendor's cries; and even the traditional conventional sounds used to summon animals or to give them commands.

(1965: 3)

Myth will be discussed in more detail in the context of religion, and there are too many others to explore them all here, but a few of these oral literature styles will highlight the variety and social importance of specialized linguistic performances.

Proverbs

In many societies, much "conventional wisdom" is stored in proverbs and other such traditional sayings.

IMAGE 4.4 Herbert Jim, a contemporary Seminole (Native American storyteller).

They tend to be brief, pithy, and often metaphorical. American English is full of them—"A penny saved is a penny earned," "A leopard can't change its spots," and so on. Other societies have their own culturally specific sayings as well as socially appropriate occasions for using them. Ilongot *purung* or Wana *kiyori* would incorporate apt proverbs, as well as original metaphors. John Messenger noted that the Anang in Nigeria employed proverbs for a variety of purposes, including entertainment and education, but also more serious ones like rituals and court hearings. Particularly in the traditional courts known as *esop*, Anang litigants "take every opportunity to display their eloquence and constantly employ adages" (Messenger, 1965: 303–304). A well-met proverb could make the case and determine the outcome of the proceedings. Of course, many of these maxims do not make much sense outside of their cultural context, for example:

"If a dog plucks palm fruits from a cluster, he does not fear a porcupine."
"A single partridge flying through the bush leaves no path."
"If you visit the home of the toads, stoop."
"The crayfish is bent because it is sick."

Africa has a particularly rich tradition of proverbs, but anthropologists and folklorists have also documented them in Lebanon (R. Parker, 1958), Japan (Storm, 1992), Vietnam (Nguyen, Foulks, and Carlin, 1991), Sicily (Giovannini, 1978), and virtually every part of the world. Boas even collected proverbs from South Africa in 1922 (Boas and Simango, 1922).

Riddles

Like a proverb, a riddle "seems to depend on *metaphor*, on a kind of poetic comparison drawn between the thing actually described and the referent to be guessed" (De Caro, 1986: 178). In contemporary American society, riddles are mostly told for fun and most often by or to children. However, in other societies they can have other and more serious functions. De Caro identified six contexts in which riddling takes place across cultures, including leisure, education (for instance, the famous Buddhist *koan*), courting and mating, greeting, initiations and funerals, and folk narrative. In Dusun society, riddles

See Chapter 10

Paralanguage
the qualities that speakers
can add to language to
modify the factual or social
meaning of speech, such as
tone of voice, volume,
pitch, speed and cadence,
and "non-linguistic" sounds
like grunts and snickers

Vocalizations
non-linguistic sounds that
can accompany and affect
the meaning of speech

Kinesics
the study of how body
movements are used to
communicate social
information, sometimes
referred to as "body
language"

Bauman, Richard. 2001.
"Verbal Art in
Performance." In
Alessandro Duranti, Ed.
*Linguistic Anthropology: A
Reader*. Malden, MA and
Oxford: Blackwell
Publishing. 165–188.

Proxemics
the study of how cultures
use personal space (or
"proximity")

could be combative as well as humiliating, and Turkish society used riddles in festivals such as weddings and actually had professional riddlers and neighborhood riddling teams.

P. D. Beuchat (1957) told that the Bantu of Africa made riddles for fun and to demonstrate intelligence and wit. The riddles were characteristically short verbal analogies that required a "solution" or answer, like:

"I have built my house without any door." Answer: an egg.
"The little hole full of grass litter." Answer: the teeth.
"Two little holes that refuse to be filled; there enter people, oxen, goats, and other things." Answer: eyes.

Ritual languages

In many societies, one or more specialized linguistic genre(s) may serve specific purposes. Joel Sherzer (1983), for instance, documented three quite distinct speaking styles in Kuna society in Panama, associated with a particular ritual activity and distinguished from everyday speech or *tule kaya*. Political or chiefly speech (*sakla kaya*), curing song or "stick doll language" (*suar miimi kaya*), and girl's puberty rite language (*kantule kaya*) each had different pace and tone qualities, as well as specialized vocabularies and other aspects of increasing formality. Latin served the same general purpose in medieval Europe, conveying a gravity that ordinary vernacular languages did not. The use of archaic forms like "thee" and "thou" in English still confers an artistic and even religious aura. Richard Bauman (2001) proposed eight characteristics or "devices" that set specialized or ritualized speech apart from everyday talk: unique "codes" including archaic or esoteric terms, formulas like conventional openings and closings (e.g. "Once upon a time"), figurative language like metaphors, stylistic alternatives like rhyme or repetition, patterns of tempo or stress or pitch, "paralinguistic" usages (see below), overt appeals to tradition, and "disclaimers of performance."

Paralanguage and non-verbal language

Not all of human communication, or even of language, is verbal, and verbal language is not limited to its words or morphemes. Nonverbal gestures of various kinds can have meaning independent of spoken language, and they can be added to alter the meaning of speech. At the same time, the ways that speakers modulate speech can also affect its meaning.

Paralanguage includes the vocal features that shape the delivery of spoken language, such as tone, pitch, speed, rhythm, and volume. Saying the same thing rapidly or slowly, or in a high- or low-pitched voice, can change its meaning. Some specialized forms of speech, like the Kuna ways of speaking mentioned above, are associated with particular paralinguistic variations. We can also communicate emotion and sincerity through voice qualities, as well as advanced skills like irony and sarcasm. Other paralinguistic features include sounds that are not strictly linguistic but that convey meaning; called **vocalizations**, some examples are "um" and "shhh" and "tsk tsk."

The vocal apparatus is not the only part of humans involved in the construction of meaning, including linguistic meaning. The entire human body can be a meaning-conveying medium. **Kinesics** is the general name for the bodily movements or gestures that augment and modify verbal communication (sometimes called "body language"). Among kinesics issues are facial expressions, hand gestures, and the physical distance between speakers. For example, a wink in America can suggest dishonesty or conspiracy between speakers. Raised eyebrows indicate surprise, and lowered ones can express doubt or displeasure. In some societies there is a more or less complete "language" of hand signs, as in the Warlpiri system known as *rdaka rdaka* (literally, "hand hand"). There are hand signs for many common words, used by hunters to maintain silence, by mourners when certain words are forbidden, and most widely by women. In many other societies, there are less complete but still important culturally relative gestures.

Finally, **proxemics** refers to the use of personal space in interactions. Different societies maintain different degrees of physical distance between members, depending on their relationship. American casual speakers keep a 24-inch or so zone between them, while Japanese maintain more distance and Middle Easterners less (the latter may

BOX 4.2 GESTURES ACROSS CULTURES

Like so much else, gestures are culturally relative; the same gesture can have a different and even opposite meaning in different cultures. For instance (based on Axtell, 1991):

Sticking out your tongue is an insult in the U.S. but a greeting in Tibet.

In the U.S., the thumb and forefinger circle means "OK," but in Russia, Germany, and Brazil it is an insult. In Japan it is the sign for money (a round coin).

In Holland, tapping your forefinger on your forehead means "You are stupid."

In Iran and Australia, the "thumbs up" signal is rude.

In Bulgaria, Greece, Turkey, Iran, and Bengal, nodding your head means "no" and shaking your head means "yes."

In England, the two-fingered "V" gesture is an insult if the back of the hand is facing the audience; in that case, it means "Up yours."

even hold hands, as we noted at the opening of the first chapter). Diverging from these standard distances can communicate intimacy, respect, avoidance, or invasiveness depending on the culture and the distance.

IMAGE 4.5 Body language and personal space: Arab men hold hands as a gesture of friendship.

Language change, loss, and competition

Like everything else in the cultural world, language is dynamic, constantly changing, and available for humans to manipulate and compete over and through. One important aspect of real-world language use is multilingualism in many societies. In places from Belgium to New Guinea, multiple languages co-exist, with various relationships, from cooperative to hostile. "Linguistic nationalism" can threaten to pull societies apart, as in Canada, where the French-speaking Quebecois have tried several times to pass a referendum separating Quebec from Canada to form their own officially French-speaking country. When two languages share a social space, the choice of language may be a "political" or "symbolic" statement, as Edmund Leach (1954) noted in Burma: Which language you speak, at any given time or habitually, can indicate "whose side you are on." Even within a single language, there may be two or more forms treated as "high" and "low" or "prestigious" and "common." This phenomenon is known as **diglossia** and consists of distinctions of function (say, lower form for "popular" or casual uses and higher form for official or formal uses) as well as class and stratification.

In situations of sustained and, particularly, unbalanced culture contact, changes may occur to one or both of the contact languages. Often a simplified working version of the dominant language, showing certain features of the subordinated

LIVING SPACE AS RITUAL COMMUNICATION

Diglossia
the use of two varieties of a language by members of a society for distinct functions or by distinct groups or classes of people

OJIBWE COMMUNICATIVE PRACTICES

BOX 4.3   CLASSICAL AND VERNACULAR ARABIC

"One of the most distinctive features of the Arab world is that Classical Arabic coexists with such national vernaculars as Egyptian, Syrian, Jordanian, and so on" (Haeri, 2000: 63), which is no surprise, since the language has over two hundred million speakers across many countries. Classical Arabic "is the language of writing, education, and administration, while the latter are the media of oral exchange, nonprint media, poetry, and plays" (63). Arabic speakers call the high version of their language *al-lugha al-'arabiyya al-fusha* or "the eloquent Arabic language," but significantly, according to Niloofar Haeri, "there is no community of native speakers of Classical Arabic" (64). The classic form lives most importantly in the Qur'an and in literary texts. As with other language situations, there are gender differences, with men preferring more than women to use markers of Classical Arabic such as its sounds and words while speaking in vernacular Arabic. More un-expectedly, while upper classes are typically perceived to be the "best" speakers of standard varieties, in the case of Arabic "often the higher one's social class, the less likely it is that one will learn [Classical Arabic] well" (68). This odd fact is related to colonialism and the dominance of English and French culture and language: "Upper class Egyptians, for example, generally attend foreign language schools—these are mostly missionary schools—and although multilingualism is a mark of their class, Classical Arabic is not necessarily one of the languages they learn" (68). Historically, the belief in the idea that the Qur'an is the word of God has made its translation controversial. This is especially the case in Arab countries where "the Qur'an has never been translated into any of the Arabic vernaculars" (75), unlike the aggressive translation projects for the Christian scriptures.

(Thanks to Niloofar Haeri for providing critique and correction to the origin version of this box.)

Anti-language
a speech style used by individuals or groups in the performance of roles opposing or inverting the society outside of their group

Pidgin
a simplified version of a language that is usually used for limited purposes, such as trade and economic interactions, by non-native speakers of the language (as in Melanesian pidgin versions of English); usually an incomplete language that is not the "first" language of any group

Creole
a pidgin language that has become elaborated into a multi-functional language and distributed into a first language of the community

language, will emerge for basic purposes like trade. Such a hybrid language is called a **pidgin** and tends to have a reduced vocabulary and grammar; a pidgin is also not the first or primary language of either party. However, over time a pidgin may become more sophisticated and multi-functional, even becoming the first language of a community. When a new or hybrid language has achieved this level of sophistication and adoption, it is called a **creole**. Another possible and common consequence of language contact is language loss, which can occur when the members of a speech community adopt a foreign language to the exclusion of their previous one, voluntarily or not. Young people may cease learning it, and elders may be the last to speak it. In the worst cases, the entire language-bearing society dies or is exterminated.

Finally, language may be a focus of struggle between two societies, communities, or subcultures, or it may be a medium for staking out distinct and competitive or resistant identities vis-à-vis the dominant society. Technical or subcultural jargons or argots can signal differentiation from or even rejection of other segments of society. Halliday

(1976) coined the term "**anti-language**" to refer to the most dramatic form of this behavior, a speech style (specialized phonetics, vocabulary, grammar, or pragmatics) used by individuals or groups in the performance of roles opposing or inverting the society outside of their group.

LANGUAGE ACQUISITION AND THE LINGUISTIC RELATIVITY HYPOTHESIS

It seems evident that language is not "in the brain" at birth; if language was innate, all humans ought to speak the same language. It also seems evident that there is something in or about the human brain that extracts or constructs language from experienced speech, some neurological capacity to acquire and use language. There is nothing contradictory in accepting both of these realities. Whatever the biological substrate, different societies speak different languages; language is relative to a particular society. However, theorists like Edward Sapir and Benjamin Lee Whorf went much beyond that obvious truth. They suggested that not just the words and the sounds, but the very minds that produce those words and sounds are quite different. As Whorf wrote:

> the background linguistic system (in other words, the grammar) of each language is not merely a reproducing instrument for voicing ideas but rather is itself the shaper of ideas, the program and guide for the individual's mental activity, for his analysis of impressions, for his synthesis of his mental stock in trade. Formulation of ideas is not an independent process, strictly rational in the old sense, but is part of a particular grammar, and differs, from slightly to greatly, between different grammars. We dissect nature along lines laid down by our native languages. The categories and types that we isolate from the world of phenomena we do not find there because they stare every observer in the face; on the contrary, the world is presented in a kaleidoscopic flux of impressions which has to be organized by our minds—and this means largely by the linguistic systems in our minds.
>
> (1940: 231)

Edward Sapir, one of the great early professional anthropologists, joined Whorf in this assessment of the role and power of language. As he said:

> Human beings do not live in the objective world alone nor alone in the world of social activity as ordinarily understood, but are very much at the mercy of the particular language which has become the medium of expression for their society. It is quite an illusion to imagine that one adjusts to reality essentially without the use of language and that language is merely an incidental means of solving specific problems of communication or reflection. The fact of the matter is that the "real world" is to a large extent unconsciously built up on the language habits of the group. No two languages are ever sufficiently similar to be considered as representing the same social reality. The worlds in which different societies live are distinct worlds, not merely the same world with different labels attached.
>
> (1949:162)

This quotation describes what is known as the **linguistic relativity hypothesis** or the Sapir-Whorf hypothesis. The idea is that a language is not just a list of words for things. It is also a code for concepts, ideas, relationships, categories (like "food" or "weed" or "drug"), and even values. Humans are not born with any vocabulary, nor are we born with any such concepts, ideas, relationships, categories, or values. Then, as we acquire the "linguistic code" of our society's language, we acquire these concepts, ideas, relationships, and so on. If so, speakers of different languages (especially radically different ones) internalize different concepts, ideas, relationships, categories, and values and subsequently interpret the world through them. In the ultimate formulation of the hypothesis, speakers of different languages live in very different mental worlds. As Whorf defined it, then, the linguistic relativity hypothesis

> means, in informal terms, that users of markedly different grammars are pointed by their grammars toward different types of observations and different evaluations of externally similar acts of observation, and hence are not equivalent as observers but must arrive at somewhat different views of the world.
>
> (1956: 221)

This is clearly a controversial suggestion and can probably be taken too far. Some concepts, like causality or space for instance, can at least partially arise from embodied experience in the physical world. Yet even in these "basic" concepts, some cultural acquisition and variation can and does occur.

Attempts to test the linguistic relativity hypothesis empirically have yielded mixed results. One area of testing has been color perception and terminology. While some cultures have as few as two color terms (essentially "black" and "white"), many have no more than four. Does the presence or absence of color terms affect the actual perception of color? The comparative work of Berlin and Kay (1969) suggested not: They discovered what they regarded as a set of standard hues that most (but not all) societies recognize and name, as well as a universal sequence of named hues, starting (and sometimes ending) with black and white, followed by red, then yellow or green, then blue. But the fact that not all societies get beyond black and white, and that many do not get beyond black and white and red and yellow, makes the research inconclusive.

Whorf, Benjamin Lee. 1956. *Language, Thought, and Reality: Selected Writings of Benjamin Lee Whorf.* Cambridge: The Massachusetts Institute of Technology Press.

Linguistic relativity hypothesis
the claim that language is not only a medium for communication about experience but actually a more or less powerful constituent of that experience; language consists of concepts, relations, and values, and speakers of different languages approach and interpret reality through different sets of concepts, relations, and values (also known as the Sapir-Whorf hypothesis)

A much more recent experiment, however, suggests the power of the linguistic effect on thought. Ross, Xun, and Wilson (2002) studied bilingual Chinese-Canadians on a series of psychological and personality items. Some individuals were given the test in Chinese, and others were given the same questions in English. An even more powerful version of this investigation was conducted by Ramirez-Esparza et al. (2006), in which they surveyed the same bilingual English-Spanish individuals twice, once in each language. Both studies found that the language of response affected the responses. Chinese-born individuals writing in Chinese showed significantly more typically Chinese views and self-perceptions than the same population writing in English. Likewise, English-Spanish bilinguals evinced personality traits more consistent with Spanish speakers when functioning in Spanish and more consistent with English speakers when functioning in English. Ramirez-Esparza et al. attribute the results to "cultural frame switching," a phenomenon in which individuals "change their interpretations of the world, depending upon their internalized cultures, in response to cues in their environment . . . as subtle as language" (2006: 20). Ross et al. go so far as to propose that "East-Asian and Western identities are stored in separate knowledge structures . . . in bicultural individuals, with each structure activated by its associated language" (2002: 1048).

Chapter 10

The effect of language on experience is most immediate and obvious in the area of social and cultural concepts, which may have no correlate at all in other cultures. The concepts may be embedded in language, or they may be lexical items themselves. As an embedded case, one cannot speak Japanese well without learning to make and express major culturally specific social distinctions, as mentioned above; likewise, in Ilongot or Wana society, the use or understanding of different speech styles attunes a speaker to egalitarianism and fluid social roles. Even more interestingly, and perhaps troublingly, a team of psychologists headed by Albert Costa recently determined that "people tend to make systematically different judgments when they face a moral dilemma in a foreign language than in their native language" (Costa et al., 2014: 1). They acknowledge the common belief that moral thinking is purely rational and principled and should not depend on the language of the moral question but conclude that common belief is wrong: Language does matter.

On the other hand, there are some ideas and concepts conveyed by words in any given language and culture that are divergent, if not absent altogether, from others (see "semantic range" above). The Warlpiri religious concept of *jukurrpa* has no equivalent in English or any other non-Aboriginal language; it is not just another name for God or heaven nor even for dreams, although its literal translation is "dream" or "dreaming." The range of this key term includes dreams as well as the creation-time at the beginning of the world, sacred designs and objects, and rituals; no single English word does or can convey all these meanings. Even when a society has words that we might render as "god" or "spirit" or "soul," we cannot assume that their meaning is identical to ours or each other's. Culturally specific words like *brahma* in Hinduism, *nirvana* in Buddhism, *diyi* ("luck") in Apache, even *jihad* in Arabic, as well as many others, cannot be simplistically translated into some supposed equivalent in another language; yet these terms and concepts are central and motivational in their societies. This presents a fascinating challenge to cross-cultural translation and understanding: The key terms and concepts of another culture, expressed in language and also in practice, may be constitutive of a very different social experience, a very different "cultural reality."

BOX 4.4 CONTEMPORARY CULTURAL CONTROVERSIES: THE POLITICS OF LANGUAGE IN THE U.S.

In George Orwell's prophetic novel *1984*, the philosophy of the regime was "Who controls the past controls the future. Who controls the present controls the past." And key to that control was language, which was why the leadership devised "Newspeak," a form of speech in which it was easy to say and think certain things and difficult or impossible to say or think others. Opinion-makers and politicians of all points on the spectrum have equally understood that language can be used not only to inform but just as effectively to persuade, motivate, and even "disinform"—usually to propagate their power or policies (hence the term "propaganda"). Sociolinguist Nicholas Subtirelu (2013) investigated the subtle use of language during U.S. congressional debates over re-authorizing the 2006 Voting Rights Act, which mandated multilingual ballots for minority languages. Opponents frequently used words like "Mexico," "foreign," "Hispanics," "immigrants," and "assimilation," while supporters were more inclined to talk in terms of "citizens," "democracy," "discrimination," "participation," and of course "rights." It would not be wrong to say that, although both sides spoke in English, they spoke different languages even as they fought over whether one language—English—was necessary to unite the society and qualify citizens to participate in its governance. What do you think?

SUMMARY

Language is both a medium of human communication and interaction and a shaping influence on that communication and interaction. Humans are not the only species that communicate, nor even communicate linguistically. However, humans have unique linguistic skills, which are also the same skills that make culture in general possible:

- symbolism
- productivity
- displacement

Language takes the form of a set of basic items and combinatory rules, from sound units to meaning units to utterances to socially appropriate speech-acts. Each of these dimensions is studied by a specific area of linguistics:

- phonology
- morphology or semantics
- syntax or grammar
- pragmatics or sociolinguistics

Language in its social production and use is much more than a list of names for things. It is a code for social information and social relationships. Any language includes a variety of specialized speech forms for different individuals and groups, different occasions, and different relationships. Language as a social phenomenon can express or determine functions such as

- changes of social status and role
- politics and power relations
- performance of specific linguistic genres, such as ritual or story-telling
- blending, stratifying, or differentiating of social groups

Language, as a set of concepts or categories, may also influence the way that humans experience and interpret, and therefore respond to, their world—both physical and social. The linguistic relativity hypothesis suggests that language mediates human thought and experience such that members of different speech communities think and experience differently. This is an area of controversy and ongoing research.

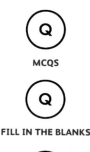

Q

MCQS

Q

FILL IN THE BLANKS

WWW

Key Terms

anti-language	honorifics	pidgin
bound morpheme	kinesics	pragmatics
competence	linguistic relativity hypothesis	productivity
creole	morpheme	proxemics
diglossia	morphology	semantic range
displacement	paralanguage	semantics
folklore	performatives	sociolinguistics
free morpheme	phoneme	syntax
grammar	phonology	vocalizations

Cultural construction of persons

Personality and gender

As in much of the world, in the southern Indian province of Tamil Nadu spirit possession is disproportionately an experience of women, particularly of young, often newly-married women. It is easy, and indeed common, to conclude that spirit possession is a product of women's marginality and victimization, some kind of (more or less self-conscious) resistance to social conditions and thus a misguided effort to escape the burdens of womanhood. The assumption is that a woman is "a self-enclosed, relentlessly conscious, and knowing subject confronting a world that is entirely external" (Ram, 2013: 86) and fairly hostile. Instead, Kalpana Ram holds that

> in entering the world of phantoms, demons, and villages goddesses in rural popular culture one is dragged into a world in which extreme human circumstances, particularly those perceived as tragic and unjust, fundamentally alter the relationship between past and present and between subject and the world.
>
> (86)

Central to the injustice against Indian women is "sundered moral relationships" (95), uncaring acts inflicted by men, other kin, or the spirits themselves.

These injustices—especially infertility, a family death, or domestic violence—*are* phantoms and ghosts, moments that refuse to "recede into the past" (105). The inability to have children is especially felt as a loss of the auspiciousness of pregnancy and motherhood, and "the situation remains dire for women from working-class and poorer classes who are stigmatized as 'infertile'" (124). Perhaps ironically, such women are believed, and believe themselves, to be plagued by female spirits: It is "the wild goddesses, their guardian deities, and the spirits of the dead who in some cases converge on every phase of a woman's life" (128). Therefore, "it is precisely the random and amoral character of capricious goddesses and demon deities that affords a little cultural respite for women" (129) who are not held entirely responsible for their own plight. However, women—even possessed women—are not completely without power, although that power might not be totally their own. Possessed women may acquire the healing capacity of spirits, becoming mediums of the very forces that afflict them. Such women can "make room" for the spirit in their selves, which equals neither a total abandonment of human consciousness and will nor a perfect preservation of that consciousness and will. What Ram calls the woman's "porous subjectivity" (147) or "intercorporeality" (145)—woman and spirit sharing the same body—allows her gradually to develop an "agency of mediumship" (154). No longer victims of spirit possession, but now spirit mediums, some women hold court as the spirit or goddess, dispensing wisdom or justice like or as the deity.

A society is a system of human individuals in some structured relationships with each other, relationships that are informed and shaped by beliefs and values and meanings. More than that, a society is a set of "kinds of persons to be," categories that organize and label humans and make their actions meaningful and appropriate. Gilbert Herdt referred to this universe of categories and meanings as a **cultural ontology**, the "local theories of being and metaphysics of the world; of having a certain kind of body and being in a certain kind of social world, which creates a certain cultural reality; and of being and knowledge combined in the practice of living" (1994: 61). Culture posits many different kinds of beings, a great number pertaining to what we would call "religion." However, a culture also contains an ontology of human beings—what kinds of humans there are, what makes them different kinds of humans, and how society treats and values them. As Herdt added,

> For a collective ontology to emerge and be transmitted across time, there must be a social condition, eventually a stable social role, that can be inhabited—marking off a clear social status position, rights and duties, with indications for the transmission of corporeal and incorporeal property and status.
>
> (60)

Through cultural categorization of innate and acquired human differences and enculturation of distributed knowledge, skill, and habit, it is fair to say that human individuals are culturally constructed, that we *become persons in the presence of culture* and that culture assigns meaning and value to different kinds of individuals. The study of the individual in cultural context raises fundamental questions about "human nature": To what extent is human behavior given by nature or shaped by culture? This is a debate that rages to this day. Two particularly important and interrelated aspects of the argument are the questions of personality and of gender. Here, as in all other areas that it surveys, anthropology finds that the answers—or at least the facts—are more complicated but at the same time more interesting than mere dualities.

CULTURES AND PERSONS, OR CULTURAL PERSONS

Each human individual lives in a complex and dynamic relation to his/her society and culture.

Cultural ontology
a society's system of notions about what kind of things (including kinds of people) exist in the world and their characteristics and social value. A socially specific way of categorizing and valuing the physical and social world

Herdt, Gilbert, Ed. 1994. *Third Sex, Third Gender: Beyond Sexual Dimorphism in Culture and History.* New York: Zone Books

See Chapter 10

IMAGE 5.1 Enculturation: Warlpiri elder men showing boys sacred knowledge and skills.

Persons are not carbon copies of culture, but neither are they utterly free agents from it. In the course of their interactions with each other and the institutions they have erected, humans develop a **personality**, which we will define rather casually as the distinctive ways of thinking, feeling, and behaving of an individual. Personality is not exactly or entirely innate: No one is born with specific ideas, beliefs, emotions, skills, and so on. Neither is personality exactly or entirely "personal" or individually unique: Members of a society share certain tendencies of thinking or feeling or behaving—in Tylor's language, capabilities and habits acquired precisely *as* members of a society.

Culture and personality then are intimately, essentially, necessarily linked. If humans are not born with it, and if humans share important and major portions of it with others around them, then where does it come from? The answer is that very much, maybe most, of it comes from outside the individual—from what other people are doing and what they teach or influence the individual to do. And the process that links these external and interpersonal realities with the internal realities of personality is enculturation. Enculturation, as discussed earlier, is the process by which an individual learns his/her society's culture—that is, by which culture gets "in" the individual. During enculturation, the ideas, beliefs, feelings, values, norms, etc. that exist before, apart from, and outside of the individual are *internalized* and become part of and "inside of" the individual. To say it once more, during enculturation, culture becomes integral to the individual's personality. The fact that, as seen earlier, acquiring culture is an active and imperfect process guarantees that individuals will not be mere cookie-cutter versions of some cultural template.

Since different cultures have different categories and definitions of persons, the anthropologist must be careful to understand theirs and not impose his/her own. One fundamental area is the concept of "self." **Self** is a key concept in Western cultures, one that is taken for granted: Self is real, everybody has one, and it ends at the surface of the individual body. According to Geertz, Western societies conceive of the self as

> a bounded, unique, more or less integrated motivational and cognitive universe, a dynamic center of awareness, emotion, judgment, and action organized into a distinctive whole and set contrastively both against other such wholes and against its social and natural background.
>
> (1974: 31)

Particularly in American culture, people are encouraged to cultivate and develop the self, to become very "self-aware" and to improve the self, through physical exercise (equating the self with the body in some way) or more often through "psychological growth" or "self-actualization." Americans even talk about their "self-image" and "self-esteem" and how it can be askew from the "reality" of the self; that is, people can imagine or see themselves to be worse than they really are or occasionally better than they really are. But if one's self-concept can be so elusive and problematic, then self is not quite as simple or self-evident as it may seem.

Two points have emerged from the cross-cultural analysis of the self. First, self is not as certain or universal as we like to think. Second, self may not be as exclusively human as we like to think. That is, not all humans may have the modern Western sense of self, and not only humans may have some sense of self. To take the first point, a fair amount of research has gone into the question of whether all societies conceive of and experience the self as Westerners do—as a bounded, enduring, private personal essence. There is at least some reason to conclude that they do not. Some versions of Buddhism teach explicitly that there is no self. *Anatta* or selflessness (not in the sense of unselfishness but literally of having no self) is a central and formal Buddhist concept: There is no "you" that endures from moment to moment, let alone for a lifetime or an eternity. Instead, in each moment the person is remade, the previous moment lighting the candle that is the "self" for the next moment. The Buddhist notion of *paṭiccasamuppāda* or "dependent origination" teaches that the self (like everything that exists) is a set of interdependent and changing relations, not a permanent fact of reality.

In other cultures, the enduring, bounded, or personal self has also been called into question. Other anthropologists have described self concepts in other societies—Dorothy Lee among the Wintu (1959), A. Irving Hallowell among the Ojibwa (1955), and Catherine Lutz among the Ifaluk

Personality
the distinctive ways of thinking, feeling, perceiving, and behaving of an individual, shaped by enculturation as individuals internalize aspects of their society's culture

Chapter 2

Self
the more or less enduring, bounded, and discrete part of an individual's identity or personality, and the reflexive awareness of this aspect of oneself

Lee, Dorothy. 1959. *Freedom and Culture*. Englewood Cliffs NJ: Prentice-Hall, Inc.

Lutz, Catherine A. 1998. *Unnatural Emotions: Everyday Sentiments on a Micronesian Atoll and Their Challenge to Western Theory*. Chicago and London: The University of Chicago Press.

OF MOUNTAINS AND MEN: CONCEPTS OF PERSONHOOD AMONG THE BOLIVIAN QOLLAHUAYAH

(1998), to name but a few. Based on Wintu linguistic practices, Lee suggested that the Wintu did not share the Western sense of "an established separate self." Rather, "a Wintu self is identical with the parts of his body and is not related to them as 'other' so long as they are physically part of him" (135). Nor was the self concept nearly as crucial for the Wintu: "with the Wintu the universe is not centered in the self" (138). Likewise, Lutz' study of Ifaluk indicated for these Pacific islanders "the person is first and foremost a social creature and only secondarily, and in a limited way, an autonomous individual" or distinct self; the Ifaluk "are oriented toward each other rather than toward an inner world of individually constituted goals and thoughts" (1998: 81). Therefore, they think of themselves as "more public, social, and relational, and necessarily more dyadic than we do" (82).

Research also indicates that the self is more malleable, porous, and "distributed" than we ordinarily imagine. The well-known "Stockholm Syndrome," in which kidnap victims or captives come, sometimes remarkably quickly, to identify and empathize with their captors illustrates that one's attitudes and values are not set in stone but are fairly easily manipulated. Further, the enduring sense of self appears to need constant reinforcement; disrupt this process (with sleep deprivation, disturbances of natural rhythms, detachment from friends and family and everything familiar, and disinformation from "re-programmers") and the self quickly collapses and can be re-shaped by the right techniques. Many societies, like the Indians of Tamil Nadu above, also conceive the self as relatively porous and penetrable, with "external" material—sometimes literally other people, other species, and the land itself—being part of the person while "internal" material or personality is projected out into the social and natural environment. Most profoundly, Alfred Gell argued that a person is not completely contained within the body, that "persons may be 'distributed,' i.e. all their 'parts' are not physically attached, but are distributed around the ambience" (1998: 106). With art objects primarily in mind—but also with deep implications for religion—Gell opined that humans (and other persons) put something of themselves in the things they do and make, like trace evidence at a crime scene, rendering a "person" as "a dispersed category of material objects, traces, and leaving . . . which, in aggregate, testify to the agency," biography, and

personality of the individual—who is now not so in-divisible (222–223).

Finally, the self may not be uniquely human. Just as anthropologists find "a little culture" in closely related species, so we find "a little self" in these same beings. The question is whether a non-human animal can have an experience of "I"— an awareness of what is and is not its particular individuality. In 1970 the psychologist Gordon Gallup conducted experiments to determine if chimpanzees have a sense of self. He set chimps in front of a mirror, and eventually they discovered that the image in the glass was "themselves": They related their movements to the movements in the mirror, and they even began to examine themselves for the first time, looking at parts of themselves that they had never seen before, like their ears and the inside of their mouths. Once the animals had become familiar with themselves, Gallup made subtle changes in their appearance, like putting a spot of paint on their foreheads. In front of the mirror, they quickly realized that "they" were different and explored the spot, touching it and sniffing their fingers to study the change to themselves. Chimps that had never seen a mirror before did not react to the spot at all; they did not have a sufficient sense of self. Other experiments have suggested that chimps may also have intersubjectivity—that is, an awareness that other beings have minds and even what may be in those minds. Chimps that are shown the secret hiding place of a key to locked-up food, and then shown humans who behave as if they do not know where the key is, will guide the humans to the key with facial and hand gestures, indicating that they know that they know what the humans do not know and what the humans need to know it.

Blank slates, elementary ideas, and human nature

The quintessential question of all social sciences and humanities is, what does it mean to be human? The two major competing perspectives in Western civilization have been "idealism" (that ideas are in us from birth) and "empiricism" (that experience shapes or fills our mind or personality over time). This dichotomy is popularly known as "nature-versus-nurture." The empiricist or nurture position

BOX 5.1   KNOWING OTHERS' MINDS IN THE PACIFIC

In various Pacific Island societies, "the avoidance of verbally speculating about the intentions, motives, and internal states of others has been reported" (B. Schieffelin, 2008: 431). Cultural anthropologists, psychologists, and linguists have dubbed this phenomenon *the opacity of other minds*, that is, the attitude that it is impossible, undesirable, or impolite to presume what other people are thinking. In the southern highlands of Papua New Guinea, Bosavi children, like children everywhere, "are explicitly socialized into culturally preferred patterns of speaking, feeling, and thinking" (432), which includes among the Bosavi learning "explicitly . . . not to verbally guess at or express others' unvoiced intentions and unclear meanings" (433). In verbal interactions, adults do not elaborate on children's sentences or attempt to interpret them; rather they encourage the youngsters to explain their own feelings. For instance, if a child cries or misbehaves, adults do not ask, "Are you hungry?" or "Are you sick?" but instead, "*Ge oba?*" or "What's with you?" And although people are enculturated to express sympathy, speakers do not give reasons for their sympathetic words: "Everyone gets the point, without verbally speculating about another's desires, internal states or intentions" (435). One reason for the Bosavi attitude toward others' minds is their concept of ownership. It is important to learn "who things belong to, and whether or not one has a right to just take those things," and another person's "unexpressed or inarticulate thoughts and desires" are considered that person's property; "Just as one does not take and use things that are not theirs to take, one does not speak others' thoughts, ones that they have not themselves articulated. Thoughts and desires are one's own" (435). More generally still, privacy and indirect speech are important to the Bosavi, who incorporate into their verbal interactions

bale to ("turned over words"), metaphors, allusion, connotations, lexical substitutes and forms of obfuscation and poetic devices. These speech forms have a surface as well as an underneath (*ha:g*), or meaning, which, according to context, may be concealed to some, but not to all.

(435)

is associated with the analogy of the *tabula rasa*, the blank slate, which is inscribed by experience. The idealist or nature position would then be associated with a full slate of information given by blood or genes or brains.

Psychology and anthropology were born at roughly the same time, attempting to answer roughly the same questions. Psychology quickly became the study of the "inner" life of individual humans, of that allegedly secret and invisible realm of "mind." Meanwhile, anthropology was coming at the question of human nature and the universal structures of mind from a different angle. One of the first important anthropological ideas was offered by Adolph Bastian (1826–1905), who proposed the term *elementargedanken* for the elementary thoughts or ideas that he believed were found in all humans in all places and times. The *elementargedanken*, few in number and universal, were expressed in local forms at various times and places as *volkergedanken* or folk ideas. Thus, Warlpiri or the Bosavi or Indians or Americans would have local expressions of language, religion, kinship, etc., but underneath these particular manifestations was a common shared humanity that merely "came out" in different ways due to local environmental or historical circumstances. One phrase to describe this notion was the "**psychic unity of humanity**," the claim that all humans share the same basic psychological processes. Lucien Lévy-Bruhl (1857–1939), on the other hand, argued that there were two radically different ways of being and thinking among humans—the modern or rational mentality as opposed to what he called a "**primitive mentality**" that was prelogical and mystical or mythical. How else, he wondered, could we explain the "odd" and ultimately "false" things that people did or thought in "primitive" societies? Lévy-Bruhl eventually withdrew his concept of primitive mentality, but ideas like it have persisted over the years to

Psychic unity of humanity the position that all humans share a single set of mental processes, even if they think or believe different things; rejects the notion of primitive mentality

Primitive mentality according to Lévy-Bruhl, a way of thinking characteristic of "primitive societies" in which individuals cannot understand cause and effect and do not distinguish one object from another (e.g. they believe that an animal can be a person)

distinguish (to the outsider) rational from irrational (symbolic? false?) beliefs and behaviors. Both Sigmund Freud and Carl Jung, for instance, posited that human minds operated on two different principles—for Freud, a primary or irrational "pleasure" principle (wish fulfillment) and a secondary or rational "reality" principle. For both, the irrational principle was associated with dreams, children, neurosis, and "primitive cultures."

The psychoanalytic influence on anthropology

Freud and Jung exerted an important influence on early anthropology. Jung was particularly interested in non-Western and non-modern societies, and both thinkers placed great emphasis on symbols. Freud, the senior of the two, explicitly linked culture (including art and religion) to depth psychology, roughly as a "symptom" of mental, including unconscious, forces. But he also made a number of claims that inspired early anthropologists to employ or test his theories. Two critical claims were the universality of mental phenomena (like the Oedipus complex) and the central role of childhood (both childhood experiences and childrearing practices).

A number of anthropologists took psychoanalytic concepts and tools seriously—and literally into the field. Géza Róheim, for instance, explored the Oedipus complex among Australian Aboriginals, using myth and ritual to psychoanalyze entire societies. Bronislaw Malinowski (1927) tested Freud's claim of a universal (male) Oedipal complex in the Trobriand Islands, arguing that it was not universal but rather a product of particular social arrangements: Freud's patriarchal Austrian society might generate such anxiety, but in a matrilineal society like that of the Trobriand Islanders, fathers did not occupy such a central place in boys' mental lives. A. Irving Hallowell took the Rorschach "inkblots" and other psychological tests along on his studies of the Ojibwa, on the premise that personality structure "is a psychological dimension of human societies that is directly relevant to the functioning of a human social order" (1955: 32). Hallowell used the Rorschach images to measure the thoughts, emotions, and sense of self of the Ojibwa, as well as other "projective tests" like

the Thematic Apperception Test (TAT) or the Draw-a-Person test, which are intended to get the subject to "fill in" or "project" his/her personality into the picture or story. Hallowell assumed that "a human being always thinks, feels, perceives, and acts as a socialized *person* who must inevitably share psychological characteristics with his fellows" (39).

American "culture and personality"

The United States is where the seed of **psychological anthropology** took firmest root. Recall that modern anthropology emerged in the early 1900s, when social changes were occurring in Western societies, not the least of which were the first battles in the "sexual revolution." So, when Margaret Mead (1901–1978) conducted the fieldwork that would culminate in her book *Coming of Age in Samoa: A Psychological Study of Primitive Youth for Western Civilization* (1928), it is clear not only that she was doing psychologically inspired research, but that she intended it to have ramifications for Western society. She expected to find that the maturation process as we know it, in particular the turbulence of adolescence, was not a universal one but a culturally particular one. In Samoans (specifically Samoan adolescent girls), she claimed to find the happy, sexually free, well-adjusted youths that she believed Americans could and should be. The implication was not only that humans are psychologically quite plastic—that there are few if any real universals—but that Westerners could stand to learn a thing or two from other, in some ways "better," societies. (Mead's work came under intense fire from Derek Freeman (1983), who argued that her methods were inadequate, her conclusions wrong, and her agenda too overt.)

Closely behind Mead came another influential female anthropologist who wrote the most widely read book ever published in the field, *Patterns of Culture* (1934b). Ruth Benedict (1887–1948) was perhaps even more explicitly psychological in her approach and interests and became a leading force in the culture-and-personality school. In *Patterns of Culture* she treated three different societies as each a unique and complete "configuration." A society, she concluded, has a culture with specific values and ideals, and it aims to construct—and generally succeeds at constructing—individuals who possess

---

www.rorschachinkblottest.com/

Psychological anthropology

the specialty within anthropology that examines the relationship between culture and the individual, that is, the mutual interactions of cultural processes and mental and psychological processes and the cultural variability of psychological experiences such as dreams, emotions, and mental illness

Mead, Margaret. 1928. *Coming of Age in Samoa: A Psychological Study of Primitive Youth for Western Civilization*. New York: W. W. Morrow.

Malinowski, Bronislaw. 1927. *Sex and Repression in Savage Society*. Chicago: The University of Chicago Press.

Benedict, Ruth. 1934. *Patterns of Culture*. New York: The New American Library.

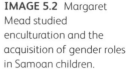

IMAGE 5.2 Margaret Mead studied enculturation and the acquisition of gender roles in Samoan children.

those values and ideals. While the process of individual-construction is not perfect (a certain "range" of personalities emerges in the end), it is effective enough to produce a recognizable "type" of person or personality that is distinctly "Kwakiutl" or "Zuni" or "Dobuan"—or, by implication, American. Thus she could sum up a culture with a few key personality or temperament traits, such as "egocentric," "individualistic," and "ecstatic" for the Kwakiutl, "restrained" and "non-individualistic" for the Zuni, and "fearful" and "paranoid" for the Dobuans. It might be instructive to think of what key personality traits you would attribute to your own society.

On the assumption, then, that human personality is culturally but not infinitely variable, early- and mid-twentieth century anthropologists often sought to describe and explain the particular personality configuration(s) or type(s) in particular societies. One important concept was **basic personality**, used to refer to the "the effective adaptive tools of the individual which are common to every individual in the society" (Kardiner, 1939: 237). This idea was pursued by a collaboration between anthropologists like Ralph Linton and psychologists like Abram Kardiner, resulting in

Kardiner's *The Individual and His Society: The Psychodynamics of Primitive Social Organization* (1939) and *The Psychological Frontiers of Society* (1945), which included contributions from Linton, Cora Du Bois, and James West. The mechanisms unifying culture and personality in this approach were institutions (defined as "a fixed mode of thought or behavior which can be communicated, which enjoys common acceptance and the infringement of or deviation from which creates some disturbance in the individual or group" [1945: 24]) and childrearing.

A similar term was **national character**, which tended to be applied to modern state-level societies, as in Benedict's World War II famous study of Japanese "national character" (1946). Several important studies of national character were composed, including Benedict's (1946) report on the Japanese, *The Chrysanthemum and the Sword: Patterns of Japanese Culture*, and Geoffrey Gorer and John Rickman's (1950) *The People of Great Russia: A Psychological Study*, often ridiculed for the so-called "swaddling hypothesis" that explained all of Russian personality in terms of wrapping babies too tightly and thereby teaching them to be passive.

Such interests led anthropologists to examine individuals more closely, to identify the connections

National character
the purported personality traits shared by an entire society or country; the term was usually applied to modern societies and countries like the United States, China, Japan, or the Soviet Union

Basic personality
the psychological traits common to most or all of the members of a society

Kardiner, Abram. 1939. *The Individual and His Society: The Psychodynamics of Primitive Social Organization*. New York: Columbia University Press.

Universal ——————→ Primary Institutions ——————→ Basic Personality ——————→ Secondary Institutions
Psychological   (family structures,   (culture, religion,
Structures   basic disciplines,   folklore, arts)
                           childrearing practices)

FIGURE 5.1 The relation between culture and personality (based on Kardiner, 1945)

Modal personality
according to Du Bois, the statistically most common personality traits in a society

BIOGRAPHY AND AUTOBIOGRAPHY IN ANTHROPOLOGY

Ethnopsychology
the psychological "theory" or understanding used by any particularly society, including its ideas about and uses of emotions, dreams, mental illness, and personhood most generally

THE SCIENTIFIC ANTHROPOLOGICAL STUDY OF MIND

THE ETHNOPSYCHOLOGY OF VIOLENCE OR NONVIOLENCE

between personal experience and personality. One outcome was a set of biographical studies, such as Leo Simmons' (1942) account of the life of the Hopi man Sun Chief. However, these more intimate studies, especially Cora Du Bois' portraits of *The People of Alor*, soon showed that all individuals in a society did not share a single personality, nor did their childhood experiences map one-to-one to their adult personalities. In reaction, Du Bois suggested the concept of **modal personality**, a statistical notion identifying "central tendencies in the personalities of a *group* of people" (1960: xix)—that is, the most commonly occurring personality traits, although not necessarily universally shared ones.

Contemporary psychological anthropology

Cultural anthropology has largely abandoned such grandiose projects; indeed, for a time, psychological anthropology largely fell out of favor in the discipline. However, recent decades have opened new avenues of investigation in the relationship between individual thoughts and feelings and culture and society. Cognitive anthropology, also known as ethnoscience or componential analysis, attempted to get at what members of a society actually had "in their minds." Claude Lévi-Strauss revived psychoanalytic thinking and blended it with linguistics, describing social phenomena from kinship systems to religious myths as products of a "deep grammar" of mental processes.

Additionally, anthropologists have discovered other personality-oriented subjects to explore. One of these is emotions, which are commonly viewed as *natural, physical, and subjective*—as "private" and therefore inaccessible to observers (like anthropologists) and "factual," sometimes bodily states like a racing heart or a tearing eye. Catherine Lutz further suggested that Western society generally considers emotions irrational, uncontrollable (we are "carried away" by our feelings), dangerous, and

stereotypically female. But not all societies share this conception of emotions nor, so it seems, even the same emotions. Indeed, Lutz insisted that other societies have not only different emotional traits, but different emotional or psychological "theories" or understandings, what she called **ethnopsychology**. She claimed that the Ifaluk experienced a number of emotions that are not quite translatable into Western categories. Among these were *fago*, which denoted compassion and love and sadness simultaneously, especially in reaction to the suffering or need of others; it could not be translated as "love," for instance, since it had no romantic connotations, and it implied an inequality or dependence not always included in "love." *Song,* another Ifaluk emotional concept, referred to anger of a particular form, "justifiable anger" or "righteous indignation," and some people were more entitled to feel and express this emotion than others, notably chiefs and parents. *Metagu* or "fear/anxiety" was seen as a positive emotion and social force: "fear is what keeps people good" (1998: 201).

Other observers have commented on the meaning and social use of emotions in other societies. According to Edward Schieffelin (1983), anger, sadness, and shame played a special role, and form a special nexus of emotions, in Kaluli cultural life. Ward Keeler (1983) re-examined the Javanese feeling of *lek*, which Geertz characterized as "stage fright" but which Keeler likened more to "respectful self-restraint" as a consequence of social-status differences. Perhaps most suggestively, Lila Abu-Lughod (1985) reported that emotions such as *tahashshum* (embarrassment, modesty, or shame) among Egyptian Bedouins not only had strategic functions—as they did in Kaluli, Javanese, and Western societies—but that the distinction between "real" and "conventional" or "private" and "public" emotions cannot be sustained. Some of the most intimate feelings in Bedouin life were communicated in conventional media like songs and poems; that is, even private emotions were conventionalized.

Anthropologists have also studied the diverse cultural meaning and importance of dreams and other altered states of consciousness. This includes, as we saw at the outset of the chapter, possession and trance states—which are sometimes seen as undesirable and sometimes, as in the case of shamans or other religious specialists, highly desirable. For many societies, dreams have been important sources of cultural information and experience. Australian Aboriginal societies placed a high premium on dreams as access to sacred knowledge—songs, dances, symbols, and stories. Among the Mehinaku of Brazil, dreams were believed to be real experiences of the "eye soul" (one of many souls of a person, including the "shadow" and the "sweat soul," the latter of which transformed into a fox upon death). While asleep, the eye soul went "wandering" (*etanowakatapai*), and people explained that the "experiences of the soul in the course of a dream are the result of its contact with the souls of other villagers, who are also wandering about" (Gregor, 1981: 711). From the point of view of Mehinaku dream theory, then, "a dream is as much the soul's experience as the dreamer's, who receives it only from afar"—in other words, Mehinaku understood their dreams to be "separate from" themselves, literally the experience of a detachable part of themselves.

Finally, anthropologists have documented cultural diversity in the prevalence and meaning of mental illness across cultures. First, as Ruth Benedict (1934a) asserted decades ago, what is abnormal or "mentally ill" in one society might not be so regarded in another; further, different societies explain abnormality or deviance in different ways. For example, Elialilia Okello and Solvig Ekblad, writing in the journal *Transcultural Psychiatry*, report that the Baganda of Uganda interpret what Western medicine would call depression as a problem of

> thinking too much and [refer to it] as an *illness of thoughts*. This illness is seen as a nonchronic condition caused by psychosocial, economic and spiritual factors. When depression becomes recurrent or episodic and has psychotic features, as is the case with bipolar illness, the belief about its cause changes and is regarded to be a clan illness "*byekika*," usually caused by *Misambwa*/clan gods or *Mizimu*/ancestral spirits.
>
> (2006: 306)

Meanwhile, Mexicans and Mexican Americans are alarmed by *susto*, a condition characterized by restlessness during sleep, listlessness, loss of appetite, and depression, which is understood as the effect of "soul loss" or the departure of some non-material substance or essence or spirit as the result of fright (Glazer et al., 2004). Clearly, these ethnopsychological concepts have profound implications for people doing counseling or therapy with members of diverse societies.

See Chapter 10

See Chapter 16

THE CONSTRUCTION OF GENDERED PERSONS

Wherever we find humans, we find male and female. **Sexual dimorphism** (the occurrence of two discrete body forms based on sex) would seem to be a natural, biological, and universal feature of human existence. American culture in particular and Western culture in general tends to reinforce this impression: There are two kinds of humans—men and women—and two proper codes of behavior—male and female. A person is born a man or a woman, remains so for life, and acts accordingly. Even if things were as simple and universal as this, it would still be within the power of culture to "culturize" the physical differences, with relative values, meanings, and role assignments for the sexes. There is cross-cultural evidence to suggest that here too things are even more complicated.

Surveying the cultures of the world, anthropologists find exceptions to all of the familiar gender notions. Not all societies believe that there are only two kinds, even two *physical* kinds, of humans. Not all believe that one's sex is immutably set at birth. And not all assign the same names, tasks, or values along the same sex-line divisions. This is an even clearer case of cultural ontology, each specific society's understanding of what kinds of beings, including human beings, exist, what qualities they possess, and how society should use those differences. As an introductory example, Will Roscoe (1994) told us that traditional Zuni culture held that a child's physical sex was a social achievement—that is, that it required social action (in the form of rituals and offerings) to ensure that a child had any sex at all, let alone a particular one, and that a child's sex was not firmly fixed until birth, if not later; if a woman fell asleep during

Sexual dimorphism
the occurrence of two physically distinct forms of a species, based on sexual characteristics as well as non-sexual ones such as body size

Gender
the cultural categories and concepts relating to sexually distinct bodies, sexual preference, sexual identity, and sexual norms

labor, the baby's sex might change. So the "settling" of a person's physical sex was the result of culture, not nature.

Further, a person's sex is not always determined in the same way (in particular, by what genitals they possess) or in a binary way. In fact, there are several related but independent variables in the arena of sex and gender, including sexual anatomy, sexual identity (what sex one "feels like" or "identifies with"), sexual preference (what sex one wants to have sex with, and how), and **gender**. By gender we typically mean the social or cultural characteristics—rules, roles, tasks, values, and meanings—that are assigned to people on the basis of (some or another) sexual characteristics. But if sex is not exactly a natural fact, then gender certainly is not. Indeed,

---

BOX 5.2   THE FLUID GENDER COSMOS OF THE NAVAJO

According to Carolyn Epple, Western terminology is inadequate for comprehending Navajo or Diné conceptualizations of sex and gender. A male *nádleehí* (see below), for instance,

> may (to varying degrees) wear women's clothing; participate in activities associated with women, such as cooking and washing; and have sexual relations with other men. In general this configuration of "other-gender" behaviors has been treated as a single phenomenon across cultures and such individuals have been termed "berdache."
>
> (1998: 267)

However, collapsing the *nádleehí* and other "third genders" into one Western category ignores "the variability across Native American cultures and [leaves] unexamined the relevance of gender and sexuality" (268). Indeed, "the role of *nádleehí*—and possibly of others who share assumed commonalities—is not one of gender at all" (273); "gender" in this sense is a foreign Western concept. In Navajo understanding, *Sa'ah Naaghai Bik'eh Hozho* (the natural order)

> is male and female and organizes everything as male and female; it is a living cycle and organizes everything as a cycle; it interconnects everything; through that interconnectedness it cycles everything into everything; and it is an ongoing cycle, since each male or female has the other (i.e., female or male, respectively) into which it can cycle.
>
> (276)

In other words, nature itself is male-female: "Everything exists in terms of this arrangement: humans, air, and water as well as less tangible things like thought or emotions. All males and females are themselves both male and female" (277). Reality is also a "continuous cycling of male and female into each other," even at the individual level; the familiar notion that there is such a "thing" as maleness or femaleness—in dress, in work, in sexuality—"is at odds with many Navajos' understandings" which hold that "masculine and feminine are not as completely separate or mutually exclusive as is usually assumed" (278). Even more,

> Because everything exists as both male and female, gender valuation to many Navajos is largely situational, even when it appears in combination with seemingly fixed attributes such as genitalia. While anatomy is often the basis for female or male social, familial, and kinship roles, from another perspective each sex's genitalia also belongs to the opposite sex.... Since what is male or what is female may not be definite, there is no basis for determining whether the individual has the personality aspects, occupations, attire, and other features of only one gender or of both.
>
> (278–279)

Roscoe defines gender as "a multidimensional category of personhood encompassing a distinct pattern of social and cultural differences. Gender categories often draw on perceptions of anatomical and physiological differences between bodies, but these perceptions are always mediated by cultural categories and meanings" (341).

The rise of feminist anthropology

In one of the key documents of feminist anthropology, *Toward an Anthropology of Women*, Rayna Reiter asserted that anthropology operated for most of its history with a male bias—in fact, a "double male bias," adding "the bias we received if the society we study expresses male dominance" to "the bias we bring to our research" (1975b: 13). In fact, the book was explicitly intended as a corrective to the male-centric nature of anthropology until the 1970s and firmly placed "its roots in the women's movement" (11).

Although a number of important women contributed to the formation of anthropology, as noted previously, still they were trained by, and the questions and problems of anthropology were perceived as largely driven by, men. The last straw for many female anthropologists was a volume titled *Man the Hunter* (Lee and DeVore, 1968), which featured essays on the evolution of humanity and culture. As evaluated by Sally Slocum, also writing in *Toward an Anthropology of Women*, the thesis of *Man the Hunter* was that the "biology, psychology, and customs that separate us from the apes—all of these we owe to the hunters of time past" (1975: 38). But since this hunting behavior "is strictly male" (39), it follows that females contributed little to the development of the species or its cultures and at the extreme that "females are scarcely human" (38).

A series of responses followed, including Reiter's collection as well as *Woman, Culture, and Society* (Rosaldo and Lamphere, 1974) and *Woman the Gatherer* (Dahlberg, 1981). Female anthropologists also conducted fieldwork to ask questions or to collect data ignored by men. For instance, Annette Weiner went back to the site of Malinowski's classic ethnography, the Trobriand Islands, where she explicitly took women's activities and objects "as seriously as any kind of male wealth" and

concluded that women were "active participants in the exchange system, and thus I accord them equal place beside" the men (1983: 11). Mary Douglas in *Purity and Danger* (1966) added that concepts of "pollution" do not necessarily imply inferiority but rather mark social categories and boundaries: Women do not pollute men because women are *bad*, but rather because women and their activities, tools, and bodies belong in one category and men and men's activities, tools, and bodies belong in another. For many cultures, violations of categories are inherently dangerous and chaotic. The husband and wife team of Yolanda and Robert Murphy, in *Women of the Forest* (1974), argued that gender *segregation* does not mean gender *inequality or oppression* and that the women of Mundurucu society were actually relatively free and happy, despite the Mundurucu ideology of male superiority. (This conclusion has been questioned on the basis of physical threats to women, including beating and rape.)

Reiter, Rayna, Ed. 1975b. *Toward an Anthropology of Women*. New York and London: Monthly Review Press.

Gender divisions and differences

Even in societies that simply and firmly assign human beings to one of two sex or gender categories, there is no absolute reason why those two categories should be segregated or valued unequally. Yet, Michelle Rosaldo asserted that "what is perhaps most striking and surprising is the fact that male, as opposed to female, activities are always recognized as predominantly important, and cultural systems give authority and value to the roles and activities of men" (1974: 19). This is not entirely universally true, but it is widespread enough to be striking. Several students of Iroquois culture, for instance, have commented on the power and status of women in that society, but more often than not women and women's activities have been held in lower esteem than men's—sometimes extremely so.

Rosaldo's explanation for this fact was to distinguish between the "domestic" and "public" spheres of a society. Women, she suggested, are typically consigned to a private or domestic space (the household, etc.), based partly on an essentialist view of their "nurturing" tendencies, which is closed off from the economically and politically important public space where men function. As appealing and intuitive as this notion is, other

See Chapter 7

IMAGE 5.3 Muslim women in "purdah" or veil.

THE OPPRESSION OF WOMEN ACROSS CULTURES

observers have questioned it. Sherry Ortner (1974) opined that women are consistently associated with "nature" and its lower biological and emotional functions (like childbirth and childcare), while men are associated with the higher achievements of "culture." On the other hand, Cynthia Nelson (1974) contended that women in the Middle East, one of the more patriarchal culture areas, exercise more power in the public cultural sphere than is usually appreciated. She named such prominent roles as marriage mediator, counselor to her sons, and sorceress/magician/healer as effective positions of power, not to mention their control over food, hospitality, and the family's reputation and honor, as well as over other women via informal friendships and formal women's organizations.

Reiter (1975a) took the case a step further. In the French village she examined, there was not a public and private segregation at all. Rather, there was a "sexual geography" of the village, such that men occupied and used certain spaces at certain times and women occupied and used some of those same spaces at other times. Women did predominantly inhabit the home and a few other locations, such as the three shops in the village as well as the church (where no "self-respecting man" was willing to be seen), and most of their interests and activities centered on the family. Men, who did

almost all of the outside-the-home labor, claimed the village square, the cafés, and the mayor's office in the evenings. However, Reiter noticed that when the men were working in the fields at midday, "The village is then in female hands" (257). Even more, women did not feel downtrodden or inferior at all. Rather, she depicted them as viewing men "as overgrown children strutting around and holding onto places and roles that are really quite silly; these have less value than their own homes and roles as family-cores. They even consider men's space to be inferior to their own" (258).

It might be useful to take the advice of these researchers and consider the relations between the sexes more in terms of a "gendered geography" than a simple and complete division or opposition. This geography can be and often is literally spatial. Herdt (1987) noted that the Sambia of New Guinea, a highly sex-segregated society, had separate buildings and even separate footpaths for men and women. However, this geographic exclusion can also be and probably more often is conceptual or cognitive, that is, in terms of knowledge and language than space. For instance, until a few decades ago it was widely believed that men in Australian Aboriginal societies had all of the ritual knowledge and responsibility; earlier studies concentrated male rituals and statuses. However, a new generation of anthropologists like Diane Bell (1993) discovered a whole parallel world of religious knowledge and ritual activity among women, which led others to explore the relations to groups and to land, which individuals can trace through fathers or mothers.

One of the more well-studied domains of gender diversity is in language. Many attempts, both popular and scholarly, have investigated how men and women communicate, including whimsical associations between the sexes and different planets (Mars for men, Venus for women [Gray, 1992]). Daniel Maltz and Ruth Borker (1996) summarized the state of the research into cross-gender communication, which determined that women ask more questions, interject more conversation-promoting utterances like "uh huh" and "yes," and allow themselves to be interrupted, encourage responses, and use interactional pronouns like "you" and "we." Men are more likely to interrupt, to argue, to ignore the other's comments, to try to control the topic, and to offer opinions or declarations. Robin Lakoff (1975) among others interpreted this as an effect of male domination and female subordination in society. Maltz and Borker proposed, instead, that men and women constitute "different sociolinguistic subcultures, having learned to do different things with words in a conversation" (1996: 84). Boys and girls, they argued, learn to speak differently "because of the very different social contexts in which they learn how to carry on friendly conversation" (87). Why there are divergent male and female conversational contexts, they do not explain.

While not universal by any means, there is evidence of linguistic segregation by sex and gender across cultures. In many societies, the "status" or "high" styles or genres of language are the exclusive province of males. The Wana *kiyori* form previously mentioned was used solely by men, as was the *kabary* style that comprises formal Malagasy; in fact, Elinor Ochs (1996) said that skilled speech and traditional speech types, distinguished by indirectness, was a skill of men, while plain speech, distinguished by directness, was associated with women. Finally, in the Hindi Fijian village studied by Donald Brenneis (1984), the "high" or "sweet" mode of speech called *parbacan*, used for religious occasions and characterized by indirectness, more traditional (Sanskrit) vocabulary, and a more complex grammar was the unique province of men.

The construction of masculinity

Much of the attention in the discussion of gender focuses on women, which is an important corrective to the disregard in much of the past literature. However, in any gender system, men are a gender too, and their gender identity is just as culturally constructed as women's. In fact, in some ways it appears to be more precarious. This is suggested by the fact that, in many societies, there is either an explicit belief or an implicit message that men are "made" whereas women are "born." To put this another way, there is a recurring cross-cultural theme that girls naturally mature into women but that boys must be "made" into men: Femininity is seen as a natural fact, but masculinity as a social achievement. David Gilmore, in his cross-cultural study of masculinity, claimed that there is a "deep structure of masculinity" in which "true manhood is a precious and elusive status beyond mere maleness, a hortatory image that men and boys aspire to and that their culture demands of them as a measure of belonging" (1990: 17). In this view, manhood (rather than mere biological maleness) is an embattled status, a struggle against boyhood (and womanhood) that requires constant proving and testing in the form of fighting, competition, sexual prowess, economic success, and whatever a particular society values in its males.

One of the persistent manifestations of this struggle for manhood is male initiation rituals. In Aboriginal Australia, boys were "made into men" through physical operations—circumcision, subincision (cutting a slit along the underside of the penis), scarification, nose perforation, or tooth removal—which took place over a series of ceremonies covering many years. The Gisu of Africa performed a ritual to instill the manly virtue of *lirima* in youths, and the headhunt was the culmination of the path to maleness for the Philippines Ilongot. This is not to say that female-oriented rituals never occur; of course they do, including scarification and **female circumcision**. Such practices seem to occur more widely in reference to men, but both sexes can be identified and even "created" by alterations of the body, which give individuals the culturally correct physical features for their sex. Harold Garfinkel (1967), sociologist and founder of ethnomethodology, referred to modified sex organs as "cultural genitals," in which

Female circumcision also known as female genital mutilation; the practice of cutting off some or all of a female's external genitalia, for purposes of "beauty" or the regulation of sexual sensations

See Chapter 4

See Chapter 4

BOX 5.3   SEX AND THE BUSINESSMAN IN CONTEMPORARY CHINA

In modern China, as in many parts of the world, bars and clubs are places where important business connections and deals are made. In such sites, "sex consumption serves as an institution for the pre-selection test and bonding activity that ensure social trust in the alliance" between men, with the female hostess or server (*xiaojie*) functioning "to redeem or recover men's masculinity" (Zheng, 2009: 105). It is crucial first to understand the cultural ontology of male sexuality in China. *Jing* is the name for the stuff of maleness, "both a substance (sperm) and an intangible energy" (116). It is "the most essential element for sustaining men's life and vitality" but is also in finite supply, so men try to conserve it and spend it wisely, which means not wasting it all on wives. Indeed, men use the phrase "turning in the grain tax" to refer to having sex with their wives. Instead, they think that "copulating with as many women as possible, especially with virgins, helped nourish their seminal essence and life vitality" (117). Businessmen naturally seek sexual conquests during their gatherings and meetings at bars. But it is not exactly sexual pleasure, or even sexual intercourse, that drives the men; rather, they aim to be seen by other men—potential business partners—as desirable to women and in control of themselves. Their goal is "to demonstrate a rational, 'cool' masculinity by conquering the emotions of female servers, thereby proving their own emotional self-control and ability to manipulate the emotion of others" (106). In the process, men learn which other men are worth doing business with: "By observing how others conduct sex consumption, they assess each other's moral qualities and business competence" (137), discovering who is or is not "rational, reliable, and trustworthy" (138).

physical facts like the possession of genitalia become "cultural facts" either through interpretation or alteration of them. I, for instance, was told to keep it a secret from the Aboriginal men if I was uncircumcised, since only circumcised men were fully men and eligible to see the most secret of male rituals.

One practice that has featured in the ritual conception of men in some cultures is what the Western world would call "ritual homosexuality."

IMAGE 5.4 In many societies, men must endure tests and ordeals to achieve adult masculinity.

(The very term suggests the problem with imposing foreign cultural categories—a foreign cultural ontology—on another society.) For example, in a variety of Melanesian societies, boys were occasionally or routinely exposed to the genitals and even semen of their elders, usually young-adult men. The Etoro (Kelly, 1977) and the Sambia (Herdt, 1987) had young boys ingest semen by oral sex performed on adolescent males, while the Kaluli introduced semen by anal sex, and the Onabasulu by manual stimulation of males onto the skin of boys. It is interesting that these societies found each other's practices offensive: The Kaluli disapproved of the Etoro behavior and vice versa (Kelly, 1977: 16).

For the Sambia, ritualized and routine juvenile homosexuality was (it has since stopped) an acceptable and necessary part of their gender creation, based on their unique cultural ontology of maleness and femaleness. In other unrelated cultures, including ancient Sparta, male homosexuality served other functions, including the establishment of corporate spirit within armies. Men in Sparta, as in Sambia culture and elsewhere, were not "habitual" or exclusive homosexuals; in fact, Spartan men married and had children, and Sambians "graduated" from homosexuality to an adolescent bisexuality to adult heterosexuality. It is not the case in all cultures that homosexuality is a total and permanent identity or "lifestyle"; it may be a temporary situation or a cultural performance that does not define the man nor constitute an alternative or deviant gender role.

The construction of "alternate" genders

Attitudes, practices, and beliefs regarding sex, sexuality, and gender—indeed the very categories on which these ideas and behaviors are based—vary across cultures. Readers might be prepared to learn, then, that not all cultures share the notion of two and only two sexes or genders at all. In fact, Thomas Laqueur (1990) insisted that the idea of two sexes and genders is actually recent in Western cultures; until the eighteenth century, there was only *one* sex—male—and females were regarded as incomplete or damaged males (Freud's theories echo this sentiment, with his "penis envy" notion).

On the other hand, a story told by Plato in his *Symposium* relates that in the beginning there were three sexes, each dual—one androgynous (male/female), one male/male, and one female/female—which were split in half by the gods, sending each person in search of his or "other half" (which might be the "opposite" sex or the "same" sex).

Be that as it may, in more than a few cultures there are categories of third or even fourth genders—and even sexes—based on beliefs and concepts that may not exist in other cultures. A few examples of such identities include:

Berdache. In many Native American societies there is or was a tradition of males who adopted certain female roles and traits. In fact, Roscoe (1994) indicates that nearly 150 societies had the third gender, and almost half of those had a fourth gender for women playing more masculine roles. Early Western observers deemed them "transvestites" or "homosexuals," partly judgmentally and partly because those were the only categories the observers possessed. However, within the societies, **berdaches** were members of a distinct and often highly regarded gender. Some were assigned to the category based on physical features, particularly hermaphrodite genitals. Others chose the role. One of the best cases of a berdache institution is the Navajo *nádleehí* (see Box 5.2 above), "one who changes continuously." The Navajo *nádleehí* was greatly respected, active as a religious specialist and often given control of the family's wealth. They performed female economic roles and might dress as males, females, or neither. The Mohave *alyha* and the Lakota *winkte* are two of the better known examples (see Roscoe, 1998: 213–247 for a more complete listing). Commonly, berdache status was not believed to be about bodies at all, but about spirit—about having "two spirits," both male and female, in one body—and Two Spirit is a preferred term today.

Eunuch. The common image of **eunuchs** is castrated males in ancient and medieval societies who were assigned specific roles and tasks, most famously guarding the harems of polygamist leaders. However, eunuchs were not always castrated; they might be sterile or celibate or simply lacking in sexual desire. The defining feature of the eunuch status was not absence of male parts, but absence of "manliness," based on their

Laqueur, Thomas. 1990. *Making Sex: Body and Gender from the Greeks to Freud*. Cambridge, MA: Harvard University Press.

THE CONSTRUCTION OF MALENESS IN SAMBIA CULTURE

Berdache
a "third gender" found in many Native American societies, in which biological men adopt some of the norms usually associated with women

Eunuch
a gender category involving non-sexual individuals (usually men), who may be castrated or merely celibate, sterile, or lacking sexual desire

non-generativity (i.e. they would not or could not have children). Kathryn Ringrose (1994) indicated that they were a legitimate third gender, neither male nor female, and that they performed functions that neither males nor females could do. Interestingly, these jobs often involved positions of mediation and transaction across boundaries, such as doorkeepers, guards, messengers, servants, secretaries, and masters of ceremonies—suggesting that their own anomalous circumstances made them fit for dealing with anomalous boundary-crossing circumstances.

Hijra. In northern India, a virtual subsociety of individuals regarded as "neither man nor woman"—but also "man plus woman"—exists and participates in the greater society (Nanda, 1999). A **hijra** or Aravani may be born with male or hermaphroditic body parts; either way, they share the quality of impotence. The ultimate mark of a true *hijra*, though, is to have the male genitals removed completely (in a ritual called *nirvana*), so that the person truly is neither man nor woman, but a third distinct gender. *Hijras* typically live in communal groups under the leadership of a guru or teacher, forming a surrogate kinship system. Local groups are organized into "houses" (of which Nanda reported seven with names and histories and rules); each house has a regional leader or *naik*, and the regional leaders occasionally meet at the national level. *Hijras* are most known for their musical

performances at weddings and births. Ironically to Westerners, *hijras* as nonsexual beings and ascetics are associated in Hindu tradition with fertility and procreation. They are sexually ambiguous, but in a culturally specific way: The god Shiva possesses androgynous traits and is ascetic, blurring the Western lines not only between male and female, but between sexuality and asceticism.

Travesti. In Brazil, there is a type of effeminate male who actively attempts to achieve more female-like physical features and often works as a male prostitute. They are not transsexuals and do not claim to be women; rather, they say that they want to be "feminine" or "like women" (Kulick, 1997). To that end, they take female hormones and get surgery to modify their bodies to a more culturally appropriate female shape. They are often appreciated for their beauty, by female standards. They do not, however, get sex-change operations, since they do not want to be women or to lose their male genitals. Sexually, they act as receivers of anal sex with men, but never as penetrators. Don Kulick asserted that *travesti* do not constitute a third gender, but rather represent the Brazilian dualistic view of gender identity—two genders, "men" and "not-men" (including women and *travestis*), based not on bodies but on behavior. Specifically, behavior is partly the role in sexual intercourse (men penetrate, non-men are penetrated) and partly the more general qualities of dress, manner, etc. A "real man"

Hijra

a "third gender" in India, in which biological men renounce their sexuality (and often their sexual organs) and become socially neither male or female

Nanda, Serena. 1999. *Neither Man nor Woman: The Hijras of India*, 2nd ed. Belmont CA: Wadsworth Publishing Company

Travesti

an alternate gender role in Brazil in which males take on certain physical traits and sexual behaviors typically associated with females

IMAGE 5.5 *Hijras* in India often sing and dance at weddings and childbirths.

BOX 5.4   THE CONSTRUCTION OF COMPETING MALE TRANSGENDERS ON TAHITI

On Tahiti and nearby islands, two different discourses of transgender males co-exist and increasingly clash. *Mahu* is regarded as an indigenous concept meaning "half-man, half-woman" and indicates more gender than sexuality. Importantly, a *mahu* may be male-bodied or female-bodied: Female-bodied *mahu* "are commonly described as behaving 'in the manner of men,'" while male-bodied *mahu* . . . are commonly described as behaving 'in the manner of women'" (Elliston, 2014: 35). Again, the behavior at stake is less sexual activity than gendered labor: For instance, male-bodied *mahu* typically "engage in forms of labor coded as feminine: sewing, craft making, hairdressing, service work at hotels and restaurants, pink-collar office work, and childcare" (35). These men also adopt other feminine styles in appearance and speech such as women's clothing and female "gesture, stance, intonation patterns, voice pitch," and so forth (35). This focus on gendered behavior rather than sexuality makes it possible for most other Polynesians to be "remarkably accepting" of the role (36) and to ignore "*mahu* sexual practices altogether" (34). Yet, Deborah Elliston finds that "the vast majority of *mahu* are sexually involved with men" (38). On the other hand, *raerae* "are male-bodied, femininity-performing, men-desiring subjects" who, significantly, only "entered the Polynesian scene of sexual/gender possibility within the past forty or so years" (33). Elliston relates the emergence of the *raerae* concept to the arrival of Western ideas—and Western men—in the 1960s. Some *mahu* realized that "the more they 'feminized' themselves, the more successful they were in attracting these foreigners" (41). In fact, she claims that the majority of sex workers in French Polynesia today are not women, but *raerae*, and since their clients are often Western men, the particular femininity of the *raerae* "participates far more in modernist fantasies of (white) femininity than it does in local gender iconography" (45), including short skirts and high heels. Most fascinatingly, *mahu* mark themselves as different from, and superior to, *raerae* on the basis that *mahu* are more "traditional," while *raerae* assert their difference and superiority by condemning *mahu* as "hypocrites and cowards for 'hiding' their feminine side, not showing it in public, and . . . concealing from others the sexual desires for and relation with men" that they both share (47).

could have sex with a *travesti* and remain a real man, as long as he was the penetrator. In fact, *travestis* thought it would be offensive to have sex with each other, since they were the "same kind."

There are a few documented cases of "cross-gender" female roles across cultures. Eric Schwimmer (1984) mentioned female transvestism in four Melanesian societies. A number of Native American societies had female correlates of the male berdache status, including the Mohave *hwame* status. René Gremaux (1994) described the custom of the "sworn virgin" by which southeast European women could become "social males." One process involved a biological female renouncing her female-ness in adulthood, often via a vow of abstention from sex and marriage, as in the "sworn virgin" tradition of Albania. A second process involved the decision of the parents to raise a baby girl as a son,

giving her access to property and inheritance and even training her as a soldier (especially when the family had no sons). Back in 1941, Oscar Lewis documented the "manly-hearted woman" or *ninauposkitzipxpe* among the North Piegan (Native American) people. Only married women could aspire to the status, which expressed stereotypically male personalities and behavior, including "aggressiveness, independence, ambition, boldness and sexuality" (1941: 175); in public, they joked, teased, and freely expressed their opinions with the men, and their husbands took pride in their confidence and style.

Finally and not surprisingly, modernization and globalization have left impressions on cultural conceptions of sex and gender. In the "transcultural junctures created by science, modernization, and development programs" (Pigg and Adams,

IS THERE A JAPANESE "GAY IDENTITY"?

2005: 21), foreign, especially Western, notions of sex and gender have circulated around the globe. The media for these cultural notions and images include of course movies and music, but also political discourse about human rights and even scientific discourse about contraception, abortion, homosexuality, sexually transmitted diseases, and other "sexual health" issues. This supposedly neutral "medicalization" of sexuality has affected local concepts and practices in disparate ways. Readers might recall that the government of Iran recently denied that homosexuality even exists in Iran. Meanwhile, according to Lawrence Cohen (2005), the Western or "cosmopolitan" category of "gay" has been introduced into India, vying with traditional categories like *hijra* or *kothi*. Likewise, Vinh-Kim Nguyen finds that the "new version of the 'facts of life'" is reorganizing male–female and male–male relationships in the Ivory Coast (2005: 245), and ideas of women's rights and practices like birth control are sparking reconstructions of the role of women, the nature of marriage, and the understanding of "morality" from Russia and India to China and Africa—and the West as well.

BOX 5.5   CONTEMPORARY CULTURAL CONTROVERSIES: DO MUSLIM WOMEN NEED SAVING?

Since the attacks on the United States on September 11, 2001 and the emergence of global Islamic terrorism, the custom in many (but not all) Islamic societies of "the veil" has become an icon of cultural difference. Well-meaning Americans and other Westerners often feel that we need to "save" Muslim women from the oppression of the veil and general gender segregation. And no doubt women have suffered under some Islamic regimes, like the Taliban of Afghanistan. But Lila Abu-Lughod noticed that more than a few contemporary Muslim women have *chosen* to wear some version of the veil (sometimes a simple headscarf or *hijab*, sometimes a full covering or *burqa*), even if those women were raised or have lived in "modern" and "liberated" cultures. Also, the custom of the veil has different meanings for different women: Some see it as an act of faith, even a religious duty, while for others it is modesty or privacy, or a marker of identity, or sheer tradition. Lughod insisted that "we need to work against the reductive interpretation of veiling as the quintessential sign of women's unfreedom, even if we object to state imposition of this form" and that "we must take care not to reduce the diverse situations and attitudes of millions of Muslim women to a single item of clothing" (2002: 786). Rather than thinking in terms of "saving" them, she advised that we "use a more egalitarian language of alliances, coalitions, and solidarity," working together toward "making the world a more just place" (788).

What do you think?

SUMMARY

Human beings are individuals, but they do and must learn to be particular kinds of individuals, and this occurs under the influence of culture. Psychological anthropology bridges the gap between the poles of "nature" and "nurture"—humans have an individual and a species nature, which is nurtured in specific ways to achieve specific outcomes.

- Enculturation is the process that links the individual to his/her society and its expected and desired psychological and behavioral characteristics.
- Personality is the individual product or precipitate of a person's experience in a social context, based on more or less explicit and intentional practices aimed at raising the proper kind(s) of people.

■ Modal personality is the cumulative or statistical result, the most common personality traits in a society, where personality traits may or will be distributed according to factors like age, sex, class, etc.

Every society contains in the final analysis a unique cultural ontology or theory or system of what kinds of entities and beings—human and otherwise—exist, what their natures are, and how society should respond to them.

■ Some societies, but not all necessarily, posit a "self" that distinguishes the individual.
■ Humans may not be the only species capable of "self" awareness, any more than we are the only capable of "language" or "culture."

Part of a society's ontology includes its sex and gender system. A society may

■ identify two sexes or genders based on physical traits,
■ identify two sexes or genders based on other than physical traits, or
■ identify three or more sexes or genders based on physical or other than physical traits.

That is, human individuals come with particular physical or bodily configurations, but how society interprets and values—culturizes—those physical facts is relative.

MCQS

FILL IN THE BLANKS

WWW

Key Terms

basic personality	*hijra*	self
berdache	modal personality	sexual dimorphism
cultural ontology	national character	*travesti*
ethnopsychology	personality	
eunuch	primitive mentality	
female circumcision	psychic unity of humanity	
gender	psychological anthropology	

6 Individuals and identities
Race and ethnicity

In the American Southeast lives a group called the Melungeons. Or do they? Although travelers and journalists have reported on the mysterious Melungeons since the late 1800s, "consistently treated as one of Appalachia's best-kept secrets" (Schrift, 2013: 15), according to Melissa Schrift, no one actually identified as Melungeon until surprisingly recently. Indeed, she contends that it is "more productive to conceptualize the Melungeon story as a regional legend that, similar to the structure of all legends, is a loosely structured narrative with an appealing story, a basis in actual belief, and a cultural message" (23). No one is even certain where the Melungeons came from or what their physical traits are. Some claimed that they were Native Americans; others said they were Portuguese or Turks. Most likely a corruption of the French word *mélange* for "mixture," the name "Melungeon" is probably an invented term for individuals who were of racially mixed ancestry in a time and place where racial mixing was a serious social problem. Persons with the physical appearance of mixed races were typically condemned as "lazy, immoral, illiterate, filthy, violent, superstitious, defiant, cowardly, mysterious, and primitive" (41); understandably, people tended

to disavow a mixed or Melungeon identity, and there was no traditional "community" or "society" of Melungeons. Things began to change, though, in the 1960s, when locals in Hancock County, Tennessee produced an outdoor play about regional history called *Walk Toward the Sunset*. The play offered a vision of Melungeonness, even if that vision was only folklore and hearsay elevated to art. Nevertheless, some folks who had never been Melungeon before subsequently "became Melungeon," claiming Melungeon ancestry as adults despite the lack of any history or memory of being Melungeon as children. As Schrift writes, "individuals do not recall being Melungeon before they chose to do so as adults" (91). This did not prevent them from forming the Melungeon Heritage Association, and a 1994 book by Brent Kennedy titled *The Melungeons* helped to secure the identity, so that by the 1990s, Melungeons declared themselves to be "a multiethnic group of people believed to have some mixture of European, Native American, and African ancestry" (Schrift, 2013: 90). Schrift rightly sees this outcome as a process in which the *category* of Melungeon predated and facilitated the *identity* of Melungeon—that is, in which the category created the identity, not vice versa.

Human beings belong to a single species. However, it is an incredibly diverse species, behaviorally and physically—a "polytypic species," one that comes in a variety of different forms. Long before anthropology existed, people were trying to make sense of this diversity, and one enduring concept invented by Western societies to categorize and explain human diversity is race. Anthropology itself adopted the race concept before it adopted the culture concept. More recently, observers advanced the concept of "ethnic group" to refer to the same, or sometimes quite different, human variables. Both terms, but especially race, have a troubled history, fraught with confusion and abuse. Both terms, like gender, are also ways to classify humans and, even more importantly, to assign value and tasks to humans. In other words, like gender, race and **ethnicity** are examples of an ontology or a taxonomy, a classification and evaluation system. As anthropologists, we are indeed interested in human difference—the characteristics of distinct human groups—but we are equally if not more interested in the systems by which those groups are conceived, the relations between those groups, and the social

practices by which, and the social purposes for which, those groups and relations are created, perpetuated, contested, or changed.

THE ANTHROPOLOGY OF RACE

Every English speaker has a general sense of what race means: physical differences (usually and especially surface differences, like skin color) between humans, or more often between major "types" or divisions, even "breeds," of the human species, generally geographically separated, and the groups characterized by those differences. Although race thus relates to physical or biological factors, there is a wide (though not quite universal) consensus that races are not "real" or "objective" divisions, but are rather social constructs. As Audrey Smedley asserted, the "reality of race" resides in "a set of beliefs and attitudes about human differences, not the differences themselves" (1999: xi). This is not to claim that there are no differences between human individuals or groups—there obviously are—but rather to draw

See Chapter 3

Ethnicity
the phenomenon of organizing around some aspect of shared culture to integrate an identity group, differentiate it from other groups, and compete in a multi-ethnic context for resources

Smedley, Audrey. 1999. *Race in North America: Origin and Evolution of a Worldview*, 2nd ed. Boulder CO: Westview Press.

IMAGE 6.1 Western tourists in Africa inevitably take their preconceptions with them.

attention to the fact that the differences that matter and precisely how and why they matter are cultural and not natural issues. Smedley explained that biological variations between groups of human beings

> have no social meanings except what we humans give them. This is what is meant when we claim that races are culturally constructed. It is the social meanings imposed on the varying human populations that we must investigate to understand race.
>
> (xii)

It is easy to show that race is a slippery and problematic term: For instance, when a "black" person and a "white" person have a child, what race is the child? And does it matter which parent is of which race? Does it matter exactly what the child looks like, that is, how "black" or "white" s/he appears? The talented "black" golfer Tiger Woods has publicly stated that he is not "black" since his ancestry includes Africa, Caucasian, Asian, and Native American; he even invented a new race-term for himself—Cablinasian—despite the fact that most Americans still consider him "black."

The truth is that different societies, or even the same society at different times in its history, have answered these questions differently. Part of the problem is that the term "race" has been chronically imprecisely defined, if it has been defined at all. Francis Collins, the head of the Human Genome Project, urges that

> it is essential to point out that "race" and "ethnicity" are terms without generally agreed-upon definitions. Both terms carry complex connotations that reflect culture, history, socioeconomic and political status, as well as a variably important connection to ancestral geographic origins.
>
> (2004: S 13)

Brazilian anthropologists Sergio Pena and Telma de Souza Birchal insist that race is not a scientific idea; rather, "the notion of race has been imported from the common sense to science since its appearance" (2005–2006: 3).

Five obvious and fatal objections to the "naturalness" of race have been raised. First, no one has been able to specify exactly how many races there are. Common estimates range from three to five or as many as nine. Second, race classifications

See Chapter 12

select certain physical characteristics (most often skin color) and not others on which to base the categories, and it is not clarified how and why these particular traits were chosen as the relevant ones: Why skin color instead of blood type or height or shoe size? Third, and related to the first two, the classifications, evaluations, and applications of race change over time. For example, not so long ago English speakers used (and sometimes still use) the term "race" in reference to "the French race" or "the Scandinavian race" or "the Jewish race" or "the Arab race" or even "the human race." Groups that never regarded themselves as a single identity ("the Native American race") are subsumed under one category, as are people who are physically quite diverse, like the "Hispanic race" which includes "white" people, "black" people, "Indian" people, and every conceivable mixture of these and more. Fourth, researchers have calculated that there is more physical and genetic variation *within* race groups than between them: According to Richard Lewontin (1972), for the eight race categories he considered, 85.4 percent of genetic diversity was found inside the categories and only 6.3 percent between the categories. Fifth and finally, race classifications have not always, if ever, been content to stop at physical characteristics, but have attributed psychological, emotional, intellectual, and even moral qualities to the purported races as well. For instance, Madison Grant opined in 1916 that "moral, intellectual, and spiritual attributes are as persistent as physical characters and are transmitted substantially unchanged from generation to generation" (226).

The evolution of the race concept

According to Dante Puzzo, a historian of Western ideas, race (and its evil concomitant racism) "is a modern conception, for prior to the sixteenth century there was virtually nothing in the life and thought of the West that can be described as racist" (1964: 579). Michael Banton (1987) found that the word "race" did not appear in English until 1508. However, as Europeans acquired more experience with peoples from other parts of the world, and as they acquired power over those peoples, differences in body and behavior became more interesting to them—and frequently became intertwined for them.

The familiar system of race categories emerged in the work of Carolus Linnaeus (1707–1778), the great naturalist and classifier. In the first edition of his *Systema Naturae* published in 1740, he divided the human species into four subtypes based on color—white, black, red, and yellow. By the tenth edition in 1758–1759, these types had evolved into Homo europaeus, Homo afer, Homo americanus, and Homo asiaticus, acquiring not only geographical but (often quite offensive) mental and behavioral features. For instance, *Homo europaeus* he characterized as "white, sanguine, muscular. Hair flowing, long. Eyes blue. Gentle, acute, inventive. Covered with close vestments. Governed by laws," while *Homo afer* was "black, phlegmatic, relaxed. Hair black, frizzled. Skin silky. Nose flat. Lips tumid. Women without shame. Mammae lactate profusely. Crafty, indolent, negligent. Anoints himself with grease. Governed by caprice." Native Americans, or *Homo americanus*, were distinct for being "reddish, choleric, erect. Hair black, straight, thick; nostrils wide; face harsh; beard scanty. Obstinate, merry, free. Paints himself with fine red lines. Regulated by customs." Finally, Asians, or *Homo asiaticus*, were "sallow, melancholy, stiff. Hair black. Eyes dark. Severe, haughty, avaricious. Covered with loose garments. Ruled by opinions" (quoted in Slotkin, 1965: 177–178). The pseudoscientific system was only worsened by the inclusion of other imaginary species of humanity such as *Homo ferus*, a hairy and mute quadruped, and *Homo monstrosus*, a monster-race of cavemen who roamed the world at night.

The elastic quality of race categories is apparent in the work of Johann Friedrich Blumenbach (1752–1840), who proposed the standard four races in his 1770 *On the Natural Variety of Mankind* —European (for whom he introduced the term "Caucasian"), African, American, and Asian. Later he added a fifth race, Malayan, for southern Asian people. Blumenbach also made several important qualifications to his race system, not the least of which was that each of the "five principal races" was actually composed of "one or more nations which are distinguished by their more or less striking structure from the rest of those of the same division. Thus the Hindoos [sic] might be separated as particular subvarieties from the Caucasian; the Chinese and Japanese from the Mongolian; the Hottentots from the Ethiopian," and so on (quoted in Slotkin, 1965: 189). In other words, he admitted considerable variation *within* "primary races." Also, he conceded that races were not entirely discrete: Although the race-types were "so many different species of man, yet when the matter is thoroughly considered, you see that all do so run into one another, and that one variety of mankind does so sensibly pass into the other, that you cannot mark out the limits between them" (189). Finally and most consequentially, the races were not only distinguished, but ranked in terms of antiquity and perfection, the first race in time and quality being the white, Caucasian one. As the original, "primeval" form of humanity, Caucasians were the most "beautiful," at the middle of a spectrum of races with Asians and Africans at the opposite extremes, Americans and Indians intermediate between Caucasians and Asians, and Malayans intermediate between Caucasians and Africans. The non-Caucasian races were deemed a product of *degeneration* from the first, ideal type and the admixture of the higher and lower types.

Race typologies multiplied and morphed over the centuries. George Cuvier (1769–1832) managed to condense them to three—Caucasian, Mongolian, and Negroid—with white Caucasians as the optimal form of humanity and black Negroids as "the most degraded race among men, whose forms approach nearest to those of the inferior animals, and whose intellect has not yet arrived at the establishment of any regular form of government, nor at anything which has the least appearance of systematic knowledge" (quoted in Green, 1959: 235). Most whimsically of all, Carl Gustav Carus (1789–1869) designed a four-race system consisting of Day People (Caucasian), Eastern Twilight People (Mongolians, Malayans, Hindus, Turks, and Slavs), Western Twilight People (American Indians), and Night People (Africans and Australians).

Measuring and managing mankind

The failure to achieve any accord on the number or nature of races, yet the persistence with which theorists have sought racial systems, alerts us to the drive toward race typing in Western societies: While thinkers have not settled on a uniform race classification, they have consistently believed that such classification was possible and important. None seemed to stop and ask the question that

BOX 6.1   RACE, CLASS, AND OTHERNESS IN PERU

As in most of the colonized world, concepts of race in Peru were initially "used as a way to classify phenotype differences between conquistadors and the conquered" and turned into a barrier "granting legitimacy to the relationship of domination imposed by the conquest" (Gómez-Pellón, 2014: 16). The most salient distinction was between "the so-called Spanish *lineages*" and the native peoples or *indios*. Racializing practice continues in Peru today, "with a typology that basically corresponds to the original existence of three segments: Indians, *criollos* or whites, and mestizos," that is, people of mixed white and Indian descent;

> Apart from these main categories, there are others, like Negroes, mulattos [mixed white and black ancestry], Asians, and so on, which represent smaller population groups. The three traditional categories: Indians, mestizos, and whites, [sic] are the ones that essentially form the Peruvian nation, although not to the same degree.
>
> (20–21)

Significantly, up to three-quarters of Peruvians identify as mestizo, giving weight to the claim that Peru is a truly racially mixed and perhaps racially integrated society. Yet Eloy Gómez-Pellón argues that race is a complicated concept in Peru and much of Latin America. "The most striking thing about Peru," he writes, "is that the typical ascriptions are not strictly related to phenotypes" or outward physical appearance. "On the contrary, a large part of the population of Peru appears to share certain phenotype traits and yet the people are assigned to different 'racial' categories without any apparent correspondence" (24). As much as or more than overt biological features, the Peruvian race system is based on culture and class and on "the conservation of privileges" of certain members of the society (20). For instance, "an indigenous individual is not indigenous because of certain biological traits, but because this individual lives in a peasant or indigenous community" (28) and disproportionately suffers from poverty and lack of education. At times, race has been linked to language or even clothing or customs like "chewing coca or walking barefoot" (22). Conversely, white or *criollo* status tends to imply higher wealth and social status: Predictably, individuals with lighter skin "are expected to enjoy high status," but this association works both ways, as "the higher the status of the person, the whiter they look, no matter what the real color of their skin is, like a strange optical illusion" (29). Gómez-Pellón concludes that in Peru

> status and roles associated with [race] are unrelated to aspects of the phenotype; the taxonomies classifying individuals according to the phenotype are so diffuse that a single person may be assigned to different phenotype categories; an individual may change phenotype status through social mobility; that racial mixing has been surprisingly intense in the past and the present, because, although it is not generally regarded as positive, neither does it arouse strong disapproval; and that the boundaries between Indians, mestizos, and whites, and any others that might be added, are indeterminate from all points of view.
>
> (31)

Sherwood Washburn (1963) posed only in the 1960s: What is a race classification for? What is its social origin and—still more significantly—its social function or effect?

The question of why people want and need to identify races and to build race classifications is indeed the central anthropological question of race. Several scholars have directed attention less toward race itself or any particular race system than toward what we could call "racial thinking," understood as

> the (erroneous) belief that humanity is divided into scientifically observable, homogeneous, and mutually distinct biological "types." Importantly, it assumes that these types exist transhistorically, that is, that these categories exist . . . as natural facts, and that these categories existed throughout time, whether people in a particular era realized it or not.
>
> (Eissenstat, 2005: 239–240)

More crucial than the concept of race for describing physical differences between kinds of humans, then, is the use of those descriptions for *explaining and justifying* certain behaviors of and relationships between these kinds.

It cannot be overemphasized that Western societies developed their racial thinking in the context of political and cultural domination over non-Western societies. Far beyond the neutral or pure-scientific activity of cataloging and organizing human physical variety (a not illegitimate project), Western travelers and theorists were led to ask why the people they encountered acted and thought in unfamiliar (and often to Western eyes nonsensical or reprehensible) ways. And as this contact became increasingly exploitative, including conquest and slavery, Westerners were further led to ponder why these other people were so "weak" or "backward" or "inferior." One possible and appealing answer was a sort of biological determinism—that humans with particular biological traits also had particular behavioral or mental traits that inhibited their "progress." The persistence of "backward" or "inferior" behavioral and psychological qualities after exposure to the "superior" ways of the West, and the failure of these other peoples to "improve" and "succeed" in the Western sense, gave rise to the notion that physical characteristics were a sign and a cause of mental and even moral deficiencies— most critically, that the physical and the mental and moral were inseparably connected and that both were innate and permanent.

Thus the conventional English-language, especially North American, concept of race arose, with its five key components (Smedley, 1999: 28):

1. A race is an "exclusive and discrete biological" entity.

2. Races are fundamentally unequal, and the relations between races are necessarily hierarchical (some are "better" than others).
3. "The outer physical characteristics" of races are "but surface manifestations of inner realities [such as] behavioral, intellectual, temperamental, moral, and other qualities."
4. All of the qualities of a race are "natural" and genetically inherited—and inherited as a single indivisible bundle.
5. Therefore, the differences and hierarchies between races are immutable, "fixed and unalterable, [and] could never be bridged or transcended."

In the end, race was not simply a classification of human physical differences, but a *bio-moral* judgment (Wolf, 1994) on certain types of humans who were ranked inherently and eternally "higher" or "lower" than other types of humans. Race thinking accomplished the valuable task of "naturalizing" political, economic, and cultural status or class inequalities and ascribing them as intrinsic properties of the victims of these inequalities.

The obvious task then was to specify and quantify these natural differences. Accordingly, the nineteenth century became the great era of measuring mankind. In fact, in his study of the science of race, John Haller proposed that the "hallmark of anthropology in the nineteenth century was anthropometry" (1971: 7). **Anthropometry** was and is a practice of measuring the bodies of human beings for the purpose of describing individual and collective physical characteristics. In itself, recording people's height and weight and head size is neither unacceptable nor absurd; however, the generalizations and interpretations of this research could be problematic, distasteful, and patently false.

Certain traits emerged as central to Western race classification, including hair form and color, skin color, eye form and color, nose form, face form, overall height and body form, and especially head size and shape. One of the earliest measurable traits was **facial angle**, or roughly the amount that the lower face and jaw protrudes, deviating from the ideal flat face of the ideal Caucasian. It was noticed that apes and even more so dogs and other animals had very acute facial angles, which was linked to their lower intelligence; by extension, humans with acute facial angles (resulting from sloping foreheads

See Chapter 12

THE EVERYDAY LANGUAGE OF WHITE RACISM

Anthropometry
the measurement of human bodies to determine individual and group ("racial") physical characteristics

Facial angle
a concept in anthropometry that measures the shape of the face from the forehead to the bridge of the nose, on the assumption that sharper angles indicate "more primitive" kinds of humans

Miscegenation

a term for the undesirable effects of the mixing of different genetic types or populations, especially race groups. Often refers to the very notion of mixing the races

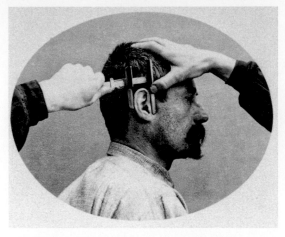

IMAGE 6.2 Anthropometry—measuring racialized bodies.

or prominent jaws or lips) were deemed more animalistic and less intelligent. Darker skin color was also taken as a lower and more primitive feature, as was short stature or especially long or short limbs.

However, the major factor then, as for many people today, was the head and brain: "Scientific" measures like brain volume and cephalic index purported to quantify racial inequalities. **Cephalic index**, introduced by the great neurologist Paul Broca, was a ratio of the width of the head from ear to ear relative to the depth of the head from front to back; a higher index suggested a rounder head and a superior intelligence. Determining brain volume was fairly straight-forward, on the assumption that larger brains meant greater intelligence. Happily for scientific racists, Caucasians scored well on both tests, with a cephalic index and a brain weight and volume higher than all other races. Samuel Morton ranked the brains of races in the descending order of Caucasian, Mongoloid, Malay, Native American, and African, further arguing that brains had not altered in four thousand years and thus could be deemed fixed and permanent. In the skull and in numerous other characteristics, Africans consistently ranked lowest, indicating to racial thinkers "a far closer relationship to the ape" than any other human species (Haller, 1971: 34).

The implications of such racial thinking are clear: If some races were naturally and permanently higher or lower than others, then it made little sense to preach the equality of races or to attempt to raise the lower races. It even seemed reasonable

Cephalic index

a measurement of the skull/ brain volume and shape, based on a ratio of the width of the head from ear to ear relative to the depth of the head from front to back

to subordinate and restrict the lower ones, and certainly interbreeding (**miscegenation**) was to be avoided as deleterious to the more perfect races— or, ironically, sometimes to be promoted as a means to "improve" the more degraded ones. Nineteenth and early-twentieth century racial thinking was thus an ideal justification for slavery, segregation, colonialism, and genocide. Influential figures like Edward Drinker Cope insisted that the "inferior character of the Negro mind in the scale of evolution made him unfit for American citizenship" (Haller, 1971: 198), while Nathaniel Southgate Shaler went so far as to excuse lynching as a legitimate form of race self-defense (184–185).

It should be noted, in conclusion, that biological-deterministic, bio-moral explanations and recommendations were not limited to race groups. In the nineteenth and even more so in the twentieth century, biological causes were often proposed for behavioral, temperamental, moral, or social phenomena. Measurements of brain size, cephalic index, and facial angle, or less "scientific" attributes like stature and skin color, were applied to the new immigrants arriving in the United States from eastern and southern Europe around 1900— Caucasians all, by the standard typology. Various immigrant groups were regarded as congenitally prone to drunkenness or idleness or crime or violence. Predictably, all sorts of vices and social improprieties were explained in biological terms, including poverty: Some people, it was held, were naturally unable to compete or succeed, and a few social engineers went so far as to recommend that the poor not be allowed to breed, since poverty was a transmissible condition. Criminals were subjected to bio-moral analyses, on the hope that a "criminal type" might be identified that would make capture and punishment of outlaws easier (a kind of biological "profiling"). Mental illness was often associated with physical imperfections and therefore with physical therapies: The "insane" were often thought to be animal-like in their insensitivity to heat, cold, pain, and exhaustion (which is not even true of animals), and somatic "cures" like bleeding, blistering, near-drowning, swinging and spinning, or immobilization were practiced. This attitude extended to those with disabilities, like the deaf who were also regarded as lacking sense or intelligence, like wild animals, and were not allowed to vote in the United States until the early 1800s.

BOX 6.2   THE POLITICS OF RACIALLY CORRECT DOLLS

Race is not only a cultural concept but, in more than one way, a cultural industry: Society produces and circulates categories and judgments of race, as well as the material manifestations and representations of race. One example, explored by Elizabeth Chin, is "racially-correct dolls," that is, toys that are intended, probably benignly, to be inclusive and positive: A little girl should be able, so the argument goes, to play with a doll that looks like her. In 1991, Mattel, the manufacturer of Barbie, introduced "minority" versions of their toy, with darker skin, African-American facial features and hair, and names like Shani, Asha, and Nichelle. Ironically, while the dolls were no doubt meant to be racially aware, they had the effect of "fixing racial boundaries more firmly" (1999: 305); that is, generalizations or stereotypes were not questioned but assumed, reproduced, and marketed. Other companies joined Mattel in offering ethnic dolls, including Shindana and Olmec, but Chin insisted that most such initiatives continue to take race as a given; they do not "significantly transform the understanding of race, or even racism" (310). They exemplify "an attempt to turn racism on its head but not an attempt to re-imagine race itself" (317). Interestingly, Chin argued that the little girls who owned dolls, including Barbies, were more "keenly aware of the complexity of race" (317), as indicated in a variety of ways. First, they did not find white Barbie as oppressive as toymakers might presume; further, they had ways of "ethnicizing" white Barbies, for instance by styling their hair in "ethnic" ways. Even more, the girls sometimes rejected the manufacturers' racial designations, like identifying Shani not as African American but as Native American. Thus, the children were actively refashioning race traits and categories, while the toymakers were simply repackaging the same old traits and categories.

Advocates of the eugenics movement like Victoria Woodhull echoed the sentiments of the racial eugenists when she insisted that all such people, "imbeciles, criminals, paupers, and the otherwise unfit . . . must not be bred."

THE MODERN ANTHROPOLOGICAL CRITIQUE OF RACE

The confusions, abuses, and outright falsehoods surrounding racial thinking could not forever escape criticism, and cultural anthropology contributed significantly to this critique. The elaboration of the anthropological concept of "culture" combined with the growing body of observational data of non-Western peoples and the inclusive and relativistic attitude of anthropology provided it with a unique and authoritative perspective from which to judge the discourse of race.

One of the first and strongest voices to challenge racial thinking was Franz Boas. Much of his work specifically targeted the reigning ideas and practices of race, as in his 1928 *Anthropology and Modern Life*, as well as his 1940 *Race, Language, and Culture* and

his 1945 *Race and Democratic Society*. Starting from the premise that there "is little clarity in regard to the term 'race'" (1928: 19), he took the key step of separating physical from psychological and cultural phenomena, concluding that "it is well-nigh impossible to determine with certainty the hereditary traits in mental behavior" (50). Rather, the variability of intelligence and personality within a group, and the rapidity and ease with which individuals change in new circumstances, convinced him that "cultural experience" was as important as if not more important than "racial descent."

Having placed experience above biology for explaining behavior, he went further to unpack the race concept itself. A race was not a closed, fixed physical type, but something more akin to a family line, with its common but by no means immutable traits; mix in other family lines and the race-type dissolves. Still worse, a race is not a homogeneous unit, but a vague division of humanity with much internal variety: Obviously not all Caucasians or *Homo europaeus* have blond hair and blue eyes, and the alleged "race traits" of any race are a statistical abstraction from a diverse distribution of features. At best, the stereotype of a race is the *extreme or*

Eugenics
the scientific practice of "improving" a population or species by selective breeding or genetic engineering, to breed out "bad" traits and breed in "good" ones

ideal form, but these extreme forms "are not pure racial types. We do not know how much their descendants may vary from themselves and what their ancestry may have been" (22–23). Most devastating of all, Boas asserted that physical traits, as much as mental and behavioral ones, are plastic and subject to environmental pressures, not fixed permanent inheritances. Some of his most influential (and controversial) research argued that the children and grandchildren of immigrants differed measurably from their ancestors in head shape, cephalic index, and height and conformed more to the standards of their newly-adopted land—indicating that "race traits" were highly changeable and only appeared stable as long as environmental conditions remained the same.

Under the tutelage of Boas, anthropology was academically and politically active on the subject of race, even condemning Nazi racism in a 1938 resolution that stated that anthropology "provides no scientific basis for discrimination against any people on the ground of racial inferiority, religious affiliation or linguistic heritage" (American Anthropological Association, 1939: 30). Melville Herskovits attacked racism against African Americans directly in *The Myth of the Negro Past*, which refuted five lies about the "Negro race": that they "are naturally of a child-like character"; that they are unintelligent since "only the poorer stock of Africa was enslaved"; that because slaves came

from all parts of Africa, they had no common culture; that whatever culture they did have was "so savage and relatively so low in the scale of human civilization" that they would have quickly given it up; and that "the Negro is thus a man without a past"—and presumably therefore only a man (and woman) with a racial body (1958: 1–2).

But arguably the most vociferous opponent of racial thinking was Ashley Montagu, who called it "man's most dangerous myth," not only an error, but a tragedy (1945: 1). Races in the everyday sense do not exist, he asserted, as it is a fact "that all human beings are so much mixed with regard to origin that between different groups of individuals intergradation and 'overlapping' of physical characters is the rule" (3). Worse still, as we have seen, the concept of race implies much more than physical similarity, but "a compound of physical, mental, personality, and cultural traits which determine the behavior of individuals inheriting this alleged compound" (6). However, "Such a conception of 'race' has no basis in scientific fact or in any other kind of demonstrable fact. It is a pure myth, and it is the tragic myth of our tragic era" (8).

For Montagu, racial thinking was a way of translating cultural differences into biological differences; the real and crucial issues are status and caste issues, in which resources, opportunities, and social value are differentially assigned to groups and then these groups are "closed" to each

Herskovits, Melville J. 1958 [1941]. *The Myth of the Negro Past*. Boston: Beacon Press.

Montagu, M. F. Ashley. 1945. *Man's Most Dangerous Myth: The Fallacy of Race*, 2nd ed. New York: Columbia University Press.

BOAS ON PHYSICAL CHANGES IN THE DESCENDANTS OF IMMIGRANTS

IMAGE 6.3 Children in central Australian Aboriginal societies have straight, often blond, hair, challenging the simple racial categories of the West.

other spatially (by segregation) and sexually (by rules of **endogamy**). Race is thus, he concluded,

> a term for a social problem which is created by special types of social condition and by such special conditions alone. In terms of social relations so-called 'race problems' are, in the modern world, essentially of the nature of caste problems.
>
> (67)

In a racial system, physical characteristics "are merely the pegs upon which culturally generated hostilities are made to hang" (66). Accordingly, following a suggestion in the 1935 book *We Europeans* by Julian Huxley and A. C. Haddon, Montagu advocated the use of the term "ethnic group" (see below) to name these socially and culturally distinguished collections of humans—and rejection of the term "race" completely.

Like Montagu, Frank Livingstone insisted on the "non-existence" of races in the human species, claiming that "there are excellent arguments for abandoning the concept of race with reference to the living populations of *Homo sapiens*" (1962: 279). The physical anthropologist Sherwood Washburn, who raised the central question of the purpose of race classifications, seconded the analysis that race is a cultural construction and that there is "no possibility of studying human raciation, the process of race formation, without studying human culture" (1963: 522). The physical evidence tells us that there are "no three primary races, no three major groups. The idea of three primary races stems from nineteenth-century typology" (523). Rather, "Since races are open systems which are intergrading, the number of races will depend on the purpose of the classification" (524)—or, if no social purpose is served

Endogamy
the marriage principle in which an individual marries someone who is in the same cultural category as him/herself (e.g. marrying someone in your own race or religion)

IMAGE 6.4 Human faces of many races.

by it, no racial distinction might be made in the first place.

These and many other anthropologists have deflated the concept of race as a natural, objective, scientific tool and have redirected attention to the social phenomenon that Manning Nash called the "ideology of race." Recognizing that the "non-existence" of races in the natural and objective sense does not mean the non-existence or irrelevance of race as a cultural force, Nash defined race ideology as

> a system of ideas which interprets and defines the meanings of racial differences, real or imagined, in terms of some system of cultural values. The ideology of race is always normative: it ranks differences as better or worse, superior or inferior, desirable or undesirable, and as modifiable or unmodifiable. Like all ideologies, the ideology of race implies a call to action; it embodies a political and social program; it is a demand that something be done.
>
> (1962: 285)

Perhaps we should add that it is also a justification for things that are already being done, such as discrimination, slavery, or genocide.

Nash went beyond the identification of race ideology to theorizing about when such an ideology will appear, for not all societies in all times have possessed it. A race ideology, he hypothesized, is likely to coalesce when there is a conflict between two or more groups distinguishable in physical terms; when there is a division of labor based on this distinction which results in the "subordination or systematic deprivation of one group"; when the subordinate group resists or refuses its subordination; and interestingly when there is dissent within the dominant group over the "prevailing facts of disprivilege" (288). In such conditions, the ideology of race serves not only to subjugate the "lower race" but to justify to the "dominant race" its own advantages and privileges. If he is correct, then the appearance and elaboration of a race system should come *after* the social inequalities which it explains, legitimates, and perpetuates rather than before.

THE ANTHROPOLOGY OF ETHNICITY

Most English-speakers are not only familiar with the concept of ethnicity or ethnic group, but commonly conflate it with race, as in "race and ethnicity" or "racial and ethnic groups." Many may consider the two terms synonymous, although they are not. Nevertheless, race and ethnicity are closely related in certain ways. Both are practices for categorizing people—by physical characteristics for "race" and by cultural or historical and geographical characteristics for "ethnicity." Often, a group that shares physical traits also shares cultural ones; as just discussed, racialist thinkers tended to link the behaviors of the group causally to its biology, while anthropologists realize today that behavior is learned and shared and, therefore, that groups of people who are genetically related will tend to interact more and to share more cultural characteristics as well. Furthermore, like races, ethnic groups are not objective or natural "things," but social concepts with social meaning and function. Accordingly, as with race, anthropological attention has shifted from the reputed traits of particular ethnic groups to the relations between these groups (frequently competitive and sometimes combative, including discrimination, oppression, and genocide) and to the processes by which the groups are formed and sustained.

When Huxley and Haddon proposed "ethnic group" as a replacement for "race," they were explicitly reviving a very old notion, one employed by the ancient historian and traveler Herodotus, who "found human beings divided into a number of groups, *ethnea*, and the *ethnos* forms his practical basis of classification" (Huxley and Haddon, 1935: 30). However, the term *ethnos*, roughly translated as "a people," "a nation," or "a cultural group" (and incorporated into anthropology in terms like ethnology, ethnography, and various subdisciplines such as ethnobotany and ethnopsychology) was then as today a vague concept:

> Thus, his *ethnos* is at times a tribe, at times a political unit, at times a larger grouping, and in using the word he guards himself against treating either type of unit as necessarily or even probably of common descent.
>
> (31)

So the root *ethnos* and the English words derived from it, including "ethnic group" and "ethnicity," entered the language with wide but various and uncertain meaning; they could refer to diverse kinds of groups with imprecise features and porous boundaries. Even so, or perhaps for exactly that reason, the concept of "ethnic group" has stuck and even grown in popular and scholarly usage. Max Weber wrote about it in the early twentieth century, defining the term as a human group

> that entertain[s] a subjective belief in their common descent because of similarities of physical type or of customs or both, or because of memories of colonization and migration; this belief must be important for the propagation of group formation; conversely, it does not matter whether or not an objective blood relationship exists.
>
> (1968: 389)

Notice in this definition that physical and cultural traits are still both included, yet neither is necessarily "real": Membership in an ethnic group, he asserted, is distinct "precisely by being a presumed identity, not a group with concrete social action. . . . [Ethnicity] does not constitute a group; it merely facilitates group formation of any kind, particularly in the political sphere" (389). This led Weber to three crucial realizations about ethnic groups: First, that they need not be very culturally different from each other (that is, a small cultural difference is sufficient to construct an "ethnic" difference); second, that they need not be very internally culturally homogeneous (that is, there may be considerable diversity *within* the ethnic group); and third, that any cultural trait—language, religion, clothing, cuisine, and so on—can suffice to distinguish one ethnic group from another.

Since the re-introduction of "ethnic group" by Weber and by Huxley and Haddon (and the later invention of the noun "ethnicity"), the concept has become essential to discussions of and developments in human group relations. While there is no single authoritative definition for ethnic group or ethnicity, the definitions that have been offered share important common features and indicate important cultural processes. Thus, ethnicity has been defined as the "subjective symbolic or emblematic use of any aspect of culture [by members of a group], in order to differentiate themselves from other groups" (DeVos, 1975: 16) or as the

> character, quality, or condition of ethnic group membership, based on an identity with and/or consciousness of group belonging that is

differentiated from others by symbolic "markers" (including cultural, biological, or territorial), and is rooted in bonds to a shared past and perceived ethnic interests.

> (Burgess, 1978: 270)

Rather than crafting definitions, another and more fruitful course is to identify the characteristics of the groups that are produced. Fredrik Barth suggested that an ethnic group has four key qualities: It is "largely biologically self-perpetuating" generally through endogamous marriage, "shares fundamental cultural values," "makes up a field of communication and interaction," and "has a membership which identifies itself, and is identified by others, as constituting a category distinguishable from other categories of the same order" (1969: 10–11). Andrew Greeley offered a list of six features of an ethnic group:

> "(1) A presumed consciousness of kind rooted in a sense of common origin.
> (2) Sufficient territorial concentration to make it possible for members of the group to interact with each other most of the time and to reduce to a minimum interaction with members of other ethnic groups.
> (3) A sharing of ideals and values by members of the ethnic group.
> (4) Strong moralistic fervor for such ideals and values, combined with a sense of being persecuted by those who do not share them and hence are not members of the ethnic group.
> (5) Distrust of those who are outside the ethnic group, combined with massive ignorance of them.
> (6) Finally, a strong tendency in members of an ethnic group to view themselves and their circle as the whole of reality, or at least the whole of reality that matters."
>
> (1971: 120–121)

Ethnic culture, ethnic boundary, and ethnic mobilization

Whether or not all ethnic groups possess all the qualities highlighted by Greeley, such analyses raise two relevant points. First, ethnicity and ethnic groups bring together a set of powerful forces,

Weber, Max. 1968. *Economy and Society*, Vol. 1. Guenther Roth and Claus Wittich, Eds. New York: Bedminster Press.

BOX 6.3   WHO IS AN UZBEK?

The existence of a country in Central Asia called Uzbekistan suggests a simple answer to the question of Uzbek identity: An Uzbek is a person who lives in Uzbekistan. The first problem is that not all Uzbeks live in Uzbekistan and not only Uzbeks live in Uzbekistan. Uzbeks "form a significant minority, often a local majority, in all neighboring states" such as Tajikistan, Kazakhstan, Kyrgyzstan, and Turkmenistan (Finke, 2014: 7). Simultaneously, Tajiks, Kazaks, Kyrgyz, Turkmen, and a dizzying array of other groups including Arabs and Russians reside in Uzbekistan. In Central Asia as in all of the world, political boundaries do not match social or ethnic boundaries. But the problem of Uzbek identity is much bigger. The idea of "Uzbekness," writes Peter Finke, is "flexible" and "acknowledges regional variation and the possibility of membership by voluntary decision" (2). Indeed, the term "Uzbek" has not had an immutable meaning over time: Although the name has been used for centuries, "it did not refer to the ancestors of those who are called Uzbeks today"; more, "the genetic predecessors of the contemporary Uzbeks did not belong to a single named group and possibly lacked a strong sense of belonging" (1). Contrary to the presumption of ancient distinct social groups, Central Asia has long been a region of movement and mixture, as groups with varying cultures, languages, and religions invaded and settled. The ancestors of today's Uzbeks—various Turkic-speaking peoples—probably arrived after the sixth century CE, but only became known as Uzbeks in the 1400s. At least as important as "ethnic" terms was the distinction "between the nomadic pastoralists (including Kazaks, Kyrgyz, and Turkmens) and the sedentary agriculturalists, the predecessors of modern Uzbeks and Tajiks" (45). The cultural similarity between Uzbeks and Tajiks had consequences even after the conquest by the Russian empire and then the Soviet Union, which imposed "national delimitation" on the region, requiring "every individual to decide on one ethnic category to be attached to" (47). Some people thereby became officially Uzbek, but Finke's research in four regions of the oddly-shaped state finds quite diverse attitudes toward Uzbek identity due to environmental, historical, and cultural factors. In Bukhara, "Uzbeks and Tajiks become a single, inclusive bilingual entity where internal differentiations are basically nonexistent and insistently denied" (65). Intermarriage between Uzbeks and Tajiks is common, and many Uzbeks "could be called—and sometimes call themselves—half-Tajiks, and vice versa" (83). At the same time, "most Tajiks actively deny being Tajik in an ethnic sense and insist on being considered Uzbek with a different dominant language" (94). With their history of intermarriage, Uzbeks in Bukhara do not base their identity on genealogy (that is, an ancient line of Uzbek ancestry) and certainly do not consider themselves a "race." They do not lack a concept of ethnicity; they simply do not apply it to themselves, reserving it for the other groups such as Kazaks and Turkmen. Elsewhere, like the Khorezm region, which is divided by a national boundary with Turkmenistan, marriage to non-Uzbeks is uncommon and ethnic identity is stronger: Each alleged ethnic group "is acknowledged as having its own patterns and is not expected to change them" (140). In the distant eastern panhandle of the Ferghana Valley, which is almost entirely encircled by Kyrgyzstan, Uzbeks are so diverse that some "feel closer to Tajiks than to Uzbeks of a different kind" (178), and many are actually uncertain of their "ethnic identity"; one man said, "I suppose I am Uzbek, but I would have to check my passport to tell you for sure" (179).

Nash, Manning. 1989. *The Cauldron of Ethnicity in the Modern World*. Chicago: The University of Chicago Press.

summarized by Manning Nash (1989) as "blood, bed, and cult," to which we might add "soil" or "land" as well. In other words, there is, to some extent, a biological or genetic component: An ethnic group may be endogamous or in-marrying, so that the group is more or less genetically "closed."

Some ethnic groups place a strong value on marrying within the group, and some practically or even legally prohibit marriage outside the group. When ethnic groups are thus sexually isolated, they necessarily come to share a biological bond with each other, like a family; some go so far as avowing an ineffable and almost mystical "essence" that sets them apart from—and often above—other groups. Pierre van den Berghe has likened ethnic groups to extended kin groups: An ethnic group, he posited, always contains at least a core "made up of people who know themselves to be related to each other by a double network of ties of descent and marriage. Ethnicity is thus defined in the last analysis by *common descent*" (1987: 24). Still, he admitted that, "in many cases, the common descent ascribed to an ethny [his term for ethnic group] is fictive. In fact, in *most* cases, it is at least *partly* fictive" (27). We should conclude that ethnicity is based not so much on ancestry as on "a myth of ancestry" (Horowitz, 1985: 52), which may involve stories of the origin and struggles of the group.

The mention of myth brings us to Nash's "cult," which here means not just religious belief (although certainly religious belief too), but all of the cultural factors that unite the group and which serve more than instrumental functions for the group. Orlando Patterson explicitly stated that certain aspects of its culture have "the functions of . . . rituals for the group—the ways in which they are used to maintain group cohesiveness, to sustain and enhance identity, and to establish social networks and communicative patterns" (1975: 305). Finally, "soil" or "land" is important literally and symbolically—literally as a place for the group to live and as a physical and territorial boundary around the group, and symbolically as a homeland where formative events occurred or whether the forefathers lived and died.

The problem of ethnicity and ethnic groups can perhaps then be distilled to two issues—the *culture* of the group and the *boundaries* that enclose the group; both serve to distinguish and often segregate groups from each other. To begin, ethnicity is "about" culture, in the same way that race is "about" biology. However, in the same way that biological difference does not make straight-forward or exclusive race classifications possible, cultural difference does not make straight-forward or exclusive ethnic classifications possible. First, as DeVos noted earlier, an ethnic group does not use *all* of its culture in defining its ethnic identity; in fact, as Weber taught long ago, an ethnic group is not different in every cultural regard from neighboring groups. In Rwanda, the Hutu and the Tutsi speak the same language, while in Northern Ireland

the Protestants and the Catholics belong to the same major religion (Christianity). Any ethnic group is unlike other groups in some ways, but like other groups in other ways.

Furthermore, there is potentially considerable cultural variation *within* an ethnic group. Anthropological studies of supposed African "tribes" in the 1940s illustrated conclusively that many such groups were highly internally heterogeneous and frequently appeared "to be an amalgam of different peoples, each aware of its unique origin and history" (Fortes and Evans-Pritchard, 1940: 26). Dunbar Moodie likewise maintains that the "tribal identity" of many African tribes is a recent development, greatly shaped by colonialism. Before European intervention, lower-level collectivities like "homestead and lineage groupings, more or less structured into chiefdoms . . . were the standard forms of social organization" (Moodie, 2005: 320). "Tribes" and "tribalism" were to a significant extent products of colonial administration, with Europeans introducing the notion of tribe (as some primordial, distinct, culturally-bounded system) and even creating "tribal authorities" like "chiefs" for "tribes" that had never had chiefs before. Finally, the circulation of labor, especially the migration of men to cities, induced them to organize and to find native leaders in totally non-traditional ways, inventing "ethnicity" or "tribal identity" in the process. Predictably, then, some groups like the Xhosa are highly diverse, even amalgamations of numerous peoples such as Thembu, Bomvana, Mfengu, and Mpondo, to name just a few. In other words, not only the "races" but the "native tribes" of South Africa are at least partly constructions of modern forces. Anthropologists refer to this process as **ethnogenesis**, the construction of ethnic identity out of the "raw material" of culture and history.

For these reasons, Fredrik Barth redirected anthropologists away from the "contents" or cultures of particular ethnic groups and toward the boundaries between them, which emphasizes the fact that ethnicity is a relationship and process. Criticizing the notion that there really are discrete "aggregates of people who essentially share a common culture" (1969: 9)—aggregates that can be identified by a trait-list of cultural characteristics (a specific language, religion, history, name, territory, and such)—Barth instructed that the key to ethnicity and ethnic groups is "the ethnic

See Chapters 13 and 15

Ethnogenesis

the process by which ethnic groups come into being and attain their cultural characteristics

Barth, Fredrik, Ed. 1969.
*Ethnic Groups and
Boundaries*. Boston: Little,
Brown & Co.

boundary that defines the group, not the cultural stuff that it encloses" (15). This shift in focus allows us to see that ethnicity is a form of social organization, not merely a fact of timeless and immutable cultural difference. It therefore compels us to analyze the processes by which groups develop and preserve boundaries, even while individuals or culture-traits within the boundary change over time. Finally and critically, it answers a question implied by DeVos' definition above: If ethnicity is the use of aspects of

BOX 6.4   THE BETAWI, THE AUTHENTIC PEOPLE OF JAVA?

Americans consider themselves the authentic people of the United States, even if there was no such thing as an "American" until a couple of centuries ago and even though Americans are a hybrid of many different nationalities, ethnicities, and races. In other words, "authentic identities" do not have to be old or pure, and "national identity is not the opposite of ethnic identity," concludes Jacqueline Knörr (2014) in her study of the new "authentic people" of Java, the main island in Indonesia. The *Orang Betawi* (Betawi people) have come to be understood as the original population of the region of the capital city of Jakarta, yet a population that is simultaneously overtly and self-consciously new, composite, and transethnic. The very name "Betawi," derived from the Dutch colonial city of Batavia, is our first clue to the origin of this "authentic" ethnicity. According to Knörr, the first inhabitants of the area that became Batavia and eventually Jakarta were largely displaced and replaced by slave laborers from many different sources; data from a 1679 census indicate that these diverse groups were not enumerated, but were lumped together and gradually morphed into "a new, shared, culture and identity and their own dialect, *Omong Betawi*," with Islam a crucial mortar to hold this new "people" together (2014: 53). By the early twentieth century and the arrival of new immigrants to the city, the Betawi began "to consolidate and organize themselves politically and culturally as *suku bangsa*, as a native ethnic group" (60), albeit a marginalized and mostly lower-class group. Finally, after Indonesian independence, Betawi identity and culture began to receive more official attention and support for "the potential offered by Betawi culture, history, and identity as a means of strengthening both transethnic Jakartan and national identity" (69). In other words, it was claimed that "Betawi culture is of significance for all Indonesians" because "it represents the indigenous and traditional culture of the Indonesian capital" (70). Even as Betawi culture is promoted as the heritage of "all people in Jakarta" and potentially in Indonesia, Knörr also notes the substantial diversity within the Betawi category. For instance, the Betawi Kota are the most modern and urban subgroup, while the Betawi Udik are regarded as the most "traditional" despite the facts that they only recently embraced the name and that other Betawi groups "did not recognize the Betawi Udik as genuine Betawi either" (105). Then there are the Betawi Pinggir, recognized as "the Betawi who practice the purest form and have the most profound understanding of Islam" (103). Indeed, Islam is important to the identity of the Betawi and of the state of Indonesia, and a "large part of the Indo-Arabic population considers itself and is considered by others as part of the Betawi" (109), but this does not preclude the possibility of Christian Betawi like the Christians of the rice-growing village of Kampung Sawah. Finally, not all Betawi are poor or low-status, as evinced by the five families of *bangsawan* Betawi who use genealogies "to prove aristocratic descent and illustrate that the heirs of the aristocracy are in no way descended from slaves and others in the service of the colonial rulers" (126). Finally, the Betawi category is not only extremely diverse, but also extremely porous and absorptive, allowing other peoples like the Batak to "become" Betawi. It is this very potential to absorb and unify the myriad societies and cultures of Indonesia's many islands that gives the label its appeal. Leaders of the state appreciate the Betawi category "as a model for forging common identity on a background of diversity.... They represent as an ethnic group what Indonesians are supposed to represent as a nation" (164)—namely, a kind of unity in diversity, an *e pluribus unum*, as the United States has claimed of itself too.

a culture, why are *some* aspects used and not others, and what are they used for? In this new view, particular elements of culture function as "markers," "signs," "flags," or "badges" of membership and non-membership, of inclusion and exclusion. Even more, members who "wear" the markers signal their solidarity with other members—and their preparedness for common action.

In the final analysis, ethnicity is a style of social action, specifically and usually political and economic action. An ethnic group may be an identity group, but it is also, in most cases, an interest group and often a competitive group. Ethnic groups do not exist in isolation; a group by itself is not an ethnic group in the proper sense. Two or more ethnic groups share a social space, where they are in some particular (if shifting) social, political, or economic relation to each other. Like races, they are or were commonly separated by territory or neighborhood, class or profession, and politics or power—and unequally at that. While ethnicity does not imply hierarchy as inherently as race, in practice it often has precisely that effect. So ethnicity can be a means to press the group into action, to mobilize it to strive for some goal, which can include or entail "closing ranks" and acting jointly *as* a group and *in the interests of* the group.

Types of ethnic organization and mobilization

Since ethnicity does not refer to any specific and universal kind of cultural difference or cultural goal, it follows that ethnic groups come in many diverse forms and relations to each other. In fact, not all cultural groups are fully and equally organized and "incorporated" *as* ethnic groups; in a word, not every cultural difference is the basis for an ethnic difference or an ethnic group. Thomas Hylland Eriksen (2002: 43) proposed that, at the lowest level of awareness and mobilization, an ethnic label might be no more than a "category," a name to call certain people or for a certain people to call themselves. When such people begin to interact in terms of their common identity, they constitute a "network." Once the group becomes not only organized, but goal oriented, it transforms into an "association," and when that association develops a territorial base, it evolves into a

"community." Not all (potential) ethnic groups, of course, achieve this complete evolution.

Among groups that attain ethnic awareness and organization, there is still great diversity. Eriksen (2002: 14–15) offered five different types of ethnic groups and relations:

(1) urban ethnic minorities (usually as the result of migration)
(2) indigenous peoples (usually as the result of colonialism and conquest)
(3) proto-nations, that is, groups that "claim that they are entitled to their own nation-state"
(4) ethnic groups in plural societies
(5) post-slavery minorities

Ted Robert Gurr and Barbara Harff (1994: 15–23) gave a similar but somewhat different analysis, including four types, which they called:

(1) ethnonationalists, "relatively large and regionally concentrated ethnic groups that live within the boundaries of one state or of several adjacent states; their modern political movements are directed toward achieving greater autonomy or independent statehood"
(2) indigenous peoples, "the descendants of the original inhabitants of conquered or colonized regions"
(3) communal contenders, "ethnic groups whose main political aim is not to gain autonomy but is, rather, to share power in the central government of modern states"
(4) ethnoclasses, "culturally distinct minorities who occupy distinct social strata and have specialized economic roles in the societies in which they now live. They are, in other words, ethnic groups who resemble classes."

The spectrum of intergroup relations between races and ethnic groups

The characteristics of race and ethnic groups are less interesting or important than the relations between these groups. In fact, it is appropriate and useful to think of racial and ethnic relations as a subset of group relations more generally, whether those relations are based on race, ethnicity, gender, age, class, or any other criteria. It is never the

Eriksen, Thomas Hylland. 2002 [1993]. *Ethnicity and Nationalism: Anthropological Perspectives*. London: Pluto Press.

differences between groups that matter as much as the social and cultural meanings of those differences and the relationships and inequalities between the bearers of the group "markers."

First and foremost, race and ethnic systems are not only methods for classifying and explaining human differences, but for establishing (more or less) sharp and permanent separation between the groups distinguished by these differences. In a word, the concepts and practices of race and ethnicity create "distance" between socially defined and socially defended bounded groups. There are various ways to conceptualize and quantify this "social distance," such as the Social Distance Scale developed by Emory Bogardus (1933), a set of questions to test the willingness of people to enter into relationships (from superficial to intimate) with members of other groups. At the minimal level of acceptance, the scale asks whether the subject is willing to allow group X to inhabit or even visit his/her country; at increasingly intimate levels, questions assess whether the subject would accept members of group X in his/her town, neighborhood, workplace, circle of friends, or very family (through intermarriage). Obviously, the more exclusions raised against a group, the greater the "social distance" between the group in question and one's own.

But the relations between groups are not merely individualistic and subjective. There are large-scale, structural relationships as well, ones that persist despite the attitudes and actions of particular individuals. George Simpson and Milton Yinger (1972) constructed a useful typology of group relations, comprising six types arrayed from relatively benign to highly malignant:

Assimilation: the process by which a group loses some or all of its unique characteristics and adopts the characteristics of another or the dominant group. **Cultural assimilation** refers specifically to the loss of distinctive cultural traits, such as language or religion, while **racial assimilation** occurs when the physical traits of a group are lost through intermarriage. (Some analysts have also proposed a category of **social** or **structural assimilation** for groups that are integrated into the society—say, sharing the same jobs or the same neighborhoods—whether or not they share the same culture. Significantly, a group may be culturally assimilated, that is, possess more or less the qualities

of another or the dominant culture, but still not be socially assimilated.)

Pluralism: the coexistence in the same country or society of groups with distinct cultures. Rather than adopting a foreign or dominant culture, a group retains some distinct behaviors or values, possibly as a source of ethnic or racial pride, and may even maintain loyalty to their group (or, if migrants, to their former homeland) rather than to the wider society in which they live. (Other theorists have recommended distinguishing cultural from structural pluralism as well.)

Legal protection of minorities: Since the personal interactions and attitudes between groups may be influenced by discrimination and hostility, a society may institute formal protections for the rights of subordinated groups. Examples would include the 1964 Civil Rights Act in the United States and the 1965 Race Relations Act in the United Kingdom, followed by many other measures to attempt to guarantee equality between groups and to reduce or eliminate the prejudice and animosity against disadvantaged groups.

Population transfer: a policy or practice of physically moving groups from one location to another, ostensibly to reduce tensions and hostilities. For instance, Native Americans were "removed" from parts of the Southeast in 1830 and resettled in "Indian country" (present-day Oklahoma) for their (and white Southerners') benefit; the surviving "reservation" system in the U.S. or "reserve" system in Australia is a product of such policies. At the partition of India in 1948, large populations were also transferred to the "correct" side of the India–Pakistan (i.e. Hindu–Muslim) border.

Continued subjugation: Dominant groups may have no desire, and no awareness of a need, to change the subordinate position of other groups in the society or country. In such cases, the dominant group may institutionalize hierarchical relations (like slavery or ghetto neighborhoods), pass laws and adopt entire systems of exclusion (like segregation in the U.S. or *apartheid* in South Africa), or even use force to suppress groups and any resistance they might organize.

Pluralism
the co-existence of multiple social and cultural groups in the same society or state

Assimilation
the social process by which individuals and groups are absorbed into another, usually dominant, cultural group

Cultural assimilation
a type of assimilation which refers specifically to the loss of distinctive cultural traits, such as language or religion

Racial assimilation
a form of assimilation in which the physical traits of a group are lost through intermarriage

Social or structural assimilation
a form of assimilation in which groups are integrated into the society (for instance, sharing the same jobs or the same neighborhoods), whether or not they share the same culture

IMAGE 6.5 Racial divisions, racial tensions, and racial violence were high during the apartheid era of South Africa.

Extermination: The "final solution" to racial and ethnic "problems" may be the physical destruction of disfavored groups. Also known as **genocide**, the most familiar case is the killing of millions of Jews by Nazi Germany in the 1940s, but many other instances have been recorded in history (and no doubt many more unrecorded), including the eradication of Armenians by Turkey, of Hottentots by Dutch settlers in South Africa, of Aboriginals by Euro-Australians, and of Native Americans by Euro-Americans. Short of all-out extermination of ethnic groups is the outbreak of "ethnic conflict."

Genocide
the destruction of a group or society by harming, killing, or preventing the birth of its members

See Chapter 11

See Chapter 13

BOX 6.5   DEAFWORLD: THE CULTURE OF THE DEAF

Most people do not think of the disabled as a cultural group; however, many among the nearly one million deaf and nearly eight million hearing-impaired Americans disagree. Indeed, as Owen Wrigley stressed in his *The Politics of Deafness*, at least some representatives of the deaf community "vigorously refuse the identity label 'disabled,' seeing themselves strictly as a linguistic minority" (1996: 7–8), even as "a distinct 'ethnic identity'" (13). They promulgate a conception of deafness not as a physical deficit but as a cultural difference. No doubt many a reader will find this use of "ethnic" and "cultural" to be a stretch of those terms: How is it that "a group of people who do not have any distinctive religion, clothing, or diet—or even inhabit a particular geographical space they call their own—could be called 'cultural'" (Padden and Humphries, 2005: 1)? And while the use of these terms does at first appear to challenge or distort them, in reality the anthropological value of "ethnicity" and "culture" does not lie in any particular "distinctive" marker or location, but rather in the creation and transmission of beliefs, practices, values, and relations. True, not all deaf (or, as some prefer, Deaf) are born deaf, nor is deafness passed from person to person in the deaf community. All the same, there is a Deaf community, sometimes named Deafworld or even "Deaf country," with its own traditions, most especially its (sign) language. American Sign Language (ASL) is more than a manual version of spoken English; it has its own style (characterized by candor and directness), its own practices for greetings, leave-takings, attention-getting, turn-taking, and so on, and even its own literature of stories, poems, plays, and jokes (Lane, Hoffmeister, and Bahan, 1996). It has a social network with social institutions, from clubs to schools and colleges (most prominently Gallaudet University), and national and international organizations, like the National Association of the Deaf, the American Athletic Association of the Deaf, the National Theater of the Deaf, and the World Federation of the Deaf. More than a few members of Deafworld are protective of their unique identity, some going so far as to demand that members use ASL and not try to "pass" as Hearing by reading lips; the most militant citizens of Deafworld reject hearing aids and surgery on the basis that such efforts are genocidal—akin to forcing black people to change their bodies to conform to white biological standards.

See Chapters 12, 13, and 15

We will encounter other examples of racial and ethnic groups, relations, and problems in future chapters, particularly the Hutu and Tutsi, the Serbs and Bosnian Muslims, and various indigenous peoples.

RACE AND ETHNICITY IN CROSS-CULTURAL PERSPECTIVE: CASE STUDIES

See Chapters 11

BOX 6.6   CONTEMPORARY CULTURAL CONTROVERSIES: THE EXPULSION OF BLACK CHEROKEES

On August 22, 2011, the Supreme Court of the Cherokee nation, based in Oklahoma, ruled that it was legal to expel the African-descended members of the tribe. But what is an "African-descended Cherokee" in the first place? Before the 1830s, the Cherokee occupied the southeastern area of the United States, from present-day Kentucky to Georgia. After Europeans settled and claimed the territory, the Cherokee were especially successful at adopting aspects of American life. They generated their own writing system and began printing their own newspaper. Some also owned their own plantations, complete with their own African slaves. In the 1830s, the Cherokee along with neighboring tribes were forced to evacuate, in what is widely known as the "Trail of Tears," bringing their black slaves with them. According to the 2000 census, there were more than 300,000 Cherokees in the U.S., including 2,800 so-called "Freedmen," the descendants of those Africans, some of whom had intermarried with the Native Americans; there may be 25,000 more Freedmen who could potentially qualify as tribal members. However, the Cherokee court's decision prevents their enrollment in the tribe and disqualifies existing members, making them ineligible for the benefits that pertain to Native Americans, like free health care, educational programs, and of course a share in tribal wealth. The tribe claims the right to regulate its membership, while black Cherokee call it racism and apartheid. What do you think?

SUMMARY

Like gender, race and ethnicity are cultural interpretations and utilizations of "facts," namely the facts of physical and behavioral difference, respectively. Racial and ethnic classifications are ways in which popular opinion—and scholarly analysis—in some cultures have made sense, and made use, of human difference.

Race has been an especially salient concept in Western societies, imposing a purportedly scientific order on the human physical variation. However, efforts to make race more scientific only made it more problematic. Ultimately, the imprecision and disagreement in the practice of race categorization, together with the discovery of the role of learning independent of biological inheritance, leads anthropology to criticize the notion of race and to focus on the social creation and function of racial thinking and racial systems.

For some observers, ethnic categories take a place alongside, or take the place of, racial categories. Ostensibly based on cultural, historical, and actual kinship characteristics, ethnic groups have proved to be every bit as vague and socially constructed—and socially exploited—as race groups. Cultural differences are actually not always great between ethnic groups, and the relationships between groups emerge as more crucial than the cultural qualities within groups. Accordingly, a number of different kinds of ethnic groups, and of relations between such groups, have been identified, from segregation and violent conflict to peaceful co-existence and amalgamation. Still, race and ethnicity continue to be salient organizational concepts in the modern world.

Q

MCQS

Q

FILL IN THE BLANKS

WWW

Key Terms

anthropometry

assimilation

cephalic index

cultural assimilation

endogamy

ethnicity

ethnogenesis

eugenics

facial angle

genocide

miscegenation

pluralism

racial assimilation

social or structural assimilation

Seeing culture as a whole #1

Western expatriates in the new Chinese economy

People have long circulated from one society, country, or continent to another. Westerners are most familiar with the migration of non-Western people to Europe or the United States, although we often forget that some of the world's greatest migrations were from one Western site (Europe) to another Western site (the U.S.). Recently, even the flow of Chinese people to Western locations like America and Europe has slowed or reversed: Due to the expansion of the Chinese economy and the weakness of Western economies, Chinese immigration has declined, and some Chinese residents of Western countries have actually returned to their homeland (Tsui, 2011).

More fascinating and important still is the global population flow in the opposite direction, of Western citizens migrating to China in search of economic opportunities. Again, the outflow of Westerners to the non-West is not without precedent: The era of colonialism saw extensive, sometimes temporary but sometimes permanent, emigration from Europe or the United States to Africa, India, East Asia, and the Pacific Islands as missionaries, administrators, soldiers, and settlers.

Like the Western émigrés before them, the Westerners in twenty-first-century China do not fit the stereotype of the poor desperate labor migrant. Rather, they tend to be educated and professional, what Angela Lehmann calls "middling migrants" who are neither impoverished nor elite. Further, such individuals "are disconnected neither from the past as an expatriate in post-colonial Asia, nor from the future as a lifestyle migrant or a potential international elite. The middling migrant is situated locally and interacts with particular people on a daily basis" (Lehmann, 2013: 7).

Americans, Europeans, Australians, and others come to contemporary China voluntarily and for their own personal reasons, and the encounters they have and the relationships they form (or fail to form) are highly contextualized, including this specific globalized moment in history. From the Western cultural perspective, it is the concept of individualism that drives many Westerners to seek a place in China, although not all of them are motivated to seek China in particular. Western culture has certainly long envisioned the detached individual bravely constructing a solo career or biography, but the individual has never been more isolated and portable than today. Thus, Lehmann finds that the "major themes" of the expatriates' lives "concern a common narrative of fragility and anomie" (19). The first of these themes, she contends, involves

> accounts of anxiety and disillusionment with home. A common feeling of precariousness or instability in terms of the workplace, career, relationships, community and meaning was spoken about by many Western people in Xiamen. The second theme addresses accounts of relationships to time and place in terms of motivations to leave home.
>
> (19)

Most of the expatriates "spoke about the decision to leave home as a desire for 'time out' from an otherwise routine life-path" (36); indeed, perhaps the fundamental issue for these travelers is *freedom*, both in terms of choosing a life-course outside the ordinary and of being free from conventional social restraints while abroad. "Once in Xiamen," she writes, "previous cultural signifiers of identity, social rank and structure were stripped of the social meanings they held in the past" (46). Whether expressed in metaphors of childhood or wilderness, Westerners often find this experience very liberating; in fact, "life could become somewhat hedonistic and ecstatic for liminal Xiameners" (56), as if they were on an extended holiday.

Even so, humans cannot live in an indefinite or even prolonged state of suspension, nor is the experience of life outside ordinary statuses and structures entirely pleasant. Lehmann discovers that sensations of "fear and difference" are relevant to how expatriates perform "the situating of selves within a moral landscape" (64). Reasonably, she asserts that much of the freedom felt by expatriates is related to their "awareness of cultural difference" (66)—often specifically including judgments of the dirt and lack of hygiene in China—which have certain effects on the psyches of the migrants, for instance teaching them patience. More, freedom does not preclude structure among the expatriate community, with differential status associated with length of time in the country and with familiar social practices like gossip, secrecy, and trust. She even discovers some formal organizations like the International Christian Fellowship.

One of the most interesting insights from the lives of Westerners in China is the role of gender and race in the experience—and the surprising connection between the two variables, that is, the manner in which "gender became 'racialized' and race became 'genderized'" (115). For one thing, Chinese gender roles and relations are often disparaged by the white migrants. More fascinating still is the difference between the lives of Western men and women in China, with the Western men easily finding Chinese girlfriends (the likes of whom, according to Lehmann, would have been unattainable by many of the men in their own countries), while the Western women cannot attract the attention of either white or Chinese men. Since the white women "perceived that they were remote from the sexual gaze of both Western and Chinese men" (120), some complained of feeling desexualized, but this very fact often leads to a growth in their self-confidence and independence from men. Of course, Lehmann also notes that many men bring their wives to China with them, but the gendered quality of in-country experience is real even for these "trailing spouses," who often do not have jobs like their husbands to fill their days.

Transnational life clearly complicates the concept of "home," which, as other studies of migration and diaspora have shown, "is conceptualized here as a multi-tiered and flexible category which refers not only to the city or region one belongs to but also to a wider notion of national belonging, and wider still, to a notion of being from 'the West'" (134). The home country is commonly an object of nostalgia, but migrants also cannot help but see their country of origin in a new light, and for most individuals, Lehmann claims, "a return to a stable, constant home was impossible" (149) after their disjunctive experience abroad.

In the end, Lehmann argues that the lives of Western middling migrants in China

> suggest that models of "rootless cosmopolitans" are part of a much larger and more complex story. While vulnerability and the weakening of social structures do occur as a part of global mobility, this vulnerability provides the conditions for the reconstruction of place-centered notions of power, structure and community.
>
> (153)

Since there can be no doubt that migration will only increase in the globalized neoliberal world, and that this migration will be multi-directional and impermanent, it is critically important that we research the persons, processes, and experiences involved.

Economics

Humans, nature, and social organization

In 2011, Juan complained to his union, the "radical" Confederación Nacional del Trabajo (CNT), about the working conditions, pay, and management treatment in the Spanish iron and steel firm where he worked. Not only were workers cheated out of wages and subjected to unrealistic production expectations, but they were sometimes shifted temporarily to work in other cities. When the company learned of the complaint, it first spied on Juan and other employees, documenting infractions on the shop floor. Disgruntled workers were then called individually to meet with management; Miguel was fired for "low productivity" (although he had always received good evaluations), and Juan was suspended for fifty days without pay, while a third union member named Lucas was pressured so severely by the company that he became depressed and took sick leave for several months. Not finished with its response, the company sent eight more workers to the North African city of Ceuta and refused to meet with the union. When CNT ordered a general strike, "management intensified its intimidation campaign. The director called all the workers separately trying to convince them to leave the union" (Roca and Rodriguez, 2014: 65), fully understanding that employees are weaker individually than collectively. The strategy succeeded: Before the strike could occur, the relocated workers agreed to their transfer—and even received improvements in their working conditions—and a court ruled that Miguel's termination was legal, even though the judge admitted that it was unfair. Emboldened by the decision, the company also fired Juan, Lucas, "and another two members of the strike committee" (65). The episode, according to Beltrán Roca and Lluis Rodriguez, illustrates how corporations can counter worker power by isolating employees from each other and their organizations, making their employment insecure, promoting "flexible" labor relations (like short-term contract work), and of course influencing public opinion against unions and trouble-making workers.

All societies face a fundamental challenge—to feed and clothe and otherwise provision their members based on the available resources in their environment. Different societies have met this challenge in different ways, but all shared one factor in common: They solved the problem of survival socially. It might be possible for humans to satisfy their needs alone, but it would be difficult and is essentially never done. So humans produce, prepare, distribute, and consume goods and services in groups, and the means by which they do so will have ramifications for those groups. The economic practices of a society are significantly influenced by the physical possibilities of their environment (the amount and quality of land, water, plants and animals, and other materials), and those practices that emerge will significantly influence other aspects of the culture—not in a deterministic, cause-and-effect way, but in specific and observable ways. Further, economic facts are seldom purely "practical"; they also have value and prestige and even symbolic and ritual significance that affect the social meaning of the products and of the relationships within which those products are made, distributed, and used.

See Chapter 1

ECONOMY AND CULTURE, OR ECONOMY *AS* CULTURE

"The project of economics needs to be rescued from the economists," wrote Hart, Laville, and Cattani (2010: 5), but their opinion was only a more provocative restatement of what anthropologists had been saying for nearly a century. The mention of economics usually conjures up images of factories, money, markets, banks, and many other familiar ideas and institutions. However, the origin of the word "economics," from the Greek *oikonomikos*, referred to the more modest matter of household management. By the nineteenth century, "economics" or "the economy" came to be seen and analyzed as a distinct, formal, even relatively impersonal subject, as in Adam Smith's seminal 1776 volume *The Wealth of Nations*. In the classical economic tradition, as James Carrier put it in *A Handbook of Economic Anthropology*, economic life is widely understood "in terms of the sorts of mental calculus that people use and the decisions that they make (for example, utility maximization)" (2005: 4), a calculus that is in principle individual, rational, and self-interested.

Rather than simply decision-making, Carrier continues, anthropologists are interested in "the substance of the activity" (4) that we call economic, which includes the actual practices and relationships that comprise economics as well as the objects that emerge from these practices and relationships. In a word, "economic anthropologists tend to situate things like markets or other forms of

Adaptation
changes in a system, including a species, in response to changes in its context or environment so as to make that system or species more fit to survive in the context or environment

circulations, or production or consumption, in larger social and cultural frames, in order to see how [they] affect and are affected by other areas of life" (4). Keith Hart has been adamant about what he called "the human economy," a term "intended to remind readers that the economy is made and remade by people in their everyday lives" (Hart, Laville, and Cattani, 2010: 4).

An anthropological perspective on economics, then, emphasizes that not all societies do economics in the same way (cross-cultural comparison) and that the economic ideas, practices, and institutions of a society will be integrated with its total culture (holism). In fact, Chris Hann and Keith Hart insist that an anthropological approach to economics arose in the 1800s precisely "to test the claim" that an economic system "must be founded on the principles that underpinned a Western industrial society striving for universality. . . . Anthropology was the most inclusive way of thinking about economic possibilities" (2011: 1).

Understanding the connection between economics, culture, and the environment begins with the notion of adaptation. **Adaptation** is the process by which humans (or any species) fit themselves into and interact with their surroundings. Although humans adapt physically like all other beings, the most interesting human adaptation takes the form of behavioral modification. So human cultural adaptation responds to the environment that a group or society inhabits. An environment is a particular combination of physical factors—climate, water and food supplies, natural resources, large-scale natural formations (rivers, mountains), etc. These factors will set constraints (technology notwithstanding) on the society; in other words, the environment will set the fundamental terms of *what is possible and what is necessary* for the people living in it. The environment is a challenge that must be met. Yet "nature" is not a completely independent variable: Through culture, humans bring the world of nature within the world of culture, *culturizing* nature and integrating it into the cultural system. In the process, both culture and nature are mutually reshaped.

Therefore, two quite different environments can pose surprisingly similar adaptive challenges. For instance, few environmental settings seem less alike than a desert and the arctic, yet some of the conditions they present to humans or any life-forms located there are actually comparable. There is little liquid water as well as a relatively short supply and variety of potential foods and of potential tool-making and building materials. Plant life is scarce, so agriculture is virtually impossible, so similar strategies must be adopted. At the same time, a single environment may allow diverse economic and cultural responses.

The first problem, then, for humans is and will always be how to transform their environment into the things that they need to support their life, which is the economic problem. If we think again now about how to model the relations between the domains of culture, we would want to start with an environment and then establish a means of livelihood that is adapted to that environment. That is, if we were to "build" a culture from the "ground up," the environment would be the ground, and the "base" of the culture would be the part that "touches the ground." It is the economic system that not only metaphorically but literally makes contact with the earth and its resources and converts them into human-usable goods. If the economy is the ground-floor of culture, shaped by the environment, then the economy likewise shapes the floors of culture constructed upon it. Of course, this is not a purely one-way process; rather there is a feedback relation between the upper and lower levels too: The upper floors exert pressure on the lower ones in particular ways, and once they have been formed, they will influence the levels "below" them, such that the politics or the religion can affect the economics and even the very environment. There is, in the final analysis, a reciprocal or mutual relationship, but one in which the economic adaptation is still the base or core.

Of course, no society sits isolated in its environment; there is the inevitable presence of neighboring societies, which may have more or less impact on the society in question. In some cases, there may be neutral or friendly exchange relations between the two (or more), while in others there may be competitive or hostile relations. Societies may be completely surrounded or even engulfed by a larger and dominant society, and they may be highly dependent on these external social structures. The society itself, finally, may be more internally complex, with multiple "layers" or subgroups or classes or even subcultures in various (and often unequal) relations with each other. All modern societies are and many pre-modern societies were actually composite systems of social groupings in diverse and problematic arrangements.

At any rate, a society's life begins with its practical, productive activities, which can be referred to as its **means of production**. The means of production is the tasks, the tools, and the knowledge and skills that humans use to get their daily bread (or kangaroo or whatever). It is labor and all that is required for labor. This may be as simple as picking a nut off a tree or as elaborate as working in an office or on an assembly line. Humans must engage in productive, practical, material activity in order to survive.

However, work cannot be done in social isolation—not in isolation from other humans, nor in isolation from other facets of society. Economic activity is always social—with and for other people too. Therefore, the **mode of production** leads to and generates some **relations of production**—that is, ways that humans organize themselves to get the work done and the products distributed and used. The general factors involved in the relations of production include division of labor, ownership, "property," power, often class, and usually the family, as well as sharing and selling and the status or prestige that comes with having, consuming, displaying, giving the goods and services. These relations give shape and content to the rest of society. These two features—mode and relations of production—in tandem make up what we would call the economy of a society.

FROM "PRIMITIVE ECONOMIES" . . .

During its formative years, anthropology was most focused on "primitive economies," pondering "whether the economic behavior of 'savages' was underpinned by the same notions of efficiency and 'rationality' that were taken to motivate economic action in the West" (Hann and Hart, 2011: 2). As late as 1940, this preoccupation was apparent in the title of Melville Herskovits' *The Economic Life of Primitive Peoples*. At the same time, as Raymond Firth opined in his *Themes in Economic Anthropology*, first published in 1967, "economists have tended to ignore these 'simpler' societies" (2004: 2), giving economists and economic anthropologists surprisingly little in common.

Means of production
the activities and tools that a society employs to satisfy its material needs; the form of "work" or "labor" that is performed in a society

Mode of production
in Marxist theory, the combination of the productive forces and the relations of production that defines the economy and society at a particular place in and time in history

Relations of production
in Marxist theory, the social roles and relationships that are generated by the mode of production, including such things as class, ownership, "management," and in some lines of thinking, "family"

See Chapter 13

Early anthropology therefore put very much emphasis on the production phase of the economy, considerable emphasis on the distribution phase, and less emphasis on the consumption phase. Eventually the discipline settled on a typology of four pre-modern production systems and three systems of distribution. Nature, of course, hates typologies, so we will see exceptions to and hybrids of these four basic systems below; also, there is a fair amount of variation within the systems. Finally, because of culture contact and modernization, no present-day society practices any pure "primitive economy," although aspects of these systems may still exist.

Systems of production

If economics is the "base" of culture, then production is the "base of the base," the first level of the first layer. Productive practices and relations shape other domains of culture. The standard four types of production systems are:

■ foraging
■ pastoralism
■ horticulture
■ intensive agriculture

In analyzing any actual society's economic system, anthropologists want to accomplish two things.

First, we want to understand their means of production and how it is anchored to the environment(s) they dwell in. Second and more importantly, we want to see what kind of culture and social order they produce—what specific relationships, values, beliefs, and so on flow from the economic base and how those things are related to and shaped by their economic activities. We should detect regular patterns of economics and culture—things that tend to go together and things that do not or cannot go together. That is, we should see patterns emerge that link particular types of economic factors with particular types of non-economic (kinship, political, and even religious) factors.

Foraging

Foraging was the first human production system. Also known as "hunting and gathering," all humans practiced and depended on it from the very first societies until some ten to twelve thousand years ago. Even since that time, when other production systems emerged and spread, foraging continued in at least some places—and occasionally in contact with other later systems—until quite recently. Originally practiced in all environments, during the past few millennia it has tended to be relegated to the most marginal environments where other systems are not possible or where societies based

PRE-MODERN PRODUCTION
SYSTEMS: CASE STUDIES

Foraging
Also known as hunting and
gathering, the production of
food by collecting wild
(undomesticated) animals
and plants

IMAGE 7.1 Koya
hunter from central
India.

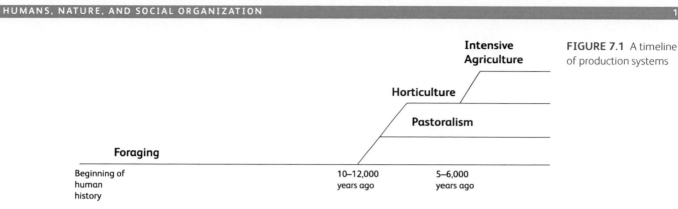

FIGURE 7.1 A timeline of production systems

on other systems cannot or have not chosen to penetrate. Examples of recent and well-known foraging societies include the !Kung or Ju/hoansi of the African Kalahari, all Australian Aboriginal societies, and the various Inuit or Eskimo peoples of the Arctic. While their environments could be quite different, the economic adaptations they made to them tended be quite similar.

The foraging mode of production involved minimal technologies for hunting wild animals and collecting wild plants. Although it appears to entail the least transformation of the environment, still transformation it was. Foraging peoples had to apply technology, skill, and knowledge to their natural environment in order to make the benefits of that environment usable or "edible" for them. In some cases, as in Australia, foragers routinely burned the landscape, undoubtedly affecting the local plant and animal life.

Foraging typically developed a **division of labor** between the hunting/animal work, normally assigned to men, and the gathering/plant work, the typical province of women. The Warlpiri in the Central Desert of Australia tended to follow this pattern, although with two warnings. First, not all "animal work" was necessarily viewed as hunting; catching small lizards and insects might be done by women or children. Second, a man might "gather" materials of particular interest to him, such as bush tobacco. So, even here the gender division was not absolute.

Ernestine Friedl (1975; 1978) identified three other foraging arrangements. In one, men hunted and both men and women gathered; the Hadza people of Tanzania (Woodburn, 1968) and a few other societies were organized this way. In a second variation, men and women shared both hunting and gathering. Estioko-Griffin and Griffin (2002)

described the Agta of the Philippines as nearly undivided in economic activities by sex: Women participated in the same productive behaviors as men, including hunting and fishing, and they gathered plants irregularly and only when more desirable food was not at hand. The Mbuti pygmies of the Congo forest (Turnbull, 1962) also worked together, male and female, to net game. In the third style, men hunted, but women processed the catch of the men.

Because women's labor often produced a large proportion (if not the bulk) of the group's food, there tended to be relative gender equality in foraging societies. In fact, they tended to be generally egalitarian, due to the inability of any individual to accumulate a surplus or to possess skills that other people did not. Concepts of "ownership" or "private property" were often limited if not lacking, particularly in regard to land. Foraging environments often prohibited economic surpluses, since there was not enough food available to accumulate it, and foraging values usually discouraged a person from trying to become superior to or richer than anyone else; values of sharing within the community provided no opportunity to hoard personal wealth. Some status differences existed, based on age, skill, ritual knowledge, and sometimes gender, but these statuses were often more interdependent than stratified. Without wealth and power differences, formal leadership and especially "government" were absent and unnecessary.

In marginal environments where food supplies were limited and unpredictable, local groups tended to be small; in many instances, the residential group was only a dozen or less, or at most a few dozen, and ordinarily composed of kin. There was simply not enough food and water to support large populations, so the society was usually dispersed

Turnbull, Colin. 1962. *The Forest People*. New York: Simon & Schuster.

Division of labor
the differentiation of the economy into a set of distinct production tasks, which are assigned to different individuals, groups, or classes, usually creating economic and political inequalities

Friedl, Ernestine. 1975. *Women and Men*. New York: Holt, Rinehart, and Winston.

over a large territory and would only assemble in times of plenty or for special occasions like rituals. This means that groups also tended to be mobile, lacking permanent settlements or houses and moving continuously in search of provisions within an established "range" or territory.

Because foragers lived in such intimate contact with their environment, they tended to have a major emotional and spiritual connection to animals, plants, and places. Typically the land itself was alive or was the handiwork of supernatural beings. They often regarded themselves and animals, plants, and places as sharing a spiritual essence, even a kinship tie.

Since generosity and equality were the general rule, the occurrence of conflict and violence was limited. Therefore, foragers tended to be comparatively peaceful peoples. This is not to say that conflicts and even violent outbursts never happened, but these usually occurred over ritual matters or marriage or other personal issues and were usually settled ritually, even if that ritual involved some symbolic or real violence.

Pastoralism

Around ten to twelve thousand years ago, one or more human groups in one or more locations discovered that they could control certain animal species. Instead of having to roam in search of their food sources, they could bring the sources home to them—in a word, **domestication**. This is sometimes referred to as the **Neolithic** ("New Stone" age) revolution, which was revolutionary not only for how humans produced food, but for every aspect of their cultures and social relationships, as well as for the species they fed on. The revolution of domestication actually culminated in not one but two new economic systems. The first that we will describe is pastoralism. **Pastoralism**, from the word "pasture," is the production of food predominantly from domesticated animals, that is, herding or "ranching." Thus, the primary work to be done was tending and exploiting—milking, bleeding, and slaughtering—such animals as cattle, sheep, goats, llamas, horses, pigs, and other smaller creatures, depending on the locally available species.

In the vast majority of these societies—and they were spread across the world, from the grasslands of East Africa to the mountains of Central Asia

IMAGE 7.2 Tuareg pastoralist with his camels, North Africa.

and the plains of North America—the ownership and control of herd animals was the prerogative of men. Women and children often performed the day-to-day work of tending the animals, but men decided when one would be slaughtered or traded or sold. Consequently, pastoralism was a man's world, and the gender division of labor devolved into gender inequality. Men's status was much higher than women's in typical pastoral societies. Men were usually the heads of family and household; again, women might wield real "domestic" power in the home, but their political power was reduced compared to men.

Since a man's herd was his surplus and therefore his wealth, he usually tried to avoid killing his animals, but rather consumed them in "sustainable" ways, such as drinking their milk or blood. Herds in some cases might be quite large; Klima reported that the average Barabaig (east Africa) cattle herd was around seventy head, and a very large herd could number more than five hundred. A larger herd meant wealth, and wealth meant

Domestication
the process of modification of plants or animals to establish human control over them, leading to agriculture and pastoralism

Neolithic
the "New Stone" age, beginning around ten thousand to twelve thousand years ago with the first animal and plant domestication

Pastoralism
a productive system based on domesticated animals as the main source of food

differential access to status and social opportunities. In Barabaig society, a man "who is successful in raising a large herd of cattle is socially recognized as being more knowledgeable and powerful than a person with a small herd" (Klima, 1970: 32), and the man who was poor in cattle might have to work for a wealthier man. "Leaders" then could emerge, with some power to command the efforts and allegiances of other men, at least members of their family, lineage, village, or tribe. Formal government was still often lacking, but the rudiments or precursors of government were observable.

One valuable opportunity open to the man rich in cattle was marriage—the ability to marry well or to marry often. A wealthy Barabaig man would have four or more wives and many sons. And he would also actively seek to increase his animal holdings through a variety of social institutions, such as the *gefuryed* in which a man would lend a bull to another man in exchange for rights to the future calf of his trading partner's cow. Klima also noted that men were not above deliberately manipulating and exploiting these arrangements for their benefit. Another way of adding to one's wealth was by marrying his daughters or sisters to men with mighty herds in exchange for a payment in cattle.

The existence of some surplus and a larger and more dependable food supply led to larger societies as a whole, sometimes with hundreds or even thousands of people (some of the enormous and important societies in history like the Mongols were pastoralists). On the other hand, not all pastoral societies were huge, and they often still had to disperse into smaller local communities. And migratory patterns, sometimes called transhumance, often had to continue, as herds required new sources of land, water, and pasturage. So pastoralists may or may not have achieved settlements in semi-permanent villages.

The presence of "wealth on the hoof," in tandem with the requirement for access to land and the dominance of males and maleness in society, almost inevitably led to a more aggressive personality than anything found in foraging societies. Pastoralists could fight to control water and pasture resources; they could raid other societies and steal their herds or defend their own herds from theft. They could also steal women or clash over previous marriage exchanges and grievances about unsolved property disputes. Sometimes they fought just to

display their toughness, honor, and power. In fact, some of the most violent and war-like pre-modern peoples have been pastoralists, and it was pastoralists who were often most effective in fighting off the colonial advances of the Europeans, while foragers were easily defeated and decimated.

See Chapter 12

Understandably, pastoral attitudes and values reverberated through their religions as well. They tended to have male gods (often sky-gods) like the male god of the ancient pastoral Hebrews. Such pastoral gods often required sacrifices, particularly of male animals, killed and roasted for the gods' pleasure. The gods too were war-like and authorized the people to raid and fight, and human males of course held the leading roles like priest, oracle, or diviner.

Finally, being mobile, aggressive, and organized, pastoralists also tended to encounter other, including non-pastoral, peoples. In some instances, like the Bedouins of North Africa, they became the "traders" and entrepreneurs (literally, "between-carriers") of goods over long distances. In other instances, they fought and often conquered their neighbors. Sometimes, they virtually exterminated other peoples; alternatively, they ruled them from afar, extracted wealth from them in the form of tribute, or even settled among them as a dominant class or caste. The impact of the pastoral Mongols on Eurasian society, especially China and Russia, cannot be overestimated. In Europe, it was pastoral tribes like the Germanic peoples who came to populate much of the continent, and it was pastoral tribes that finally toppled the Roman Empire. Similarly, pastoral peoples were on the move in India (the "Aryans"), the Middle East, and Africa, and many of today's "composite" societies like Rwanda and Burundi are products of this historic meeting. Even in the United States the classic confrontation between the "cattlemen" or pastoralists and the "sod busters" or farmers largely shaped the life of the western region.

See Chapter 8

Interestingly, the dividing line between foraging and pastoralism was not clear or absolute. In his study of Melanesian societies, Paul Sillitoe stated that some societies raised their pig herds as essentially domesticated animals, while others left "their creatures more to forage and root for themselves"; the latter also did not so much breed animals as allow animals to breed in the wild. This "unsupervised" form of "pig herding" led Sillitoe to conclude that "it is sometimes difficult to decide whether a group preys on wild pigs or herds semi-domesticated ones" (1998: 47).

Horticulture

The other economic system to evolve out of domestication involved the production of domesticated plants or **horticulture**, defined as farming without the use of technologies like the plow, irrigation, fertilizer, or draft animals. The absence of these inputs tended to limit outputs and to prevent the permanent use of farmlands, since the soil became exhausted of nutrients after a few years' tilling. Horticulture was once practiced in a wide variety of climate types, but has recently been found most often in and is most suited for hilly inland areas and for tropical environments, like the rainforests of New Guinea or the Amazon, where soils are relatively thin, rainfall is fairly dependable, and growth rates are high enough that displaced wild vegetation can quickly recover.

In such environments, one of the more common strategies of horticulture was and still is "**slash-and-burn**" or **swidden** farming. In this technique, future fields are cleared of vegetation by cutting away brush and "slashing" trees to cause

them to die and dry out; some time later, the horticulturists return and set fire to all of the undergrowth, clearing the field for planting while restoring the nutrients in the native plants back to the soil in the form of ash. Sowing the fields can be as simple of tossing a few seeds into holes poked by digging sticks or can be more complex and labor intensive. Either way, stumps, rocks, and other debris are usually left in place; no attempt is made to plow the fields or to contour the land in any appreciable way. That is, the farmers basically work around the obstacles in their fields. As you might imagine, a horticultural community would need to have a number of such areas in various states of readiness, from "in production" to recently burned to recently slashed to fallow. After two or three harvests, the fertility of the land is often depleted, and it is necessary to allow it to "return to nature," only to be slashed and burned again in the future.

Horticultural labor can be assigned to members in various ways; one common division of labor is for men do the heavy work of clearing the land while women do the planting and harvesting. The Dani of New Guinea were an example of this classic pattern (Heider, 1979), but this labor arrangement is by no means universal. Among the Semai of Malaysia the women and children slashed the trees

Horticulture

a production system based on low-technology farming or gardening, without the use of plows, draft animals, irrigation, or fertilizers

Slash-and-burn

a horticultural practice in which trees and underbrush are cut, left to dry, and then burned as preparation for planting a garden. Also known as *swidden*

Swidden

see *slash-and-burn*

IMAGE 7.3 Slash-and-burn is a common technique of horticulture.

before the men chopped them down; then men and boys made the planting-holes, and women and children followed behind placing the seeds in the holes (Dentan, 1968). The Yanomamo (South America) reserved both forest-clearing and planting for men (Chagnon, 1992). And the Konyak Nagas of India had a very mixed system: Older men and women would clear the undergrowth while younger men did the slashing. Then men sowed rice and millet, with women coming after to cover the grains with earth. Boys and girls weeded together, and men and women harvested together (Von Fuerer-Haimendorf, 1969).

The diversity of productive relationships within horticultural societies guaranteed a diversity of cultural systems emerging from them. For instance, in some cases land was private property, in other cases not. The Konyak Nagas maintained very old links with ancestral lands, and almost all farm plots were individually owned; in fact, one person would own multiple scattered plots, as many as two hundred and fifty in the extreme case. Among the Semai, there was no permanent ownership of land; the "owner" of a tract was simply the person or family who cleared and presently used it. If they abandoned or simply neglected it for too long, others would move in and occupy it (but still not acquire "title" to it); the same was true of houses.

The relationship with and productivity of the land also affected settlement or mobility. Some societies built fairly permanent villages and farmed the land in the vicinity on some kind of rotation. Other societies moved frequently to open new land and establish new temporary residences for a few months or years. Likewise, cultural values and practices like gender stratification and violence were diverse. The Iroquois (eastern North America) represented one of the most female-centered societies on record (J. K. Brown, 1975).

At the other end of the spectrum, some horticultural societies, like the Sambia, maintained tense and profoundly unequal, even segregated, relations between the sexes. The Yanomamo were also highly male-dominated. Even so, overall horticulture was likely to provide prominent female status: According to one analysis, more than one-fourth of horticultural societies assigned children primarily to their mother's kin group, compared to ten percent of foraging groups and even less of

pastoral and intensive agricultural societies (Lenski and Lenski, 1982).

Violence varied as well but somewhat independently from other variables. The Yanomamo reportedly were male-dominated in their economics and their gender roles and also war-like, and the Semai were egalitarian in their economics and their gender roles and peaceful. However, the Iroquois and many other societies mixed these traits in many combinations: Some were male-dominated but non-violent, while (more commonly) others were not male-dominated but violent.

Even such "low intensity" farming could produce a noticeable surplus, allowing for larger societies—often multiple local communities or villages—and enhanced notions of, and competition for, wealth, power, and prestige. Horticultural societies sometimes developed elaborate ranking and stratification systems and even "governments," up to chiefs and other political institutions. They certainly had more problems to solve and disputes to settle, with larger populations living in closer contact. The weaknesses or vulnerabilities of horticulture were compensated by the new opportunities it offered. Among these opportunities was one of the prerequisites for further cultural elaboration—specialization. A small number of people could be "freed" from food production due to the surplus that others provided, permitting them to practice other activities and develop new skills and techniques, including pottery, weaving, metalworking as well as more full-time religious and artistic roles such as priestcraft, and even "time-keeping" (the builders of Stonehenge were, after all, horticulturists).

Speaking of priestcraft, religion tended to reflect the realities and values of horticulture, often focused on fertility and the cycle of natural processes, from the "birth" (planting) to "death" of the plants. Gods or spirits of various species or natural forces (rain, sun, etc.) or moments in the planting cycle were important for organizing economic activity, as was an awareness of the timing of the seasons. So, for instance, knowledge of the solstices appeared, along with "calendrical" (annual) rituals to demarcate them and the key activities undertaken around those times. A "harvest" ritual (not unlike Thanksgiving in the U.S.) was common, or even a ritual recognizing the "season of death" (not unlike Halloween in the U.S. or the *Dia de los Muertos*

Chagnon, Napoleon. 1992. *Yanomamo*, 4th ed. Fort Worth, TX: Harcourt Brace College Publishers.

See Chapter 5

in Mexico) at the end of the farming season. The winter solstice (late December), when the days started to get longer in the Northern Hemisphere, and the spring equinox (late March) were both commonly associated with birth or rebirth and moments for important rituals. Note that the two major Christian holidays fall at precisely those times.

Sillitoe also found that the line between foraging and horticulture was not always certain. The Gidra and Kiwai people of New Guinea engaged in "limited management of plant resources" (1998: 27), for instance claiming sago and coconut palm trees but only minimally tending them until harvest-time. Men might "dig them up and replant them elsewhere or leave them to self-propagate into dense stands." "There is not much difference between these activities and those of nearby Australian Aboriginals, customarily labeled hunter-gatherers," Sillitoe concluded (27).

Intensive agriculture

Intensive agriculture
high-input, high-yield
farming on permanent
farmlands through the use
of technologies like
irrigation, fertilizer,
pesticide, and the plow

Approximately five or six thousand years ago, a second revolution in economics and culture occurred that eventually had even more profound and lasting effects on the species and the planet. **Intensive agriculture** is high-input, high-yield farming employing such technologies as the plow, irrigation, fertilizer, and draft animals (all the ones missing from horticulture), allowing for something else that horticulture cannot provide—permanent farmlands. Given this "base," intensive agriculture made possible not only more of what we have seen before, but entirely new dimensions of culture not previously possible.

The most obvious difference between horti-culture and intensive agriculture is the vast surpluses achievable with the latter; farmers were able to produce crops—sometimes two or three per year in extremely well-watered locations like Bali—sufficient to feed enormous populations, measuring into the tens of thousands even in ancient times and into the hundreds of millions today. The earliest environments for this new practice were frequently river valleys, which provided the requisite water and alluvial soils; however, not every early intensive agricultural society lived along a river (for instance, the Inca and Aztec). Rather, what intensive agricultural environments seemed to share was a restricted amount of productive land, such that the only possible response to increasing populations was intensification of production.

The work of early intensive agriculture was arduous and incessant and required the efforts

IMAGE 7.4 Intensive agriculture societies use all available land, as in Nepal where hillsides are cut into terraces.

of the entire farming family; men, women, and children alike were enlisted as farm labor. However, in contrast to horticulture, ownership and control of land, production, and surplus was usually concentrated in the hands of men, leading back to a male-centered and male-dominated society. Fathers tend to be heads of families, and membership, inheritance, and such issues were settled among and between males. This male pre-eminence, together with the accumulation of sometimes vast surpluses, made raiding, plunder, and inter-society aggression attractive. Accordingly, intensive agricultural societies tended and tend to be war-like, even promoting a social institution of professional soldiers on permanent military stand-by.

In fact, a key aspect of the form of society made possible—and probably necessary—by intensive agriculture was a high degree of social differentiation and social specialization. First of all, the enormous surpluses translated to enormous differences in wealth and power; while most people were still food-producers (which was true until very recently), a small but important class of wealth-expropriators existed to "rule" and "manage" the economy and society. This class constituted and constitutes an elite or an actual government over the equally new political institution, the territorial state. There might be other classes intermediate between the elite and the agricultural **peasants**, the latter now not independent subsistence producers but providers of surplus to a "center" of society. As this suggests, the second possibility of intensive agriculture was an elaboration of the number of different kinds of jobs to do or different kinds of people to be. In addition to peasants and rulers, there could be professional priests, scribes, craftsmen, artisans, and naturally soldiers. All of this variation was financed by the surplus production of the laboring classes, often including slaves.

Where intensive agriculture first appeared—in the Middle East (so-called "Mesopotamia"), Egypt, India, and China—we find a new type of society and culture normally referred to as **civilization**. Civilization is a social formation centered on, although not exclusively consisting of large, densely populated communities or "cities." Most of the population still lived in the hinterland, but the power and decision-making for the society emanated from the city; it was the "seat of power." Along with, or perhaps because of, cities came a constellation of new skills, technologies, and species of knowledge. Among these were the state, the first writing systems, mathematics, monumental architecture (e.g. pyramids and palaces), and representational art.

Another new institution created by intensive agriculture was the market (see below), a location and institution for exchanging goods based on their economic value. Eventually money was invented to symbolize that value and facilitate exchange. And to make the market function, a professional class of merchants evolved, who extracted a share of the value in order to mediate the exchange. This market, and the long-range trading that sustained it, introduced a circulation not only of goods, but of ideas and cultures, as travelers from distant lands brought their produce and their languages, religions, and other cultural elements to the city. Cities thus, from the beginning, were sites for the mixing and transmitting of culture and thereby for the creation of new cultures and of new cultural awareness like "cosmopolitanism" (*cosmos* for "world" or "universe," and *polis* for "city") and "multiculturalism"—and ultimately globalization.

Religion predictably reflected social changes on the ground in these societies. Just as economics and politics were "centralized," so religion and the "spiritual realm" could become centralized too. There was often a single "high god" or a pantheon of gods (like the Greek Olympian gods) of the city or civilization that was believed to own and control the affairs of the society. The human rulers and the god or gods might be in close communication—or in the case of ancient Egypt, be one and the same. Professional priests ran the cult of the god(s) from the city center, collecting tribute (what we would call taxes) for the benefit of the god(s), which was used to fund all of the activities of the society. The god(s) was(were) often judgmental and war-like, identical to the rulers themselves, who sat in judgment over the people and led the "defense" of society. Religion was so central to the function and identity of many of these ancient civilizations that have been referred to as "temple communities."

Systems of distribution

Once goods are produced, there is the task of distributing them to the people who need them—or

ANTHROPOLOGIES OF
CLASS

See Chapters 9 and 13

Peasant
an out-of-favor term for rural and agricultural peoples who live in but are peripheral to a centralized and often urbanized society. The peasants provide the food for the society but generally have the least power and wealth in the society

Civilization
a form of society based on cities as the centers of administration and the focus of social life, usually dependent on intensive agriculture in the surrounding countryside

at least the people who will consume them, which is not necessarily the same thing. Unlike the tendency for a society to have a single dominant system of production, it may have more than one distribution system or all three systems in operation simultaneously, sometimes in different realms of the culture. Anthropologists generally follow the eminent economist Karl Polanyi (1957) in identifying three distribution systems:

- reciprocity
- redistribution
- market exchange

Reciprocity

Reciprocity is an informal type of back-and-forth exchanging, of giving and taking. Since all exchange involves some amount of give-and-take, we might do better to think of it as a style of exchange in which individuals or groups of relatively equal power and status, and who know each other personally, mutually give and take goods as part of and as a commentary on their ongoing social relationship. Reciprocity really exists in three sub-forms, namely:

1. Generalized reciprocity, in which goods are given without any particular calculation of the value of the goods or any particular expectation for a "return" of equal value in any particular time frame. That is, if I have something to give, I give it, not worrying whether I will receive something in exchange any time soon, but assuming that, if you have something to give, you will give it. The person who does not share, or who demands credit or acclaim for doing so, is simply impolite and socially inappropriate. Clearly, this type of sharing will only occur between people who know and trust each other and who have a long-term social relationship—during which "reciprocity" will eventually and generally be achieved. One example was the *hxaro* of the foraging !Kung or Ju/hoansi, a "delayed form of nonequivalent gift exchange" that had the effect of "circulating goods, lubricating social relations, and maintaining ecological balance" (R. Lee, 1984: 97). Every visit between individuals and communities was an occasion for starting new

or completing old *hxaro* trades. Givers would downplay the quality of their gift with comments like "I couldn't find a really good thing, I just brought you this" (100). What was important, and explicitly so, was not the object itself but the social relationship between the participants: Ju/hoansi understood that a deficient reciprocation "could mean a *hxaro* partner was losing interest in maintaining the relationship and was allowing it to lapse" (101).

2. Balanced reciprocity, in which goods are given with some calculation of their value and some expectation of an equal return within some reasonable time. It still entails a long-term and meaningful relationship between the exchangers, but ordinarily transpires between individuals who are not quite as close as those who would do generalized reciprocity; after all, you would not give a friend or loved one a gift and then impatiently wait for an equal return.

3. Negative reciprocity, in which goods are given with calculation of their value and also with an expectation or intention of receiving more value than one gives. Perhaps the most famous and well-researched example of negative reciprocity is the "kula" institution described by Malinowski in Melanesia. Men traveled great distances at considerable bother and risk in order to trade necklaces and armbands with their partners, each man hoping to receive the "best" necklace for his armband or vice versa. However, the point was not to get and hold a piece, but to get it, display it, and eventually trade it for an even more prized piece. This way, a man achieved and expressed his status in society, his skill as a trader, and ultimately, if all went well, his elevation to "kula master." Still, in the end, his success depended not only on his tough bargaining and skillful manipulation of the game, but on his relationships with other traders who could just as easily pass their prestigious objects to other partners.

Redistribution

One of the key characteristics of reciprocity is that it has no "center." No one person or group controls or oversees the exchange. In **redistribution**, on the other hand, a center is implicit and necessary, and

Reciprocity
a form of exchange that involves giving and receiving between relative equals and as part of a larger ongoing social relationship

Redistribution
a form of exchange that involves collection of surplus or wealth by a "central" individual, group, or institution that controls how the wealth is redistributed and used

the social implications of this fact are serious. Redistribution can be defined as exchange in which wealth is collected by a central person, group, or institution who (or which) then hands it out to the people who need it or "spends" it for purposes that are (ideally) beneficial to all in the exchange arrangement but which also reflect the power and interests of the distributor.

A classic example of redistribution also comes from Melanesia, where a "big man" might gather a redistribution system around himself. A man was not born a big man, even if his father was one. Rather, this was a status that each man had to gain individually. The point was to develop a coterie of followers who would turn their surplus over to you, which you could redistribute according to the needs and interests of the system. So, a potential big man first had to generate his own surplus, which he displayed and gave away in a very public gesture resembling a party. If his hard work and generosity were seen and appreciated, others might opt to associate themselves with him; like finding a good "patron," it was always desirable to attach oneself to a powerful and generous man. The more people who joined his "team" and contributed their surplus, the more the big man could display and redistribute. Eventually, he might become the center of an important and powerful exchange network. Like a feudal lord (another center of redistribution), his favor was valuable and his support good or even necessary, and a follower was likely to return deference for various kinds of benefits.

In intensive agricultural and industrial societies, redistribution is an important function of the political authorities. Whether this takes the form of king or priest or state, the center can compel and even coerce participation in the form of taxes or tithes or other expropriation of private wealth. This wealth goes to "social services" (like unemployment or retirement benefits), but also to large-scale projects individuals could not afford alone (like roads), to "security" systems like the police or military, and to finance the government itself, which often enough meant (and means) the luxurious lifestyle of the leaders.

Market exchange

Market exchange was the last of the three distribution systems to appear historically and is not the only system even in "modern" societies. However, it is increasingly defining the modern world and penetrating and displacing other systems. In Western society, when people practice reciprocity or redistribution, it is still usually in terms of goods and services acquired by market practices (e.g. gifts bought at the store and paid for by money).

We can think of market exchange as distribution that involves a specialized location or institution—the "market"—where people bring their goods or their symbols of wealth (like money) for the purpose of exchange based on self-interest and maximization of value ("profit") determined by "supply and demand," and where ongoing social relationships are reduced, not significant, or an actual impediment to exchange. Although the market has been the main preoccupation of economists since Adam Smith's 1776 *The Wealth of Nations*, modernity or capitalism hardly invented the market principle; ancient intensive agricultural societies generally had markets, and many traditional African horticulturists, for instance, held markets but on a more limited scale and schedule. Villages might organize a "market day" once every several days, at which time people gathered to exchange foods or handicrafts or whatever they produced. After market day, people would not do market exchange until the next market day, leaving lots of occasion for reciprocity or redistribution.

Classical economic theory also envisions markets are basically, even ideally, impersonal practices (verging on forces of nature). Contemporary economists, like anthropologists, realize that markets are social institutions made and perpetuated by human actions. In pre-modern market behavior, it was of course true that people usually knew each other and interacted over long periods of time. In modern Western and global market behavior, participants may know the people they "buy from" or "sell to" or even that they develop a personal relationship with them. Humans are humans and tend to form social bonds over time. This can facilitate the market "deal," as trust can grow between traders. However, in capitalist society, friendship is not enough, which is why formal devices like contracts and courts exist. On the other hand, as many people have discovered, "doing business" with friends or family can be a vexing undertaking.

Market exchange
a form of distribution based on the use of a specialized location (the "market place") and relatively impersonal principles of supply and demand and the pursuit of profit

IMAGE 7.5 Modern markets, like this one in downtown Tokyo, can generate great wealth.

BOX 7.1   THE MORALITY OF MARKETS IN WEST AFRICA

One of the generally unquestioned tenets of classical economic thinking is that individuals engage in market activity essentially to maximize their profit and money—that is, to achieve "accumulation" of capital. However, Paul Clough's research among the Islamic Hausa people of West Africa indicates that "polygamous marriage and the relationship of patronage and trading friendship have deflected a potential agrarian capitalist transition into a distinctive pattern of noncapitalist accumulation" (2014: 60) that results in a non-Western kind of market morality. Part of the matter is that Islam discourages *riba* (often translated as "interest") or deriving profit without effort. Even more, Hausa traders pursue an exceptional path of mutuality, of "accumulating together" (53) that is set within—and often converted into—personal and even kin relationships. One such relationship is "trading friends" (*abokanan ciniki*), which often grows out of previous close friendship; loans in particular are typically extended to friends whose *hali* or "character" was already known. In other words, friendships are transformed into business relationships, and vice versa: Business relationships are often transformed into friendships or actual family bonds. For instance, people may enter into *biki* partnerships by agreeing "to make donations of money, grain or other goods at each other's naming and wedding ceremonies" (184); at the extreme, trading friends marry their offspring to each other, thus ensuring access to each other's goods, credit, and labor. The ultimate goal of market activity and wealth accumulation is marriage: A wife, or better yet, multiple wives, is "a crucial dimension of 'wealth' (*dukiya*) in the eyes of men and women" (64). In fact, the word *dukiya* means much more than cash wealth but also refers to "wives and children and their provisioning; social relations which included friends, patrons and clients," and of course, all of the familiar "economic" resources like land, equipment, animals, and money (64). In a word, men trade in the market not so much so that they can be rich as that they can be married. Finally but importantly, the practice of Islam in Hausa society is a powerful economic factor. First, conversion to Islam allows men "to enter Muslim trading networks and use the profits therefrom to hire labor and purchase land" (55). Second, Islam removes women from public life including "most forms of farm labor," thereby increasing "the prestige of polygyny among men, for it signified a man's capacity to maintain more than one wife" (46). Likewise for women, "entry into a polygynous marriage for the first time often increased their economic security and social prestige, since a man's capacity to have more than one wife depended on his income" (46). As Clough concludes, not money but (polygynous) marriage "is a core value shared by farmer-traders on both the production-oriented and trade-oriented paths to wealth acquisition. It generates a particular kind of enterprise, in which household, cliental, and capital management are merged" (368). As in all market systems, there "is competition. However, the notion of competition is heavily qualified by the idea of cooperation. The boundary between the domestic and the extradomestic is blurred" (376), establishing a "paradigm of social action, moral obligation, and collective desire" (377).

Again, the market principle does not depend on money or even on capitalism. Capitalism is one way of doing markets (even communists "went to the market" to buy bread), and money is a convenient "medium" or symbol of wealth and value: It is easier to carry some money to the market than some corn, and of course "service" workers like teachers do not produce material goods to take to market anyhow. Nevertheless, money and capitalist modes of production and exchange are increasingly pervading the economic and social world—not just in the U.S. or the West, but globally—and they appear to be the future (at least the short-to-mid-range future) of economics and culture.

... TO ECONOMIC ANTHROPOLOGY

A sign of the times, Herskovits revised his 1940 book on "primitive economies" in 1952 under the new title, *Economic Anthropology: A Study of Comparative Economics*. In the preface he explained that the change "represents a reorientation in point of view that goes far beyond the question of mere terminology" (1952: v). Not only was it no longer acceptable to talk about "primitive" people or societies, but the interests of economic anthropology had graduated far beyond the old typologies of production and distribution. As further evidence of the growth of economic anthropology, the topics covered in the ensuing chapters included business, credit, and value; money and wealth; capital formation; and government. Most remarkably, he concluded that

> practically every economic mechanism and institution known to us is found somewhere in the nonliterate world. Division of labor and the specialization this represents, the multitudinous

forms of money, the various aids to business such as credit and interest, the investment in labor-power and other resources in capital goods—all these, so important in our own culture, have been found to exist in numerous non-machine, nonliterate economies.

(488)

Accordingly, economic anthropology has matured into an anthropological study of all elements of complex economies, including industrialization and the corporation; work; money, credit, and finance; and the "informal" economy.

Industrialism

In the last few centuries, changes in agricultural techniques together with technological advances have spawned a new kind of production based on "industry" or machine-generated energy and machine-produced goods. Indeed, anthropology and sociology were born during and largely because of the "industrial revolution" that was wreaking profound changes on Western societies and on the non-Western societies integrated into their empires to feed their industrial needs. It was nineteenth-century industrial capitalism that inspired Karl Marx to formulate his theory of societies or "social formations" as effects of material and economic forces; Émile Durkheim and Max Weber also discussed **industrialism** as a momentous change in human relations and organization.

The key new institution in industrialism is "the factory," which is a site of productive activity, but also a set of social roles, attitudes, values, and symbols. As a concentration of workers occasioned by a concentration of machinery, the factory tends to create large dense population centers; of course,

See Chapter 11

Industrialism
an economic and social system based on the production of large quantities of inexpensive manufactured goods and the concentration of employment in urban factories

as we saw above, "the city" existed before industrialism, and some experts estimate that cities like imperial Rome reached a population of one million. Nevertheless, industrialism led to the growth of more cities and larger cities than previously seen, achieved through rural-to-urban migration and even international migration—that is, large-scale population transfers.

One effect of the factory system is a separation of productive functions from other social functions—in a word, the separation of "work" from "home." Inside the factory, according to the historian E. P. Thompson (1967), new social habits of time (e.g. a preoccupation with clocks and schedules) and work-discipline have to be mastered and managed, many of which were resisted by rural people unaccustomed to the demands of the city and factory. Beyond the factory walls, the effects of industrialization on society are profound: Durkheim theorized that an entirely new kind of social organization, the "organic" society with its elaborate division of labor, interdependent classes, and fundamentally economic or practical motivations, emerged, while Weber believed that industry was one facet of a more general process of "modernization" that also featured urbanization, bureaucracy, and even secularization (the reduction or disappearance of religion). Marx reasoned that industrial capitalism was necessarily destructive of traditional society: It depends on "creative destruction" and the continuous revolutionizing of the means of production, such that "all that is solid melts into air."

Anthropology joined the discussion of industrialism somewhat later than the classical sociologists, but emphasized the diversity and cultural relativism of the new production system. Some of the first works of urban anthropology were inspired by the impact of colonial industrialism in Africa, particularly in the so-called "copperbelt" region. At the same time, some anthropologists were conducting participant observation inside factories, describing their processes and concepts. Our main discovery has been that there is more than one path or process of industrialism and that the relationship between industrial and "traditional" society is complex and variable.

For example, Morton Klass investigated the effects of a bicycle factory near a village in West Bengal in the 1970s. To be sure, Bengali industrial centers, like many others, were "overcrowded" with

all the attendant problems of "disease, crowded slums, filth, poor sanitation and water, crime, and so on" (1978: 8). But the factory did not simply erode traditional identities and organization, nor was it experienced as entirely negative. The factory managers were not even village people, but already urbanized Indians. And while most of the laborers did come from the village, their pre-industrial social and religious identities and practices did not suddenly disappear. Rather, for example, the pre-industrial caste system not only continued but served as an important organizing principle of the factory, members of the same caste often "cluster[ing] together in particular factory departments or activities" (219). Pre-industrial religion also adapted, with a minor god named Bissokormo, the patron-spirit of men who work with tools, assuming more importance. And of course many workers regarded the factory as a distinct improvement over the labor, social conditions, and uncertainty of the farm.

Industrialism is often associated with smaller families, but the assumption that industrialism necessarily damages families is unjustified. David Kertzer found, for instance, that industrialization in the Italian community of Caselecchio di Reno actually *strengthened* the nuclear family. In the mid-1800s, fifteen percent of children under the age of fifteen did not live with their parents but rather as "servants or apprentices in the homes of others"; by 1921, this number had fallen to three percent, largely as a result of factory work for poor families (1987: 154). "Far from tearing children away from a nurturing parental family environment, industrialization often permitted children to grow up in their parental household to an extent that would not have otherwise been possible" (158), he concluded.

Finally, Aihwa Ong, like others, has explored the symbolic and religious effects of industrialism. Malaysian factories, as in many places, have tended to hire young women, who are often stereotypically valued for their dexterity and patience as well as their shyness, obedience, and deference (that is, they take orders well and do not complain) (1988: 33). However, "when young peasant women began to leave the kampung [village] and enter the unknown worlds of urban boarding schools and foreign factories, the incidence of spirit possession seems to have become more common among them" (32). Ong concluded that these outbreaks of spirit

URBAN ANTHROPOLOGY

possession—in which women-workers "explode into demonic screaming and rage on the shop floor" (28)—

> may be taken as expressions both of fear and of resistance against the multiple violations of moral boundaries in the modern factory. They are acts of rebellion, symbolizing what cannot be spoken directly, calling for a renegotiation of obligations between the management and workers.
>
> (38)

Anthropology of work and the corporation

In the first chapter we mentioned that anthropology has been studying the modern workplace since at least W. Lloyd Warner's research in the Western Electric Company in the 1930s. Since then, a section of the American Anthropological Association, the Society for the Anthropology of Work, and its journal, *Anthropology of Work Review*, have kept professional attention on the subject. Recent field projects have examined the work of Turkish-Dutch police officers (Mutsaers, 2014), Syrian delivery workers (Monroe, 2014), women on Wall Street (Fisher, 2012), American cheesemakers (Paxson, 2013), and Brazilian exotic dancers in New York (Maia, 2012), to name but a few.

In pre-industrial economies, anthropologists have investigated the gender and caste division of work. For instance, among the Cheyenne of the American Great Plains, women made all of the clothing, did the tanning, made pottery, and performed the task of "quilling" or embroidering clothes with porcupine quills. The prestigious women's Quiller's Society existed for the latter purpose. On the other hand, one of the most cross-culturally common aspects of labor is its association with a particular social or ethnic group or "caste." In Africa, metalwork, leatherwork, woodwork, and music and entertainment were typically caste occupations; many societies, claimed Tal Tamari, had castes for weaving, several different kinds of metalwork, epic poetry, and clowning, and "blacksmiths, leatherworkers, and woodworkers, as well as bards, have specific musical and dance repertoires" (1991: 224–225). India of course is most famous for its intricate system of caste professions.

In industrial and post-industrial societies, a prominent social institution is the corporation, and anthropologists have been documenting its form and function for several decades. A 1979 essay by June Nash on "The Anthropology of the Multinational Corporation" was a turning point in the discipline, highlighting the internal structure (the "corporate culture") and the external impact of corporations. To be sure, corporations are not unique to late-modern industrial societies; they were part of colonialism, and many indigenous societies have founded corporations—or actually incorporated themselves *as* businesses.

An entire special issue of the journal *Current Anthropology* (April 2011) was dedicated to the "social life" of the corporation and the diversity of "corporate forms." In the United States and elsewhere, the corporation is a legal "person" with rights and responsibilities—what Guldbrandsen and Holland (2001) called a "super-citizen" because it is so much more powerful than the average person. Corporations hire us, manufacture our goods, influence our laws, shape our culture, and affect virtually every part of our lives. More profoundly, as James Ferguson argued, corporate persons see the world in particular ways—in ways that are at once more local (specific to the corporation and its managers and shareholders) and more translocal (across political boundaries and national markets) than ordinary citizens.

Anthropology of money, finance, and banking

Finally, anthropologists cannot help but appreciate the complex webs of financial instruments and institutions that entangle individuals and societies. A key element of modern economies is money, although George Dalton reminded us in 1965 that even some "primitive" societies had a form of money, if only for certain purposes; also unlike modern "impersonal and commercial" money, "primitive money frequently has pedigree and personality, sacred uses, or moral and emotional connotations" (1965: 44). Keith Hart, an energetic scholar and vociferous critic of modern economies and economics (see above and below), and Horacio

ANTHROPOLOGY OF WORK

INDUSTRIALIZATION AND SOCIAL TRANSFORMATION IN CONTEMPORARY CHINA

See Chapters 12 and 15

See Chapter 1

ANTHROPOLOGY OF THE CORPORATION

Ortiz assert in their new review article that anthropology has only been on the trail of contemporary monetary systems and practices since the 1980s and still struggles to integrate its participant observation style of research with global and historical forces.

Certainly questions of the origin, diversity, and effects of money are important, but money cannot be understood in social isolation. It depends on and circulates between major institutions, including governments (states), corporations, and financial institutions such as banks, insurance companies, credit companies, and many others. Accordingly, anthropologists have begun to study banks and bankers, like Joris Luyendijk (2011) who spent time among the financiers in the City of London. Four years later, Paul Durrenberger and Gísli Pálsson (2015) led an interdisciplinary team analyzing the meltdown of Iceland's banking and financial system, which was hit particularly hard by the great recession of 2008. Inexperience in international finance together with exuberance and overconfidence made the system vulnerable, overconfidence partly fed by the country's pride in its swashbuckling Viking heritage and its perception of its modern-day banking professionals as *útrásarvíkingur* or

See Chapter 14

"Business Vikings." Rising to the challenge of grappling with history, David Graeber published in 2011 his massive *Debt: The First 5,000 Years*.

At the opposite end of the social spectrum, anthropologists have also described the small-scale, face-to-face encounters with credit and debt. For instance, Detlev Krige describes local all-male savings clubs in the poor township of Soweto, South Africa, which "have played an important role for working-class neighborhoods in mobilizing collective credit and savings, retaining flows of monies within township communities and practicing solidarity and mutuality in a hostile environment" (2015: 63). Significantly, these clubs have begun doing more business with formal institutions like banks, which are happy to handle their cash. In the rich world, law professor Linda Coco contributes a chapter to a volume on the anthropology of wealth and power, describing the legal process of individual bankruptcy in the United States and the culture that demonizes the bankrupt person as a social and moral failure in a way that "obscures far more degenerate neoliberal economic and social policies that strive for accumulation by imposing debt structures on actors at the local, national, and international levels" (2014: 41).

BOX 7.2 THE INFORMAL ECONOMY IN THE GLOBAL ECONOMY: MEXICAN BEACH VENDORS

Informal economy
according to Keith Hart, the marginal, unofficial, even illicit zone of the economy, consisting mainly of work that is impermanent, irregular (not full-time), and not guaranteeing a fixed wage

Every system generates a marginal, unofficial, even illicit zone, and that includes the market system (with its "black market"). Keith Hart is credited with coining the term **informal economy** to refer to such marginal activity in otherwise formal economies, by which he essentially meant work that is impermanent, irregular (not full-time), or not guaranteeing a fixed wage. Some behaviors that he classified in the informal economy are illegal, including receiving stolen goods, loaning money at exorbitant interest, drug-peddling, prostitution, smuggling, and so forth (1973: 69). Informal is not necessarily illegal, and much informal economic activity is legal but disreputable (such as begging or panhandling) or legal and reputable (such as street vending or running a small business). The World Bank, recognizing the informal economy as work and income that is partly or completely outside regulation and taxation, actually takes a relatively positive attitude toward it, insisting that it reduces labor costs and offers opportunities when the formal economy is inadequate (i.e. in situations of high unemployment), but also complaining that it harms tax revenues and undermines laws. The World Bank also finds that the informal economy is a major and vital component of poor and developing economies, and indeed, Busani Mpofu (2015: 39) estimates that informal work or vending occupies eighty percent of Zimbabwe's labor force. Many anthropological studies have investigated the informal practice of street vending, including Tamar Diana Wilson's research on the vendors serving the tourist beaches of Mexico. These "petty capitalists" are commonly people who have little education, few job skills, and hail from discriminated social groups like indigenous societies, also thus often lacking knowledge of the dominant language. Predictably, many such individuals engage in selling trinkets, snacks, and souvenirs on the beach because they have no other options. Interestingly, though, some vendors, especially men, actually choose and prefer this lifestyle and even contradict the stereotype: "relatively well educated men find informal self-employment to their liking whereas women may find themselves self-employed for lack of other opportunities or because they are forced by necessity into often part-time income-generating activities" (Wilson, 2012: 41). Also, some participate in beach vending because it is a multigenerational family business. Finally and significantly, informal does not mean detached from or contrary to the formal global economy. First, beach vendors depend on all of the forces and technologies of global tourism to bring them a clientele. Second, other forces of globalization or neoliberalism often push them into the trade by driving them off of their ancestral land or enmeshing them in the cash economy. Third, they provide a service to the tourists, who are sometimes happy to purchase cheap or useful items (like sunglasses) on the beach. Last, they are the end-link in a global "commodity chain": The t-shirts, tablecloths, silver jewelry, towels and blankets, serapes, fans, glasses, bags, etc. that they sell have often been manufactured in other parts of Mexico or other parts of the world, and vendors buy these products of global capitalism to resell for a small profit on the beach (83–84).

CONSUMPTION AS CULTURAL PRACTICE

The third and most neglected phase of any economic system is consumption, the actual use of goods and services. It has received less attention in anthropology at least partly because it has received less attention in Western economic thinking in general: As Gregory expressed, "The consumption sphere is very much a subordinate sphere under capitalism, and as such was not subjected to any systematic analysis by the classical economists. . . . The methods of consumption under capitalism are disorganized relative to the methods of production" (1982: 75–76). Many cultural anthropology textbooks make little or no mention of it, which is regrettable, not only because it too is a cultural activity, but because it is such an important part of modern societies.

Anthropologists in the field have not ignored consumption, and a few prominent economic theorists have given it some thought. Marx, who was most concerned with the "mode of production," did also identify a "mode of consumption," but it was a secondary issue for him that received little elaboration beyond the distinction between subsistence consumption and luxury consumption, associated with the working class and the owning class respectively. The first scholar to take consumption seriously was perhaps Thorstein Veblen,

whose *Theory of the Leisure Class: An Economic Study of Institutions* (originally published in 1899) introduced the concept of "conspicuous consumption." Veblen's idea was that the drive to consume certain kinds of goods was based on the desire to create and display differences between people and on the capacity of goods to do so. In other words, products do not just have "uses," but they also have "values," and the people who possess—and can display—certain items have *their* social value enhanced as well. He imagined that the upper classes set the tone in a society, which the lower classes tried to emulate in order to acquire some of the status and prestige of their betters. One of the marks of high status in the past, he argued, had been leisure itself (free time and freedom from labor), but now it was material objects.

While the study of consumption has progressed since then, a theory of consumption really has not appeared. To my knowledge, there is no system or typology of consumption available, comparable to those of production and distribution discussed above; there is certainly no standard typology common to textbooks. We can begin to lay out some of the issues that would be part of any systematic anthropological study of consumption. First, consumption entails a variety of sub-processes, from acquisition to preparation to presentation to use. This leads to a series of research questions:

- Who acquires goods and services for consumption by the group, and how and where (i.e. the cultural phenomenon of "shopping")?
- Who prepares items for consumption, and how?
- How and why are products presented or displayed to potential consumers—and to potential audiences?
- When (for instance, at what time of day or on what occasions) and by whom are particular goods consumed?
- How are goods consumed in ritual contexts?
- Are different products consumed by different types of people, and are they consumed in different ways?
- Who can consume together, and who cannot?
- How does consumption perform, perpetuate, and comment on social relationships and institutions? How can consumption be used to challenge and change social relationships and institutions?

The essence of an anthropology of consumption is that consumables are not neutral things, even when they are minimally processed natural commodities (like kangaroo meat). Food itself, as Roland Barthes asserts, "is not only a collection of products that can be used for statistical or nutritional studies. It is also, and at the same time, a system of communication, a body of images, a protocol of usages, situations, and behaviors" (1997: 21). That is, like all other parts of culture, consumable goods are *symbols* with meanings and effects. Any object— food, clothing, a house, a car—"sums up and transmits a situation; it constitutes information; it signifies" (21).

Mary Douglas was one of the first anthropologists to consider consumption seriously. In her famous essay "Deciphering a Meal," she discussed the social construction of various kinds of food-sharing. Central to her analysis was the distinction between the categories of "meal" and "drinks." Anyone in Western society knows that "having drinks" is a more casual social matter than "having dinner." The social dynamic involved is "intimacy and distance": "The meal expresses close friendship. Those we only know at drinks we know less intimately" (1972: 66).

Since food is such a ready medium for observing consumption, let us remain with it. The Barabaig,

ADVENTURES IN EATING

Douglas, Mary. 1972. "Deciphering a Meal." *Daedalus* 101 (1): 61–81.

pastoralists from earlier in the chapter, consumed milk, but the preferences of the sexes differed: Men liked raw milk, whereas women preferred churned or curdled milk. More significantly, a husband lived and ate in his own room in his homestead, apart from wives and children. A wife cooked in her room (*ged*) and delivered the food to his room (*huland*); if he had multiple wives, each woman cooked for him in turn, and he had to eat the same amount from each or cause dissension in his family (Klima, 1970: 37).

The idea that food is more than food, and that goods are more than goods, is a common one, and it is closely tied to individual and group identity and status. In the village of Gopalpur, as in many parts of India, humans were classified according to social and spiritual qualities. One of the manifestations of the caste system was restrictions on who could sit with and eat with whom. The various castes or *jatis* did not "eat together," although this had a culturally specific meaning: It applied to certain kinds of foods more than others (especially rice) and to certain acts more than others (especially eating off the same plate or bowl and sitting in a line to do so). Thus, different castes could eat together if they used separate plates and either faced each other or at a slant, but then by their cultural definition, they were not "eating together" (Beals, 1980).

As Douglas opined, consumption speaks to basic cultural notions of categorization—what is food, and what kinds of foods are there? The Garo, straddling the border of India and Bangladesh, have a distinct vocabulary and clear preferences for the taste of food:

> The major tastes that are recognized include *chia* (sweet), *kaa* (bitter), *spaka* (neither sweet nor bitter but in between), *mesenga* (sour), *jalik* (chili hot or burningness). Of these tastes, *chia* or sweetness is a taste most preferred in uncooked food, snacks and fruits. . . . *Kaa* or bitterness and *mesenga* or sourness are two tastes which are preferred for main meals.
>
> (Marak, 2014: 39)

However, the favorite flavor of the Garo is hotness/ burningness: "All Garo meals are perceived to be tasty when chilies are added to get a burning sensation"; otherwise the food is judged as watery or tasteless (40). Rice (*mi*) is an absolutely essential component of Garo diet and of a satisfying Garo meal: "A Garo is always 'hungry' if he has not consumed rice, even though he might have had a large quantity of other cereals" (39–40). Indeed, "Have you eaten rice?" is a common Garo greeting, and no Garo host would offer a feast without including rice (74).

Consumables like food also have religious and ritual significance. Ceremonial occasions not only tend to call for different food behaviors (such as feasts and sacrifices), but for different foods; Americans eat more turkey at Thanksgiving than any other time of year. One of the best-known food regulation systems in Western civilization is the Torah and Old Testament proscription against shellfish and various other potential foods. Douglas (1966) analyzed this too as related to categorization (e.g. animals that chew their cud and split the hoof versus those that do not), some of which are fit to eat and some of which are not. Similar to Jewish *kosher* restrictions are Islamic *halal* (literally, "allowed") rules, which forbid pork, alcohol, and other substances and actions. The Hua of Papua New Guinea not only had rules for what foods could and could not be eaten by different kinds of people, but believed that food transmitted a spiritual

substance called *nu* (Meigs, 1984). *Nu* was present in foodstuffs and all material, including human beings, and was passed between people directly by physical contact as well as indirectly through food exchanges.

Food is not the only realm of consumption studied by anthropologists. Boas' student, Alfred Kroeber (1919), used fashions in clothing to make basic points about the process of culture change. Karen Tranberg Hansen (2004) recently surveyed a century of "anthropological perspectives on clothing, fashion, and culture." One topic of special interest in clothing is Muslim women's dress, which many in the West perceive as restrictive and fashionless. Yet, Muslim women have found ways to be pious and fashionable at the same time, and designers and retailers like Artizara (www.artizara.com) and Muslima Wear (muslimawear.com) have emerged to serve that market.

Finally, of course, homes and home furnishings carry charged cultural messages, as Veblen explained. In contemporary Macedonia, ethnic Albanians (predominantly Muslims) are often more prosperous than native Macedonians, as Albanians are more likely to migrate to and make their fortunes in Western Europe or the United States. When they

PIOUS, MODEST, AND FASHIONABLE: CLOTHING FOR THE MODERN URBAN MUSLIM WOMAN

IMAGE 7.6 Meat and other goods produced in conformity to Islamic religious norms of consumption are classified and sold as *halal*.

BOX 7.3   REAL PEOPLE AND FAKE BRANDS: CLOTHING BETWEEN TURKEY AND ROMANIA

In the contemporary world of conspicuous consumption, brand names are valuable. Famous brands attract sales for the manufacturers and convey status for the consumers and, in the case of clothing, the wearers. We tend to think—and manufacturers want us to think—that fake brands are inauthentic at best, inferior at worst, but as Magdalena Crăciun contends, some fakes are of comparable quality and not really "fake," but rather damaged originals, overstock, or copies made on the side. In Turkey, one site of the global production of clothing, it is sometimes the same factories that make "originals" and "fakes," blurring the line between the two categories. At the workshop level, Turkish shop owners take orders from celebrated Western labels but often end up with excess inventory, which they sell to wholesalers or retailers. "One could easily claim these products were originals: the same fabrics, patterns, stitches, and packaging were used for the garments as for the originals" (Crăciun, 2014: 50). Some manufacturers intentionally produce a separate line of lower-quality items to sell to "those less discerning customers . . . in search of fashionable but cheap garments" (51). At the retail level, store owners like Ismail know that they are selling "counterfeits," some of which are overstock of the authentic item, some of which are rejected by the big companies for "some tiny invisible defects," and some of which "were manufactured on the same premises and with the same materials as the originals" (56). Rather than feeling like a criminal, Ismail believes that selling "imitations could be seen as something good, a way of helping the poor, facilitating their access to products they coveted, but could not possibly afford because of the exaggerated prices practiced by the brands" (57). He even considers his business "a form of free advertisement" for the big brands. Many of these items are shipped to Eastern Europe, where Romanians shop for and wear them with a mixture of pride and embarrassment. Some like fakes for their "affordability and availability," while others are more concerned with the materiality, the physical quality and comfort, of the clothes than with the fancy label. Still others are quite proud of their fake goods: The shoppers view them as "new garments for smart thrifty consumers" (94), and they are rather pleased with their cleverness in getting a fake for a low price, the fakeness of the item being "completely disregarded" (98).

BOX 7.4   CONTEMPORARY CULTURAL CONTROVERSIES: STUDYING CONSUMPTION OR MANIPULATING CONSUMPTION?

Modern market practices have not only come to dominate economic activity in industrialized Western societies, but have become worldwide forces, shaping a national and global "buyosphere" (Hine, 2003). The power of market concepts and behaviors to reconfigure social relations has been noted, from Max Weber's seminal study of the relation between capitalism and Protestantism to anthropologist Daniel Miller's *A Theory of Shopping* (1998). One of the most ubiquitous aspects of contemporary consumption, economies, and societies is advertising, the deliberate attempt to encourage buying through shaping desires, tastes, and the meaning of goods and services. Anthropologists have certainly studied advertising, such as McCabe and Malefyt's (2010) evaluation of the ad campaigns of Cadillac and Infiniti, or Brian Moeran's (1996) study of a Japanese advertising agency. Others, including Timothy de Waal Malefyt himself, have gone further and participated in the creation of ad campaigns, using anthropological knowledge and methods to advise companies how to better market their wares to the public. Malefyt and co-author Robert Morais recommend that "universities can and should do more to train anthropologists for work in the corporate world" and that "anthropology departments should partner with business schools and offer joint MA/MBA and PhD/MBA degrees" (Malefyt and Morais, 2012: 152). What do you think?

return, they "display their wealth by purchasing commodities such as clothes, cars, and, notably, decorations for the interiors and exteriors of their houses" (Dimova, 2013: 57–58), including furniture that Rozita Dimova characterizes as "baroque"— plush, ornate objects (some literally made by a company called Barok). This conspicuous consumption declares their "modernity" and marks them from their Macedonian hosts, who are often galled by their own relative poverty in their own country.

SUMMARY

Every society has an economic dimension to its culture, even if it does not have factories and money and supermarkets. Those are specific ways of doing an economy, not the definition of economy. An economy is the practices and institutions, and the associated beliefs and values and roles, involved in transforming the environment into usable products for humans. As such, the economic behaviors of a society will dramatically influence other aspects of the society, including how humans organize themselves and assign tasks and values and meanings to work, objects, and humans themselves.

In its first decades, anthropologists focused on "primitive economies," identifying and analyzing four major production systems (although a specific society's economy may combine or modify them in various ways):

- foraging
- pastoralism
- horticulture
- intensive agriculture

Three major distribution systems, which may co-exist in a society, have also been described:

- reciprocity
- redistribution
- market exchange

In the later twentieth century, an "economic anthropology" matured, jettisoning its preoccupation with "primitive economies" and applying anthropological concepts and methods to modern economic processes and institutions including work, the corporation, money and finance, and the informal economy.

Finally, although it is has not been studied and systematized as extensively as other economic questions, consumption has been recognized as a cultural concept and practice in which the roles, values, statuses, and meanings of goods and social relationships and situations converge in the actual use of cultural products.

MCQS

FILL IN THE BLANKS

WWW

Key Terms

adaptation	informal economy	peasant
civilization	intensive agriculture	reciprocity
division of labor	market exchange	redistribution
domestication	means of production	relations of production
foraging	mode of production	slash-and-burn
horticulture	neolithic	swidden
industrialism	pastoralism	

8 Kinship and non-kin organization

Creating social groups

The Na or Mosuo, an ethnic group in western China, traditionally had no institution of—indeed, no term for—marriage. It was considered undesirable, even anti-social, to enter into such an exclusive, emotionally intense, and volatile relationship as a marriage. According to Cai Hua, the Na were a firmly matrilineal society, in which women controlled the household, did the bulk of the productive labor, and maintained remarkable social and sexual freedom. Women (and men) "freely engage in sexual relations with several partners and change them whenever they so desire" (Hua, 2001: 20). The preferred arrangement was called *nana sésé* or "furtive visit," in which the man snuck into the woman's house (supposedly undetected by her family). In some instances the man might offer small gifts to his paramour, but there was no assumption of a long-term bond, and if a child was conceived, the man had no responsibility for it. The idea and word "father" was literally lacking among the Mosuo: "I have not found any term that would cover the notion of father in the Na language" (20). Likewise, "Na vocabulary cannot directly signify the terms: fiancé, engagement, wedding, marriage, to marry, to wed, and to divorce" (303). Children were raised and remained in their mother's home,

and leaving that home to cohabitate alone with a partner was deemed bad behavior.

There is no society on earth in which humans live, work, and fill all of their needs in isolation from each other; such would be the very opposite of a society. Rather, humans build relationships and groups to accomplish their ends and enjoy their lives. The kinds of relationships and groups they can form are incredibly diverse, but they form them for various and particular reasons, love and reproduction being just two. Humans also cooperatively produce and distribute and consume wealth, establish residences, solve problems and exercise power, and create and perpetuate identities. The solitary individual could not make or perpetuate these social arrangements and institutions. It is groups of people who share in tasks, results, and interests.

There are many types of human groups, including crowds and classrooms. Each has its own dynamics and its own "culture." However, the most socially significant groups are what we can call **corporate groups**, collectivities that act and to an extent think as a single "body" (*corps*) in regard to such practical concerns as production, distribution, consumption, ownership, decision-making,

Corporate group
a social group that shares some degree of practical interest, identity, residence, and destiny

residence, inheritance, and ultimately identity or destiny. They are the ones who see themselves as "in this together," who "look out for each other," who "face the future as one." Accordingly, family or kinship is one way to provide this structure, but hardly the only way. In this chapter, then, we will consider the cross-cultural possibilities and necessities of kinship—the diverse ways in which people can arrange themselves into "family" groups and assign those groups not only tasks but meaning—and we will investigate other social principles and relationships that supplement if not replace kinship for organizing society.

CORPORATE GROUPS: THE FUNDAMENTAL STRUCTURE OF HUMAN SOCIETIES

A society is not just a group of humans, but a group of groups, a structured constellation of collectivities. The most important and enduring of these are corporate groups. Corporate groups are the basic organizational and functional units of a society. The kinds of functions they provide vary by the society and by the specific corporate group, but they can include such things as:

Regulating behavior or establishing rights for members, as well as between members of disparate groups. Like a business corporation, each group is a system of interrelated roles, with rules for their interaction.

Owning property. A corporate group is often if not ordinarily an ownership entity, collectively possessing rights or title to land, buildings, wealth, and other resources.

Producing and distributing wealth. A corporate group is frequently a "work" group, which accomplishes productive tasks together and shares the fruits of that labor among the members.

Inheriting property. A corporate group often aims to keep its wealth and resources within the group when members pass away. Thus, it may establish a sequence of ownership and rights for the transference of property from current to future members.

Consuming and residing. A corporate group, since it may produce and distribute together, may also consume together. It may give members a place to eat or to sleep (although it is not necessary that all of the functions of the members are conducted together).

Providing for the social and emotional needs of members. The individuals in corporate groups have needs other than physical and material ones, and the group may satisfy those needs through meaningful social interactions, camaraderie, and even affection.

Creating a sense of identity. A corporate group regularly shapes the sense of self of the members, giving them a common "name" and a feeling of belonging to something greater and more enduring than themselves. This identity can translate into a sense of destiny as well—that they have a future *as* a collectivity and will collectively face that future.

Perpetuating the group over time. Any group has a future only if it can perpetuate itself. Corporate groups have various mechanisms for obtaining new members (reproduction, adoption, capture, hiring, etc.) and inculcating them with the skills or values of the group. Perpetuating groups often entails perpetuating social statuses—and status differences. In other words, poor or subordinate groups tend to reproduce poverty or subordination, and rich or powerful groups tend to reproduce wealth and power.

Establishing alliances between groups. Societies also provide mechanisms for making (and breaking) relationships between groups with different members, interests, and identities. Corporate groups can enter or find themselves in diverse connections with each other, over the short or long term. These relations can be mutually beneficial, mutually exploitative, or beneficial for one and exploitative for the other.

Any society consists of a network of such corporate groups, some deeply important, some trivial, and no single corporate group must fulfill all of these functions. Such groups can consequently be constructed on the basis of any number of natural or cultural characteristics of their members. Of the wide array of possible corporate foundations, we

Residence
the kinship principle concerning where people live, especially after marriage, and therefore what kinds of residential and corporate groups are found in the society and what tasks and values they are assigned

IMAGE 8.1 Two mothers and their children from the Samantha tribe, India.

Marriage

a socially recognized relationship between two (or more) people that establishes a kin-based group and that provides norms and roles for residence, property ownership and inheritance, labor, sexual relations, and childrearing

FAMILIES AND FACTIONS IN SICILY

Descent

the kinship principle of tracing membership in a kin-based corporate group through a sequence of ancestors

can distinguish two general types: groups that are based on kinship ties or relations and those that are based on other, non-kinship qualities or characteristics. In any society, both of these types of groups will co-exist, and any particular individual is simultaneously a member of one (or more than one) kinship group as well as multiple non-kinship groups. This creates bonds with kin and non-kin alike, often of different types and functions and sometimes competing or conflicting with each other.

KINSHIP-BASED CORPORATE GROUPS

"For seventy-five years the subject of kinship has occupied a special and important position in social anthropology," wrote Radcliffe-Brown almost seventy-five years ago (1941: 1). As early as 1871, Lewis Henry Morgan realized that kinship consisted of two very different kinds of factors, which we commonly distinguish as "blood relations" (technically, consanguinity) and "in-law" or marital relations (affinity). In 1924, W. H. R. Rivers added the crucial observation that kinship cannot be reckoned merely in terms of the "facts" of blood ties: Even fatherhood and motherhood, he declared, "depend, not on procreation and parturition, but on social convention, and it is evident that blood-relationship is quite inadequate as a means of defining kinship" (1996: 52). Further, as the present chapter claims, kinship is only one example of what

he called "social grouping," including also political, occupational, religious, gender, race, ethnic, and national categories.

Anthropologists analyze any kinship system as a product of three interconnected principles or concepts, namely:

■ **marriage**
■ **residence**
■ **descent**

Marriage might be thought of as the "horizontal" principle, which links individuals (and groups) together and establishes new groups. Residence is the geographic or spatial principle, the site where people actually live or perform their corporate activities. Descent constitutes the "vertical" or temporal principle, linking individuals and groups through time and "down" between the generations. Each of these principles or concepts comes in diverse forms and in various combinations, giving the society's kinship system its unique contours.

Marriage

Marriage is the first step in constructing kinship-based corporate groups. Marriage brings together individuals from different kin groups and binds them into one, or the other, or a new group. As always, anthropologists must build a definition that is inclusive, not simply impose their own cultural notion of marriage on all societies and assume that how their culture does marriage *really is* marriage and that if another culture does it differently, theirs is not "really marriage." Even in Western societies, marriage is a contentious issue. Is marriage only between a man and a woman? That is, can members of the same sex marry? Is marriage between only one man and only one woman? Is marriage only between two *living* people?

Marriage across cultures has certain core characteristics but a great degree of flexibility. Wherever it is found, it is a socially recognized relationship between (two or more) individuals and often between their families as well. It has enduring if not permanent qualities, and it establishes various kinds of rights and obligations. Marriage can and usually does include economic functions (shared labor or other productive activities, distribution and consumption, ownership, inheritance, and so on), political functions (establishment and enforcement of rules, decision-making, and problem-solving for members), and of course sexual and reproductive functions. Societies universally culturize the physical act of sex by elaborating rules and norms for who, how, when, where, and so on. In some societies, this is more critical than others: Some have fairly lax norms about sex and "fidelity" (including "premarital" sex) and some have harsh restrictions, down to premarital virginity sanctioned with the death penalty. The most common "rule" across human societies is the famous **incest taboo**, that members of the same "family" do not ordinarily have sexual access to each other, although again, "family" is a highly diverse term.

One of the key aspects of marriage relates to children. Children are of course necessary in order to expand and perpetuate a kinship group. Childbearing is an important function of marriage in virtually all societies, although not of all marriages, since many married people choose not to have children. It goes without saying that marriage is not necessary for making babies—it is again a way that society culturizes the biological function of reproduction. Many societies do deem that marriage is a prerequisite to produce "socially acceptable" or

Incest taboo
the nearly universal rule against marrying or having sex with kin

---

BOX 8.1   MARRIED FOR A DAY . . . OR AN HOUR: TEMPORARY MARRIAGE IN IRAN

Although it is controversial even in their own country, Shahla Haeri reports that contemporary Iran has a form of temporary marriage called *mut'a*, defined as "a contract, *'aqd*, in which a man and an unmarried woman decide how long they want to stay married to each other, and how much money is to be given to the temporary wife" (2014: 1). The specified duration may be as long as ninety-nine years and as short as an hour. Interestingly, rather than declining in recent years, the practice has received official support under the Shi'ite regime: *Mut'a* "actually is perceived to combat corruption and immorality," and "the more religiously inclined Iranians view it as a divinely rewarded activity" (6) that earns *savab* or religious merit. To comprehend this unusual institution, we must grasp Muslim concepts of marriage and sexuality. Haeri asserts that Shi'a Muslims view marriage "as a 'contract of exchange' that involves 'a sort of ownership'" (ix)—specifically a man's ownership of a woman's sexuality and quite literally her vagina. Further, sex and pleasure are considered quite natural, but must also be socially regulated; premarital and extramarital sex are disdained, but sexual abstinence is also regarded as abnormal, especially for men. So, rather than commit "adultery" or "fornication," men are allowed to contract short-term marriages to satisfy their sexual desires. Temporary *mut'a* marriages are distinguished from permanent marriages (*nikah*) because permanent marriage creates not only sexual ownership, but also "bonds of affinal kinship" (35) and ultimately children. Looking more deeply into the practice, Haeri finds that there is also a form of nonsexual *mut'a* that simply permits men and women to mix socially without the strictures of gender seclusion; thus, a couple may enter a temporary marriage so that they can travel together or inhabit the same space. Finally, while it is appealing to see temporary marriage as exploiting women, Haeri discovers that the motivations of women to choose the institution are diverse and complex, from their own sexual desires to the wish for male companionship and a home to, admittedly, the financial advantages.

WHAT'S LOVE GOT TO DO WITH IT? AN ANTHROPOLOGY OF LOVE

Social reproduction
the maintenance and perpetuation of society beyond mere childbearing, including enculturation and teaching of members to take their place in society and day-to-day activities to allow members of society to perform their specified tasks (including what is sometimes called "housework")

Exogamy
the marriage principle in which an individual marries someone who is not in the same cultural category as him/herself (e.g. marrying someone of a different sex or gender)

Endogamy
the marriage principle in which an individual marries someone who is in the same cultural category as him/herself (e.g. marrying someone in your own race or religion)

THE WARLPIRI SUBSECTION SYSTEM

"legitimate" children. But birth is hardly the end of the member-making process. Children must be cared for and instructed, that is, *enculturated*, which is a typical though never exclusive function of family. Children must learn the social and practical skills they need to participate in society—from language and "manners" to gender roles and economic skills. Some societies feature full-time professional institutions to contribute to this process (like schools), but the family is always a place where it occurs first if not most. We can think, more broadly, of the care and teaching of children as one crucial part of the general concern of **social reproduction**, that is, reproducing social groups and institutions over time, including over generations.

Another major and often overlooked element of social reproduction is the reproduction of labor. In the short term, laborers must be prepared for the next day's labor. The marriage relationship and resultant family is where much of this work occurs, including feeding the laborers, cleaning their clothes, providing them a place to sleep, and so on. In the "anthropology of housework," researchers in recent decades have investigated the various activities that are required to insure that the group and the society can continue from day to day—activities that are overwhelmingly associated with women but have become more problematic in societies where women are also wage laborers.

Finally, marriage can be effective in establishing alliances between families. Practices like arranged marriage and marriage exchanges suggest that marriage is often more than a relationship between the individuals entering into the bond. Often, and explicitly in many cases, the marriage is actually a relationship or alliance between families. Royal marriages in European history were frequently quite self-conscious in their intentions to unify powerful or rich "houses" or noble families, and entire countries have been created through such marriages. On a more mundane level, families may seek to marry their children to other specific families for economic, political, or status reasons. The alliance between families may be more important to both sides than the particular marriage at hand, as indicated by ways in which they may strive to sustain the alliance even if the marriage fails in some way.

We should not ignore the pleasant emotional potential of marriage for partners. Neither should we overestimate it. In Western societies, love is regarded as the best reason and reward for marriage, but this opinion is not universally shared. Many marriages cross-culturally are arranged, often between individuals who may not even know each other, let alone love each other. If the marriage grows into love, that is wonderful, but the marriage does not depend on it. Westerners tend to privilege the romantic aspect of marriage, but not all societies share this infatuation with love. Some actually consider love undesirable or inappropriate in marriage, since marriage is serious social business, while love can be so intense and volatile.

Who to marry?

The first question that a society's marriage system must address is whom one can or should marry (that is, who is an eligible partner), which leads to a basic distinction between **exogamy** and **endogamy**. These terms are elusive, because they do not refer to a society as a whole, but to groups or categories within society: Any particular marriage will be exogamous in regard to some groups and categories, and endogamous in regard to others. Most simply, exogamy (*exo* for "outside" and *gamy* for "marriage") means marriage to someone who is "outside" of (not a member of) one's own group or category, while endogamy (*endo* for "inside") means marriage to someone who is "inside" or a member of one's group or category. For instance, most societies have an exogamous rule or preference—even a quite strong one, sometimes a formal or "legal" one—in regard to sex or gender: You should marry someone who is not a member of your own gender—while almost all societies observe basic kin-group exogamy, that you should not marry someone who is a member of your kin group. Similarly, there is a tendency (more or less explicit or formal) toward endogamy in terms of age or social class or race and ethnicity or religion or locality. For instance, although the U.S. does not have a "race endogamy" law, in times and places in the past it did, and most American marriages today are still racially endogamous, even if most Americans do not disapprove of interracial marriages.

IMAGE 8.2 A traditional wedding ceremony on the island of Vanuatu.

How many to marry?

Within the general limitations of exogamy and endogamy, societies ordinarily specify how many people an individual can marry. There are fundamentally only two choices (one or more than one), but anthropologists refine this distinction, identifying three systems:

Monogamy (*mono* for "one")—the individual can only marry one person. The most common form is heterosexual monogamy, one man married to one woman; homosexual marriage of course could also be monogamous. We should also acknowledge what we might call **"serial" monogamy**, in which a person can have only one spouse at a time, but may have several spouses over a lifetime. Modern Americans on average marry more than once in their lives; American monogamy then prohibits multiple *simultaneous* marriages, but allows multiple *consecutive* marriages.

Polygyny (*poly* for "many" and *gyn* for "woman")—a man may or should marry two or more women. While this seems abnormal, even perverse, to many Westerners, it is in fact the most common marriage rule or preference cross-culturally. Somewhere

between seventy and eighty percent of the world's known societies have condoned multiple wives for men. This can be seen as, and often is, a means of male domination or at least a manifestation of male status and power. However, women are not always the helpless victims of polygyny; women in many societies welcome co-wives into the home (or sometimes a homestead consisting of multiple households, one for each woman and her children) for purposes of shared housework, female companionship, and division among them of the husband's sexual demands. Women often feel that it is bad for a woman to sit alone in the household, and "first wives" may go so far as to play a role in selecting co-wives for their husbands. Men may marry sisters, termed **sororal polygyny**, which promises (but does not guarantee) more domestic tranquility. Finally, in many polygynous societies, one or a few dominant males may monopolize the women, leaving other men with one wife or none. The Tiwi of Melville and Bathurst Islands north of Australia, a foraging society in which a few old men monopolized the young women, found an ingenious solution: A man was not allowed to marry at all until he reached the age of thirty or more, and his first wife would usually be an older woman, widowed from her own previous marriage to a

Monogamy
the marriage rule in which an individual may have only one spouse

Serial monogamy
the marriage practice of having only one spouse at a time but perhaps having more than one spouse, at different times, during one's life

Polygyny
the marriage rule in which a man can or should marry two or more women

Sororal polygyny
the marriage practice in which a man marries two or more sisters

much older man. Thus, every man and every woman married several times at various stages of life to spouses at various stages of their own lives (C. W. M. Hart and Pilling, 1960).

Polyandry
the marriage rule in which a woman can or should marry two or more men

Polyandry (*andro* for "man")—a woman may or should marry two or more men. This marriage form is particularly rare, observed in less than one percent of known societies, including the Toda of southern India, the Pacific Island Marquesans, and the Tibetans. Often, a woman will marry a set of brothers, bearing children for all of them. The children may be assigned "social fatherhood" to the senior brother, since physical fatherhood cannot be known and is culturally irrelevant, or social fatherhood may be assigned to various husbands for various children. The "problem" of paternity might be one reason why polyandry is so rare.

Arranged marriage
a practice in which family members (often parents) choose the partner for marriageable youths, sometimes with little or no input from or option for the partners themselves

How is wealth involved in marriage?

A third question in marriage is how precisely individuals establish the relationship. In some societies, the procedure was as informal as a man leaving gifts of food or other goods at the household of a woman; if she accepted the gifts and welcomed him in, they took up residence and were recognized as married. Among the Cheyenne, a man announced

Hypergamy
the marriage practice of marrying "up" with a spouse in a higher status, class, or caste than oneself

to his kin his desire to marry. If they approved, they would gather wealth and deliver it to the woman's parents. If her kin accepted the pairing, the wealth was distributed among her family, and the following day her kin would return gifts of equal value (Hoebel, 1960).

However, in many societies marriage is a much more elaborate affair that occupies the interest of entire families if not entire communities. Many societies traditionally practiced—and many still practice today—**arranged marriage**, in which the families of prospective marriage partners make the selection and plan the event. The partners may not know each other at all, may never have even seen each other, and typically do not "date" before the marriage; unchaperoned dating is a unique characteristic of Western courtship and a relatively modern one at that. Arranged marriages illustrate quite clearly not only that marriage is an alliance-building institution in many cases, but also that it is a device and field for male social dominance, as men plan marriages for their sons and daughters. Especially in situations of **hypergamy** (*hyper* for "up" or "high"), families may be seeking to raise their overall social status by marrying their daughter to a richer or more prestigious family, which may expose their women to potential abuse and even death.

BOX 8.2   THE POLITICS OF MARRIAGE AMONG THE KALASHA

Three thousand Kalasha—non-Muslims in a sea of Islam—live in the northwest of Pakistan. One of the ways in which they declare their difference from surrounding Muslim peoples is their endorsement of love-marriages, as opposed to the arranged marriages customary in neighboring societies. Indeed, although many Kalasha marriages too are arranged, at least initially, Wynne Maggi contends that the "cultural right that young Kalasha people claim to translate love and longing into marriage, unique in this very conservative region, is a central marker of Kalasha ethnicity" (2006: 82). It is not the only marker, however: The Kalasha themselves assert that "our women are free," and they express their freedom by dressing brightly, dancing and singing in public, even drinking wine and showing their faces without a veil (86). This female freedom extends into marriage: Women can decide to leave a marriage, and husbands "are well aware that they have a few short years to win their 'little wife's' affection and loyalty" (84). This is why the men and their kin ply the wives with gifts, from food treats to consumer goods. Because they respect their children's choices, parents often submit to their children's love-preferences even when a marriage arrangement has been negotiated, but when the parents do not, the young lovers have the cultural option to elope. But young people have one other weapon they can use against intransigent parents—the threat of conversion to Islam.

By converting, the couple would escape the authority of their parents and of Kalasha traditions. They would be married by a mullah and bound in a new moral community. Converting to Islam is a desperate act, because it is irrevocable—but for this very reason it is an effective threat that gives young lovers powerful leverage in these emotionally charged situations.

(87–88)

Thus, unhappy parents are likely to capitulate to their children's wishes for a love-match, rather than lose them altogether to a foreign religion. One wonders how real this threat is, however, since the young lovers would be giving up so much—including the woman's cherished freedom—in order to get their way in marriage.

Marriages, whether arranged or not, often are accompanied or even accomplished by property exchanges. This signals both the economic and contractual and the alliance aspects of marriage. Of course, while in American society there are minor wealth exchanges at weddings (e.g. guests bring gifts), some societies hand over substantial amounts of wealth in planning or consummating a marriage. The main forms this can take are:

Bridewealth or **brideprice**—In this practice, a man gives wealth to the bride's family, usually her male kin, in order to make the marriage. Nearly half of all recorded societies have done this, and it correlates to male social power and prestige, since men are not only giving and receiving wealth, but women are often not included in the negotiations nor are they recipients of the wealth themselves. This can sometimes be construed as "buying a wife," virtually treating women like property. However, more often it is viewed as compensation to the woman's family for the loss that her departure will mean—particularly, loss of her production (household work) and of her reproduction (the children she will bear). The woman's status in her marital family is often quite low, at least until she bears a child, preferably a son. However, in some cases today even a child does not enhance her status much. Bridewealth is especially closely associated with pastoral societies, where men dominate and have transferable wealth to offer, namely their herds. Thus, a man will typically offer a woman's male relatives a certain number of animals in exchange for her hand in marriage, and a father may search for the best bridewealth offer for his daughter, meaning that men with much wealth will be able to arrange more and "better" marriages

for themselves and their sons than less wealthy men can.

Bride service—In societies where men are expected to give something in exchange but real "wealth" does not exist, they may be required to provide service instead. For example, in foraging societies a man may be obligated to bring meat from his hunts to the woman's family for a period of years before the marriage is considered fully made or before he can remove her to his family. The Torah or Old Testament story of Jacob and his efforts to marry Rachel is an example of the institution of bride service, wherein he was asked to labor for her father (Laban, his own mother's brother, making Rachel his first cousin; see Genesis 29) before he could marry her.

Dowry—Much less commonly, the woman's family gives wealth to the man in order to make the marriage; in a few cases, the wealth may go the couple or even to the woman herself. In some societies this is interpreted as an "early inheritance" of her parents' property; however, when the wealth is transferred to her husband or his parents, it is hard to see how this constitutes an inheritance to her. In fact, the system of dowry can be a real disadvantage to the woman and her family and can be yet another path to male domination; not surprisingly, it is found in societies, like pre-revolutionary China, parts of India, and even the U.S. in the past, where men were or are dominant. The heavy burden of providing a dowry can make parents averse to having female children; as one advertisement for an India abortion clinic starkly framed it, "Pay 500 rupees now [for an abortion] or 50,000 in 18 years [for a dowry]" (Sen, 2002). China's government has

Bride service
the marriage wealth-exchange practice in which a man must labor for his wife's kin for some period of time before he may assume rights over his wife

Bridewealth/bride price
the marriage wealth-exchange practice in which a man or his family must pay an amount of property to his wife's kin before he may assume rights over his wife

Dowry
the marriage wealth-exchange practice in which the woman's family is required to provide the husband with property (money, land, household goods, etc.) in order to make the marriage

Sen, Mala. 2002. *Death by Fire: Sati, Dowry Death, and Female Infanticide in Modern India*. New Brunswick, NJ: Rutgers University Press.

IMAGE 8.3 Great amounts of wealth may be displayed and transferred in dowry or bridewealth.

Evans-Pritchard, E. E. 1951. *Kinship and Marriage among the Nuer.* New York: Oxford University Press

Levirate

a marriage practice in which the brother of a deceased man is expected to marry his brother's widow

Sororate

a marriage practice in which a woman is expected to marry the husband of her sister in the event of the married sister's death

outlawed extravagant dowries (although they still occur), which place an exorbitant drain on parents and highly discourage raising daughters.

It is worth mentioning a few other notable marriage practices that put the institution in perspective. The **levirate** specifically entails that another man from the groom's family, ideally a brother, should marry the widow if her husband dies. This practice tends to be associated with male-dominated societies and families and with the high value of male children; in fact, in many cases any children issuing from the "second marriage" may still be attributed to the first (dead) husband. The practice also says something about the contractual and alliance nature of marriage, where the alliance outlives its human members. The **sororate** is the opposite, in which a widower is provided with a sister or other female relative of his dead wife. In so-called "ghost marriage" among the Nuer of East Africa, a woman could be married to a man who had already died, particularly if he died young without children. As her ghost-husband, any children she later had (not by him, obviously) were looked upon as his children, who would continue his male line

and perform rituals and ceremonies for him (Evans-Pritchard, 1951). As a final example, among at least upper-caste Newars of Nepal, girls are put through a series of two (or three, depending on what qualifies) marriages, beginning with *Ihi* marriage while still pre-pubescent. During a three-day ritual, young girls are married to a *bel* fruit, symbolic of Vishnu or the Buddha. While occasionally derided as a mock marriage, Gutschow, Michaels, and Bau insist that it is a quite important initiation ritual introducing a girl to her lineage before her marriage to a man permanently transfers her to his lineage. At least as meaningfully, Newar parents claim that once a female is married to a god she can never become a widow, even if her human husband dies. "Consequently, the 'real' marriage with a human groom is regarded (at the time of *Ihi*) as a secondary marriage" (Gutschow, Michaels, and Bau, 2008: 158), and a girl who has not undergone *Ihi* may have a hard time finding a human spouse. In between *Ihi* and human marriage, girls also undertake a twelve-day seclusion, called *Barha chuyega* or *Barha tayegu*, which some observers consider another marriage (to the sun) between their divine and human weddings.

Residence

The second principle of kinship systems concerns who actually lives together in local domestic groups. Residence is not essential for corporate behavior, but it definitely is a convenience; furthermore, people who form a residential unit will almost necessarily act corporately. We can thus think of residence as the spatial or geographic element of kinship.

Anthropologists make a distinction between a family or kindred and a household. A **family** or **kindred** is roughly all the people to whom a person considers him/herself related by blood or marriage. It is not probably or even possibly a residential group, since it is too large and dispersed to live in one house, or even one compound or neighborhood. A **household** is all the people who live together "under one roof" and act corporately within that residence. Obviously just as not all of a family or kindred shares one household, not all of the people who share a household need be family or kindred; people can and do live in non-kin residential groups, as when a set of roommates shares a house or apartment. They may still be corporate in the sense of preparing and consuming food, owning property, and sharing responsibility for expenses, though they are not related by kinship.

Nevertheless, kinship and residence tend to overlap, and most residential groups or households are also kin groups. Anthropologists, therefore, regard residence as one of the building blocks not only of kinship but of corporateness in general. The kinds of corporate residential groups formed by residence practices will significantly shape society. There is a finite set of possibilities, although they can be mixed and modified in various ways.

Patrilocality or **virilocality** (*patri* for "father" or *viri* for "man"). The vast majority of societies (approaching seventy percent) typically settled married couples in or near the residence of the husband and his family. Men brought their wives into the household, and women left their childhood homes to reside in their husband's household. The resulting household consisted of related men (fathers and sons, brothers, uncles and nephews, and so on) and their in-marrying wives as well as the children born to the spouses. They might all live in one big house, perhaps with separate corners or cooking areas for marital groups, or perhaps in

separate houses in a family "compound." Either way, patrilocality tended to enhance male status and power, since daughters left their own household to move into their husband's. Thus, men remained to own and control the property, whereas women lived in places where they did not own and control much of anything. Worse yet, women were sometimes distantly separated from the male kinsmen who could protect and defend them; alone in their husband's household, surrounded by his male kin, women were at a distinct disadvantage.

Matrilocality or **uxorilocality** (*matri* for "mother" or *uxori* for "wife"). A much smaller percentage (less than fifteen percent) of societies advocated that people live in or near the residence of the woman and her family. Women brought their husbands into the home, and men departed for their wives' homes. Here, the resulting household contained related women (mothers and daughters, sisters, and so on) and their in-marrying husbands plus their joint children. This practice tended to enhance female status, since women tended to own and control the property, land, and wealth. Men were separated from their own families and allies and cast among related females, and their access to wealth and property might depend on their wife's family. Such an arrangement would be conducive to horticultural economies, where women often formed important land-holding and farm-laboring corporate groups.

Avunculocality (*avuncu* for "uncle"). In a small number of societies (perhaps four percent), married people preferentially lived with or near the man's mother's brother. This was essentially an adaptation to male property rights in a society that traced group membership through women (see below). In such a system, a man's maternal uncle was a kinsman in a way that his paternal uncle was not; the effect was to live with the most important male relative in the kinship universe.

Ambilocality (*ambi* for "both" or "either"). Somewhat more often (nine percent), married people were either free to choose which household to live with or elected to divide their time between the two households. This was a useful adaptation for societies that lived in difficult environments or low-yield economies, which gave them maximal

Kindred

an ego-centered (that is, reckoned from the perspective of some particular individual) category of persons related by kinship, especially in bilateral societies, including members from "both sides" of the family in older and younger generations

Household

all of the people who live in the same house or compound of houses and act for some or all purposes as a corporate group

Multilocal

the residence practice of living with or near the wife's family after marriage

Avunculocal

a residence practice in which a married couple lives with or near an uncle, often a mother's brother

Patrilocal

the residence practice of living with or near the husband's family after marriage

Ambilocal

a residence practice in which individuals may live after marriage with both "sides" of the family (perhaps alternating between them), or optionally with one or the other flexibility in their living arrangements. One place we might expect to find it, then, was in foraging societies, where nuclear families may need to travel and camp with the man's family at certain times and the woman's family at others.

Neolocal

the residence practice in which married people start their own household apart from their parents' or families' households

Neolocality (*neo* for "new"). In a surprisingly small minority of societies (five percent), married people preferred or were expected to start a new household on their own, apart from either family. While this is the norm in most Western societies, that fact simply reinforces the conclusion that Western ways are often quite exceptional among the cultures of the world. Neolocal residence tends to produce small households, since kindreds split into nuclear units. It further requires a fair amount of wealth—and wealth in the hands of young people—since it is not cheap to own and furnish a home for each marital couple. Accordingly, neolocal residence is suited to intensive agriculture and perhaps even more to industrial and post-industrial societies. Not only are individuals and nuclear families fairly rich and independent, but labor needs to be mobile, since the family may be called upon to relocate in search of work. Neolocal households also maximize consumption, since each household requires a complete set of furnishings.

Within these ideal types, considerable variation and complication exists. According to their ethnographers, neither the Ulithi (Pacific Islands) nor the Dani (New Guinea) had residential nuclear families. The Ulithi nuclear family was not a "commensal" group, that is, they did not eat together; eating arrangements and living arrangements did not coincide in any serious way (Lessa, 1966). Heider asserted that the Dani lived in multi-family compounds and that it was

> hopeless even to try to generalize about the composition's population. One can find

unrelated nuclear families, polygynous families, families extended vertically into three or even four generations or laterally with siblings and cousins, as well as the odd singleton unrelated to anyone.

(1979: 76)

Cheyenne nuclear or conjugal families were organized into what Hoebel (1960) called kindreds, which were matrilocal groups that camped together; these kindreds were further aggregated into "bands," of which there were ten, each of which would set up camp in its own area when the whole society gathered.

Descent

Descent is the third principle in a kinship system, the vertical or chronological relationship between the generations, "coming down" from parents to children and beyond. In this sense, descent is a physical fact; children really are related to their parents and their ancestors. However, what societies choose to do with it—how they employ it to create corporate groups—is cultural and therefore culturally relative.

Societies can create all kinds of different kinship arrangements, but anthropologists have found that they can represent the entire spectrum of such relationships with a kit of only a few symbols and abbreviations. In fact, only six are required to represent most kinship relationships (see Figure 8.1).

So, in order to diagram a simple nuclear family, we can draw a triangle linked to a circle by two parallel lines, with a descent line down to one or more children, which can "branch" as often as necessary. In order to show siblings for the parents, we can draw branches above them; and in order to show multiple generations (say, the grandparents or

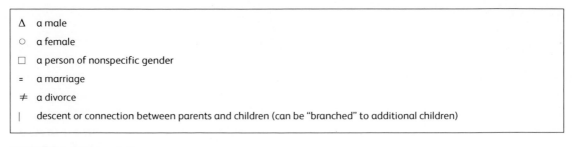

FIGURE 8.1 Kinship notation

M	for mother	Z	for sister	FZS	for father's sister's son
F	for father	H	for husband	MBW	for mother's brother's wife
S	for son	W	for wife	FF	for father's father
D	for daughter	MBD	for mother's brother's daughter	and so on	
B	for brother				

FIGURE 8.2 Kinship abbreviations

grandchildren), we can add descent lines above or below the nuclear generations depicted. To represent a deceased kinsperson, anthropologists place a slash mark through that person's symbol.

It is also useful to have abbreviations for the "absolute" relationships between people, rather than invoking ethnocentric and loaded kinship terms like "uncle" or "cousin." For more complex and inclusive kinship diagrams, we can describe literal relationships with a limited set of letters (see Figure 8.2).

With this notation, it is possible to distinguish relationships like "father's brother" (FB) or "mother's brother" (MB) instead of "uncle"—which might be an important difference in a society. Likewise, it is possible to distinguish precisely between "cousins"—"father's brother's son" (FBS) versus "mother's sister's daughter" (MZD)—or any other combination of relationships.

All societies use descent in at least some way to assign children to parents and to assign children and their parents to corporate groups. However, not all societies institutionalize descent into exclusive groups such that an individual belongs to one group and not another. When such exclusive groups are present, anthropologists call them descent groups. The easiest and most common way for a society to do this is through **unilineal descent**, that is, tracing a single "line" of related ancestors based on a shared characteristic, particularly sex. Not all, but a majority (around sixty percent), of societies utilize the concept of unilineal descent to create corporate groups that include some people and exclude others. The disadvantage of such systems is that they do exclude some kin; the advantage is that they sharply identify who is and who is not a "member" of the group. The two obvious alternatives of unilineal descent are patrilineal and matrilineal:

Patrilineal descent—Membership in the kin corporate group is reckoned through a line of male ancestors. That is to say, children belong to their father's corporate group or **lineage**. They of course know who their mother is, and they recognize her as a close relative, but she is not a member of "their group" in the same sense as their father. All siblings will belong to the same group since they all have the same father. All other relatives who can trace their relationships through the same line of related men are also members of the lineage. So, all of the father's brothers (FB) are lineage members, as are all of their children (FBS and FBD alike). Females belong to the lineage too, but they do not perpetuate it: A woman's children belong to *their* father's (her husband's) lineage, not her own. Anglo-Americans do not have a formal lineage system, but they do inherit their surname "patrilineally," at least traditionally. Of unilineal descent systems, this is by far the most common (eighty-five percent).

Matrilineal descent—Membership in the kin corporate group is traced through a line of female ancestors. In a reverse image of the patrilineal system, children belong to their mother's group or matrilineage. Siblings belong to the same lineage, but only females will continue it; a man's children belong to their mother's lineage. Since the father is not part of his children's lineage, the most important male relative may be the mother's brother (MB), their maternal uncle, who is a member of their matrilineage. However, the MB's own children will not be part of the lineage; they will belong to his wife's lineage. This is a much less common way of reckoning descent (fifteen percent), but makes sense in societies where female-centered families occur. Ulithi practiced a matrilineal descent system, in which lineages owned land and houses, maintained cooking hearths, and attended to their own ghosts at their own shrines; curiously, they also practiced patrilocal residence.

Lineage
a kinship-based corporate group composed of members related by descent from a known ancestor

Matrilineal descent
a descent system in which lineage relations are traced through a line of related females. Children belong to their mother's corporate group

Unilineal descent
a principle in which individuals trace their ancestry through a "line" of related kin (typically a male or a female line) such that some "blood" relatives are included in the descent group or lineage and other relatives are excluded from it

Patrilineal descent
a descent system in which lineage relations are traced through a line of related males. Children belong to their father's corporate group

IMAGE 8.4 Individuals belong to their mother's kinship group in matrilineal societies.

Double descent

the kinship practice of reckoning one's membership in kinship-based corporate groups through two lines of descent, ordinarily the mother's and the father's

Ambilineal descent

a descent system in which individuals trace their membership through both "sides" or "lines" of the family, or optionally through one or the other

Bilateral descent

relating to both "sides," as in a kinship system, in which individuals regard kin related to the mother and to the father as socially equivalent

Clan

a kinship group, sometimes an assortment of lineages, that can trace its descent back to a common ancestor

Phratry

a kinship-based corporate group composed of two or more clans that recognize common ancestry

Moiety

one of the "halves" of a society, when kin groups are combined in such a way as to create a binary division within society

In a few rare instances, societies may use the descent relationship to create corporate groups, but not in a unilineal manner. We refer to such systems as **double descent**, where an individual belongs to both mother's and father's groups, sometimes for different purposes. For example, among the Yako of Nigeria, people obtained access to land and forest goods through their father's line, but access to other kinds of resources (such as animals and money) through their mother's. About five percent of societies did this.

Two other possibilities include **ambilineal descent**, in which, like ambilocal residence, children may be assigned to either group by their parents or may move freely between groups during their lifetimes, and **bilateral descent**, in which children are considered to belong to both "sides" of their family equally. Ambilineal descent, also like ambilocal residence, provides the most flexibility for individuals and families. Bilateral descent, which is the standard Anglo-American form, does not create "lines" of kin at all, but rather "sides" of families and makes the least distinction between them. Some individuals might prefer their mother's or father's side, but there is no institutionalized distinction. Like neolocal residence, this form of kinship provides the most independence and mobility.

It is possible for societies to extend the descent principle for assembling even larger and more inclusive kinship groupings. The term **clan** is sometimes used to name a corporate group of related lineages, often one that cannot actually specify all of the lineal links between the members; the "founding" member may not be remembered or may be "mythical" (a spirit or animal, for instance). When two or more clans are conjoined, we have a **phratry**. And in a few cases, the various kin groups of a society may be agglomerated into two halves such that the entire society is bifurcated for at least some (perhaps ritual) purposes. We refer to such a "half of a society," the highest possible level of corporateness short of an entire society, as a **moiety,** which is commonly exogamous.

These institutions can also be surprisingly diverse. Dani society contained fifty clan-like entities, which were not territorial but did share corporate interests in marriage and ritual. These clans were combined into two named patrimoieties, called *Wida* and *Waija*. The moieties were exogamous, but strangely all children were born into the *Wida* side; around puberty, children of the other moiety were transferred to it (Heider, 1979: 64). Barabaig patrilineages were organized into clans called *dosht* that Klima (1970) described as territorial "mutual aid societies" that looked after their members (39). The sixty or so named clans were mostly autonomous, sharing few interests or institutions, and were divided into two types (not moieties), the five priestly *Daremgadyeg* clans and the fifty-five secular or "commoner" *Homat'k* clans.

Kinship terminologies

Since societies vary so widely in how they understand and use kinship relations, it figures that they would vary in how they reference kin. Every society has a set of kinship terms or names, like the English "father," "mother," "uncle," "cousin," etc. What one society calls a "cousin" might not be called, or treated like, a cousin in another. The physical relationships that underlie any set of terms are the same; how those "blood" or physical relationships are valued and used diverges greatly by culture.

There is an almost infinite variety of permutations on kinship terminology, but anthropologists have identified six basic systems, which are modified or customized according to societies' local needs and interests. Use the following kinship chart to make sense of these systems described below.

1. **Hawaiian.** This common (about one-third of societies) terminology is nearly the simplest possible one, in which a very limited set of terms is used to make a very limited set of distinctions. There are only four main terms— two for the parent's generation (one male, one female, approximately equivalent to "father" and "mother") and two for one's own generation (again, one male, one female, roughly "brother" and "sister"). So, what English speakers would call "uncle" (both MB and FB) would be called by the same term as father (F in the figure), "aunt" (MZ and FZ) would be called by the same term as mother (M in the figure), and all "cousins" would be called by the terms for brother and sister.

2. **Omaha.** This system represents a patrilineal naming convention. Parallel-cousins are called by the same term as brothers and sisters, but cross-cousins are called by different terms. Even more, cross-cousins on the mother's side are called by different terms—the same

as for B and H, respectively—than ones on the father's side. Finally, father's brothers is called the same term as father, and mother's sisters is called by the same term as mother, but father's sisters and mother's brothers are called by different terms, roughly equivalent to "aunt" and "uncle."

3. **Crow.** The Crow system is the prototype of a matrilineal naming convention. The same basic logic applies as in the Omaha, but in mirror reversal. Mother and MZ are termed the same, father and FB are termed the same, and FZ and MB each get a unique term. Parallel cousins are all called "brother" or "sister," and FZ's children are referred to by the same term as FB and FZ.

4. **Iroquois.** This system is similar to the two unilineal systems above, with one major exception. Cross-cousins on both sides (MB's children and FZ's children) are called by the same two terms—essentially, what we might translate as "male cousin" and "female cousin." Parallel cousins are still designated as "brother" and "sister."

5. **Sudanese.** This "descriptive" system is the hardest to commit to memory but the easiest to understand. It makes the most possible distinctions, using a different term for each relationship and collapsing no relationships into others; MB is not the same as FB, etc., and every possible variation of "cousin" is given a different name (that is, FBS and FZS are termed differently, ad infinitum).

6. **Eskimo.** Fairly uncommon, at about ten percent of societies, is the system that most resembles the Anglo-American one. No distinctions are made between cross- and parallel-cousins (that is, between sides of the family) nor between their parents. FB and MB are called by the same term (like "uncle"), as are FZ and MZ (like "aunt"). All cousins are distinguished by only one feature, sex (and in

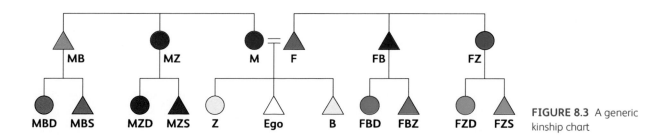

FIGURE 8.3 A generic kinship chart

English, not even by that—there are no English words that distinguish "male cousin" from "female cousin," like the French *cousin* and *cousine* or the Spanish *primo* and *prima*). The key kinship unit based on the terminology is the nuclear family.

We can think of a kinship terminology as a kind of language or code for important cultural aspects of family and kinship. The key is to appreciate that different societies have reasons to make the terminological distinctions that they do. Rather than naming people, they are naming relationships: The "cousin" relationship or the "uncle" relationship indicates a certain kind of role, feeling, and even social duty. If an individual calls two different people by the same term, then that individual's role toward them should be the same and their role toward him/her should be the same. On the other hand, if an individual calls two different people by two different terms, then his/her and their roles should be different. This is what we mean by "collapsing" different kin into the same term: If I call MB and FB by the same term, then they are culturally equivalent for me. I know they are not the same person, but what is important is how I am supposed to act toward them and they toward me. And if I call MB and FB by different terms, that indicates a culturally relevant distinction between those two kinsmen.

Some of the information that is "coded" into a system of terms—or more significantly, the statuses they name—includes:

- Generation—are they in my own, my parents', my children's generation, etc.?
- Sex or gender—are they male or female? Or, in some cases, are they the same sex as me or the opposite sex from me (i.e. relative gender)? For instance, Ulithi did not have terms that meant "brother" or "sister," but rather "sibling of my sex" or "sibling not of my sex."
- Blood vs. marriage—are they kin by descent or by marriage? In the American system, members do not even distinguish between, say, mother's brother and mother's sister's husband.
- Side of the family—are they on the mother's side or the father's side? That is not a terribly important distinction in American society. However, when laterality becomes lineality, it

is important in a society to know which side the kinsman falls on. This is seen in the Omaha and Crow systems, where who is "in my lineage" and who is not is a serious concern.
- Age or relative age—are they older or younger? Or are they older or younger than me? Warlpiri, for example, has separate terms for older brother (*papardi*) and younger brother (*kukurnu*).
- Marital status—are they married, single, widowed?

In other words, the "logic" of a kinship system can be decoded—the kinship terminology can be "read"—if we realize what social and kinship distinctions are made and are central in a society. Or, by reading the system, we can decipher what distinctions are made and central. In the U.S., for instance, the same terms apply identically to both sides of the family. Americans do not privilege age seniority, so they do not encode that distinction. If a society does make meaningful distinctions (like lineage-mates versus non-lineage-mates), it must and will have a way to talk about them.

NON-KINSHIP-BASED CORPORATE GROUPS

The "facts" and principles of marriage, residence, and descent exist in (nearly) all societies, and those societies use them—in unique and creative ways—to assign people to groups and to give those groups common tasks, interests, and identity. We might think that this would be enough structure for a society, but even in the smallest societies, other groupings are created too. Why would a society go on to elaborate non-kinship corporate groups in addition to kin groups? There are probably at least three reasons:

1. Kinship-based corporate groups might not be large enough or dispersed enough to handle all the tasks and "corporate duties" desired in a society.
2. Kinship-based corporate groups alone might tend to fragment society into identity and interest groups with little in common, turning them into competitive or even conflictual groups. Of course, this can happen anyhow, but a society may benefit from "cross-cutting" groups that bring together members of

divergent kinship groups in various kinds of non-kinship collectivities. Such cross-cutting or "vertical" groups provide more social "glue" or integration.

3. Other non-kinship kinds of traits and identities exist, so individuals tend to identify with them, and societies tend to exploit them. In other words, all humans have characteristics besides kinship that they share with other people and by which they can be classified and organized.

There are many such traits or categories available in any society and many ways to exploit them where they are found. Among these traits and categories are race and ethnicity (discussed in Chapter 6), sex and gender (discussed in Chapter 5), age, class, nationality, and many others, including ones that do not even exist in most Western societies, such as nobility or royalty.

The rest of the chapter will explore sex and gender corporate groups in more detail, adding a discussion of age groups and the widely-overlooked phenomenon of "friendship."

Sex and gender

As noted in previous chapters, the most universal and fundamental social distinction across cultures is sex or gender: the gender division of labor for example assembles the sexes into production groups, like hunters or gatherers. Among the Abkhasians of Georgia, a country in the Caucasus and formerly part of the Soviet Union, local men gathered in voluntary work cooperatives or *kiaraz* ("self-help") to tend each other's fields in order of need (ripeness of crop, weediness of land, etc.). According to Sula Benet (1974), each task that the *kiaraz* performed had a name and a song, and the group would divide into teams to compete in races and contests during work breaks; also, if it passed a widow's land, it would tend her fields for her. Finally, the group also functioned as a militia and as a law court, with powers to confiscate property or even assign the death penalty.

In other societies, men and women each have their particular spaces and prerogatives. One particularly common institution is the "men's house," where men may spend their day, conduct rituals, and sometimes even eat and sleep. The West African Poro men's ritual association maintained a house in various villages, which was an abode of ancestor spirits and powerful religious forces and "medicines." Among the Mundurucu of Amazonia, the men's house or *eksa* was "the residence of all males above about thirteen years of age," and the home of the *karoko* or sacred flutes (Murphy and Murphy, 1974: 82), which no woman dared touch on pain of rape. The Konyak Nagas in India also had a men's house, or *ban*, which functioned as a

See Chapter 7

See Chapter 6

See Chapter 5

IMAGE 8.5 At age fifteen, a Mexican girl would traditionally celebrate her *quinceanera*, at which she is introduced to adult society.

dormitory for older boys and unmarried men. Actually, each village might have several of these, associated with a neighborhood or ward of the village; some were large and ornate, with fancy carvings and a large drum or gong. Women were not totally forbidden from entering and in fact did enter on ceremonial occasions. Otherwise, the *ban* was corporate in many ways, including social, economic, legal, and ritual. It held joint ownership of land as well as of "symbolic property" like songs, dances, and decorations; it cultivated land together, defended and avenged its interests, and collected wealth for tribute. It also made up the core of the political system, sending officials (*niengba*) from each *ban* to sit with the chief as a village council, while other officers (*benba*) conducted rituals and sacrifices. Women also had a site, the *yo*, that served as a dormitory for young unmarried girls (Von Fuerer-Haimendorf, 1969).

See Chapter 10

The Cheyenne offered an assortment of military associations for men. In the early nineteenth century there were five named associations (Fox, Elk, Shield, Dog, and Bow-String or "Contrary"), with two more added later (Wolf and Crazy Dogs). Young males were free to join any of the groups, which were not formally stratified (although they might rise and fall in prestige based on their achievements). Each group was essentially a private army, with its own symbols, dances, songs, history, and internal organization; they could in fact conduct private raids and wars or act together as a tribal police force and army (Hoebel, 1960).

See Chapter 5

Not all societies have demonstrated the same degree of segregation and stratification between the sexes, but some degree of camaraderie between sex-mates is common if not universal. From the National Organization of Women or the League of Women Voters to sex-specific sports teams to the modern "women's spirituality" movement, women in modern societies often meet and act corporately, as do men, who have done so for a very long time in their "old boy's networks" and "smoke-filled rooms."

Age

Like sex and gender and race, age refers to a physical fact—the number of years that a person has been alive. However, that physical fact is subject to the same kind of cultural elaboration and construction as the facts behind sex and gender and race. Yet, age has often been a neglected variable in the analysis of societies, although it is universal and almost always very significant for social organization.

In English-speaking societies, there is a terminology for age-categories, allegedly naming real biological phases like "infancy," "childhood," "adolescence," "adulthood," and so on. These categories are also commonly associated with age appropriate norms, roles, and institutions—for instance, childhood with school, adulthood with marriage and work, or old age with retirement. Over the past century, a distinct "youth culture" has developed in many societies, characterized by ways of talking, dressing, and behaving. And many societies mark the transition from one stage of life to another with ceremonies and rituals, or "rites of passage." From the Jewish tradition of *bar mitzvah* for boys to the Australian Aboriginal (and other) ceremony of circumcision, rituals especially relate to the attainment of adulthood; recall that some societies, like the Sambia, believed that a boy could not become a man "naturally" but only through cultural and ritual intervention.

Margaret Mead was one of the first to comment that societies did not conceive and experience age and the maturation process alike. "Adolescence," she concluded in *Coming of Age in Samoa*, did not exactly exist among the Samoans and thus was a cultural concept more than a biological fact. According to Margaret Booth, the African Swazi likewise have no indigenous word for adolescence. Instead, for males, roughly age eight to seventeen is called *lijele* and age seventeen to twenty-seven is called *lijaha* or *libungu*, while for females the categories are different again and more articulate, with age eight to fifteen dubbed *litshitshane*, fifteen to seventeen *lichikiza*, seventeen to twenty-one *ingcugce*, twenty-one to twenty-four *makoti* or *umlobokati*, and twenty-four to fifty-five *umfati* (2003: 225). Significantly, under the impact of Western contact, Christian missionization, and modern schooling, Swazi people are being introduced to the idea of adolescence, although not all yet accept the notion. Adolescence was also being introduced to Inuit peoples in the 1990s as a result of population growth and concentration in towns, increased economic security, and exposure to Canadian and American cultural influences—not only images of modern youths, but institutions like

IMAGE 8.6 Members of the *moran* or warrior age set among the Samburu of Kenya.

the school. Consequently, there has been a rise of "a large adolescent peer group which now dominates the social/recreational activities of young people" (Condon, 1990: 266); Inuit teenagers, like their southern peers, "spend most of their time interacting with friends and peers, both in and out of school, and very little time in the company of parents and other adults" (273).

Anthropologists have gone on to note that other societies have constructed, labeled, and defined age categories in diverse ways. Classical Hinduism, for instance, divided life into four stages or *ashramas*—*Brahmacharya* (to age twenty-five), the (celibate) student phase; *Grihastha* (prime adulthood), the time of marriage and family life, oriented toward the production of wealth and the reproduction of children; *Vanaprashta* (beginning around age fifty), when a man (but ordinarily not a woman) could and should renounce home and family and take up residence in a modest hut in the forest, engaging in solitary prayer; *Sannyasin*, the last stage of life when a man became a wandering ascetic with no worldly attachments, devoted full-time to his eventual death and hopeful release from reincarnation.

A famous institution of age-based corporateness in many societies is the so-called **age grade system**. Particularly common in pastoral societies, boys might be assigned in their early childhood to an **age set** along with their age-mates. At a certain age, depending on the society, they moved together as a group into the next stage or grade of life, sometimes given new labors to perform, new tools to use, and even new names. The transition between grades might be ritualized, especially the transition to the grade of adult, which was often the grade of warriors. The Maasai (east Africa) possessed a basic system with three grades, roughly equivalent to "youth," "warrior" (*moran*), and "elder." Males in the *moran* grade lived apart in a *manyatta* where they acted as the standing army of the society (Leakey, 1930).

The Dinka (east Africa) held an initiation ceremony for males around age sixteen, at which time they were assigned to an age set with a designated "father" for the group who named it, thus bringing it into existence. During the initiation, boys received deep cuts across their foreheads and moved into a separate village for several months. They received new rights, including the right to dance and flirt with girls, as well as new responsibilities, including adult expectations of courage and aggressiveness tempered with dignity and self-control. Most importantly, they became warriors. As they matured they remained forever connected to their age set, although its corporateness faded over time; marriage weakened it, as corporateness was transferred to the kin unit, and by old age it had almost disappeared. Women also had age sets, but they ceased to act corporately at marriage (Deng, 1972).

The Hidatsa, a people of the Northern Plains of North America, had formal age grades for both

Age grade system
a non-kinship-based corporate system in which members, usually of one sex, are organized into groups or "grades" according to age and assigned roles and values as a group

Age set
a division or subset of a society based on shared age characteristics, as determined by the age grade system of that society

men and women in which the latter were at least as important as the former. As a horticultural, matrilocal, and matrilineal society, they put more emphasis on women than many other societies. Accordingly, there were four named grades for women (each with a male counterpart), starting with the "Skunk Society" at age twelve and extending to about twenty, whose main role was to dance after successful wars. Young married women (age twenty to thirty) moved into the "Enemy Society," which also had responsibilities following wars. From age thirty to forty women joined the "Goose Society," a prestigious level concerned with fertility, farming success, and the annual return of migratory birds. Women who attained seniority were eligible for the "White Buffalo Society," charged with caring for certain sacred objects (medicine bundles) and with bringing the buffalo to the people. Altogether, this system not only conferred status on women, but served as a social network through which they enjoyed guidance while youths and comradeship and support while adults.

While a great deal of anthropological attention has been paid to childhood and youth as the formative period of enculturation—for instance, Beatrice Whiting's (1963) edited cross-cultural comparison, *Six Cultures: Studies of Child Rearing*—anthropologists have considered every life-stage, including old age. Barbara Myerhoff's (1978) moving portrait of a Jewish community center depicted the day-to-day encounters and dramas of elders in California. Maurice Bloch told that among the Zafimaniry of Madagascar, as among probably all societies, elderhood "is a status but it is also a style of behavior"; in the Zafimaniry case,

> This is marked by posture and linguistic code. He tends to speak very quietly, using formalized and fixed language which is highly decorated and full of quotations and proverbs. When an elder speaks he addresses nobody, apparently not caring if he is heard or not, ignoring the fact that others may be speaking at the same time since a specific linguistic exchange would negate the almost other-worldly character of what he is saying.
>
> (1998: 183)

And while we might say that old people slow down in general, Bloch found that the Zafimaniry believe that people "dry" as they age, young people being especially "wet" and unformed, until they dessicate in old age, eventually hardening "like an inanimate object" (184) and "becoming merged with the fixed, hardening, and beautifying house" (183). Indeed, Bloch contended that the house was a primary cultural symbol and material manifestation of culture and kinship: Young unmarried people were not associated with a house and spent much of their time (especially the males) in the forest, but married adults settled down in a house, and elders literally *became* the house.

One of the underappreciated factors of culture is the inevitable tension between generations: Youths want to and must usurp the position of adults, while adults may hold onto their position and privilege to the disadvantage of youths. Among the formerly hunter-gatherer and egalitarian Lanoh of Malaysia, age is perhaps "the most important structural principle" (Dallos, 2011: 141), and one way that older men exercise power over younger ones is through their control of the younger men's marriage prospects and labor—that is, their authority over women, wealth, and work. (Dallos adds that traditionally the Lanoh did not even have a word for marriage and that their unions were "short-lived and ephemeral" [61].) The Lanoh say that a future husband should "pay something back" to his wife's kin: "During courtship younger men demonstrate this willingness by giving gifts of food (usually meat) to their prospective bride, who then passes these on to her parents" (186). Parents are keenly interested in the activities of the young couple, as this knowledge "offers them a sense of control, as well as the prospect of benefiting from the labors of young men in the future."

> Yet, these expectations are usually never realized, because, once married, sons-in-law become notoriously unreliable. . . . Since elders can only count on younger men while they are courting their daughters, it is therefore advantageous for competing leaders to keep their prospective sons-in-law in perpetual courtship. . . . Thus, by guarding their elder daughters competing leaders not only ensured a source of additional labor within their households, they also secured the help of younger suitors.
>
> (188–189)

In a word, fathers dangled their daughters like temptations to strong young men, overcoming the

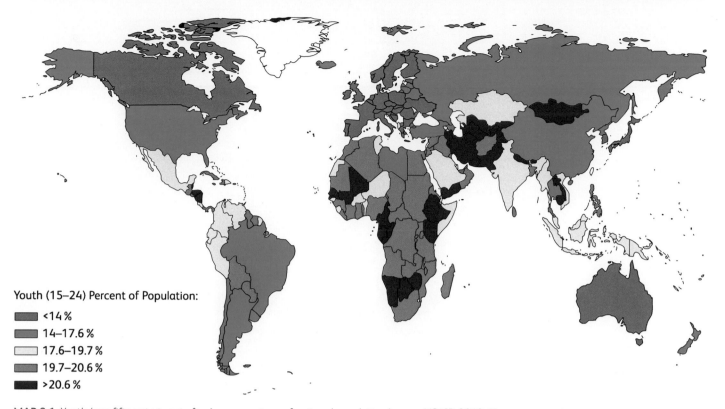

Youth (15–24) Percent of Population:

- <14 %
- 14–17.6 %
- 17.6–19.7 %
- 19.7–20.6 %
- >20.6 %

MAP 8.1 Youth (age fifteen to twenty-four) as percentage of national population (source: USAID 2012: 5)

limitations of their own age and channeling the work of those men into serving the elders. In this type of bride service, as well as other taboos and expectations (including military service), older men consume the fruit of young men's labor.

These struggles between generations are especially important today, since many societies are experiencing rapid population growth with a so-called "youth bulge." In extreme cases, nearly half of the population—forty-six percent in Afghanistan, forty-eight percent in Angola, forty-eight percent in Uganda (www.kff.org/global-indicator/population-under-age-15)—is under age fifteen. Understandably, such societies struggle to find education, jobs, and housing for this burgeoning young demographic, which is also and therefore prone to unrest, delinquency, crime, and political and religious extremism.

BOX 8.3   WHAT TO DO WITH YOUNG PEOPLE? THE YOUTH BULGE IN TAJIKISTAN

In Tajikistan, "seniority is one of the main principles of organization" (Roche, 2014: 103), which applies equally between parents and children and between elder and younger brothers. This is particularly challenging in a society that had the highest fertility rate in the former Soviet Union, that is experiencing a youth bulge today, and whose youths have lived through civil war and modernization. According to Sophie Roche, more than a third (35.3 percent) of Tajik males qualify for the category "youth" by the local definition of the term, which includes age fourteen to twenty-five and is known as *javon* or *bacha*. *Javon* (literally "young") has a "political connotation," she explains, while *bacha* ("unmarried boy") suggests "men behaving in a 'wild and undomesticated' manner" (4). The stage of *javon* is followed by *mardak*, a period of increasing maturity including marriage; in these years, men "are expected to use their labor to serve the family and community" (6). Only after age thirty-five or forty does a man achieve full maturity; during this mature phase (*kamolod*), men work until around age sixty, at which point they are expected to retire, assuming the role of " a wise and oft-consulted person" (6)—as their sons pick up the slack of productive labor for the elderly parents. Hence, in a word (and not uniquely to Tajiks), Roche says that the challenge is "domesticating" those immature and often wild youths who are seen alternatively or even simultaneously as "victims, actors, and troublemakers" (86). Many institutions have been established to harness and direct the energy of youths, from pre-Soviet *madrasas* (Islamic schools), to Soviet-era Komsomol (short for Young Communists League) and of course the army, to post-Soviet organizations like the Youth Union of Tajikistan and the Committee for Youth, Sports, and Tourism. Work itself is a domesticating and disciplining activity, although it also creates tensions between generations and between siblings. The relationship of siblingship, Roche rightly notes, has not received sufficient attention, but it is especially important in Tajik society, where the eldest son is expected to accept the burdens of the family and aging parents "while the youngest son inherits the family compound and therefore remains in the parental household, with all the other siblings eventually moving out" (112). Not surprisingly, eldest sons sometimes resent their situation, as middle sons enjoy the most freedom and youngest sons get the most reward. More, Tajiks increasingly migrate out of the country for work, where they accumulate more wealth and suffer fewer restrictions— and to escape parental and social authority. Even marriage does not always have the desired settling effect: Tajikistan's civil war in the 1990s, added to migration and modernization, enabled youths to shake free from many of the traditional and institutional constraints of marriage, and "parents have so far not regained full control over their children's marriages, as is demonstrated by the amount of effort parents have to put into persuading their sons to marry" (186). The state has entered the generational fray, attempting to manage youths through organizations but also through more subtle methods such as official categories, school, and military service. Ultimately, Roche concludes, by asserting the power to define, categorize, and administer youths, "the state devalues young people's attempts to demand rights" (215).

Friendship

See Chapter 7

If there is a relationship and organizational principle that has been truly overlooked in social science, it is friendship. Many scholars have regarded it as trivial, while others have dismissed it as merely Western or as entirely private and unstructured and therefore beyond the reach or concern of anthropology. However, as Martine Guichard insists in her introduction to a new edited volume on friendship in Africa, friendship "is a socially constructed form of relationship governed by norms serving as cultural scripts from among whom to choose friends, how to act toward them, and what is appropriate to expect from them" (2014: 2).

Part of the problem with appreciating friendship has been the assumption "that 'real' friendship is a non-kin relationship" (21) in societies where kinship is the essential factor and friendship is either absent, insignificant, or limited to kin.

Fortunately, a small but growing literature on cross-cultural friendship is upsetting many assumptions and finding that friendship and kinship are distinct relationships, although they can certainly overlap—and even transform into one another, as in the case of West African market traders discussed previously.

One of the first studies of non-Western friendship was Evans-Pritchard's 1933 essay on Zande blood-brotherhood:

> a pact or alliance formed between two persons by a ritual act in which each swallows the blood of the other. . . . It may bind only the two participants to certain obligations, or it may also involve the social groups of which they are members.
>
> (1933: 369)

A form of friendship was found in pre-modern India by Owen Lynch, regarded as one of the five "primary emotions," specifically *sakhya bhaba* or "friendship between friends" (1990: 18).

A reason why friendship has been so mysterious to scholars is the assumption that "true friendship" must be "disinterested," that is, it must be entered without the pursuit of financial or social gain. In many places like Sardinia, locals may say that "truly disinterested friendship is a very rare and precious thing, maybe even non-existent" (Sorge, 2009: 4); in its stead is offered "hospitality" between families and between strangers. Yet although "the host-guest relationship is at first based on mistrust," over time "the guest eventually comes to offer the possibility of disinterested friendship" (6). Another well-known example of a relationship that combines friendship and interest is *guanxi* in China. Meaning "relationship," *guanxi* refers to "the social connections built primarily upon shared identities such as native place, kinship, or attending the same school. *Guanxi* is seen as ubiquitous in 'getting things done' in China and among Overseas Chinese" (Smart, 1999: 120). People accept such an alliance for practical reasons, and it comes with specific and strict rights and responsibilities, including gift-giving and mutual assistance. And *guanxi* is one among a set of non-kinship voluntary identities like *tongxue* (shared education or "classmates"), *tongshi* (shared work experience or "co-worker"), and *tongzhi* (political affiliation or "comrade" and party member). Friendship was even listed among the five key relationships in the fifth century BCE document *Doctrine of the Mean*.

The case of the Moose and the Fulbe in contemporary Burkina Faso illustrates the complexities and interconnections of kinship and friendship in a multi-ethnic context. The Moose, predominantly farmers, recognize a variety of non-kin allegiances, such as *reementaaga* ("comradeship that develops between neighbors growing up together"), *tudentaaga* ("a friendship-like relation reinforcing bonds within the context of associations and migration, or trade networks"), and *zoodo* (a highly emotional and intimate bond that nevertheless comes with concrete expectations) (Breusers, 2014: 76–77). Preferably, friends should be non-kin and even prior strangers, since friendship is a pathway and prelude to exchanging women and "an intermediary phase that transforms strangerhood into kinship" (78). The pastoral Fulbe likewise cement friendship (*yiggiraagu*) with each other, often by entrusting cattle to each other's herds, and woman-exchange between friends is much simpler than among the Moose. Most interestingly, there are a number of institutions for creating links between Moose and Fulbe. One is the "host" relationship, in which individuals become frequent visitors to another person's home. The Moose also sometimes entrust their cattle to Fulbe, and people say, "Before a Moaga [singular of Moose] entrusts a Pullo [singular of Fulbe] with an animal, there must first be friendship; he does not bring his cattle to a Pullo without knowing him first" (82). Last but not least, to protect their children from evil spirits, the Moose may symbolically "sell" the child to a Pullo.

ANTHROPOLOGY OF FRIENDSHIP

BOX 8.4   CONTEMPORARY CULTURAL CONTROVERSIES: THE SEXUAL BENEFIT OF FRIENDSHIP

One of the many benefits of friendship in modern societies is "friends with benefits," which the *Urban Dictionary* defines as "two friends who have a sexual relationship without being emotionally involved. Typically two good friends who have casual sex without a monogamous relationship or any kind of commitment" (quoted in Garcia et al., 2012: 163). This is a unique—and to many adults, troubling—twist to both the friendship and the sexual relationships, yet it is more common than some might think: One study found that sixty percent of college students have engaged in friends-with-benefits behavior at least once. Most often the sex ended but the friendship endured, but almost ten percent of the time the sexual relationship evolved into a romantic one. While some observers consider this situation an exploitation of gullible women, Hanna Rosin (2012) opines that it actually gives women considerable freedom and allows college students to concentrate on their educations and future careers without the distraction of dating and boyfriends. What do you think?

SUMMARY

A society must assign names, identities, roles, interests, and statuses to individuals. This entails establishing and perpetuating corporate groups. Kinship is one universal way of making and maintaining such groups, but not the only way. A kinship system is a confluence of three principles:

- marriage
- residence
- descent

Within each of these principles are multiple sub-issues with considerable area for diversity in each (e.g. who to marry, how many to marry, etc.), and the forms they take and the interconnections they make significantly shape the experience of the society, in particular gender, domestic, and property relations.

In addition to kinship principles, non-kinship characteristics and commonalities can be and widely are used to create corporate groups and allot tasks, roles, and social meaning and values. Some of the traits that humans share and that can be used to build groups and categories are sex and gender, age, and race and ethnicity. Race and ethnicity have been discussed previously, but sex and gender is a common cross-cultural premise for constructing associations and social spaces, and age is an underappreciated variable in social organization. Finally, friendship and other non-kin bonds are found across cultures, and friendship often combines a voluntary emotional connection with practical interests and advantages and is sometimes converted into kinship (or sexual) relations.

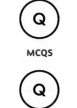

MCQS

FILL IN THE BLANKS

WWW

Key Terms

age grade system	dowry	monogamy
age set	endogamy	neolocal
ambilineal descent	exogamy	patrilineal descent
ambilocal	household	patrilocal
arranged marriage	hypergamy	phratry
avunculocal	incest taboo	polyandry
bilateral descent	kindred	polygyny
bride service	levirate	residence
bridewealth/brideprice	lineage	serial monogamy
clan	marriage	social reproduction
corporate group	matrilineal descent	sororal polygyny
descent	matrilocal	sororate
double descent	moiety	unilineal descent

Politics
Social order and social control

With its legacy of corruption, violence, racism, and poverty, Haiti has long been judged a failed state, or at least an exceedingly weak one, without the will, power, or financial resources to improve the lives of its citizens. Twentieth-century Haiti experienced a series of unstable governments, at least two dictators (François Duvalier and his son Jean-Claude), military occupation by the United States between 1915 and 1934, the overthrow of democratically elected Jean-Bertrand Aristide, and Aristide's return to power with the assistance of American troops. A major earthquake in 2010 added to the country's misery. Given the perceived hopelessness of formal Haitian politics, many foreign governments and international agencies have chosen to bypass it more or less altogether in favor of non-governmental organizations (NGOs), designed and financed to provide many of the services that the state cannot. In effect, NGOs "became parallel states," concludes Mark Schuller (2012: 6), whose research focuses on two NGOs offering support for Haitian women, particularly vulnerable to the violence, disease, and poverty of the island. Although locally based, both organizations were born out of foreign initiatives— *Fanm Tet Ansanm* as an American government

program and *Sove Lavi* as a United Nations effort. For a variety of reasons, including their leadership, their office location and internal politics, and their relationship to their financial backers, the two agencies have very different characters. *Fanm Tet Ansanm* is more engaged with the local community and encourages more participation, while *Sove Lavi* is more formal and bureaucratic, keeping more distance from its clients. Yet the reality is that both groups feel that they are often driven by the interests and policies of donors and outside institutions and that they only "carry heavy rocks" (71)—that is, do the difficult work—but do not make key decisions. Both NGOs, and all such organizations, are caught between their clients "below" and their benefactors or bosses "above." Humanitarian work thus involves a web of international actors, "including recipients of services, NGO staff, directors, other NGOs, the Haitian government, and donor agencies" (9), established ostensibly to help people in need but for other purposes as well, including as vehicles of American foreign policy. Schuller argues that such programs often do not benefit local people or actually make their lives more unpredictable and dependent; he critiques the global network of NGOs as "trickle-down imperialism" (176) and

IMAGE 9.1 A Haitian woman talks with an employee from an organization set up to help transform waste into resources.

encourages the empowerment of the Haitian state to serve its own citizens.

The ancient philosopher Aristotle called humans a "political" species because humans live in ordered societies and only reach their fullest individual and collective potential in such societies. The word "politics" itself derives from the ancient Greek *polis* or "city," referring to the proper organization of the city or city-state for the good of its citizens. Not all societies, of course, have lived in cities, nor have they possessed formal governments or written law or police forces and armies. Yet humans have all lived in orderly social groups.

Politics broadly conceived, then, refers to the cultural ideas, norms, values, and practices that regulate how people interact in an orderly and (more or less) mutually beneficial manner. This may involve formal, specialized, and large-scale institutions, like a congress or parliament, where the rules and laws of the society are formulated and propagated; it may involve informal, generalized, and nearly socially invisible norms and relationships that do not appear "political" at first glance. In most—or all—cases, it will involve both, and often the latter more than the former.

Like economics and kinship in prior chapters, and religion in the next chapter, politics has been a subject for anthropology from its earliest days, as in Henry Sumner Maine's 1861 *Ancient Law* and 1883 *On Early Law and Custom*. Eventually, according to Georges Balandier, a "political anthropology" or anthropology of politics emerged, seeking "to transcend particular political experiences and doctrines"—especially those of Western societies—and to find "properties common to all political

organizations in all their historical and geographic diversity" (1970: 1). Characteristically this originally meant a focus on "primitive" political systems, but by the 1970s at the latest, political anthropology recognized its project as separating "the political" from so-called "historical societies" and formal states, comparing political systems across all societies, and documenting "the processes of the formation and transformation of political systems" over time (4–5). Naturally and appropriately, anthropology's attention has turned usefully to contemporary political processes and how they impact particular peoples and societies.

SOCIAL CONTROL: THE FUNCTIONS OF POLITICS

Anthropologists, sociologists, and political scientists alike realize that the most fundamental aspect of society is *social organization* or *social control*. In the normal course of social living, various kinds of problems and challenges arise that demand attention and resolution, if people are to continue to live harmoniously, if at all. These issues include:

- decision-making
- norm/rule/law creation
- dispute resolution
- norm/rule/law enforcement
- deviance punishment
- social integration
- defense of community and society
- aggression and offense against other communities and societies

Social control then consists of the range of types and sources of pressures that can be brought to bear on individuals and groups to get them to do what the society demands and expects of them. In its more sinister guise, which often enough actually exists in the human world, social control is the imposition of one person's or group's will on others—inducing members of society (the ones under the "political control" of the dominant person or group) to do what the "leadership" wants them to do. In other more benign instances, it is simply what is necessary for successful communal co-existence.

Social control can take two very different though related forms. Before any particular

MAINTAINING SOCIAL ORDER AND SOCIAL HARMONY

Social control
the political and general social function of getting members of a group to conform to expectations and rules and to obey authorities. Includes inculcating of social values as well as punishment of deviance from expectations

individual is born, the rules, norms, groups, and institutions of society already exist, and humans, for the most part, conform to them. Therefore, the people who came before us and enculturated us into social expectations are the agents and embodiment of the society and its rules, norms and so on. Being "before" and "outside of" each new member of the society, they operate as **agents of social control**, and every society abounds with them. They consist of such roles or positions as parents, peers, priests, professors, police, prison guards, parole officers, and presidents and prime ministers. Together they achieve the function of **externalized control**. When a person does "right," these agents provide positive responses, but when a person does "wrong," the agents administer negative feedback, from instruction to punishment. Hopefully and usually, the individual gets the idea and voluntarily conforms to expectations, accepting and even believing in them. Nevertheless, in every society in some way or another, agents of social control stand over society to ensure compliance.

As just implied, though, during the enculturation process and throughout subsequent experience, people absorb their society's rules, norms, values, beliefs, and so forth; this external cultural content gets "inside" the individual and becomes part of his/her personality. In essence, then, enculturation is the first and most important political process: Acquiring culture means internalizing, embodying, the society's organization. The intended and generally accomplished result is **internalized control**, such that the individual controls his/her own behavior in conformity with rules or norms or standards. This is by far the most efficient form of social control, since no society can have a guard monitoring every member at every moment. Fortunately, most people most of the time do not require monitoring to ensure their compliance. They conform because they have been con-formed or constructed by society.

However, internalized social control is not total, nor is it totally effective. Individuals are not carbon copies of their society, nor are they robots that mindlessly enact culture. There are many reasons for this. For instance, given the "guided reinvention" quality of culture, it is possible that the individual may be exposed to all the normal rules and pressures and still not learn or internalize the preferred things; s/he might learn or construct an idiosyncratic lesson from cultural experience. Additionally, the individual may be exposed to "abnormal" experiences, like violence or abuse in home life, internalizing a lesson that society would prefers/he not. Individuals may even be enculturated into what some researchers call a "culture of deviance" (for instance, a gang or a criminal environment), in which they acquire "alternate norms" that are deviant by society's standard, but "normal" for the subculture. Finally, an individual may internalize all the right norms and values but find that social circumstances do not allow him/her to conduct normal, socially appropriate behavior. As an example, one may possess the "good" values of hard work and frugality and such but find oneself in a class or race or ethnic or gender situation where these values do not apply or "work"—where, for example, opportunities for employment or education are absent or blocked.

Sanctions

Agents of social control apply externalized control, and encourage members of society to practice the discipline that leads to internalized control, through the administration of **sanctions**. English-speakers tend to think of sanctions as negative pressures: When the U.S. imposes sanctions on a country like Cuba or North Korea, a punishment is intended, which is intended to impel the belligerent country to change its behavior in more favorable (from the sanctioning agent's point of view) directions. In reality, there are both positive and negative sanctions. Sanctions are merely reactions or responses by others that are intended to affect the sanctioned individual's or group's behavior. Positive sanctions intend to inspire the individual to repeat "good" behavior, while negative sanctions aim to discourage "bad" behavior.

Sanctions can also be more or less formal. A **formal sanction** is one that is explicit, even "official," and perhaps written down; normally it applies to more serious social infractions, and usually members know exactly what behaviors will unleash it, exactly what the consequences will be, and exactly which agents of social control have the right to administer it. An **informal sanction** is more vague, implicit, and usually not written down. Individuals may have some general sense of what

See Chapter 2

Agents of social control
individuals, groups, or institutions that play a part in instilling social norms in members and protecting and perpetuating those norms through the use of their powers and sanctions

Externalized control
the source of social control that lies outside of the individual, in the form of individuals, groups, and institutions with the power to sanction behavior, such as parents, teachers, police, governments, etc.

Sanction
any type of social pressure in the form of "reward" or "punishment" that can be imposed on people to influence and control their behavior

See Chapter 5

Internalized control
a form or source of social control in which individuals make themselves conform to social expectations through the internalization of rules and norms; by enculturation, social rules and norms become part of the personalities of members

Formal sanction
a method of social control employing rewards and punishments that are explicit and well-known, often written down, and administered by special agents of control who possess the authority to administer them (such as police or courts)

Informal sanction
a "reward" or "punishment" that is widely understood in a society but not precisely defined, usually not written down, and for which no specialized role exists to administer the sanction

Positive Formal	Negative Formal
Reward, prize, promotion, eternal life in heaven	Prison, fine, execution, expulsion, excommunication, eternal torment in hell
Positive Informal	**Negative Informal**
Praise, friendly expressions and gestures, inclusion	Insult, criticism, gossip, ridicule, rude expressions and gestures, ostracism

FIGURE 9.1 Sanctions: formal and informal, positive and negative

behaviors produce what sanctions, but there may be no specialized agents to impose them. In fact, the right to impose informal sanctions might exist for every member of society.

There are then four possible varieties of sanctions—positive formal, negative formal, positive informal, and negative informal (see Figure 9.1)—not all of which are always recognized as "political." However, in the sense of seeking to establish and maintain social control, they are all political.

The point here is that, while formal social control or official "politics" is the most visible, it is hardly the only—perhaps not even the main—avenue through which political functions are accomplished. All humans are "politicking" each other all the time, reacting to each other's behavior with praise or condemnation and administering,

and having administered to them, sanctions intended to shape the flow of behavior. In other words, politics is not just something that governments do. Politics in any society is mostly informal and interpersonal and only secondarily formal and institutional. Ordinarily, only when the pervasive informal political processes fail do we resort to the formal and institutional side of politics. That is, as we will discuss below, government is only one expression of an omnipresent "governmentality" located in many sites throughout society.

Power

Sanctions are one manifestation of the general phenomenon of *power*. Anthropologically, power is

IMAGE 9.2 Power is not only situated in governments but in many informal sites in society.

not merely physical force and usually does not require or take that form. Rather, we can think of power as ability of a person or group or institution *to influence and affect the course and outcome of social interactions*. Again, this control could perhaps be (at least temporarily) achieved through the sheer physical strength or some related quality of the powerful person, group, or institution, but anthropology joins the other social sciences in emphasizing power as a social relationship. In other words, power is never entirely "in" the power-figure or leader, but is "between" him/her/it and the subjects of that power, who are—to some extent— accomplices of power. Physical force or violence is not necessary if members of society *grant* power to the power-figure and actually internalize the concepts and relations of power.

The classic sociologist Max Weber was one of the first to understand the social nature of power and its three forms or sources—authority, persuasion, and coercion. **Authority** can be thought of, and is experienced as, "legitimate" power, power that a person or group or institution possesses and uses "rightfully"; Morton Fried defined it precisely as "the ability to channel the behavior of others in the absence of the threat or use of sanctions" (1967. 13). Followers recognize the authority's right to this power and respect and obey it. Such authority derives from a variety of sources, including physical strength but more often skill or knowledge, age, education, charisma, or formal office.

Illustrating the institutionalization of authority apart from the individual, an **office** is a defined position or role of power in a society. "Police officer" is an office, as is "teacher" or "boss" or "president." The power belongs to the role, not the individual; any person who occupies the office has the authority; of course, how the person attains the office is a significant question. As long as the individual occupies the role or position, s/he exercises the authority of the office; however, when the office is lost or vacated, the power is lost too.

Weber also reminded us that authority emanates from the "rational-legal" processes of the system, including documents like constitutions as well as credentials, regulations, and written laws. More interesting and ineffable is *charisma*, which in fact is experienced as a quality of the power-figure. It is a certain kind of attraction, even "grace," a

personal magnetism that draws people to the charismatic leader and encourages them to submit to and follow him/her. Weber borrowed the concept from religion (Christianity in particular: Some Christians expressly consider themselves "charismatics" because they feel the personal power of Jesus or God) to account for the "extraordinary" qualities of certain political authorities. And no discussion of charisma or of politics in general would be complete without an acknowledgement of what observers have called the pleasure of being a follower, of surrendering one's individuality and will and participating in something beyond oneself, something important or transcendent, like a country or a religion.

Finally, Weber contrasted charisma to routine and institutional politics and society: Precisely because charisma is personal, it is supposedly ephemeral and non-institutional. But anthropologists have found that charisma can be cultivated— as in the "cult of personality" promoted by parties and rulers from Joseph Stalin to Kim Jong-Un and Saddam Hussein—and can survive the death of the charismatic leader. Certainly Christianity has endured after the loss of its original charismatic figure, capturing the charisma of Jesus in institutions like the Catholic Church, in many subsequent charismatic preachers, and even in material objects like icons. More recently, Yoram Bilu explained how the charisma of Rabbi Menachem Mendel Scheerson survived his passing in 1994. Head of the Habad-Lubavitch Hasidic movement, his death did not end the movement or even his place in it; rather, for his followers, "he continues to live, invisible but intact, in '770,' his abode and movement's epicenter, located at 770 Eastern Parkway, Crown Heights, Brooklyn" (Bilu, 2013: 214). From that space, his "phantom charisma" emanates in the form of portraits and photographs, videos, books, and objects that he owned, as well as daily routines and ongoing encounters with him through "dreams, near-death and out-of-body experiences, visions, and apparitions" (226).

Up, down, and sideways: modern anthropology traces the paths of power

Like other social sciences, anthropology has a historical preoccupation with weaker or poorer

Authority
legitimate power or power that an individual, group, or institution is felt to rightly possess and exercise on the grounds of age, knowledge, office, and such

Fried, Morton H. 1967. *The Evolution of Political Society: An Essay in Political Anthropology*. New York: Random House.

Office
a more or less formal social position with specific rights and responsibilities; one source of "political" authority and social control

Hymes, Dell, Ed. 1972 [1969]. *Reinventing Anthropology.* New York: Random House, Inc.

See Chapter 7

Persuasion

a source of social and political power, based on the ability to move people to agree with or obey the persuader. Often exercised through linguistic skill (e.g. the ability to give a good speech) and the manipulation of resources and social relationships

See Chapter 4

Geertz, Clifford. 1980. *Negara: The Theatre State in Nineteenth-Century Bali.* Princeton, NJ: Princeton University Press.

Coercion

power based on the threat or use of force

Symbolic capital

"resources" that humans can use to influence situations and affect other people's behavior that are not "material" or "economic"; these can include knowledge, social relationships or debts, prestige, and so on

elements of society—what has sometimes been called the "subaltern" or lower-other. This has particularly translated to a focus on indigenous peoples, the lower class, non-white populations, and such marginalized and underprivileged types. Surely these individuals and groups deserve our full consideration, but as Laura Nader insisted in her memorable essay "Up the Anthropologist— Perspectives from Studying Up," in a discipline-altering volume titled *Reinventing Anthropology,* power and the society it constructs cannot be understood by merely studying "down." She urged us to apply anthropological perspectives equally to corporations, bureaucracies, government agencies, banks, law firms, and all the sites where power is situated and practiced. We saw some of the fruits of this suggestion in the discussion of the anthropology of money, banking, and the corporation in Chapter 7, as well as immediately above in the remarks about charisma and leadership.

Nader's recommendation draws us to Weber's two other forms or sources of power, namely **persuasion** and **coercion**. Persuasion is power based on one's ability to influence or manipulate people into obedience or compliance, typically through skillful use of language or control of resources. One of the most familiar forms of persuasion is "talking people into" the persuader's will. In all societies, there are specific linguistic skills of oratory or "speech-making" that give certain individuals more persuasive power than others. In the United States, "political speaking" is a special and highly elaborated and valued style of language, and leaders who can speak "well" are more effective—ultimately "more powerful"—than those who cannot.

The other foundation of persuasion is control or manipulation of cultural resources. These resources can include money or property; if someone is rich—or, say, the boss—then people may tend to find his/her opinions and directions more compelling than other people's. The "big man" discussed below has persuasive power by virtue of his central position in the redistribution system. A teacher has a certain persuasive power by virtue of his/her control over grades. However, persuasive power may not necessarily involve "economic" resources, but may rest on what Pierre Bourdieu (1977) called cultural or symbolic capital. **Symbolic capital** refers to meaningful cultural

"assets" like flags, uniforms, robes, and white coats along with impressive titles, key words and concepts (in the U.S., "freedom" or "rights"), specific bits of cultural knowledge, myths, rituals, and so on. Across cultures, members of royal lines have demonstrated and reproduced their power through ritual performances like coronations, state marriages, and state funerals. Clifford Geertz claimed that precolonial Bali took this principle to an extreme, establishing a "theater state" in which the rituals and demonstrations were the very basis and expression of power. Politics itself was display and acting:

> the kings and princes were the impresarios, the priests the directors, and the peasants the supporting cast, stage crew, and audience. The stupendous cremations, tooth filings, temple dedications, pilgrimages, and blood sacrifices, mobilizing hundreds and even thousands of people and great quantities of wealth, were not means to particular ends: they were the ends themselves, they were what the state was for. Court ceremonialism was the driving force of court politics; and mass ritual was not a device to shore up the state, but rather the state, even in its final gasp, was a device for the enactment of mass ritual. Power served pomp, not pomp power.
>
> (1980: 13)

Contemporary politicians often criticize their opponents for engaging in "political theater" without realizing (or maybe without admitting) that all politics is theater, or at least cultural performance, to an extent.

When all else fails—or often in conjunction with other sources of power—a would-be leader can resort to coercion, the threat or use of force or violence. There is no doubt that coercion can escalate as the authority and persuasive power of the political leader decline, but it is probably not correct to see them as antithetical and foreign principles. A police officer combines authority, persuasion, and coercion in his/her power, and most members of a society recognize some form of "legitimate force," whether in the criminal justice system, in the military, or in personal self-defense.

As the sole basis of power, coercion can be very effective in the short term: If a police officer needs to subdue a suspect, physical force—up to and including deadly force—can accomplish the task. However, coercion alone cannot control a society indefinitely, and even coercive leaders attempt to project an aura of legitimacy on themselves and their actions. They may suggest that they are eliminating a threat to the society, preserving "law and order," or actually improving the society in some way. The leaders of the French Revolution, particularly in the period known as the Terror, explicitly employed violence and terror (the term "terror" or "terrorism" was invented at that moment) as a political device. For the higher purpose of creating a perfect society, deadly violence was a valid method or tool, as Maximilien Robespierre stated:

> We desire an order of things in which all base and cruel feelings are suppressed by the laws, and all beneficent and generous feelings evoked; in which ambition means the desire to merit glory and to serve one's country. In which distinctions arise only from equality itself . . .; in which all minds are enlarged by the continued conviction of republican sentiments and by the endeavor to win the respect of a great people. . . .
>
> We must crush both the internal and foreign enemies of the Republic, or perish with it. And in this situation, the first maxim of your policy should be to guide the people by reason and repress the enemies of the people by terror.
>
> (quoted in Gershoy, 1957: 159–160)

Coercion can and often does include guillotines and clubs and dogs, but there is also "soft coercion," as anthropologists, political scientists, and interrogators and advertisers have discovered. People do not have to be beaten or threatened to have their behavior largely determined for them. There are ways to bend them to another's will, from "strong" soft coercion like sleep deprivation, starvation, cold-water dousings, and emotional and informational manipulation, to "weak" soft coercion like invasive advertising, product placement, and a host of marketing tricks that opinion-shapers have learned from decades of close observation of consumer habits and tendencies. Human voting behavior, buying behavior, and most other forms of behavior can be shaped quite effectively—and without the victim's knowledge—through much more subtle devices than torture. In fact, often such

devices only work, or at least work best, when they are not seen or felt at all. Some of these techniques might perhaps belong in the persuasion category, but when options are denied or hidden, they begin to cross over into coercion, albeit "soft" coercion.

In the early twentieth century, Marxist thinker Antonio Gramsci taught us that some power is actually invisible, so taken for granted that it is unrecognized as power at all. He used the term "hegemony" to refer to this omnipresent but largely unseen influence. For Gramsci, government was the official apparatus of political power and enforcement, while hegemony constituted the

> "spontaneous" consent given by the great masses of the population to the general direction imposed on social life by the dominant fundamental group [i.e. the dominant class]; this consent is "historically" caused by the prestige (and consequent confidence) which the dominant group enjoys because of its position and function in the world of production.
>
> (1971: 12)

In a word, hegemony is "naturalized" power—or at least power that followers experience as natural. One of the most important processes for the construction and inculcation of this social consciousness, Gramsci insisted, is education, which is intended "to raise the great mass of the population to a particular cultural and moral level, a level (or type) which corresponds to the needs of the productive forces for development, and hence to the interests of the ruling class" (258).

In reminding us to study "up," Nader was in no way demanding that we abandon studying "down." Indeed, in tracking power up,

> we would sooner or later need to study down as well. We are not dealing with an either/or proposition; we need simply to realize when it is useful or crucial in terms of the problem to extend the domain of study up, down, or sideways.
>
> (1972: 292)

Anthropologists were quick to respond to the call to study up, but it took longer to practice—or even comprehend—studying "sideways." Studying sideways means investigating people, groups, and institutions at a comparable or parallel level of power, that is, paying attention to *others like ourselves,* which for anthropologists amounts to other professionals and "experts" and other disciplines and institutions that produce cultural knowledge, such as *advertisers, consultants, journalists, writers, artists,* and *scholars in "think tanks."* The contributors to the recent volume *Up, Down, and Sideways: Anthropologists Trace the Pathways of Power* (Stryker and González, 2014) rise to the challenge, reporting on and from power-sites including courts, clinics, bureaucracies (with its dreaded "meetings"), government agencies, and international organizations. In another new collection dedicated to Ulf Hannerz, a preeminent anthropologist of the modern world (see Box 9.1), studying sideways includes interviewing Irish novelists and conducting fieldwork at the Center for Global Development, a Washington, DC think tank (Eriksen, Garsten, and Randeria, 2015).

THE ANTHROPOLOGY OF POLITICAL SYSTEMS

As in the domains of economics and kinship, anthropologists have identified a variety of formal political systems, which can be organized along a

---

BOX 9.1   SEEING POWER AND BEING POWER: NEWS MEDIA IN REMOTE ARGENTINA

An underappreciated site and practice of power is the news media—so much so that in the late 1700s the press was dubbed the "Fourth Estate," in addition to the three formal estates of French society (the nobility, the clergy, and the commoners). It has long been known that journalists not only report the news, but to an extent make the news, and they are certainly an important influence on public knowledge and public opinion. Anthropologists like Ulf Hannerz, whose work has evolved from urban anthropology to the study of "cosmopolitans" or "transnationals" (those people who have a more international or global perspective and identity), have noted that journalism and anthropology have much in common: They "share the condition of being in a transnational contact zone, engaged in reporting, representing, interpreting—generally, managing meaning across distances" (Hannerz, 2002: 58). Hannerz and others have done participant observation among journalists, studying "sideways" these fellow travelers and writers, shedding light on the organization of the newsroom, the culture of news production and writing, and the experiences of individual journalists. Indeed, an entire special issue of the journal *Ethnography* (volume 7, issue 1) was dedicated to the "worlds of journalism," with articles on Palestinian journalists, news coverage in India, the state press in Ghana, and Western institutions such as Euronews and the World Trade Organization. However, the power of the media can be much more literal, as in the town of Puerto Iguazú, a remote part of Argentina "historically neglected by the central government," prone to "water shortages, power cuts, natural gas and fuel scarcity, impassable roads, and squatter settlements" (Jusionyte, 2014: 151). The local media, like Cable Video Imagen (CVI), keep a watchful eye and a critical discourse on the failures of the state (for more on the state, see below), highlighting problems and demanding solutions. Much more, though, CVI steps in to solve problems itself: As one of the co-owners of the enterprise said, "We help the people a lot. What the state does not do, we do as the media. And not only us—all the media in Iguazú" (169). CVI "works like an office of social services" (170), organizing various campaigns throughout the year "to distribute food products, clothes, toys, and more to residents in a big televised public event" (171). For squatters in unofficial and illegal settlements, CVI helped to hook them into the electrical power grid and advocated for them to the government. Finally, CVI called on the government to provide more security, including lights and surveillance cameras; interestingly, meanwhile CVI already had its own camera on a tall antenna, with "the ability to zoom into particular streets and buildings. Live images were extensively used in the morning and afternoon television shows and in between programs" (175). In a word, in the absence of an effective state, the local media not only cajoled the state to act, but in ways *acted like a state*, producing "state effects by patching up inconsistencies in infrastructure and imposing competing or overlapping layers of security regimes" (176).

rough continuum in terms of their **level of political integration**. By this phrase, we mean the extent to which politics "integrates" or "makes one out of" a society, which can be expressed as a product of at least five variables:

1. Size of society. A small society is less integrated than a large one, since more people, groups, and institutions are "made one" and incorporated into a single polity or political community in a large one than a small one. Size of society may be measured in terms of population or in terms of the number of local groups (families, villages, towns, etc.) encompassed by the political system.

2. Complexity of society. A society that contains internal differentiations, such as class distinctions, is more integrated or requires more integration than one that does not. This internal complexity can also include multiple linguistic, religious, racial, or ethnic communities.

3. Centralization of power. If power is dispersed widely or evenly through society, there is little political integration. The more that power is concentrated into a few hands, the more integrated the system.

4. Amount of coercion. The more force that is available to the political system and its agents, the more integrated the society.

5. Formality of power. The more explicit and specialized the agents and institutions of power and politics are, the more integrated the system. Societies in which rules, sanctions, and roles of enforcement are implicit or embedded in other non-political relationships and institutions are less integrated.

Different anthropologists have proposed different typologies for a "range" or "spectrum" of political systems. Morton Fried, for instance, suggested four types, including egalitarian, rank, stratified, and state societies. An egalitarian society is "one in which there are as many positions of prestige in any given age-sex grade as there are persons capable of filling them" (1967: 33); that is, political power is not limited to a few individuals in an exclusive way. A rank society emerges

> when there are fewer positions of valued status than persons capable of filling them. A rank society has means of limiting the access of its members to status positions that they would otherwise hold on the basis of sex, age, or personal attributes.
>
> (52)

Individuals must then compete for rank. A stratified society "is one in which members of the same sex and equivalent age status do not have equal access to the basic resources that sustain life," and this unequal access is formalized into hierarchical (and often hereditary) strata or classes (186). Finally, a state is "the complex of institutions by means of which the power of the society is organized on a basis superior to kinship" (229). Put another way, a state is "a collection of specialized institutions and agencies, some formal and others informal, that maintains an order of stratification" (235) and thus strives for and defends its "sovereignty" or "monopoly of permanent control over a population and an area" (237).

Despite the utility of this typology, the one advanced by Elman Service in his 1962 book *Primitive Social Organization* has achieved the widest adoption. No typology is, of course, true or perfect, but since Service's is the best known, it is the one we will discuss in more detail.

Band

The **band** is the lowest level of political integration. Bands tended to comprise a remarkably small number of people over a very local area, sometimes no more than a handful and seldom more than a hundred or so, typically averaging between thirty and fifty. This number was clearly too small to constitute an entire society; instead, bands tended to be local subunits of societies, dispersed over the

Level of political integration
the extent to which political institutions unite a group of people into a single political entity, as measured by the size of the society, the complexity of the society, the formality and centralization of political rules and roles, and the amount of coercive force available to political leaders

Band
a political system or "level of political integration" where small, autonomous, and typically leaderless groups constitute local segments of a decentralized society

Service, Elman R. 1962. *Primitive Social Organization: An Evolutionary Perspective.* New York: Random House.

PRE-MODERN POLITICAL SYSTEMS: CASE STUDIES

BAND   TRIBE   CHIEFDOM   STATE

Least   Most
integrated   integrated

FIGURE 9.2 Political systems by level of political integration (following Service 1962)

territorial range of the society. Essentially a residential subset of a society, it was often simply an extended family that moved and camped on its own.

The decentralization of power was manifested in two ways. First, within the band, there was no single individual with a great amount of power compared to other members. Since the "political" and residential group was essentially a kinship group, kinship organization and power was synonymous with political organization and power. Elders, often both male and female, exercised nominally more power than youngsters, but this power was limited to authority and persuasion (with occasional coercion) and was not very extensive. It was basically "head of the household" power, like any parent or elder would enjoy. Actually, it may have been less than most parents and elders enjoy: Many band-level societies, like the Australian Aboriginals, the Ju/hoansi, or Inuit (Eskimo) societies, did little in the way of disciplining or controlling the behavior of children, often explicitly believing that young humans lacked the "reason" or maturity to take instruction and discipline. Some, like the Semai, found it positively offensive to be told what to do.

See Chapter 12

The highest position of leadership in bands has been dubbed the "headman," but this is often a foreign concept, and such a man had little formal power. His authority came from age, kinship relationships, experience and knowledge, and perhaps spiritual or ritual prowess. Members of the band deferred to him in decision-making, but they were not bound to follow him and could follow other members whose authority exceeded the headman in specific arenas like hunting. And the headman's power was overtly circumscribed. The general and often self-conscious ethic was to maintain equality between individuals; any man who tried to get too "big" was reminded in no uncertain terms that he was out of line. This phenomenon, known as a **leveling mechanism**, intentionally prevents anyone from becoming more important, dominant, or prestigious than anyone else.

The general absence of coercion made band membership fluid and transient. People moved and resided together while it was desirable to do so. Personal disputes commonly led to leaving or completely "disbanding" the group. The

Leveling mechanism
a practice to establish or re-establish social equality or parity, usually by "bringing down" individuals or groups that threaten to get "above" or "better than" others

environment also played a prominent part in the life of bands. Bands lived dispersed mostly because it was necessary, their environments being difficult and relatively unproductive. In times of plenty, multiple bands might gather and reside together for a while, often conducting their ritual affairs. However, these larger aggregations were always short-lived, either through environmental constraints or the social frictions they cause, and soon bands disbanded and headed their separate ways.

Just as there was little power within the band, there was little power above the band level, that is, little to coordinate or integrate disparate bands. There was no "pan-band" or "super-band" leadership. Bands usually shared kinship or non-kin ties (for example, members of the same family or ritual-group might cross bands), and of course they shared a common language and religion and culture, but that was as far as inter-band cooperation went. This lack of higher level integration, which served them well enough in their traditional circumstances, was often a severe handicap upon contact with Western societies; band societies were unable to mount an organized resistance to colonial invaders and were often swept aside like wildlife—which is often how the invaders regarded them—in the path of settlement and development.

Not surprisingly, the fluid, egalitarian, unspecialized, non-integrated ways of the band fit most closely with the foraging mode of production. Foraging peoples typically organized themselves into band systems, or rather, foraging organization *was* band organization. Especially in less productive environments, groups had to be small and dispersed, each band hunting and gathering within a specific "country" inside the society's territory. The band was typically a family unit, among whom distribution of food and other goods was accomplished mainly through reciprocity, although some long-distance trading might be conducted. Kinship expectations, economic exigencies, and religious beliefs and values tended to shape and integrate the society and accomplish the political functions.

Actually, in Service's original formulation, he distinguished (following Julian Steward's earlier ecological analysis) between the patrilocal band (the smallest type, basically a male-centered exogamous kin group), the composite band (lacking band exogamy or definite residence rules, therefore "more of an expedient agglomeration than a structured society [1962: 60]), and the anomalous band (a fragmented system that did not fit into either category).

Tribe

Non-anthropologists often use the word "tribe" to designate any small-scale, traditional society (such as the "Warlpiri tribe" or the "Ju/hoansi tribe"), but this is technically incorrect. A tribe is a very particular kind of society or polity; some pre-modern peoples lived in tribe-level societies and some did not. The word derives from ancient Roman politics, which divided the population into *tribua* or political and economic units (which paid taxes or "tribute" as a group). In contemporary anthropology, we use **tribe** to refer to a small-scale—but larger than band—political system, often encompassing multiple local residential groups that lose some of their local autonomy in a larger polity, with some at least incipient overarching political institutions. The organization of tribes may not be very extensive or very recognizably "political," but we witness what can justifiably be called "pan-tribal" politics.

Tribe-level politics is associated most closely with pastoralism and horticulture, which, as we know, yielded larger economic surpluses, more populous and settled social units, and more specialization of labor and other roles than foraging economies. They also produced more social inequalities and disputes (over property and the uses of property, such as bridewealth). The net result was more interpersonal friction in the society together with comparatively ranked or stratified individuals or groups who began to add other kinds of power than authority to their means of social control.

These new means of social control were what we meant above by "incipient overarching political institutions." There was usually nothing in tribe-level integration that equates to the Western conception of "government," but individuals or groups or institutions were able to exert various kinds of power on various grounds across one or more communities within a tribe, up to and including the entire tribal population. Some of the possible forms that tribal political institutions could take were:

- Age grade system and age sets. In some tribal settings, especially East African pastoralism, the male age grade system constituted a political arrangement. Men in the warrior set provided the defensive and "law enforcement" arm of politics, while the elder set provided the decision-making or problem-settling branch.
- Council of elders. Even in the absence of a formal age grade system, elder members of the tribe, sometimes as representatives of families, lineages, clans, or villages, met as an ad hoc decision-making or problem-settling body. This council was not a full-time government but only assembled when there was a specific pan-tribal issue to address. At other times, disparate families, lineages, clans, or villages handled their own affairs.
- Descent groups. As just mentioned, kinship corporate groups could serve a political function, perhaps by providing representatives to some political body. Another way that descent groups, like lineages and clans, could contribute to political integration was by having members resident in diverse local communities or villages. In this way, the group could preside over issues that concerned more than one local community and give some structure to the wider social life of the tribe. Specific families or lineages might function as "segments" of a larger kinship corporate group, making for what we call a segmentary lineage system. As with the council of elders, for the most part each lineage segment functioned autonomously, but when an inter-segment problem arose, or an external threat challenged multiple segments, they could pull together at least temporarily, although they tended to fall apart again when the problem was solved or the threat was past.
- The "big man." The big man was a type of tribal leader whose power flowed from his central position in the redistribution system. Redistribution was only possible in economic settings of greater surplus and greater control of that surplus. The big man did not in most cases have formal, permanent, or coercive power, but he did have both authority and persuasion. He was in a constant status competition with other rivals who may have their own entourage and their own power

Tribe

a political system or level of integration in which multiple local communities may be organized into a single system but in which political power is still relatively informal and usually flows from institutions that are not specifically political (such as elders, lineages, age sets, religious specialists, and so on)

See Chapter 7

within the tribe—the very essence of a rank system. Collectively, the various big men in a village or tribe provided an amount of political structure to the society.

■ Common interest groups. These non-kinship corporate groups could also add political structure to a society. Like the Cheyenne warrior clubs, they were often law enforcers and agents of social control, although not quite a "government." Still, their existence and the sanctions they could impose—including physical force—made them potent intra-society and inter-society political forces. Cheyenne warrior clubs, for example, were "police" of the buffalo hunts as well as private armies for defense of their own interests as well as the whole tribe (when they acted in unison).

■ Religious specialists. In many tribal societies, men or women of distinguished religious or spiritual power and skill had a substantial political role to play. These specialists, who were usually "part-time", could act as mediators, "consultants" (like oracles and diviners, whom individuals might consult before making important decisions), problem-solvers, and sanctuaries to whom disputants and defendants could turn to get temporary protection from violence until a more pro-social solution could be found to arguments or "crimes" (crimes sometimes including murder).

Chiefdom

a political system or "level of integration" in which a central office, often hereditary, possesses formal political power and social prestige through some degree of redistributive control over surplus and the ability to organize and manage labor

See Chapter 10

IMAGE 9.3 In many societies, religious specialists like this *mara'acame* of the Huichol Indians provide political leadership.

What these and similar roles, institutions, and mechanisms have in common is: (1) they were "political" even while they also arose and drew power from other aspects of culture (economics, kinship, non-kin corporateness, and religion); (2) they were part-time or ad hoc (that is, they only assembled or served when needed, unlike a permanent full-time sitting government); and (3) their ability to dictate decisions and solutions to the society and its members was fairly circumscribed. Such was the nature of politics in societies of only limited size, surplus, wealth, and socioeconomic and power distinctions.

Chiefdom

In larger and higher-surplus pastoral and horticultural societies, a more formal, full-time, and recognizably "political" system could develop, which anthropologists refer to as a **chiefdom**. A chiefdom is a polity usually consisting of multiple local communities over which an individual or a hierarchy of individuals exercises authority, persuasion, and at least some coercion. Since the chief and his "court" are full-time political specialists, they will be exempted from economic and productive activity, so obviously the economic system of the society must be productive enough to support this new "ruling class." Sometimes the role of chief is a ritual or ceremonial one; in other situations, it is a distinctly political one.

Besides—and based on—the economic aspect of chiefdom-level integration, the system depends on a clear, consistent, and often hereditary conception of rank, in which individuals, families, lineages, even entire villages or sets of villages are more or less literally and explicitly "ordered" from first to last in a prestige and power ladder (a kind of "pecking order"). Chiefs of course come from the "premier" families or lineages of society or control the premier resources of the society. This phenomenon should be familiar to Westerners in the case of European royal families: The next king or queen of England will, for example, come from the current ruling family (the Windsors), who are regarded as "higher" in some way than even other royal families (the dukes and earls and princes, etc.), let alone the "commoners." This is why royalty is often addressed as "your highness." Pre-modern

IMAGE 9.4 The king or Asantehene of the Ashanti Kingdom (present-day Ghana).

and feudal European society was an elaborate set of ranked individuals and families, with middle-level office-holders in the system both a "lord" to somebody below them and a "serf" or "client" to somebody above them (a higher lord and ultimately the king).

The African countries of Rwanda and Burundi before colonialism were traditional chiefdoms, with a multi-layered hierarchy of small chiefs leading up to the paramount chief, who approximated a king. There were chiefs of villages, chiefs of particular hills, chiefs of districts, and chiefs of other chiefs, in interlocking allegiance and competition with each other. Individuals and families "below" a particular chief would pay gifts to their chief, who used that wealth both to "take care of his people" and to pay his own gifts to his higher chief. The paramount chief accepted gifts from the chiefs immediately below him, who accepted gifts from the chiefs below them, and so on, so that ultimately everyone was contributing indirectly to the paramount chief. When Europeans encountered this system, they found it quite convenient to exploit and manipulate for their own purposes, actually in some ways *increasing* chiefly power rather than dismantling it.

Chiefdoms are thus definitely more formal and explicit political relationships than anything we have seen before. Chiefs are not always such overt political and economic masters of their societies—in some societies, the chief is a symbolic or even ritual figure, perhaps even one who did not venture out of his "royal" compound and whose existence and health supposedly symbolized and determined the fate of the society—but most of the time their concrete effect on society is unquestionable. Chiefs obviously live off of the surplus of the economy, and they can in many cases compel (although this compulsion often takes the form of personal or religious obligation) contribution to it. A chief often "holds court," where important decisions are made and important problems are settled: "Subjects" will "come to court" to get a hearing and a decision. The chief frequently even maintains a fighting force loyal to him, which he uses for external aggression as well as control of his own people. Some large and advanced chiefdoms, like the one on traditional Hawaii, have shaded into the next and final level of integration, the state.

State

The highest level of political integration (so far) is the **state**, which is the system with which Westerners

State

a political system or level of integration in which a formal centralized government has power over a delimited territory to make and enforce laws, to establish currency and collect taxes, and to maintain an army and declare war

are most familiar and under which they—and essentially all people of the world ultimately—live. By state, anthropologists do not mean the units like New York or Texas or California that Americans ordinarily call "states." These are not states in the anthropological and political science sense, but rather administrative divisions or sub-polities of the state (although, because of unique American history, "states" like New York retain some of the qualities of anthropological states). Rather, the U.S. is a state, the United Kingdom is a state, Mexico, Canada, Australia, Japan, France, Russia, Nigeria, India, and the other countries that one finds on political maps are states.

A state is a centralized political system with a formal government that has monopolistic power or "sovereignty" over a specific territory, including the power to make and enforce laws, to print money and collect taxes, and to maintain an army and declare war. A state is sovereign, that is, it is self-ruling or autonomous; there is no higher political power to which it must answer, certainly not the United Nations. (In fact, the United Nations might be better named the "United States," since all of its members are states, not nations.) States are the legitimate actors on the world political stage; while

there are some inter-state political bodies today (for instance, NATO or indeed the UN), they do not really function like states and are not sovereign like states. The European Union (EU) is the closest thing to an actual trans-state or inter-state polity.

States, which can reach great size (up to hundreds of millions of people), depend on the most productive economic practices, namely intensive agriculture and industrialism. In fact, the first states (albeit small ones, merely independent cities or city-states) appeared with the emergence of intensive agriculture in places like Mesopotamia, Egypt, India, and China, and later in Central America and Peru. What all of these societies had in common was a highly productive economy controlled by a powerful central government, often integrating military and religious power for the purpose of controlling territory and wealth. The size and density of society, especially the new social phenomenon called the "city" plus the elaborate stratification and specialization of society, was possible only because the new food-production methods were incredibly productive, yielding more than enough food for the farmers themselves. There was subsequently enough for a significant number of non-productive "specialists," including political

See Chapter 13

IMAGE 9.5 State-level political systems, like the German one headed by Chancellor Angela Merkel (pictured here) combine power and pageantry to control large, complex, and wealthy societies.

leaders, religious authorities, and soldiers. Not surprisingly, with the stockpiles of surplus in these societies and the male-dominated and hierarchical organization of politics, war was an inevitable and regular outcome.

State leaders still depend on their position as the center of the economic system, in which they can command not only production and labor, but the contribution of that production and labor in the form of taxes or tribute or labor on "public" projects like palaces, pyramids, roads, and city walls. In addition, the market plays a key role in state

societies, and the state may exercise power over the market as well; the earliest cities and states were also market societies. Certainly modern Western and Western-style governments manage their market economies (despite the ideology of "free markets") with centrally controlled monetary and banking institutions, like the Federal Reserve and the Federal Deposit Insurance Corporation, as well as domestic subsidies and international trade policies. States make rules and regulations for market players, tax those players, and protect them from players from other states.

BOX 9.2   THE LIFE OF POLICY WITHIN AND ACROSS STATES

One of the neglected powers or prerogatives of states is "policy," which is developed and implemented by governments to shape laws, institutions, and ultimately the behavior of its citizens. The Business Dictionary (www.businessdictionary.com/definition/policy.html) defines policy as "the basic principles by which a government is guided" and "the declared objectives that a government or party seeks to achieve and preserve in the interest of national community." In a word, policy is the outline that structures law and institutional practice, even as those laws and practices actualize the policy. Catherine Kingfisher explores "the social life of policy" (2013: 1), arguing that policy is "a power-laden artifact and architect of culture" (3) that simultaneously influences and is influenced by culture. Further, as she traces the path of policy within the institutions of a state and between states, she finds that it is "produced not only officially but also in myriad unofficial ways" (3). The particular issue at hand is welfare reform, which has been a major project of Western states since the 1990s. Kingfisher begins in Aotearoa (the indigenous name for New Zealand), where—as in the U.S. and elsewhere—poor single mothers were often demonized as "lazy and likely to cheat the system" (27). Finance minister Ruth Richardson proposed a number of changes to the welfare system, including "major cuts to the value of welfare benefits, tighter targeting and eligibility requirements, the introduction of user fees for health care services, and the virtual elimination of housing subsidies" (31). This was followed by the 1996 Tax Reduction and Social Policy Bill, requiring recipients to hone their work skills and accept any job offered to them on threat of losing their benefits. This so-called "New Zealand Model" gained international life when a previous finance minister, Roger Douglas, went into private business with "a cadre of former New Zealand government officials, academics, and activists crisscrossing the globe to sell—or warn of the dangers of—the NZ Model" (39). One client was the Canadian province of Alberta. But western Canada is a very different place, historically, culturally, and environmentally, than New Zealand, so Kingfisher finds that "those involved in the New Zealand-Alberta exchange were highly selective in what they paid attention to with regard to both the architecture and temporal unfolding of the NZ Model" (58). The outcome, at the policy level, "was a disjunctive constellation of bits and pieces from the here and the elsewhere," since "certain aspects of the NZ Model ... were completely suited to the Alberta context [while] others ... were not , and so were elided" (59). The life of policy becomes still more complicated when it is translated into practice in the welfare offices where recipients encounter the state face-to-face. Even when welfare officials were committed to the policies, they necessarily had to convert general principles into specific actions, replacing the "one-size-fits-all abstract individual of official policy with a more nuanced each-individual-is-unique approach" (91). Their actual decisions blended:

> bits and pieces of current policy mandates and bits and pieces of previous mandates, articulated with aspects of wider cultural systems of meaning and structures of sentiment, understandings (albeit partial and incomplete) of the exigencies of clients' lives, and adaptations to (and simultaneous constructions of) the parameters of their own institutional lives and identities.
>
> (101)

Matters got still more complicated at the level of service providers like food programs, training and education services, and homeless and battered-women's shelters, where the policy translated by office-dwellers had to be retranslated into real assistance. Finally, Kingfisher chases policy down to the level of the recipients, the poor women, who had to translate all of it into a way to feed their children and protect themselves from abusive men.

SOCIAL MEMORY AND THE STATE

Not all states have seen their primary business as business. In fact, the first states were probably more religious than they were economic institutions. The early Mesopotamian cities were "temple communities" where the priests and kings lived and which not only served as the religious and ritual center of society, but lived off of the religious contributions of outlying rural inhabitants. This raises a critical point, which concerns the "legitimation" of this new social arrangement. Why would laborers, who work hard out in the countryside, participate in a system in which their labor and wealth is expropriated from them—in fact, in which they often constitute a poor and lower or "peasant" class? One answer to this question is religion. As the political power was centralized in the city and its ruler(s), so the religious power was centralized as well, and the two were closely allied. The king was often the chief priest or, in the case of ancient Egypt, a living god himself; in pre-modern Europe kings claimed to rule by "divine right," while in China the emperor supposedly enjoyed the "mandate of heaven." The diffuse and spiritualized religion of earlier societies became a centralized and ritualized religion of state power and prestige. Subjects participated in the political system because that was what the god(s) ordained; religion became a source of authority for the (new) political institutions.

State political integration is comparatively new to the human world, not a natural fact, but a distinctly social and relative construction. No states existed before five or six thousand years ago, and many states have come and gone since then. States tend to emerge from social practices like war and political and cultural expansion; the early modern European states coalesced as local or regional rulers began to exercise their power and authority over larger areas and integrate them into a single political, economic, and cultural system, through means like a common currency, language, and set of weights and measures. Local communities and polities often resisted—and continue to resist—this "unification" and centralization. Even today, there are disputes (some of international proportions) over what is or is not a state. Tibet is one example: Many Tibetans consider their land a sovereign state, but China regards it as an historical part of China. Probably the most ominous debate is over the status of Taiwan, which was settled by refugees from Nationalist China when the Communists took control of the mainland in 1949. Today, Taiwan is less than a state but more than a territory of a larger state, with mutual defense treaties with the United States. However, China sees Taiwan as a rogue and separatist province of China (much as the U.S. saw the southern Confederacy during the Civil War) and intends to reintegrate it someday. When that day comes, there will be serious international ramifications.

State politics can take many forms, from monarchy and totalitarianism to democracy, with many economic arrangements from capitalist to socialist and communist. These are all merely ways of organizing state power and function. All of them—Mesopotamian and Greek city-states, empires, kingdoms, constitutional monarchies, capitalist democracies, socialist democracies, communist "people's republics," brutal autocracies, and even theocracies—finally have much more in common with each other than with bands and tribes and chiefdoms. None of them contemplates doing away with borders, laws, capitals, taxes, or armies. Rather, they merely value different ways of arranging those social and political realities. Whether the state is one person (France's King Louis XIV famously uttering, "I am the state") or "we the people" (as declared in the U.S. Constitution), states aim to perpetuate themselves as they regulate the people who fall within their territory and thus their jurisdiction.

STATE SEEING, STATE BEING

A state, like any other institution, is not just an assortment of human beings, but a social entity with its own "life," its own interests, practices, and ways of seeing and being. James Scott said as much in his *Seeing Like a State*, in which he contended that one of the primary goals of the modern state is "legibility," its capacity to "read" the society and thus understand and manage it. The pre-modern state, by contrast, was

> particularly blind: it knew precious little about its subjects, their wealth, their landholdings and yields, their location, their very identity. It lacked anything like a detailed "map" of its terrain and its people. It lacked, for the most part, a measure, a metric, that would allow it to "translate" what it knew into a common standard necessary for a synoptic view.
>
> (1998: 2)

Legibility, which features but is hardly limited to mapping, "provides the capacity for large-scale social engineering" (5) based on what Scott called "a pernicious combination of four elements" (4). The first is "the administrative ordering of nature and society," made possible through "the concept of citizenship" and detailed knowledge of those citizens; the second is the modern ideology of "scientific and technical progress" and "the rational design of social order commensurate with the scientific understanding of natural laws" (4), which is after all what social science is all about. The third and fourth elements are more sinister yet—"an authoritarian state that is willing and able to use the full weight of its coercive power" to achieve its

---

BOX 9.3   BEING THE STATE—AND RESISTING THE STATE—IN THE REPUBLIC OF GEORGIA

Although the state is not just a collection of people, neither is it some abstraction independent of people. A state requires human individuals to "perform" it, to "impersonate" it (that is, to give it personal embodied form), and to make it real. In the former Soviet Republic of Georgia, as everywhere, this means wearing the state's uniform and doing its business—enforcing its law, enacting its policy, fighting its wars, and so on. At the same time, according to Florian Mühlfried, people may "guard against the state," seeking to reduce their dependency on it, to exclude some objects, places, or practices from its invasive gaze, and therefore to maintain boundaries between themselves and the state that "open up 'room for maneuver' and allow for 'flexible citizenship'" (2014: 6–9). Mühlfried's focus is the Tushetians, a small nationality or ethnic group in northeast Georgia who were pressured to integrate first into the Soviet Union and then independent Georgia. Under both regimes, politics was "experienced as something that descends upon the people, increasing their vulnerability and chances for profit alike," but above all the state and citizenship were obligatory, "experienced as fate, as the very fact of belonging to a state [which] is non-negotiable and has palpable and sometimes fatal implications for daily life" (63). Some Tushetians have put themselves at the service of the state, "being the state" by lending their bodies as state employees, police officers, soldiers, and such. Others, though, exploit the fact that "the state is not everywhere" (69), finding and preserving those corners of culture that the state has not subdued. This includes certain places like mountain regions and religious shrines, along with local and ethnic knowledge and practices. In the end, Mühlfried holds that citizenship produces "ambivalent, fuzzy, and confusing results," since it combines "participation and entitlement" with the fact "of yielding one's sovereignty, of divesting one's subjectivity. Citizenship is a world where intentionality and the loss of it are intertwined to an inseparable extent" (162).

**CITIZENSHIP AND BEING
THE STATE IN
CONTEMPORARY CHINA**

**Non-governmental
organization (NGO)**

any non-profit, voluntary
citizens' group organized on
a local, national, or
international level. Task-
oriented and driven by
people with a common
interest, NGOs perform a
variety of service and
humanitarian functions,
bring citizen concerns to
governments, advocate and
monitor policies, and
encourage political
participation through
provision of information.

See Chapter 15

Governmentality

as formulated by Michel
Foucault, the assorted
practices, institutions,
instruments, and discourses
of power by means of which
a "government" (state) or
any other political entity
can manage a population
and manage to get that
population to manage itself

World Association of
Non-Governmental
Organizations worldwide
NGO directory: http://www.
wango.org/resources.
aspx?section=ngodir

vision, and "a prostrate civil society that lacks the capacity to resist these plans" (5).

One of the gifts that a state bestows on its constituents is "citizenship": Residents of the state are citizens, not merely subjects, of the state. But as historian Karen Kern (2011) pointed out, in the late Ottoman Empire, citizenship is also a burden; citizens have certain rights, to be sure, but they also have certain obligations, not the least of which are obedience, tax payment, and a willingness to sacrifice—even die—for the state. Citizenship integrates residents more totally into the state, asking not only for their loyalty, but for their participation, for citizens *to enact or perform the state themselves, to become agents of the state.*

GOVERNMENTALITY: POWER BEYOND THE STATE

The anthropological analysis of the state as a social form has yielded two crucial insights—first, that the state is not a single "thing," but a bundle of concepts, institutions, and practices, and second, that the state is not the sole site of these concepts, institutions, and practices. As Carole Nagengast (1994) put it, the state shares the political field with "sub-state" actors (class, race, ethnic, religious groups) and with "superstates" or trans-state actors (e.g. global Islam, communism, or regional "families" of related societies or states often called "civilizations").

One of the key thinkers on the practices of the state—and the distribution or diffusion of those practices—is Michel Foucault, who advanced the notion of **governmentality**. Governmentality is not synonymous with government; rather, Foucault argued that modern "state" government was one recent variation of governmentality. Governmentality refers more generally to the forms of power that political actors of all sorts can marshal and manipulate, including not only the obvious tools of laws, police, courts, and armies, but more subtle and widely-diffused

methods of examination and evaluation; techniques of notation, numeration, and calculation; accounting procedures; routines for the timing and spacing of activities in specific locations; presentational forms such as tables and graphs; formulas for the organization of

work; standardized tactics for the training and implantation of habits; pedagogic, therapeutic, and punitive techniques of reformulation and cure; architectural forms in which interventions take place (i.e. classrooms and prisons); and professional vocabularies.

(Lemke, 2007: 50)

States clearly do not enjoy a monopoly on governmentality. First, all cultural institutions possess some amount and methods of governmentality, including corporations and colleges. Second, non-state and especially sub-state groups or categories may claim aspects of governmentality for themselves: Ethnic or racial or class groups may contest the power of the state or even seize some of the functions commonly associated with the state. For instance, the "terrorist" organization Hamas also provides social services for the Palestinians of Gaza and operates schools, orphanages, health care facilities, soup kitchens, and sports leagues. Third and most remarkably, non-state institutions have been intentionally created to assume some of the roles customarily associated with states.

One important expression of non-state governmentality is the **non-governmental organization** (NGO), defined by the NGO Global Network (www.ngo.org) as

> any non-profit, voluntary citizens' group which is organized on a local, national or international level. Task-oriented and driven by people with a common interest, NGOs perform a variety of service and humanitarian functions, bring citizen concerns to governments, advocate and monitor policies and encourage political participation through provision of information. Some are organized around specific issues, such as human rights, environment or health. They provide analysis and expertise, serve as early warning mechanisms and help monitor and implement international agreements.

Some examples of NGOs include the World Wildlife Fund and Doctors Without Borders (not to mention the two Haitian NGOs at the opening of this chapter); there are many, many other special-interest NGOs, working in areas such as child protection, hunger and poverty, human rights, women's rights, peace, and so forth. The result is a

IMAGE 9.6 A complex web of non-governmental organizations provides much of the governmental structure of the modern world.

thick web of national, regional, and international governmentality

The relations of governmentality between states and non-state institutions are complex but critical. Non-state institutions can influence state policy through public opinion, political action, and even violence. As in the case of NGOs in Haiti, such institutions can actually assume some of the functions of government, at which point "it becomes only too clear that NGOs are not as 'NG' as they might wish us to believe. Indeed, the World Bank baldly refers to what they call BONGOS (bank-organized NGOs) and even GONGOs (government-organized NGOs)" (Ferguson and Gupta, 2002: 993). Indeed, the World Bank itself is an example

of an inter-governmental organization (IGO) established *by states* to provide certain services of governmentality for states around the globe.

In short, then, the concept of governmentality redirects our focus from the "thing" called the state to the techniques of power that states *and other entities* can administer—that is, "practices instead of object, strategies instead of function, and technologies instead of institution" (Lemke, 2007: 58). This takes the anthropology of power and politics to new places, for instance to what James Scott (1990) has called the "hidden transcripts" of power, a notion akin to Gramsci's "hegemony." Recently, though, attention has turned to a specific technique of governmentality, the audit. In 2000, Marilyn Strathern edited a volume examining **audit culture** in a discussion centering on academic institutions but equally applicable beyond them. Derived from the root for "hearing," an audit is a practice of monitoring, of checking results, of accountability. Cris Shore and Susan Wright, writing in Strathern's anthology, explicitly linked auditing and audit culture to governmentality as "a relationship of power between scrutinizer and observed," which depends on cultural concepts and norms—an audit "repertoire"—including "'public inspection,' 'submission to scrutiny,' 'rendering visible,' and 'measures of performance'" (2000: 59). Associated with the rise of the audit culture are the view of the audited person or group "as a deper-sonalized unit of economic resource whose pro-ductivity and performance must constantly be measured and enhanced" (62), a change in the subjective experience of the audited person toward *self-monitoring*, and "the creation of new categories of experts including 'educational development consultants,' 'quality assurance officers,' 'staff development trainers,' and 'teaching quality asses-sors'" (62). All of these can be seen quite justifiably as micro-governmentality processes.

See Chapter 14

Audit culture
a system of power between scrutinizer and observed which depends on cultural concepts and norms an audit "repertoire" including "public inspection," "submission to scrutiny," "rendering visible," and "measures of performance"

BOX 9.4   AUDIT CULTURE IN CONTEMPORARY CHINA

The concept of audit culture, and indeed of governmentality, is most often applied to "neoliberal" governments and economies, but there is no reason in principle why it should be so restricted. Yan Hairong found that contemporary China is undergoing its own audit culture revolution in regard to *suzhi* or "quality," a term that "facilitates exploitation" of Chinese workers "*and* makes it invisible"

See Chapter 14

(2003: 494). As Yan portrayed it, there is a veritable crisis of *suzhi* in modern China, with newspapers complaining of "the low suzhi of peasants [which] has become an excuse for many things not getting done or not getting done well"; President Jiang Zeming himself stressed the need for "cultivating millions of high-suzhi laborers and skilled technicians" (495). Yan asserted that "what suzhi *is* eludes precise definition," but that it seems to concern both "'hardware,' or embodied physical quality, and 'software,' which referred to a wide range of cultural qualities (*wenhua suzhi*), including psychological quality (*xinli suzhi*) and quality of consciousness (*sixiang suzhi*)" (496). Of course, before suzhi can be "improved," it must be quantified and measured, and "the most quantifiable index of suzhi is . . . wages," but other measures "include various kinds of psychological and practical ability tests and IQ tests offered by popular magazines" (497). Thus, as in all other instances of audit-culture governmentality, individuals are monitored and evaluated by authorities *and are encouraged to monitor and evaluate themselves.*

AN ANTHROPOLOGY OF WAR

Turney-High, Harry H. 1971. *Primitive War: Its Practice and Concepts.* Columbia: University of South Carolina Press.

Politics refers to both internal or domestic (intra-society or intra-state) social control and external or inter-society or inter-state social control, and one of the most important external or "foreign" political relations is war. It is by no means the only relationship between any two societies (many live in peace, or in tense mutual co-existence, or in occasional brief outbreaks of conflict, like raids and border skirmishes), nor is war the only form of political violence, which includes feuds, persecution, genocide, ethnic conflict, and others. There are those who might assert that an anthropology of war is unnecessary (war being simply a natural and instinctive trait of humans) or impossible (war being not a social phenomenon, but the *breakdown* of society). But of course, whatever the status of the first claim, it is untrue that war is the absence or failure of social life or politics; after all, according to Carl von Clausewitz' classic formulation, war is the continuation of politics by other (deadly) means.

Anthropologists have, not surprisingly, devoted some attention to war. Malinowski himself wrote an essay entitled "An Anthropological Analysis of War" in which he defined it as "an armed contest between two independent political units, by means of organized military force, in the pursuit of a tribal or national policy" (1964: 247). Such an activity clearly requires at least two societies or states, with political interests and goals ("policies") and with sufficient social and political organization to field an army and prosecute an extended struggle.

Harry Turney-High therefore distinguished between what he called "modern" or "true" war and "primitive" or pre-modern or tribal war. True war, he insisted, entails tactical operations, command and control processes, "the ability to conduct a campaign for the reduction of enemy resistance if the first battle fails" (in other words, the ability to support a protracted military conflict, which involves a military institution like an army), a collective motive rather than a personal one, and "an adequate supply," which requires the organization of the entire society for the purpose and provisioning of war (1971: 30). By these standards, most pre-modern inter-society violence did not rise to the level of war. Combat practices of the Plains Indians of North America, who were more interested in "counting coup" by striking an enemy and retreating or stealing an enemy's horse than conquering or exterminating the enemy, would disqualify them. Raids or attacks motivated by personal interests like vengeance, jealousy, theft, or suspected witchcraft would also not constitute war; a classic example would be the Ok of highlands New Guinea, for whom "war" consisted of

small-scale ambushes and raids, which probably produce the majority of casualties, as well as the rarer large-scale confrontations . . . and battles that are circumscribed by rules and conventions, such as the use of traditional fighting grounds. Confrontations or "nothing fights" escalate to all-out fighting with heavy casualties only infrequently. The proximate cause of particular incidents is the perceived need to retaliate for past wrongs summarized in the phrase *blood revenge*, often the murder or putative murder (by sorcery) of a group member by members of a neighboring group.

(Morren, 1984: 173)

Such are the reasons that Turney-High regarded the pre-modern fighter as more of a "warrior" than a "soldier," the latter being a disciplined member of a sustained military project.

That war is a social institution or phenomenon is also evidenced by the amount of social support that it demands. This includes not only the logistics of war—the recruitment of large numbers of soldiers, the contributions of the non-combatants to the "war effort," the military and political decision-making systems, and the supply procedures to keep the armies fed and fueled in the field. As Turney-High rightly acknowledged, war depends on the social acceptance of war, constructed and maintained through warrior values, attitudes, norms, and rules. Among the martial values are high-minded principles like honor, bravery, patriotism, and self-defense and lower-minded ones like vengeance and the acquisition of war profits and trophies. Until very recently, war was typically seen as a glorious and manly undertaking; war preparedness is still a virtue, and participation in war is still widely regarded as "service to one's country." And, contrary to the image of war as anti-social chaos, there are

indeed "rules of war" (codified in institutions like the Geneva Conventions) and standards for a "just war," such as not harming non-combatants and not torturing war prisoners.

War is orderly; moreover, war can be constitutive of social order. Malinowski actually concluded—and he was by no means alone in this conclusion—that war produced the very state itself. The demands of centralization, administration and decision-making, and recruitment and morale, required an institution like the state. And we can go far beyond Malinowski's view: War creates or sustains many other institutions, not the least of which are armies, war colleges, defense contractors, research institutes, hospitals, veterans' affairs offices, not to mention holidays (from Bastille Day to Veterans Day), parades, monuments, and many more.

Finally, we cannot overlook the cultural, even mythical, quality of war. War itself is a cultural or ideological practice, one that plays upon and activates the deepest meanings of a society. Journalist Chris Hedges has gone so far as to stress, as his book is titled, that war is a force that gives us meaning: "It can give us purpose, meaning, a reason for living. Only when we are in the midst of conflict does the shallowness and vapidness of much of our lives become apparent" (2002: 3). At such times, individuals transcend the individual existence and truly become part of a grander, sometimes even cosmic, endeavor.

ANTHROPOLOGISTS AT WAR: THE HUMAN TERRAIN SYSTEM

BOX 9.5   CONTEMPORARY CULTURAL CONTROVERSIES: ANTHROPOLOGY OF WAR VERSUS ANTHROPOLOGY IN WAR

Montgomery McFate, an anthropologist and professor at the U.S. Naval War College, helped develop the Human Terrain System for the United States Army. According to "The Human Terrain Team Handbook," military commanders and planners "require insight into cultures, perceptions, values, beliefs, interests, and decision-making processes of individuals and groups" with whom they are at war (U.S Department of Defense, 2008: 3). For this purpose, Human Terrain Teams consisting of five to nine members are proposed to gather data using "classic anthropological and sociological methods such as semi-structured and open-ended interviews, polling and surveys, text analysis, and participant observation" (4). This is hardly the first time that anthropologists have been recruited for a war effort: Ruth Benedict examined Japanese culture and personality during the Second World War, and William Howells was a lieutenant in the Office of Naval Intelligence before teaching at Harvard University from 1954. Joy Rodhe (2013) documents a wide array of anthropological and social scientific collaboration with the government during the Cold War, to understand and prevent "insurgency." Some anthropologists have leapt at the opportunity, while others are deeply troubled by this meshing of social science and war. What do you think?

SUMMARY

Political functions must be fulfilled in all societies, but not all have distinct and formal political institutions, separate from the economic and kinship and non-kin and religious roles and institutions of the society. The various functions can be encapsulated into social order and social control. Social control is achieved by a combination of externalized and internalized controls.

The agents of social control who make up the external controls have a variety of sanctions at their disposal, and, while formal agents can and do impose heavy pressures for proper behavior, most sanctions are informal and personal. In fact, all members of a society are informal agents of social control on each other.

Politics is the exercise of power, with different sources and different qualities—authority (including charisma), persuasion, and coercion. Power can be institutional and highly visible, or it can be hegemonic and relatively invisible. Anthropologists have learned to investigate power by studying power relations up, down, and sideways.

Therefore, based on their level of political integration, including the types and roles of power, political systems can be distinguished into

- band
- tribe
- chiefdom
- state

In the twenty-first-century world, states are not the only actors on the world stage. Many of the powers and functions of the state have been shared by, transferred to, or usurped by non-state groups or organizations, showing that governmentality is a set of practices that can be diffused through and layered in a society or in the entire international community. Governmentality directs attention away from "state" or "government" to power and the distribution and practices of power.

Finally, war is an endemic, if not entirely inevitable, aspect of modern politics. Contrary to the sense that war is anti-social, anthropologists have discovered that war tends to be, even needs to be, socially organized and that war can even produce elements of culture and society.

Q

MCQS

Q

FILL IN THE BLANKS

www

Key Terms

agents of social control	formal sanction	office
audit culture	governmentality	persuasion
authority	informal sanction	sanction
band	internalized control	social control
chiefdom	level of political integration	state
coercion	leveling mechanism	symbolic capital
externalized control	non-governmental organization	tribe

Religion

Interacting with the non-human world

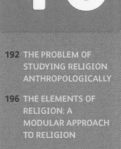

In the Democratic Republic of Congo (formerly Zaire), "nearly everybody claims to be a Christian" (Pype, 2012: 32), although Christianity sits uncomfortably alongside other religions, especially traditional religions. Worse, it sits uncomfortably alongside the "heat" of the city, with its materialism and its sexuality, confusion, and uncertainty. Pentecostalism in Kinshasa, the capital city, adopts the conventional dualistic division of modern urban society into the good godly part and the bad ungodly part, with "a strong belief in the demonization of quotidian life and an invisible battle . . . between God . . . and the Devil" (38). This struggle between good and evil plays out throughout the society, including on television, in the form of Pentecostal melodramas. Acting troupes that produce these shows are essentially churches or ministries and therefore worry deeply about who is or is not a "real Christian" as opposed to merely a "carnal Christian" or "Christian of the flesh." The melodramas themselves are almost invariably morality plays of some sort, depicting the threats of modern city life with stock characters like the "bad girl," "an adolescent girl with occult powers who does not belong to the earthly realm of reality but inhabits a demonic world" (211). The serials also function as witchcraft accusations and wider condemnations of traditional religion, the power of the elders, and the immorality of the city. Not surprisingly, "Pentecostal melodramas frequently end with confessions" (163) and the victory of Christians over the forces of darkness. For the actors, the experiences are more than fictional, but quite real, so individuals are sometimes hesitant to play evil characters, and before filming begins, the performers attend "special prayer sessions at which participating members not only seek inspiration but also solicit spiritual guidance and protection" (131). It is not only the actors who need protection against the forces that they portray and potentially unleash; audiences also express "a fear of becoming bewitched while watching the actors perform dances originating in the dark world" (145) or otherwise bringing these evil beings and forces to life.

Religion has been a focal topic for anthropology from its earliest days: It was the main subject of E. B. Tylor's founding document, his 1871 *Primitive Culture*, and the entire content of James George Frazer's epochal comparative mythology, *The Golden Bough* (first published in 1890 but greatly expanded over the years). Scholars and the general

IMAGE 10.1 Preacher at a Pentecostal church in the Democratic Republic of Congo.

See Chapter 5

public alike have been fascinated with religion, for its color and pageantry as well as for its strangeness and for what it potentially reveals about the human mind (sometimes prejudicially construed as "primitive mentality" or irrationality) and about the world beyond humans.

The anthropology of religion emerged from nineteenth-century curiosity about comparative religion and the evolution of religious beliefs and institutions (in parallel with interest in political, kinship, and economic institutions, as we have seen). Research into ancient and Eastern religions, like William Robertson Smith's 1889 *Lectures on the Religion of the Semites*, or Max Müller's translations of Hindu texts, led to questions about "primitive" religion, but anthropology has long since shed its obsession with primitive religion (and politics and economics) and opened itself to the diversity of religions, including world religions such as Christianity and Islam. Contrary to the nineteenth- and early-twentieth-century prediction that religion would fade into irrelevance, it is a vital force in the modern world and one that highlights all of the essential qualities and processes of culture.

THE PROBLEM OF STUDYING RELIGION ANTHROPOLOGICALLY

The anthropological approach to religion, as to all other facets of culture, requires a cross-cultural, holistic, and relativistic perspective. That is, we must consider all the variations of religion found among humans, search for the interconnections between religion and the rest of culture (not the least of which are language, politics, and gender), and understand and judge religion only in the terms of the society in which we find it and never merely our own. This is more difficult for religion than for other facets of culture, precisely because religion *does* seem to deal with the "real" in ways that the rest of culture does not. That is, it is hard to imagine someone (at least someone with any level of anthropological awareness) saying that their language, economic practice, or political system is "true." Language, economy, or politics is easily recognized as culturally relative; it makes no sense to claim that English is "truer" or "better" than Spanish, Japanese, or Warlpiri or that states are "truer" than bands. However, people are much more comfortable asserting that their religion is true—and often uncomfortable with challenges to the truth of their religion. Robertson Smith was accused of heresy and libel for daring to study religion like just any other subject.

Early (and not so early) researchers were attracted to but at the same time distanced themselves from the religious beliefs and practices they viewed and reported, in a way that is unusual if not unthinkable for most cultural behaviors. For example, Frazer testified that "I look upon [the myths collected in *The Golden Bough*] not merely as false but as preposterous and absurd" (1958: vii). Of magic he concluded that "every single profession and claim put forward by the magician as such is false" (53). Evans-Pritchard, writing on witchcraft among the Azande of Africa, asserted: "Witches, as the Azande conceive them, cannot exist" (1937: 63); the great Radcliffe-Brown himself added that religious rituals are "based on erroneous belief" and that "the natives are mistaken" because "the rites do not actually do what they are believed to do" (1965: 44). They follow a long tradition, back to the ancient historian Herodotus, who wrote: "My duty is to report all that is said, but I am not obliged to believe it all" (1942: 556).

It is obviously not an anthropological attitude to refute, let alone to disparage as "absurd," another culture's ideas and behaviors. Religion, then, has proven to be a place where relativism and objectivity are most elusive. Fortunately, Radcliffe-Brown, following the founding sociologist Émile Durkheim in his seminal book *The Elementary Forms of the Religious Life*, advised that anthropologists should not inspect religions for their truth but for "the contribution that they make to the formation and maintenance of a social order" (1965: 154). Truth is frankly irrelevant to that function.

What is relevant to anthropologists is what people do and say in (or as) religion—that is, their practices and their language. For anthropology, religion is *practiced* more than it is *believed* (long ago, R. R. Marett famously declared that religion "is, fundamentally, a mode of social behavior" [1909: xi] and "something not so much thought out as danced out" [xxxi]), and anthropologists have gone so far as to question the applicability of the concept of "belief" to all religions. Rodney Needham contended that the very notion of "belief" is culturally relative and that not all cultures use it with the same meaning, if at all. "We have discovered grounds to conclude that the concept of belief is not expressed in all languages," therefore "we are not sharing their apprehension and are not understanding their thought if we foist this typically Western distinction on to them" when they do not possess it themselves (1972: 175).

Treating religion like language impresses the relativity of religion upon us. Among other things, a religion consists of a vocabulary, each word of which has a semantic range that may not be shared with other religions. Familiar "religious" words like

"spirit," "soul," "heaven," "hell," and even "god" or "religion" may not occur in other religions or may have very different meanings in them. The same holds, and is easier to see, in regard to unfamiliar religious words including *karma* or *nirvana* or *jukurrpa* or *kwoth*. No one would assume those terms to be cross-culturally universal, and no one would think to adopt them as supposedly neutral analytical tools to describe other religions.

Defining religion

The first problem in the anthropological study of religion is determining what religion is, that is, defining religion. E. B. Tylor offered what he considered to be the "minimal" or simplest possible definition—*belief in spiritual beings*. But as terse as it is, it faces at least one problem: It introduces another term, "spiritual being," that requires a definition. If the phrase means "being without a physical body," then not all religions agree; sometimes religious beings have or can assume bodies. In classical Islam, beings known as *jinn* were said to possess bodies of light or fire and to take the shape of animals (El-Zein, 2009).

Since Tylor's day, anthropologists have suggested a plethora of definitions for religion, sometimes emphasizing belief, sometimes behavior, sometimes myth or ritual, and so on. They are too numerous to count or recount here, but three influential ones include the following:

a unified system of beliefs and practices relative to sacred things, that is to say, things set aside and forbidden—beliefs and practices which unite into one single moral community called a Church, all those who adhere to them.
(Durkheim, 1965 [1915]: 62)

a set of rituals, rationalized by myth, which mobilizes supernatural powers for the purpose of achieving or preventing transformations of state in man and nature.
(Wallace, 1966: 107)

a system of symbols which act to establish powerful, pervasive, and long-lasting moods and motivations in men by formulating conceptions of a general order of existence and clothing these conceptions with such an aura

Evans-Pritchard, E. E. 1937. *Witchcraft, Oracles, and Magic Among the Azande*. New York: Oxford University Press.

Durkheim, Émile. 1965 [1915]. *The Elementary Forms of the Religious Life*. New York: The Free Press.

Needham, Rodney. 1972. *Belief, Language, and Experience*. Chicago: The University of Chicago Press.

Wallace, Anthony. 1966. *Religion: An Anthropological View*. New York: Random House.

See Chapter 4

See Chapter 5

of factuality that the moods and motivations seem uniquely realistic.

(Geertz 1973: 90)

No doubt religion is ideas, practices, rituals, morality, and community: each definition captures something of its complexity. Simultaneously, religion has no monopoly on ideas, practices, rituals, morality, and community, which are common to all cultural institutions and social relations. The difference seems to be the inclusion of new kinds of entities in these institutions and relations, entities that we can only call *persons* too. Thus Robin Horton reasoned that when we are talking about religion

> we are dealing with action directed towards objects which are believed to respond in terms of certain categories—in our own culture those of purpose, intelligence, and emotion—which are also the distinctive categories for the description of human action. The application of these categories leads us to say that such objects are "personified". . . . In short, Religion can be looked upon as an extension of the field of people's social relationships beyond the confines of purely human society.
>
> (1960: 211)

That is, religion appears to rest on the conception of non-human personhood, of the existence of *other-than-human* persons who share with humans what we call "**agency**." Agency is the capacity to possess mind, will, personality, or intentionality (i.e. to act with intention or plan rather than to be a passive object of someone else's will). Agency also implies *efficacy*, the capacity to have an impact on the world, to have an effect, to get things done.

Other-than-human persons are different from mere things; humans can and must treat them with consideration, even respect, as they would any person. Most importantly, other-than-human persons call for, perhaps demand, a *social relationship*. They may have a language (usually ours) and can be contacted and influenced. They may have emotions, likes and dislikes, and needs. They may expect or require gifts and offer gifts in exchange— that is, basic reciprocity. They may even be part of the kinship system, named and regarded as parents or grandparents.

The classic statement of non-human personhood came in A. Irving Hallowell's description of Ojibwa culture. In their language, grammatical markers distinguish animate beings from inanimate objects, but some inanimate objects to Westerners, like stones, are categorized as animate by the Ojibwa. When Hallowell asked if all stones are animate, one old man answered, "No! But *some* are" (1976: 362). Going deeper, Hallowell realized that trees, pots, pipes, and the sun and moon or thunder were seen as animate and believed to speak and

IMAGE 10.2 Religions convey belief and meaning in symbols, like this golden Buddha in Thailand.

BOX 10.1 THE GLASTONBURY GODDESS

"The Goddess is alive in Glastonbury, visible for all to see in the shapes of the sacred landscape," declares the Glastonbury Goddess Temple (www.goddesstemple.co.uk) in the United Kingdom. Tracing its spiritual history to King Arthur, the magical island of Avalon, and pre-Christian British religion, the Goddess Temple is the abode of deities in the form of "willow wickerwork statues who are venerated, spoken with, petitioned, and said . . . to 'embody' the Goddess" (Whitehead, 2013: 76). While devotees of the Goddess may say that the figures represent her, they also say that she is "present in" them and in the surrounding land. Like the Goddess, the Nine Morgens are materialized in wicker statues and possess healing powers. Even more, followers assert that they "sometimes move, that their facial expressions change, and that 'things' occur around them" (77). The Goddess statue is routinely dressed and decorated "to display colors corresponding with one of the eight points in the ritual year" (78), but she is present not only in that wicker body, but in other objects and images too: One female artist (the Goddess' worshippers are predominantly women) painted a picture of the Goddess and asserted that "it took roughly three days after the painting was finished for the Goddess to 'settle in' (her words) to the image," after which the image was seen "as containing and embodying the Goddess" (81). The Goddess is also taken in procession (see www.youtube.com/watch?v=msxgiUwFvtA for a video of the 2013 event), as Christian icons and statues often are, and when she returns to her temple home, women place items like earrings, stone, seashells, and pictures on or near her, kissing their own fingers and transferring the kiss to the figure. In the temple, the Goddess also receives offerings from devotees "in times of hardship or need, in thanks, or simple celebration of her" (86). And in these actions and the round of rituals, "intimate, day-to-day relationships with the Goddess figure and the Nine Morgens can take on 'real' interactions" (88). Believers claim that each statue has its own personality and changing mood—"sometimes they look pissy or serious, and sometimes they look happy and pleased"—and ultimately they are more than symbols of the divine persons. "the statues are the Morgens" (88).

listen. They were called "grandfather" and viewed as sources of power or blessing for humans. At the extreme, Hallowell concluded that everything was personal for them: "any concept of *impersonal* 'natural' forces is totally foreign to Ojibwa thought" (367). If so, then, there was no such thing as "natural" apart from "social"—and therefore no such thing as "supernatural" apart from "natural." In a word, the recognition of objects and phenomena "as other-than-human persons exemplifies a world view in which a natural-supernatural dichotomy has no place" (368).

Functions of religion

Why do humans have such a thing as religion, and what does it do for them? We can identify a diverse set of potential functions, each of which spawns a particular theoretical perspective on religion.

Malinowski emphasized religion's role in filling individual needs, especially psychological or emotional needs, such as comfort, hope, perhaps love, definitely a sense of control, and relief from fear and despair. Radcliffe-Brown, in his theory of structural functionalism, insisted that society has its own needs, particularly the need for cohesion, solidarity, integration, and perpetuation. So, in times of crisis, or just in the ordinary course of events, people might drift apart or even blow apart, ending "society" altogether. Religion's shared beliefs, shared values, and shared activities (prayers, rituals, sacrifices, etc.) not only provide things to do together to get through the hard times, but make them more alike, give them a sense of shared identity and shared destiny. Partly this position is derived from Durkheim, who focused on the social force that results from ritual behavior, creating almost a "group mind," a collective conscience, or at least a common experience.

MEET SAINT ANTHONY OF PADUA, CHALK PERSON

Surveying these and other functions of religion, we can condense them into three main categories:

1. Explanation, especially of origins or causes. Humans wonder why things are as they are. How did the world start? How did humans start? How did society start? Most religions not only provide a cosmogony (ideas about the creation of the world), but speculate on the origin of specific cultural issues, like marriage, language, technology, politics, and so on. Religions also explain why things happen in the present: Why do we get sick? Why do bad things happen to us? Why do we die? In some societies, much if not all of sickness and misfortune is attributed to religious causes, as was true in Western society not so very long ago and still is for some people.

2. Control, both of culture and of nature. Religion has, in all societies, an inherently political function, to guide human behavior in certain directions; which direction in particular depends on the society and religion. So, religion provides rules and standards, sometimes quite explicit and formal ones (like the Judeo-Christian "Ten Commandments"), sometimes implicit and informal ones. It also provides models or paradigms of behavior: Christians are taught to imitate Christ (many determine their behavior by asking WWJD—what would Jesus do?), Muslims hold up Muhammad as the paragon of human virtue, and the Buddha is the archetype for Buddhists. Finally, religion adds sanctions and the agents and institutions (human and non-human) to impose those sanctions, from sickness or misfortune to excommunication and eternal damnation. Religion even asserts itself as a means to control the physical world, including the human body. Religion may offer practices to affect the wind and the rain, the fertility of land or animals, and the health of humans: Curing rituals, after all, are intended to combat illness, and "black magic" is intended to harm one's enemies.

3. Legitimation, of cultural and natural facts. Humans appear to need to legitimate or justify the arrangements of society and nature to themselves, that is, not merely to explain why some fact exists (like death or kingship), but *why it should exist, why it is right and good.* Why

is it not only true but proper that women suffer in childbirth? Why is it not only true but desirable to have a king? Christianity has answered these questions with doctrines like the sin of Eve and the divine right of kings. In each case, either a spirit or ancestor set the precedent, or a supernatural figure made the choice. All religions meet the challenge of legitimating the reigning order by containing some element of "order-establishment" or "culture-establishment." This is the **charter** function of religion as identified by Malinowski (see below): It acts as the guideline or authority or "charter" by which humans organize themselves in particular ways and follow particular standards. Of course, there are many types of legitimation, such as popular opinion or majority vote. But religious legitimation is superior to mere social legitimation, since the religious beings or forces—the "authors" of the religiously given order—have the "authority" to create order and are not subject to the imperfections and indecisions of humans.

In terms of these three functions, religion is often seen as a generally conservative force. Yet, with its rules, authorities, and institutions all in place, it can also be a powerful medium for change and protest—for adjusting to, challenging, resisting, and creating social relations. As we will see below, often the first change or resistance movements in a society take a religious form, and many of the most important movements for cultural change in the world today are religious in character.

THE ELEMENTS OF RELIGION: A MODULAR APPROACH TO RELIGION

Another emerging anthropological and general social science attitude toward religion is that it is a basically composite or modular phenomenon. That is, rather than struggling to identify the one "essence" or universal feature of religion, it is more useful and accurate to analyze what religion is "made of." Actually, a half-century ago, Anthony Wallace (1966) proposed that religion is not a "thing" or single unitary phenomenon, but instead a composite of elementary building blocks, erected upon the "supernatural premise" that super-human

CONSTRUCTION OF RELIGIOUS EXPERIENCE

See Chapters 11 and 15

beings or forces exist. He identified thirteen "categories of religious behavior" (such as prayer, music, myth, sacrifice, physical "exercises," etc.) that are combined in particular ways in any given religion. These are further combined into religious or "cult" *institutions,* which are finally combined into *a religion.* Thus religion is "essentially a summative notion and cannot be taken uncritically to imply that one single unifying, internally coherent, carefully programmed set of rituals and beliefs characterizes the religious behavior or the society or is equally followed by all its members" (78).

Contemporary scholars like Pascal Boyer (2001) and Scott Atran (2002) developed the modular approach in a new direction. Boyer for instance posited that religion is not so much a composite of behaviors as a "by-product" of "mental systems and capacities that are there anyway, religious concepts or not" (311). Boyer, Atran, and a host of scholars from multiple disciplines represent what has come to be known as the cognitive-evolutionary theory of religion, that religion is just a specific manifestation of general human mental

and social tendencies—the same ones that make culture possible—including agency detection (paying attention to other persons, or what is known as "theory of mind"), emotional attachment, and so forth. If this view is valid (and there is much evidence for it), then the "notion of religion as a special domain is not just unfounded but in fact rather ethnocentric" (311).

Because religion is modular, it is not entirely useful or even possible to speak of "types" of religion in the way that we previously specified types of economic production or marriage or formal politics. Any actual religion may contain elements or modules of different alleged "types" of religion, and some may contain certain elements while lacking other elements (for example, ritual versus prayer). It is also important to appreciate, as Wallace, Boyer, and Atran do, that the religious modules have non-religious correlates, that is, that there is nothing uniquely "religious" about them: There is religious ritual and non-religious ritual, religious feasting and non-religious feasting, religious and non-religious music or narratives, etc. The great

BOX 10.2   RELIGION, NATIONALISM, AND VIOLENCE IN EASTERN EUROPEAN PAGANISM

For most Americans, paganism is a benign (although perhaps un-Christian) religion of femininity and earth-worship. In other settings, it is decidedly different. In contemporary Russia and Eastern Europe, paganism often gets attached to militant nationalism and even anti-ethnic violence. Victor Shnirelman notes two forms of paganism in Russia, one with a "less politicized folklorist" quality, and the other with a "highly politicized national-patriotic" nature (2013: 63). For the nationalists, "Russian nationalism is the actual creed and . . . Pagan beliefs and symbols legitimate the implementation of ethnic Russian rule and discrimination against non-Russians" (65). This has led, unhappily, to an alliance between pagans and right-wing, including neo-Nazi (skinhead), organizations like the Union of Slavic Communities of the Slavic Native Faith. The pagan-nationalist movement can turn to actual violence against ethnic minorities as well as against Christian churches, which they view as false and foreign. Thus Shnirelman invites us to perceive Russian neopaganism "as both an ideology . . . and as a fighting practice" (73) based on the concept of *the sacred nation.* Interestingly, one other cultural resource that gets mixed with pagan-nationalist religion is popular music, especially heavy metal. Pagan metal bands are the most prominent in Eastern Europe, particularly in the former communist countries of Russia, Belarus, Ukraine, Lithuania, Poland, and Bulgaria. On the dark end of the hard rock spectrum, Benjamin Hedge Olson finds the origins of National Socialist Black Metal (NSBM) in Scandinavian countries; with its message that "the present is sick and degraded; the past was glorious and vital; the present must be destroyed and/or escaped in order to attain a meaningful existence" (2013: 137), Eastern Europe has developed "one of the most vibrant, fanatic and racist black metal scenes in the world" (146), although the United States "has become one of the most prolific producers of NSBM in the last ten years" (140).

psychologist William James confessed that religious emotions are merely human emotions directed at religious objects or persons. Furthermore, because religion like all culture is modular, non-religious modules—such as politics, race, technology, and popular culture—can attach to religion, resulting in some surprising and even disturbing outcomes.

Religious entities: beings and forces

Among the most fundamental building blocks of a religion are the specific entities that it posits as real. This area is often referred to as the "beliefs" of the religion, but that term is misleading and potentially ethnocentric, as we noted above. There are two general subcategories of religious entities—beings and forces—which can and often do appear together in any actual religion.

Beings

Tylor's minimal definition of religion referred to spiritual beings. In familiar Western-Christian thinking, a spiritual being is a person without a body. The concept clearly and meaningfully separates agency or personhood from materiality. However, it is not true that all cultures and religions conceive religious beings as completely immaterial (that is, oppose "spirit" and "body") or necessarily distinguish human beings from religious beings. In some traditions, "spiritual" beings have, or at least at times, assume physical bodies, and humans may transform into spiritual beings, while spiritual beings may become human. The boundary between humans and other-than-human persons is porous in many if not all religions.

One of the most persistent ideas across cultures is that humans themselves have a spiritual part or parts, which co-habits with the body to some extent and which survives the body after death. In the Christian tradition, the **soul** is an eternal, immaterial, indivisible, personal (that is, it preserves the individual's personality) entity. Not all religions have such a concept, and those that have it often have very different notions about it. According to the Buddhist teaching of *anatta* or "no soul," the human spiritual part is not a permanent unchanging essence but rather is in constant flux. Other religions speak of multiple souls or a soul with multiple

parts. The Tausug of the Philippines said that humans were composed of four parts: the body, the mind, the "liver" or emotion, and the "soul." The soul also had four parts: the transcendent soul, which was all-good and always in the spiritual realm, even while one was alive; the life-soul, which was related to the blood and attached to the body but which wandered from the body in dreams; the breath, which was the essence of life and always attached to the body; and the spirit-soul, the person's "shadow" (Kiefer, 1972). The Dusun of Borneo mentioned seven soul-parts, one inside the other, the smallest the width of the little finger and the largest the thickness of the thumb. They were not born full-sized but grew as the body grew. The six "outside" souls or *magalugulu* were visible in human form, but the innermost soul or *gadagada* was formless and invisible (Williams, 1965).

The spiritual fate of deceased humans also varies from society to society. Among the Navajo, a **ghost** was the evil part of a dead person, so there were no good ghosts by definition (Downs, 1972). In his renowned study of Burmese religion (1978), Melford Spiro found that the dead could become *leikpya* if they did not receive a proper funeral or if they were powerful and ambitious people in their lifetime (like government officials), in which case they haunted their former house or village. In other cases, humans may be dead but still "active" in the physical world, as in the case of the vampire or the zombie, both of whom are dead individuals who have somehow been reanimated but without a soul.

In other cases, dead people may carry on as **ancestor spirits**, who may be benevolent or malevolent. It is not always correct to speak of "ancestor worship," since not all societies worshipped their dead ancestors, or even particularly liked them. The !Kung or Ju/hoansi understood their ancestors as ultimately responsible for all misfortune, as the deceased were lonely and pulled on their kin from beyond. For the Dinka of Sudan as for many peoples with strong lineage systems, the clan spirits or *yieth* were their prime concern, even more so than their god and their "independent spirits" or *jak*. *Yieth* spirits tended to be "partial [to humans] and protective," but they could also be punitive, in which case they recruited the *jak* to do their dirty work. In other words, "there is much crisscrossing in which spirits protect or injure people with justification, or as their whims may dictate" (Deng,

Ghost
a religious or spiritual being, generally regarded to be the disembodied spiritual part of a deceased human

Spiro, Melford. 1978 [1967]. *Burmese Supernaturalism*, expanded ed. Philadelphia: Institute for the Study of Human Issues.

Ancestor spirits
the spirits of dead family members who are believed to continue to reside near and interact with their living kin

Soul
a religious concept of a non-material component or components of a living human; it is widely believed that a soul survives the death of the body, at least temporarily, and continues in another form of existence

1972: 123). Most fascinatingly, in 1936 J. H. Driberg made the apt observation that "ancestor religions" in Africa were not particularly "religious"; rather, respect for the dead ancestors was simply an extension of respect for the living elders. He warned that "no African 'prays' to his dead grandfather any more than he 'prays' to his living father" (1936: 6).

If humans have or can become spiritual beings, it stands to reason that other things could also have or be spirits. Perhaps the most common of these are the "nature spirits," the spirits that are or are in plants and animals and natural objects and natural forces. **Animism**, derived from the Latin *anima* for "alive" or "moving" (as in "animate"), is the general conception that non-human beings have spiritual parts too. It is not always the case that every non-human thing is "animated"; recall that the Ojibwa told Hallowell that some stones are persons and some are not. Also, in any society some animal and plant species might be spiritual, while others were merely natural beings. In the past, the term **totemism** was frequently used to name the spiritual relationship between non-human beings and human individuals or groups (families, clans, villages, etc.), but the word is not much used today. ("Totem" is another case of applying a word from one society   in this case, Ojibwa—to other religions.)

The animistic spirits of plants and animals and so on could be individual or collective—that is, each individual being may have a spirit, or there may be a spirit of the species (say, a generic "bear spirit"). Ainu religion contained a vast number of spirits; in fact, they regarded all species (and practically all objects) as "soul-owning." Even artifacts like tools and utensils had souls. Accordingly, those beings and objects had to be treated with respect, like the "people" they were. Hunting thus was never a purely "practical" activity, since it involved interacting with spirits that could anger and withdraw cooperation; in other words, hunting was seen as a kind of "reciprocity" between humans and animals and spirits. Also, at the end of its "life" a soul-owning being—human or otherwise—deserved a decent burial. For animals, a proper location, a bone pile or *keyohniusi*, was maintained for each species, and even household objects had a "final resting place." Rituals had to be performed as part of the disposal, "since their negligence brings forth much suffering, mostly in the form of illness" (Ohnuki-Tierney, 1974: 87).

The spirits could be named and well known or only vaguely and collectively known. Sometimes they were associated with specific locations or physical objects; sometimes they were diffuse and amorphous. They may be good, bad, or indifferent from a human point of view; they may be helpful, harmful, mischievous, or even unaware of their effect on humans. The Burmese villagers in Spiro's research told him about three categories of *nat* spirits. The first were native spirits that resided in trees and hills and fields and bodies of water; they guarded their domains, were "petty and irascible," and overall made the world a more dangerous place (Spiro, 1978: 47). The second category were the *devas* or Buddhist spirits, who were good and moral. The higher *devas* were too distant to be matters of ritual or speculation, but the lower *devas* took a positive interest in humans, since they were the spirits of former especially pious humans, bridging all four types of beings—humans, ancestors, spirits, and gods. Finally, the "thirty-seven *nats*" were regarded as evil.

A final type of religious being is a god. There is no universal definition for a god, but they tend to be extremely powerful, usually creative, and comparatively remote spiritual beings. Many societies that recognized gods (and not all did) did not attempt to communicate or relate directly to those gods because they were so distant, but rather approached them through lower-level spiritual intermediaries. !Kung or Ju/hoansi religion, for instance, contained two gods, a high god, *Gao Na*, and a lower god, *Kauha*, although most human attention was directed to the ancestors. Across religions, some gods were highly personal and moral, while others were not. The sky god of the Konyak Nagas intervened in the moral affairs of humans; the god of the Azande, named *Mboli* or *Mbori*, was morally neutral and uninvolved in human moral business. The Semai of Malaysia regarded their god as "a vicious ludicrous monster" (Dentan, 2008: 74) and "a stupid, incontinent, violent dupe" (84) that they simultaneously feared and ridiculed.

A religion that focuses primarily on god(s) is called a **theism** (from the Greek *theo-* or *deo-* for "god," which also gives English the word "deity"). In any particular theism there may be one god (**monotheism**) or multiple gods (**polytheism**), and gods ordinarily co-exist in a religion with human

Animism
a type of religious belief in which natural objects (animals, plants, hills, lakes, the moon, etc.) and forces (wind, rain, etc.) have spiritual components that interact socially with humans

Totemism
a religious conception that human individuals or groups have a symbolic or spiritual connection with particular natural species, objects, or phenomena

Theism
the religious belief in one or more gods

Monotheism
the form of theism that includes belief in only one god or goddess

Polytheism
the religious belief in two or more gods

STORIES OF SPIRIT AND ANIMAL IN AINU CULTURE AND RELIGION

spirits, nature spirits, ancestor spirits, and other supernatural entities (like angels or devils or *jinn*). Ancient Greek religion is a familiar example of polytheism, with its "pantheon" (from *pan-* for "all") of gods residing on Mount Olympus. The Greek gods were not always good or "moral" (some of them did very reprehensible things, even in Greek eyes), nor were they always eternal or immortal (many Greek gods were born, often from other Greek gods, and many died). Judaism, Christianity, and Islam constitute the dominant monotheisms in the world, although there are other smaller and newer religions that hold the notion of a single god (like Baha'i). The notion of a relatively impersonal god, perhaps one who created the universe and then took no moral interest in it, is called **deism**; many colonial American leaders considered themselves deists, and Azande theism resembled deism.

Forces

Some religions feature impersonal spiritual forces—powers that do not necessarily have an individual "mind" or "will"—instead of or in addition to personal beings. Often these forces are like spiritual water or electricity—a (super)naturally occurring power that exists in and flows through the physical world. The common name given to this religious conception is **animatism**.

The classic example of a spiritual force is *mana*, as understood in numerous Pacific Island cultures. Mana was an energy that presented itself in material objects, including people, but was not inherent in them; it was a potentiality or efficacy granted by the spirits or ancestors. A person who knew how to use and accumulate mana possessed luck, strength, and virtue; a person without mana was destined to be unlucky, weak, and unsuccessful. Another example is the Chinese principle of *chi*. Chi follows its *tao* or "way" or "path," flowing like water; water is the most frequent analogy for it. Thus, the person who would live well should go with the *tao*, leading to such insights in the ancient text *Tao Te Ching* as "Do nothing and leave nothing undone" or "The best ruler is he who rules least." Many aspects of traditional Chinese culture were governed by the idea of *chi*, from diet to medicine (e.g. acupuncture opens the flow of *chi* in the body) to architecture and home furnishing (*feng shui* is the art of arranging living space to maximize the flow of *chi*).

Along with their gods and ancestors, the !Kung or Ju/hoansi also had a concept of spiritual energy called *n/um*, a

> substance that lies in the pit of the stomach of men and women . . . and becomes active during a healing dance. The !Kung believe that the movements of the dancers heat the *n/um* up and when it boils it rises up the spinal cord and explodes in the brain.
>
> (Richard Lee, 1984: 109)

The Ju/hoansi shaman (see below) mastered this force and called upon it in healing rituals to transfer power and wellness to patients. On the other hand, the Apache force known as *diyi* was not perfectly impersonal. *Diyi* had some "personal" attributes, including the ability to seek out specific people to attach to (individuals could also seek *diyi*) and to feel anger, which could of course harm humans (Basso, 1970).

Religious specialists

As in all walks of life, there are some individuals who have more ability or power in religion than others. This facility may come from knowledge, skill, practice, training, personal experience, office, or such factors. Hence, when the layman has a problem or an interest to which religion applies, s/he can turn to a specialist for assistance or intervention. It is again common for scholars to label specific "types" of religious specialists, but actual specialists often combine various functions or tasks associated with a particular "type" or perform only some of the functions or tasks so associated. Therefore, it is probably more helpful to address the religious tasks than the supposed specialist types.

Healing

One task that all societies desire is curing illness, and long ago—in his 1924 *Medicine, Magic, and Religion*—W. H. R. Rivers taught that medicine and religion or magic are so intertwined in many cultures that they could not be easily or meaningfully separated. The healing of disease or injury through ritual, speech (chant, prayer, etc.), spirit possession, and other religious means is usually associated with the role of the **shaman** (yet another case of

Deism
the form of theism or belief in god(s) that posits a creator god that does not take an active role or moral interest in human affairs

Animatism
a type of religious belief in which impersonal spiritual forces exist in the world and affect human life and behavior

Shaman
a religious specialist, often part-time, who has personal power, based on unique life experiences or apprenticeship to a senior shaman, to communicate, interact, and sometimes struggle with supernatural beings or forces. Often a healer

See Chapter 16

IMAGE 10.3 Ganakwe bushman dancing into a trance.

borrowing a concept from one society—this time, the Tungus of Siberia—to apply to other religions). The unique and important quality of shamans is that they tend to be understood as spiritually powerful individuals, that is to say, their specialist talents came from some personal religious abilities.

A potential shaman usually showed a propensity toward shamanic abilities early in life, such as talent for singing or facility to enter into trances or have visions. Once identified, the aspiring shaman often then became an apprentice to a senior shaman, who instructed the novice. This training commonly consisted of ordeals like sleep deprivation, long hours of chanting, drug ingestion, seclusion, quests of various kinds, and other difficult and even painful experiences. One common factor in becoming a full-fledged shaman was acquiring a helper-spirit or "spirit familiar," which would show the trainee things that cannot be known any other way.

Ju/hoansi healers (simply called *n/um kausi* or "master/owner of *n/um*") were called upon when a member of the band was sick or troubled. The healer (most were male) began his work by singing and chanting until he fell into a trance; his body collapsed on the ground because his "soul" had left it and was sojourning in the spiritual dimension. The entranced master regained his senses and conducted "operations" that included rubbing his own sweat on the patient, which was thought to contain the "boiling energy" of *n/um* (see above). In Australian Aboriginal societies, healers would often accomplish their cures by removing objects—like stones or feathers—from the body of the victim. (In many cultures, shamans themselves were thought to have supernatural objects in their bodies, which may be implanted as part of their training.) Elsewhere, healers were said to visit spirits while in trance and either question them or on occasion fight them; a shaman really could be a spiritual warrior.

Healers often combined "spiritual" and more mundane techniques, including herbal medicine. They also sometimes specialized in only part of the curing process. Among the Thai village Buddhists studied by Stanley Tambiah (1970), the religious-medical division of labor included the *mau song* or diagnostician, the *mau ya* or herbalist, the *mau tham* or exorcist, the *tiam* or exorcist of major spirits in the case of severe illness, and the *mau mau* or finder of lost property.

Tambiah, Stanley J. 1970. *Buddhism and the Spirit Cults in North-East Thailand.* London: Cambridge University Press.

IMAGE 10.4 Shamanism is a common religious idea and practice across cultures.

Priest

a religious specialist, often full-time, who is trained in a religious tradition and acts as a functionary of a religious institution to lead ritual and perpetuate the religious institution

Leading ritual

A different task is leading or performing rituals for members of the society, including birth, marriage, funeral, and other culturally appropriate rites. The familiar term for the ritual performer is the **priest**. In contrast to the healer or shaman, the priest is often a full-time specialist occupying a formal office achieved by mastery of a body of knowledge and practice followed by "ordination" by a religious institution or structure that has the power and authority to invest priests. Priests may or may not be powerful individuals—some are quite ordinary people—but they hold a powerful office. As such, they represent the institution in which they belong, rather than being independent and informal practitioners like shamans.

A priestly office, while not always hereditary, may have a hereditary component. In various societies there are priestly lineages or classes, most formally the Brahmin caste in Hinduism. In traditional Judaism the Levite line provided the priests of the group. In Barabaig society, five of the clans were priestly (the *Daremgadyeg*), and fifty-five of the clans were purely secular. So, priesthood tends to be associated with social stratification as

well as institutionalization or formalization of religion and the conflation of religious with political power. Priests, especially in larger, richer, and more centralized societies, tend to be full-time employees of the religious establishment (depending on a considerable surplus to support them), and they often exercise secular or political power as well as religious. The most formal and elaborate system of priests, which once did wield secular power as the head of a state (and still officially exists as a state, albeit a very small one), is the Catholic Church, with the Pope as paramount priest.

As with healers or shamans, ritual leaders or priests may combine tasks or distribute tasks. Among the Nuer, weddings, funerals, adoptions, and initiations, as well as rites for the *colwic* (dead human) spirits, called for a "master of ceremonies" or *gwan buthni*. Sacrifices were conducted by the famous *kuaar twac* or *kuaar muan*, the leopard-skin or earth priest. And a panoply of priests or "owners" shared ritual duties, including the *kuaar/gwan yika* (priest/owner of the mat, who arbitrated between in-laws in the case of death during childbirth), the *kuaar/gwan muot* (priest/owner of the spear, who performed war and hunting rituals), the *kuaar/gwan pini* (priest/owner of water, who protected against floods), and more. According to Barbara Myerhoff (1974), the *mara'akame* among the Huichol of Mexico combined the functions of shaman/healer and priest/leader, using his spiritual powers to diagnose and cure sickness while also presiding over the annual ceremonial cycle and guiding people on the "peyote hunt" pilgrimage.

Communicating with spirits

Humans face the daunting task of communicating with other-than-human persons when we cannot be sure if those religious beings are listening or even present. A variety of spiritual communicators or mediums offer their services across cultures and religions, such as the **diviner** or **oracle**, who practiced many techniques to read or interpret the will of spirits. Astrology has traditionally been a divining activity, looking for traces of "divine" communication in the stars. Any number of other kinds of signs have been read for spiritual messages, from tea leaves and coins to the bones or entrails of animals; a diviner may put a question or request to the spirits, then kill and study the body of an animal for indications of an answer. The Barabaig diviner or *sitetehid* manipulated a pile of stones and examined the patterns for messages, usually involving witches or angry ancestor spirits, although he did not actually perform the cure, which was turned over to another specialist. Probably the most famous oracle in Western history was the Greek oracle at Delphi, where citizens—including kings, generals, and philosophers—would ask advice from young priestesses who gave cryptic responses while in a trance. Decisions to go to war and other epoch-making decisions were sometimes made in this way.

In Judaism, Christianity, and Islam the most important medium is the **prophet**, an individual who receives direct communication from the spirits, often involuntarily (recall how Moses and other Hebrew prophets were reluctant to take on the role), and is then charged to pass that knowledge along to other humans. Judaism provides a long sequence of prophets, and Muhammad is revered among Muslims for being not only a prophet, but "the seal of prophets"—the final and authoritative one. His prophecy, received as a recitation or *Qur'an* directly from Allah and the angels, was intended to complete and correct all previous prophecies. Obviously, though, there are those who think that new prophets continue to appear, both inside and outside the Judeo-Christian-Muslim world. For example, the Church of Latter-day Saints (Mormons) teaches that all of its contemporary leaders are "apostles and prophets" (http://www.mormon.org/faq/present-day-prophet).

Doing harm

Also as in every walk of life, some people use their spiritual powers for malignant purposes, to harm other people or their property. **Sorcerers** were generally people believed to exercise spiritual power, typically for the worse, through specific "technical" means. That is, sorcery might be classed as a subset of magic, which is commonly understood as an instrumental action in which certain gestures or behaviors automatically lead to certain results. The line between magic and religion is thin and controversial, and we will not explore it here; there is no doubt that there is much magic in any religion and some religion in all magic, but we can perhaps distinguish them usefully, as anthropologists from Frazer and Malinowski have attempted to do. Frazer in particular made a further distinction, between what he called contagious magic and sympathetic or imitative magic. **Contagious magic** is the spiritual consequence of bringing two things together, sometimes literally touching. For example, if I do some kind of ceremonial act on or store up some kind of spiritual power in a wand or other object and touch you with it, that power will be transferred to you. Australian Aboriginal sorcerers would focus their power through a magical bone, which they would point at a victim to "shoot" the magic at them. The use of a piece of a person's hair or fingernail on a "voodoo doll" follows the same logic: The body part was in contact with the person, so there is still a magical connection. **Sympathetic** or imitative **magic** relies on some similarity between the action or the object and its target; so, if people want to make rain, they might pour water onto the ground, simulating rain. Or, if they want to guarantee fertility, they might incorporate a particularly fertile animal (perhaps a rabbit, or a symbol of fertility, like an egg) into their technique. In all of these behaviors, the idea is that the behavior is sufficient to achieve the result. The sorcerer, then, can be regarded as a person who performs such activities ordinarily for the purpose of evil or harm.

Sorcerer
a religious specialist who uses techniques, including spells and potions, to achieve supernatural effects

Diviner
a religious specialist who uses one of many techniques to "read" information from the supernatural world

Oracle
a religious specialist (or any religious object or process) with the power to forecast the future or answer questions through communication with or manipulation of supernatural forces

Contagious magic
the belief and practice that objects that come in contact with each other have some supernatural connection with each other

Prophet
a human who speaks for or receives messages from spirits

Sympathetic magic
the belief and practice that objects that have something in common with each other (e.g. same shape or texture) have some supernatural connection with each other

Witch

a religious specialist, often conceived as a human with a supernatural ability to harm others, sometimes through possession of an unnatural bodily organ or an unnatural personality; sometimes viewed as an anti-social and even anti-human type who causes misfortune out of excessive greed, anger, or jealousy

An Apache sorcerer had to learn the techniques of negative magic, and most sorcerers were men, since men were thought to feel more *kedn* or hatred than women. Potential sorcerers would have to pay a senior expert, usually a maternal kinsman, for the knowledge and skills, which took three main forms—making and administering poisons, casting spells, and shooting objects "into" the victim's body. The result of successful sorcery was a specific set of symptoms that struck suddenly and without warning; further, the corpses of victims were distinguished by "swollen tongues and bluish markings around the face and neck. They are also reported to decompose at an unusually rapid rate" (Basso, 1970: 76). On the African island of Mayotte, sorcerers worked through evil spirits, "hiring" them to do harm; the greatest sorcerers met spirits in person and used the souls of the recently deceased. Michael Lambek explained that the cure for sorcery was to find and remove

a small, rotting cloth packet filled with dirt, nail clippings, hair, broken glass, and the like from either the body of the patient, his house floor, or the ground of his compound or fields. This packet of dirt is the physical representation of the harm caused by the spirit itself.

(1981: 44).

The other classic role of malevolence is the **witch** (although modern day Wiccans would beg to differ with that characterization). Many societies were and are quite sure that witches are at work in the community. As a cultural concept, witchcraft is very diverse, but the common thread is that witches are held responsible for bad things that happen to people—often all bad things. In his seminal study of witchcraft, Evans-Pritchard argued that the Azande of the Sudan saw the action of witches everywhere; essentially every illness, misfortune, or unpleasantness was caused by witchcraft. Some societies held that a witch was a person with an innate, even anatomical, power to do harm; the witch may have an extra organ in his/her chest containing negative spiritual power, or the witch's emotions simply radiated some malevolent force. Witch power may actually be involuntary to the witch, at least initially; they may simply exude negativity in ways that even they did not understand or control. The Kaguru also said that witches (*wahai*) were congenitally evil people, the ontological opposite of normal human beings (Beidelman, 1971). Or they may practice, sharpen, and intentionally employ their power for their benefit, especially against rivals, including rival witches. The Swazi of Africa lumped witches together with sorcerers as *batsakatsi* or "evil-doers." On the other

---

BOX 10.3   THE DIVISION OF RELIGIOUS LABOR IN A NEPALI FUNERAL

The major types and tasks of specialists hardly exhaust the diversity of the work to be done in religion. In their richly illustrated (complete with a DVD) ethnography of a Newar funeral ritual in Nepal, Niels Gutschow and Axel Michaels (2005) reveal just how many roles are part of ceremonial business. Naturally, Hindu Brahmin priests, forty-three of whom live in the town of Bhaktapur, lead or conduct various rites, from offerings to the *sapindikarana* ritual to merge the deceased with the ancestors. For Buddhist sub-castes among the Newar, Buddhist priests are involved. Beyond these two standard priesthoods, astrologers (*Josi*) and Tantric priests (*Karmacarya*) "perform preparatory functions in a number of rituals" (2005: 41): The former (who also determines auspicious days for rites and does some healing) assists the Brahmin, while the latter oversees the cooking of rice. The *Tini* perform purification actions involving fire, the *cyah* offer services at the pyre for cremation, and the *Cala* act as torch bearers and cymbal players. The *Bha* or funeral priest handles some of the more polluting work of the funeral, freeing the pure Brahmins from such corruption. *Pasi* washermen clean the clothes of the mourners, who are then entrusted to the *Nau* or barber for further purification. Finally, there is any number of tailors, musicians, cooks, sweepers, and cleaners—some known collectively as *Jugi* who "literally absorb the food that is offered to the *preta* [deceased spirit] on the seventh day after death" (49)—who contribute their labor to a funeral.

hand, the Menomini of North America said that witches were not antisocial deviants but rather the group in society with the most power and prestige, namely the elders: "social control is achieved . . . by the threat of witchcraft by power figures rather than through accusation of the witch by the community" (Spindler and Spindler, 1971: 73). Thus, the power of witches and sorcerers was not necessarily immoral; sometimes they felt themselves to be the victims of selfishness, envy, or other moral violations.

ADDITIONAL ELEMENTS OF RELIGION: OBJECTS, RITUAL, AND LANGUAGE

Religion is practiced in many forms and "stored" or materialized in many sites other than beings, forces, and specialists. Many of these sites can rightfully be called symbols because they "stand for" the beings or forces or convey meaning in some way. "Symbol" is a problematic term, though, since members of a religion may not see their objects, activities, and utterances as symbolic at all. For a Warlpiri, a *churinga* stone or board is not a symbol of an ancestral spirit but a *manifestation* of that spirit, an embodiment of the spirit. The same is true for the *torma* or dough bodies that Sherpas craft for visiting Buddhist deities.

The academic study of religion, partly influenced by (especially Protestant) Christianity, has tended to overlook the centrality of material objects and physical places in religion, on the assumption that religion is "really" about immaterial and otherworldly matters. But even the most otherworldly religions must take some visible and palpable form, and the appreciation of this fact is evident in a scholarly journal dedicated to religious "things," titled *Material Religion: The Journal of Objects, Art and Belief*. Every religion, for instance, has sacred spaces, either sacralized by humans or by the spirits who inhabit(ed) them. A ceremonial ground, a mountain, a building, or an entire city may be a sacred space. All religions contain sacred or powerful objects, such as the medicine arrows of the Cheyenne and carvings, paintings, masks and many other examples across cultures. Relics (pieces of the bodies of important human figures) have religious value in some societies. Individual followers may use various objects to facilitate their

prayer as well as their fortune and health, from rosaries and prayer wheels to amulets and charms. And, as with the Glastonbury Goddess or the chalk Saint Anthony of Padua, not to mention entire traditions of icons, statues (including important traditions in the Catholic and Eastern Orthodox Christian churches), and fetishes, religions may claim that gods, spirits, or ancestors are literally present in physical objects.

Ritual: religion enacted

Religion, you will recall, is not only or mainly thought and believed, but also danced—or generally more embodied and enacted. Religious action is usually dubbed "ritual," but ritual is not an exclusively religious phenomenon; humans engage in many secular rituals such as greetings or graduations, and even animals have rituals (mating rituals, fighting rituals, etc.). A **ritual** is a highly stylized and formalized behavior pattern that is thought to be effective if performed properly. In this sense, most or all of culture is ritualistic, insofar as it specifies the appropriate and expected sequence of social behavior. Ritual was characterized by the philosopher John Skorupski in his study of anthropology as part of the *interaction code*, which he defines as behavior intended "to establish or maintain (or destroy) an equilibrium, or mutual agreement, among the people involved in an interaction as to their relative standing or roles, and their reciprocal commitments and obligations" (1976: 77). Interaction between humans is routinized by the elaboration of an interaction code that contains such elements as honor and politeness. Naturally, the interaction system extends to other-than-human persons too, with whom humans likewise want to establish and maintain agreement and to honor reciprocal commitments and obligations—and with whom the stakes of interaction are unusually high.

Religious rituals can take many forms, and Wallace (1966) suggested a typology, including

■ technical rituals—rituals that are intended to achieve certain specific ends, like divination or rites of intensification (see below)
■ therapeutic or anti-therapeutic rituals—rituals that are intended to cure illness and misfortune

THE MORAL POWER OF WITCHCRAFT AMONG THE SUKUMA OF TANZANIA

Ritual
any type of formal, repetitive behavior that is felt to have significance beyond the actions themselves; in particular, religious ritual is often composed of symbols, re-enacts supernatural or mythical events, and is believed to have efficacy if performed correctly

Skorupski, John. 1976. *Symbol and Theory: A Philosophical Study of Theories of Religion in Social Anthropology*. Cambridge: Cambridge University Press.

Liminality

the condition of being "in between" or "on the margins" of social roles, in particular of being in transition (as during ritual) between one social role and another

See Chapter 15

Turner, Victor W. 1969. *The Ritual Process: Structure and Anti-Structure*. Chicago: Aldine Publishing.

Rite of passage

a form of ritual intended to accompany or accomplish a change of status or role of the participants, such as initiation (change from youth to adult) or marriage

Rite of intensification

a form of ritual in which members of the society are brought into greater communion, in which social bonds are intensified

such as shamanic healing or to cause it such as sorcery and witchcraft

- ideological rituals—rituals that are intended to express or achieve social goals, including rites of passage (see below), taboos, and rituals of rebellion or transgression (e.g. carnival)
- salvation rituals—rituals that are intended to work changes in individuals, particularly at moments of personal crisis, such as spirit possession or mystical experiences
- revitalization rituals—rituals that are intended to work changes in society, particularly at moments of social crisis

Victor Turner (1969; 1981) added an analysis of what he called the "ritual process," which follows a common pattern or progression. Turner noticed that many rituals have a recurrent structure, in which individuals are transformed—socially or even physically—from one condition or status to another. Following Arnold van Gennup's suggestion, he called these **rites of passage**, indicating that the subjects "pass" from one social state to another. Familiar rites of passage include weddings, initiations, and (at least in some interpretations) funerals. Participants are moved from one social position or status (e.g. single, juvenile, alive) to another (e.g. married, adult, dead).

The key to the process of ritual passage is the detachment of the subject-person from his or her previous role or status and reassignment to a new role or status. However, "in between" there is a critical period of "rolelessness," of non-identity or undifferentiated status, which Turner called **liminality**. In the liminal phase, the person is neither this nor that, but is between statuses and therefore without status. For most Western or Christian rituals, this moment is usually fleeting, but some religions or rituals sustain it for a long period. In Australian Aboriginal initiations, boys or young men would be isolated from society for weeks or months, following a ritual "capture" that was treated and mourned like a death. During the isolation they might undergo deprivations like silence and nakedness, as well as physical operations like circumcision, while also learning about or at least being exposed to sacred knowledge and objects. Upon their return to society, they were "new people"; symbolically, the boy died and a man was made in his place, with an altered body to mark his transformation.

Not all rituals are rites of passage; some are **rites of intensification**, which are practiced to "intensify" nature or society at specific times or on a regular schedule. One reason for intensifying nature is to guarantee or increase the fertility of plants, animals, and even humans (leading to what are sometimes called "increase rituals"). Thus, a society may perform a ritual to increase the number, health, or reproductive capacity of wild species or

IMAGE 10.5 Warlpiri women lead girls in a dance ritual.

domesticated herds. A rite for intensifying society might occur after a crisis or shock that threatens to disorient or even disintegrate society, such as a natural disaster, a death, or a defeat in war. The ritual could unite people as a society and strengthen the bonds between them. Some rites of intensification are ad hoc, while others are "calendrical," that is, part of a society's ritual calendar. For farmers, a harvest will occur every year around the same time, so a harvest ritual can occur every year around the same time. Americans find remnants of this in the observance of Halloween, a version of a harvest (and death, which is often associated with the harvest and the approach of winter) festival. Some American rituals combine natural and historical occurrences (Thanksgiving), while some are purely historical (Fourth of July).

Religious language: myth

When most people think of religious language, they think of "myth," and most academic investigation of religious language has focused on myth. Anthropologically, **myth** does not mean an error or lie; rather, a myth is simply a religious narrative, a story of sacred events that has some explanatory value or spiritual power. That is, a myth tends to be an account of how some aspect of the world—the universe as a whole, the earth or the society's particular environment, human beings, or social institutions, for example—came into existence. The origin may be an act of god(s), animal or plant spirits, or human ancestors ("culture heroes") and can be as diverse across cultures as possibly imagined.

Myths are a way in which members of a society communicate their ideas about the sacred and about their own "holy history"; as such, myths are a manifestation of the general human tendency of narration, of turning our lives and worlds into stories. Humans are story-telling beings, that is, we aim to "make sense" of the flow of events and facts by organizing the details into a continuous and meaningful narrative. Myths then are "instructional" in the strongest possible sense of the word: They put "structure in" thought and social life. Malinowski called them "charters" or "models" for how humans should live their lives today in one of the most quoted passages in anthropology:

Studied alive, myth . . . is not symbolic, but a direct expression of its subject matter; it is not an explanation in satisfaction of a scientific interest, but a narrative resurrection of a primeval reality, told in satisfaction of deep religious wants, moral cravings, social submissions, assertions, even practical requirements. Myth fulfills in primitive culture an indispensable function; it expresses, enhances, and codifies belief; it safeguards and enforces morality; it vouches for the efficiency of ritual and contains practical rules for the guidance of man. Myth is thus a vital ingredient of human civilization; it is not an idle tale, but a hard-worked active force; it is not an intellectual explanation or an artistic imagery, but a pragmatic charter of primitive faith and moral wisdom.

(1948: 101)

Religious language: prayer

Myth, or narrative in general, is not the only form of religious language. **Prayer** is speech directed specifically to religious beings. The form and intent of prayer depends intimately on the nature of the being who is prayed to. Prayer can be casual and spontaneous, like ordinary speech, or it can be highly formulaic (think, for instance, of the Christian "Lord's Prayer"). One of the most developed traditions of prayer is found among the Navajo: "prayers are considered to be complex ritual acts whose performances engage and are informed by elements of mythology and the cultural contexts in which they are performed" (Gill, 1981: xxii). In fact, this context is critical, since any particular prayer can be used in different ways with different meanings, for instance "in one context to request and effect a smooth and healthy birth and in another to request and effect rainfall in a period of drought" (xxiii). Even more, each prayer type has a standard structure of elements in a particular order. For example, an Enemyway prayer, which is part of a ritual to expel a foreign evil, opens with a place reference, which is followed by naming one or more sacred beings called Holy People, then a section asking for the removal of the evil force, and finally one or more references to an eventual state of blessing.

Myth
a narrative, usually of the activities of supernatural beings, often telling of how some or all of the natural or social world was established. In addition to an explanation of origins, it also provides a "charter" or model for how humans should live today

Malinowski, Bronislaw. 1948. *Magic, Science, and Religion and Other Essays.* Garden City, NY: Doubleday Anchor Books.

Prayer
a form of linguistic religious ritual in which humans are believed to speak and interact with supernatural beings

Gill, Sam D. 1981. *Sacred Words: A Study of Navajo Religion and Prayer.* Westport, CT: Greenwood Press.

Religious language: ritual languages and other speech acts

See Chapter 4

**EVANGELICAL CHRISTIAN
CONVERSION AS
LANGUAGE LEARNING**

Many linguistic genres besides myth and prayer are incorporated into religious observance. Among these are chants, spells, curses, and songs. Christian-influenced scholars sometimes neglect these forms on the grounds that they are too "superstitious" or "magical" or too rote and repetitive. For instance, devotees of Hare Krishna (more accurately, the International Society for Krishna Consciousness) repeat and sing, "*Hare Krishna, Hare Krishna, Krishna Krishna, Hare Hare, Hare Rama, Hare Rama, Rama Rama, Hare Hare.*" Some Japanese (Nichiren) Buddhists find great power in chanting, *Nam(u)-myoho-renge-kyo*, and Hindu meditators may focus on the single sound *Om*. Michael Pye (2015) argues that chanting has historically been a more important activity than meditation in Buddhism. In her unique study of American fundamentalist Baptists, Susan Harding (1987) stressed two specific speech-forms—preaching and witnessing.

Finally, in many societies, one way of indicating the special and "set-apart" nature of religious behavior is through the use of forms of speech not used at any other time. For instance, until the Second Vatican Council (1962–1965), the Catholic mass was performed exclusively in Latin, the language of religion and "high culture," and reformers like Martin Luther met with great resistance in efforts to translate the Bible into vernacular languages. Likewise, Muslim tradition demands that the *Qur'an* should only be read and recited in Arabic.

As we mentioned already, special speech styles and formats are distinguishable by unique properties, including vocabularies that are not employed in any other type of speech, voice qualities (like chanting or singing), the use of metaphor, and specific formulas such as standard openings or endings. Recall the previous discussion of Joel Sherzer's research on Kuna "ways of speaking," including *suar miimi kaya* (so-called "stick doll language" associated with curing rituals) and *kantule kaya* (used in girl's puberty rites). *Suar miimi kaya* is spoken to carved wooden dolls that serve as mediators between healers and spirits, while *kantule kaya* is directed to the spirit most closely related to girls' puberty. Each Kuna speech-form differs so far from the other (and from everyday speech and

"chief" language) in phonology, vocabulary, grammar, and style (i.e. speed of speech or inclusion or exclusion of vowels or entire syllables) that they are nearly situation-specific dialects.

Language may not even need to be heard or understood to be effective. Many traditions encourage members to wear a bit of scripture as a charm or amulet. The Islamized Berti of Sudan sewed a few words from the *Qur'an* into a leather bag or strip of cloth to counteract sorcery—and sometimes to perform it (Holy, 1991). Even more interestingly, they would write verses of scripture with chalk on a wooden slate and then wash the words off and drink the *Qur'an*-infused water. Stanley Tambiah noticed that laymen in the Thai Buddhist village (and sometimes Buddhist monks themselves) could not understand the words that were chanted—or were not present to hear them at all—but they were certain that the words were powerful and meritorious, an attitude that he called "the virtue of listening without understanding" (1970: 196). Meanwhile, Katherine Swancutt's (2012) Mongolian informants are convinced that words in the form of gossip (*khel am*) circulate around the society and gather strength, until they do the same harm as intentional curses.

RELIGION, RELIGIONS, OR RELIGIOUS FIELD?

We noted above that there are Hindu Newars and Buddhist Newars in Nepal, but some Newars claim to be both Hindu and Buddhist, which has led some observers to judge that they are either confused about their religious identity or possess a corrupted identity. In contrast, David Gellner reasoned that the notion of a single exclusive religious identity is "a Judeo-Christian definition of religion and religious allegiances, which hinders comprehension of Asian realities" (1992: 42). From the Newar—and many another society's—perspective, it is neither contradictory nor confused to follow two religions at once. For practical purposes, to the Newar "the terms 'Hindu' and 'Buddhist' are almost irrelevant. When Newars seek an urgent cure for some worldly ill, they usually do not stop to consider whether it is Hindu or Buddhist" (68).

Religions of course seldom have a monopoly on a society—many religions co-exist, in various and sometimes fractious relations with each other in all societies—but ethnographic evidence suggests that religions have monopolistic claims on individuals much less than we tend to believe. The notion of mutually exclusive "religions" or "religious identities" is an assumption born of Western-Christian ideals, of both the Christian desire for "conversion" and a total break with past identities and of the Western drive to categorize and label religions (and everything else). Anthropologists have come to the position that it is more valuable and precise to speak of a "religious field" in which multiple religions interact, compete, overlap, or blend in complex and specific ways.

Tambiah described this phenomenon in Thailand decades ago, where Buddhist monks shared the village religious scene with a specialist called *paahm*, from the Hindu term "Brahmin." Young men almost all entered the Buddhist monastery and received training as a *bhikkhus*, earning merit and performing funeral rites for their elders. Most men left the priesthood, though, and some assumed the role of *paahm* in their later life, conducting rituals for marriage and other occasions most associated with youth. In other words, the two ritual roles were reciprocal. Further, Buddhist and pre-Buddhist spirits and cosmologies shared the village, and four distinct ritual complexes not only co-existed but were "linked together in a *single total field*" (1970: 2).

Michael Carrithers called this situation "polytropy" ("many-turning"), defined as "the sense in which people turn toward many sources for their spiritual sustenance, hope, relief, or defense" (2000: 834). He considered it characteristic of India, but it is hardly unique to that country. Adam Yuet Chau reports a similar practice in China, where funerals may involve the participation of Buddhist monks or nuns, Daoist priests, and Confucian officials. Not only do the Chinese indulge in "Confucian-Buddhist-Daoist polytropy," but many ordinary Chinese people do not consider themselves "members" of a religion, but rather feel "free to employ a Confucian, Buddhist, or Daoist to conduct rituals" (2012: 89). The point was not to "belong to" a religion, but to maximize the efficacy of rituals. In his study of Chinese immigrants in New York, Kenneth Guest (2003) likewise chronicled religious diversity, including Catholic and Protestant Christianity in addition to "Eastern" religions;

within those "Eastern" religions were institutions like the Temple of Heavenly Thanksgiving, classified as "Daoist" although it featured both Daoist and Buddhist deities together with Confucius. In Japan, Michael Pye notes that pilgrimage trails may link Buddhist and Shinto sites into one spiritual journey.

If religious polytropy and complex religious fields are typical in the East, they are not unknown even in the more monotheistic and exclusivistic West. At the very least, a religion may contain a "high" or official version and one or more "low" or popular versions, for instance, official Catholic doctrine and ritual as opposed to the religiosity of ordinary parishioners. Sometimes these levels of religion interact in interesting and productive ways, as when Greek villagers began to revere medieval figures named Rafaíl and Nikólaos after their remains were discovered and after locals began to have dreams and visions of them. At first the Greek Orthodox Church was skeptical, dismissing the experiences as "a sign of imagination and credulity" and the rantings of "simple people and above all women" (Rey, 2012: 84). Eventually, though, the established church accepted the local claim and absorbed the historical characters into its body of saints, making the formerly popular the now-official.

Even Islam, commonly criticized for its intolerance (see below), manifests instances of religious co-existence and cooperation. John Bowen (2010) examines how Muslims not only seek to live in Western societies like France, but how they struggle to construct, for instance, a "French Islam," to adapt Islam to France while adapting French practices and institutions to Islam. Even more, Muslims and non-Muslims sometimes share sacred space, as at the Sveti Bogorodista Prechista monastery in Macedonia. Officially an Orthodox Christian site, Muslims also visit the monastery because it "is a healing place that is known to work" (Bowman, 2010: 208), especially when Muslims are afflicted by "Christian demons" that "can be driven out only by beneficent Christian powers" (206).

Of course, Christian powers—sacred or secular—are not always beneficent. In Europe and the United States, there are significant streams of anti-Muslim sentiment, even what has been called Islamophobia. In the United Kingdom, the English Defence League opposes the "Islamicization" of English society, sometimes violently. In the Solomon

Islands, some Christian leaders worry "that Islam threatened the national unity that results from a shared Christian faith and may undermine post-conflict reconciliation work that is being carried out in Christian idioms" (McDougall, 2009: 483). In Papua New Guinea some Christian organizations actually demanded a ban on Islam through a constitutional amendment limiting freedom of religion. Whether or not that initiative succeeds, Islam, Christianity, and many other religions will continue to cohabitate in complicated and tumultuous religious fields.

RELIGION AND THE EVERYDAY

Finally, a popular assumption is that religion is a separate phenomenon from mundane culture—and often from the material world itself—something that occupies its own unique sites (literal and figurative) in the society. However, anthropology insists that religion is not and cannot be limited to essentially "religious" times and places; instead, religion flows out into the wider culture as the wider culture flows into religion. As Marion Bowman and Ülo Valk phrase it, religion "cannot be neatly compartmentalized into the theoretical containers of academic discourse" (2012: 2)—or of the official discourse of religions themselves.

Since anthropologists care about how people actually practice religion, not just about official or scriptural religious doctrines, we increasingly appreciate how religion pervades and shapes the small, mundane, everyday aspects of social life. Indeed, religion can be and often is so pervasive and taken-for-granted that members of a society have religious "moods and motivations" without realizing that those ideas and feelings are specifically religious. A short list of the social sites in which individuals may encounter and practice religion includes:

- bodily habits—religions often influence how we inhabit our bodies, including how we wear our hair or facial hair (e.g. Muslim beards and Jewish earlocks), how we dress, and even how we stand or bow
- eating habits—most if not all religions have regulations on what may be eaten by whom, as well as rules for feasting or fasting (e.g. Muslim Ramadan) and ritual occasions of consumption
- sexual behavior—most if not all religions add regulations on sex, such as with whom, in what positions, within what institutions (e.g. marriage), etc.
- timekeeping—many religions organize time in religion-specific ways, from calendar systems originating at key moments (e.g. the birth of Christ, Muhammad's flight to Medina) to weekly cycles and "sabbath" days to specific annual holidays ("holy-days")

IMAGE 10.6 A sacred site: the inside of a spirit-house in Papua New Guinea.

- personal names—religions tend to reproduce the names of figures in their history in the naming practices of living members (e.g. Mathew, Mark, John, Daniel, Mary, Rebecca, etc. in Christianity and Judaism; Muhammad, Ali, Hussein, etc. in Islam; and so forth)
- place names—religions tend to reproduce the names of significant places, so that members inhabit the sacred landscape wherever they may live (e.g. Bethlehem, Pennsylvania; New Canaan, Connecticut; Corpus Christi, Texas).

In these and many other ways, religion provides less a belief system for members to accept than an experience for members to absorb. In a word, a religion is a lifeway more than a creed.

SECULAR AND SECULARIZATION: LOSS OF RELIGION OR CHANGE OF RELIGION?

BOX 10.4 CONTEMPORARY CULTURAL CONTROVERSIES: IS ISLAM INHERENTLY VIOLENT?

Scholars, religious partisans (anti-Muslim or anti-religion), and the general public alike have condemned Islam as inherently and irredeemably violent. Franklin Graham, son of the evangelist Billy Graham, called it "a very violent form of faith" (www.youtube.com/watch?v= kvzQHJ3Cba4), and Pat Robertson asserted that violence is "latent" in Islam because Muhammad and his followers were "warriors" (www.youtube.com/watch?v=RSelDNQgngU). But it is not only evangelical Christians who accuse Islam of innate violence: Vocal atheist Sam Harris contends that "Islamic fundamentalism" is simply an outcome of the fundamentals of Islam (www.youtube.com/watch?v=kMFsO58hXVM). Even serious scholars have doubted whether Islam is compatible with democracy, tolerance, and human rights—all this despite the fact that most Muslims are peaceful (at least, as peaceful as followers of any other religion), that even some "traditionalists" like Salafists are more interested in piety than politics, and that there are actually liberal and secular Muslims and Muslim organizations like *Hizb 'Almani* (Secular Party), and *Tuyyur al-'Almani* (Movement for Secularism), and the Institution for the Secularization of Islamic Society (www.centerforinquiry.net/isis), not to mention secular regimes in Tunisia, Egypt, and Turkey. What do you think?

SUMMARY

Religion is part of human culture, but it presents unique problems for anthropology, not only because both members of societies and anthropologists themselves often take it more seriously and literally than other parts, but because it poses profound challenges to the terms and concepts that we use to understand and analyze cross-cultural belief and behavior. An authoritative definition is difficult to determine, but an essential feature is that it includes conceptions of nonhuman and superhuman beings and forces that are in social and cultural relationships with humans. Society and its prerogatives and meanings are thus expanded to include humans and other kinds of "persons."

Religious ideas and practices help to explain, control, and legitimize the social and natural world. They also, like myths, linguistic "performatives," and rites of passage, are meant to affect the human and nonhuman world and to bring about actual changes in individuals, society, and the universe.

A religion is a composite of various modules or building-blocks of ideas, practices, tasks, and institutions. Among these modules or elements are:

- "spiritual" being(s) or force(s)
- roles or tasks for human specialists

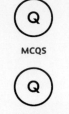

MCQS

FILL IN THE BLANKS

WWW

- behavioral or "ritual" activity
- language or religious speech, usually as part of—or itself being—ritual activity

Within the category of beings and forces is a wide variety of overlapping conceptions, with permeable boundaries, such that humans can become spirits or demons or even gods and vice versa. Some beings and forces are intimately known, while others are vague and amorphous. Multiple religions also share the "religious field" of a society, in diverse interrelationships.

Finally, religion is integrated within the wider culture, shaping and being shaped by that culture. Since anthropologists are interested in how individuals and groups really understand and practice religion, we explore how religion enters and influences everyday life.

Key Terms

ancestor spirit	myth	shaman
animatism	oracle	sorcerer
animism	polytheism	soul
contagious magic	prayer	sympathetic magic
deism	priest	theism
diviner	prophet	totemism
ghost	rite of intensification	witch
liminality	rite of passage	
monotheism	ritual	

Seeing culture as a whole #2

A holistic approach to Boko Haram and "Islamic violence"

In spring 2014, Boko Haram surged into the public eye with its abduction of more than two hundred girls from a school in northern Nigeria. To most observers, Boko Haram—which means roughly "Western education is forbidden" in the Hausa language—epitomizes Islamic extremism and terrorism, and they might think even more so if they knew that the proper name of the group is *Jama'atu Ahlus Sunnah Lid Da'awati Wal Jihad* or People Committed to the Prophet's Teachings for Propagation and Jihad (M. Smith, 2014: 80). As reprehensible as the kidnapping of schoolgirls and their forced conversion, marriage, or enslavement are, journalist Mike Smith, political scientist Abdul Raufu Mustapha, and the anonymous author of an article in the *Journal of Religion in Africa* concur that "the religious and temporal dimensions should be equally taken into account" (Anonymous, 2012: 118) in understanding the movement. In other words, a holistic anthropological perspective is necessary.

Mustapha insists that three factors must be considered in the rise and career of Boko Haram. The first of these is certainly religion, since the militants believe that they are doing "God's work" (2014: 167). The organization is an instance of a wider movement in Islam called Salafism, based on the concept of *salafiyyah*, the "ancestors" or "early years," referring to Muhammad and his first generation of followers. Salafism tends toward a literalist interpretation of the Qur'an and the sayings and precedents (*sunnah*) of Muhammad: If the scriptures or the Prophet condoned slavery or execution of apostates, Smith says, then those actions are deemed legal today. Further, all three writers remind us that West Africa has a long history of Islamic activism and of reproaching members of other sects for false religion. Mustapha adds that Boko Haram is driven by religious vengeance: If one of its followers is killed, then they feel justified to kill in reaction, including suicide bombing and "the ritualistic slaughter of their victims as if in some manner these were some sacrifices to Allah" (169). One of their slogans, Mustapha reports, is "Killing is believing" (169).

But religion never exists in isolation from its cultural and historical context, including translocal, regional, and even global forces. One of the temporal contributors to Boko Haram's violence and that of other extremist groups is economic. In northern Nigeria, "poverty is an important factor in radicalization not just because radical groups offer a possible economic prospect for deprived unemployed *individual* youths, but also because relative poverty fuels a sense of *group* resentment" (173). Despite its oil wealth, Nigeria has not delivered prosperity to its people, and the north has been particularly neglected: The predominantly Muslim north suffers from more poverty and more intense poverty than the rest of the country, simultaneously experiencing greater class inequality as the rich minority towers over the impoverished majority. Combined with the "youth bulge" of young Nigerians without jobs or economic hope, these conditions are primed for political instability and ideological extremism. In a word, Boko Haram's very existence and its violence "must therefore be understood, not just in context of its extremist doctrinal positions, but also in the more immediate context of poverty, inequality, and alienation" (176).

As predicted, the third source of Boko Haram is political. Mustapha identifies three specific political problems in Nigeria. The first is "the collapse of the surveillance and control functions of local state institutions, including those of traditional authorities, making it practically possible for the unhindered mobilization of disaffected youth" (177). From the ground level, Smith describes the fecklessness of the army and police and therefore the state's inability to impose law and order in the north. Surely the feeble response of security forces to the abduction of the girls illustrated the relative powerlessness of the state. Worse, the Nigerian army has been accused of rampant corruption and violence itself, instilling no trust among the people.

The second political factor stressed by Mustapha is "the nature of the sub-national elite political competition" (178) including ethnic and tribal and individual and party rivalry. Nigeria was created by colonialism, cobbling together the Christian south and the Muslim north, throwing together dozens of ethnic and tribal groups inside ill-defined and porous borders. The history of post-independence Nigeria is a series of military coups and failed governments. And regional politics cannot be discounted either: Smith mentions the influence of Islamic militants elsewhere in Africa, especially nearby Mali where French troops had to dislodge an insurgency that temporarily captured much of its territory. A recent article in *The Atlantic* warned that Mali and West Africa are on the verge of becoming Islam's "new terrorist training ground" (Dreazen, 2013).

The third political factor is "the adverse incorporation of unemployed youths into patron-client political networks at all levels of the Nigerian federation" (179). In the absence of attractive economic and political options, and with no "trust in the normal processes of governance," young men "have become available for recruitment into other forms of mobilization, including religious extremist groups" that offer them gifts and services in exchange for loyalty and violent action (180).

Even this brief analysis of Boko Haram shows that multiple cultural variables interact to construct and perpetuate what, to many minds, is simply a "religious" problem. But as Samuli Schielke rightly asserts, "there is too much Islam in the anthropology of Islam" and not enough appreciation of "the existential and pragmatic sensibilities of living a life in a complex and often troubling world" (2010: 1). If anthropology still places too much emphasis on Islam when it comes to violence committed by Muslims, how much more do the general public, pundits, and politicians need to consider the economic, political, and demographic factors that spark and spur contemporary violence?

Cultural dynamics
Tradition and change

BUDDHISM GETS A SOUL IN CHINA

Buddhism was born in India some 2,600 years ago, although it hardly exists anymore in its country of birth. Soon it was carried by merchants and missionaries to Southeast Asia, Tibet, and China, where it was adapted to the local language and culture. Buddhism arrived in Japan via China a thousand years later, where it quickly proliferated into many sects and blended with Japanese culture, producing many Japanese Buddhisms and what Japanese call *shinbutsu shugo* or "the syncretization of *kami* (local gods/spirits) and buddhas" (Nelson, 2013: 32). In the nineteenth century, Buddhism was attacked as not a traditional religion, but "a 'foreign' religion" and was "forcibly separated" from "the government's newly reorganized religion of choice, Shinto" (37). Yet John Nelson reports that "traditional" Buddhism has continued to adjust to modern culture in the twenty-first century. Since it can no longer depend on people maintaining hereditary links to the religion and seeking its spiritual services, "traditional" Buddhism has become creative, even experimental. Some Buddhist priests and temples have become involved in social welfare and "Buddhist-inspired activism" such as collecting money for the poor or assisting in disaster relief. Others have begun to offer funeral and burial

services for pets, while one has opened a temple in a shopping center (ambitiously named Everyone's Temple), and another runs a bar (the Osaka Vows Bar) where the drinks have Buddhist names like "the hell of lust" and "the priest's shaven head." Yet another sponsors "lectures, concerts, theater performances" (118) and other entertainments, while most remarkably one temple features an "all-woman cabaret dancing group": "In sequined but skimpy costumes with feather head ornaments and high heels, they performed a line dance routine titled 'Light of the Buddha,' which ended with synchronized high kicks" (168). Clearly even an ancient and otherworldly system like Buddhism is prone to and capable of modernization and change.

Cultural anthropology is the study of the diversity of human behavior in the present, but this definition hardly conveys the depth or the urgency of the discipline. Even worse, anthropology has long had, and often helped perpetuate, a reputation for being exclusively concerned with small, remote, or traditional societies. The influential A. R. Radcliffe-Brown actually described anthropology not so long ago as "the study of what are called primitive or backward people" (1965: 2). Aside from the fact that "primitive" and "backward" are

IMAGE 11.1 Buddhists praying and taking collections for earthquake victims in Kyoto, Japan.

Malinowski, Bronislaw. 1945. *The Dynamics of Culture Change: An Inquiry into Race Relations in Africa*. New Haven and London: Yale University Press.

Tradition
some practice or idea or object that is (at least believed to be) continuous or associated with "the past"; a tradition may be very ancient or very recent, but as an ideological element it is often assumed to be important, authentic, and even "superior" to non-traditional (especially foreign) practices, ideas, and objects

Linton, Ralph, Ed. 1945. *The Science of Man in the World Crisis*. New York: Columbia University Press.

harsh and judgmental terms which we avoid today, the statement itself is false in the twenty-first century and has been for decades—if it was ever true. If anthropology were seriously to consider itself, or to be considered, the science of the primitive and the traditional, then it would be finished, since there are no primitive or purely traditional people in the world to study. On the other hand, new "**traditions**" (like Buddhist cabaret) are emerging all the time, and diversity remains and thrives, giving anthropology an endless supply of cultural phenomena to investigate, along with the basic processes of culture and tradition themselves.

If modern professional anthropology, marked by the innovations of Boas and Malinowski, could maintain an innocent and naïve attitude toward culture and tradition through the first half of the twentieth century (and on close inspection, it did not always), it certainly had shed that attitude by the second half. As early as 1945 (the end of World War II), books like *The Science of Man in the World Crisis* (Linton, 1945) and Malinowski's own *The Dynamics of Culture Change* (1945) illustrated that the discipline had become aware of the changes that were occurring in their chosen subject-societies, in the world around them, and in the discipline itself.

Stanley Diamond, in anthropology's soul-searching phase in the late 1960s and early 1970s, finally recast it as "the study of man in crisis by man in crisis" (1972: 401). This is profoundly true and profoundly important but not really new. In a certain sense, the human world has always been in crisis in some way or another, whether it was Native Americans confronting the first European invaders, ancient Israelites confronting the first Roman conquerors, or Neandertals confronting the first Homo sapiens.

So, anthropology has changed, and *had* to change, because the groups that it aims to study have changed. It has also come to see change as not corruption or de-traditionalization, but as an inherent part of the cultural process, of the dynamic nature of culture and human ways of living. And it has, as a result of these realizations, taken a look at itself in new ways and come away from the experience better for it.

THE TRADITION OF TRADITION

Many people (and perhaps a few anthropologists) still think of anthropology as the study of traditional cultures. Outside of anthropology, the word "tradition" has acquired major cultural and political significance, as American citizens, for instance, debate issues of "traditional marriage" or "traditional values," etc. "Tradition" is not just a term or concept of interest to anthropologists, but to the general public as well, and in fact it is an anthropological concept because it is a general concept, not unlike "belief" or even "culture," as we have seen in past chapters. Anthropology is, or at least has been, a product of its own culture too.

The discussion of traditional culture—or the discussion of culture *in terms of tradition*—is not so much false as vacuous. What precisely is tradition? It implies something that exists and continues "from way back" or "following old ways." "Traditional," therefore, suggests continuity with the past, something that is rooted in and consistent with the past. But of course, no societies today are carrying on the past exactly as it was. First, no society is a living fossil, and no person inhabits the past; all existing societies live in the present. Second, no society is or ever has been in such complete isolation from the "outside world" that it did not have some exposure to other societies and incorporate some elements of those other cultures in its own. Certainly many if not all of these societies have absorbed influences from the "modern" world, like automobiles and cell phones and blue jeans. But they have also absorbed influences from neighboring "traditional peoples" that were "changing" them long before the "modern world" arrived.

There is a third issue that makes the term and idea of tradition even more problematic: If "tradition" refers to the past, then which particular moment of the past and which particular parts of that moment? When we think for instance of the traditional cuisine of Italy, we probably think of pasta and tomato sauce. And indeed, for the last few hundred years, pasta and tomato sauce have been staples of the Italian kitchen—but only for the last few hundred years. A mere five hundred years ago, these dishes were not and could not have been Italian traditions. Tomatoes were not native to Europe; rather, they were domesticated by ancient Mesoamericans and introduced to Europe only after contact following 1492. Even pasta was not a local creation of Europe, but was developed in China and brought to the attention of Europeans through the voyages of Marco Polo and others in

the 1300s and 1400s. Travelers carried the practice of noodle-making back to Europe, modified it using local ingredients (wheat instead of rice), and invented pasta. Later, tomato sauces were added to create a "traditional" cuisine that had never existed before.

We could multiply examples infinitely. When, say, Protestant Christians talk about their "religious traditions," those traditions cannot extend back more than five hundred years, since Protestantism only originated in the early 1500s—and particular denominations much later. And "Christian tradition" as such cannot reach back more than two thousand years, since there was no Christianity before that time. Every tradition has its starting point, before which it could not be "traditional," and when it was first introduced, it was not traditional but innovative, even radical.

The only conclusion is that, like so much else in culture, *tradition is relative*. It is relative to the particular society or cultural domain at hand (that is, there are Christian traditions and Jewish traditions and Muslim traditions and Warlpiri traditions, etc.). It is relative to the particular time-period to which "traditionalists" point (fifty years ago, five hundred years ago, five thousand years ago?). And it is relative to the particular elements of that time-period the "traditionalists" want to emphasize, remember, or revive. In other words, when Americans talk about preserving or returning to "traditional values," they usually mean not only a specific time-period—usually the 1950s, certainly not the 1850s or 1750s—but only certain aspects of that period. Presumably, they are not talking about returning to racial segregation or black-and-white television. And presumably, they are not talking about living without cell phones and computers and modern medicine. They are, in other words, picking and choosing from among the shards of the past to imagine a "traditional culture."

For anthropology and its sister-disciplines, folklore and religious studies, tradition is not what it used to be. Dan Ben-Amos commented three decades ago that people tend to take "tradition" to mean specific cultural content—stories, songs, scriptures, etc.—that has existed, unchanged, from time immemorial. In contrast, he urged that "tradition" is a process, namely "the dynamics of transmission of cultural heritage from generation to generation" (1984: 116), which includes the ways

IMAGE 11.2 Halloween in the United States is an invented tradition combining very old and general harvest and spirit practices with newer and uniquely American elements.

TANGO: A NATIONAL TRADITION OF ARGENTINA?

and contexts in which it is performed and reproduced. The great folklorist Ruth Finnegan went further, insisting that since people must practice or use a "tradition" for it to persist, then "this actual *usage* may be as liable to exploit, to modify, or to play with tradition as to follow it blindly. Traditions, it has become clear, are constantly open to change" (1991: 112). This opens such anthropological questions as "'traditional' in what sense? is it necessarily old? or collectively composed? or passed on passively without individual manipulation? *who* created it in whole or in part? how has its editing and interpretation affected the evidence, and with what assumptions or for what purpose?" (113)—not to mention for whose benefit and at whose cost? Within religion, the matter is equally serious. Richard Heitzenrater explained that the "truth" of a religious tradition might depend less on facts of history than on "the willing reception and critical practice of the tradition in the present in a fashion that is . . . meaningful and relevant . . . to those who continue to hold and practice the tradition" (2002: 637). The survival, even authority, of the tradition "depends upon the regularity of its repetition," and "'[g]ood' traditions are those that give continuing special meaning to self-conscious

identity. They have built-in biases, developed, practiced, passed on, and accepted down through the years" (637). Finally, the eminent Bible scholar Walter Brueggemann made "tradition" a verb— traditioning—in describing "the work of tradition," the process or action of formulating, transmitting, interpreting, and employing tradition that always and necessarily involves "imaginative remembering" (2003: 7). "The traditioning process is endless and open-ended" (11), so even a tradition like the Old Testament is never fixed or finished.

Ultimately, there is no such thing as a "traditional" culture—not today and probably not ever— because the very meaning of the term is so vague and relative. If by "traditional" we mean "living in some primordial unchanged condition," then the idea is not just wrong but nonsensical: No society lives as it did "in the beginning." Significantly, anthropology too has its "traditions." Doing fieldwork and writing ethnographies are anthropological traditions. Focusing on small-scale and remote societies is an anthropological tradition. And treating these societies as if they were "traditional" is an anthropological tradition. It has even been argued that the very notions of "society" and "culture" are anthropological traditions (Kuper, 1988;

BOX 11.1 THE (RE)INVENTION OF A NATIONAL TRADITION: THE SCOTTISH SMALLPIPES

The "smallpipes" or small indoor bagpipes may be a "traditional" instrument in Scotland, but "between the middle of the nineteenth century and the early 1980s, museums were just about the only place in Scotland where they might be found with any consistency" (Power, 2013: 68). Several types of bagpipes had existed before the integration of Scotland into the United Kingdom in 1707, but most were lost because politics and war "largely destroyed the population that had supported bagpipes"; ironically, the familiar large "highland pipes" survived only because they were adopted by the British army, which led piping "to become stylized, regimented, heavily literate, proscribed and highly technically accomplished" (69). In the 1970s and 1980s, the smallpipes began to make a comeback, which renowned piper Iain MacInnes called a "genuine revival, mixed with more than a hint of reinvention. No one would claim that the low-pitch pipes which dominated the early years of the revival have much in common with eighteenth-century instruments" (quoted in Power, 2013: 69). For instance, instrument maker Hamish Moore designs his smallpipes to play "an older, rhythmic style of Scottish music" in contemporary spaces like "the pub, the public dining room, the kitchen, the stage, the studio" (75). The very act of crafting the smallpipes again after many years

> rejects many of the cultural changes that took place in Scotland after the 1706–7 Acts of Union. . . . His performance of Scottish traditional music in this context is thus a performance of his commitment to Scottish community and oral culture in a contemporary context.
>
> (76)

The act of fashioning and playing the instrument is then "a way to resist hegemonic power of one sort or another—a regretted historical discourse, the power of an uncaring and foreign state, or the depredation of commodified, mass-mediatized culture" (72).

Wagner, 1975). It is well to recall that anthropology emerged at a specific place and time with specific interests.

Because the nineteenth-century Western anthropological project focused on cultural history and the origin and evolution of institutions, it required examples or "survivals" of past cultural eras to describe, categorize, and compare, and because the researchers who arrived to study the "primitive societies" necessarily had no data on the prior state of those societies, it was easy and natural to conclude or assume that they had no history, that they were living "in some primordial unchanged condition." More, it was useful: Only if those remote societies were preserved fossils of a lost cultural past could they play their role as representatives of former and lower cultures. Eric Wolf, in his epic treatise on the contact between Europeans and non-Europeans, made light of this notion in the title of his book, *Europe and the People without History*

(1982). In reaction to the dearth of historical information and of the obvious excesses of the historical and evolutionary approach, Malinowski and Boas advised on avoiding historical questions at all, probably perpetuating the impression that non-European societies really were ahistorical and static.

Surprisingly, Malinowski, the father of supposedly ahistorical "functionalism," is wrongly accused of being indifferent to history and change. In fact, he was one of the first major scholars to draw attention to both. In his previously mentioned *The Dynamics of Culture Change,* he declared:

> The figment of the "uncontaminated" Native has to be dropped from research in field and study. The cogent reason for this is that the "uncontaminated" Native does not exist anywhere. The man of science has to study what is, and not what might have been.
>
> (1961: 2–3).

See Chapter 3

He added:

- "The scientific anthropologist must be the anthropologist of the changing Native. Why? Because what exists nowadays is not a primitive culture in isolation but one in contact and process of change" (6).

- "The nature of culture change is determined by factors and circumstances which cannot be assessed by the study of either [European or traditional] culture alone. . . . The clash and interplay of the two cultures produce new things" (25).

- "To the student of culture change, what really matters is not the objectively true past, scientifically reconstructed and all-important to the antiquarian, but the psychological reality of today" (29).

- "[T]he retrospective vision, however erroneous, is more important than the myth unknown or forgotten by old informants" (31).

- "What the 'old men of the tribe' tell us about the past can never be scientific or historical truth, since it is always affected by sentiment, by retrospective regrets and longings" (154).

- "[E]lements of the old culture . . . are being revived with a secondary, almost ethnographic interest in racial history, customary law, and the artistic and intellectual achievements of their race. . . . This sophisticated nationalism or tribalism can still draw full strength from the enormous residues of old tradition" (158).

Later anthropologists took this insight much further, pondering whether the very concepts of "culture" and "society" might be impositions on social reality. Edmund Leach was perhaps the first to question the objectivity of terms like "society," calling clearly-bounded, isolated, and stable societies an "academic fiction": The anthropologist, he wrote, "has often only managed to discern the existence of [a society] because he took it as axiomatic that this kind of cultural entity must exist" (1954: 291). This awareness led to a flood of publications with titles like *Reinventing Anthropology* (Hymes, 1972), *The Invention of Culture* (Wagner, 1975), *The Invention of Primitive Society* (Kuper, 1988), and ultimately, *The Invention of Tradition* (Hobsbawn and Ranger, 1983). Roy Wagner, for instance, argued that we assume culture to be "a

concrete entity, a 'thing' that has rules, 'works' in a certain way, and can be learned" and then go out and find what we expected to find (1975: 8). Kuper opined that the concept of society, especially primitive society, supported certain preconceptions and prejudices of Europeans of their day in regard to their own origins and to the relation of cultural "essentials" to identity. In other words,

> the idea of primitive society fed the common belief that societies were based either on blood or on soil, and that these principles of descent and territoriality may be equated with race and citizenship, the contrasting components of every imperialism and every nationalism.
>
> (1988: 9)

Since those days of the "crisis in anthropology," brought about partly by the crisis in the subject peoples of anthropology, the discipline has become even more self-reflective. Anthropology itself is not as "traditional" as it once was, just as the societies we examine are not as traditional either. Multiple scholars including James Clifford and George Marcus (1986), George Marcus and Michael Fischer (1986), Vincent Crapanzano (1992), and most scathingly, Sandall (2001) in his *The Culture Cult* have questioned the objectivity, the scientific-ness, and even the motivations of anthropologists and others who use "traditional culture" for various purposes. Clifford and Marcus in particular pointed to the "literary" and even poetic quality of anthropological works, which are "fictions" or "narratives" instead of or in addition to "factual accounts," and Sandall savagely criticized the romantic and destructive "designer tribalism" that he perceived in much professional and popular thinking about culture. What all of these authors, and the entire history of anthropology and the encounter with cultural difference, illustrate is that the description of, analysis of, and participation in culture and culture change are much more problematic and subjective—in the end, more human—than once thought.

CULTURAL DYNAMICS: THE PROCESSES OF CULTURAL CHANGE

As a consequence of this professional self-critique, anthropologists have become "less likely to think of

Clifford, James and George Marcus, Eds. 1986. *Writing Culture: The Poetics and Politics of Ethnography.* Berkeley: University of California Press.

Hymes, Dell, Ed. 1972 [1969]. *Reinventing Anthropology.* New York: Random House, Inc.

Wagner, Roy. 1975. *The Invention of Culture.* Englewood Cliffs, NJ: Prentice-Hall, Inc.

Kuper, Adam. 1988. *The Invention of Primitive Society: Transformations of an Illusion.* London: Routledge.

Hobsbawm, Eric and Terence Ranger, Eds. 1983. *The Invention of Tradition.* Cambridge: Cambridge University Press.

'culture' in terms of bounded, fully integrated, and static systems, and they are more inclined to ponder cultural processes, dynamics, and conflicts grounded in uneven fields of power that cross the contested boundaries of nation-states and peoples" (Harrison, 2008: 7). This is why it is unprofitable to speak of "culture change" as if it is foreign, almost unnatural or hostile, to "traditional culture." In fact, cultural change is a constant and natural quality of culture, not something that only appeared in recent years or centuries with colonialism and globalization to disrupt tradition. Just as a living body does not stay the same throughout its lifetime, neither does a society or culture. This is why we will talk about the processes of culture change under the more general heading of *cultural dynamics*—dynamics meaning action, practice, movement, growth, and generation. Culture never stands still, but continuously moves and develops. Any actual culture is a complicated and sometimes contradictory fusion of continuity and change.

Innovation and diffusion

What the "original" form of culture was, or where it came from, we will probably never know. Primate studies offer some indication of what pre-cultural or proto-cultural but highly social and imitative beings are like, but non-human primates are just that—not human. So their study can answer some questions, but not the most fundamental question: What is human culture, and how did humans get it? Therefore, a better question to ask is, what are the means by which cultural novelty enters a society? Arguably, cultures do tend to be conservative in the sense that they try to preserve and reproduce what they have done in the past. However, new elements also enter cultures, or else we would all still be sitting in caves making stone tools—which were themselves cultural novelties at first.

There are two main sources of novelty in any society—innovation and diffusion. **Innovation** is the ultimate source of all cultural novelty: At some point in time, somebody has to think of or start doing something different. An innovation (meaning "to make or do new") can be an invention or a discovery, in the form of a **primary innovation** (the development of a completely new principle or object) or a **secondary innovation** (a novel application or combination of already-existing principles or objects, i.e. using old components in new arrangements, such as attaching wires and vacuum tubes to construct a television). In whatever form, innovation is internal to the society: A member of the society invents and introduces it.

Innovation tends to be an initially small-scale process. In other words, most if not all innovations (perhaps less so today, in the age of research teams) tend to be the work or inspiration of a single person or at most a small group of people. When fire was first made and controlled, or plants and animals were first domesticated, or the wheel was first invented, it was quite probably discovered by one person or a few people. We know that when a new religion like Buddhism or Christianity originates, it tends to be the idea of one or at most a few individuals, with a single founding figure like Buddha or Jesus. Others of course helped shape and promote it (like Paul in the case of Christianity), but the original innovators were most often lone individuals.

Innovation may be the ultimate source of culture change, but it is not the most common source. Humans are very inventive, to be sure, but humans are above all else imitative. Most Americans speak English not because Americans invented English, but because the English language was carried to America by English-speakers. This process is **diffusion**, the spread of some cultural practice—an idea, an object or technology, a word or symbol or meaning, etc.—from one society to another.

Diffusion is orders of magnitude more common than innovation. There is good reason to believe that humans, for instance, invented writing at most three or four times in human history, and almost all of them quite long ago. But virtually all societies write today. That is because not only the notion of writing but a specific notation for writing diffused from another society to theirs; that is why there are so few major scripts or writing systems in the world today.

Whether the immediate source of novelty is innovation or diffusion, the introduction of the new cultural element is not the end of the story but just the beginning. For, if Sequoyah or anyone else "invents" a new word or language or religion or clothing style or cuisine, is it culture now? What makes something "culture"? The simple criterion is

See Chapter 13

ANTHROPOLOGY AND THE "GREAT TRANSFORMATION"

Diffusion
the spread of a cultural trait (object, idea, practice, institution) from one society to another

See Chapter 2

Innovation
the invention or discovery of a new cultural concept, idea, behavior, or object

Primary innovation
the invention or discovery of a totally original cultural item, as opposed to *secondary innovation*

Secondary innovation
an invention or discovery that uses or combines existing ideas, objects, or techniques in novel arrangements

BOX 11.2   THE INVENTION OF CHEROKEE WRITING

One of the only, if not the only, case of the invention of a writing system in recorded history (since recorded history could not start until writing existed) occurred in the 1800s among the Cherokee. According to the Manataka American Indian Council, a man named Sequoyah single-handedly developed a system for writing the Cherokee language (although an ancient legend tells of a lost script). Sequoyah was born between two cultures himself, with a Cherokee mother named Wu-the and a white father named Nathaniel Gist or Guest. He was raised in Cherokee society, married a Cherokee woman, and learned to craft iron and silver. He also was exposed to the American practice of writing, although he supposedly never learned to read and write in English; however, he did witness the phenomenon of making marks on paper to represent sounds. Between 1809 and 1821 he worked on a set of language symbols for Cherokee and finally introduced it in 1821. It was not an alphabet but a syllabary, with "letters" for syllables rather than for individual sounds or phonemes. The Cherokee elders accepted the system after a demonstration by Sequoyah, and by 1825 the Bible and several other documents including religious and legal writings had been rendered into the new script. In 1828, after acquiring their own printing press, the Cherokee Nation began to produce their own newspaper, *Tsa la gi Tsu lehisanunhi* or "Cherokee Phoenix," with parallel columns of Cherokee and English. Whether this case constitutes an innovation or a diffusion, or something in between, is open to interpretation.

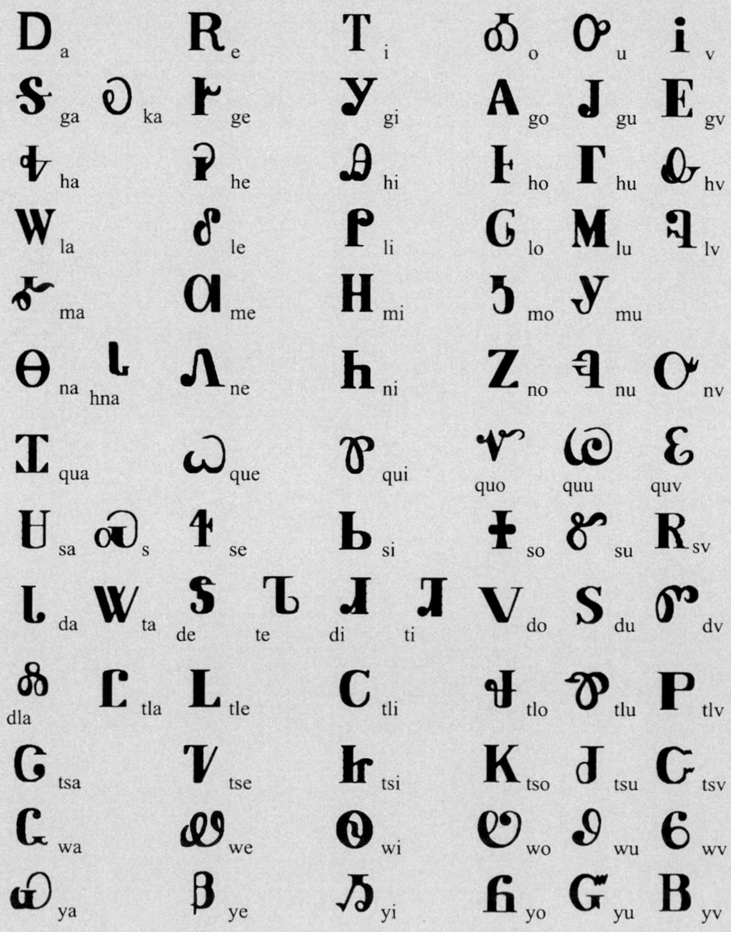

FIGURE 11.1 The Cherokee Syllabary

learned and shared behavior. So, if someone starts a new language or religion, it is not cultural unless and until other people observe it, adopt it, practice it, and transmit it to others, especially their children. If no one ever learns and shares the innovation or diffusion, it never achieves "cultural" status. But as soon as it is learned and shared, it is cultural.

There is, as we said elsewhere, no precise quantifiable limit to culture; it is not necessary that all or even most or any specific percentage of the population adopts the new behavior. Every innovation or diffusion starts as "individual peculiarities" on Linton's spectrum of the distribution of culture. If it never catches on or spreads any further, then it remains a peculiarity and eventually disappears. If it spreads a little further, it can become a cultural specialty; a little further and it could achieve the rank of an alternative. If it becomes widely known and practiced, it may become a new "universal" within that society. Of course, any particular cultural item can settle at one of these stages and remain there, or even begin to decline again. Similarly, a cultural practice of age and prestige, even a universal one, can over time fade until it becomes a peculiarity or vanishes completely.

So the question is what makes a cultural novelty "catch on" or not. Or, in more technical terms, after an innovation or diffusion is introduced to a society, a process begins, which can end in any of three outcomes: acceptance, rejection, or acceptance-with-modification. Probably most cultural innovations fail, and virtually all deviate from their original form before they are widely distributed. Some of the factors that affect the course of new phenomena are:

- how well it fits with already-existing preferences and tastes
- what local materials or ingredients are available
- how difficult or expensive it will be to implement
- what symbolic or social meaning or value exists in society
- how well it performs relative to competing items already in the culture
- how much it enhances or threatens other aspects of the culture
- how much power those who resist the change can muster

- whether it is perceived as "foreign"
- the status of the innovator or diffuser

The basic issue in any case of adoption of cultural novelty is whether it fits with the prevailing culture. For example, if Americans do not like to eat insects, then there is small chance that a new dish based on grasshoppers or cockroaches will gain very wide acceptance. If a society prefers that men wear pants and women wear dresses, then a dress for men will probably not succeed; this could also be a matter of symbolic or social meaning—of a behavior "appropriate for" one type of person but not another. One common factor is local tastes and ingredients; when I cook international foods, I often substitute exotic ingredients with local ones that I already have in my kitchen. When I was in Japan some years ago, I found a pizza restaurant in my neighborhood that served not only pepperoni pizza and sausage pizza but seaweed pizza and shrimp pizza. The Japanese restaurateurs had simply adapted pizza to local tastes, using local ingredients, to make a "Japanese pizza."

The issue of expense or difficulty is illustrated well in the American resistance to the metric system. As useful and precise as it is, the changes involved in trying to convert the entire society and economy to another system of measure make it prohibitively difficult. Every machine, every tool, every cup and container, every thermometer would have to be replaced, at great cost for material and learning. It is easier just to leave things as they are. The English typewriter keyboard is another prime example. The familiar "QWERTY" keyboard (so named for the row of keys across the upper left) was in fact allegedly designed to be intentionally inconvenient. In the days of mechanical typewriters, fast typists could jam the keys since they could type faster than the machine could respond. It was necessary to slow down these speed typists to compensate for the limitations of the device. Today, electronic keyboards have no such mechanical limitations, so more "natural" keyboards, including the proposed Dvorak style, could be effectively used. However, again, the cost of replacement and of retraining would be so exorbitant that nobody seriously considers a change. The lesson is that cultural elements are not always chosen or preserved because they are the best, but because they are the most familiar or the "easiest" in the sense of requiring the least bother.

See Chapter 2

THE INVENTION OF AN AMERICAN TRADITION: THANKSGIVING

BOX 11.3   STONE VERSUS STEEL AXES IN AN ABORIGINAL SOCIETY

Because culture is holistically integrated, it can and often does happen that a modification in one area of culture, even a small one, can have ramifications, frequently unexpected and sometimes serious, in other areas. The Yir Yoront of Cape York Peninsula, northeast Australia, used stone axes long before contact with Europeans. The tools were relatively easy to make, and men (but not women or children) could produce them for themselves. Women in fact were the primary users of the tools, for chopping firewood; however, men owned and kept them, and women or youths had to ask a man's permission to use one and return it promptly. Lauriston Sharp (1952) wrote that access to axes was part of a general status system in which people were ranked by age, sex, and clan membership. The ax was a symbol of masculine power, an important trade good for establishing interpersonal relations, and a ritual object. When European Australians arrived and introduced steel axes, one might think that the impact would be minimal—perhaps cutting down more trees with less effort. However, the effects rippled through the society, from gender and political relations to religion. Aboriginals could not make their own steel axes, so they were dependent for them on whites, especially administrators and missionaries. Aboriginals who interacted with whites—and were perceived as "good" Aboriginals by the whites—had better access to the technology. This meant that older and more "traditional" men were more often excluded. Further, whites often gave the tools directly to women or children, unaware of, unconcerned about, or actively opposed to the gender segregation in the culture. Women and youths were freed from dependence on men for the property, depriving men of a practical and symbolic expression of power. Exchange relations between the Yir Yoront and other tribes broke down, as the Yir Yoront could not acquire steel axes from them and did not desire to trade steel axes to them. Sharp argued that the greatest effects were in the arena of "ideas, sentiments, and values," which radiated rapidly and contributed to the "collapse" of their society. Concepts of ownership, status, and even religion, myth, and ritual underwent stresses and transformations, "hacking," as he concluded, "at the supports of the entire cultural system" (22).

Cultural loss

Cultural loss
the process by which elements of a culture disappear over time, through natural or environmental changes, social pressures, or individual choices

Deculturation
see *cultural loss*

Ideally, innovation or diffusion would result in at worst a substitution of one cultural practice for another and at most an addition to the cultural repertoire, a new specialty or alternative. However, culture does not proceed by addition and substitution alone, but also by subtraction. In some cases, cultural elements are lost and not replaced by anything. The net result is an impoverishment of culture. It is important to remember that culture only exists so long as somebody is learning it, practicing it, and transmitting it. When that process stops, culture ceases to be. This is why **culture loss** is sometimes also known as **deculturation**.

This is a major problem in the world today, especially in the context of the sharing of culture between the generations. In many societies, young people often have little interest in the ways of the elders. Among the Gaguju people of Australia, as told

in a National Geographic program entitled "Australia's Twilight of the Dreamtime," there are no longer enough men who know the traditional dances to conduct them in the old way; the Gaguju must invite men from other tribes to fill the required roles. The cause is a combination of the interests of the young and the decisions of the old. The young often do not care much about traditions, and frequently they are not even available much of the time due to new demands of school or work and new opportunities for travel and play (not to mention plagues like alcohol and drugs). At the same time, the elders assess the readiness of the next generation before they transfer their secret-sacred knowledge. In Australia, religious knowledge is not for just anyone, and only men who are properly initiated and committed to and advanced in the traditions can receive it. If the elders never consider the youngsters qualified to have the knowledge, then the elders will keep it to themselves, and when they die it will die with them.

From the perspective of the young, there is sometimes a voluntary or involuntary detachment from their culture. In a changing and modernizing world, the young may see little use for or value in "traditional" knowledge or skills, from hunting or horticulture to music, language, or religion. On the other hand, outside agents may intentionally or unintentionally interrupt the culture-transfer process, as with boarding schools, separation of families, and even forced adoptions. In some cases, other groups or classes, including the government under which a society lives, have explicitly forbidden the use of some or all parts of a culture; for example, in the second half of the twentieth century, Turkish authorities outlawed the use of Kurdish language and symbols in an effort to eliminate not only Kurdish culture, but even Kurdish identity.

All of these things have already happened in many parts of the world to many parts of culture—and in some cases, to entire cultures. By some counts there are hundreds of traditional languages that are endangered today, and we can never know how many have already become extinct. An alarming number of languages are on the verge of disappearance, some with less than one hundred surviving speakers. The Ainu language, spoken by natives of northern Japan, is one of the worst cases: With the youngest remaining speaker already sixty-five years old in the 1990s, such a language has little future

It is of course not just language that is in the process of being lost. Religions, music, and other kinds of irreplaceable knowledge, including potentially important botanical and medicinal knowledge, are in danger. When these cultural possessions are dead, some will "live on" in the ethnographies of anthropologists, but some will be lost to humanity forever.

Acculturation

Enculturation is the process of acquiring one's culture, ordinarily as a child, in interaction with other members of one's society. **Acculturation** as a word sounds very similar, and conceptually it is very similar, but with a profound twist. Acculturation can be thought of as the acquisition of (some or all of) a second culture other than one's own, although this is too simple to be completely accurate: In the case of Sequoyah, which culture was "his own" culture? In a way, having two cultures might sound like a good thing, a kind of "multiculturalism" or cultural "bilingualism." And no doubt in some cases and in some ways it is a good thing. However, it can also be disruptive, and it can be coercive. In essence, acculturation is the process of culture change that

See Chapter 15

See Chapter 13

Acculturation
the process of acquiring a "second culture," usually as an effect of sustained and imbalanced contact between two societies. Members of the "weaker" society are compelled to adopt aspects of the dominant society

IMAGE 11.3 Foragers are often forced to settle down, as in these concrete houses built for the formerly nomadic Warlpiri.

occurs as a result of intense and sustained contact between two societies. Whenever there is such contact, there is going to be a circulation or flow of culture (and sometimes genes too) between the two societies; after all, that is how Europe got noodles and gunpowder and the compass and the zero and tomatoes and potatoes. Cultural exchange can bring benefits for both sides.

However, one crucial issue in acculturation is the power differential between the two societies. In such cases, the smaller or weaker society is usually changed much more profoundly than the larger or more powerful one, although both are changed some. When the first English settlers arrived at Massachusetts Bay, there is no doubt that they learned some critical things from the Native Americans, and there are many elements of Indian culture in Euro-American culture today. Even so, no one can dispute that the changes for Native American societies were immeasurably greater and more negative than for the European immigrants.

One of the fascinating aspects of acculturation is that it is often extremely personal. That is, it is less true to say that a society is acculturated than that individual people are acculturated. Usually the first to feel the pressure are those in the most intimate and prolonged contact with the foreigners, including those engaged in trade or in political relationships. Others who feel the clutch of acculturation earliest are the children of mixed couples, like Sequoyah, who find themselves physically and culturally "in between." Sometimes referred to in the early anthropological literature as "marginal people," they often experience the personal sting of acculturation by being partly in each culture but not completely in either. They are the harbingers of the future.

As members of the dominated society (which may actually be larger demographically, as in the case of India under British rule) succumb to the pressures and lures of the new society, they may become in some ways more like this new society—that is, assimilate to it. They may learn its language, adopt some of its practices (clothing, firearms, and alcohol are three familiar ones), and in various ways emulate the new models. This process is partly natural and spontaneous, but it is also sometimes artificial and compulsory. In such cases, we can rightly speak of repressive acculturation or forced acculturation.

See Chapter 6

There are many known (and probably even more unknown) instances of forced acculturation. They are basically implementations of ethnocentric beliefs and attitudes. The activity of missionaries is one of the prime examples. Missionaries often did good work, bringing food and even peace to conflicting societies. However, the "mission" behind these works was always to change the society, most obviously (but not exclusively) its religion. Missionaries naturally would attempt to introduce foreign beliefs into the society, but they would often do so by ridiculing, condemning, or even punishing the "traditionalists" or at least by favoring the "converts." They were not above using the influence of their resources, including food and water, as weapons in this conversion effort, nor did they refrain from using corporal punishment or destroying native religious artifacts and buildings. In some places, missions became virtual prisons, from which natives were not permitted to leave once they arrived and where the missionary's will was law (see Tinker, 1993). Obviously, too, the missionary's interests were not limited to religion as such, seeing as how all the domains of culture are integrated and that religion provides the rules and the sanctions for conduct in other regards. So, missionaries often imposed their (that is, Western or European) values and practices in the areas of kinship, gender roles, language, and economics on the local people too, forbidding, for instance, polygyny or child marriages or nakedness or gender equality or nomadism, etc.

In addition to (and often connected to) the missionaries were the institutions of education, most notably boarding schools. In America and Australia as elsewhere, native—and especially mixed-race—children were rounded up into these schools, sometimes by force, where they were compelled to change their appearance, their language, and their religion and where they were expected to receive "civilization and Christianity" including a new name, a "modern" education, and a trade. (The feature film *Rabbit-Proof Fence* is a splendid portrayal of this process in early twentieth-century Australia.) Boys were taught conventional white male roles and girls conventional white female ones. No matter what, they were subjected to acculturation pressures which neither they nor their parents could resist and which the dominant society thoroughly approved. Often, at the end of their stay, the children were turned back out into

IMAGE 11.4 Native American children were often acculturated through the use of boarding schools, like the Carlisle School.

the bigger world, where they did not have the skills and knowledge to be Indians or Aboriginals nor the acceptance to be whites. They were literally marginalized.

These more overt methods to acculturate American Indian and Australian Aboriginal children were not the only ones employed. Children were sometimes actually seized from their parents and placed in white foster homes, to give them the benefits of white culture. And other more indirect means were used too, some of which were ostensibly in the natives' "best interests." For example, in 1887, after most Native American societies had been pacified and placed on reservations, some white Americans thought they were doing the

Indians a favor (while others had different motivations) by breaking up communal tribal land and assigning it as private property to individual people or families. Known as "allotment," the intention was not only to turn Native Americans into private landowners and farmers like other Americans, but also to tear down any communal identity and to destroy any vestiges of traditional economies and politics. After all, people could not practice foraging or pastoralism on sixteen acres of land. Individual Indians on their little plots would cease thinking of themselves as "Indians" and assimilate to the white "individual land-holder" model (and "excess" land could be sold to or seized by non-Indians).

BOX 11.4   ACCULTURATING THE "INTERNAL OTHER": CHANGING PEASANTS INTO CITIZENS IN CONTEMPORARY CHINA

Intentional acculturation targets the "other," but that other need not be a member of a completely separate society. In American "assimilation," non-white races and lower classes have been perennially subjected to acculturation into white and middle-class values and culture, often through explicit programs like Head Start (early-childhood education) or even efforts to teach adults not only job skills but the proper way to dress and behave in the workplace. Predictably, while China has been experiencing one of the largest population shifts in human history—with rural people migrating in droves to cities

See Chapter 6

and cities expanding into formerly rural land—villagers "form an internal other that is both the antithesis and the condition of possibility" for centers like Shenzhen (Bach, 2010: 448). Between 1980 and 2006, Jonathan Bach reports, the population of Shenzhen grew by twenty-seven percent annually, and this astronomical growth has relied not only on in-migration from the countryside, but on incorporating the countryside, resulting in two hundred and forty-one "villages in the city" that persist as urban villages "discursively and spatially long after their legal status was forcibly changed from rural to urban" (423). Although these villages-cum-neighborhoods were officially declared urban in 1992, "they continue to have an emotional and evocative power in linking Shenzhen's land and history to a different space and time" (423). Likewise, the urbanites of Shenzhen perceive the internal villagers as other; to them, "Shenzhen is a civilized city, and civilization is urban, urbane, orderly. Villages are uncivilized, messy, disorderly, and removing these 'dirty, chaotic, and backward' spaces is akin to removing 'the city's cancers'" (425). Transformation of villages and villagers into cities and city-dwellers is also akin to acculturation. The process formally began in 1992 when villages were re-categorized as urban residents; their village committees were converted into shareholding corporations, usually led by a Communist party secretary. It continued with the civilizing of space, specifically forbidding and destroying informal and illicit buildings: "the demolishing of illegal migrant housing was a central part of the campaign to improve the conduct, outlook, and 'correct values' of zone residents," replacing ramshackle structures with malls, supermarkets, and entertainment centers (444). Residents were even treated to a written message on a poster "backlit in purple with three black circles containing, respectively, a T-shirt, a handbag, and a plate with a knife and fork"—surely three signs of modernity—as well as "the English word *civilized* in white letters" and the slogan "Civilization is a taste" (*Wenming ye shi yizhong pinwei*) in Chinese (445). Yet Bach notes that the development of the city would not be possible without its urban villagers, who provide not only much of its labor, but also much of its housing. Those subjected to acculturation are also recruited into the workforce of the acculturating society—whether it is colonized peoples or the lower class—and Bach justifiably argues that urban villagers-turned-landlords house up to half of the residents of some parts of the city. If these informal neighborhoods were "to be destroyed overnight—something theoretically within the power of the government to do—the city would need to provide housing for nearly a million people"; ironically, the persistence of unregulated urban villages "enabled the municipal government to avoid taking responsibility for social, economic, and infrastructural development in these villages" (433), which was no accident. Bach concludes that "the de facto reliance of the city on the informal provision of housing and services"—the deliberately incomplete acculturation of villagers and taming of villages—"is less an unintended consequence than part of what one city official told me was Shenzhen's secret of success—the implementing of policies without paying for them, or as he phrased it, 'building the city at no cost'" (434).

Genocide and ethnocide

Acculturation can be forceful and repressive, but it tends to leave people alive, more or less. However, when one society desires and seeks the complete eradication of another people, this is known as **genocide** (from the Greek *gens* for "a people or group" and *cide* for "kill"). Genocide as a practice has been formally recognized and defined by the United Nations, which described it in Article II of the 1948 UN Genocide Convention as "acts committed with intent to destroy, in whole or in part, a national, ethnical, racial, or religious group, as such:

Genocide

the destruction of a group or society by harming, killing, or preventing the birth of its members

(a) Killing members of the group;
(b) Causing serious bodily or mental harm to members of the group;
(c) Deliberately inflicting on the group conditions of life calculated to bring about its physical destruction in whole or in part;
(d) Imposing measures intended to prevent births within the group;
(e) Forcibly transferring children of the group to another group.

By this definition, there have been many genocides over human history, most occurring in ancient times, but plenty in recent history. It is indisputable that many societies and their cultures have vanished from the earth or had their remnants absorbed into other larger societies, without a trace or a memory. In modern times, the Nazi "final solution" against European Jews is the very face of genocide for most people, but it is by no means the only one. Around the turn of the twentieth century, the Turks committed genocide against the Armenians, while in the 1990s the Serbs conducted "ethnic cleansing" against Bosnian Muslims in Yugoslavia, and the Hutus killed vast numbers of Tutsis in Rwanda.

The first or stereotypical impression of genocide is violence against "them," outsiders to a society or members of other societies. However, "them" is a relative term too, and some societies, or at least contingents within societies, have committed what we could call "auto-genocide" against what we would normally think of as their own people. Cambodia under the Khmer Rouge party and then government is perhaps the most familiar instance. Pol Pot, the head of the Communist Khmer Rouge (as told in the popular media, like the movie *The Killing Fields*), was responsible for the death of up to a third of the population of his own country under various programs aimed at forced culture change. That is, in order to realize the desired communist workers' utopia, "enemies of the revolution" and counter-revolutionaries had to die,

and this tended to include the intelligentsia, the urban population, and anyone who disagreed with official policy.

Genocide can be effective, but it is horribly expensive, messy, and unpopular; while the world does not always rush to stop it, it does usually condemn it. Genocide leaves evidence, in the form of corpses. However, it is not necessary to kill people in order to achieve the same basic result—the elimination of a social group. A much "cleaner" method that has proven just as effective is ethnocide. **Ethnocide** (from the Greek *ethnos* for "a culture or way of life") means destroying the culture or institutions of a group rather than the people. It often masquerades as any other "educational" endeavor. The missions and boarding schools described above could and perhaps should be understood as ethnocidal projects and are often viewed as such by the indigenous people. The goal was, and was sometimes even stated as, the eradication of one kind of person and the replacement with another kind. This sentiment was expressed directly in the late nineteenth-century American slogan, "Kill the Indian to save the man." This meant erasing the Indian-ness from Indian people, so that they would become "regular Americans," like the acculturation of Chinese villagers discussed above. And many white Americans thought they were doing the Indians a favor—giving them a

GENOCIDE IN RWANDA 1994

Ethnocide
the destruction of a group's culture, without necessarily killing any of the members of the culture

IMAGE 11.5 A newspaper image protesting political oppression in Mongolia. The main text reads "Don't forget . . . This repression shouldn't be repeated."

"modern" culture by means of which they could participate in broader American society and life.

Unlike genocide, ethnocide leaves living victims. The aftermath is people who look like Indians or Aboriginals, etc., but who do not act, think, or live like them. They are, culturally, indistinguishable from the dominant society. They have in effect been deculturated and then re-enculturated as members of the dominant society. The consequences can be and have been so abrupt, however, that some people refer to ethnocide as "cultural genocide."

Directed change

As we have acknowledged, culture change is inevitable in situations of culture contact, which has been the normal condition of human societies as long as there have been human societies. Even without that contact, individuals or groups continuously modify their cultures. Environmental changes may call for new behavioral adaptations, over the short or long term. Innovations introduce new material, and re-interpretations shift the meaning of previous material. The mere passing of generations brings new individuals with new perspectives on their "traditions." In all of these ways, culture change is normal and natural. Cultures are always "in process."

Even in situations of culture contact, the changes induced are often unplanned, spontaneous, and uncoordinated. People observe this or that, transfer this or that, accept or modify or reject this or that in the normal course of cultural development without any specific goals in mind and without anybody dominating or driving the process. However, sometimes this change is not spontaneous and voluntary at all, and more and more in the modern world, such change is highly planned and even highly coercive.

Let us define **directed change**, then, as planned, coordinated, and sustained efforts to make changes to part or all of a culture. There are two directions from which this initiative may come. In one case, changes are imposed "from the outside," by a foreign society that is aiming to change the culture of another society for the benefit of the former (and occasionally, at least the perception of the benefit of the latter). In the other case, changes

are imposed "from the inside," by one element (class, religion, race, ethnic group, etc.) or region (e.g. urban versus rural, north versus south) of a society on another element or region of the same society. This distinction can be a little blurred, however, since in practice, "on the ground," it might not be quite clear when a group or society is "inside" or "outside." This too can be relative. When the United States wanted to encourage settlers into the Oklahoma territory in the nineteenth century, this could be regarded as promoting changes *inside American society and territory* or as imposing changes *on non-American, namely, Indian societies.* Or, in actuality, it can and should be regarded as both simultaneously, depending on the point of view. The same would be the situation in discussions of "developing" the Amazon rainforest, which is inside and under the control of the Brazilian state but also inhabited by societies that do not identify themselves as "Brazilian," as well as in many other parts of the world.

For our purposes, directed change will come in four major, world-historical manifestations, which will comprise the remainder of this book. The first is colonialism, a prime example of directed change from the outside; although modern European colonialism began as a piece-meal and even accidental project, it eventually coalesced into a very intentional and organized enterprise, with profound international repercussions that are still felt today. The second is nationalism, a type of cultural and political movement to unify and empower a social group, often with the ultimate goal of achieving sovereign political power and an independent state for the group. Closely associated with nationalism is ethnicity, a different but related form of cultural movement that may have political or other goals. The third is development, usually conceived as coordinated changes to the economy of a (most often poor) society, often along with or for the purpose of changes in the standard and quality of life as well. Development is an example of directed change that can come from the outside or the inside, and often both simultaneously, since states frequently propose and direct development efforts within their territory with the assistance (financial and technical) of foreign states, corporations, or organizations. It increasingly takes the form of globalization or neoliberalism. The fourth and final is what we will call generally "revitalization

See Chapter 12

See Chapter 13

Directed change
a cultural process in which internal or external agents make more or less intentional, coordinated, and sustained modifications or reforms to a society and culture

See Chapter 14

IMAGE 11.6
Inculturation is a common way for religions to find a place in a new society.

movements," including efforts to "reform" elements or institutions of a society as well as initiatives (particularly in the case of small, indigenous groups) to protect and preserve and in some instances revive cultural practices. These revitalization movements often, but not always, emphasize "tradition" but in a modern and "nontraditional" way and are not above using nontraditional media (like the internet) to achieve their objectives. All in all, they and the other types of directed change illustrate the power and pervasiveness of cultural innovation and diffusion and of the "invention of tradition"—which can become a "real tradition" tomorrow.

See Chapter 15

BOX 11.5 CONTEMPORARY CULTURAL CONTROVERSIES: INCULTURATION AND RELIGIOUS CHANGE

Anthropology does not have a monopoly on the culture concept, nor can we control how it is used. For individuals and institutions seeking to impose cultural change, the concept of culture is indeed very useful, and Christian missionaries are among the most ardent agents of religious change. Missionaries and scholars of missiology (the study of missionary practices) have produced books like Paul Hiebert's 1986 *Anthropological Insights for Missionaries*, 1994 *Anthropological Reflections on Missiological Issues*, and 2008 *Transforming Worldviews: An Anthropological Understanding of How People Change*, as well as Charles Kraft's 1997 *Anthropology for Christian Witness*, to name but a few. The Catholic Church has been particularly thoughtful about culture and religion, overtly promoting the notion of "inculturation" or "the recognition that faith must become culture, if it is to be fully received and lived" (Shorter, 1988: xi). Alwyn Shorter, a prominent theorist of inculturation, directly discussed culture and acculturation, but he rejected acculturation as "cultural domination." He also dismissed syncretism— mixing Christianity with local religion—as a compromise on Catholic truth. The beginning of real inculturation is translating Catholic doctrines and practices into local languages and cultures, as well as the reciprocal process of absorbing some local elements into Catholicism—not, to be sure, to change Catholicism, but to produce locally meaningful Catholicisms and a more inclusive world Catholicism. The ultimate goal, of course, is "that the Christian message transforms a culture. It is also the case that Christianity is transformed by culture, not in a way that falsifies the message, but in a way in which the message is formulated and interpreted anew" (14). Many anthropologists are understandably apprehensive about this application of anthropological concepts; meanwhile, many Christians are apprehensive about this modification to Christianity, even while non-Western Christians are modifying Christianity on their own. What do you think?

SUMMARY

Anthropology has often been thought of, and thought of itself, as the study of "traditional societies," but no society today is perfectly "traditional," and "tradition" is a relative concept in itself. Anthropology has grown and changed, as the societies that interest it have grown and changed, into the study of cultural processes by which human groups adjust to changing internal and external realities, including contact with societies that are very different from and in very unequal power relationships with them. As it has done so, anthropology has become more self-aware of its own practices and of the entire project of conceptualizing and describing cultures.

Cultures are never static and unchanging. Even when they appear "continuous," this is an achievement of ongoing active cultural processes. In fact, every culture at every moment of its existence is a complicated alloy of continuity and change, and that is normal. Some of the processes that function in the dynamics of culture are:

- innovation
- diffusion
- cultural loss or deculturation
- acculturation
- genocide and ethnocide
- directed change

Whatever the original source of the cultural novelty, a process of circulation and distribution within the society is begun, which can end in three general outcomes:

- acceptance
- rejection
- acceptance with modification

It is also possible that the new cultural element may achieve a certain limited distribution and "stall" there. Culture, thus, emerges as a living system of elements that are differentially distributed throughout the society and moving (growing or shrinking) within that society. This process is often spontaneous and unintentional, or even unnoticed, but it can—and in the modern world, increasingly is—very intentional as well as very contentious.

Q

MCQS

Q

FILL IN THE BLANKS

WWW

Key Terms

acculturation	directed change	primary innovation
cultural loss	ethnocide	secondary innovation
deculturation	genocide	tradition
diffusion	innovation	

Colonialism and the origin of globalization

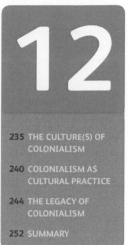

When Captain James Cook arrived at the Hawaiian Islands in 1778, a complex society already existed there. Humans had probably inhabited the islands for almost fifteen hundred years, bringing a cultural and physical mixture from various Pacific islands. Within a decade of Cook's "discovery" of Hawaii, American ships used it as a waypoint on route to Asia. Meanwhile, by 1810 King Kamehameha I successfully unified the island chain into a single kingdom while holding off the encroaching Westerners who sought to harvest Hawaii's rich sandalwood resources. However, after his death in 1819, American and European traders penetrated the islands, and a year later Christian missionaries from the United States arrived as well. But the colonial era for Hawaii really began with the development of sugar plantations, the first established by American William Hopper in 1835. Interestingly, missionaries like Amos Starr Cooke often switched their work from Christianity to sugar. But sugar production was labor intensive, so as early as 1868, Japanese contract laborers were imported to the islands; Koreans were eventually hired after 1903 and Filipinos after 1907. A British citizen, George Paulet, had tried to seize the islands from Kamehameha III in 1843, but it was a group of American businessmen, in conjunction with the American government and military, who finally overthrew the Hawaiian kingdom in 1893. Despite the fact that an 1876 treaty had recognized Hawaii's sovereignty, with sugar production increasing tenfold over twenty years, the islands had become too valuable to resist. In 1898, the same year that the U.S. seized the Philippines and Cuba from Spain, it annexed Hawaii. Hawaii's prizes also included an excellent harbor, Pearl Harbor, and soon a thriving new industry—pineapples. James Dole came to Honolulu in 1899, where his cousin Sanford Dole happened to be the governor since the 1893 coup. By 1907. Dole was canning pineapples for the American market, and in 1922 he managed to buy the entire island of Lana'i, which became a 200,000-acre pineapple plantation. With such profound economic and military interests in the islands, it was a small step to Hawaii's admission as the fiftieth state of the U.S. in 1959, only shortly after Alaska, another recently colonized territory.

The nearly five-hundred-year long enterprise of European colonialism profoundly changed the world. Peoples who had never been in contact with another society so extraordinarily different and so extremely remote were more or less suddenly

IMAGE 12.1 The proclamation of the independent "Republic of Hawaii," with American missionary Sanford Dole as president, after the overthrow of the Hawaiian monarchy.

drawn into a system of global proportions and interconnections. However, the phenomena of culture contact, culture change, and unequal cultural relationships introduced by Europeans or modern colonialism were not completely novel. Muslim traders had long since reached Southeast Asia, and entrepreneurs from India worked in Africa. Even the Aboriginals on the northern shore of Australia had been in contact with Macassan or Malay fishermen who came annually to trawl the waters off the continent. Complex, hierarchical, and multi-cultural societies and empires had risen and fallen throughout history, and no area of the earth was exempt from culture contact and the effects of long-distance trade and unequal power relations. In fact, societies that are associated with one "traditional" area or way of life, such as the Cheyenne of the plains of North America, have frequently been shown by historical, archaeological, and ethnographic evidence to have reached these places and social patterns only comparatively recently in time (obviously, there was no horse-riding culture in the American Plains before the European introduction of horses).

Modern colonialism in a certain sense continued long-standing and familiar cultural processes of innovation, diffusion, acculturation, etc. In ways it merely escalated and intensified these processes, while in other ways it was radically different. For the first time, cultural contacts and political and economic relationships were not merely local or regional, but truly global. The impact on the local societies too was complex and contradictory: Sometimes it appeared to freeze their "traditional" cultures at a particular moment in time, while also altering those traditions or even destroying them and generating new ones. Even before modern colonialism, it would be false to insist that indigenous societies were static or could be meaningfully described and understood in isolation. However, by five hundred years ago we see the seeds of contemporary globalization, in which distant societies would become enmeshed economically, politically, technologically, and "culturally." Societies were increasingly integrated into national, regional, and ultimately global systems in which the events, decisions, and policies of any one society, state, or region could now affect other and perhaps all societies. In fact, that wider social context *became part of their contemporary culture.*

THE CULTURE(S) OF COLONIALISM

In 1492, when Christopher Columbus and his expedition made landfall in the "New World," an unprecedented expansion and acceleration of cultural forces was already underway that would come to be known as **colonialism**. Colonialism, as a world-system of occupation and exploitation of foreign territories within the political economy of Europe, and eventually as a world-system of territorial empire, was to have unprecedented effects. Yet, the practice of establishing and controlling colonies was not new at all. In fact, colonies are not even unique to humans. The word "colony" comes from the Latin *colonia* which derives from *colonus* or "farmer," which further derives from *colere* or "to cultivate" (also related to the root of the term "culture"). A **colony** is a segment of a population that moves into and occupies a new territory; as such, there can be not only colonies of humans, but of animals, trees, or bacteria. To "colonize" is merely to expand into areas previously unoccupied by the population, and the offshoot of the original population that pioneers this new occupation is the colony.

So fifteenth- and sixteenth-century Europeans did not invent colonization. Societies were colonizing new lands in the ancient and prehistoric past. Greek cities colonized the Mediterranean coast, planting colonies of Greeks as far afield as present-day Turkey and Spain. When Alexander the Great swept through the Middle East and Central Asia, he intentionally left behind colonies, often named Alexandria, with the full complement of Greek social, intellectual, and artistic institutions. Polynesian peoples colonized Hawaii after settling other Pacific Islands, and modern-day European societies themselves are the product of multiple waves of colonization of the continent, from the first Homo sapiens who displaced the Neandertals to Greek and Roman and Germanic, Slavic, Celtic, Nordic, and other peoples (again refuting the "pure race" illusion of Europeans). Later, these products of ancient colonizations reached out to colonize a world that had itself been shaped by successive waves of occupation.

As James Clifford reminded us, "Everyone's on the move, and has been for centuries" (1997: 2). Therefore, the anthropological "study of colonialism erases the boundaries between anthropology and history or literary studies" (Pels, 1997: 163), even as it erases boundaries between different societies— simultaneously creating new boundaries. The worldwide phenomenon that was sparked by the explorations of early-modern wanderers was to evolve into something unmatched in scale and impact, since no society had ever flung its colonies so broadly nor wrought such grand changes on the colonized regions. And gradually it was to shift from mere colonization to a deliberate and sustained policy of colonialism. Colonialism eventually became a form of directed change, a deliberate and concerted attempt to place settlements in new territories for the purpose of economic and political domination of those territories and of the peoples who already live there. This domination was, of course, primarily for the benefit of the transplanted foreigners (the colonists) or ultimately of the "mother country" from which the colonists were sent, rather than of the local indigenous people. In fact, the interests of the colonists and the locals or "indigenous peoples" were usually if not invariably at odds, leading to serious and often violent conflict.

The diversity of colonialism

An anthropology of colonialism would stress its diversity and its relativism, as well as its integration with various aspects of culture. In 1972, Ronald Horvath distinguished colonialism, as a type of "intergroup domination in which settlers in significant number migrate permanently to the colony from the colonizing power," from imperialism, which involved few if any settlers (1972: 50). While that is probably not the salient difference, he did make the valid observation that some colonies included many settlers while others included few. He added that in either case, the relation between local inhabitants and colonial invaders could take the shape of extermination of the locals, assimilation of the locals to the colonial culture, or "relative equilibrium" in an integrated or segregated society (see Furnivall on "plural society" below).

A more fruitful approach has been to identify the variables that shaped different styles or

Colonialism
the more or less organized system of occupation and exploitation of foreign territories through settlement and conquest, especially as practiced by Western states since 1492

Colony
a segment of a population (not exclusively a human population) that moves into and occupies territory not previously occupied by the population, often displacing or subduing the previous occupants

See Chapter 15

See Chapter 6

Colonies of settlement colonies to which many foreigners immigrate, sometimes such that they and their descendants become the majority population of the territory

Colonies of exploitation colonies to which few foreigners immigrate but the territory is still used for its resources, wealth, labor, markets, and/or strategic location

experiences of colonialism, depending on precisely who or what did the colonizing and on how the power of colonialism was organized. For instance, there was an important difference between *direct rule* and *indirect rule*. With direct rule, a Western state directly intervened in local society, conquering the territory with state armies and administering the territory with state bureaucrats (governors, tax collectors, police and judges, and missionaries acting on behalf of the state). Direct rule was not the only or most common practice, though, especially in the early stages of colonialism: Often direct governmental intervention came later, after the area had been occupied by settlers or merchants, whose lives and property had then to be defended by the state. Even when Western states could project power directly into foreign regions, they frequently chose to practice indirect rule, in which they would co-opt native authorities to participate in the governance of the colony. Indirect rule was cheaper and often more effective, since the native people in the colony still took orders from "traditional" leaders, who in turn took orders from Western states. In a word, "traditional" leaders became partners in the colonial enterprise, although they

were not equal partners, nor were they necessarily entirely traditional.

In most colonies, relatively few Westerners immigrated. Therefore we can distinguish between **colonies of settlement** and **colonies of exploitation**. In the former, large numbers of foreign colonists flocked into the colonies, sometimes to the point where they outnumbered the native population. The United States is a classic case of a colony of settlement (actually several colonies of settlement that eventually united into a single polity); other colonies of settlement included Canada, Australia, New Zealand, South Africa, and Southern Rhodesia (Zimbabwe today), although the European population never reached majority status in the last two. Typically they at first identified with, and ruled in the interests of, the mother country, but eventually they became more locally minded, even striving (and fighting) for local independence. Unlike colonies of settlement, colonies of exploitation never acquired large European populations, sometimes because the climate was unwelcoming, sometimes because large-scale settlement was too expensive, and sometimes because it was simply unnecessary. After all, if the purpose of

IMAGE 12.2 Indirect rule involved creating partnerships between European colonizers and local people, including recruitment of native soldiers into colonial armies, as depicted here in Rwanda.

the colony was cheap supplies of primary products like cotton or rubber or coffee, the colonizers did not need or perhaps even want a lot of settlers.

In some cases the conventional notion of colonialism as a governmental undertaking is not accurate at all. Many colonies were actually corporate projects, managed not by governments and not by individuals or families, but by corporations, charted companies founded to trade with other countries and societies. Among the most famous of these are the Dutch East India Company and the British East India Company; in the Western hemisphere, the Hudson Bay Company operated in Canada, and the Virginia Company was responsible for the settlement of Jamestown in 1607. The key to remember is that colonialism was about trade and profit first and foremost, and corporations then and since have been the primary mechanism of business. But profit is an effect and a cause of power, and many of these early trading companies eventually began to exert real political power over non-Western territories—enforcing civil and criminal law, negotiating with local rulers, and maintaining armies and fighting battles as if they were states. In many ways, they were multinational corporate colonial states.

When Western powers could not totally conquer a society, **spheres of influence** often resulted. This was particularly the case in China, which was simply too large and too integrated to be controlled in its entirety or by any single foreign power. In such cases, the local society was weakened to the point that it could not prevent foreign interference and penetration, and chunks of territory were occupied or dominated by various foreign powers. Hong Kong, which was only transferred back to China from the United Kingdom in 1997, was one such chunk; other states including France, Germany, Japan, and the United States claimed their pieces or "spheres," in which foreign law and culture was more or less formally instituted (known as "extraterritoriality").

Finally, **internal colonialism** was—and in some cases still is—a situation in which one group or region dominates the land, population, and resources of another region or group within "the same" state. The United States prior to the Civil War has been described as a case of internal colonialism, with the industrial North exploiting the agrarian South, and after the war the North

militarily occupied the South. Brazil and its exploitation of the Amazonian region for the benefit of the urban eastern and southern regions could be another example, as could England with its historical domination of Scottish, Welsh, and Irish lands and people. The term has also been used to refer to the process by which colonized people internalize the values and practices of the colonizer, thus participating in their own colonization. Interestingly, on many occasions non-Western societies began to adopt aspects of Western culture before they were actually colonized. Sometimes these changes came through pre-colonial cultural, financial, or military influence (as when Japan eagerly embraced many aspects of Western society after being "opened" by American warships in 1854): Reformers in these societies either wanted to become "modern" like Europeans and Americans or to acquire the tools of power and prosperity to ward off colonial advances.

Diverse eras, diverse agents

The colonial experience also diverged according to the era in which it was practiced. When Europe launched its colonial adventure, just prior to 1500, it was still a relatively weak continent in comparison to the great empires of the day—Ottoman, Chinese, Mughal (Indian), and others—with humble goals and capabilities. Also, its geographic range was fairly limited: Parts of North and South America came under its sway, as did the "East Indies" or the so-called Spice Islands (largely, present-day Indonesia) and a very few coastal patches of Africa and India. This phase, sometimes called **mercantilism**, focused essentially on trade monopolies between states and their colonies and the accumulation of wealth, particularly gold. Colonies were often like remote farms and mines for the mother country to harvest and tap.

Many of these early mercantile colonies achieved independence from their overlords in the mid- to late-1800s. Subsequently, European colonialism reconstituted in a modern and more systematic and exploitative form, which we will call **imperialism**. Imperialism sought more than the old colonialism ever did, including territorial possession, efficient administration, and enhanced wealth production and extraction, all related to the

CORPORATIONS AND COLONIALISM

COLONIZING EGYPT

Sphere of influence
in European colonial practice, an area of foreign territory where the power and authority of one European state was recognized

Internal colonialism
the practice in which a society (usually a state) penetrates and occupies territory within its jurisdiction (normally inside its borders) but that contains peoples who do not identify as and with the occupying society. In some usages, it can also refer to the condition in which colonized peoples internalize (in their minds and personalities) the institutions and values of colonialism

Mercantilism
an early modern European economic and political system in which wealth and power were determined by possession of gold and a favorable balance of trade with each other

Imperialism
the pursuit of territorial and political domination of foreign lands and peoples (building an "empire"), known since ancient history but reaching its greatest extent in the late phase of European colonialism

political competitions between the "Great Powers" of Europe and their industrial and military needs and interests. In this later period, the final and complete occupation of the world was accomplished, with enormous colonial holdings, especially for England, in Africa, India, Asia, and the Middle East. For instance, following the Congress of Berlin in 1884–1885, a "scramble for Africa" commenced, which led within a few years to the carving of what King Leopold of Belgium dubbed the "magnificent Africa cake," every "piece" of which was colonized except Ethiopia and Liberia—and Liberia had been founded by the American Colonization Society in 1821 in the first place.

The most obvious difference between colonial experiences depended on the culture and policies of the specific colonizer. Spain naturally implanted Spanish culture, the Spanish language, and Catholicism, while England brought British culture, the English language, English common law, and Anglican and other Protestant Christianity. However, the fact that Spanish colonialism came relatively early and English colonialism relatively late meant that the two states practiced distinctly different styles of colonialism, basically "different *levels of colonialism*" defined as "the extent to which a colonizing power installs economic, political, and sociocultural institutions in a colonized territory" (Lange, Mahoney, and vom Hau, 2006: 1414). For instance, Spanish settlers and authorities "concentrated colonial institutions in those areas that were the most populous and most politically and economically developed at the beginning of the colonial epoch," exploiting them and leaving behind "predatory states and dysfunctional markets"; in comparison, the British "pursued comparatively limited settlement and institutional transformation in the more populous and more politically and economically developed precolonial areas" (1414). The contrast between England and France, the primary rivals of later colonialism, is even more interesting. It has often been commented that France perceived its colonialism as part of a noble "civilizing mission" (*mission civilisatrice*), raising the natives from their primitive, savage condition. More, France treated its colonies (like Mauritius; see Box 12.3 below) as overseas parts of France and its colonized peoples as (at least potentially) Frenchmen and Frenchwomen. England, on the other hand, mainly sought to rule

and profit from its colonies, not absorbing the territories and peoples into the English state and certainly not imagining that they were English people. As political scientist William Miles puts it, "When the French colonize, they try to turn their subjects into Frenchmen themselves. When the British colonize, they take what they want, take off when they've finished, and let their former colonies fend for themselves" (2014: 115). The difference meant that England could imagine and assist eventual colonial independence, whereas France intended to hold colonial lands the way that the United States holds Hawaii or Alaska.

Finally, it should be apparent by now that colonialism involved a diverse cast of characters, not merely states and their functionaries. Many "agents of colonialism" played a role—often conflicting roles—in the colonial project, pursuing diverse interests that were only later coordinated and integrated into a few great empires. Explorers obviously were often the first foreigners to set foot on non-Western lands, to map them, report information back to the home country, and claim the territories in the name of the home country. Sometimes arriving with the explorers, and soon traveling and exploring on their own, were the missionaries. One of the most energetic missionary groups was The Society of Jesus, best known as the Jesuits. By the late 1500s and early 1600s, missionaries—Catholic and later Protestant—were blazing trails to the interior of the Americas, often ahead of explorers and other colonizers. While they imposed many changes on indigenous cultures, they often did important descriptive work too, in places where acculturation and cultural loss sometimes made subsequent study difficult or impossible. One of their main contributions was in the area of language, which they studied principally for the purpose of translating the Christian scriptures into local languages; still, some of those linguistic analyses—dictionaries, grammars, and translated documents—are the oldest or only records of native cultures.

Not far behind the explorers and the missionaries were the traders, planters, and administrators. Some traders were individual men (and occasionally women) who came to exchange goods with the native populations. They often lived relatively "native" lives, acculturating to native ways to the point of wearing native clothing, speaking

BOX 12.1 GERMANY, COLONIALISM, AND "INNER COLONIZATION"

Germany was a relative latecomer to the colonial game, only entering the scramble for colonies in the 1880s, almost four centuries later than Spain and three centuries later than England (Germany was not unified into a single state until 1871). Nor did the German colonial presence last long: The country was stripped of its overseas possessions after World War I. In that short time, though, German colonialism "manifested itself differently in each of its colonies" from Africa to the Pacific;

> parallel institutions in the various colonies enacted different policies regarding issues such as intermarriage, citizenship and property rights and...the source of these differences can be traced back to local variations in ethnographic practices that preceded the official act of state-driven colonization.

> (Kopp, 2011: 155)

In some places conquest was especially brutal, as in German Southwest Africa (Namibia today), where a genocidal war was fought against the local Herero and Nama peoples. Although many historians and anthropologists agree that genocide and the destruction of difference are inherent in colonialism, elsewhere and overall, German colonialism was focused neither on annihilation nor on civilization; instead—and more like England than France—Germany's interest was basically financial, "mainly concerned with economic exploitation, profit, formal rule, and subjugation" (Pogge von Strandmann, 2011: 202). In a word, as Theodor Leutwin admitted, "The main purpose of all colonization is, if one leaves all made-up idealism and humanitarianism aside, a business" (quoted in Pogge von Strandmann, 2011: 202). Accordingly, Germany adopted the approach of allowing corporations to do most of the initial work of colonialism. One more variation on German colonialism, although not utterly unique, was the focus on continental Europe. Of course, Greece, Rome, and other states had built impressive empires on European soil, and England had colonized Ireland in the 1600s. But Kristin Kopp contends that Germany considered Eastern Europe a colonial space long before the Nazis came to power. Germany applied the same colonial lens to Poland as to Africa, judging the Polish people to be "uncivilized" and hardly capable of modernization and development, fit only for labor, expulsion, or extermination. This racialization and dehumanization of Poles and Slavic peoples generally came to a crescendo under Hitler's rule, which some scholars see as a continuation of colonial thinking and a modern theater of European empire-building.

native languages, and occasionally marrying native women. They thus often produced the first generation of mixed-blood children. Other traders were employees of large corporations, as mentioned above. They merely wanted to make money but were compelled (at least at first) to deal with local authorities and observe local customs.

Where land was good and plentiful, planters or settlers soon arrived, and administrators (from governors and regents to accountants and tax collectors), as well as soldiers to secure peace and obedience, were usually not far behind. While governments often did not take much interest until the colonies were functioning and profitable, it was inevitable that European law and power would eventually prevail in these colonies and that even the natives themselves would be brought under their jurisdiction. In some cases this involved military campaigns to "pacify" restless and resistant locals; in other cases, or at the same time, formal "inter-governmental" relations with the locals were often established, including formal treaties between governments and indigenous leaders. This practice was most common in English territories and the United States, where treaties still significantly shape U.S.–Indian relations today, setting the precedent of Indian tribal sovereignty.

**A U.S. INDIAN TREATY—
THE TREATY OF
CANANDAIGUA 1794**

IMAGE 12.3 Colonialism was a political and personal relationship between colonizers—like the British officer depicted here in colonial India—and colonized.

COLONIALISM AS CULTURAL PRACTICE

As a cultural phenomenon, anthropology sees colonialism not only holistically and relativistically, but as a form of practice—specific (although diverse and changing) behaviors and tactics. At the most fundamental level, as noted in the case of Germany above, its goals were economic (the enrichment of the colonialist society and of the colonists who emigrated to the colonies) and political (the empowerment of the colonialist society through expansion of its dominion and blockage of expansion by its rivals).

Accordingly, colonialist or imperialist regimes sought wealth, first portable wealth that they could expropriate and carry back to their home countries. Much of early colonialism was committed to finding a sea route to the riches of Asia, and when Columbus set off for the "Indies," his eyes were fixed on gold (along with God, government, and glory). Later expeditions to the Americas criss-crossed the continent searching for El Dorado, the legendary city and society of gold. Where gold was found—either in use or at the source—it was theirs for the taking. How all of this appeared to the native peoples of the Americas is captured in *The Indian Chronicles*: "I believe the gold makes them crazy. . . . That is truly their god. Gold is more important to them than their own people. . . . The Castilla [Spanish] worship only one God, his name is Gold" (Barreiro, 1993: 191). But they also worshipped silver, which was extracted from mining regions like Potosí, Bolivia, modifying the local labor system

known as *mita* to conscript thousands of locals—and soon African slaves—to labor in the mines.

Other valuable trade goods also made for lucrative business, including spices like cinnamon, ginger, nutmeg, unique scented woods, silks and porcelains, and products that would become staples of Western life like coffee and tea. Long overland routes and hostile Muslim competitors cut into profits, though, so Europeans dreamed of making their own connections to the source, "cutting out the middleman" and maximizing their profits. Accessing and controlling the sources of goods involved finding and, where possible, taking possession of, farms, mines, forests, and any other means of production. In other words, trade soon became domination, and domination soon became conquest.

Probably the most valuable resource was land itself. Colonizers claimed and occupied land and put it to whatever use they could discover or develop there. In the process, colonizers sought to justify this expropriation of native land, morally and legally. Two principles—"legal fictions" if you will—designed to solve the problem were the "doctrine of discovery" and the notion of *terra nullius*. The **doctrine of discovery** stipulated that any state that could discover and claim a hitherto unknown or unclaimed land could have undisputed title to it. The doctrine of discovery therefore gave the discovering power the first right of occupation if there were no previous inhabitants. If there were inhabitants, the discovering power had the first right to trade with them and to negotiate political relations with them, normally taking the form of

Doctrine of discovery the European colonial principle that the state that "discovered" or arrived first in a new territory had the right to occupy and administer it without interference from other states

subordination or war. The idea of **terra nullius**, Latin for "empty land," suggested that the lands discovered and claimed by Europeans were unoccupied and therefore available to anyone who could squat on them. If it could not be argued that the land was vacant, it could be argued that it was void of *human beings* (a racial argument) or of *civilized* human beings, the mark of civilization being permanent settlements and cultivated farmland after the European fashion. Natives who were foragers or nomads were treated as little more than "beasts of the field," who did not own the lands they wandered and foraged on. Since such people never established title to the land, original title could be claimed by the European arrivals. In other cases, title to land could be created by treaty, which extinguished native claims and invented the first "deed" for it.

In many locations, colonizers acquired more land than they could possibly work themselves. So the system needed more than the dispossessed property of the natives; it needed their labor too. Hence, native labor became a valuable commodity, since it produced great wealth at little or no cost. Indians were "employed" in the mines or farms or ports of the Americas, and in more powerful and resistant societies (like African and Indonesian ones), increasingly imbalanced and exploitative relations were established, with the workers converted into European employees and serfs. Europeans devised many tactics to create the labor they desired, including force and enslavement. The system of *corvée* labor required that every able-bodied person provide a certain number of days or months of work each year. Large private farms or plantations were quick to appear. In Spanish territories, these farms were known as *encomiendas* and *haciendas* (in Portuguese Brazil, the name was *fazendas*). An *encomienda* was essentially a grant of land to conquerors and explorers, much like medieval estates; as such, control of land meant control of the people and wealth on the land. Therefore, unlucky Indians who were organized into *encomiendas* found themselves changed into serfs who owed labor and tribute to their new lords. This institution was eventually replaced by a more modern but thereby more exploitative arrangement called the *hacienda*. A **hacienda** was less feudal, but was truly owned by the *hacendados*, who acquired workers or tenants through indebtedness and

sharecropping. Mines and other interests were organized on basically the same principles: Europeans controlled or owned, and natives worked. In many cases, the natives failed to do the work satisfactorily, either because the ordeals of the work simply killed them or because they could escape and run away. This led to the introduction of a new institution—slavery. African slaves were collected (with the cooperation of African rulers and entrepreneurs) and sold to plantation owners throughout the Americas. Of course, Europeans did not invent slavery, and long after they abolished it, other societies continued (and continue today) to practice it, but the scale of the European slave trade was truly unique. Also, Africans were not the only peoples to be enslaved. In a practice known as **blackbirding**, European sailors would land on small Pacific islands and carry off virtually the entire populations to work on some far-off colonial project in India or Southeast Asia.

A clever device for raising money and recruiting labor was taxation. European colonialists introduced taxation in their colonies for two reasons. One was to pay the administrative costs of the colony itself. Colonies were not always profitable ventures; colonialism was inefficient compared to some of the more "modern" means of exploitation. Rather than bearing theses costs themselves, the colonializers shifted the burden to the natives. Arguably, some improvements in the quality of life were subsidized this way, including schools and hospitals, but none of it was the choice of the natives. Yet another reason for taxation was to compel natives to participate in the colonial economy. The colonial administration would order that all inhabitants had to pay a cash tax on their houses, their livestock, their own heads, and so on. Lacking cash, the locals had no option but to engage in wage labor for European businesses. So colonialists got the natives' land, their wealth, their work, and at least some of their wages.

The colonization of everyday life

While colonialism was ultimately about power and profit, those goals cannot be divorced from the wider culture and the everyday habits of the people affected. John and Jean Comaroff have described how colonialism in southern Africa involved

Terra nullius
the colonial doctrine of "empty land," that colonized land was empty of human inhabitants and therefore could be claimed and settled by colonists

Blackbirding
the colonial practice of abducting the populations of areas, often islands, and resettling them as a labor force in some other part of the world

Corvée
a colonial practice in which local people were required to provide a period of labor to the administration as a sort of "tax"

See Chapter 14

Encomienda
in Latin American colonial history, a grant of land to a conqueror and explorer, much like medieval estates, which gave the grant-holder control over the land and inhabitants

Hacienda
the Spanish colonial practice in which land was granted as private property and in which these estates were run both for subsistence production and for the production of cash and export crops

CRIMINAL CASTES AND SALVATION SOLDIERS IN COLONIAL INDIA

IMAGE 12.4 Colonialism typically involved the military defeat and conquest of native peoples, like these Apache women held captive by American soldiers.

changes to and domination of the political and economic aspects of subject societies, together with religion and other cultural habits like dress, speech, marriage, gender roles, and so on—what Jean Comaroff called "the signs and structures of everyday life" (1985: 80). Therefore, the religious conversion process was designed to effect a change in these signs and structures, a "revolution in habits," "a quest to refurnish the mundane: to focus human endeavor on the humble scapes of the everyday, of the 'here-and-now' in which the narrative of Protestant redemption took on its contemporary form" (Comaroff and Comaroff, 1991: 9). They also characterized this struggle as "an epic of the ordinary" and "the everyday as epiphany":

> [I]t was precisely by means of the residual, naturalized quality of habit that power takes up residence in culture, insinuating itself, apparently without agency, in the texture of a life-world. This, we believe, is why recasting mundane, routine practices has been so vital to all manner of social reformers, colonial missionaries among them.
>
> (31)

One important site was farming techniques. Missionaries offered a model for "civilized cultivation" in the form of the "mission garden"; a major aspect of this new model was a reversal of traditional gender roles, in which women had done the bulk of horticultural work. The plow became a potent symbol of Western-style farming; fences introduced conceptions of "enclosure" and property; and inequality of output, related to intensity of labor, generated Western-style differences in wealth and status as their reward. But economic change went beyond horticulture to new institutions like markets and money. Modern labor and cash were part of a new "moral economy," stigmatizing idleness and "primitive production" and promoting "the kind of upright industry and lifestyle that would dissolve [tradition's] dirt" (189).

Yet more mundane areas like clothing and household practices were valued for their civilizing effects. Clothes not only meant covering heathen nakedness, but teaching locals the proper wear and care of these articles; native clothing, it seemed to colonists, was dirty, too "natural," and lacked the necessary markers of social—especially gender—distinctions. For this purpose, old used clothes were shipped from England to clothe, and thereby transform, the pagan body, teaching them shame and pride at the same time. And as already suggested, proper (that is, Western-Christian) gender behavior was essential: Women needed to be covered modestly and re-assigned to the home. Home became a "domestic" sphere, which became woman's sphere, where she would sit, sew, and serve. But the traditional native house would not do; the house and the community had to be transformed from what the Europeans perceived as "a wild array of small, featureless huts scattered across the countryside" (282). Missionary houses and buildings again acted as the model: With right angles, specialized spaces (e.g. a room for eating, a room for sleeping, etc.), doors and locks for privacy, and modern furniture, the mission structures "became a diorama" for how people should live (292). The collection of residences that became the "town" differentiated public from private spaces, all set in a universe of square blocks and broad streets. In these and many ways, the foreigners were doing much more than bringing a new religion; they were "teaching [them] to build a world" (296), one in which civilization itself was expressed "in squares and straight lines" (127).

Managing the body, scheduling the tribe: colonial governmentality

John and Jean Comaroff convincingly showed that colonialism was about more than economics and politics in the narrow sense. It entailed power in the wider sense of the term, what Anupama Rao and Steven Pierce (2006) call "disciplining 'uncivilized' people" (4) through coercion and violence, but also through manipulation of lifestyles, experience, and the very body. Elsewhere we discussed these pervasive techniques of power as *governmentality*, and David Scott related this concept to colonialism to identify "colonial governmentality," that is, "the practices, modalities, and projects through which *the varied forms of Europe's insertion* into the lives of the colonized were constructed and organized" (1995: 193).

Consistent with the emphasis on the embodiment of culture, anthropology views colonialism as power applied to the natives' bodies, as *bio-power*: "Colonialism was and is an inherently corporeal enterprise," consisting of "the subtle and yet palpable pressures brought to bear on colonial subjects to 'normalize' and 'civilize' their daily lives" (Boddy, 2011: 119). As the Comaroffs stressed, the naked native body had to be clothed, and the dirty native body had to be cleaned. "Wild" and "irrational" native practices, especially religions, had to be domesticated, if not discontinued altogether. The natives' bodies were exposed to colonial force through compulsory labor, not to mention whips, chains, and—especially in Belgium's vast Congo colony—amputations. Even the tastes and sentiments of indigenous peoples were refashioned: Native Americans were taught the fear and shame

of good Christians, "to shed copious tears of repentance" (Rubin, 2013: 7), while Taiwanese under Japanese colonialism learned to associate Japanese cuisine with modernization and high status (Wu, 2015). Naturally, anything that smacked of immorality or obscenity to colonizers—from polygamy and child marriage to disposing of dead bodies by any means other than burial—was strongly opposed (see e.g. Deana Heath [2010] *Purifying Empire: Obscenity and the Politics of Moral Regulation in Britain, India, and Australia*).

But governmentality involves more than the immediate control of bodies. It entails all the modern forms of administration such as categorization, measurement, documentation, and monitoring. The celebrated nineteenth-century linguist Max Müller dubbed this process "classify and conquer" (quoted in Chidester, 2013: 59). Local peoples were assigned to named "tribes" or "races" or "religions," ideally imposing exclusive identities where complex overlapping and shifting identities often previously reigned. In the United States, "membership" in a Native society was (and is) determined by the placement of one's name on an official tribal roll. Under British rule, culture and class in India were conflated by categorizing the *Adivasis* or "original inhabitants" as "Depressed Classes" and "Scheduled Tribes and Castes"; the 1950 Indian Constitution recognized 744 scheduled tribes, defined as groups with "indications of primitive traits; distinctive culture; shyness of contact with the community at large; geographical isolation; and backwardness" (tribal.nic.in/Content/IntroductionScheduledTribes.aspx).

See Chapter 9

Colonial governmentality mixed steps to improve administrative efficiency with imposition of cultural norms and expectations. For instance, in Rwanda's Kigali province, the number of chiefs was reduced, from 119 to five, and pre-colonial patron–client relations were replaced by wage labor. Elsewhere "traditional" social organization was invented for colonial convenience, like the allegedly authentic landowning descent groups named *tokatoka* on Fiji. In more than a few cases, new names and cultural markers were introduced, often construed as "races" (see below): The Gude people in French Cameroon became Djimi, while the Higis were reclassified as Kapsiki (Miles, 2014: 24). It has even been claimed that the very category "Hindu" was created in colonial India to categorize all those

INVENTING TRADITION IN COLONIAL FIJI

people who were not classified as Christian, Muslim, or Buddhist—and then these Indians were assumed to *be* Hindus, although they might observe Hindu, Buddhist, and other practices. At the extreme, and revisiting the techniques of embodied governmentality, native peoples were frequently collected into camps, neighborhoods, or mission compounds—like the *reducciones* in Spanish territories, where Native Americans were ordered to labor to feed the soldiers and priests who surveilled them or the similar "praying towns" in early New England.

THE LEGACY OF COLONIALISM

Eventually, formal colonialism came to an end, and the entities that were formerly—ranging from a few decades or a few centuries—colonies became "independent." This does not mean, of course, that everything returned to pre-colonial conditions, nor that everything had a happy ending. It certainly does not mean that external and global forces ceased to impact and indeed to be intimately enmeshed with local groups and cultures. In some ways, new intercultural relations emerged that were not all that different from the colonial relationships. The one thing that would never again be true, if it ever was, is the possibility of thinking in terms of bounded and discrete societies in isolation from each other.

The experience of colonialism left enduring marks on societies around the globe, and many of their effects are still felt today. Some of the changes introduced by colonial practices are environmental, some are cultural, others are demographic, and still others are "economic" and "political" in the familiar sense. All of them concern not only anthropologists, but citizens of those countries and the entire world.

Depopulation

In all colonial settings, there was extensive loss of life. In some, huge numbers of native people died from diseases like smallpox, syphilis, and other plagues that were new to those societies. Some estimates suggest that as much as ninety percent of the Native American population died in the early decades of contact, many before they ever saw a white person. Where disease did not ravage the local people, war often did. Many colonized people fought long and hard battles to resist European invasion; however, in practically every case, European military technology was superior to local weapons, and where weapons alone could not suffice, economic and political pressures eventually overwhelmed the peoples. In many places, there were declared wars prosecuted by professional soldiers, including the "Indian wars" in the United

TABLE 12.1   Dates of independence from colonialism, selected countries

First (mercantile) phase		Second (imperialist) phase	
United States	1776	Iraq	1932
Brazil	1815	Jordan, Syria, Lebanon	1946
Peru	1821	India, Pakistan	1947
Mexico	1821	Indonesia	1949
Argentina	1815	Ghana (Gold Coast)	1957
Bolivia	1825	Mali, Niger, Chad	1960
Venezuela	1830	Sudan	1956
Guatemala	1838	Nigeria, Cameroon, Senegal	1960
Honduras	1838	Libya	1951
El Salvador	1838	Zaire/Congo	1960
Costa Rica	1838	Malaysia	1963
Chile	1818	Algeria	1962
Ecuador	1803	Kenya	1963
Paraguay	1811	Angola, Mozambique	1975
Uruguay	1828	Zimbabwe	1980

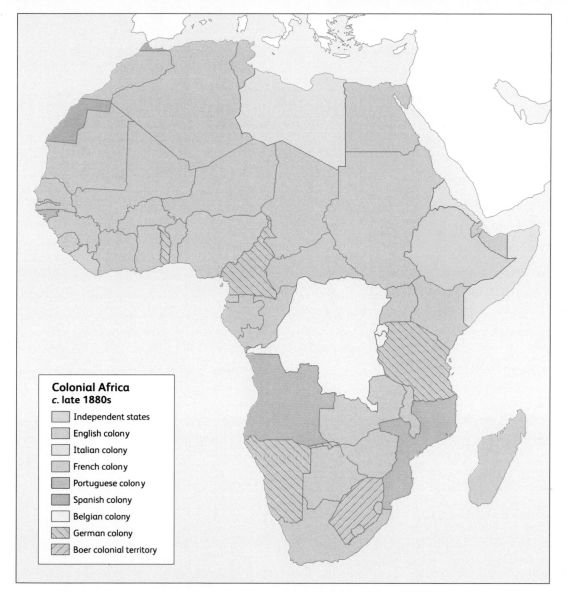

MAP 12.1 Colonial Africa

States. However, an untold number of native people died from unofficial and small-scale violence perpetrated by settlers. In Africa, armed homesteaders often killed locals in "self-defense" when those locals attempted to defend their land.

In Australia, which was entirely inhabited by band-level foraging societies, English settlers often considered the Aboriginals little more than vermin to be exterminated, like any other native wildlife that obstructed farming and ranching. Massacres happened from the first days of Australian settlement (1788) until the early 1900s. When settlement ships arrived with the original eight hundred or so English convicts, it took only a year for an Aboriginal leader, Pemulwuy, to be captured and beheaded.

As Euro-Australians pushed into central Australia, they encountered more foragers occupying land in "non-productive" ways and displaced them. The settlers who followed, with the aid of the territorial police, "protected" white interests against the predations of the Aboriginals, who merely defended their land and culture. By the mid-1800s, the era of massacres was well under way. Entire Aboriginal communities were rounded up and executed for the deaths of whites or of the cattle of whites, regardless of whether those particular Aboriginals were the culprits or not. Some of the most notorious killings occurred fairly recently, like the 1928 Coniston massacre, in which police and settlers killed fifty-one Aboriginals (most of them probably innocent

IMAGE 12.5 Well into the twentieth century, Australian Aboriginals were often arrested and chained.

of any wrong-doing). In the same year, police captured another whole society of Aboriginal hunters, chained them by the neck, and killed all of them except three women. Neck chaining persisted in Australia until 1960.

From Africa and other locations as well, large populations were deported into slavery. It is estimated that as many as thirty million Africans were removed, mostly bound for South America, although many fewer than that number ever arrived alive. "Blackbirding," as we noted above, wiped out whole island societies. And where slavery as such was not practiced, people were often transferred from one area to another as labor, like the Tamils of India who were imported into Malaysia and highland Ceylon (Sri Lanka) as plantation workers. Finally, many native people died from the living conditions in the colonies, including poor diet, alcoholism, internecine fighting, seizure of women and children, the difficulty of making culturally correct marriages, and the sheer hopelessness that comes with the destruction of one's way of life.

Acculturation and deculturation

Native peoples were often unable to practice their pre-colonial cultures, due to inadvertent factors or intentional policy. Indigenous societies, especially foragers and pastoralists, were often settled more or less forcibly in villages. Efforts were made to convert all locals into wage laborers and tax payers, and all production was integrated into the colonial and global economy, bound for export rather than

local consumption. Furthermore, if people were compelled to toil on plantations or in mines, there was little time reserved for traditional social or religious activities, which were often discouraged or forbidden anyhow. When men were required to travel long distances for work, traditional family structures suffered and occasionally collapsed. Kinship practices were altered, often by law, particularly when it came to matters of sex and marriage. Western-style marriage and sexual rules were enforced on natives, and European gender roles were imposed, often to the impoverishment of women who in some cases enjoyed better status before colonialism. Western-style education, boarding schools, and separation of native children from their parents and societies interrupted cultural transmission and introduced competing values and institutions. Religion was a particular target for change and "conversion," discrediting local spirits and gods and co-opting or prohibiting local practices and institutions. Often, key artifacts and symbols were appropriated or "collected" by travelers, traders, and magistrates. Finally, particularly in colonies of settlement, indigenous societies were literally swamped by Westerners, although even a small number of settlers could radically reshape cultural relations.

Environmental degradation and declining living conditions

In many colonial settings, the rapacious exploitation of local resources and labor wrought extensive environmental damage. Entire forests were cut down (and are still being cut down) to make room for farms and towns, for export of timber, and for the production of charcoal. Erosion and pollution followed. Squalid shantytowns rose up, often where local people had never congregated in large numbers before. In places where indigenous people had always lived in small mobile groups, settlement only aggravated their social and physical complaints and caused despoliation of the land. Colonial officials did make certain attempts to clean up the messes they made, such as establishing hospitals—but these institutions were often further vehicles for conveying Western ideas, values, and practices. Ironically, one unintended and undesired consequence of this humanitarianism was a population explosion. People who improved their infant mortality rates and life expectancies but did not curb their reproduction soon found themselves with up to a ten percent annual population growth rate, resulting in doubling the population every seven years or so. In the villages, the land—already expropriated by colonial interests—simply could not support the burden of population growth. People had no choice but to gather in burgeoning new cities, without the infrastructure or economy to handle such large inflows. Millions of people migrated and still migrate to cities, where they live as fringe-dwellers and squatters without adequate (or sometimes any) fresh water, sewerage, electricity, and other amenities, consuming the environment on a profligate scale. Forests get denuded for firewood, farmland is overworked to the point of exhaustion, and water and food supplies become inadequate or prohibitively expensive, as evidenced by the worldwide food riots of 2008. Meanwhile, communicable disease (like dysentery and malaria and most recently AIDS) run rampant. Still the population grows, composed of people with lots of complaints and little to lose—a recipe for political disaster.

BOX 12.2 MANAGING THE COLONIAL FOREST IN NIGERIA

Part of modern governmentality is environmental management, including "scientific forestry." England established a forest department in colonial Nigeria in 1899 to "increase the yield of existing known products by safeguarding them from damaging methods which might result in their extinction" (von Hellermann, 2013: 12). Scientific forestry represented an effort "to rationalize forests" through plans that "regulated logging activities and tree regeneration programs in government-controlled forests, resulting in the systematic transformation of forests into more regimented collections of trees nearing foresters' ideal of the *Normalbaum* (the 'normal' tree)" (12). The threats to wood resources not only emanated from colonial exploitation but, and sometimes especially, from "traditional" practices, which were deemed irrational and unscientific. The first strategy, from 1901, was the creation of reserves, and the 1916 Forest Ordinance set aside twenty-five percent of Nigeria's land "to meet present and future timber needs" (52). In the 1920s, a new system developed in Burma was introduced to Africa; known as *taungya* farming, it was soon denounced as "a means of destroying the forest" (126). Since it did not achieve its goals, the reserve system was abandoned by the 1930s in response to demands for land by both small-scale Nigerian farmers and large-scale plantations. Worse, Pauline von Hellermann reckons that none of these policies took pre-colonial culture or their own unintended consequences into consideration. First, much of pre-colonial Nigeria was not virgin forest, but mixed-use land with trees, farms, and villages; further, "disease, warfare and slave trade" leading to depopulation had turned previously "more savanna-like conditions" into forest, which was presumed to be primordial (42). More problematically, before colonialism the local king or *oba* had been "the nominal owner of the land," although communities enjoyed great freedom to occupy and use the land, but the colonial system transferred the majority of land to government control. Consequently, "the *oba* became more literally 'the owner of the land' than he had been before" (60), centralizing decision-making and thus making land "more easily available for large-scale plantation projects than community land" and "a source of patronage for politicians" (81). The sad outcome was more destruction of the forests, not less.

Forced resettlement

Part of colonial policy was to compel local people to live according to patterns that met the economic and political needs of colonialism. In particular, colonizers (and contemporary state-level government) detested nomads and tried as aggressively as they could to settle them. Nomads like foragers and pastoralists were hard to control, to count, and to tax. They occupied large tracts of land but produced little of value to the colonial economy. Whether in America, Australia, Africa, or Amazonia, their land was a prime attraction to settlers and entrepreneurs who meet little opposition to exploiting those untapped resources. So, these societies were particular targets for "pacification" and acculturation efforts, when they were not, like many Aboriginal or many American Indian societies, simply exterminated. In addition to forced settlement of nomadic peoples, wholesale population transfers were conducted, moving people to where colonial interests wanted them. Colonial administrations would shift populations, either to fill jobs or to populate "underpopulated" regions. And as in other cases, this policy did not end with the colonial era; under Indonesia's *transmigrasi* program in the 1960s and 1970s, people from high-density areas like the city of Jakarta were encouraged to relocate to less-dense lands like Sumatra and Kalimantan (Borneo). Of course, the destinations were seldom if ever *unpopulated*, and such human transfers tended to create social conflicts. As long as there was a net improvement on the balance sheet of the colony or state, other considerations were secondary.

Creation of "plural societies" and mixing of cultures

One of the most enduring and significant characteristics of colonies was their *artificiality*. Before colonialism, the political entities that became colonies usually did not exist. The colonies were "artificial" in the sense that someone (a foreign power) drew lines on a map or cobbled together conquered territories to create administrative boundaries. Suddenly there was a thing called, for example, Gambia, where there was no such polity before. However, the political aspect of this colonial artificiality is less profound than the social aspect.

Not only had there never been a state called Gambia, but there had never been a society that called itself Gambian. After all, Gambia is the name for a river, not for a people. The peoples living near the Gambia River had various cultures, languages, and religions—almost two dozen of them. There was no such thing as "Gambian culture" or "Gambian language." So colonies like Gambia (or Nigeria or Congo or virtually all of them) were created with little knowledge of—and quite frankly, little concern for—which people were circumscribed by its borders. The borders were administrative, not cultural. Colonial policy was sometimes explicitly to seize territory and, as much as possible, rule it as if there were no people there at all. The result was that, in virtually all colonies, diverse peoples were thrust together in unprecedented and uncomfortable ways.

This non-traditional creation and management of multicultural social systems posed a managerial problem. J. S. Furnivall wrote one of the most important and influential studies on the subject, *Colonial Policy and Practice* (1956), in which he analyzed the social realities of two colonies, Burma and the Dutch East Indies (Indonesia). What he noted was that these colonies were by no means homogeneous—made up of one kind of people—but highly heterogeneous and "enclaved."

In other words, the groups were not fully or even nearly integrated, but rather occupied very discrete social, and in some instances physical, spaces in the colony. In Burma, he found, in addition to the "Burmese" (who themselves were a diverse group), Indians, Chinese, and of course Europeans, as well as "mixed blood" individuals of every combination. In fact, the north-central Kokang region of Burma had actually been part of China until 1897, when the staggering Chinese government surrendered it to England, which subsequently attached it to the colony of Burma. Today, ninety percent of inhabitants of Kokang are Chinese.

To describe this common colonial situation, Furnivall coined the term **"plural society,"** which has two characteristics. The first or political characteristic of a plural society is that it contains multiple cultural or social sections that "mix but do not combine." They live side by side in the same political unit but do not form an integrated "society" in any significant way. Social and political life is

---

Furnivall, J. S. 1956. *Colonial Policy and Practice: A Comparative Study of Burma and Netherlands India.* New York: New York University Press.

See Chapter 14

See Chapter 13

Plural society
a society that contains various cultural groups; such groups often occupy "niches" in the broader social system, such that the groups do not interact with each other except in limited and often mutually exploitative ways

**Colonial
Boundary**

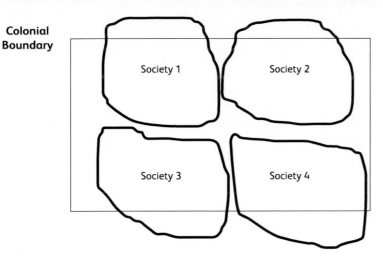

Society 1

Society 2

Society 3

Society 4

FIGURE 12.1 A hypothetical
colonial boundary, in relation to
societies within

therefore "atomized" or fragmented: The cultural sections of the society are not coherent groups themselves. but mere "aggregates of individuals." Each "is a crowd and not a community." An explanation for this fact is the second or economic characteristic of plural societies, that is, that they are purely economic arrangements, not true societies or cultures at all. In what he called "the process of the survival of the cheapest," market forces function "to eliminate all non-economic values," leaving only economic interests and relations with no other common social interests or causes (299). Society is stripped of cultural significance, and only jobs and money drive the system or unify people.

BOX 12.3   THE PLURAL SOCIETY OF COLONIAL—AND CONTEMPORARY—MAURITIUS

Political scientist William Miles calls the Indian Ocean "an overly ignored area" (2104: 189) that covers fourteen percent of the earth's surface, falls between the cultural regions of Africa and India, and contains eight island states formerly colonized by England or France—or both. Among these former colonies is tiny Mauritius (2,040 square kilometers), composed of several islands and part of the wider Mascarene Islands. The main island, called Mauritius, was actually uninhabited until the Dutch founded a colony in 1638. In 1715 France occupied the abandoned colony, which was ceded to England in 1810. Such transfers of colonies were remarkably common: Dutch New Amsterdam became British New York in 1664, England acquired Quebec from France in 1763 and Ceylon from the Dutch in 1815 (after Holland wrested it from Portugal), and the United States, as mentioned, seized the Philippines and Cuba from Spain in 1898. Although European colonial policy was mostly competitive, occasionally it was cooperative. In the South Pacific, Britain and France jointly administered the islands of New Hebrides or Vanuatu under an agreement called the condominium, and on Mauritius, French settlers were allowed to retain their land, language, and law after British conquest. Thus, "a strong Franco-Mauritian elite stamp preserved and expanded Francophonie" (193), not only among French settlers but also their African slave laborers, who developed an Afro-French creole language and culture. The abolition of slavery by England in 1835 did not end the need for workers, who were imported from India, soon outnumbering Africans. Additionally, tens of thousands of Chinese traders and businessmen came to the island. But Miles stresses that British, French, African, Indian, and Chinese do not exhaust the diversity of the colony. There was and is also "subethnic and religious diversity" (203): Among Hindu Indians caste and language differences existed, and some Indians were Muslim. Finally, the territorial carve-up also featured the preservation of French colonialism on the neighboring island of Réunion, which eventually became one of the overseas departments of France, and the detachment of the atoll of Diego Garcia, which was transferred to the United States as a naval base, its entire population moved to Mauritius.

Introduction of race-concept and racism

See Chapter 6

Race, at least in the way that it is understood and practiced in Western societies, is not a concept shared by all societies. When colonizers began to have prolonged contact with non-Western peoples, their reactions to those people were not at first entirely negative. Columbus was rather impressed with the appearance and personality of the natives he saw. Even Captain James Cook, one of the first Europeans to lay eyes on Australian Aboriginals, commented in the 1770s that they were tranquil, non-materialistic, and happy people (Reed, 1969: 136). However, as European domination of these peoples became more absolute, it became more common to berate them as, if not reduce them to, abject savages worthy of no better treatment than conquest and subjugation. The social Darwinism of the time suggested the natural inequality of peoples, evidenced by the "success" of some and the "failure" of others. However, it could be argued that Western racism was not so much a cause as an *effect* of colonialism. How else to justify the conduct and policies of colonializers toward the native peoples? If the natives were inferior—a lower race, a primitive species, a sort of half-human, half-animal—then what better consideration did they deserve? Racism in this sense indicated the dissonant feelings of the conquerors and their attempt to assuage these feelings by rationalizing their behavior.

If racism helped the whites to legitimize colonialism, it did not benefit the locals. It exposed them to previously unknown levels of cruelty and exploitation. But even more, it penetrated their own thinking about the identity of and relations between groups, with profound consequences. In some colonies, Europeans found certain peoples with whom they felt more affinity than others; the Tutsi in Rwanda, the Sikhs in northern India, and the Sinhalese in Sri Lanka are three examples. The Tutsi were the dominant segment of Rwandan society. A chiefly class or caste, they were ascribed physical traits as well—taller, thinner, and more "Caucasian" in some ways. The Hutu were seen as more "African" or Bantu. Accordingly, the European opinion of the Hutu was much lower. One colonial observer in 1925 characterized the Hutu as "generally short and thick-set with a big head, a jovial expression, a wide nose and enormous lips," whereas the Tutsi

Maquet, Jacques. 1961. *The Premise of Inequality in Rwanda: A Study of Political Relations in a Central African Kingdom*. London: Oxford University Press.

has nothing of the negro, apart from his color. He is usually very tall. . . . He is very thin. . . . His features are very fine: a high brow, thin nose and fine lips framing beautiful shining teeth. Batutsi women are usually lighter-skinned than their husbands, very slender and pretty in their youth, although they tend to thicken with age.

(quoted in Prunier, 1995: 6)

It was claimed that each kind had a racially specific personality too: Hutu tended to be "hardworking, not very clever, extrovert, irascible, unmannerly, obedient"—suitable to the lower class they occupied—while the Tutsi were "intelligent (in the sense of astute in political intrigues), capable of command, refined, courageous, and cruel"(Maquet, 1961: 164). The 1925 observer went so far as to applaud the Tutsi for displaying "a refinement of feelings which is rare among primitive peoples" (Prunier, 1995: 6). Not surprisingly, the Tutsi were preferred by the European colonializers for political service and education. This created a new dimension of difference and animosity between them and the Hutu majority (around eight-five percent), which could only make for trouble at a later date.

The same was true in colonial Ceylon (Sri Lanka), where the dominant Buddhist Sinhalese, whose history and mythology told of a northern India origin, absorbed the British concept of and preference for "Aryan" peoples, which they fancied themselves. They used this distinction against the south Indian, non-Aryan or "Dravidian" Hindu Tamils on the island to assert their own similarity to the Europeans and their superiority to the minority Tamils. The Sinhalese came to regard themselves as a race in the European sense and as a higher race than their fellow natives, introducing again a new type and degree of distinction between the two local groups. As the Sinhalese apologist Dharmapala put it:

the Aryan race is the only race with noble customs handed down from tradition . . . [therefore] the Sinhalese [who are Aryans] should cultivate ancient codes of conduct. Aryan customs and Aryan dresses and ornaments. . . . The Sinhalese first came to this country from Bengal and the Bengalis are superior in their intelligence to other communities in India.

(quoted in Dharmadasa, 1992: 145–146)

Racism, then, was not only a virulent force in relations between white colonizers and non-white colonized peoples, but also often enough between various non-white peoples themselves. In fact, the concept of race and its inherent hierarchy helped to exacerbate inter-group differences and hostilities when such differences already existed or sometimes to invent the very notion of disparate native "peoples" where no such distinctions had previously existed. This too would bear fruit long after colonialism ended.

Loss of economic independence

Native peoples were no longer free to make their own decisions about labor, production, distribution, or the use of resources; they now worked within systems of which they had no control and often little understanding. Land, resources, and other means of production were taken into foreign hands, and this would not change with mere political "independence." Even if the colonial administration went home, this did not mean that ownership and control of land and resources suddenly—if ever—reverted back to the natives. In reality, it was not governments that owned and controlled most of the wealth and property, but companies and individuals, and these did not give up their power, or even leave the territory, when colonialism officially ceased. Also, naturally, since they did not want the competition, most colonial regimes discouraged the development of local industry. Colonies had few factories or other facilities to produce manufactured goods. Colonies were essentially suppliers of primary goods or raw materials in an extractive economy, which were transported to Western factories for processing into finished goods and then sold back to the colonies. And since "value-added" goods (like manufactures) are almost always more expensive than raw materials, colonized peoples lost on both ends of the transaction. Finally, colonies were often "specialized" in one or a few products for which each particular colony was best suited; farming colonies were often marshaled into **monoculture** agriculture, in which one single crop constituted the main if not the sole product of the colony, particularly if the crop could not be grown in Europe, such as sugar, coffee, tea, rubber, cocoa, bananas, and so on (hence the term "banana republic"). This left the colony vulnerable to food dependency, as well as to international prices and demand; a drop in prices or demand could impoverish an entire colony and its people.

Monoculture
the specialization of production of only one crop or product for which a territory is particularly suited. This can involve food crops like corn or rice, or raw materials like lumber, coffee, rubber, tea, and so on

Chapter 14

BOX 12.4 CONTEMPORARY CULTURAL CONTROVERSIES: IS ANTHROPOLOGY COLONIALISM?

Since about 1970, anthropologists have wrestled with the historical relationship between our discipline and the practice of colonialism. As acknowledged in Chapter 2, anthropology was born during and from the colonial encounter; thus, Talal Asad argued that "the basic reality" that made early anthropology "a feasible and effective enterprise was the power relationship between dominating (European) and dominated (non-European) cultures" (1979: 91). An even angrier William Willis redefined anthropology as "the social science that studies dominated colored peoples—and their ancestors—living outside the boundaries of modern white societies" (1974: 123). This sentiment is shared by many non-Western people, including scholars like Linda Tuhiwai Smith, a Ngati Awa/Ngait Porou (Maori of New Zealand) writer who condemned cultural research in the strongest terms:

See Chapter 2

> From the vantage point of the colonized, a position from which I write, and choose to privilege, the term 'research' is inextricably linked to European imperialism and colonialism. The word itself, 'research,' is probably one of the dirtiest words in the Indigenous world's vocabulary. When mentioned in many indigenous contexts, it stirs up silence, it conjures up bad memories, it raises a smile that is knowing and distrustful.
>
> (1999: 1)

What do you think?

SUMMARY

The spread of colonies into new territories is not a uniquely modern or exclusively human phenomenon, but modern colonialism (from the fifteenth to the twentieth centuries) escalated the process and its impact to unknown levels. It not only brought far-flung societies into prolonged contact with each other, but began the centuries-long project of linking all societies into a truly global cultural network, a project that is just now reaching its fulfillment. Anthropologists who had previously looked for discrete, homogeneous, and static "traditional societies," began to understand that societies are often internally complex and even contradictory, that discrete boundaries are often lacking, and that even "traditional" societies had their histories—of which Western colonialism and even anthropology itself would now and forever more be parts.

The goals and tactics of colonialism varied by time period, colonizing power, colonized area, and other such factors, but tended to include expropriation of wealth, seizure and management of land and resources, organization of native labor and taxation of that labor, all in the interests of Western and global markets and geopolitics. Beyond these macro-scale processes, anthropology also examines the diversity of local colonial practices, including the disciplining of the native body and the classification and surveillance of peoples that has been called colonial governmentality.

These interests and the political and economic institutions that were instated to achieve them imposed extensive changes on colonized societies, many of which did not disappear when colonialism officially ended. These changes included

- depopulation
- acculturation and deculturation
- environmental degradation and declining living conditions
- forced settlement
- creation of "plural societies" with artificial boundaries
- the concept of race and racism
- loss of economic independence

At the most extreme, but not uncommonly, old cultures and identities were given new interpretations and valuations, or new cultures and identities were invented outright from a combination of indigenous cultural materials, colonial imperatives, and human imagination.

Q

MCQS

Q

FILL IN THE BLANKS

WWW

Key Terms

blackbirding

colonialism

colonies of exploitation

colonies of settlement

colony

corvée

doctrine of discovery

encomienda

hacienda

imperialism

internal colonialism

mercantilism

monoculture

plural society

sphere of influence

terra nullius

Politics in the postcolonial world
Nation-building, conflict, and borderlands

In July 2011 the world community welcomed a new state, the Republic of South Sudan, which seceded from Sudan and which itself was born from colonialism. Sudan has a long history—though arguably never as a single unified entity—dating back to the ancient kingdom of Kush, which had important relations with Egypt. By the sixth century CE, Christianity entered the vicinity, followed shortly by Islam. Over time the north became more thoroughly Islamized and Arabized than the south, where numerous tribal (especially pastoral) societies lived. Sudan began to coalesce—but still largely as two distinct territories—in the 1800s, when Ottoman Turks conquered and unified the north. The story of the modern state of Sudan only begins, however, with European colonialism: Belgium, France, and England all invaded the area and claimed parts of the future Sudan, but England emerged as the dominant power after 1898, ruling Sudan jointly with Egypt as "Anglo-Egyptian Sudan." As independence approached after World War II, England considered granting self-rule to the north, but in 1946 northern and southern Sudan were unified into a single state, to be governed from Khartoum in the north. Since independence in 1956, the integrated state of Sudan has suffered

civil war between the north and south (1955–1972), two political coups (1965 and 1969), and a second civil war starting in 1983; one specific tragedy was the violence in the western Sudan province of Darfur. In 2005, the north and south finally agreed to allow the south to hold a referendum on its political future, and that vote—held in January 2011—resulted in almost-unanimous southern support for secession. The fledgling Republic of South Sudan faced many challenges, including one of the lowest average incomes and literacy rates in the world, as well as considerable cultural and ethnic diversity (see Figure 13.1). In late 2013, this diversity erupted into conflict, as the two main tribes—Dinka and Nuer—clashed over power. President Salva Kiir (Dinka) opposed Vice President Riek Machar (Nuer), and this political rivalry soon mobilized tribes as militias, Dinkas attacking Nuer and Nuer responding in kind. At least ten thousand people have been killed and perhaps a million displaced.

Look at a political map of the world, and you see states. What you do not see is the colonial origin of the vast majority of these states: In Latin America, Africa, the Middle East, Asia, and the Pacific, state boundaries largely reflect the boundaries created

Civil war
a violent conflict within a particular state or between corporate or identity groups within the state

MAP 13.1 The ethnic
groups of northern Sudan
and southern Sudan.

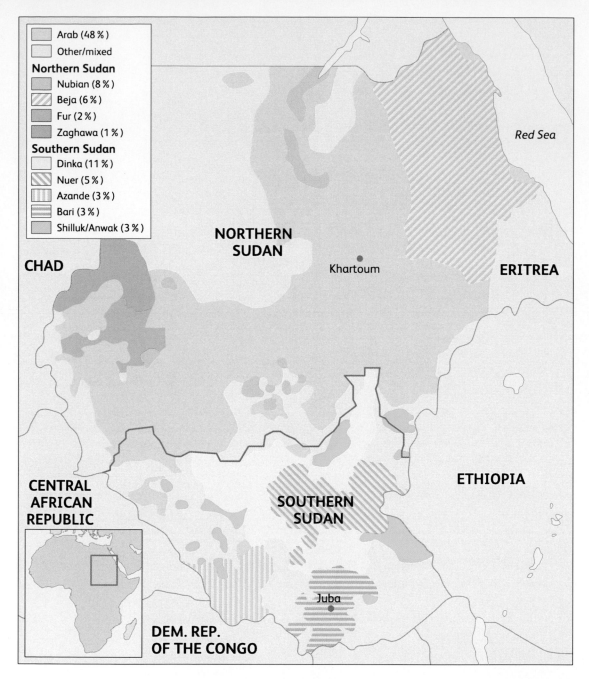

Arab (48 %)

Other/mixed

Northern Sudan

Nubian (8 %)

Beja (6 %)

Fur (2 %)

Zaghawa (1 %)

Southern Sudan

Dinka (11 %)

Nuer (5 %)

Azande (3 %)

Bari (3 %)

Shilluk/Anwak (3 %)

CHAD

NORTHERN
SUDAN

Khartoum

Red Sea

ERITREA

CENTRAL
AFRICAN
REPUBLIC

SOUTHERN
SUDAN

ETHIOPIA

Juba

DEM. REP.
OF THE CONGO

more or less arbitrarily by Western colonizers. The political boundaries on maps appear real, stable, and unambiguous too; something else you do not see is how unstable, diverse, and often ineffective those idealized states are. The final thing that you do not see is various cultural groups subordinated to or divided by those reified boundaries.

The previous chapter remarked on the colonial legacy of arbitrary and plural societies and states. The present chapter explores the political situation in these postcolonial settings, as states struggle to govern, define, and even construct themselves. Indeed, numerous scholars have commented that maps are not only products of political processes, but essential tools in the formation and legitimation of modern politics—what James Scott (1998), who will figure prominently in the discussion below, called "state simplifications" or techniques that allow the state to see, "read," and believe in itself and to convince others of its reality

See Chapter 15

and legitimacy. In actual practice, though, things are not so simple.

Finally, we must note that the term "postcolonial" is itself not so simple. It glosses a wide variety of experiences; for instance, the United States emerged from colonialism almost two hundred and fifty years ago, while Zimbabwe has been independent for only twenty-five (as of 2015). More, many of the world's peoples do not consider colonialism to be over; recently, I heard Glenn Morris, a Native American political scientist and member of the American Indian Movement, passionately argue that Native Americans are still thoroughly colonized.

POLITICS AND IDENTITY ON THE PATH TO INDEPENDENCE

Colonialism radically reorganized peoples and cultures, as colonizers seized land, compelled labor, relocated groups, and classified people in order to make colonies not only profitable but "legible" in Scott's sense of the term. But the complex and often painful nexus of politics, "traditional culture," and identity was extended and exacerbated by the end of colonialism and the subsequent attempts of postcolonial states to administer themselves. The immediate fate of the colonies after independence was largely shaped by the colony's particular path to independence. There were two main variables in this process. First, power in the postcolonial regime might befall to native peoples or to European settlers or their descendants (resulting in what has been called, derisively by native peoples, "settler states"). Second, independence might come via a more or less gradual and orderly transition or by more or less violent resistance and rebellion, with locals using force to dislodge foreign rule. These two variables provided for a diversity of anticolonial experiences, with significant consequences for post-independence politics and society.

Settler government

Independence in many cases did not mean return of power to "natives" at all, if by natives we mean descendants of the indigenous peoples. In colonies where large numbers of Europeans immigrated (like the United States), there was a sufficient population of local whites to constitute a white-dominated postcolonial government. In the United States, independence substituted rule by foreign whites with rule by domestic whites, not by Native Americans. South and Central America and parts of Africa followed the same pattern. Perhaps the most extreme case was Brazil, which first claimed independence as a kingdom when members of the Portuguese royal family resettled there after the Napoleonic wars—transplanting Portugal to Brazil. Brazil's indigenous people certainly were not part of the independence declaration nor included in the first (or any subsequent) government. However, a white majority was not necessary to hold power: In the Republic of South Africa, ten percent of the population (white) ruled ninety percent of the population (black) until about 1990. In this and similar cases, independence meant fairly little—or worse—for the colonized peoples.

See Chapter 6

Transition to native self-government

See Chapter 9

Some colonizers were more cooperative in transitioning to independence than others. As noted in the last chapter, British colonies were regarded as part of the British Empire but not part of England itself; the colonized people were subjects of England but were not and could not be "English," and so the end of colonialism was relatively unthreatening. French colonies, by contrast, were regarded as *overseas parts of France*, so independence was largely unthinkable; native resistance to colonialism equaled civil war. Other colonial powers did little or no preparation and abandoned their colonies abruptly, leaving a power vacuum that was not easily or painlessly filled, as in the case of the Belgian Congo. Others fought to the bitter end to prevent their colonies from escaping, like Portugal's prolonged wars to stop separatist movements in Angola and Mozambique until 1975.

The transitional course had common and often, in the long run, troubled contours and consequences. One of the main questions was how power would be shared by the diverse peoples of the colony. Colonies consisting of multiple cultural groups, as most were, faced dilemmas of power-sharing and sheer co-existence that involved the smallest details of life—what language(s) would be spoken, what symbols (flags, etc.) would be used, what religious holidays would be celebrated, and so on. Dividing power evenly between groups would alienate the majority group, but dividing it proportionally, or leaving it to the results of "democratic" elections, would disempower the minority group(s). Beyond that, the introduction of Western cultural, legal, economic, and educational institutions often created a small but influential class of acculturated native people who did not identify with any traditional groups but with either the colonial "nation" or with Western culture. So even gradual transition led to immediate and long-term controversies and conflicts.

There were two fundamental problems with transition to independence. First, in a sense nothing much really changed immediately after independence. Given the choice, Western colonizers preferred to transfer power to acculturated (Westernized) natives, not the more "traditional" (and often militant) elements of society. Second, the acculturated natives often did not understand or share the sentiments and interests of the more traditional citizens and were often soon replaced by more "nativistic" leaders and parties that played on communal identities and grievances. So, often enough, this first native government was truly a "transitional" one, on the way to more native—and many times, more violent—politics at the next stage. A case with long-term reverberations is Iraq, which was hammered together out of the rubble of the Ottoman Empire after 1920. England was granted a "mandate" to administer the three provinces of Basra (mostly Shi'ite Arab), Baghdad (mostly Sunni Arab), and Mosul (mostly Kurdish) as the State of Iraq. No such entity had ever existed, and some warned of its instability. The British selected a king for the new state, Faisal, who was unknown to most Iraqis (he was born in Mecca, Saudi Arabia) but sympathetic to England and the West, permitting England to retain military bases in his territory. Independence came quickly (1932), but the kingdom was overthrown in 1941, in response to which England invaded the country and restored the monarchy until another revolt in 1958 ended the pro-Western government and led to a series of coups eventually placing General Saddam Hussein in power in 1979.

IDENTITY AND POWER IN COLONIAL CEYLON (SRI LANKA)

Native resistance and rebellion

In virtually all cases, colonialism was imposed by military force and answered with organized resistance, even where a relatively generous amount of preparation for independence was allowed. From King Philip's War (1675–1676) between the Massachusetts colonists and the native Wampanoag to the Battle of Omdurman (1898) in which the British killed ten thousand fighters in Sudan—and hundreds of times in between—colonizers had to use violence to subdue colonized people. Even in India, Mohandas "Mahatma" Gandhi's principle of "passive resistance" and non-violent morality-based opposition was preceded by armed rebellion in 1857, and native protest was frequently met with deadly force, like the 1919 demonstration that was suppressed at the cost of hundreds of Indian lives; clashes continued between crowds and police into the 1930s.

In many instances, the anti-colonial resistance was fiercer. Both Arabs and Jews employed terrorist tactics against the British occupation of Palestine in the 1940s, and Algeria in the 1950s used similar methods against the French. In Vietnam, Angola, and elsewhere "guerrilla" armies fought protracted wars against European regimes to dislodge them from native homelands. And, in Vietnam and Angola as in many other colonies, communist ideology and even soldiers from other communist states defined the course of the struggle. It must be remembered that all colonial struggles in the twentieth century took place in the context of international communist revolutions and the "Cold War." Communism was attractive to colonized peoples for two reasons—as a way to distinguish themselves from their European oppressors and as a "language" or "theory" of resistance and of the political and cultural future after victory. European/Western culture was equated to capitalism, which was equated to colonialism and oppression by many colonized peoples—that is, capitalism seemed naturally to lead to or include colonialism. As non-Westerners, the rebels would then naturally be non-capitalists and non-colonialists, and the opposite or antithesis of capitalism was seen to be communism. More importantly, communist states such as the Soviet Union and the People's Republic of China (and their satellites) actively supported such independence movements. This is why Cuban soldiers fought alongside

IMAGE 13.1 Colonized people often used force to end the occupation of their land, as in the Algerian War where Algerians sought independence from France (1954–1962).

Angolan rebels against Portuguese colonizers in the 1970s, why China sent armies into North Korea to oppose American forces in the 1950s, and why the USSR supplied North Vietnam in its war.

For many, resistance and rebellion not only were but had to be violent processes. Practically speaking, the superior power of colonizing states meant that they would not withdraw without a fight. Theoretically or philosophically speaking, colonized peoples, especially when inspired by communist ideology, saw violent **revolution** as the completion of the predicted world system and also as a kind of "cleansing" of the souls of the colonized. No one represents this position better than Afro-Caribbean writer and revolutionary Frantz Fanon, author of *The Wretched of the Earth* (1963). In this

influential book, he maintained that "decolonization is always a violent phenomenon" (35) because colonialism itself is violence. The colonizer's and colonized's "first encounter was marked by violence and their existence together—that is to say the exploitation of the native by the settler—was carried on by dint of a great array of bayonets and cannons" (36). The violence perpetrated against them, he advocated, "will be claimed and taken over by the native at the moment when, deciding to embody history in his own person, he surges into forbidden quarters" (40):

To break up the colonial world does not mean that after the frontiers have been abolished lines of communication will be set up between

Revolution

a more or less sudden, complete, and often violent movement to change a political or social system

Fanon, Frantz. 1963. *The Wretched of the Earth.* Constance Farrington, trans. New York: Grove Press, Inc.

state

a political system or level of integration in which a formal centralized government has power over a delimited territory to make and enforce laws, to establish currency and collect taxes, and to maintain an army and declare war

Country

commonly used as a synonym for "nation" or "state," more properly refers to the territory that a society or polity inhabits

Nation

a corporate group that shares an identity based on such traits as history, culture, territory, etc. and that recognizes a shared political destiny. A group that is politically mobilized to achieve certain goals, usually including political recognition, rights, and sometimes an independent state

Nationalism

a social movement to achieve recognition, rights, and sometimes an independent state for a nation

See Chapter 15

Self-determination

the concept that groups with a distinct culture and identity have a right to choose their own political arrangements and their own collective destiny

See Chapter 14

Anderson, Benedict. 1983. *Imagined Communities: Reflections of the Origin and Spread of Nationalism.* London: Verso.

the two zones. The destruction of the colonial world is no more and no less than the abolition of one zone, its burial in the depths of the earth or its expulsion from the country.

(41)

POLITICS AND CULTURE IN POSTCOLONIAL STATES

Whatever the process, the formal system of colonialism eventually ended, posing the question of what would follow. A return to pre-colonial conditions— the dissolution of the colony and its replacement with "traditional" social and political systems—was virtually impossible and never happened in reality. Instead, the colonial polity, regardless of its form and composition, almost always became a sovereign polity, a "state." In fact, the entire colonial enterprise, from first conquest and settlement to independence struggle, essentially guaranteed this outcome. Where a colony had been founded (artificially, even irrationally), social, economic, and political institutions were established—schools, markets, transportation systems, courts, etc.— which would not disappear overnight. Furthermore, legislatures and parties were organized, especially when a peaceful transition was planned, such that the colony was intentionally groomed to become a state, with a functioning central government and usually the same borders, the same multicultural makeup, and even the same name as before. Little would in actuality change. In fact, Fanon quoted the president of the new state of Gabon, a former French colony in Africa, who said to officials in Paris, "Gabon is independent, but between Gabon and France nothing has changed; everything goes on as before" (67).

The key problem faced by what were dubbed the "new states," aside from the economic conditions that perpetuated its poverty and dependence, was the mixed and confused demographic composition of plural societies now expected to govern themselves. In a word, there was a fundamental mismatch between the state and its population. A state, as discussed in Chapter 9, is merely a political system with a centralized government empowered to exercise certain authority over a bounded territory. There is no particular assumption about who lives in and under the state and its government.

European states had taken centuries to coalesce out of the fragments of petty kingdoms and principalities and regional village and tribal cultures, and the process had not been peaceful—nor complete, as the ongoing struggles of the Basques and Irish, to name only two, attest. In the "new states," this was a keen problem because the internal diversity was even greater and fresher, and the time-scale to achieve unity was shorter.

The terms state, nation, and country are often used synonymously in English, but anthropologists make some careful and useful distinctions. A **state** is, strictly speaking, nothing but a political system. **Country** refers to the *territory* that a group (state or non-state) occupies. A **nation** (from the Latin *nasci* for "to be born") is some group of humans who identify *as* a group, frequently using the idioms of birth and kinship. The three concepts need not be, and routinely are not, coterminous. Simply drawing a line around a congeries of fragmented and bruised social groups and calling it a state does not ensure state unity or legitimacy.

In other words, a state is politics, but a nation is people—or more accurately, *a people*. However, most political scientists agree that a people is not equivalent to a nation; not just every society is a nation. Most political scientists agree that a nation entails not only a certain amount of cultural commonality but also self-awareness and political mobilization. Nations are often not only the actors of but *the products of* **nationalism**, a political movement to achieve recognition, rights, and sometimes sovereignty for a people or society. More, a nation is not only a construction of mobilization but, as Benedict Anderson insisted, of imagination. He defined a nation as "an imagined community—and imagined as both inherently limited and sovereign" (1983: 6)—that is, limited in terms of who belongs and who does not and sovereign as worthy and capable of **self-determination**, the freedom to govern itself and practice its culture. The nation is imagined, he continued, "because the members of even the smallest nation will never know most of their fellow-members, meet them or even hear of them, yet in the minds of each lives the image of their communion" (6). But this imagination is not spontaneous; he revealed that it was achieved through techniques such as printing and reading—creating a community of shared knowledge and memories—

not to mention self-conscious celebration of culture and, again, mapping.

Building the nation, imagining the state

By the 1960s anthropologists and others thought they were witnessing a transformation, an "integrative revolution," in which old pre-state identities were being swapped for new "modern"

and "national" ones (e.g. Geertz, 1963). This has been called "nation-building" and refers to the shift of corporateness from local, "tribal" levels to the translocal and state level; as such it is probably better understood as *state-building*.

The crux of the issue, as mentioned, is the mismatch between state and nation. In the modern world, the political ideal is the **nation-state**, which does align politics with culture and identity. A nation-state is a state that consists of all of and only one nation, or a nation that has its own state

Geertz, Clifford, Ed. 1963. *Old Societies and New States: The Quest for Modernity in Asia and Africa.* New York: The Free Press.

Nation-state
in modern political thought, the ideal form of state in which the state contains only and all of one nation, or in which a nation has its own territorial state

BOX 13.1   NATIONHOOD AND SUFFERING IN CONTEMPORARY CROATIA

The Croats are one of the main peoples involved in the implosion of the plural state of Yugoslavia in the 1990s and the nasty three-way war with Serbs and Bosnian Muslims. Like other southern Slavs, they probably migrated to the Balkans in the seventh century. They struggled with larger and more powerful neighbors for centuries, including the Byzantine, Ottoman, and Austrian empires. Although they speak the same language as Serbs (Serbo-Croatian), they write with a different script (Latin versus Cyrillic), reflecting their Catholicism versus Serb Eastern Orthodoxy. During the nineteenth-century era of European nationalism, the Croats, like other Slavic peoples, began to think of themselves as a *nacija* or nation, although there was controversy about the contours of the nation: Some Serb thinkers claimed that Croats were merely Catholic Serbs, while Croat nationalists like Ante Starcevic and Josip Frank countered that all southern Slavs were actually Croats. Submerging their differences, several peoples joined to form Yugoslavia (originally called the Kingdom of Serbs, Croats and Slovenes) after World War I, but Croat nationalism did not end; rather, some nationalists felt betrayed by the creation of a Serb-dominated centralized state, and organizations like the Croatian Peasant Party kept the dream alive. During World War II, an independent Croat state under the ultranationalist fascist Ustasha party enjoyed a short life, but independence was declared again in 1991 and achieved after a war with Yugoslavia. This long historical experience resulted in a specific shape of Croatian nationalism, captured in the phrase, "*mali narod, velika nepravda*"—"small nation, great suffering" (Schäuble, 2014: 11). Michaela Schäuble finds—and not uniquely to Croats—that central to their identity is the sense that the nation "has been systematically persecuted, has suffered more than any other, and is consequently innocent of any injustice or crime" (10). Especially along its marginalized Dalmatian coast, Croats maintain the self-image "of a small, victimized country with the greatness to overcome oppression and to fight heroically for its independence" (52). This national imagination is ritually re-enacted in the *Sinjska Alka*, an annual celebration of the defeat of the Turkish army in 1715. Locals portray the glorious footsoldiers and knights, wearing traditional folk costumes, brandishing flintlock rifles, and sporting big mustaches in a performance of masculinity. But Croatia's specialness is marked in other ways, including an alleged sighting of the Virgin Mary in 1983, "consecrating and symbolically putting the land under the Virgin's protection" (106). And certainly, a century of war has left a landscape littered with battlegrounds and memorials, constant reminders of the nation's suffering and survival—and more essentially, "of who is and who is not a perpetrator, who suffered the most..., who made the most sacrifices, who has to bewail most casualties, and, eventually, who will emerge as the victor of history" (137). In the meantime, many Croats feel victimized once again by the European Union and the domination of the capital city, Zagreb, over the countryside and villages of the "real Croats."

Multinational state

a state that contains some or all of two or more distinct nations or cultural groups

Multi-state nation

a nation or cultural group that is divided across two or more state borders

(territory and government). But the fact is that *few if any states are nation-states*. Most states and nations find themselves in more contradictory and tortuous relationships. The most common is the **multinational state**, in which two or more (and sometimes many more) nations share the same state. Most modern states are multinational states, including virtually all of the states born from colonialism. Another and often parallel situation is the **multi-state nation**, in which one nation is split across two or more states, with parts of the nation living in different states. This was also a regular outcome of colonialism, in which political boundaries were drawn with little knowledge of or interest in social or cultural identities.

What many would-be state builders failed (and fail) to grasp is that a state—a successful, *legitimate* state—is more than territory and government. Indeed, Akhil Gupta and Aradhana Sharma remind us that states "as cultural artifacts" (2006: 278) are also imagined: "The state has to be imagined no less than the nation, and for many of the same reasons" (280), especially when it is new, unprecedented, and fairly unsatisfactory. People need to know, to see, and to believe in the state, when it is unfamiliar, distant, and often unfair or ineffective.

Nation/state-building obviously entails not only establishing the institutions of state but of constructing and proffering a state identity—that is, ideally inventing a nation that *is* coterminous with the state. Anthropologists appreciate that this is a thoroughly cultural undertaking, as did the Renaissance state-builder Machiavelli, who urged a ruler to exploit cultural traditions and religious symbols to justify their power and inspire loyalty (or fear) in their followers. There are many potential sites for the construction and dissemination of a state "national" culture and identity, perhaps the most influential of which is the school: The state can inject its self-imagination into the curriculum, the history and literature and civics. Like Anderson indicated, the state also seeks to create a single public sphere, shaped by media and literacy, which often requires a single common "national" language. Memorials, holidays, celebrations, parades, museums—these and more are forms of collective memory and nation/state-building.

In some instances, state authorities have leaned on culture more explicitly. Kevin Birth stresses music and carnival as critical to the daunting task

See Chapter 6

of unifying the diverse peoples of Trinidad and Tobago, where the post-independence government "emphasized the institutionalization of musical and cultural competitions in order to invoke and inspire national unity" (2008: 43). By sponsoring carnival performances and "Best Village Competitions," the state aspires to make a kind of "cultural nationalism" out of music, focusing on the distinctive calypso instrument, the steel drum or "pan." In Zaire (presently the Democratic Republic of Congo), dictator Mobutu Sese Seko coopted popular music, especially rumba, to win support for his regime while "the musicians successful under these conditions ended up unwittingly reproducing the organizational and symbolic mechanisms that would make Mobutu one of the most hated and feared political leaders in modern African history" (Bob White, 2008: 24). Insisting that "happy are those who sing and dance" (24), Mobutu's cultural policy featured the promotion of traditional clothing, African personal names, and marches, rallies, and meetings. Bob White asserts that Mobutu commanded people to dance and sing for the state, "to move their bodies as an expression of loyalty to the corrupt regime" (78), and ordered musicians to write and perform songs praising the state.

Competing imaginations: ethnicity and other sub-state and trans-state identities

The state may try to fashion the imagination of its citizenry, but other rival imaginations challenge the state, often with much greater antiquity and authenticity than official state discourse. In fact, sub-state (national, tribal, racial, religious, etc.) groups sometimes resent the exploitation of their cultures for state use.

In modern plural societies, pre-state and sub-state identities are frequently understood as or converted into "ethnic" identities. Recall that George DeVos (1975) defined ethnicity as the symbolic subjective use of culture to manufacture identity-and-interest groups and to distinguish between groups, in a context of competition for social resources. Ethnicity, in short, is a "boundary creating" and a "boundary maintaining" phenomenon (Barth, 1969), which is only necessary or possible when multiple groups share the same social-political space—which is common if not universal in postcolonial, globalized contexts.

The main issue is that cultural difference alone does not make an "ethnic group," any more than it makes a "nation." An **ethnic group** is a construction out of the raw materials, if you will, of culture, which must be first imagined and then performed and achieved. Rwanda is an enlightening example, where colonial discourses and post-independence politics mobilized groups into "ethnic" and "racial" groups. Prior to colonialism, our best information suggests that Hutus and Tutsis did not conceive of themselves as ethnic groups or races. European interlopers classified them as members of the "Hutu race" or "Tutsi race," which widened existing social or caste differences. As independence approached, the majority of Hutus perceived their political exclusion as contradictory to the principles of democracy, so the first step toward ethnicity was formation of an "ethnic" Hutu political party, TRAFIRO, in 1956. One year later, a set of Hutu intellectuals issued their "Manifesto of the Bahutu,"

demanding the political and economic emancipation of the Hutu people. When Gregoire Kayibanda, the future prime minister of Rwanda, founded the *Parti du Mouvement de l'Émancipation Hutu* (PARMEHUTU) in 1959, the Tutsis responded with a supposedly "national" Rwandan party, *Union Nationale Rwandaise*, but their (cynical) call for "national unity" did not prevent Hutu nationalism. Rather, "ethnic" relations worsened until the genocidal "ethnic" war of 1994.

In new postcolonial states where political institutions and state or national identities were still in formation, like Rwanda, pre-state and sub-state groups found much to compete over, and cultural and historical differences were easy rallying points and tools or weapons in the competition. Ripe prizes of land, wealth, political power, education, jobs, housing, and mere pride and prestige were available to groups that could claim them and legitimate their claims *as groups* with an authentic and historical right to them. Anthropology and other Western discourses of culture and identity contributed to this "**identity politics**," characterized

Barth, Fredrik, Ed. 1969. *Ethnic Groups and Boundaries*. Boston: Little, Brown & Co.

Ethnic group

a corporate group based on some shared cultural traits language, religion, history, etc. and finds itself in competition with other groups for wealth, power, opportunity, and recognition. An ethnic group shares an identity and a destiny and therefore competes as a group

Identity politics

the organization and mobilization of groups and parties on the basis of shared cultural characteristics, such that these groups and parties are seen to share an "identity" and to pursue economic, political, and cultural goals for and in the name of those who share that identity

IMAGE 13.2 During the 1994 genocide, Ugandan fisherman found themselves pulling dozens of bodies out of Lake Victoria. The badly decomposed bodies had traveled hundreds of miles by river from Rwanda.

by Kauffman as "the belief that identity itself—its elaboration, expression, or affirmation—is and should be a fundamental focus of political work" (1990: 67). As such, ethnicity is cultural politics twice over: first in using culture for political purposes, and second for fomenting the political strategy that culture *can and should* be used for political purposes.

Ethnicity as a political device requires a cultural difference, but it also requires a demand or claim and a (real or perceived) grievance or injustice. As a social imagination, it further requires a sense of the past, of "tradition," but we already understand that "tradition" is relative and labile. Tradition is never merely "the past remembered," but is always a combination of remembering, forgetting, interpreting, and inventing "the past." Ethnic groups tend to look backward for signs or symbols or indicators of their "authentic" identity or culture. Like the Croats above, they find these in stories and myths, in historic battles (both victories and losses), and customs and practices (often long lost). However, no group does or can remember all of its past; some forget spontaneously, and some forget strategically. Sinhalese in Sri Lanka "remember" that they were the first people to settle the island but forget that there were also historical Tamil kingdoms and rulers and that maybe Tamils were there before. Serbs remember that their traditional homeland was the area of Kosovo but forget that most Serbs abandoned it over six hundred years ago.

Ethnicity is not only non-state identity and imagination competing in and for the state. Indeed, the state is assaulted "from below" and "from above" by an array of cultural and political identities. At the sub-state level, races, classes, religions, parties, and ideologies may advance their own interests and identities in contrast or opposition to the state; for instance, after the invasion of Iraq in 2003, Sunnis and Shias—Muslims and Arabs both—clashed over power, and in many places, the lower classes, often in concert with disadvantaged ethnic groups and indigenous peoples, have challenged the state. At the trans-state level, many of the same forces operate across state boundaries and even internationally. Communism was a trans-state class-based ideology that defied the political structures of all capitalist states, while al-Qaeda is an international religion-based movement (with "franchises" in several states). *Négritude* was a translocal movement of the mid-1900s, primarily among Africans in French colonies, to assert a distinct and united global black identity.

Fighting for and against the state

The state clearly does not enjoy a monopoly on identity or culture; nor, more than occasionally, does it enjoy a monopoly on force. Differences in and competitions based on culture, identity, and interest frequently escalate into real violence, which

IMAGE 13.3 A mural in Ulster, Northern Ireland depicting the "struggle" of loyalists against Irish Catholic nationalists.

sees subordinated groups struggling to seize a share of the state and its spoils, to seize control of the state altogether, or to escape the state and perhaps form a state of their own.

The most familiar version of culture-related violence within states is "ethnic conflict," in which cultural groups or "nations" mobilize militias to fight each other or the state. It is critical to understand, if it is not already clear, that the state is not and arguably never can be a neutral entity. It is always *somebody's* state, representing the interests and institutionalizing the power of some particular group, if only "the people" (also an imaginary category that is constructed and often exclusive: The French revolutionaries of the 1790s imagined themselves "the people" just as the Bolsheviks in revolutionary Russia fancied themselves "the people") but more likely a specific class, race, ethnicity, etc. Ethnic conflict, then, often pits a subordinate ethnic group (like the Hutus in Rwanda, the Tamils in Sri Lanka, or the Croats in Yugoslavia) against a dominant ruling ethnic group (like the Tutsis, Sinhalese, or Serbs, respectively).

Sometimes the goal of conflict is cultural survival and autonomy for the bellicose group or a share of the resources (land, jobs, housing,

education, and so forth) of the state. Sometimes, as with the Hutus, the goal is to capture the state. Sometimes, perhaps after these other aims have failed, the goal is **secession**, the complete break with the existing state to establish a separate sovereign territory or state (also known as "**separatist movements**"). The Tamil movement in Sri Lanka aspired to an independent Tamil state on the island, to be called Tamil Eelam. Successful postcolonial separatist movements have included Bangladesh (from Pakistan), Eritrea (from Ethiopia), and of course South Sudan; unsuccessful ones, at least so far, are more numerous, including Biafra (from Nigeria), Khalistan (Sikh homeland, from India), and of course the Confederacy (from the United States). For a startling list of contemporary separatist movements, see http://en.wikipedia.org/wiki/Lists_of_active_separatist_movements.

As the reference to the United States indicates, secession is not limited to non-Western and recently decolonized states. French-speaking Quebec has voted repeatedly on seceding from Canada, while Scotland narrowly rejected (fifty-five percent to forty-five percent) a referendum to separate from the United Kingdom in late 2014; around the same time, the overwhelming majority (eighty percent)

Secession
the act of separating from a state or such structured political entity to exercise self-rule

Separatist movement
a social movement that has as its goal the cultural or political disengagement of two groups or societies, often struggling to detach its territory from a multicultural or plural state and establish its own state

A CASE OF ETHNIC CONFLICT: THE KURDS

IMAGE 13.4
Independence supporters on the streets of Barcelona during the National Day of Catalonia.

of people in Catalonia, a northeastern province of Spain, supported independence and allegedly intend to carry out that wish. In the United States, there is a lively Hawaiian sovereignty movement, and several counties recently considered seceding from California and Colorado.

Because of all this internal friction, states are often compelled to use repression to maintain the power of the dominant group or even to hold the state together. Again, "the state" is frequently a cover for the power of one ethnic group, race, tribe, class, etc., which may feel little common identity with and feel free to use force against other restless groups. Modern-day Syria is a classic case, with the minority Alawites governing an unruly mix of nationalities and sects. And, as in Syria, the state commonly uses military power against "its own people"—although the oppressed and oppressive groups may identify as essentially different peoples.

At the extreme, state oppression crosses the line into **state terrorism**, in which states use virtually the same illicit tactics as other terrorists against their citizens. Some of the most savage violence of the century was committed by "left-wing" movements with goals of radical social change. Under the communist Khmer Rouge party led by Pol Pot, up to one-third of the population—deemed corrupt and counter-revolutionary "enemies of the people"—was killed in a project of utterly remaking Cambodian society. On the other hand, the perception of such threats often sparked extraordinary "right-wing" violence. Argentina's "dirty war" in the 1970s is a good illustration. From the 1960s there had been a violent leftist guerrilla movement that targeted police, soldiers, government officials, business figures, journalists, and scholars; former President General Pedro Eugenio Aramburu himself was kidnapped and executed. Rightist paramilitary groups formed to oppose these actions, like *Asociacion Anticomunista Argentina*, employing virtually identical methods as the leftists. A military coup brought a right-wing government to power in 1976, which "perpetuated and carefully fed the myth of a subversive threat, *even after the armed left had been virtually annihilated in the field*" (Suarez-Orozco, 1992: 232). The regime soon developed a "paranoid ethos" that saw Argentina at the center of an international attack on Western civilization and that gave rise to metaphors of "cleansing" and "curing" the society of dirty or unhealthy influences. Among these influences were the ten to thirty thousand citizens who "disappeared" during the period.

State terrorism

the use of force and terror by a state government against its own people either a particular group or minority within the state or the entire population

---

BOX 13.2   TRANSITIONAL JUSTICE IN GUATEMALA

One of the crucial issues of the modern age is that when outbreaks of violence, even genocidal violence, end, people must find ways to live together. One strategy, or set of strategies, that has been devised and implemented is transitional justice, understood as "the process of redressing past wrongs committed in states shifting from a violent, authoritarian past toward a more liberal, democratic future" (Hinton, 2010: 2). This noble and ambitious goal has been pursued through a number of means including truth commissions, trials, "lustration (administrative purges of those associated with the prior regime), memorialization, and reparation programs" (4). And, as Alexander Hinton emphasizes, transitional justice initiatives must take into account the local circumstances—the local institutions and understandings, the specific situations and players, and the particular political context—which makes the pursuit of justice not only difficult but "often quite messy" (17). In Rwanda, for instance, transitional justice has been sought through a combination of international tribunals, foreign courts, and a traditional legal dispute-resolution mechanism called a *gacaca*. And despite its best intentions, transitional justice often fails to bear results, partly because victims may be afraid to make public their grievances or because perpetrators are beyond the reach of the proceedings. Victoria Sanford and Martha Lincoln, writing about Guatemala, call this "impunity" and find that the government officials who were responsible for atrocities during three decades of violence have not met justice. In 1996 the Guatemalan Army made peace with the Guatemalan National Revolutionary Union, and a Commission for Historical Clarification was established. The Commission reported in 1999 that 626 villages had been destroyed, over 200,000 people killed or "disappeared," and 1.5 million others displaced; further, of the documented human rights violations, ninety-three percent were committed by the Army and only four percent by the revolutionaries (2010: 70). However, despite the fact that a court ordered the arrest of numerous generals and other officials, these war criminals "continue to make public justifications and/or deny any knowledge of human rights violations" and "none of them have been jailed" (71). Instead, the level of violence *since the peace* has rivaled the war era, with 20,943 registered killings in five years (72). Sanford and Lincoln are particularly alarmed at what they call "feminicide" or the killing of women—seldom if ever combatants—and, even more, "state responsibility for these murders, whether through the commission of the actual killing, tolerance of the perpetrators' acts of violence, or omission of state responsibility to ensure the safety of its female citizens" (86). For instance, they tell the story of Claudia Isabel who was killed in August 2005 and whose killer has never been found—and is unlikely to be found, given the terrible mishandling of the crime scene and investigation. Organizations like the Forensic Anthropology Foundation (www.fafg.org/Ingles/paginas/FAFG.html) help recover and identify victims to begin the justice—and the grieving—process.

The weak or failed state

In summary, while the states on a standard political map seem well-defined and well-ordered, in reality many states are weak and ineffective, to the point of being labeled "failed states." Somalia is often offered as a textbook failed state, in which no orderly governance structure exists at all; since the fall of Muammar Qaddafi in 2011, Libya has been essentially stateless, as rival factions vie for power. Haiti is also widely condemned as a weak or failed state.

There are many reasons why postcolonial (and not only postcolonial) states are weak or failed, including

- poverty, resulting in low taxation and little state revenue
- corruption, including stealing from public funds and accepting bribes
- ineffectual or absent political institutions, such as police, courts, and army, preventing the state from imposing the rule of law
- heavy expenditure on weapons, for use against citizens and neighbors: According to the World Bank (data.worldbank.org/indicator/MS.MIL. XPND.GD.ZS), between 2010 and 2014 the United States spent 3.6 percent of GDP on defense, Yemen 3.9 percent, Angola 4.9 percent, Algeria five percent, and Oman a staggering 11.6 percent

- military domination of society, with a propensity to military coups: The army dominates Egypt and Pakistan; Brazil experienced military coups in 1931, 1945, and 1964; coups in Thailand occurred in 1951, 1976, 1991, 2006, and 2014

The Fund for Peace (global.fundforpeace.org) calculates an annual Fragile States Index, scoring states on a 120-point system based on population pressures, poverty, group grievances, factionalized elites, refugees, security and human rights, and legitimacy of the state. According to the most recent results (Table 13.1), the most fragile states are predominantly African, along with Afghanistan, Haiti, and Pakistan; the most stable states are European.

The United States ranked twentieth in stability (35.4), between France and Singapore; the United Kingdom was eighteenth (34.3).

See Chapter 9

WHERE STATES CANNOT REACH— OR SEE: POLITICS AND IDENTITY BEYOND THE STATE

Another fallacious assumption is that every part of the world is controlled by a state (ideally one and only one state) and that states project their power evenly throughout their territory, up to their very edges. In reality, some places are claimed by more than one state (for instance, China claims many

TABLE 13.1   Most fragile and most stable states, 2014 (source: Fragile States Index)

Ten Most Fragile States		Ten Most Stable States	
South Sudan	112.9	Finland	18.7
Somalia	112.6	Sweden	21.4
Central African Republic	110.6	Denmark	22.8
Democratic Republic of Congo	110.2	Norway	23.0
Sudan	110.1	Switzerland	23.3
Chad	108.7	New Zealand	24.1
Afghanistan	106.5	Luxembourg	24.6
Yemen	105.4	Iceland	25.9
Haiti	104.3	Ireland	26.1
Pakistan	103.0	Australia	26.3

See Chapter 9

Clifford, James. 1994. "Diasporas." *Cultural Anthropology* 9 (3): 302–338.

Diaspora
the dispersion of a social group from its historical homeland (often applied specifically to the Jewish community)

See Chapter 14

small islands that are simultaneously claimed by Japan, Vietnam, and other countries), and some regions inside states are actually not firmly under state control. Anbar province is western Iraq is famously lawless (and its capital, Ramadi, fell to ISIS/Islamic State in May 2015), and we noted the absence of the state in remote areas of Argentina. Mountainous regions are notoriously difficult to administer, although unruly neighborhoods can occur in the middle of cities. As we will see, states are not the bounded containers of people that we often presume: People flow across boundaries in search of work or safety in ways that undermine the state's ability to manage or "read" those populations. Finally, besides being weak or absent in some places, states in general are in retreat from some of their conventional functions such as regulation and social services, due to budgetary constraints but also the bundle of policies known as neoliberalism, which increasingly surrender governmental roles to market forces and non-state actors like corporations.

Diasporas

Whatever geographical isolation existed between societies ended long ago with the advent of long-distance travel and trade. In fact, the spatial boundaries between societies were never permanent and impenetrable: Objects, ideas, genes, and people always flowed across social boundaries, whether in Aboriginal Australia, Native America, or pre-modern Europe. James Clifford, who wrote extensively about the cultural circulation and movement,

noted that there is an "unruly crowd" of concepts relating to "the contact zones of nations, cultures, and regions: terms such as *border, travel, creolization, transculturation, hybridity*, and *diaspora*" (1994: 302). In short, the old "localizing strategies" of anthropology, aimed at assigning one person or artifact or practice to one society or culture occupying one homeland is hopelessly obsolete.

One particularly common and important circumstance is **diaspora**, the dispersion of a cultural group across multiple social territories and states, potentially even globally. As coined by the ancient Greeks, diaspora (from *speiro* for "to sow" and *dia* for "over") referred to the generally voluntarily movement of Greek settlers into the islands and remote mainlands of the Mediterranean. Other and later diasporas were often involuntary. Whatever their form and motivation, Clifford regarded the key characteristics of diaspora to be "a history of dispersal, myths/memories of the homeland, alienation in the host (bad host?) country, desire for eventual return, ongoing support of the homeland, and a collective identity importantly defined by this relationship" (305).

There are obviously multiple ways for a society to find itself in a diaspora. One, as with the ancient Jews, is forced eviction from their land and transplantation into another land; another, as with the modern Africans, is an international trade and trafficking in humans, transporting them afar for labor. In other cases, members of a society may voluntarily migrate—permanently or cyclically—in search of work or other advantages. People may also flee their homeland to escape natural disasters (droughts, floods, etc.) or, more frequently, wars—

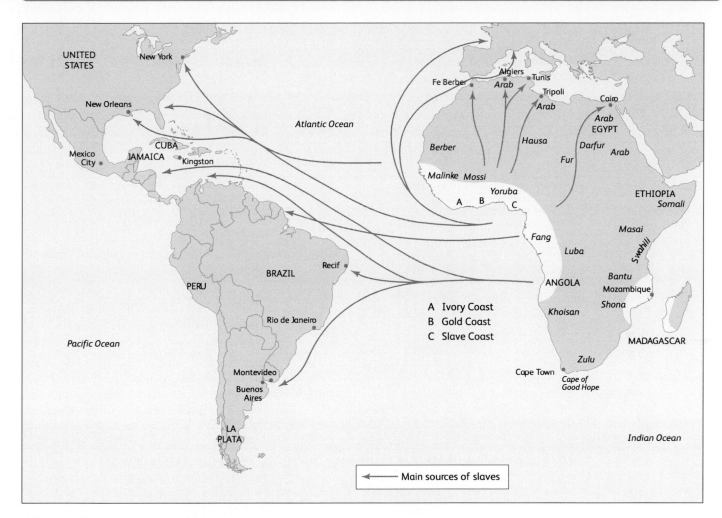

MAP 13.2 African diaspora/slave routes

in which case they become not only a diaspora but a refugee population (see below). They may, finally, become diasporic through the drawing of political or state borders, which divide the people without the people actually moving. Robin Cohen (1997) distinguished between *victim, labor, trade, imperial*, and *cultural* diasporas, with the spread of British settlers and colonists around the world an example of the imperial type.

Many, many societies exist in a diaspora today, including Chinese, Armenians, Asian Indians, Sikhs, Tamils, Somalis, and an endless list of others. Ultimately, it may be true that virtually all societies are to some degree diasporic, their members tossed around the world—increasingly so with expanding globalization and incessant political conflict. Indeed, André Levy emphasized that diasporas

evolve within transnational politics and are related to them, individuals within the diasporic scene are influenced by such politics. . . . [Therefore] the "larger picture" of transnationalism and global processes affects and even transforms the informants' lives and, by implication, shapes the ethnographer's perspectives.

(2000: 146)

Refugees

In a world of dwindling resources, escalating globalizing pressures, and seemingly continuous hostility, it is no wonder that a considerable number of people are displaced from their homes and

CULTURES IN EXILE: RWANDANS, CAMBODIANS, AND ANTHROPOLOGISTS.

cultures. As noted above, people "leave home" for a number of reasons, from job opportunities to natural disasters to political oppression and war in their region, creating a significant international flow of refugees. In a certain sense, refugee status is one kind of, or one process in, diaspora.

The United Nations High Commissioner for Refugees, created by international agreement in 1951, defined a refugee in its founding document as a person who

> owing to well-founded fear of being persecuted for reasons of race, religion, nationality, membership of a particular social group or political opinion, is outside the country of his nationality and is unable or, owing to such fear, is unwilling to avail himself of the protection of that country; or who, not having a nationality and being outside the country of his former habitual residence as a result of such events, is unable or, owing to such fear, is unwilling to return to it.

www.unhcr.org   (2007b: 17)

While this definition focuses on political displacement, the UNHCR has added other categories of displaced persons or "persons of concern," including

- asylum-seekers—"persons who have applied for asylum or refugee status, but who have not yet received a final decision on their application" (2007a: 16)
- internally displaced persons (IDPs)—those "who have been forced or obliged to flee or to leave their homes or places of habitual residence, in particular as a result of or in order to avoid the effects of armed conflict, situations of generalized violence, violations of human rights or natural- or human-made disasters, and who have not crossed an international border" (16)
- returnees—"displaced populations (mainly refugees and IDPs) who have returned to their country or place of origin," who are to be reintegrated into their former homeland (17)
- stateless persons—people who are "not considered as a national by any State under the operation of its law" (17)

Applying these criteria, the UNHCR reported that there were 51.2 million forcibly displaced persons at the end of 2013, including 16.7 million refugees, 1.2 million asylum-seekers, 33.3 million internally displaced persons, and ten million stateless persons. Fully 10.7 million people were displaced in

IMAGE 13.5 A refugee camp in Somalia, east Africa.

2013 alone, the largest number coming from Syria, Democratic Republic of Congo, Myanmar, Afghanistan, and Iraq.

While the sheer scale of the refugee problem rightly attracts scholarly attention, anthropology takes an interest in quite specific ways. First, as Harrell-Bond and Voutira suggested, refugee status—living apart from one's land and society, often in poverty and squalor, frequently unwelcome and disliked in their host country—requires that displaced persons "adapt to radically new social and material conditions. Documenting and interpreting the variety and diversity [of such responses] is the work of anthropology" (1992: 7). Further, the international relief effort directed at refugees itself forms a social system, what they called "the machinery of humanitarian assistance." For studying the humanitarian response itself, then—that is, how aid is doled out, how refugee camps are administered, how the goals and policies of assistance are determined and implemented—"anthropologists' insights into power, and their expertise on the structure of authority, place them in an advantageous position." Anthropology can advise policy-makers, investigate the needs of refugees, and assess the impact of assistance programs on the recipients. Harrell-Bond's own study of the humanitarian system, *Imposing Aid: Emergency Assistance to Refugees* (1986), is a model for such research.

Anthropology can also examine the forces that drive people from their homes. War is one obvious cause; natural disasters are another. However, as we will discuss later, human-made but not intentionally violent conditions can force many people into refugee and exile status, including resettlement programs (explicitly to move them from one place to another) and development schemes (incidentally requiring them to move). Dam projects, for instance, in India and elsewhere have flooded vast tracts of land and with it entire villages; the current Three Gorges project in China promises to do so on an epic scale.

Finally and most significantly for anthropology, the processes that create and perpetuate refugee status also lay bare some of the most basic processes that create, perpetuate, re-interpret, and modify culture itself. As Harrell-Bond and Voutira explained, and as can be observed in diasporas and other forms of modern transnational community,

One of the gains for anthropology in studying refugees is that it offers the chance to record the processes of social change, not merely as a process of transition within a cultural enclave, but in the dramatic context of uprootedness where a people's quest for survival becomes a model of social change.

(1992: 9)

One of the most fascinating and profound aspects of this change-and-survival process is the manipulation of culture and tradition—of memory and history themselves—for specific purposes and in reaction to specific pressures for dispersed and displaced groups. Indeed, the

> creation of a shared history, a founding myth, is such a common phenomenon among both refugees and others forced from home that it needs probing. It has powerful creative functions, but is no sign that the uprooted have put their experience behind them and moved on to other things. . . . Resettlement does not wipe out memory, but rather provides a medium through which it is reworked, and the memory of shared experience of uprooting helps to create new forms of identity.
>
> (Colson, 2003: 9)

A number of anthropologists have accepted the challenge to study how culture and memory function in refugee and other diasporic communities, perhaps most famously Liisa Malkki (1995) in her fieldwork in a Rwandan refugee camp who found that residents engage in a kind of mythico-history intended not to remember the "facts" of the past but to select, marshal, and employ history, tradition, and culture to understand and solve problems of their current social predicament.

Borderlands

As refugees, migrants, tourists, and other transnationals (including journalists and anthropologists) pour across state borders, these very borders reveal their porosity and their inadequacy as barriers between societies and cultures. It also becomes clearer that borders are cultural constructs, obviously not physical facts that ensure citizenship and prevent movement. In the words of Sondra

TOWARD AN ANTHROPOLOGY OF HUMAN RIGHTS

Harrell-Bond, Barbara E. 1986. *Imposing Aid: Emergency Assistance to Refugees*. Oxford: Oxford University Press.

See Chapter 14

Malkki, Liisa. 1995. *Purity and Exile: Violence, Memory, and National Cosmology among Hutu Refugees in Tanzania*. Chicago and London: The University of Chicago Press.

Hausner and Jeevan Sharma, a border is not a thing, but rather "a range of technologies, sociocultural instruments, and personnel that define and patrol it" (2013: 96). This insight urges us to apply the anthropological perspective to borders as well as the states that they allegedly circumscribe.

That state borders are artificial, often arbitrary, and contestable (and frequently contested) has been amply demonstrated. That borders are also techniques by which states "see" their own and other people and know themselves and are known in the global system of states is also true. But historian Willem van Schendel insists that this fact demands an "anthropology of frayed edges" instead of a "geography of lines," investigating "the human relations that create, maintain, undermine, and evade borders" (2013: 269). Due to colonialism, borders often do not respect peoples and nations; one of the most dramatic examples is the phenomenon of *chhitmahals* in India and Bangladesh, "islands of territory belonging to one country surrounded by the territory of the other," of which there are one hundred and twenty-three patches of India inside Bangladesh and seventy-four fragments of Bangladesh inside India (Gellner, 2013: 9). At the same time, peoples and nations do not respect borders.

All of this has led to an anthropological focus on *borderlands* as cultural sites and cultural processes in their own right. Especially but not exclusively in South and Southeast Asia, observers have lately "discarded the unified state-oriented approach to shed light on issues of borderlands," according to Wen-Chin Chang (2014: 14), abandoning the notion that borderlands are irrelevant compared to states or are "associated with periphery, wasteland, backwardness, and lawlessness" (12). More than anything else, what borderlands are really associated with is *diversity and movement*. As David Gellner stresses, in borderlands, "repeated movement is taken for granted. Rootedness to a place since time immemorial is not particularly valued" (2013: 14), which challenges one of the fundamental premises of classical anthropology.

Few have done as much to put borderlands on the map, if you will, as James Scott, who also introduced the notion of "legibility" by states of their populations and territories. In his recent *The Art of Not Being Governed*, he too concentrates on the highlands of Southeast Asia, which he claims is not only a distinct culture area relative to centralized civilizations and modern states, but has long been a "zone of refuge" for individuals and groups actively evading these powerful centers. Suggestively, he calls the region a "shatter zone," where "the human shards of state formation and rivalry accumulated willy nilly, creating regions of bewildering ethnic and linguistic complexity"; not unique to central Asia, such shatter zones "are found wherever the expansion of states, empires slave-trading, and wars, as well as natural disasters, have driven large numbers of people to seek refuge in out-of-the-way places" (2009: 7–8). Colonialism of course sought to harness these peoples for labor and to bind them to a single place, and postcolonial states "have tried to bring such peoples under their routine administration, to encourage and, more rarely, to insist upon linguistic, cultural, and religious alignment with the majority population at the state core" (12). Nevertheless, and to the consternation and confusion of states, the borderland peoples "spill promiscuously across national frontiers, generating multiple identities and possible foci of irredentism or secession. Weak valley states have permitted, or rather tolerated, a certain degree of autonomy when they had little choice" (11).

States, borders, and illegality

It is not surprising, as Chang mentioned, that borderlands are often zones of illegal activity. By their very nature, borderlands are difficult for states to "see" and to control, and among the prime illegal activities on and across borders are smuggling (including drug trafficking) and undocumented immigration.

Because the outlawed cross-border traffic in goods and people has become such a crucial issue, anthropologists have paid attention to "illegality" in borderlands. States of course may attempt to stop illegal trade and border-crossing, but they may also turn a blind eye toward it; in fact, Rebecca Galemba (2013) makes the salient point that ignoring illegal border activity allows the state to preserve the fiction of borders and of state sovereignty and legibility. Of course, on their borders, "states may be both present—often with regard to boundary enforcing and policing—and absent—in terms of providing services and responding to citizens"

BOX 13.3 A CULTURE OF MOBILITY IN THE CHINA/BURMA BORDERLAND

The previous chapter mentioned how a historical part of western China was transferred to Burma in the colonial era. While this territory officially moved between colonies and states, people in the region have been on the move for much longer. Wen-Chin Chang informs us that mule caravans have been traveling between Yunnan and northern Southeast Asia for over two thousand years, generating a "mule caravan culture" (*mabang wenhua*) that crisscrossed future states. Yunnan province was not absorbed by China until around 1300 CE. For the next three hundred years Chinese migrated or were resettled in the vicinity, growing to the majority by the 1600s. This population shift did not inhibit mobility and trade but rather encouraged it; "Transborder commerce continued to expand" in the late pre-modern and colonial period (2014: 4), to which was added a flood of Chinese after the Communist revolution of 1949. Fleeing members of the army of defeated Nationalist China, the Kuomintang (KMT), re-formed as guerrilla units in the borderland, and some of them moved on to northern Thailand in the 1960s, attracting civilians with them. Subsequently, "KMT forces carried out transborder trade between Thailand and Burma," leaving little distinction between soldiers and traders (6). More recently, Chang reports, Yunnanese Chinese have drifted into major cities like Yangon (former Rangoon) and "continually extended their migration routes from upper mainland Southeast Asia to overseas domains (e.g., Taiwan, Hong Kong, Gaungzhou, Japan, Malaysia, and Singapore)" (8). Indeed, Chang's main project in her book is to document the lives of individuals for whom this supposed borderland region is "a central area for transnational trade from which smuggled goods were further distributed to widespread locations" (174). Occupying what she calls a "transnational popular realm," they move back and forth across local borders—sometimes eluding state authorities, sometimes fighting them, and sometimes collaborating with them. And the specific mobility patterns and transnational connections depend on the particularities of cultural identity: For instance, for Yunnanese Muslims, the paths may lead to the Middle East.

IMAGE 13.6 An undocumented immigrant is apprehended in Arizona near the Mexican border.

(2013: 276), like the United States both blocking and arresting border-crossers and rescuing and assisting them. At the extreme, but not uncommonly, state officials may actually benefit "from collaborating with locals and smugglers"; in Galemba's field site of the Mexico–Guatemala border,

> some officials received local protection from being chased out by angry residents wielding sticks; many received gifts of gasoline and soda; and most received substantial bribes. Others were suspected of being involved with the drug traffickers and gangs they were charged with combating.
>
> (275)

To be sure, illegality is not restricted to borderlands. Illegal activities can and do occur anywhere within the state, including urban pockets where gangs operate. Indeed, in the opinion of former American gang member Sanyika Shakur (1993), gangs are mini-states, collecting revenue, defending territory, and waging war. Galemba notes that labeling an activity as illegal "enhances vulnerability; legitimizes exploitation, and justifies accumulation, extraction, and violence" (276), often precisely making certain behaviors invisible. A good but unfortunate example is illegal employment of migrant laborers in China. Sarah Swider asserts that one-third of migrant workers participate in the construction industry, the majority in informal or illegal arrangements; modern China would not exist without them. Those who sign contracts with employers or agents may be hidden—virtually imprisoned—in the workplace, making them invisible to the state but also restricting their movement and exposing them to abuses like non-payment. Those engaged in what she calls "embedded employment," hired through ethnic networks and communities, "are less vulnerable in relation to their employers [but] more vulnerable in relation to the state" (2015: 51), which may harass, arrest, or deport them. Finally, those who find work as day laborers through "street labor markets" are the most likely to be "beaten, jailed, placed in work camps, fined and/or returned 'home' by the police and urban security officers" (53).

What illegality, borderlands, and all of the challenges and threats to the governmentality of states reveal is that "state power . . . is always unstable," that the state "is continually both experienced and undone through the *illegibility* of its own practices, documents, and words" (Asad, 2004: 279) and that, whatever states may say and whatever maps may suggest, anthropologists "must turn to the pervasive uncertainty of the law *everywhere* and to the arbitrariness of the authority that seeks to make law certain" (287).

BOX 13.4   CONTEMPORARY CULTURAL CONTROVERSIES: BEDOUIN REFUGEES IN ISRAEL

One group's claim to territory or sovereignty often excludes and disadvantages another. According to the Association for Civil Rights in Israel (www.acri.org.il),

> Since its establishment in 1948, Israel has ignored the Bedouin's historical presence in the region and has sought to transfer and concentrate the population into a small geographic area in the northeastern Negev—in order to confine their living space and free up the most fertile areas of the Negev for Jewish agricultural settlement. The state continues to deny recognition to the Bedouin villages and to deny the villagers their right to their own soil, which they have lived upon and worked for decades.

Up to thirty thousand Bedouin residents are targeted for evacuation and relocation to towns, and many others have already had their land seized and their economy undermined. Some will receive compensation, but only if they can provide documentation of ownership—something that most indigenous peoples of the world do not possess. What do you think?

SUMMARY

Colonialism created a stable-looking map that masks a highly volatile and unstable assortment of states and peoples in plural societies with contested and porous boundaries. The processes by which colonialism ended in any single colony set the tone for immediate political opportunities or challenges, in terms of

- settler states versus native rule
- gradual transition to independence or violent resistance and rebellion.

Decolonization frequently yielded a temporary transitional state and a struggle for political control and cultural definition in the future. Communism was often an attractive element in the battle against colonialism because it seemed to offer an explanation or theory of colonialism and anti-colonial resistance as well as a plan for the future.

The "new states" formed from independence movements faced the distinction between state, nation, and nation-state. Virtually none of them were nation-states but rather

- multinational states and/or
- multi-state nations.

This reality called for explicit policies of "nation-building" and provided conditions of cultural competition and conflict between groups sharing the state. In these contests, culture itself became a useful tool for contrasting groups from each other and making and legitimizing demands. Out of "traditional" cultures came cultural movements like nationalism and ethnicity, with their varying cultural bases and goals, including sometimes secession and sovereignty. These conflicts all too often escalated into real shooting wars, with sometimes genocidal consequences. Some of the results of anthropological significance have been

- ethnic conflicts
- diaspora
- refugees
- borderlands with their characteristic trans-state mobility and illegality.

These painful contemporary developments call for a re-examination of concepts like culture and identity—for a re-examination of the concepts and practices of anthropology.

MCQS

FILL IN THE BLANKS

Key Terms

civil war	multi-state nation	self-determination
country	nation	separatist movement
diaspora	nation-state	state
ethnic group	nationalism	state terrorism
identity politics	revolution	
multinational state	secession	

14 Economics in the postcolonial world

Development, modernization, and globalization

See Chapter 7

No society has experienced more rapid and exceptional development than China. In one lifetime, China has gone from a closed communist system to a market-friendly economy with double-digit growth containing (in 2014) ninety-five of the *Fortune* Global 500 companies and producing (in 2011) seventy percent of the world's cellphones and ninety-one percent of its personal computers. Like the earlier modernization of Europe, the U.S., and Japan, Chinese development is associated with industrialization, urbanization, massive population movement, environmental damage and pollution, increased inequality, and some calls for more democracy; unlike other recently developing countries, China has not depended on foreign aid and loans. Transformations in China's economy, landscape, and society are deeply interrelated. Entire multi-million population cities have sprouted, and poorer remote regions like the west have been "the target of on-going efforts at development . . . intended to both unleash the potential of the region and to decrease migration flows towards the richer coastal areas which put a strain on the services and infrastructure of China's megacities" (Lora-Wainwright, 2012: 8). In the process, some villagers

have lost their home but not their land; some have lost much or all of their land but not their home; and some still have both their home and their land, but they predict they will be moved in the near future.

(2012: 9)

Sadly, in order to frustrate rural unity and demands of higher compensation for their losses, Anna Lora-Wainwright reports that the secretary of one village "took family heads one-by-one to a local hotel where, accompanied by township and county officials, they signed compensation agreements"—a classic "divide and rule strategy, undermining any potential efforts to collectively oppose unfair and unequal distribution of benefits while marginalizing those who refuse to sign" (9). More, officials perceive villagers as *needing* modernization and improvement, as "lacking 'quality' and legal awareness; as uncollaborative and stuck in their ways; as selfish and unable to put the national good before their own," and as "unwilling to rely on themselves" (9). The representatives of the state naturally see themselves "as champions of 'national benefit'" and even as the weak and injured party in the interactions (10). Meanwhile, in the cities, poverty—"an

IMAGE 14.1 China's cities, including Beijing (pictured), face serious air pollution with the development of industry.

unavoidable condition of the market economy" (Cho, 2012: 188)—leads to another division, between poor urbanites with state-granted rights and poor rural migrants without. Accordingly, urbanites identified *with* the state and *against* their fellow citizens.

When the formal relationship of colonialism ended, former colonies became independent states. However, as we have already discussed, many negative effects of the colonial period lingered long past this independence, up to the present day. Some of these effects are primarily political. Others are more fundamentally economic—involving ownership of wealth and resources, production, distribution, and the international system of trade—although these are not entirely separable from politics. Ownership and control of productive resources confers political power, and political power grants influence over the economy. The legacy of economic relations during and after independence indicates that political independence does not equal economic independence, and it certainly does not equal economic prosperity.

This chapter examines the ongoing economic challenges facing the newly independent states and the societies within them as they recover from colonialism. It also looks at some of the policies and practices intended to "correct" or "improve" the

economy and society, often referred to as "development." Finally, it highlights the mixed effects of contemporary development activities and globalization, not only at the state level, but at the level of the small indigenous groups within those states. As emphasized in the earlier chapter on economics and throughout this book, societies seldom if ever dwelt in total economic isolation. But with the arrival of colonialism and then state and global cultural processes, it is impossible to understand the situation in any society—even small and allegedly "traditional" ones—apart from wider forces. At the same time, we consider the contribution of anthropology to understanding, delivering, and critiquing these development and culture-change activities.

See Chapter 7

WHY ECONOMIC DEPENDENCE?

The end of colonialism meant the departure of foreign administrators and armies and the establishment of an internal government with its own army. It did not always mean changes in the economic realities on the ground; often independence was intentionally meant *not* to change those realities. If a colony had a large number of landless people before independence, it still had them afterward. If it had an economy dependent on **primary production** (producing raw materials rather than manufactured goods), it still had such an economy afterward. And if non-local or non-indigenous individuals or corporations owned and controlled resources and wealth before independence, they still did afterward. In fact, because political independence was a change of relations between governments (new state and former colonizer) and not necessarily between individuals or classes or businesses, it often could not address those other issues, at least not initially.

There are a number of reasons why economic conditions changed more slowly, if at all, compared to political ones. In many former colonies, large or at least significant foreign populations remained after independence. The United States is a good example: When the U.S. became independent, power and ownership hardly reverted to the native peoples. Rather, white, European-descended landholders continued to hold land and gradually increased their holdings at the further expense of

Primary production the production of raw materials, in the form of farming, mining, foresting, etc.

See Chapter 12

See Chapter 13

Apartheid

in twentieth century South
Africa, the official policy of
separating the races within
their society legally and
socially

See Chapter 13

internal colonialism
the practice in which a
society (usually a state)
penetrates and occupies
territory within its
jurisdiction (normally inside
its borders) but that
contains peoples who do
not identify as and with the
occupying society. In some
usages, it can also refer to
the condition in which
colonized peoples
internalize (in their minds
and personalities) the
institutions and values of
colonialism

www.worldbank.org

monoculture
the specialization of
production of only one crop
or product for which a
territory is particularly
suited. This can involve
food crops like corn or rice,
or raw materials like
lumber, coffee, rubber, tea,
and so on

the native populations. Australia, Canada, and New Zealand were the same, while in South Africa local whites, a mere ten percent of the population, dominated the state long after independence in 1910 and actually enacted discriminatory laws (**apartheid**) to disenfranchise and restrict non-whites formally. When multiracial elections were held for the first time in 1994 and a black government was elected, headed by Nelson Mandela, even this did not alter basic economic facts, such as the extreme poverty of many black South Africans.

In other former colonies, with or without significant white populations, independence often was merely a transfer of power from one group of elites (white) to another (native). But, as in the cases of Sri Lanka and Rwanda, these native elites were usually enculturated to Western ways and did not challenge the status quo. In some cases, the outgoing colonizers actually set up the future government, as in Iraq. These native elites sometimes continued to take inspiration, if not direction, from former colonizers, and too often they aimed to enrich themselves by exploiting the population no less than the colonizers had done. In fact, we might call this stage in the history of "new states" **internal colonialism**, as one section of the society—sometimes a regional group, sometimes an ethnic or "national" group, sometimes just an individual and his/her family or party—ran the state for his/her/their own benefit. Zaire under Joseph Mobuto (later Mobuto Sese Seko) is a prime example, since Mobuto was reported to have accumulated $5 billion in personal wealth while his state slid into poverty, repression, and chaos.

Finally and most basically, nothing did or perhaps even could change in regard to the states' external relations with the global capitalist system. During colonialism, entire colonies had been turned into **monoculture** plantations, producing one crop (such as coffee, tea, rubber, sugar, cocoa, peanuts, etc.) for export. On the day after independence the new states did not simply plow under the coffee fields and plant food crops for local consumption—or build factories to manufacture cars and computers. Even if the resources were controlled by native peoples (which we just acknowledged was not the case), they too typically wanted or needed to perpetuate the export economy and its income stream. Worse, if the new government had wanted to alter fundamentally the economy of the state, the

process would have been difficult if not impossible for financial reasons. The new states were often quite poor, as their wealth had been systematically stripped. Even more, they still had production contracts and other economic obligations, including debts, and their only means of earning cash to pay their debts was exporting their existing products. Foreign banks, corporations, and other agencies influenced their internal economic decisions. And lastly, it cannot be overlooked that powerful forces, including the United States and European countries, pressured new states not to reform their economies (and vehemently opposed policies like land distribution to the poor or the expulsion of foreign companies), offering assistance or even convincing them that production-for-export was the road to economic freedom and success. The result is that the damage and injustices of colonialism were usually not reversed with the arrival of political independence, but were actually perpetuated by new and less overt (and also less expensive) means.

THE PATH TO UNDERDEVELOPMENT

So, colonialism left a constellation of economic legacies that would not soon be erased in most new states, if any such attempt was even made. The economic conditions of the new states were marked most conspicuously by poverty. In its 2000–2001 report, the World Bank asserted that almost half of the world's population lived on less than $2 per day and that twenty percent lived on less than $1 per day. Of these desperately poor people, 43.5 percent lived in South Asia, 24.3 percent in sub-Saharan Africa, 23.3 percent in East Asia and the Pacific, 6.5 percent in Latin America and the Caribbean, and only two percent in Europe and Central Asia (World Bank 2001: 3–4). And the situation had actually deteriorated in South Asia and sub-Saharan Africa, which in 1987 accounted for 40.1 percent and 18.4 percent, respectively, of those living on less than $1 per day.

Although global poverty has improved somewhat in the interim (see Figure 14.1), deep problems persist. The economic characteristics underlying this condition include:

■ primary production (the production of raw materials, like food, lumber, metals, fuels,

IMAGE 14.2 Many of the world's poor live in squalid conditions, like this crowded *favela* or slum in Brazil.

etc.) as the predominant element of the state economy

- a high proportion of the population engaged in agricultural activities
- low incomes, individually and nationally
- an unfavorable distribution of the national income, such that a small minority received or controlled most of the wealth and the vast majority were relatively—or sometimes absolutely—impoverished
- little industry
- dependence on foreign sources for money, skill, and manufactured goods
- dependence on foreign markets for their primary goods, with prices out of their control

Perhaps equally if not more significant and negative are the social consequences of these factors, affecting the quality of life in the new states:

- a mostly rural population
- very high birth and death rates, combining short life expectancies and high infant mortality with high fertility to produce a population explosion
- insufficient diets and poor nutrition

- high incidence of (preventable) diseases, both infectious and parasitic and nutrition-related
- low education and high illiteracy
- insufficient and inadequate housing and services, combined with urban overcrowding as people attempt to escape rural conditions, creating a huge urban slum-dwelling population
- often quite low status for women

A few statistics convey the scale of the problem. One common measure of the wealth and economic health of a state is **gross national product (GNP)**, roughly defined as the total value of the goods and services produced by the state, domestically and by overseas investment. However, since it is deceptive to compare the production of a large state with that of a small state, a more meaningful figure is **GNP per capita** or the GNP divided by the population, which calculates how much wealth is produced per inhabitant. This does not mean that every person in the state actually earns this much income per year; some have much more and much less, making the distribution of this wealth a critical issue. Also, individuals may have access to other forms of livelihood than cash, such as subsistence agriculture, but these other forms will not ordinarily allow

Gross national product (GNP)
the total value of goods and services produced by a society or state

Gross national product per capita
the GNP of a state divided by its population

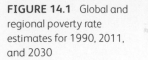

FIGURE 14.1 Global and regional poverty rate estimates for 1990, 2011, and 2030

(Source: World Bank 2015: 3)

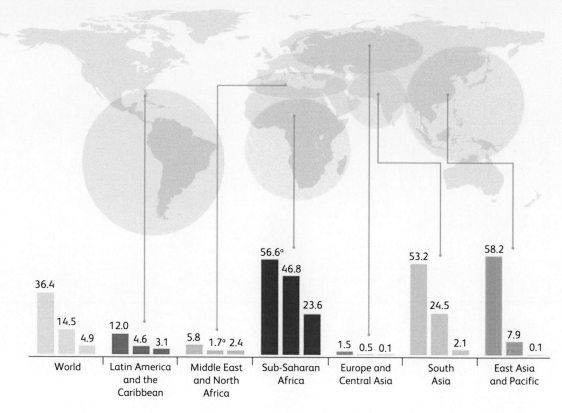

them to participate in the cash-based economy, where they can acquire manufactured goods, medical care, and education.

From this information it is clear that the "richest" states in the world are Western or Westernized states, while the "poorest" states in the world are non-Western states. In fact, all of the lowest ten state economies are found in Africa. But average income figures do not tell the whole story, since the average may be quite high while large proportions of people live in poverty. Therefore, we must also consider income distribution. The poorest states also have some of the worst inequalities of wealth.

The measure of living conditions in a state is not economic alone; we must also consider

TABLE 14.1   GNP per capita 2013, in dollars

Highest 10 Countries		Lowest 10 Countries	
Norway	102,610	Burundi	260
Switzerland	90,760	Malawi	270
Qatar	86,790	Central African Republic	320
Luxembourg	69,900	Niger	400
Australia	65,390	Liberia	410
Sweden	61,680	Democratic Republic of Congo	430
Denmark	61,680	Madagascar	440
Singapore	54,040	Guinea	460
United States	53,470	Ethiopia	470
Canada	52,200	Eritrea	490

Source: World Bank

Note: The World Bank method calculates gross national income, based on purchasing power parity.

Note: This listing does not include states for which precise dollar amounts were unavailable, as well as extremely small polities.

indicators that measure health, education, and other quality-of-life variables. Infant mortality (the rate of death of infants before one year of age) and life expectancy (the average length of life) are two telling indicators.

TABLE 14.2   Infant mortality (per 1,000 births), 2014 estimated

Lowest 10 States		Highest 10 States	
Monaco	1.81	Afghanistan	117.23
Japan	2.13	Mali	104.34
Bermuda	2.48	Somalia	100.14
Norway	2.48	Central African Republic	92.86
Singapore	2.53	Guinea-Bissau	90.92
Sweden	2.60	Chad	90.30
Czech Republic	2.63	Niger	86.27
Hong Kong	2.73	Angola	79.99
Iceland	3.15	Burkina Faso	76.80
France	3.31	Nigeria	74.09

Source: CIA World Factbook

The next fourteen highest infant death rates were also in African states. Note that the United States was not among the ten best states for infant mortality; its rate was 6.17, fifty-sixth in the world and *a decline* from 6.06 in 2011. The United Kingdom suffered from a rate of 4.44. The situation at the other end of life is no better for Africa, as illustrated by average life expectancy.

TABLE 14.3   Life expectancy, in years, 2014 estimated

Highest 10 States		Lowest 10 States	
Monaco	89.57	Chad	49.44
Japan	84.46	South Africa	49.56
Singapore	84.38	Guinea-Bissau	49.87
Switzerland	82.39	Afghanistan	50.54
Australia	82.07	Swaziland	50.54
Italy	82.03	Central African Republic	51.35
Sweden	81.89	Somalia	51.58
Canada	81.67	Zambia	51.83
France	81.66	Namibia	51.85
Norway	81.60	Gabon	52.06

Source: CIA World Factbook

The U.S. occupied forty-second place, with 79.56 years, and the United Kingdom twenty-ninth, with 80.42, which is still about twice the life span of some African states. Indeed, the next twenty-seven lowest life expectancies after Gabon were all found in Africa, followed by Haiti. While longevity is not necessarily a proof of quality of life, it can only be surmised that people who live half as long do not live as well. On measures of education, literacy, health, access to clean water, and women's rights, the picture remains consistent. For instance, the United Nations calculates a Human Development Index as a composite score of the "livability" of various states based on life expectancy, adult literacy, school enrollment, educational attainment, and per capital national income. On this data, the most livable and least livable states in the world are shown in Table 14.4.

TABLE 14.4   Most and least livable states, Human Development Index 2013

Most	Least
1. Norway	1. Niger
2. Australia	2. Democratic Republic of Congo
3. Switzerland	3. Central African Republic
4. Netherlands	4. Chad
5. United States	5. Sierra Leone
6. Germany	6. Eritrea
7. New Zealand	7. Burkina Faso
8. Canada	8. Burundi
9. Singapore	9. Guinea
10. Denmark	10. Mozambique

Relative poverty
the possession of less money than others in the same society, or the inability to afford the standard of living of more comfortable individuals or that is believed to be possible or appropriate

Absolute poverty
a level of income below what is required to have a decent standard of living, sometimes measured at less than $US 1 per day

Global apartheid
the de facto division of the world's states into rich, powerful, majority-white states and poor, weak and dependent majority-non-white states

Modernization theory
the theory that the improvement of economic and social conditions in poor states entails the creation of "modern" (generally understood as Western-like) institutions, values, and habits; also, the specific processes or policies by which this form of social change can occur; W. W. Rostow offers one of the most complete and well-known modernization theories

Rostow, W. W. 1965. *The Stages of Economic Growth: A Non-Communist Manifesto.* New York: Cambridge University Press.

True to form, all of the "best places to live" were Western or Westernized, and all of the "worst" were non-Western states—in fact, all in Africa. And the next eight least livable were African states, followed by Afghanistan and Haiti and then eight more in Africa. Incidentally, the United Kingdom ranked as the fourteenth most livable state.

This international "lower class" of states has other distinct—and unsettling—characteristics. A line drawn to separate the poorest states from the richest highlights two facts. The first is that there is a "north/south" aspect to the inequality, such that virtually all of the poorest states lie in the Southern Hemisphere or at least south of the rich states. Second, virtually all of the poorest states are majority non-white—Asian, African, and other non-European. It is as if the apartheid system mentioned above applies to between states too—as if there is a color-based stratification of states and not just of races within states. This phenomenon has been termed **global apartheid**, which does not suggest a deliberate or formal or legal system of international racial discrimination, but rather a (for the most part) unintentional and informal or situational outcome based on historical, environmental, political, and economic factors.

Another way to look at the distinction between the rich and the poor states is in terms of level of development, with "developed" states versus "undeveloped" or "underdeveloped" or "less developed" states. The "developed" category tends to have exactly the opposite characteristics of the dependent states listed above; by contrast they tend to enjoy:

- high GNP and income
- wealth often comparatively evenly distributed

- agriculture as a very small (as little as two percent) part of the economy
- manufacturing ("secondary sector") and services ("tertiary sector") as the bulk of the economy
- high rates of urbanization
- high life expectancy, low birth and death rates
- adequate food supplies, mostly self-sufficient
- generally good health care, high education and literacy, and adequate social services and standard of living
- relatively high women's status

Because of these traits, developed states are for the most part able to meet the needs of their populations. While there are of course poor and hungry people in the richest of states, the proportion of these people is low, and this poverty is relative rather than absolute. That is, in conditions of **relative poverty**, poor people do not have as much food or as many comforts as others in their society, while in **absolute poverty** poor people do not have enough food and other resources to live reasonably if at all. Famine and starvation are common sights.

Underdevelopment and processes of accumulation

Global poverty and inequality and its amelioration have been matters of interest for scholars and politicians. It is fair to say that poverty and inequality cannot be solved unless it is understood. An early and dominant perspective in the twentieth century was "modernization theory." Argued most effectively by W. W. Rostow (1965), **modernization**

theory saw the fault for underdevelopment as internal to poor societies, in particular their "backward" values and practices. In their pre-modern condition, such societies purportedly had economies that were stagnant, due fundamentally to a "traditional culture" promoting values and attitudes that presented roadblocks to development. Tradition bred a kind of "cultural inertia" in which nothing changes, no one takes any risks, people simply repeat old behaviors, and there is no growth. Before development could occur, culture change must occur, including new attitudes and beliefs about progress, planning for the future, risk-taking and entrepreneurship, education, and individuality and the freedom and right to accumulate private property and wealth. Only after these cultural changes could the economy "take off," with individuals building the economic structures necessary for a modern economy—starting businesses and making, saving, and investing money. The measure of successful development was economic growth, and a society and economy reached "maturity" when it achieved "self-sustained growth": Like an airplane, it stayed aloft and continued to climb, borne by industrialization, technology, and modern culture. The ultimate goal was "high mass consumption," an economy and society that resembles the West.

In fact, Rostow, a political economist, based his model on the experience of the West, where modern high-growth economies emerged from old feudal pre-capitalist systems. According to Marx, key to this process was **primitive accumulation**, the historical process "by which large swaths of the population are violently divorced from their traditional means of self-sufficiency" (www.marxists. org/glossary/terms/p/r.htm). Marx considered this a "brutal, expropriative process," even a form of robbery, exemplified by "enclosure" of common or unused land (e.g. by fencing) and conversion of that land to private property, which the few could then accumulate *as wealth*. In so doing, ordinary people were wrenched and excluded from their land, transformed into a "floating mass" of poor potential "free" laborers. Significantly, Michael Webber sees the same thing happening in China since 1980, characterized by "the transformation of state and collective enterprises into capital, the peasants' loss of land through various forms of dispossession, and the voluntary migration of peasants from agriculture to industrial pursuits"

(2008: 299). In other words, Rostow appeared to be positing the necessity of primitive accumulation as the first step toward development and modernization.

Others have seen modern Western society as less the cure than the cause of global poverty. André Gunder Frank, writing primarily about the Latin American experience, insisted that the rise of the Western capitalist system, especially colonialism, created underdevelopment in the first place; his thesis is known as **dependency theory**. In his 1966 article "The Development of Underdevelopment" and his 1979 book *Dependent Accumulation and Underdevelopment*, he argued that underdevelopment was not the "traditional" or pre-contact condition of most of the world. Instead, the underdevelopment in present-day states was the product of historical and ongoing economic and political relationships between what he called the "metropoles" (roughly the colonizer-societies like England, France, etc.) and the "satellites" (essentially the colonies).

In the course of "underdeveloping" or "de-developing" the dependent satellites, wealth and resources flowed from colonies, enriching the colonizing states—which Frank dubbed **dependent accumulation**. Essentially, as the West got richer, the rest got poorer. On this model, underdevelopment then is not the "native condition" of today's poor states, but is the consequence of Western development, both of which emerged from colonialism. As we saw, colonialism stripped traditional peoples of their wealth, dispossessed them of their land, deprived them of their own labor and the fruits of that labor, entangled them in the interests of foreign societies, bled them in the form of taxes, and rendered them dependent on foreign products to replace their lost self-sufficiency. In the cases of small, less politically integrated societies (bands, tribes, and even some chiefdoms) this was a simple process: Colonizers arrived with weapons, religious convictions, economic institutions, and adequate populations to overpower natives and compel their participation in the new regime.

But of course not all pre-colonial societies were living in "tribal" arrangements. India and China had highly advanced states, and they and parts of Africa had flourishing traditions of enterprise and mass production (although not modern industrial mass production) long before Europeans arrived. In addition to the colonial methods previously

---

Dependency theory
the theory of "Third World" underdevelopment that attributes the poverty and weakness of certain states to their ongoing unfavorable relationship to richer and more powerful states. Poor or weak states continue to be dependent on rich or powerful (mostly Western) states for capital, manufactured goods, and other key economic resources

Frank, André Gunder. 1979. *Dependent Accumulation and Underdevelopment*. New York and London: Monthly Review Press.

Primitive accumulation
according to Marx, the process by which precapitalist modes of production such as feudalism and slavery were transformed into the capitalist mode of production, by forcibly, even brutally, separating people from common resources like land and converting those resources into private property owned by the few

See Chapter 12

Dependent accumulation
according to Andre Gunder Frank, the colonial process by which colonies became poorer as colonizers became richer, since colonizers expropriated and accumulated the wealth of colonies for themselves

described, colonizers devised more muscular means to crack open and exploit these societies. Native industries had to be defeated, sometimes by unfair competition (for example, dumping products onto their markets at unnaturally low prices), sometimes by creating hostile financial and business environments. The British textile industry, for instance, could not compete with Indian producers at first and had to suppress and destroy it before they could underdevelop India and render it dependent. African native trading and financial institutions also had to be crushed.

China presents a yet more dramatic and shameful case of the de-development of a thriving society, since unlike India it was a unified empire. After travelers like Marco Polo reached China, Chinese goods such as silk and porcelain became highly prized by European consumers. China was happy to sell to but reluctant to buy from Europe, creating an unpleasant trade deficit. European inventors worked furiously to discover the secrets of Chinese silk, porcelain, and other goods and to find a product that China would purchase, until they stumbled upon opium. In the early 1800s, Western traders began to unload opium on Chinese markets, at great profit and with destructive consequences for Chinese society. The government of China banned the opium trade, but England fought a war (1839–1842) to protect its drug market. This first major defeat for China opened it to further exploitation, resulting in territorial loss (Hong Kong was ceded away by treaty, a treaty that only expired in 1997) and more war (a second "opium war" was waged by England and France in 1856–1860). Eventually, Beijing was occupied, and the carve-up of Chinese territory began.

DEVELOPMENT: SOLUTION AND PROBLEM

From the middle of the twentieth century, the dominant answer to the problem of poverty and inequality was **development**. Development is a form of directed change intended to correct the inadequacies and failures of existing economic systems—their poverty, dependence on primary production, lack of industry, and low standard of living. Development then consists of planned and coordinated efforts, usually by the government of a

state, but sometimes by agents outside of the state, to change or improve the economy of the state—and as necessary the culture of the state—so as provide greater wealth and a higher standard of living.

Various social scientists, including historians, political scientists, and economists, have offered various definitions or conceptualizations of development, generally recognizing that economic change cannot occur without more widespread cultural and social change. Gunnar Myrdal (1968: 1869) characterized it simply as "upward movement of the entire social system" and not just the economy (although "upward" is a vague and relative term). Wilbert Moore called it the "total transformation of a traditional or pre-modern society into the types of technology and associated social organization that characterize the 'advanced,' economically prosperous, and relatively politically stable nations of the Western world" (1963: 93). Surveying various definitions, David Apter (1968) identified some common elements: differentiation or increasing specialization of roles, stability or the ability to institute changes without causing greater problems, choice or the freedom of innovation and flexibility, and emulation or the imitation of foreign or Western models.

Riall Nolan, a contemporary anthropologist involved in development issues, viewed development as "attempts to improve the conditions of life for people, focusing on raising standards of living, building local capacity, and encouraging local participation and decision making. Development almost always involves multiple groups, and therefore, multiple cultural perspectives" (2002: 309). This reminds us that development, like any other initiative of directed change, is ideally first and foremost about people. The 1986 U.N. General Assembly's Declaration on the Right to Development (GA Res 41/128) related development to "human rights and fundamental freedoms." Furthermore, since development is about changing how people live and work, it is also cultural to the core: It introduces new cultural ideas and practices and brings cultures into contact in critical ways—not only Western and non-Western cultures, but various disparate cultures within the zone in development. It cannot be conceived as a sheer economic or political process and takes place at multiple social levels simultaneously, including individual, household/family/kin group, community, nation/state, and international/global.

Myrdal, Gunnar. 1968. *Asian Drama: An Inquiry into the Poverty of Nations.* New York: Pantheon.

Nolan, Riall. 2002. *Development Anthropology: Encounters in the Real World.* Boulder, CO: Westview Press.

Development

a form of directed change in which a state tries to change its internal economy and society, and/or foreign states and institutions try to change it, to promote economic growth, industrialize and urbanize, and ideally achieve a higher standard of living for its inhabitants

Development planning and projects

In its classic form, development is conceived as something that a society, ordinarily a state and its government, chooses to do and thus directs at "itself." We say "itself" in quotation marks because, as we have seen and will explore again below, the state and its dominant group(s) may target areas that are within its jurisdiction but not inhabited by those groups themselves or entirely integrated into the state political/economic system. At any rate, development ordinarily entails large-scale, planned, and sustained decision-making and implementation. It is also one manifestation of what Tania Murray Li calls "the will to improve," an attitude found in colonialism and modern Western states and inherited by postcolonial states. The "will to improve" empowers governments to "problematize" their populations by "identifying deficiencies that need to be rectified"—problems like "underdevelopment" or "backwardness"—and "rendering technical" those problems, that is, bringing them within the domain of experts who allegedly can fix people through well-conceived and well-managed change (2007: 7). The outcome, says Li following David Ludden (1992), is a "development regime" characterized by

> (1) ruling powers that claim progress as a goal, (2) a "people" whose conditions must be improved, (3) an ideology of science that proffers principles and techniques to effect and measure progress, and (4) self-declared, enlightened leaders who would use state power for development and compete for power with claims of their ability to effect progress. Like their colonial predecessors, contemporary national development regimes sometimes resort to violence to achieve their objectives.
>
> (Li, 2007: 15–16)

Perhaps the first thing to understand is that development is business—big business. It starts, as all rational economic decision-making does, with the perception of a problem to solve. It then entails the formulation of a **development policy**, the broad principles or goals of the effort. Among the common development goals are "economic growth," especially as measured by rising GNP. Some states adopted the policy of **import substitution**, in which they aimed to produce domestically what

they previously imported from abroad (i.e. substituting local production for foreign-made products). Since 1980, development policies have turned toward what is called **structural adjustment**, a bundle of economic and social modifications including, according to the World Health Organization (www.who.int/trade/glossary/story084/en/),

> currency devaluation, managed balance of payments, reduction of government services through public spending cuts/budget deficit cuts, reducing tax on high earners, reducing inflation, wage suppression, privatization, lower tariffs on imports and tighter monetary policy, increased free trade, cuts in social spending, and business deregulation.

These modifications were precursors to what has become known as neoliberalism, to which we return below.

A state's development policy dictates the specific **development projects** that it will undertake. Development projects are pinpointed actions that the state takes to achieve its development goals, expected to deliver specific returns and ideally serve as the basis for additional development beyond the scope of the project itself. This means that such projects tend to emphasize "infrastructure" that provides multiple benefits, a platform for subsequent development, and ultimately self-sustaining economic growth. Some of the preferred development projects include:

1. energy projects, especially as hydroelectric dams if appropriate rivers are available
2. transportation projects, especially roads and railroads
3. agricultural projects, to increase the yield of agriculture or open up new land for farming
4. settlement projects, to move people to less-populous or under-producing territories or to move people off of territories that are marked for "development" (e.g. flooding from a dam project)
5. industrial projects, to increase (or in many cases start) the manufacturing sector of the economy and provide a new source of export income and local self-sufficiency

In a sense, the fifth type is the ultimate goal of development, but it is not possible without the

Development policy
the general priorities and decisions set by a state or by development agencies to achieve economic, political, and social goals

Import substitution
a development policy aimed at producing domestically what the state or society currently imports from other states, i.e. substituting its own local products for imported products

Structural adjustment
a set of policies designed to reduce government control over development specifically and economic activity more generally, including "opening" or "freeing" local markets to foreign goods, eliminating economic protections like tariffs and subsidies, reducing taxes, deregulating industry, cutting government spending, and allowing the value of local currencies to "float" on international currency exchanges

Development project
a specific activity or task settled upon to achieve the economic, political, and social goals of a development policy. Such projects often include transportation, energy (especially hydro-electric), agricultural, and resettlement schemes

JAMES FERGUSON ON DEVELOPMENT AS AN "ANTI-POLITICS MACHINE"

preceding four types. There must be power to run the factories, transportation for workers and materials to get in and manufactures to get out, adequate agriculture to feed the workers while freeing laborers from farm work to shift them to factory work, and adequate income and capital for investment, which is usually skimmed off of the agricultural sector. And there must be people where the state needs them—which may or may not be where they are now and traditionally lived.

Clearly, development entails much planning, but often not the correct kind of planning; decisions have been made for economic and political reasons, but with little knowledge of or concern for the environmental or social and cultural variables and consequences of the plan. One possible solution is **social impact analysis** or **sociocultural appraisal**, which introduces the human and cultural dimension back into the planning. Such work examines the project and the areas and peoples affected, considering the appropriateness of the project, its likely impact on the various groups implicated by it, and the distribution of the benefits that accrue from it.

IRRIGATION AND AGRICULTURE IN A SENEGAL DEVELOPMENT PROJECT

THE DIVERSITY OF DEVELOPMENT DISCOURSE: ALTERNATIVES AND COUNTERS TO DEVELOPMENT IN THREE NASA (COLOMBIA) COMMUNITIES

Social impact analysis a fieldwork study of the consequences that a development project or other social-change policies have on the affected peoples

Sociocultural appraisal a study examining the *appropriateness* of a development or other social-change project, its likely *impact* on the various groups affected by it, and the distribution of the benefits that accrue from it

BOX 14.1   APPRAISING DEVELOPMENT: A ROLE FOR ANTHROPOLOGISTS

Allan Hoben (1986) and John Grayzel (1986) painted contrasting but mutually informing portraits of development projects and their relation to indigenous cultures, as well as the value of "applied anthropology." Hoben's research was fortunate to come before the project, in this case to resettle eighty thousand people from a heavily populated mountain region of Cameroon to a thinly populated plateau to the south. He discovered that there were as many as twenty-seven cultural or ethnic groups in the source region, in two clusters of cultures. The more northern cluster was distinguished by a denser population and higher fertility rate. They lived in scattered households with no villages but rather "sprawling hamlets" of twenty-five to fifty households, which were further aggregated into units of up to a thousand households. Worse yet, these non-Muslim mountaineers were looked down upon by the local Muslims as *kirdi* or "pagan, naked, poor, backward, and lack[ing] government" (180). In the target region, Hoben found seventy thousand already in residence, divided into ten or more groups with the Fulani comprising over fifty percent. As just noted, there were standing hostilities between the Muslims of the plateau and the incoming *kirdi*, and the relocation of the latter appeared to be not quite voluntary anyhow. Finally, the amount of quality land did not match the number of proposed settlers, almost guaranteeing environmental degradation and the gradual drifting of the settlers back to their home region. He therefore concluded that the project should not be undertaken, and the decision-makers took his advice. Meanwhile, Grayzel investigated a land- and cattle-management project in Mali, where the Doukoloma Forest Reserve was being developed for use by Bamana (Bambara) horticulturalists and Fulbe (Fulani) pastoralists. Here he found a cultural mismatch between the values of the project and those of the Fulbe people. Decision-makers had assumed that the people would appreciate a plan to graze and fatten their cattle for sale to the market, but they did not understand Fulbe practices. More important than owning cattle (which not all Fulbe did) was a Fulbe code of life called *pulaade* "which they guarded more fiercely than their animals" and which included notions of intelligence, beauty, wealth, and above all else independence. Intelligence, for instance, involved displays of cunning and calculation. The pursuit of beauty, especially female beauty, could lead a man to make certain economic choices, including selling his whole herd. And independence meant not taking orders from or being beholden to anybody. The project threatened all of these values: Government planning and control deprived them of their opportunity to display intelligence and was a direct affront to independence. As far as cattle went, Fulbe had never regarded them as a "fixed source of income" but rather as "convertible capital" they could accumulate or liquidate as they saw fit, including their pursuits of beauty, intelligence, and independence. What planners had failed to consider was the "aesthetic" or "emotional" core of life for people swept into projects, for which "development projects have failed and will continue to fail" (160).

Development financing

Like all major business ventures, development costs money—lots of money. Classic development emphasizes huge projects like dam construction schemes. Poor states do not have the wealth to finance such projects themselves, so they turn to various external sources of funding. Among these are foreign governments, **multilateral development institutions**, and private enterprise, including multinational corporations. Foreign governments, particularly rich Western ones, provide a certain amount of "foreign aid" for development purposes, either in the form of loans or grants. The United States, for instance, gives billions of dollars in foreign aid, although much less than previously; according to Hook (1996), in the 1950s in the heyday of development, the U.S. accounted for sixty percent of total international aid, but by the 1990s only seventeen percent. In real terms, the U.S. contribution of three percent of its GNP to foreign aid dropped to 0.1 percent in the late 1990s, lower than any major Western state. Among the institutions through which the United States funnels assistance to poor countries is the U.S. Agency for International Development (USAID)

Large corporations may elect to invest in particular places to take advantage of tax breaks, cheap labor, access to resources, or access to local markets; theirs is of course always a business decision, not a humanitarian effort.

Many multilateral development institutions were created around the end of World War II, originally to rebuild Europe. Out of a meeting held at Bretton Woods, New Hampshire in 1944, two important institutions—the International Monetary Fund (IMF) and the International Bank for Reconstruction and Development (IBRD, better known as the World Bank)—emerged. The IMF was intended primarily to assist states with balance-of-payments problems, although it also offers some advisory and technical assistance. The World Bank was designed to be just that, a bank, with deposits of cash from rich states that could be loaned for particular purposes to poor states and repaid by them.

The World Bank may be the prime mover in international development financing. Underdeveloped states come to it with formal proposals for projects, which the Bank evaluates and agrees to support or not. The Bank's decision-making process, as that of all lending and aid institutions, is affected by various internal criteria, in this case.

Multilateral development institutions
organizations like the World Bank (officially the International Bank for Reconstruction and Development) and the International Monetary Fund that were established and are funded and operated by more than government for the purpose of disbursing money, advice, and technology in the pursuit of development

IMAGE 14.3 The gleaming modern headquarters of the World Bank, one of the leading institutions of global development.

■ the control of the Bank, which is determined by the financial contribution made by the member states. The United States is by far the largest single contributor and therefore largest single influence on decisions. Up to fifty percent of the voting power in the World Bank is held by a half-dozen rich states.

■ the mission of the World Bank to lend money. It is in the business of lending, and it has annual lending targets, so it is inclined toward supporting projects rather than rejecting them.

■ the organization and staffing of the Bank. Kardam wrote in 1993 that "Sociological issues do not fit naturally into the goals and procedures of the World Bank" (1993: 1777), which was composed at that time of about seventy percent economists and most of the rest engineers. Only some fifty or sixty anthropologists and sociologists were employed there.

THE BENEFITS—AND COSTS— OF DEVELOPMENT

Finally, like any business venture, development involves the measuring and weighing of benefits and costs. There is no dispute that development can confer benefits, financial and otherwise. The question is what kinds of costs are incurred, who pays the costs, and how the benefits are distributed. Obvious costs include the expense of the projects themselves, for instance, the price of concrete to build a dam. As an economic exercise, development planners assign dollar values to costs and benefits and approve projects that appear to have a favorable cost–benefit ratio. However, there are other kinds of costs that are not always or easily factored into the calculations. There are the costs of cultural displacement, social disorganization, and acculturation or deculturation; these costs are paid much more dearly by poor, rural, and indigenous peoples whose lands are regularly coveted for development. These people often pay the cost for benefits that go to other, often distant, people, as when the afore-mentioned dam is constructed and electrical power is sent to remote cities or factories. The local people may find their land submerged, their previous way of life destroyed, their culture undermined. How does one put a number on that?

No one is unaware of the costs of development. In the film *The Price of Progress*, a World Bank official admits, "You can't have development

BOX 14.2   LOCAL SELF-DEVELOPMENT IN EGYPT

The will to improve is not the sole province of states. Many charitable and humanitarian organizations share the same mentality and discourse. As with microfinance (see below), small-scale efforts can be accomplished by local people, often representing fascinating mixtures of the traditional and the modern. For example, Sherine Hafez describes an Islamic women's organization in Egypt called al-Hilal that not only offers various services to urban women in Cairo (child care, education, charity, etc.), but also operates a "modernization" project in a poor village. In their efforts to "improve" the village it becomes clear "how modern liberal principles of development" and "the values of the secular modern are applied on a grassroots level"—not in place of Islam but in conjunction with Islam (2011: 128). While the women's motivation and their language is distinctly Islamic, their specific goals and "disciplinary techniques" (131) are recognizably modern. For instance, they want the village women to become more time-conscious, more tidy, and most of all more independent and productive. The methods they use to effect these changes are formal classes, inspections and detailed recordkeeping, material rewards, and verbal praise and reprimand. The traits and values that they set out to instill in those poor women include "punctuality, self-discipline, hygienic practices, and effective household organization and, most important, individual material production and motivation" (149). Although familiarly modern, "'Islam' was invoked in these practices every time a new concept was introduced and even when the village women attended a lesson on astronomy. A religious rhetoric was always linked to the activities and discussions" (149).

without someone getting hurt" (Claxton, 1989). Environmentalists are particularly attuned to the environmental costs, while anthropologists are particularly attuned to the cultural costs. Many observers and critics—and observers-turned-critics—like John Bodley in his *Victims of Progress* (1975; see also 1985), have chronicled the destructive consequences of development, a few of which are:

- Poverty. Ironically, while development is intended and designed to raise net economic wealth, it often has the opposite effect, at least for segments of the population. Groups whose lands and livelihoods are lost end up more impoverished than before. Wealth may be transferred from one geographic or social segment of the society or state to another, so that even improved GNP numbers do not mean prosperity for all.

- More difficult working conditions. Development often brings not only different work, but a different work ethic that demands eight or more (sometimes ten or twelve) hour workdays away from home. This work is also often more arduous and dangerous than any traditional activity; jobs like mining and manufacturing can mean more effort for proportionately less gain. Post-development economies are frequently more exploitative than pre-development ones, not less.

- Poor health. New populations in previously unpopulated or underpopulated areas, new living conditions (inadequate sanitation or clean water, overcrowding, etc.), and new practices can add up to a more unhealthy life. The gains from modern medicine are often offset by the losses to degraded health and social standards. Diet may decline; people may eat absolutely less, or they may eat less well, including overprocessed foods like sugar, flour, canned food, and junk food. "Developing" peoples regularly experience the **diseases of development**—high blood pressure, tooth decay, obesity, diabetes, and other degenerative diseases like cancer—previously unknown to them. For instance, medical anthropologist Dennis Wiedman notes that diabetes "was unknown prior to 1940 among all Oklahoma Native Americans," suddenly "reaching

epidemic proportions by the 1960s" (2012: 597) with diabetes-related death rates nearly twice as high as the national average, most directly caused by diets full of processed and fried foods accompanied by lower levels of physical activity. Parasites and bacteria may flourish; people may come into contact with previously isolated pathogens like the Ebola virus, or they may spread pathogens more effectively than ever, like the HIV virus in Africa and India.

- Loss of land and forced resettlement. States routinely look to their "least developed" regions for development schemes, which tend to be inhabited by the least efficient producers in the state—usually foragers or pastoralists—who must get out of the way of development. Lands are opened to settlers and prospectors when roads are built. Lands are submerged when dams are built. And lands are claimed by immigrating groups when poor urban people move or are moved into "lower density" areas, as in the Indonesian *transmigrasi* project in Indonesia or the Cameroon resettlement scheme above.

- Debt. Developing states can find themselves in horrendous debt to foreign institutions. Debt restricts freedom of operation and consumes future earnings. The fallout is less money for today's and tomorrow's needs. Also, as too often occurs, if a development project fails to deliver its promises, the state still holds the obligation of repayment. Poor states struggle under significant debt burdens, as much as four or five percent of their total yearly GNP. When the burden gets too great, the state may default and refuse to repay the debt, as Argentina did in late 2002. It borrowed over $800 million from the World Bank and owed more than $77 million in interest payments alone.

- Social disorder and conflict. Changes of these types and magnitude have all kinds of socially negative consequences. People under the pressures of development tend to suffer social breakdown, as their traditional orders are replaced by new orders—or sometimes what seems like no order. Crime, alcoholism, violence, suicide, juvenile delinquency, etc. appear in previously relatively well-balanced

Claxton, Nicholas. 1989. *The Price of Progress.* Oley, PA: Bullfrog Films.

Bodley, John. 1975. *Victims of Progress.* Menlo Park, CA: Cummings.

Diseases of development the lifestyle-related diseases that are common in developed industrial societies and increasingly common in developing societies, such as high-blood pressure, heart disease, diabetes, tooth decay, and obesity

Market-dominant minority

"ethnic minorities who, for widely varying reasons, tend under market conditions to dominate economically, often to a startling extent, the 'indigenous' majorities around them" (Chua, 2003: 6)

Chua, Amy. 2003. *World on Fire: How Exporting Free Market Democracy Breeds Ethnic Hatred and Global Instability.* New York: Anchor Books.

Overurbanization

the growth of large cities without the infrastructure to handle the urban populations, especially when a disproportionate amount of the state's population lives in one or a few such cities

Microfinance

an idea first promoted in the 1970s, to provide very small loans directly to poor individuals or families, for the purpose of starting or growing a small business

societies and sometimes destroy those societies. Ironically, Amy Chua (2003) suggested that the much-vaunted "free market" policies underlying much contemporary development planning can actually lead to escalated violence, when these reforms interact with multicultural societies in which there is a **market-dominant minority** that benefits disproportionately. The result can be protests and violence directed at the market reforms and the wealth of the minority, democracy and the power and rights of the majority, the minority group itself, or the majority group(s)—all of which have been witnessed in recent years.

■ Overurbanization. As people flee or are driven from rural areas, they tend to congregate in cities, which can result in **overurbanization**. In a few extreme cases, a single sprawling city may be home to ten percent or more of the entire state's population, such as Luanda, Angola (twenty percent of the state's total population), Brazzaville, Republic of Congo (thirty percent), Buenos Aires, Argentina (thirty percent), and Montevideo, Uruguay (over thirty-three percent). Cities in developing states, especially such densely populated ones, often lack the infrastructure—water, electricity, sewerage, the housing—or the jobs to support large dense populations, leaving people who were already marginalized now living on the margins of urban society, in shanty towns or squatter communities. The city of Mumbai in India houses sixty percent of its population in slums, and the United Nations has warned that one-third of the entire human population may inhabit slums by the year 2030.

■ Environmental degradation. Pollution, loss of forests, exhaustion of sometimes-fragile soils, destruction of habitat for animals, and general accumulation of the "garbage of development" can scar a state's territory almost irretrievably. Developing states often declare that they can and must "develop" their own resources, but the rate of disappearance of their and the world's valuable resources had become much more than a local problem. Developing states sometimes complain that Western states were free to exploit their own—as well as colonial—resources but that now they are being denied the same freedom.

IMAGE 14.4 This Gunjari village in India was submerged because of a dam project.

THE PASSING OF THE CLASSIC DEVELOPMENT MODEL

The classic approach to development came under a great deal of criticism, for a number of reasons: It promoted large expensive projects that often failed to deliver results (or failed altogether), it involved government bureaucracies and public money, and it perpetuated dependencies on foreign capital, technology, and culture. Even before the 1980s, Immanuel Wallerstein posited that poor, dependent, underdeveloped states were trapped in a "world system" that did not operate in their favor. According to his **world system theory** (1974), there is a "world economy" or a global economic system, composed of a **core**, **periphery**, and **semi-periphery**. The core of the world system contains, naturally, rich industrial states. But it also consists of those multilateral organizations designed to shape and control the world economy, such as the World Trade Organization (WTO), the G-7, GATT (the General Agreement on Tariffs and Trade), and the World Bank and IMF. The same few rich industrial states reappear in these institutions, gathering in diverse forums to design and manage the world economy in their own interests. Third, the core also includes major corporations, as we will emphasize below.

The periphery of the world system is the underdeveloped states, which are not invited to sit with the G-7 and do not have much clout in the World Bank. The periphery merely feeds the core and takes orders from it. It is dependent. Meanwhile, the semi-periphery is composed of the states "in the middle" or "in transition," since it is possible (though not at all easy) to move from periphery to core. States that have been successful in their industrialization, like South Korea, Brazil, Indonesia, and especially China and India, are moving from periphery to semi-periphery, while states that were formerly core like Spain and Portugal have moved out to semi-periphery. In many ways, the classic development model depends on this world system—and also perpetuates it.

Since around 1980, a number of alternatives to the classic development approach have appeared. Microfinance focuses on the small-scale assistance, while neoliberalism empowers the private sector rather than the state.

Microfinance

As noted, classic development is not only business, but *big* business, usually implicating governments, banks, large corporations, and huge sums of money in vast projects like dams and roads. The value of such projects to actual poor people is questionable, and often the damage outweighs the gains. An innovative and promising new direction in development is to make small loans, sometimes only a few dollars, directly to poor individuals and families, which they can invest in their own products or businesses. Known as **microfinance** or microcredit, it was first attempted in Brazil in the 1970s but was more formally instituted in Bangladesh by economist Muhammad Yunus (b. 1940) after he toured impoverished and war-ravaged villages. His encounters suggested that credit offered to struggling households could yield dramatic positive results. (His first loan, $27 of his own money, went to forty-two women in the village of Jobra; interestingly, many of microfinance's borrowers are women.) Since major banks were reluctant to loan such trivial amounts to "non-credit-worthy" borrowers, Yunus eventually founded his own bank, the Grameen ("village/rural") Bank, in 1983. Grameen Bank has continued to make money available to individuals and families, as well as supporting irrigation, telecommunications, and other local projects. Grameen is today one of numerous microfinance institutions that loan directly to poor rural people. Some, like Kiva, allow citizens from around the world to contribute to—and even to select specific projects or individuals to receive—small-scale self-development in needy countries.

Neoliberalism

As mentioned above, "structural adjustment" became a buzzword around 1980, indicating a sea change in ideas about development. Classic development called upon governments to lead in planning and implementing change. Structural adjustment envisioned a diminished role for government, relying instead on practices and incentives emphasizing the market. These adjustments contributed to "opening" or "freeing" local markets to goods and investment from other societies.

World system theory
the theory that explains the ongoing poverty and low standard of living in Third World states as the effect of external arrangements and relationships, specifically the global economic and political practices and institutions set up by the "core" of rich, powerful, industrialized states that function to their own advantage but to the disadvantage of the poor, weak, "peripheral" states

Wallerstein, Immanuel. 1974. *The Modern World-System: Capitalist Agriculture and the Origins of the European World-Economy in the Sixteenth Century.* New York: Academic Press.

www.wto.org/; www.imf.org/external/index.htm; www.cfr.org/international-organizations-and-alliances/group-seven-g7/p32957

Core
in dependency/world system theory, the states that make up the power-center of the world system, essentially the rich industrial states and former colonialists

Periphery
in dependency or world system theory, the societies and states that have the least wealth and power and the least influence on the practices and policies in the global economy

www.kiva.org

Semi-periphery
in Wallerstein's world system theory, the states "in the middle" of the core and the periphery or "in transition" from the periphery due to their successful development and industrialization

IMAGE 14.5 Indian women attending a presentation on microfinancing.

Neoliberalism

according to David Harvey, a theory of political economic practices that proposes that human well-being can best be advanced by liberating individual entrepreneurial freedoms and skills within an institutional framework characterized by strong private property rights, free markets, and free trade

In recent years, these policies have evolved into a concept known as **neoliberalism**, which hearkens back to the earlier notion of "liberalism" or "laissez-faire" economics. The basic idea of liberalism was to "liberate" the productive energies of individuals and businesses by reducing government interference in and regulation of the economy. Neoliberalism has since become a standard way to talk about the modern world: One group of anthropologists determined that the number of anthropological articles mentioning neoliberalism quadrupled in one year, from 2004 to 2005 (Hoffman, DeHart, and Collier, 2006: 9). David Harvey, in *A Brief History of Neoliberalism*, gave this influential characterization of neoliberalism:

> Neoliberalism is in the first instance a theory of political economic practices that proposes that human well-being can best be advanced by liberating individual entrepreneurial freedoms and skills within an institutional framework characterized by strong private property rights, free markets, and free trade. The role of the state is to create and preserve an institutional framework appropriate to such practices. The state has to guarantee, for example, the quality and integrity of money. It

> must also set up those military, defense, police, and legal structures and functions required to secure private property rights and to guarantee, by force if need be, the proper functioning of markets. Furthermore, if markets do not exist (in such areas as land, water, education, health care, social security, or environmental pollution) then they must be created, by state action if necessary. But beyond these tasks the state should not venture.

> (2005: 2)

But while it claims to serve all people equally, Harvey argues that neoliberalism tends—if not intends—to transfer power and wealth to an elite minority, providing almost colonial conditions for dependent accumulation, which he dubbed **accumulation by dispossession**. Many of its devices are indistinguishable from Frank's dependent accumulation, and signify escalations of Marx's primitive accumulation, such as

> the commodification and privatization of land and the forceful expulsion of peasant populations ([as in] Mexico and of China, where 70 million peasants are thought to have been displaced in recent times); conversion of

Accumulation by dispossession

according to David Harvey, the extraction of wealth from society and its citizens that occurs under neoliberalism, through privatization of public assets, expulsion of people from their land, national debt, slavery and forced labor, and other such tactics

various forms of property rights (common, collective, state, etc.) into exclusive private property rights (most spectacularly represented by China); suppression of rights to the commons; commodification of labor power and the suppression of alternative (indigenous) forms of production and consumption; colonial, neo-colonial, and imperial processes of appropriation of assets (including natural resources); monetization of exchange and taxation, particularly of land; the slave trade (which continues particularly in the sex industry); and usury, the national debt and, most devastating of all, the use of the credit system. . . .

(Harvey, 2005: 159)

An extraordinary example of dispossession and privatization is the decision of New Jersey Governor Chris Christie in early 2015 to sell city water systems to corporations—to essentially make municipal water private property. In Colorado, it is illegal to collect rainwater. Meanwhile, Walmart forced its way into one of Mexico's greatest cultural treasures, building a store in the shadow of the ruins of Teotihuacan.

With the state in a reduced capacity, and "class" largely discredited as a social issue, the key actors in neoliberalism become corporations. In a sense, neoliberalism is the governmentality of corporations and all of the institutions that enable global business, including states and agencies like the World Bank. Legally, corporations are "persons," and we often speak of corporations as "corporate citizens" participating in and contributing to society—although Thaddeus Guldbrandsen and Dorothy Holland (2001) called them *super-citizens* because of their dominant power compared to ordinary citizens and because of their ability to portray their private interests as general social, even popular, interests. Indeed, one of the features of neoliberal society is that more and more people put their faith in corporations while corporations gather ever more power and penetrate social life ever more thoroughly, unmaking and remaking—disorganizing and reorganizing—not only work but community and society. One new word that has been coined for the result is **precarity** (the noun form of "precarious"), in which employers shift risk and cost back to employees (e.g. by providing fewer benefits and more irregular and part-time work) while the state abandons its functions of guaranteeing services and standards of living. The result is increased vulnerability for individuals and families and, too often, increased inequality and poverty.

Precarity
the condition of vulnerability and insecurity associated with neoliberalism, as employers provide less in benefits, wages, and regular full-time work while states abandon many of their functions for regulating the economy and guaranteeing services and standards of living

NEOLIBERALISM IN MEXICO

IMAGE 14.6
Neoliberalism often exposes people to the impersonal forces of global markets. Here a woman and her daughter from the Nigerian delta stand in oily deposits resultant from a Shell oil spill.

BOX 14.3 PRECARITY IN THE AMERICAN AUTOMOBILE INDUSTRY

Saturn, a subsidiary of General Motors, billed itself as a new kind of company, "where the troubles of class conflict that characterized the 'old world' of the Detroit-area and other long-standing industrial centers had been resolved" (Kasmir, 2014: 205), where workers were well paid and part of the decision-making process. However, like many of those "old world" companies that had fled from the "Rust Belt" of northeastern and Midwestern U.S. to escape high taxes, high wages, and strong unions, Saturn built its new factory in the South (Tennessee) consistent with its "Southern Strategy" of relocating "where there was little industry and where deep-seated anti-union sentiment, racism, and racial violence were expected to keep workers unorganized" (211). Sharryn Kasmir calls this the beginning of the "long dispossession" that had workers chasing after jobs, leaving their homes and communities in the North behind and breaking—but not really remaking—social bonds. One of the first things that Saturn, like other corporations, did was to put workers, cities, and states into competition, bidding for factories and jobs and offering concessions for the privilege of hosting a factory. Saturn got employees to sign a contract separate from the national union surrendering pay and benefits, and the company squeezed the small town of Spring Hill, Tennessee for tax relief and a free road and sewage system. Even at that, Saturn declared that its decision to build was "provisional" (216), and sure enough in 2009 the plant was halted for bankruptcy reorganization, with a plan to reopen with 1,800 employees instead of the original 7,200. Meanwhile those employees had been subjected to various kinds of instability and insecurity. The apparently generous offer of cooperation with management created divisions among workers while obfuscating the real difference between labor and management. Non-union subcontractors were hired, and a two-tiered wage scale was established, paying new hires less than senior workers. The constant threat of layoffs and plant closures, known as "whipsawing," kept workers and towns nervous, competing against each other for survival. Relocation of workers fractured relationships and communities, while shift work and long commutes strained and often broke marriages. Workers became isolated from their peers, with little socializing outside of work. And host towns saw little benefit from factories, only higher rents, property taxes, and utility costs. In the end, Kasmir concludes, Saturn—and hardly only Saturn—engaged in intentional "geographic displacement, disorganization, and individualization" (242), all hallmarks of neoliberalism, in "a slow, deliberate project of capital, aided at critical junctures by the state" (244), to render workers vulnerable and pliant.

Neocolonialism
the reconstitution of dependent relationships between states in the post-colonial era, with poor states providing land, labor, and resources to richer industrial states; although invasion and military occupation may not be involved, the inequality of the relationship can lead to exploitation reminiscent of formal colonialism

NEOLIBERALISM OR NEOCOLONIALISM?: INDIA IN AFRICA

NEOLIBERAL ISLAM: DEVELOPMENT AND SPIRITUAL DEVELOPMENT IN INDONESIA

While neoliberalism and its effects have been immanent in developed countries, they have been especially pernicious in poorer underdeveloped ones, which were already dependent and precarious. Some observers and critics have likened neoliberalism to a new kind of colonialism, a **neocolonialism**, without the armies and with a new set of actors—not surprisingly China, but perhaps more surprisingly India and some Middle Eastern states—doing the colonizing. Indeed, much of this activity is happening *between* former colonies or within the "global South." It is also occurring in unexpected cultural locations, like Islam, which has shown a remarkable capacity to be pious and neoliberal simultaneously.

BOX 14.4   CONTEMPORARY CULTURAL CONTROVERSIES: IS "FAIR TRADE" FREER THAN FREE TRADE?

One proposed remedy to combine trade with justice and environmental consciousness is "fair trade," defined by Sarah Lyon as "a form of alternative trade that seeks to improve the position of disempowered small-scale farmers through trade as a means of development" (2011: 1), primarily by guaranteeing higher prices for commodities like coffee. By 1871 wealthy land owners in Guatemala became so powerful that they "enacted exploitative land and labor measures intended to promote coffee cultivation and exportation" (26). Eventually, "Guatemala became one immense plantation." After a century of such exploitation, the U.S. Agency for International Development (USAID) began in 1970 to fund the formation of rural cooperatives, partly out of fear that poverty would attract the farmers to communism. Late in the twentieth century these cooperatives started to work with American companies and international agencies like the Fairtrade Labelling Organization (FLO) to get their coffee certified, labeled, and marketed to consumers as high in quality and fair in trade. While this action did result in higher prices for their coffee, Lyon warns of several less-positive outcomes. First, she stresses that fair trade did not focus on cultural preservation and in fact imposed a number of cultural changes on local growers, both in their social organization and their environmental practices. Second, while better paid, the growers did not necessarily feel more empowered, and cooperative programs "often serve to strengthen and entrench a small group of better-off peasants without significantly benefiting large sectors of the population" (120). Most notably, in some ways participation in fair trade networks actually *increased* the dependence of local growers, enmeshing them in global webs of governmentality that audited their products and practices, intensifying "the power that northern certifiers and roasters wield over coffee production and processing" (155). And of course the whole notion of fair trade depends on American and other consumers who are willing to pay more for the cause—or at least the image—of social justice. What do you think?

See Chapter 9

SUMMARY

The arrival of political independence did not necessarily or usually bring economic independence to postcolonial states. The old economic relations of ownership, control, production, and export did not change substantially if at all, because economic and financial institutions were already in place, settlement was not reversed, and ownership did not change hands. The result was continued economic dependence on foreign individuals, corporations, governments, markets, and agencies.

The consequences of economic dependence add up to underdevelopment, characterized by

- poverty
- low standards of living, including housing, health, and education
- mainly rural populations and agricultural or "primary" production

To alleviate these problems, development has been seen as the solution, with public and private development institutions created to guide and fund the process. The business of development, premised on policies and implemented in projects, seeks to build up the infrastructure and productive capacity of a poor state to the point where economic growth and improved living standards are possible. Development planning, often undertaken by politicians, economists, and business interests, have not always considered the environmental and social impact of their ideas, which is where anthropologists can contribute and have contributed.

The general approach to development has been informed by theories and models of development and underdevelopment, including modernization theory and dependency and world systems theory, each describing its own brand of accumulation and each with its pros and cons. However, one thing that all observers can agree on is that development is, from start to finish, a cultural and not purely economic or political affair and that many of its costs have offset its benefits, including such costs as

- displacement of people
- social disorganization
- declining health and living standards for some
- acculturation and deculturation
- destruction of the environment

Alternatives to classic development such as microfinance and neoliberalism bring individuals and corporations into the process, but also draw people into global finance systems while spreading vulnerability and instability and sometimes actually increasing inequality. However, groups impacted by development and neoliberalism have begun to organize to resist or shape these forces, as we will consider further next.

Q MCQS

Q FILL IN THE BLANKS

WWW

See Chapter 15

Key Terms

absolute poverty
accumulation by dispossession
apartheid
core
dependency theory
dependent accumulation
development
development policy
development project
diseases of development
global apartheid
gross national product (GNP)
gross national product per capita
import substitution
internal colonialism
market-dominant minority
microfinance
modernization theory
monoculture
multilateral development institutions
neocolonialism
neoliberalism
overurbanization
periphery
precarity
primary production
primitive accumulation
relative poverty
semi-periphery
social impact analysis
sociocultural appraisal
structural adjustment
world system theory

Cultural survival and revival in a globalized world

It is hard to imagine anything more modern and Western than hamburgers and rock music—unless it is the chain restaurant—and one chain restaurant associated with hamburgers and rock music is the Hard Rock Café. However, as explained on the corporate website (www.hardrock.com/corporate/ownership.aspx), Hard Rock International has been owned since 2007 by the Seminole Tribe of Florida (www.semtribe.com), who also claim to be the only Native American tribe that never signed a peace treaty with the U.S. The purchase of the Hard Rock Café corporation was not the first foray of the Seminole into big business: In 1979, the tribe opened Hollywood Seminole Bingo, "the first tribally run high-stakes bingo hall in Native North America" (Cattelino, 2011: S137), which allowed them to raise the $965 million to buy Hard Rock International. While the Seminole do not operate the Hard Rock Café as a "cultural" institution (there are no Seminole symbols or artifacts in the dining areas), tribal spokesman Max Osceola, Jr. did have these words to say about the venture:

> Our ancestors sold Manhattan for trinkets. Today, with the acquisition of the Hard Rock Café, we're going to buy Manhattan back one hamburger at a time. . . . And so to provide for the Tribe, we're looking beyond the borders, the four square borders of our reservations. We're looking not just in the United States, we're looking in the world. . . . When the British had colonies all around the world they used to say, "the sun will always shine on the union jack." Well the sun will always shine on the Seminole Hard Rock. . . . We are in 45 countries now.
>
> (quoted in Cattelino, 2011: S145)

For decades or centuries, most of the world's peoples have labored under dual burdens. One burden is the system of invasion and intervention, expropriation and even extermination that was colonialism. This system affected every part of their culture and left lasting and probably permanent legacies. The other has been a "burden of silence," in which such peoples were not able or allowed to speak for themselves or were not heard when they did. Early modern anthropologists like Franz Boas and Margaret Mead felt that their duty was to "salvage" as much of "traditional" culture as possible before it all disappeared and was silenced forever. And many cultures did disappear. Others that survived, though,

IMAGE 15.1 Hard Rock Café, owned by the Seminole Tribe.

See Chapter 14

First World
a term not commonly used anymore for the rich, powerful states in the world that dominate the international political and economic arena and consist basically of the former colonial powers

Third World
a term sometimes used to refer to the economically poor, politically and militarily weak, relatively unstable, and dependent states of the world, most of which emerged from colonialism in fairly recent history

Fourth World
a collective term for the "traditional," often small-scale and indigenous non-state societies that live inside states (frequently created by colonialism) that they do not control and in which they are the minority and typically the poorest group

acquired their own voice, understood their own plight, and expressed their own perspectives on their life and culture, on colonialism and globalization, and even on anthropology itself.

As societies newly integrated by global processes struggle to come to grips with them, they respond in various important ways. At times they have retreated into or revived their "traditional" culture, while in other cases they have abandoned "tradition" and dived headlong, voluntarily or not, into "modern" culture. More likely, though, they have made modifications and interpretations—creative and complex ones—based on memory of the past, experience of the present, and anticipation of the future. We are no longer witness to "traditional culture" (if we ever were), but to an accelerating—and increasingly self-conscious and intentional—dynamism of culture, in which "culture" itself becomes a resource or discourse in a cause or movement.

VOICES FROM ANOTHER WORLD

The previous chapter contrasted the rich Western or Westernized states and the poorer mostly post-colonial states, sometimes dubbed **First World** and **Third World**, respectively. The one thing that these worlds share is that they both consist of states. However, these two categories do not capture the experience of non-state peoples like the various Native American and Australian Aboriginal societies, the !Kung or Ju/hoansi, and so many of the world's other societies that have been the conventional subject of anthropology. These groups are sometimes designated as the **Fourth World** or indigenous peoples or First Peoples. Unlike the First and Third Worlds, the Fourth World consists of the mostly small-scale, "traditional," non-state or pre-state societies that dwell within states—states that they did not create and do not control and that ordinarily do not work in their interest. Usually the original occupants of the territory held by the state, they tend to be the poorest and weakest citizens of the state—when they are granted citizenship at all (the U.S. only bestowed citizenship on Native Americans in 1924, and Australia on Aboriginals in 1967). Because they tend to be small and not highly politically integrated, they could mount limited resistance to colonialism then and to state power and global forces today.

Many of the non-state societies that existed five hundred years ago have long since vanished. Still, according to the International Work Group for

TABLE 15.1   Indigenous peoples by select country

Continent or Country	Number of Indigenous Peoples	Percent of population
Russian Federation	41 (out of more than100 ethnic groups)	0.2 %
Canada	More than 600	2.6 %
United States	566 "federally recognized tribes"	0.9 %
Mexico	68 native languages and 364 native dialects	12.7 %
Bolivia	36	41 %
Brazil	305 ethnic groups, 274 indigenous languages	0.42 %
Australia	Approximately 500	3.0 %
China	55 recognized "ethnic minorities"	8.49 %
Indonesia	1,128 recognized ethnic groups	20–30 %
Myanmar (Burma)	More than 100 ethnic groups	32 %
Bangladesh	At least 54	2 %
India	461 "scheduled tribes," up to 635 total	8.2 %
Tanzania	125–130 ethnic groups, four of which identify as indigenous peoples	1.2 % (counting only the "indigenous" Maasai, Barabaig, Hadza, and Akie)
Gabon	50	N/A
Papua New Guinea	Around 840	N/A

Source: Mikkelsen 2014

Indigenous Affairs (www.iwgia.org), there are over five thousand surviving indigenous societies, numbering more than 370 million people. IWGIA's annual report for 2014 reminds us of "the enormous pressure indigenous peoples are facing in upholding their lands, their livelihoods and, ultimately, some of the world's most fragile and biodiversity-rich ecosystems against the ever-expanding development frontier" (Mikkelsen, 2014: 12). For a more extensive list, see http://en.wikipedia.org/wiki/List_of_indigenous_peoples.

By the early 1990s, an alarming number of indigenous societies were already considered endangered—either in danger of loss of their cultural identity or of total extinction. In Venezuela, the Piaroa had declined to five hundred members, in Brazil the Uru Eu Wau Wau and the Waimiri-Atroari numbered only three hundred each, and in the U.S. the Alaskan Eyak had been reduced to one last survivor. In some cases, while the group was large, its language and culture were disappearing. The Ainu of Japan still numbered about 25,000, but fewer than one hundred of them still spoke their own language (Verrengia, 1993). In Australia, hundreds were already gone, in the U.S. less than 150 Indian languages have survived out of several hundred pre-Columbian tongues, and in Africa

about a third of today's languages (550 out of 1400) are declining, with 250 in dire conditions. Only in the Pacific region—with more than two thousand living languages—is linguistic and cultural diversity fairly secure. The United Nations (www.unesco.org/new/en/culture/themes/endangered-languages) shares the IWGIA's view that half of the world's cultures and languages are at risk of extinction.

The threats to these groups are multiple. Frequently remote, they are beyond the vision of most people within their state and the wider world. Their comparatively low population density and economic productivity makes them prime candidates for development. Their lack of modern weapons and (but not always) political integration makes armed resistance futile, and their lack of political clout makes political resistance difficult though not impossible. Their susceptibility to some of the diseases and vices of development has crippled many of them. Malaria, cholera, influenza, smallpox, AIDS, not to mention alcoholism and other social problems, have taken a great toll.

Indigenous people have lost much in the advance of colonialism, development, state integration, and globalization. These losses have involved two kinds of "property"—their land and other physical or symbolical property, such as their

See Chapter 14

IMAGE 15.2 Many indigenous societies are in danger of extinction, like the Akuntsu of South America, who are down to their last six survivors. Their numbers continue to decline.

Griaule, Marcel. 1965.
*Conversations with
Ogotemelli: An Introduction
to Dogon Religious Ideas.*
London: Oxford
University Press.

Shostak, Marjorie. 1983
[1981]. *Nisa: The Life and
Words of a !Kung Woman.*
New York: Vintage Books.

Neihardt, John G. 1961.
*Black Elk Speaks: Being the
Life Story of a Holy Man of
the Oglala Sioux.* Lincoln:
University of Nebraska
Press.

**NATIVE AMERICAN
INDEPENDENCE: THE
REPUBLIC OF LAKOTAH**

See Chapter 12

**SHERMAN ALEXIE ON
"IMAGINING THE
RESERVATION"**

artifacts, knowledge, and the very bodies of their ancestors. In former days, anthropologists and archaeologists would collect objects and human remains virtually at will and carry them away for study and storage. However, in both domains, indigenous people have made gains in re-establishing control. For instance, in 1990 the Native American Graves Protection and Repatriation Act (NAGPRA) went into effect, requiring that all federally funded organizations (including universities and museums) in the U.S. catalog their holdings of Indian human remains and artifacts, inform the societies from which the materials originated, and return the materials if requested. It also outlawed trafficking in illegal human or cultural materials. A 1992 Australian court decision called *Mabo and Others v. Queensland* declared that Eddie Mabo and his Aboriginal co-plaintiffs had property rights to their traditional homelands; instead of the presumption of *terra nullius* and state ownership, courts would have to presume native ownership unless the state could prove that there were no traditional owners or that they had voluntarily relinquished ownership (for example, through a treaty, of which there were none in Australia).

Meanwhile, individually and collectively, indigenous peoples have raised their voices, in all sorts of media. A few have even trained as anthropologists. Others have used art, song, and writing (both fiction and nonfiction) to express facts, feelings,

and fears. Chinua Achebe's 1959 *Things Fall Apart* about the traditions and contact experiences of an African society, Mary Crow Dog's 1990 biography *Lakota Woman*, Leslie Marmon Silko's 1977 *Ceremony* about Pueblo Indian life and culture, and Sherman Alexie's 1994 *The Lone Ranger and Tonto Fistfight in Heaven* about life on the reservation are just four well-known examples. Anthropologists too have found ways to assist native peoples in telling their stories and speaking to the world, as in Griaule's (1965) conversations with Dogon elder Ogotemelli, Shostak's (1983) life of the Ju/hoansi woman Nisa, or John Neihardt's (1961) account of the life and visions of Lakota elder Black Elk.

FROM CULTURE TO CULTURAL MOVEMENT

It is clear that culture was never static, closed, and homogeneous; rather, it has always been (more or less, depending on the place and time) dynamic, open, and complex and heterogeneous. As a system of *adaptation*, it only stands to reason that humans would adapt ever-changing cultural forms and expressions as circumstances or simply membership changed over time. And when circumstances changed especially rapidly or unfavorably, the form of those new adaptations would be more dramatic and total.

IMAGE 15.3 Indigenous Aymara of Bolivia marching in 2006 in support of new president Evo Morales.

Bronislaw Malinowski, despite his reputation as a functionalist and at a time when colonialism seemed ascendant, foresaw these profound cultural effects. The unprecedented cultural encounters in the twentieth century were leading to novel cultural outcomes, which were not a mere continuation of "tradition," a passive adoption of Western styles and practices, or a simple mingling of the two. Rather, the cultural changes were constructions of something original; commenting on the scene in Africa, he wrote, "They are one and all entirely new products [with] no antecedents in Europe or in African tribalism" (1961: 25), although of course the same could be said about the entire world. What he observed were "new cultural realities"—but even more, cultural developments with a new attitude toward "culture." Even when culture appeared to be changing in the direction of "tradition," he noted that the "elements of the old culture [were] being revived with a secondary, almost *ethnographic* interest in racial history, customary law, and the artistic and intellectual achievements of their race" (158, emphasis added). In other words, "natives" were becoming something like anthropologists of their own culture—which meant their "traditional culture" was already somewhat "foreign" to them.

In many of their new circumstances and relations, people (and not just indigenous people) experienced dissatisfaction and frustration, from mild to extreme. Their land, livelihood, liberty, and very lives were under attack. Often it seemed that their identity was eroding or disappearing; hence there was a widespread urge to protect or re-establish identity, on the basis of culture. But a culture or identity re-established is not quite the same as a pristine or "traditional" one. A common result was and is a "cultural movement" in which the group acts intentionally to fix, save, or restore some aspect(s) of culture. And while culture is continuously in motion, there is a major difference between "culture in motion" and "a cultural movement." Cultural movements are much more self-conscious, even "ethnographic," as the groups engaging in them experience their cultures in new ways—particularly, as "problems" and "resources." Cultural movements could be understood as yet another instance of "will to improve." Also, cultural movements tend to be more argumentative and mobilized than mere cultures-in-motion. They can be positively militant, like the effort of ISIS (Islamic

See Chapter 11

Malinowski, Bronislaw. 1961 [1945]. *The Dynamics of Culture Change: An Inquiry into Race Relations in Africa.* New Haven and London: Yale University Press.

See Chapter 14

Revitalization movement

according to Anthony Wallace (1956), the deliberate, organized, and self-conscious effort of a society to create a more satisfying culture

Wallace, Anthony F. C. 1956. "Revitalization Movements." *American Anthropologist* 58 (2): 264–281.

See Chapter 14

Syncretism

a type of revitalization movement in which elements of two or more cultural sources are blended into a new and more satisfying cultural arrangement

Cargo cult

a form of revitalization movement, most associated with early-twentieth century Pacific island societies, in which indigenous peoples adopted aspects of Western cultures and modified or abandoned aspects of pre-contact culture on the expectation of receiving shipments of wealth or "cargo," often from the dead ancestors

Worsley, Peter. 1968. *The Trumpet Shall Sound: A Study of "Cargo Cults" in Melanesia.* New York: Shocken Books.

Lawrence, Peter. 1964. *Road Belong Cargo.* Manchester: Manchester University Press.

See Chapter 2

State in Iraq and Syria) to revive the Muslim caliphate.

Cultural movements aimed at reviving or repairing a damaged culture or identity are sometimes called **revitalization movements**. Revitalization movements, as described by Anthony Wallace (1956: 265), are conscious, deliberate, and organized efforts on the part of some member(s) of a society to create a new, better, and more satisfying culture. As such, they are a special type of self-directed change. Like all other instances of change, whether arising from innovation or diffusion, revitalization efforts have certain consistent characteristics:

1. They appear at moments of cultural stress—when past ideas and actions no longer produce satisfactory results, especially when foreign influences or persons have disturbed the balance of the society.
2. They are usually the inspiration of one person or at most a few people. Certain individuals detect the "culture crisis" before others, and their inspiration often comes in the form of a dream, a vision, or a near-death experience.
3. They go through a process of acceptance, rejection, or modification. Members of the society may join or ignore the movement, and elders and traditionalists may actively oppose it. Outside forces may also oppose it as a threat to their domination.
4. They begin as unfamiliar, often "heretical" or "cultish" phenomena, but if they catch on they become "mainstream."
5. They can have unanticipated, undesired, and even undesirable consequences.
6. There may be more than one such movement occurring in the same society at any time, sometimes with opposing goals. Differing and rival movements and movement leaders may vie for the attention and loyalty of the society, each offering a solution to the society's troubles.
7. The movement, if it survives, will "routinize" and institutionalize—either as the new "mainstream" or as a more constricted alternative or specialty within the society.

Revitalization movements can take many forms. Very often, especially in their early outbreaks, they are religious in nature (see below). Subsequently or

in combination, they can take a political shape; in fact, all such movements are probably "political" in the sense that they seek to modify the order of society, including its power arrangements and norms and rules. Despite their diversity, however, there are a few recurring components or qualities of cultural or revitalization movements. Any actual movement may exhibit one or more of these features or "types."

Syncretism

Syncretism means the mixing or blending of elements from two or more cultural sources to produce a new, third, better culture or system. In a very real sense, all culture is syncretistic; humans are forever borrowing from various sources and combining them in ways to produce whatever it is they call eventually "their culture" or "their tradition." Of course, this borrowing and combining is not always deliberate or clearly recognized, but no culture, religion, or any other human activity is "pure" or "original" in any significant or meaningful way. All humans live in a melting pot of culture.

Among the most colorful syncretistic movements in the anthropological literature are the so-called "**cargo cults**" that swept through the Pacific Islands, particularly Melanesia and the southwest regions, between about 1900 and 1950 (see Lawrence, 1964; Worsley, 1968). During the two World Wars, thousands of Western soldiers came ashore and, even more remarkably, unloaded caches of goods the likes of which no local had ever seen. Islanders could have no idea where these people and their goods came from; the one thing they knew was that the strangers had a lot of "cargo" and that they never seemed to work for any of it. They stood around, marched around, sat around, but they never produced anything—yet they had this inconceivable largesse.

Cargo cults were an indigenous attempt to make sense of this new situation and, quite literally, to get some cargo for themselves. One of the first and best-known examples is the "Vailala madness" that broke out in 1917 among the Elema people of Papua. After failing to incorporate the foreigners into their native economic system of reciprocity by giving them gifts, a man named Evara began teaching that people needed to practice specific

IMAGE 15.4 Pacific Islanders adopted aspects of Western culture—including marching in formation with mock rifles—in their cargo cults.

religious observances, including trances and jerky body movement and speech, which seemed so pathological to outsiders that it was dubbed "madness." If people destroyed parts of their traditional culture and replaced them with parts of the foreign culture, Evara believed, they could conjure cargo ships of their own. Accordingly, traditional religious and ceremonial items were discarded, gardens and animals were untended or destroyed, and imitative gestures toward Western culture were made (for instance, a pretend radio was built to talk to the phantom cargo ship). Evara prophesied that these changes would call forth a ship laden with cargo piloted by their dead ancestors, who would establish a better and happier culture for the Elema. Needless to say, it did not happen.

BOX 15.1   BLENDING OLD AND NEW IN YALI'S CULT

Cargo cults tended to involve mimicking aspects of Western religious, behavioral, and moral behavior in order to access the wealth that Westerners possessed, "based on the natives' belief that European goods (cargo) . . . are not man-made but have to be obtained from a non-human or divine source" (Lawrence, 1964: 1). However, Julia Zamorska saw such movements as much more than efforts to be rich but as "ways of adaptation, adjustment to a new situation, attempts to find a new place in the changing world and ways of searching for a new definition of Melanesian culture and a redefined cultural identity of the native people" (1998: 7). Louise Morauta described the complex interplay between the native/local and the foreign/global in the so-called "Yali cult," which erupted in the Madang region of New Guinea in the 1960s. The area had a history of cargo cults reaching back to the 1920s. Yali Singha became the leader of a widespread movement, covering more than two hundred villages whose representatives followed his teachings, held meetings, and collected offerings for him. The size of Yali's movement was unusual, most previous and contemporary cargo cults (for his was not the only one in the vicinity) being smaller and more local, sometimes restricted to a single village. At the same time, Yali's movement had two contradictory features. First, it was relatively centralized, with "local bosses" answering to Yali; it was more regularized and standardized than most movements, conducted in pidgin (the hybrid of native and foreign language) rather than the indigenous language, and "not limited to traditional channels of communication" (1972: 436). Yet his followers were a distinct minority in the area: In some villages he had no supporters at all, and most villages were divided between members and non-members. Significantly, the villages where Yali had little or no support were those most effectively integrated into the colonial system, linked by roads providing jobs, schools, and hospitals. Yali was actively opposed by the local Lutheran Church as well as those who favored the colonial administration and modern economic development. Yali's influence was strongest in the more remote and less acculturated villages, where literacy and income were lower and where, most importantly, many of the precolonial practices and institutions that had provided social cohesion had broken down. Yali's movement seemed to offer not only a new means of social integration and of material success but a new political vision and identity. It was both traditional and modernizing, uniting residents of disparate villages into a regional and potentially national society; his movement exploited internal divisions within villages to "forge strong links between villages" (446), to serve the needs of a partially de-traditionalized society that sought more than cargo but also a way to relate to each other and to the outside world.

Millenarianism

a type of revitalization movement aimed at preparing for and perhaps bringing about the end of the "present era," however that era is understood, and replacing it with a new and better existence

MILLENNIUM ON THE SUBWAY: AUM SHINRIKYO

Irredentism

a revitalization movement to reclaim a lost homeland

Another example of a syncretistic movement, during which twenty or thirty million people died, was the Taiping Rebellion in China (1850–1864), one of a number of such movements after the Opium Wars and the colonial carve-up of China. The Taiping movement (from the Chinese *Taiping tien-quo* for Heavenly Kingdom of Great Peace) began with one man, Hung Xiuquan (also Hsiu-chuan), who, after a personal crisis and a near-death experience, received a series of visions of an old man (supposedly God) who warned that people had stopped worshipping him and taken to the worship of demons. Hung was to battle these demons, as he was in fact the second son of God and the younger brother of Jesus. In the 1840s, his religious community was reorganized into a holy army, and in 1851 he declared the Taiping tien-quo a theocratic state with himself as the Heavenly King. His heavenly host marched against the government, capturing the city of Nanking in 1853 and from there attacking Beijing. The imperial government resisted for a decade until Hung's death in June 1864 and the end of a conflict that claimed millions of lives in the hopes of a better day.

Millenarianism

Millenarianism (from the Latin *mille* for "thousand") is a familiar concept to Western culture and

Christianity. The point of millenarianism is not a thousand-year period (since not all cultures use base-ten), but the notion that the current time-period will end soon. Thus, **millenarianism** is based on the conception that the present era of the world (an inferior, unhappy, or wicked one) is coming to a close and that a superior era is approaching. The followers of the movement must either prepare for the coming change or actively set the change in motion.

Millenarianism is common in movements among large-scale modern societies as well as small-scale traditional ones. The cargo cults and the Taiping rebellion had millenarian aspects, as did the well-known "Ghost Dance" movement among Native Americans in the late 1800s. Ghost Dancers believed that performing the special dance and wearing particular symbols and clothing would make the dancers impervious to white weapons, bring back their dead ancestors, and ultimately restore their land and independence to them. The failed armageddons of the Aum Shinrikyo and Heaven's Gate are only two of the more recent instances.

Irredentism

Irredentism (from the Italian *irredenta* for "un-redeemed") is any movement intended to reclaim and re-occupy a lost homeland. As such, irredentism is at the heart of many ethnic conflicts in the modern world. The Tamil struggle in Sri Lanka was an irredentist movement, to (re)create and (re)occupy the homeland of Tamil Eelam. At least part of the motivation for the Yugoslavian wars of the 1990s was irredentist, Serbs reclaiming Serb territory, especially the heartland of Kosovo lost in 1389. The Zionist movement, beginning officially in the late 1800s but with much older roots, claimed as its goal the recreation of a Jewish national state in the Jewish "holy land." Zionists like Theodore Herzl, author of the 1896 *The Jewish State*, worked toward returning to their lost homeland, from which they had been dispersed for nearly two thousand years. The subsequent establishment of the modern state of Israel in Palestine in 1948 was the culmination

of this movement. Contemporary irredentists like the Jewish fundamentalist group *Gush Emunim* (The Bloc of the Faithful) not only support the recovery of their ancient homeland, but seek to expand it, ideally "from the Euphrates River in Iraq to the Brook of Egypt" (Aran, 1991: 268).

Modernism/vitalism

Modernism, also termed **vitalism**, includes movements to import and integrate alien cultural ways, in part or in total. Some societies, when they encountered Western colonial power, determined that the best course was to adopt the foreign culture, at least in its essential aspects, to empower themselves to resist and perhaps even join the

Modernism
a type of revitalization movement intended to adopt the characteristics of a foreign and "modern" society, in the process abandoning some or all of the "traditional" characteristics of the society undergoing the movement. Also termed *vitalism*

Vitalism
see *modernism*

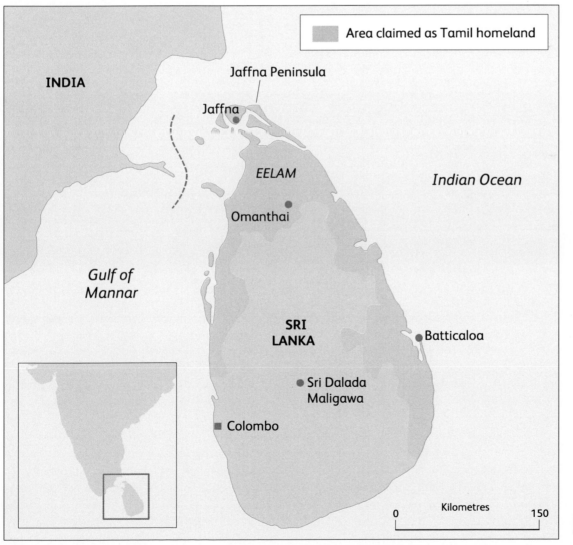

MAP 15.1 Sri Lanka and "Tamil Eelam"

See Chapters 1, 7, 9, 12, and 14

Nativism

a type of revitalization movement aimed at perpetuating, restoring, or reviving "traditional" cultural practices or characteristics, which are thought to be the source of the group's strength and to be threatened or lost

Traditionalism

a form of revitalization movement intended to preserve or restore "tradition" as that tradition is remembered or imagined by members of the movement

Fundamentalism

a type of cultural or revitalization movement in which members attempt to address perceived social problems or disadvantages by restoring the perceived "fundamentals" or oldest, most important, and most "genuine" elements of culture

international political system. Japan presents probably the best example of a successful vitalistic movement. Japan was almost completely isolated before the mid-1800s. However, its rulers watched with interest as Europeans forced the Opium Wars and then colonialism and spheres of influence on the defeated Chinese. When American Commodore Matthew Perry arrived with his flotilla of gunships in the Tokyo harbor in 1854, the Japanese shōgun accepted trade and relations with America. Very quickly, Japan began to adapt itself to this new contact, sending observers to Europe and America to study Western culture and technology, particularly railroad and military technologies. Japanese students were sent to foreign schools and colleges. English was widely learned, and Western-style music and dress were embraced. By 1868, a revolution was underway, known as the Meiji (Japanese for "enlightenment") revolution. A modern-style constitution was written, the feudal system was abolished, mass state-sponsored education was established, and concentrated efforts to industrialize and to modernize the army were made. Even symbolic signs like Western haircuts became important; instead of the long hair of the traditional samurai, barbered hair was the fashion. (A saying of the time was, "If you slap a barbered head, it rings 'civilization and enlightenment.'") This modernist/vitalist movement was so successful that, within forty years of the Meiji revolution, Japan became the first non-European state to defeat a European state in war (Russia in 1904–1905). Of course, like all vitalistic movements, there was not a wholesale replacement of local culture with foreign culture. Japan did not jettison the Japanese language, nor Japanese political, economic, or social values. Its "modernization" and industrialization pursued a distinctly Japanese path, emphasizing social duty over individualism, order over competition, and government or business cooperation over disengagement and regulation.

Vitalist/modernist movements employ all of the tactics and techniques of modern society. These include of course print, radio and television, and electronic media, as well as political organization, such as the formation of political parties. Schools and other modern cultural institutions, like museums, are part of modernist revitalization, as are arts, music, food, and other aspects of culture. One of the key modern institutions, as we have

stressed throughout this book, is the corporation. Not surprisingly, many indigenous societies have adopted the corporate form, some buying a corporation (like the Seminole), some founding corporations or even *becoming* corporations. For example, the Bafokeng Nation is a "traditional" kingdom as well as a modern enterprise, "one of South Africa's largest community-based investment companies" (Cook, 2011: S151). Not only do the Bafokeng run a complex modern political system, but Royal Bafokeng Holdings manages the society's mining interests in platinum and chrome along with a non-mining investment portfolio, totaling $4.15 billion in 2008. The Bafokeng Nation operated with a budget of $150 million in 2009, over half of which was invested in the community for infrastructure, education, and social programs (S155). A few other examples of indigenous corporations, offering their services for sale to others, include Hawaiian Native Corporation (www.hnchawaii.org), Gumula Aboriginal Corporation (www.gumala.com.au), Juluwarlu Group Aboriginal Corporation (www.yindjibarndi.org.au/ juluwarlu/index.php), Maori Mega Mall (www.themaorimegamall.com), and the many Alaskan Native Regional Corporations established since 1971 (fairbanks-alaska.com/alaska-native-corporations.htm).

Nativism/traditionalism/fundamentalism

At the opposite end of the spectrum are nativist, traditionalist, or fundamentalist movements. **Nativism, traditionalism,** or **fundamentalism** emphasizes local or "traditional" culture and values and resistance to or even elimination of alien culture and values. Unlike the Japanese, the Chinese response to colonialism was nativistic. Chinese society considered itself superior to European in every imaginable way, and they could not conceive of themselves falling prey to such backward barbarians. The emperor showed no interest in and strictly forbade European toys like trains and clocks, and the Chinese leadership was sure that it could strengthen itself by relying on completely native resources. In other words, China (and many other societies) attempted to become more "traditional." In the late twentieth and early twenty-first centuries, some societies and states have gone

BOX 15.2   KOREAN MODERNISM AGAINST JAPANESE COLONIALISM

We easily assume that religion is inherent in fundamentalism, but during Japanese colonialism in Korea (1910–1945), Christianity was a central element of modernism; indeed, Kyusik Chang explains that Korean thinkers "accepted Christianity not as a religion but as a driving force behind the country's push toward a modern society" (2014: 119). Christianity was seen as part of the modern liberal culture of the West, and "Protestantism was adopted by the leading class of the local society in P'yŏngyang Province in the context of the affinity between the new social order of civil society and commoners' traditional self-government in the region" (121). Christianity in Korea had an especially Korean quality and agenda, where the middle class "operated churches by themselves without relying on missionaries"; this same class "established modern educational institutions and began social movements" (123), opposing liberal Protestantism to Japanese domination. Organizations like Young Korean Association and Young Korean Academy were dedicated to nation-building and character-building through "a trinity of the cultural, educational and industrial, and political movements in each sector of society" (124). Marking this blend of economics and religion were two key institutions, the Society for the Promotion of Korean Production (which sought to modernize industry and promote the consumption of Korean-made products) and the YMCA. Founded in 1921, the P'yŏngyang YMCA, whose board members were also mostly supporters of the Society for the Promotion of Korean Production, saw the Christian organization as the means by which "they would build the Kingdom of God on earth, full of humanity and justice . . . and the spiritual, mental, and physical training of young men" (127). YMCA leaders like Cho Man-sik went on to found the Association of Commerce and Industry "to support the development of Korean businessmen" and reformed the Soong-in Middle School "as a commercial school dedicated to producing outstanding business minds" (130). Improving Korean living conditions, he believed, required reshaping Korean society and even individual consciousness and even physical fitness—for which he also led the Sports Association of Northwest Korea—and Korea's eventual liberation from Japanese rule would be "the first step toward the Kingdom of God on earth" (131). In sum, the "nation-building project that comprised the fostering of the public as modern individuals, the establishment of a foundation for civil society, and the organization of a public sphere in the political realm based on public opinion" all involved the perception of Christianity "as a symbol of modernity in Korea" and a driving force of that modernity (134–135).

so far as to isolate themselves totally from the outside world. Burma (or Myanmar today) is a tightly closed society, North Korea cuts itself off effectively, and Cambodia under the Khmer Rouge and Pol Pot forcibly eradicated foreign and modern influences, including urbanization, education, and eyeglasses, as portrayed in the movie *The Killing Fields*. However, as these cases illustrate, extreme nativist or isolationist societies tend to end up impoverished, paranoid, and dangerous (to others and to themselves).

Nativism/traditionalism/fundamentalism, even more so than the other types of revitalization, is a resistance movement based on difference—*the rejection of difference* as experienced in modern, foreign, or secular influences and the advancement or exaggeration of what makes the group unique or authentic. It is a way of distancing the "other" by emphasizing the "authentic." Different groups naturally find different things to oppose, but from a non-Western and postcolonial perspective, often Western culture itself is the enemy, as Hasan al-Banna, founder of the "fundamentalist" Muslim Brotherhood, said:

Just after the First World War and during my stay in Cairo, the wave of atheism and lewdness engulfed Egypt. It started the devastation of religion and morality on the pretext of individual and intellectual freedom. Nothing could stop this storm.

[Westerners introduced] their half-naked women. . ., their liquors, their theaters, their dance halls, their amusements, their stories, their newspapers, their novels, their whims, their silly games, and their vices [as well as] schools and scientific and cultural institutions in the very heart of the Islamic domain, which cast doubt and heresy into the souls of its sons and taught them how to demean themselves, disparage their religion and their fatherland, divest themselves of their traditions and beliefs, and to regard as sacred anything Western.

See Chapter 11

(quoted in Voll, 1991: 360–361)

Thus, nativist/traditionalist/fundamentalist movements see themselves as returning to the original, "traditional," pure state of their culture. The family of movements in Islam known as Salafism are good examples. Derived from the word *salafiyyah* for ancestors or early years, Salafist movements harken back to the era of Muhammad and the first Muslims, who serve as models for today's impure society. Like all nativists/traditionalists/fundamentalists, Salafists have a propensity to turn militant, but others simply promote piety and Islamic lifestyles.

One ironic fact is that nativism/traditionalism/fundamentalism is itself culturally relative and wonderfully modern. Since we now know that "tradition" is culturally relative, it is necessarily true that "militant tradition" is relative too. First, all cultures or traditions have their fundamentalisms;

BOX 15.3   "ABYSSINIAN FUNDAMENTALISM" AND ETHNIC CONFLICT IN ETHIOPIA

Nativism/traditionalism/fundamentalism is not only a kind of movement, but a kind of imagination, even fantasy, about the past and about present identity, as becomes immanent in the "ethnic" struggle between Ethiopians and Eritreans. Both Ethiopia and the coastal province of Eritrea have ancient histories, although never until recently as a single unified state. An Italian business, Rubattino Shipping Company, bought part of modern-day Eritrea in 1869–1870, and "Italian Eritrea" was founded as a colony in 1889. A boundary between Ethiopia and Eritrea was settled in a 1902 treaty, but Ethiopia claimed the region after Europeans withdrew. Conflict between the Ethiopian state and Eritrean separatists continued until 1991, when the Tigrayan People's Liberation Front (TPLF) defeated the government, dominating the state and becoming "more repressive, imprisoning and murdering opponents" (Sorenson and Matsuoka, 2001: 40). Not surprisingly, many non-Eritrean Ethiopians experienced this reversal as not only a political disaster, but as "a violation of the ancient entity that provided a sense of pride, belonging and national identity" (40), to which they applied the pre-modern name "Abyssinia." In sources like the magazine *Ethiopian Review* and online, an "Abyssinian fundamentalism" emerged, portraying "threats to Ethiopian identity as explicitly foreign, alien intrusions that disrupt appropriate relations within the national family" (44). While Ethiopia was envisioned as an authentic continuous civilization, Etrirea was condemned as inauthentic, as a product of colonial "false consciousness, a betrayal of Ethiopian identity rooted in the ancient past" (44). One Abyssinian activist, Getachew Mekasha, quoted in Sorenson and Matsuoka, declared that, "Only a return to traditional norms and values can bring a new revival of the national spirit . . . the nation feels the urgent need to rediscover itself and stop experimenting with newfangled alien ideas" (45). One past institution that some advocated was the monarchy, once again crowning an Ethiopian emperor. Fundamentalists also denied that Eritreans had any legitimate grievances against the Ethiopian state, rather seeing themselves as victims of Eritrean treachery. When fighting broke out in 1997, not only did Ethiopian authorities kill or deport thousands of Eritreans, but "Ethiopians cheered this devastation as a great national victory" (54), and many fundamentalists seemed to thirst for more violence. Like fundamentalists everywhere, Abyssinian fundamentalists "experienced a renewal of their own fantasies of national identity" by denying, opposing, and eradicating the "other" in their midst (60).

there are Christian fundamentalisms and Islamic fundamentalisms and Jewish fundamentalisms and Hindu fundamentalisms, etc. *Hindutva*, for instance, is a modern movement to claim India as the exclusive national homeland of Hindus and to impose Hindu religion and culture on the society. Further, each fundamentalist movement has different goals and picks and chooses from "the fundamentals" of its doctrine and history. Religion's relation to nativism is ambiguous: As the Korean case above indicates, religion is not always a force of anti-modernism, nor do all nativist/fundamentalist movements invoke religion. Even when a movement is undeniably religious and fundamentalist, it may still mix religion with political and modern other elements; ISIS/Islamic State has no qualms with video, the internet, or its glossy magazine *Dabiq* (see www.clarionproject.org/news/islamic-state-isis-isil-propaganda-magazine-dabiq), let alone guns and bombs.

THE FUTURE OF CULTURE, AND THE CULTURE OF THE FUTURE

Cultural movements reveal in starker contrast what the study of "normal" (or non-crisis) cultural dynamics shows: If humans make their culture, if culture is in the end a social construct, not a given fact, then humans can and will remake their culture again and again. Whether it is colonialism or development or syncretism or fundamentalism, culture is always on the move, as humans think of new things, reinterpret old things, encounter new things from other groups, and respond to new situations and circumstances. The fiction that culture is static can no longer be believed.

"Culture" and "tradition" seem oriented to the past. However, today we can see that this is more ideology than reality. Culture and tradition invoke the past, but humans are ultimately oriented toward the future. The main question for humans is always, "Who are we today and who will we be tomorrow?" A powerful answer to this question, or a key resource for thinking about the answer, is the past. As humans grapple toward and construct their future, they inevitably select, examine, and assemble the bits and shards of broken and vanished pasts to create that future—partly because those pasts constitute the lenses through which they view the present and future, and partly because those pasts constitute the primary, though not only, raw materials with which to build.

Once upon a time, and still in many locations for many individuals, the construction of culture was an "invisible," spontaneous, or unself-conscious process. Increasingly in the world today, cultural construction is conspicuous, self-conscious, and even belligerent. Individuals, groups, parties, classes, races, genders, etc. assert that the culture is theirs to make—that culture is not just a construction, nor even just a "negotiation," but a contest and struggle. In the process, many partisans have achieved Malinowski's "ethnographic" attitude toward their own culture, seeing it *as culture* and not just as what they have always been or done unproblematically.

The culture of "modernity" and after

Much of the discussion about culture today centers on the notion of "modern" culture or "modernity." Scholars have viewed Western society as in the condition of "modernity" for at least a couple of, or as many as several, centuries. Since the European Enlightenment (1700s) and arguably as far back as the Renaissance (1400s–1500s), a distinct cultural complex dubbed "modern" has been in effect, with some specific assumptions:

- Rationalism—The world, including the human/social world, is rationally knowable, and rationally controllable, because it is seen as orderly, consistent, and therefore predictable.
- Progress—The general ethos, fueled by advances in knowledge and science and by growth in economic and political power, is that things improve over time. Progress is not only desirable but inevitable.
- Optimism—Therefore, modernity is characterized by an overall positive outlook: What we do not know today we will know tomorrow, and what we know tomorrow will aid us in making a better world the day after. Particularly in the "social sciences" that arose in the 1700s and 1800s, the attitude was that, by manipulating culture, we could construct a better society composed of better people.

VARIETIES OF CHRISTIAN FUNDAMENTALISM IN THE U.S.

- Integration—The early modern period leaned toward ever larger (and happier) conglomerations of humans, including "modern" states out of disparate polities and societies. Societies that were already "integral," like England for the most part, became internally connected with new systems of canals, roads, and ultimately railroads. Other societies that were not yet integral but that shared cultural commonalities, like Germans or Italians, struggled toward integration with "culture" as their guide. Colonialism represented the largest possible integration, into a few imperial systems. The expectation was that small, independent, "traditional" identities and allegiances would give way to the larger, interdependent "modern" ones.

- Bureaucratization—Instead of the subjective and personal leadership of kings, princes, chiefs, or headmen, society would become more organized and impersonal, with various departments headed by professionals making decisions relevant to their jurisdiction and expertise. All aspects of society, from law to the economy to the family, become more "rational" and less arbitrary.

- Secularization—A final but perhaps pervasive assumption is an inherent secularization or detachment of civil society, especially the government and the economy, from religion. It was widely predicted that religion would lose its importance and perhaps disappear altogether.

These qualities have often been construed as the essence of modern culture, although anthropologists and others increasingly regard them as distinct to modern *Western* culture (see below).

Already by the late 1800s, a few sensitive types were questioning the triumph of modernity, even in the West. Nietzsche, Freud, and others began to criticize rationalism, objectivity, mass integration, and all the other conceits of modern society. They emphasized the irrational in human life (the "will to power" or the "unconscious"), and they often despaired of the homogenization that was transpiring under capitalism, democracy, and mass culture. The proof of human irrationality and of the danger of modernity seemed to come in the form of World War I (1914–1918), which shocked people more than we can comprehend today. Citizens who

prized their rationality, their progressivism, their optimism, etc. were horrified at their behavior in the trenches, at their capacity and even thirst for destruction. When the Spanish Civil War (1936–1939) and World War II (1939–1945) followed, it became increasingly more difficult to maintain the rosy predictions of modernity. In fact, it was in the arts that much of the soul-searching occurred: Artists like Picasso gave humanity disturbing irrational and emotional depictions of itself, Dali made time and space melt, and Munch captured the mood of the epoch with perhaps the best-known work of the period, his 1893 "The Scream."

By the early 1900s, some critics began to feel that the "project" of modernity had failed, replaced by a condition that could only be called "postmodern." Post-modernity, or **post-modernism**, emphasizes the irrational or unconscious, the subjective, the spontaneous and non-bureaucratic, even the superficial. It doubts progress and is considerably more pessimistic, while at the same time in a sense more "playful." Since in many versions there is no "ultimate reality," no "knowable truth," no "absolute center," all things are mere representation, surface, perspective, or image. Science becomes a "culture," history becomes a "point of view," and all things become relative, so humans can mix and match fragments of this or that culture or heritage into an ersatz creation that amuses, whether or not it informs. What *could* humans in the end communicate, since the "meaning" of the work according to the viewer may not and probably will not be the "meaning" of the author? Meaning becomes **decentered**; there is no "true" meaning, just *your* meaning or *my* meaning, and either of us can choose or create any meaning we want. The detachment gained from one's own culture breeds Malinowski's "ethnographic" perspective. Or, as Walter Truett Anderson expressed it, in the pre-modern condition humans did not choose their culture; rather, "If you choose, you are at least modern. If you know you are choosing, you are postmodern" (1990: 112).

The commodification of culture

The contemporary world is a place not only where culture is chosen and created, but also where it is commodified and consumed. A commodity is

---

Post-modernism

a form of life or way of thinking, and the theory of these, of the mid- to late-twentieth century, in which earlier notions of unity, progress, reason, and the increasing integration of peoples and societies breaks down and is replaced by pluralism, "irrationality" or emotion or tradition, de-centering, and cultural disintegration

Decentered

the absence or denial of a particular society's or culture's perspective from which to view the world, usually associated with moving away from a Western- or Euro-centric perspective. Could potentially imply the absence of any central perspective

Anderson, Walter Truett. 1990. *Reality Isn't What It Used to Be: Theatrical Politics, Ready-to-Wear Religion, Global Myths, Primitive Chic, and Other Wonders of the Postmodern World.* San Francisco: Harper & Row.

something that is bought and sold, to which a price can be attached. We easily think of clothes and food and manufactured goods as commodities; culture, it might seem, is something that you *are*, not something you buy, sell, and consume. However, not only is "the consumption of culture" a more and more common practice, but it is a prime opportunity to observe the process of the construction of culture.

In a world in which business and "the market" increasingly define human interactions, it should be no surprise that culture becomes a business as well. In fact, a "culture industry" exists to make, distribute, and sell culture. Two of its main forms are **cultural tourism** and **popular culture**. Neither is an entirely new idea, but each has become bigger, more deliberate, and more influential than ever, like all of the other intentional forms of culture we have discussed.

Cultural tourism

Cultural tourism entails seeking out a "cultural" experience as entertainment and education. Former president of the National Tourism Association, Bruce Beckham, stated that the modern American vacationer is "more into life-seeing than into sight-seeing" (K. Brown, 2000). This often means seeing someone else's life, someone exotic, someone "anthropological." The thrust of Katherine Brown's article was that cultural tourism is big business, whether it involves visiting a museum or a "heritage

exhibit" like an ethnic festival or a performance of "traditional" music or dance, etc. In fact, the National Trust for Historic Preservation helped formulate the first "strategic plan" for cultural/ heritage tourism, which it defined as "traveling to experience the places, artifacts, and activities that authentically represent the stories and people of the past and present" (Brown, 2000). The key word here is "authentically."

Naturally, if someone is going to consume culture, someone else must produce and distribute it for them. This is why there are "native dance shows" and "native arts centers" and adventure and culture camps and get-aways. In Australia, one can take an "authentic" Aboriginal excursion, complete with an Aboriginal guide, during which tourists hike in the bush, eat over a campfire, and learn to throw a boomerang; never mind that most Aboriginal peoples, like the Warlpiri, never made returning boomerangs. Australia is one of many countries that have discovered that visitors want to consume "traditional culture": A 1993 survey of international travelers indicated that almost half wanted to see Aboriginal culture and that more than one-third actually did include such an event in their itinerary. Other travelers seek out "authentic" cultural experiences on African safaris or anywhere else in the world.

The problem, of course, is that these experiences are not necessarily, if ever, "authentic." They are selected, and sometimes invented, for tourists,

Cultural tourism
the practice of "consuming" culture as a form of entertainment and education. Traveling to foreign societies to observe their ways of life (not always "traditional" but sometimes designed for the tourist) in an informal manner

Popular culture
often contrasted with "high" or "official" culture, the cultural practices and creations of "the people"; often used as a pejorative term to indicate the poor quality and low intelligence of such culture, in the contemporary world it has also become an important and vibrant form of culture, although one that is not entirely "of the people," in the sense that large corporations often create and disseminate it

IMAGE 15.5 Cultural tourists strolling through Aztec ruins in central Mexico.

Ecotourism

a form of cultural and
environmental tourism
ostensibly characterized by
responsible travel to natural
areas that conserves the
environment, sustains the
well-being of the local
people, and involves
interpretation and education

playing on Western imaginations of culture or nature. This may be especially true in **ecotourism**, defined by the International Ecotourism Society as "responsible travel to natural areas that conserves the environment, sustains the well-being of the local people, and involves interpretation and education" (www.ecotourism.org/what-is-ecotourism). However, this well-meaning activity often embodies Western notions of conservation and "nature" and "culture," while adding a component of "adventure tourism" (mountain climbing, white-water rafting, etc.). Robert Fletcher has recently written about the culture of adventure tourism, often touted as a form of sustainable development but actually commonly entailing "a basic alteration of the landscape itself to conform to the nature-culture dichotomy" (2014: 139). Ecotourism does not benefit the local people as much as it does the global tourism industry, and most ironically, indigenous-operated ecotourist lodges frequently disappoint or aggravate Western ecotourists: Foreign and Western entrepreneurs tend to understand the ecotourists' expectations better than locals do and therefore engineer more enjoyable "wild" experiences than the actual inhabitants of these allegedly wild places.

Cultural tourism, rather than being educational, may perpetuate stereotypes (who would go on an Aboriginal tour without a boomerang?) and trap people in questionable "traditions." Worse, they actually change the culture of the host-people; for instance, "native artists" begin producing small (portable) trinkets in styles that they know tourists will buy. And they expose the providers of these cultural experiences to the vagaries of foreign tastes and trends. For instance, in the memorable documentary *The Refugee Show* (Steiner, 2007), tourists travel to see Paduang society, whose women are famous for wearing stacks of metal rings around their necks. The tourists are not told that the Paduang are refugees from Myanmar/Burma living in Thailand and forced to open their villages to tourists; meanwhile the Paduang themselves complain of living in a "human zoo" and in a cultural "Disneyland."

One other important site for cultural experience and education is the museum, but museums are also cultural artifacts in their own right and typically tell one narrative about culture and history while silencing other narratives. An interesting new trend,

although problematic like all cultural tourism and modernization, is the establishment of "tribal museums," where indigenous peoples display and narrate their culture and history as they choose. Amy Lonetree describes two such locations in the United States, including the Mille Lacs Indian Museum in Minnesota (sites.mnhs.org/historic-sites/mille-lacs-indian-museum) and the Ziibiwing Indian Museum in Michigan (www.sagchip.org/ziibiwing), as well as the Smithsonian Institute's National Museum of the American Indian. She argues that tribal museums "can serve as sites of decolonization . . . through honoring indigenous knowledge and worldviews, challenging the stereotypical representations of Native people produced in the past, serving as sites of 'knowledge making and remembering' for their own communities and general public" (2012: 25), although she acknowledges that the indigenous meanings are often lost on non-indigenous visitors.

Popular culture

If indigenous societies produce "tradition for sale," America and other modern societies produce "popular culture" in abundance. Popular culture as a distinct category tends to mean three things: not "high culture" like opera or symphony, culture for sale and disposal, and culture mass-produced and mass-marketed. Western scholars have tended to disparage popular culture in comparison to high or elite culture, which is allegedly noble and non-commercial, and folk culture, which is supposedly primitive but authentic, traditional, and also non-commercial. Popular culture, made by and for ordinary people or the masses, is largely devalued as cheap, low-quality, even "ghastly" (Rosenberg, 1957: 9). And often it is. But it is also important, if only because it is a significant part of what people make, do, and think. After all, Malinowski urged us to study "the minutiae of everyday life" and "narratives, utterances, folklore and other conventional sayings and activities" in addition to the big structural aspects of culture, and popular culture is surely conventional minutia. More than this, though, it gives anthropologists important insights into contemporary society and the culture-making process.

Contemporary popular culture is related to other cultural forces and variables. It could not exist

**TOURING INDIANS:
CULTURAL TOURISM IN
CHEROKEE COUNTRY**

**BOLLYWOOD: FILM
MAKING AND CULTURE
MAKING IN INDIA**

without mass production, disposable income to buy it, leisure time to enjoy it, and a "mass society" to sell it to. Some observers have considered this a uniformly bad thing: José Ortega y Gasset famously judged that "the masses, by definition, neither should nor can direct their own personal experience, and still less rule society in general" (1932: 11). It also has social consequences, including the "leveling" of social distinctions and the establishment of a common "language" and experience—or even the creation of new communities and institutions (as *Star Wars* and *Star Trek* have done). Popular culture can be conservative or subversive. As advertising and propaganda, it can manipulate people for the enrichment and empowerment of others. At the same time, with the machinery of cultural production in their own hands—whether the printing press, the television camera, or the internet—people can comment on and protest against social institutions and offer alternative perspectives. It is not without significance that the Warlpiri, for instance, now have their own television studio (see www.pawmedia.com.au).

As trivial and banal as much of popular culture seems, like all other cultural forms it communicates meaningful messages. Underneath the transitory characters and stories are the deep myths, values, and symbols of the society. It also keeps culture alive and diffuses it locally and globally, while altering and modernizing it in fascinating ways. Christopher Scales (2012) notes that the circuit of pow wow events (see www.powwows.com) across the U.S. and Canada gives Native Americans the opportunity to perform their songs and earn income and has even spawned an indigenous recording industry. Kristin Dowell reports on the lively film and television industry among Aboriginal Canadians, which "simultaneously alters the visual landscape of Canadian media by representing Aboriginal stories on-screen and serves as a vital off-screen practice through which new forms of Aboriginal sociality and community are created and negotiated" (2013: xii). Native Canadian programming is available for viewing online through the Aboriginal Peoples Television Network (http://aptn.ca).

This last point about the real social consequences of popular culture bears emphasizing. As depicted in the video *No More Smoke Signals* (Brauning, 2009), radio station KILI 90.1 FM is a

IMAGE 15.6 The pow wow is a popular inter-tribal event.

valuable resource for the Pine Ridge Reservation, calling itself "the voice of the Lakota Nation." Hip hop music was recruited conspicuously by Yoweri Musaveni in his 1986 bid to become president of Uganda; later, when people became dissatisfied with his leadership, hip hop music became a powerful tool of protest. As Ugandan musician Oz Twelve claims, "rappers, we are the new journalists of life. . . . We do it through the beat" (Mazurek, 2009). In Brazil, Anderson Sa has used Afro-reggae music for pulling youths out of a life of poverty and crime in the favelas, as well as bringing attention to police brutality (Zimbalist and Mochary, 2007).

Four views of the future of culture

Long ago, anthropology ceased to be the "science of the primitive," the study of the "tradition." As Malinowski instructed, anthropology must be the study of what is, not an antiquarian (and essentially fanciful or impossible) reconstruction of the past. Anthropology not only can but must be relevant to seeing the possibilities for the future and the

See Chapter 14

Barber, Benjamin. 1995. *Jihad versus McWorld*. New York: Times Books.

Jihad versus McWorld
Benjamin Barber's notion that two opposing but related forces operate in the modern world, one to integrate the world into a single market dominated by a few multinational corporations, and the other to disintegrate the world into exclusivist and often hostile cultural or national groups

One-world culture
the idea that all of the peoples and cultures of the world are becoming (or should become) more similar, to the point at which all humans share a single culture. Often attributed to globalization and the universal access to technology and cultural images (like American movies), it assumes that disparate groups will continue to become more similar until all groups share the same basic values, tastes, and media

advantages and disadvantages of those various possibilities, as well as to constructing that future. Various observers have offered at least four potential visions for the future.

One-world culture

Some observers foresee a future in which humans will integrate into one vast single culture on the basis of globalization. From the first days of Western colonialism, events or decisions or consumption choices in one part of the world tied together other and potentially all parts. Decades ago people were speaking of the "global village" in which all people would be citizens (although it would more likely be a "global city" with many neighborhoods and enclaves). Developments in those decades—in trade, technology, media, and the environment—have helped to hasten the dictum to "think globally." Many people herald the coming of a single global cultural system as the inevitable, if not perfectly positive, destination of integrative processes.

There are two different versions of how a **one-world culture** might evolve. The first is a hybridization of all the world's cultures, in which societies big and small contribute toward a new system that includes, affirms, and addresses all of them. However, it seems patently unlikely that all societies would make an equal contribution to this global culture or that the contribution of some would be felt at all. What language would it speak? A polyglot of English, Spanish, Japanese, Warlpiri, and the 5,997 other world languages? Not likely. Rather, a few languages and cultures or even a single language and culture would be liable to dominate this new world. Therefore, the second version of a one-world culture is a "globalization" of one or a few dominant culture(s). The most likely candidates for global dominance at present are Western culture generally or American culture specifically, as expressed in Francis Fukuyama's *The End of History and the Last Man* (1992). In his (rather discredited) view, the one-world culture will be essentially Western democratic capitalism triumphant. Others see China poised to be a major international political, economic, and cultural force in the twentieth century, which would alter the winds of cultural change and globalization. Martin Jacques in his *When China Rules the World* (2009) predicts that China could reconfigure Wallerstein's

"world system" in major and not altogether unpleasant ways.

Jihad versus McWorld

Partly out of recognition of the obstacles to globalization, Benjamin Barber (1995) identified two opposing tendencies in the contemporary world— **Jihad versus McWorld**. "Jihad," the Arabic word for struggle, Barber adopts to stand for all of the local, tradition-oriented, frequently angry and militant, "identity-based" groups and movements in the world. It represents the fragmentation of the world, the disengagement from and even hostility toward the world system and the "integrative revolution" that scholars once applauded and declared victorious. It speaks the language of culture and tradition, but this is remembered tradition as well as aggravated, mobilized, and often armed tradition.

Barber's jihad is innately hostile to other societies in its midst and to the globalizing and modernizing influences of the world economic and cultural system. This nemesis of local identity Barber calls "McWorld." McWorld is the culture and power of the multinational corporations and their "development" discourse. These corporations include all of the famous names that modern people know so well, like Nike, Microsoft, Coca-Cola, and Disney (and others that we do not know so well). McWorld is nakedly economic or capitalist in focus, and it is culturally invasive. By nakedly economic, Barber meant that it has only one interest—profit. It is not concerned to any degree with social relationships, environmental issues, or "tradition." All of those things can be impediments to profit and are to be minimized. Corporations often come to non-Western states bearing the gift of development—jobs, income, training, "modernization," and increased GNP—but this comes with all of the costs discussed in earlier chapters and few benefits other than to the corporations themselves.

McWorld is culturally invasive in two senses— that it brings a message from another culture that is at best foreign and at worst corrosive to the host society, and that it acts, sometimes consciously, to undermine the culture of the host society. An important part of McWorld is American popular culture, embodied in Hollywood. The messages and images of the American culture and entertainment industry are seductive but also anathema to many of the values and beliefs of other societies. No wonder a few societies with the power to do so restrict or ban satellite dishes and the internet; they consider the content of this McCulture to be decadent and disruptive. That McWorld is even intentionally "hostile" toward local cultures is evident from the fundamental requirement to "adjust" a culture so the corporations, their products, and their values can penetrate it. Before a society will drink Coke, its local tastes and preferences must be changed. Before a society will wear Nikes or Mickey Mouse t-shirts, its sense of style and perceived needs must be altered.

Barber roughly equated jihad with tribalism (although militant tribalism) and McWorld with globalization. He did not equate either with democracy, cultural pluralism, or cultural relativism. It is easy to see the exclusivism in jihad: "Our" cultural group is right and good, and "yours" is wrong and bad. Groups with this mindset tend to find it undesirable if not impossible to co-exist; the only option is separation, and the path to separation is often conflict. But McWorld is exclusivist too: Microsoft tolerates but hardly enjoys having Apple in the world, and Coke and Pepsi do not like each other and both dislike local "traditional" drinks. If jihad is about separatism, McWorld is about monopoly. In jihad, choice is inconceivable: One is born a Basque or a Tamil or a Serb or a Christian, and these are inescapable, "natural" identities. In McWorld, choice is celebrated, but it is a trivial choice between this corporation or that one. The citizen or member is reduced to a consumer.

Clash of civilizations

Samuel Huntington (1996) augured a different cultural future, but one that is no more heartening and that reflects the same general cultural dynamic. In his **clash of civilizations**, Huntington suggested that the primary actors on the future stage of world history and culture will not be states or even societies. Beginning in the 1600s or 1700s, the previous agents of cultural history—individual rulers or "great men"—were replaced by "nations" and the states in which they wrapped themselves. However, these nations or states have coalesced into a few "civilizations," which Huntington defined as a sort of "super-society" or "super-culture," a family of closely related cultures that share certain basic beliefs and values, often religious.

Civilizations were there throughout the modern era; they were merely obfuscated or forgotten in the excitement of colonialism, modernization, and globalization. Western scholars believed or assumed that modern movements—communism, liberalism, progressivism, capitalism, or what have you—were or would become the true forces of cultural history, and they ignored (when they even knew about) the local "pre-modern" cultural movements and narratives suppressed by modernization. Insofar as Westerners were aware of other civilizations and their worldviews, they fully expected that Western worldviews would replace them. But as the smoke of demolished colonialism and communism clears, we see the old civilizations looming from the haze. Today and tomorrow, the world's main civilizations—Western, Christian, Islamic, Chinese, South Asian/Indian, "African," etc.—are back, although they were really never gone. And they are "back with a vengeance," as Huntington predicted that the conflicts and wars of tomorrow will be between these civilizations (for instance, "the West" versus "Islam") or along the fault-lines where they meet (for instance, the Middle East and Israel or Taiwan).

Multiple modernities

Some might find in Huntington's vision, and perhaps Barber's too, a failure of modernity, but in an important way, modernity was another Western imagination and movement like colonialism and development. Accordingly, one of the most interesting, and anthropological, commentaries on the present and future of cultures—one which explicitly opposes Huntington's and Fukuyama's analysis—has recognized multiple paths to this cultural future, multiple ways to be "modern," that is, **multiple modernities** (Eisenstadt, 2000; Hefner, 1998).

S. N. Eisenstadt noted that all of the dominant theories and predictions regarding culture assumed

> that the cultural program of modernity as it developed in modern Europe and the basic institutional constellations that emerged there would ultimately take over in all modernizing and modern societies; with the expansion of

Multiple modernities
the perspective that "modernity" as known in the Western tradition is not the only possible form of modern society, and that other societies can and will devise their own particular experience of and response to modern and global forces

Eisenstadt, S. N. 2000. "Multiple Modernities." *Daedalus* 129 (1): 1–29

Hefner, Robert W. 1998. "Multiple Modernities: Christianity, Islam, and Hinduism in a Globalizing Age." *Annual Review of Anthropology* 27: 83–104.

Huntington, Samuel. 1996. *The Clash of Civilizations and the Remaking of World Order.* New York: Simon & Schuster.

Clash of civilizations
Huntington's notion that the key forces in the future will not be societies or states but regional cultural entities (like "Western civilization" or "Islam"); within a civilization a variety of cultural attitudes are shared, but between civilizations differences of attitude and interest will breed conflict

modernity, they would prevail throughout the world.

(2000: 1)

However, as he found generally, and as Hefner found specifically concerning religion,

> The actual developments in modernizing societies have refuted the homogenizing and hegemonic assumptions of this Western program of modernity. While a general trend toward structural differentiation developed across the wide range of institutions in most of these societies . . . the ways in which these arenas were defined and organized varied greatly, in different periods of their development, giving rise to multiple institutional and ideological patterns. Significantly, these patterns did not constitute simple continuations in the modern era of traditions of their respective societies. Such patterns were distinctively modern, though greatly influenced by specific cultural premises, traditions, and historical experiences. . . . Many of the movements that developed in non-Western societies articulate strong anti-Western or even

antimodern themes, yet all were distinctively modern.

(Esienstadt, 2000: 1–2)

In other words, while Eisenstadt acknowledged elsewhere that Western civilization represents "the 'original' modernity" (1999: 284), the Western version of "modern culture" is neither the only possible one nor the only existing one. Rather, each society can and will find its own form of or response to common yet unevenly distributed global forces; the future can and will hold "attempts by various groups and movements to reappropriate and redefine the discourse of modernity in their own new terms" (Eisenstadt, 2000: 24), based on their particular pre-modern cultures, their particular experiences of modernization, and the particular choices of leaders and members alike. This perspective aligns with the notion of "glocalization", in which global processes cannot help but take locally specific shapes. In the end, then, there would not be one cultural future, not two, not even several, but many diverse and continually emerging and changing ones—precisely the sort of future that cultural anthropology should expect and is uniquely poised to understand.

See Chapter 1

BOX 15.4   CONTEMPORARY CULTURAL CONTROVERSIES: INDIGENOUS SOVEREIGNTY

For many indigenous peoples, the ultimate achievement of cultural survival would be "indigenous sovereignty." According to *Black's Law Dictionary*, sovereignty is a legal concept implying "supreme political authority" and "the self-sufficient source of political power, from which all specific political powers are derived." Some indigenous leaders claim that their people were sovereign before colonialism. Colonialism stripped them of sovereignty, which was usurped by foreign masters, and independence transferred that sovereignty to postcolonial states that continued to dismiss indigenous sovereignty. Either having never surrendered their sovereignty, or in some cases actually enshrining their sovereignty in treaties (as in the United States), activists contend that "states will have to concede part of their national sovereignty to the 'indigenous' peoples" (*Cultural Survival*, 2001), and in 2007 the United Nations adopted the Declaration on the Rights of Indigenous Peoples, pronouncing that such peoples "have the right to self-determination" to "freely determine their political status and freely pursue their economic, social, and cultural development"; as self-determining, they "have the right to autonomy or self-government in matters relating to their internal and local affairs" and "to maintain and strengthen their distinct political, legal, economic, social, and cultural institutions, while retaining their right to participate fully, if they so choose, in the political, economic, social and cultural life of the State" (2008: 4–5). Insofar as indigenous sovereignty is feasible in practice, it would mean significant modifications of the behavior and policies of states, which may explain why the U.S. was the last country in the world to endorse the Declaration, in December 2010. What do you think?

SUMMARY

While world-altering processes like colonialism, globalization, nationalism, and development have affected many peoples negatively, those peoples have not been passive victims of cultural changes. Increasingly in the contemporary world, indigenous people have raised their voices to state their demands, reclaim their cultures, and speak on their own behalf. Formerly "traditional societies" have mastered the modern tools of arts, media, politics, and organization to present formidable challenges to perceived injustices and inequalities. Along the way, anthropology has changed to reflect and study these changed cultural realities.

One of the most important aspects of culture in the twentieth and twenty-first centuries is the adaptation of culture into cultural movements intended to address some aspect of cultural frustration and dissatisfaction. A cultural movement, however, is a new kind or formation of culture itself and not merely a continuation of traditional culture or an abandonment of it. These revitalization movements have taken many shapes and are not unique to small, "traditional" societies, but are an increasing part of the life of all societies. Some of the types or qualities of movements include

- syncretism
- millenarianism
- irredentism
- modernism or vitalism
- nativism, traditionalism, or fundamentalism

All of these movements are modern manifestations of the "culture-making" phenomenon. In the post-modern world, culture is perceived more or less clearly as a product and a construction, rather than as a "thing" or an "essence." People in all sorts of societies have developed a nearly "ethnographic" or anthropological understanding of their own culture. At the same time, the processes of culture creation and consumption have expanded and accelerated, to include cultural tourism and popular culture. Where the culture of the future will take us, we cannot say. We can, however, appreciate that it will be a construction too—one emerging from multiple and contradictory forces and one to which anthropology has something to contribute as observer and participant.

MCQS

FILL IN THE BLANKS

WWW

Key Terms

cargo cult

clash of civilizations

cultural tourism

decentered

ecotourism

First World

Fourth World

fundamentalism

irredentism

Jihad versus McWorld

millenarianism

modernism

multiple modernities

nativism

one-world culture

popular culture

post-modernism

revitalization movement

syncretism

Third World

traditionalism

vitalism

16 Health, illness, body, and culture

Several hundred thousand people died in Liberia's two civil wars between 1989 and 2003, leaving the survivors scarred physically and psychologically. Sharon Abramowitz tells that a post-conflict report on Liberian mental health found that forty percent of the population suffered from depression, eleven percent from suicidal thoughts, and seven percent from substance abuse (with even higher numbers among ex-combatants). Concerned not only about the damage to its citizens but about slipping back into war, the country and the world mounted a mental health intervention to aid the "traumatized nation" (Abramowitz, 2014: 65), including not only individual trauma but "collective trauma" or "the disarticulation of the subjective, embodied person from the collective norms, social mores, and moral conduct that constitutes social order" (66). Some of the signs of collective trauma were fighting in the streets, sexual violence, and a general sense of fear and foreboding. Various international organizations such as Save the Children, the Center for Victims of Torture, the Lutheran World Federation/World Service, and Médecins du Monde (Doctors of the World) arrived with the task of "implementing trauma healing and psychosocial interventions, and through them, instilling post-

conflict *peace subjectivities*" (6, emphasis in the original). In other words, the goal was not so much curing individual mental illness as managing the society and preventing a relapse into war; in fact, some organizations actually instructed their workers "to turn away anyone with a serious mental illness" (45). The patchwork of nongovernmental organizations and individual medical professionals turned the country into what Abramowitz dubs an "interventionscape," where "flows of resources, personnel, bureaucratic protocols, administrative practices, financial mechanisms, and ethical guidelines shape the space of mental health, trauma-healing, and psychosocial intervention in the unique Liberian post-conflict landscape" (36). In the process, the Liberian people "were transformed into beneficiaries of a massive, uncoordinated, and decentralized project of humanitarian social engineering" (25)—and not only beneficiaries, since many Liberians were themselves trained as mental-health providers and as trainers of other providers, recruiting the whole society to do therapy on itself. "Trauma" became part of everyday speech, and barely trained workers swept through the country as what Abramowitz calls "a vast, informal constabulary of care" (175), offering questionable

IMAGE 16.1 A star Liberian footballer visits former child soldiers at a care center as part of a UN campaign. The focus is on reintegrating children who have been traumatized by their war experiences.

advice, blending modern medicine with folk medicine and medicine with morality.

Illness, injury, pain, and death are universal human experiences. At first glance, health seems like a purely physical matter, just as the healthy or unhealthy body seems like a purely physical object. But the ideas and concepts, the institutions, and the practices and practitioners that societies develop to deal with illness, injury, and pain are thoroughly cultural, and even notions of a healthy human body—or a human body at all—vary across cultures.

Health is thus a perfect topic for anthropological investigation and has been a prime target of anthropological research. Health illustrates the fundamental anthropological concept of embodiment, of culture applied to, inscribed on, and enacted through the body. It opens questions of cultural knowledge (such as knowledge of medicinal plants, part of **ethnobotany**) and of cultural classification (such as what counts as "disease," e.g. the American Psychiatric Association removed homosexuality from its official roster of mental illnesses in 1973). It exposes the social and cultural influences on health, from beliefs and values to

lifestyle choices (like smoking) and inequalities of class, race, and gender, as well as the health influences on society, from the cost of health care to the impact of an aging population. Finally, health is a site for the practical application of anthropological concepts and methods; many anthropologists have trained as health professionals and vice versa, and there is a long productive history of collaboration between anthropologists and the medical establishment.

TOWARD A MEDICAL ANTHROPOLOGY

As previously told, anthropology was a biological and physical science before it was a cultural one, and many of its early advocates were biologists, anatomists, and physicians. Among the most illustrious was W. H. R. Rivers, whose 1924 *Medicine, Magic, and Religion*, based on lectures given to the Royal College of Physicians of London, recognized medicine as a cultural phenomenon and as inseparably entangled with the cultural domains of magic

Ethnobotany
cultural knowledge and uses of plants, especially but not exclusively for medical purposes

See Chapter 2

Paul, Benjamin D. 1955.
*Health, Culture and
Community: Case Studies of
Public Reactions to Health
Programs*. New York:
Russell Sage Foundation.

Medical anthropology
the branch of anthropology
investigating the factors that
influence health and well-
being, the experience and
distribution of illness, the
prevention and treatment of
sickness, healing processes,
the social relations of
therapy management, and
the cultural importance and
utilization of pluralistic
medical systems

and religion. He also wrote on psychology, as in his 1920 *Instinct and the Unconscious*, and in the same year he speculated on cultural and psychological (rather than biological and infectious) explanations for the depopulation of Melanesian colonial societies in his "The Dying Out of Native Races" in the medical journal *The Lancet*. In a second book, published originally in 1926, Rivers declared:

> Medicine is a social institution. It comprises a set of beliefs and practices which only become possible when held and carried out by members of an organized society, among whom a high degree of the division of labor and specialization of the social function has come into being. Any principles and methods found to be of value in the study of social institutions in general cannot be ignored by the historian of medicine.
>
> (Rivers, 1999: 61)

Other observers also remarked on the cultural dimension of health. Erwin Ackerknecht applied Ruth Benedict's famous concept of "culture pattern" to various "primitive" medical practices, reasoning that it is

> an almost hopeless task to try to understand and evaluate the medicine of one primitive tribe while disregarding its cultural background or to explain the general phenomenon of primitive medicine by purely enumerating that in the medical field primitives use spells, prayer, blood-letting, medicine men, twins, toads, human fat and spittle, etc.
>
> (1942: 546–547)

Noting that "the practice of medicine and the practice of magic have been closely associated" throughout history, the famous anthropologist Edmund Leach insisted that modern medicine retained a certain magical quality, while "people with completely mystical conceptions of the origins of illness may still handle minor ailments in a practical common sense manner" (1949: 165).

Anthropology's relation with the medical field did not remain merely academic. According to Veena Bhasin, by the 1950s, "many anthropologists were working on problems of international health; they were employed as teachers, researchers, and administrators both in universities and in hospitals" (2007: 2). One example was Cora Du Bois, who was hired by the World Health Organization in 1950.

William Caudill is generally credited with devising the term "medical anthropology" (or "applied anthropology in medicine") in 1953, and Benjamin Paul edited one of the first medical anthropology texts, *Health, Culture and Community: Case Studies of Public Reactions to Health Programs*, in 1955.

The advances of the anthropology of health and medicine were signaled by the founding of the forerunner of the Society for Medical Anthropology (www.medanthro.net) in 1967, and by 1971 "medical anthropology" had matured sufficiently as a discipline to merit a review article by Horacio Fabrega. **Medical anthropology**, according to the Society for Medical Anthropology, is the branch of anthropology investigating

> those factors which influence health and well being (broadly defined), the experience and distribution of illness, the prevention and treatment of sickness, healing processes, the social relations of therapy management, and the cultural importance and utilization of pluralistic medical systems. The discipline of medical anthropology draws upon many different theoretical approaches. It is as attentive to popular health culture as bioscientific epidemiology, and the social construction of knowledge and politics as scientific discovery and hypothesis testing.

More succinctly, in a textbook intended for health professionals, Cecil Helman defines medical anthropology as the study of

> how people in different cultures and social groups explain the causes of ill health, the types of treatments they believe in, and to whom they turn if they do get ill. It is also the study of how these beliefs and practices relate to biological, psychological, and social changes in the human organism, in both health and disease.
>
> (2007: 1)

In a word, it is "the study of human suffering, and the steps that people take to explain and relieve that suffering."

Comparative health care systems

In the health domain as elsewhere, anthropology seeks a holistic, relativistic, and comparative or cross-cultural perspective. This can be a challenge because many of the medical practices of modern Western societies do not seem "cultural" to Western practitioners or patients, while many of the practices of pre-modern and non-Western societies do not seem exactly "medical" (again, falling more in the category of religion and magic, if not superstition and old wives' tales).

The most basic distinction that anthropologists and health professionals make is between biomedicine and ethnomedicine. **Biomedicine** is roughly synonymous with modern Western medical concepts and practices, so named because it "views disease as having a unique physical cause within the body, whether it is a microorganism causing infection, the growth of malignant cells or the failure of an organ due to repeated insults (such as alcohol consumption)" (medanth.wikispaces.com/ Biomedicine). It is, for most people, quite simply *medicine*, the "kind of legitimized, credentialed medicine practiced and recognized throughout the world by governments and licensing bodies." As the "bio" in biomedicine indicates, "biomedical understandings of disease tend to privilege the body as the only relevant environment for the understanding of the disease causation and individuals are perceived as uniquely responsible for their health." Biomedicine, in other words, is the world of operations, pharmaceuticals, and direct technical interventions on the individual body premised on scientific knowledge.

Ethnomedicine means "culture-medicine" or "the medical institutions and the manner in which peoples cope with illness and disease as a result of their cultural perspective" (medanth.wikispaces. com/ethnomedicine), but in practice tends to specify *other cultures' medical systems or beliefs*. Often the implication, if not the overt criticism, is that ethnomedicine is more primitive, less scientific, and ultimately less *true* than Western biomedicine. Also often, the assumption is that ethnomedicine is at best folk knowledge and at worst magic. Two things are true about ethnomedicine, however. First, as Leach (1949) noted, ethnomedicine also commonly focuses on the body (even if it integrates social and spiritual elements) and employs practical material means like plant remedies, massage, and such. Second, many ethnomedical traditions are quite sophisticated, like Ayurvedic (Indian) or Chinese medicine. They feature written

texts and trained specialists, and some of their practices, including acupuncture, have been adopted by Western medicine.

Aptly, Robert Hahn and Arthur Kleinman concluded that biomedicine "is an *ethnomedicine*, albeit a unique one"; it is *Western* ethnomedicine, "the product of a dialectic between culture and nature" like every other healing tradition and therefore a biocultural thought-system like every other (1983: 306). In other influential works, Kleinman elaborated the concept of "explanatory model" to account for these different medical traditions. In an article (1978) and then a book (1980), he proposed the term "explanatory model" to designate "the notions about an episode of sickness and its treatment that are employed by all those engaged in the clinical process" (1980: 105) and thereby act as "the main vehicle for the clinical construction of reality" (110). A model consists of the words, practices, roles, institutions, and instruments related to five variables in the sickness episode—etiology or cause, time and mode of onset of symptoms, pathology, course of the sickness, and treatment.

Kleinman further asserted that there were three "sectors" or "social arenas" in societies "within which sickness is experienced and reacted to," namely the *popular*, the *folk*, and the *professional* (1978: 86). The popular arena "comprises principally the family context of sickness and care, but also includes social network and community activities"; not only does the vast majority of medical care happen in this sector—in non-Western and Western societies alike—but "most decisions regarding when to seek aid in the other arenas, whom to consult, and whether to comply, along with most lay evaluations of the efficacy of treatment, are made in the popular domain" (86). The professional sector or arena "consists of professional scientific ('Western' or 'cosmopolitan') medicine and professionalized indigenous healing traditions (e.g. Chinese, Ayurvedic, Yunani, and chiropractic)" (87). Note, significantly, that Kleinman's professional sector does not equate to biomedicine. Finally, the folk sector or arena "consists of nonprofessional healing specialists" (86), which is an incredibly broad and unstable category, as any healing tradition may professionalize. He concluded that the three sectors or arenas "organize particular subsystems of socially legitimated beliefs,

Biomedicine
roughly synonymous with modern scientific Western medicine, the model that sees illness as the effect of physical and chemical causes in the individual body

Kleinman, Arthur. 1980. *Patients and Healers in the Context of Culture: An Exploration of the Borderland between Anthropology, Medicine, and Psychiatry.* Berkeley and London: University of California Press.

Ethnomedicine
healing knowledge and practices that are specific and related to particular cultures, usually construed as non-Western, "premodern," or "traditional" cultures; some analysts argue that modern scientific biomedicine is Western ethnomedicine

expectations, roles, relationships, transaction settings, and the like. These socially legitimated contexts of sickness and care, I shall refer to as separate *clinical realities*" (87), which may nevertheless overlap and interact (see below).

Healing roles

Like every area of human endeavor, health systems feature specific healing roles. In biomedicine, the familiar roles are doctor, nurse, surgeon, pharmacist, and—according to prominent sociologist Talcott Parsons—patient. In his epic *The Social System*, the functionalist Parsons imagined sickness as a kind of dysfunction and the sick person as a sort of deviant social actor; more, society actually provides an "institutionalized expectation system relative to the sick role" (1951: 436), characterized by an exemption from ordinary responsibilities (e.g. the freedom to stay home from work), an obligation to want to "get well," a notion of the patient's inability to heal on his/her own and thus accept the dependent position of being "taken care of," and a resultant duty to seek qualified help and to cooperate with those helpers.

We will have much to say about pre-modern and modern, ethnomedical and biomedical, healers below. For now, a word about the sick person is in order. First, as we have seen elsewhere, people whom society might classify as sick or disabled, like the deaf, may not identify as such and may decline "treatment"; whatever society and medicine had or has to say, many homosexuals and transsexuals reject the label of illness. In some very interesting research, Rebecca Lester finds that women with eating disorders may resist medication: "They may actively restrict their intake of medications, take them and then purge them, or hoard them and 'binge' on them" (2014: 241). Part of the problem she attributes to the discourse of medicine as food, since food is the patients' core issue; more profoundly, Lester reminds us that some eating-disorder patients are intentionally "depriving the body of what it needs to function optimally" and "maintaining a state of constant deprivation, of not allowing oneself to thrive" (248). At the deepest level, the disorder is "about feeling unworthy to exist and sustaining an existence as a non-entity while relentlessly punishing oneself for the

unforgiveable crime of remaining alive" (249). Not quite so self-negating is what many medical professionals call the "bad patient." As we will see in our discussion of hospitals below,

> a good patient is someone who does not interrupt staff routines, but complies uncritically with staff orders. The good patient takes the right kinds and doses of prescribed medicine when told to, answers questions correctly and volunteers relevant information, and does not complain or "create trouble." A bad patient is described as the opposite and does not accept staff authority or recognize their monopoly on medical knowledge.
>
> (Andersen, 2004: 2010)

In other words, some patients fail or refuse to play the sick role.

Besides the conventional doctors, nurses, etc., there is a great diversity of healing roles and traditions, most of them jumbled into the category of pre-modern, ethnomedical, "traditional" healer, or "indigenous" healer. Those ethnomedical practices are often assumed to be and disparaged as magical or spiritual, but not all are. In her review of medical anthropology, Bhasin identifies four categories of traditional healers:

1. "specialists in home remedies," commonly "elder people who do not consider themselves healers, but suggest and give plant remedies in case of illness" (2007: 13)
2. "herbal specialists," who "treat people with the help of herbs available in the vicinity. They learn the secrets of the trade from their fathers or any other expert in the required field" (13)
3. "ritual specialists and spiritual healers" who address illness "with divination and therapeutic cult rituals," often centering on spirit possession and/or spirit mediumship; healing rituals "tend to focus on symbolically encouraging and assisting the putatively natural course of the sickness or on transferring it away from the patient's body, rather than on 'treatment' or 'cure' in specific sense" (14)
4. the "magico-religious healer," who intervenes in "illness believed to be caused by supernatural forces. He exorcises evil spirits and suggests preventive measures against the attack of

THE ANTHROPOLOGIST IN THE SICK ROLE: ROBERT MURPHY'S BODY GOES SILENT

See Chapter 6

evil spirits. Charms and amulets are also recommended" (14).

Fifth, of course, is Western biomedicine.

Obviously, the specialist and the treatment in this crowded "folk arena" depend on the perceived etiology or cause of affliction. Some common cross-cultural explanatory models of sickness (and other kinds of misfortune) include malevolent or capricious spirits, sorcery, witchcraft, the "evil eye," and agitated ancestors. Such ideas almost all count as "religion" for followers of modern biomedicine. Perhaps the classic traditional or spiritual healer is the shaman, sometimes actually dubbed the "medicine man." Among the !Kung or Ju/hoansi foragers of southern Africa, the *n/um kausi* (master/owner of *n/um*) performed shamanic functions, using knowledge of and power over the spiritual and bodily substance called *n/um* to effect cures. Singing and chanting, the *n/um* situated at the base of the spine heated and boiled, rising up the spine painfully and driving the curer into trance; detaching from his own body, the shaman might struggle against the ancestors or the god *Gao Na* or wipe potent sweat on the patient.

A common practice among shamans was pulling sickness, sometimes in the form of a foreign object, out of the sufferer's body (a practice called *twe* among the Ju/hoansi) (Richard Katz, 1982). Australian Aboriginal shamans might have their own internal organs symbolically removed and replaced with new spiritually powerful ones or objects like stones; "So long as these stones remain in his body he is capable of performing the work of a medicine man" (Spencer and Gillen, 1968: 525). In a typical curing session,

See Chapter 10

> the patient lies down on the ground while the medicine man bends over and sucks vigorously at the affected part of the body, spitting out every now and then supposed pieces of wood, bone, or stone, the presence of which is believed to be causing the injury or pain.
>
> (531)

Not all shamans or "spiritual" healers treat the same complaint in the same way, and not all use

IMAGE 16.2 Yebichai, giving the medicine: Navajo shaman with participant.

AN NDEMBU RITUAL OF AFFLICTION

Turner, Victor W. 1981 [1968]. *The Drums of Affliction: A Study of Religious Processes Among the Ndembu of Zambia*. London: Hutchinson University Library for Africa.

Greenfield, Sidney M. 2008. *Spirits with Scalpels: The Culturalbiology of Religious Healing in Brazil*. Walnut Creek, CA: Left Coast Press.

exclusively "spiritual" means; in fact, we could argue that Australian Aboriginals use a distinctly "physical" technique. Francisco Javier Carod-Artal and Carolina Vázquez-Cabrera (2007) compare headache remedies in three Central and South American societies, finding that Tzeltal (Mexico) practitioners wash the patient's head with a herbal solution, while Kamayur'a (Brazil) shamans apply a herbal liquid to the eyes, and Chipaya (Bolivia) experts instruct the victim to drink their plant-based medicine. In fact, Tzeltal healers claim that ordinary headaches have purely physical causes, but if the pain persists, then the cause is witchcraft; since a headache is believed to stem from vengeance by hunted animals among the Kamayur'a, their healers combine plant substances with prayers. In his pivotal work on Ndembu (Zambia) "rituals of affliction," Victor Turner (1981) also highlighted the role of medicinal plants, not only their application, but their acquisition and preparation, all steeped in ritual practices and symbolic meanings.

Even within societies, "traditional" ethnomedical treatments vary. Among the Yoruba of Nigeria, various specialists were available to treat deafness. Herbalists more often attributed the condition to natural causes than "indigenous faith healers," who tended to see malevolent forces like witchcraft at work. Accordingly, "while the majority of herbalists prescribed a herbal ear drop, a majority of *babalawos* [diviners] and the indigenous faith healers prescribed sacrifices to appease the aggrieved parties" (Odebiyi and Togonu-Bickersteth, 1987: 645). Interestingly, though, all healers inquired into "the relationships between the deaf child's parents and the neighbors, relatives or friends, because they too believe that strained social relations can result in witchcraft," and they all considered "adherence to lineage taboos during pregnancy of the deaf child and during postnatal periods" since "a break of these taboos could result in the deaf condition" (647).

Clearly there is no essential contradiction between spiritual and natural causes and cures in many cultures, and it is wrong to equate ethnomedicine with supernaturalism. Likewise, it is wrong to blithely associate ethnomedicine *or* spiritual cure with pre-modern societies and biomedicine with modern ones. The modern United States produces its share of "faith healers" and sufferers who seek their services. Asaf Sharabi documents a

"deep healing" movement known as *teshuvah* in contemporary Israel. Starting in the 1960s, with a revival in the 1990s, healers like Rabbi Yitzchak held curing rallies once or twice a week. Opening with a sermon,

> Rabbi Yitzchak's rallies focus on giving the audience the opportunity to ask questions and request blessings. While the rabbi encourages the audience to ask questions, a considerable part of what the people talk about is their personal difficulties with medical issues, finding marital partners, and infertility; these are, in fact, openings to ask for a blessing from the rabbi.
>
> (2014: 280)

In most cases, the treatment involves performing religious actions—observing biblical commandments (including growing a beard for men), studying the Torah daily, taking a vow of silence, and so on. "The solution to a medical problem, according to Rabbi Yitzchak, is on the level of tangible performance rather than one merely requiring a change of trust or belief" (283).

Meanwhile, Sidney Greenfield tells a remarkable tale of "culturalbiology" in "Spiritist surgery" in Brazil,

> where spirits, incorporated in mediums, cut into patients with scalpels, kitchen knives, and even electric saws to remove, at times with unwashed fingers, infected materials and growths. Yet the patients are given no anesthetic, feel little if any pain, and develop no infections. They recover without complications.
>
> (2008: 9)

Health and the cultural body

In virtually all examples given, even when there is a "spiritual" component to an illness and its cure, the patient's body is a definite focus of interest and activity. Ethnomedicine is not disembodied medicine. However, the understanding of the human body differs across cultures and informs diagnosis and treatment. In short, ideas about the body are part of Kleinman's explanatory models.

In biomedicine, the human body is basically conceptualized as an organic and chemical machine, isolated from other bodies and from the social and physical environment; illness is malfunctioning of the machine, and cure is restoring normal function structurally (by repairing or removing parts) or chemically. Not all cultures and medical traditions share this view. Rather, in many cultures, the individual human body is constituted by and inseparable from social relations and physical surroundings, and its structure and function are analogous to the society and the material world.

For instance, Deborah Kaspin showed that for the agricultural Chewa of Malawi, "conceptions of the body are based on agricultural metaphors" (1996: 561), and "homologies between the farm and the body inform the management of the body" (567), including notions of health. Just as rain is critical to crops, bodily fluids and humors are basic to human life, resulting in *moyo* or "life." "Moyo is not an entity but a force, the quality of being alive and vital"; it is "concentrated in the blood, to a lesser degree in semen, and to a still lesser degree in saliva, milk, urine, and phlegm. All bodily humors contain the life force, which ebbs and flows through the course of a lifetime" (568). The human body is then a microcosm of the physical and cultural world, and "similarities between the seasons and physiological conditions reflect an overarching set of equivalences in which agricultural production and human reproduction are analogous as systems" (570).

In the Bolivian Andes, where mountains are the most prominent feature, the Qollahuayas "understand their own bodies in terms of the mountain, and they consider the mountain in terms of their anatomy" (Bastien, 1985: 598). Like a mountain with its vertical circulation of air and water, they conceive the body "as a vertically layered axis with a system of ducts through which air, blood, fat, and water flow to and from the *sonco* (heart). . . . If these fluids accumulate, they become noxious and must be purged from the body" by means of "enemas, fastings, dietary restrictions, and baths. Basically, the body is a hydraulic system with distillation, circulation, and elimination processes" (595). Sickness, then,

is a disintegration of the human body similar to the landslide on the mountain, and health is restored by feeding the complete mountain. During healing rituals, diviners create a

metaphorical image of the body when they feed the earth shrines of the mountain. Diviners serve coca, blood, and fat in thirteen scallop shells to different earth shrines, which are associated with topographical features of the three ecological levels and with anatomical parts of the human body.

(598)

Key to their health thinking are distinctions of hot/cold and wet/dry:

Hot and dry blood is symptomatic of tachycardia or thinly oxygenated blood and refers to rapidly dispersing blood with little air and fat. Cold and wet blood is symptomatic of arthritis and refers to sluggish blood that does not disperse to the muscles. Cold and dry blood is symptomatic of respiratory ailments and refers to blood with a low concentration of air and a slow rate of dispersal to the parts of the body. Corresponding to the diagnosis, herbalists prescribe an herb to regulate hydraulic forces of the blood.

(599–600)

Based on such observations, Nancy Scheper-Hughes and Margaret Lock (1987) proposed that anthropologists should think of three kinds of body in cultural practice. They distinguished the conventional body as experienced by the person "in" it as the "individual *body-self*"; seemingly self-evident, it is really a highly variable concept in terms of how its parts and functions are defined and integrated, as our examples illustrate. Second is the *social body* or "the representational uses of the body as a natural symbol with which to think about nature, society, and culture" (1987: 7). "The body in health," they opined, "offers a model of organic wholeness; the body in sickness offers a model of social disharmony, conflict, and disintegration. Reciprocally, society in 'sickness' and in 'health' offers a model for understanding the body" (7). Third, the *body politic* designates "the regulation, surveillance, and control of bodies (individual and collective) in reproduction and sexuality, in work and in leisure, in sickness and other forms of deviance and human difference"; in all societies, "the stability of the body politic rests on its ability to regulate populations (the social body) *and* to discipline individual bodies" (7). This last issue

BOX 16.1 HEALTH, HOLISM, AND THE KNOWING BODY AMONG THE CASHINAHUA

Modern biomedicine regards the body as an isolated biochemical machine, but the Western tradition has long posited a fundamental separation between body and mind, reflected in the distinct field of "mental health." Although "psychosomatic disorders" and the emerging perspectives of holistic medicine and embodied mind have challenged mind/body dualism, some societies do not draw a radical line between the body and the mind and between health states and knowledge. For the Cashinahua of Brazil and Peru, "a healthy body is one that constantly learns through the senses and expresses the accumulated knowledge in social action and speech"; "An ill body is one that no longer knows. Curing, therefore, acts to restore a person's capacity to know" (McCallum, 1996: 347). Indeed, Cecilia McCallum explained that for the Cashinahua the body is a nexus and product of a person's spirits (in the plural) and "physical, mental, and emotional capacities" including speech (348). Spirit and body are not opposed; they are hardly distinguished. Nor is mind separate from body: The Cashinahua do not even assign knowledge to the brain, and they have no word that means "mind" in contrast to body. They attribute no special role to the brain, rather conceiving knowledge to be distributed throughout the body. Each organ—"skin, hands, ears, genitals, liver, and eyes"—is "linked to a specific process of acquiring knowledge and of putting it to use in physical action" (355–356). "Thus the body integrates different kinds of knowledge acquired in a varied manner, in different body parts" (356). Not surprisingly, changes in spirit are experienced in the body, as "medical" symptoms like fainting and dizziness. Illness and ultimately death are understood as loss of knowledge, specifically of closing off connections with other people, and illness is treated with various kinds of *dau* or medicine, which is any substance "used to transform the body's capacity to know" (363). This case shows "a 'total' vision of the body is a necessary precondition for a possible 'medical anthropology'" of the Cashinahua (351)—and not only for them, since "any medical anthropology" requires "a thorough examination of . . . epistemology" or how a society knows the body (347).

See Chapters 9 and 12

relates directly to previous discussions of governmentality.

SITES OF MEDICAL PRACTICE

Anthropologists have applied their perspective and method to many specific sites of modern medical practice. Among the most obvious locations for conducting medical anthropological research is the hospital, where medical care is provided. But anthropologists have also examined how medical knowledge is transmitted in the first place and how medical professionals are created, and they have studied—and contributed to—public health and other medical initiatives.

Medical schools

Since medicine, including Western biomedicine, is cultural, individuals must acquire the knowledge and skill that qualifies them as medical professionals. In a word, they must undergo *medical enculturation* in formal settings such as medical schools. This medical knowledge and skill includes not only information about the body and its diseases, but expertise in interacting with patients, presenting cases to other physicians, perhaps conducting and writing research, and generally conforming to the culture and standards of medical professionals.

Inspired by Parsons' ideas on medicine and society, some of the earliest studies of medical training were conducted by sociologists, including Robert Merton, George Reader, and Patrician Kendall's 1957 *The Student Physician* on the social organization of medical schools, and Howard Becker, Blanche Geer, Everett Hughes, and Anselm Strauss' 1961 *Boys in White: Student Culture in Medical School*, which stressed the ritual quality of medical education with its uniforms (white lab coats), discipline, ceremonies, and ordeals. Since then, a minor industry in ethnographies of medical schools has arisen, such as Samuel Bloom's 1973

Power and Dissent in the Medical School (which was commissioned as a self-study of SUNY Downstate Medical Center), and Simon Sinclair's 1997 *Making Doctors: An Institutional Apprenticeship* (like many in the field, Sinclair was both a medical doctor and an anthropologist). Sinclair's work on medical training in London is instructive, if only because he stressed the "remarkable stability" of educational practices and experiences over more than a century (1997: 11). He reported on both official (e.g. lectures, dissections, and rounds) and unofficial (e.g. student bars and clubs) settings and interactions, finding that, like all cultural content, much of the enculturation was informal and even tacit: "Many of the most vital ways of thinking and acting are transmitted from practice to practice simply through contact of the one who is learning with the one who is teaching" (21).

In their review of ethnographies of medical schools, Scott Reeves et al. (2013: e1375) identified four themes:

- ■ "the use of critical evaluation of medical education"
- ■ "an exploration of socialization of students into the medical profession"
- ■ "the examination of students' perceptions of professionalism"
- ■ "the investigation of the role of the hidden curriculum within medical education."

The **hidden curriculum**, a standard concept in the sociology of education, refers to the unofficial or implicit messages that are embedded in teaching practices and institutions, ones that may even contradict the official or manifest curriculum. Robin Higashi et al. expose part of this hidden training in regard to the "good patient" mentioned previously. Physicians must "determine the quality and quantity of time to devote to each patient," and a decision-making scheme or "moral economy" is "taught to physicians-in-training as part of the 'hidden curriculum' in medical education" (2013: 13).

> Physicians-in-training learn to use these cultural beliefs and values to make assessments about patient worthiness, and these determinations guide decisions about the quality and quantity of care provided to each patient. Instead of money or material goods, time is the

currency that is spent and saved by physicians. As exchange for this capital, physicians may expect to receive, among other things, a sense of competence and purpose, measurable improvement in the patient's health status, and perhaps positive feedback from their superiors or from patients.

(14)

A **worthy patient** is deemed as one who is wealthier, even a colleague in the medical or other profession; other desirable traits are a patient who is "socially engaging and interactive (as opposed to unresponsive or unpleasant)," whose illness is "not caused by bad habits," and who is "motivated to do whatever was necessary to improve their condition" and "likely to make a full recovery" (20). Conversely, unworthy patients include drug addicts, the "non-adherent" or "defiant" person who does not follow instructions and even harms him/herself, the "frequent flyer" who seeks repeated care, and, sadly, the elderly: Doctors griped that "older patients were more 'needy' in a way that made interactions slow and frustrating. Several participants felt that interactions with older patients took more time and felt less productive" (19).

Anthropologists have investigated not only general practitioners but specialists too. Rachel Prentice (2013) recently researched the contemporary training of surgeons, which increasingly uses computer simulations and physical substitutes for the difficult-to-obtain and difficult-to-maintain cadavers of old. Pearl Katz (1999) further elucidated the culture of surgeons in regard to decision-making, styles of interaction (scientific, clinical, artistic, entrepreneurial), and consideration of non-medical factors in the referral process.

Hospitals

Much (but by no means all) of modern medicine happens in the hospital, which makes it a natural setting for medical anthropological research. In fact, a 2008 issue of the *Journal of Contemporary Ethnography* was dedicated to hospital-based fieldwork, on the premise that hospitals are, to say the least, "distinctive institutions" (Finke, Hunter, and Iedema, 2008: 246). As Helle Max Andersen put it, a hospital "is a bureaucracy, whose units,

Sinclair, Simon. 1997. *Making Doctors: An Institutional Apprenticeship.* Oxford and New York: Berg.

Worthy patient
sometimes also called "good patient," the patient who has the qualities desired and preferred by medical professionals, such as wealth, education, youth, cooperativeness, and a lack of bad or unhealthy habits

TODAY'S TECHNOLOGY FOR TOMORROW'S SURGEONS

Hidden curriculum
the unofficial or implicit messages that are embedded in teaching practices and institutions, ones that may even contradict the official or manifest curriculum

hierarchies and roles are defined in relation to a biomedical discourse involving specific categories of actors that sets the stage for their interaction"; yet "the role of the organizational layout in heath service delivery has largely been overlooked in studies of health care" (2004: 2003–2004). One of the first hospital ethnographies was Rose Laub Coser's 1962 *Life in the Ward*, which described an American hospital as an "exotic" place, a "tight little island" (3) apart from the normal world of society. Debbi Long, Cynthia Hunter, and Sjaak van der Geest add that hospitals

> are ultimately liminal spaces, where people are removed from their day to day lives, taken into a betwixt and between space of being diagnosed, operated upon, medicated, cleansed, etc. For many people, hospitals are places in which their previous identities as a healthy person, as a mobile person . . . are stripped bare. . . . In hospitals, medical experts determine the rites of passage undertaken.
>
> (2008: 73)

See Chapter 10

Although hospitals have specific features as cultural sites, they also share many characteristics with all bureaucracies as well as with the surrounding society. In Andersen's (2004) study in Ghana, the working conditions at the hospital reflect the resource deficiencies in the health care system in general. The buildings are deteriorating (parts of the electrical and sewage system are out of order for instance) and equipments are faulty or lacking, making it impossible to carry out even basic hospital procedures.

(2004)

Further, social rank, which is important throughout the society, is omnipresent inside the hospital; doctors and nurses are accorded high status, and some patients bring higher status than others into the hospitals, affecting the quality of care. Indeed, the African doctors practice their own version of worthy/unworthy patient "differential treatment": "some patients are treated with attentive kindness and respect while others are made to wait, are treated with impatience and discourtesy, given less information and accorded less time. They are ordered around, yelled at, accused of lying, etc." (2005). The key dividing lines between patients are their education and their general sophistication and "modern-ness": Uneducated, non-modern, or non-urban patients are "villagers," "more likely to be made to wait, to be addressed rudely and to receive treatment below formal standards" (2008).

IMAGE 16.3 Waiting room at a Japanese clinic.

BOX 16.2   LIFE IN THE WARD IN BANGLADESH

Shahaduz Zaman has written an intriguing series of works (e.g. Zaman, 2004; 2005) on medicine in Bangladesh, focusing on a public teaching hospital and particularly an orthopedic ward. As a state-run facility and therefore cheaper than its alternatives, the hospital disproportionately serves poorer clientele, who are also predominantly male and victims of violence, occupational accidents, and especially traffic accidents. As in Andersen's Ghanaian hospital, the Bangladeshi ward is a microcosm of the society, where the "physically crushed patients ... were found to be mentally crushed as well. They suffered from a host of uncertainties" (Zaman, 2004: 2027), some carried into the hospital and some generated by the hospital. Patients get little information from their doctors; instead,

> *Boka* (scolding) is one of the things that patients receive from all the staff members, from cleaners to professors, regardless of their rank. Scolding the patients and their relatives is an integral part of the ward scene; they are scolded for a multitude of reasons, especially when they do not act according to the expectations of the staff.
>
> (2028)

Like information, the hospital also provides little in the way of supplies:

> The patient must buy almost all of the medicines and other materials for daily use in the hospital. . . . Cotton, gauze, and X-ray films are irregularly available and most of the time are bought by the patients. Injectable drugs and medicines required for operation are almost never available in the ward.
>
> (2028)

Worse, life in the hospital demands a constant stream of informal payments, to the medical staff and non-medical workers like gatekeepers and elevator operators. Understandably, a patient's survival in the hospital largely depends on the assistance of relatives. Usually at least one kinsman "becomes 'attached' to the patient during the whole period of the patient's hospital stay, and plays an important role in caring for the patient. In fact, patients' family members are crucial players in the overall functioning of the ward" (2029), since there is a shortage of nurses and orderlies and since someone must purchase supplies and often administer medicines. Finally, Zaman makes the point that, although the hospital represents modern biomedicine, it must find a variety of "indigenous solutions" to its shortcomings. This includes the inventive use of non-medical hardware like bricks as weights for traction and razor blades to perform skin grafts. He concludes that the ward "carries many traits of Bangladeshi society at large" including poverty, social hierarchy, the value of family, the prevalence of violence, the invisibility of women, and creative use of materials at hand (2032).

One other enlightening and troubling example of hospital ethnography comes from the Netherlands, where Eric Vermeulen discusses decision-making in a neonatal ward. American readers may be shocked to learn that the "ward's policy is to refrain from starting life-prolonging treatment for some children. This is done when staff members consider their chances too small" (2004: 2071). There is no cultural imperative to save every newborn: "Children born under 26 weeks of gestation are not admitted to the ward, or if they are admitted, they will (at first) not receive life-prolonging treatment" (2074), and parents know this reality. Instead, a severely premature baby "is taken to the mother and father to die"; for those babies who are granted care, it is "crucial that they 'prove,' for hours or parts of a day, that they are able to breathe on their own. If they have 'proved themselves,' they are offered the treatment they need" (2076).

Hospitals are clearly places with the power of life and death. They are, more generally, places of power. Anthropologists often feel this during their fieldwork: In most settings, "the researcher occupies a more powerful position than the research subjects. Ethnography in medical settings often reverses this hierarchy and power balance. The ethnographer may be the more junior party, if not in age, at least in terms of professional and occupational status" (Pope, 2005: 1184), since our informants are cultural elites like physicians, surgeons, and hospital administrators. Luckily, many medical professionals have been quite accepting of anthropology, and more than a few have trained as anthropologists and written about anthropology for their peers.

The role of hospitals and modern medicine in colonialism has not gone unnoticed. One of the first links between colonialism and medicine was "tropical medicine," research and treatment for the sort of diseases that colonists might contract in "exotic" locales. But hospitals were key sites for the colonial project. Most basically, "the provision of medical services [was] a way of becoming involved with the local population" (Tejiirian and Simon, 2012: 128) and of introducing the natives to modern knowledge and power—what Foucault called "biopower." Hospitals and clinics were also associated with and often coupled with schools, furthering the work of "civilization" and Westernization. Finally, hospitals were vehicles for Christian missionization. Yunjae Park reveals that "Western missionaries used medicine as a way to enter and work in Korea" (2014: 156), as with the Severance Hospital, founded in 1885, where missionaries envisioned "a purely Christian hospital where missionaries could preach Christianity without restriction" (146). As in other instances of culture contact and acculturation, things did not always work as intended: Alice Street (2010) recounts that patients at a Papua New Guinean hospital would ostensibly convert to Christianity not so much out of commitment to Christian doctrine as out of desire to establish a harmonious relationship with hospital staff and their god, which hopefully would facilitate healing.

Public health and applied medical anthropology

Medical anthropology does not only analyze institutions like the hospital, but also gets out among the people to study public health. Bemoaning the "conceptual split between 'science' and 'culture'" in public health literature (2006: 1), Melissa Parker and Ian Harper call for an anthropology of public health, "which remains passionately concerned about ill-health and deprivation and the need for public policy," one that not only takes an academic stance on health, but "helps to alleviate the distress and suffering caused by infection and disease" (2). This involves fieldwork among citizens—modern urbanites and rural and indigenous people—to learn about their health beliefs and knowledge, practices, and outcomes, in regard to complaints like high blood pressure, heart disease, obesity, sexually transmitted diseases, and more.

Here too anthropology has a long tradition, dating back at least to Benjamin Paul's 1955 volume and continuing through Robert Hahn and Marcia Inborn's 1999 *Anthropology and Public Health: Bridging Differences in Culture and Society*. Very soon after Paul's pioneering work, the 1957–1962 Navajo Cornell Field Health Research Project combined doctors, nurses, and an anthropologist to assess and improve health services to the Navajo tribe. Nearly a half-century later, the Navajo Healing Project united anthropologists and medical experts not only to study the practices of medical doctors, traditional Navajo healers (of three different kinds), Navajo Christian faith healers, and Native American Church healers, but to open dialogue between them and "to produce knowledge that could be circulated back into the Navajo community in a way that could enhance health care providers' understanding of their Navajo patients" (Csordas, 2000: 466).

As concerned citizens and human beings, some medical anthropologists have transcended scholarship to become consultants or providers of public health services. In Hartford, Connecticut, anthropologist Jean Schensul founded the Institute for Community Research in 1987, which, according to its website (www.incommunityresearch.org),

conducts research in collaboration with community partners to promote justice and equity in a diverse, multiethnic, multicultural world.

We engage in and support community-based research partnerships to reverse inequities, promote positive changes in public health and education, and foster cultural conservation and development.

Robert Trotter et al. advanced a model for "rapid assessment" based on short-term fieldwork, the use of existing statistical data, and "direct involvement of community leaders and health providers" (2001: 139). Consistent with her engaged and militant anthropology, Nancy Scheper-Hughes not only returned to Brazil as an anthropologist after her stint in the country in the 1960s as a Peace Corps volunteer and health worker, but co-founded Organs Watch in 1999 to track and end illegal organ trafficking.

ANTHROPOLOGY AND MENTAL ILLNESS

Anthropology's relation with psychology and psychiatry is nearly as old and arguably stronger than its history with biology. Boas and other founders of the discipline pondered the notion of "primitive mentality," and many anthropologists were influenced by Freudian theory; psychological anthropologists like Ralph Linton collaborated with psychiatrists like Abram Kardiner. Especially American anthropology's preoccupation with personality led Edward Sapir to engage directly with psychiatry and to claim that social psychology was the "mother science" of both cultural anthropology and psychiatry; no one was more adamant that anthropology needs the psychiatrist (Sapir, 1932; 2001), since both disciplines study the "adjustment"—or maladjustment—of the individual to his/her social milieu. Margaret Mead's (1928) seminal report on childhood in Samoa was explicitly psychological in orientation, and Ruth Benedict's (1934b) *Patterns of Culture* had a clearly psychological tone.

Culture-and-personality anthropologists like Linton, Mead, and Benedict understood that individuals were not mere copies of social structures and cultural norms, but that all societies produce exceptional or "abnormal" individuals too. In her classic "Anthropology and the Abnormal," Benedict offered examples of shamanism, divination, trance,

and catalepsy as types of psychological abnormality, arguing that such abnormality is not always bad: "Culture may value and make socially available even highly unstable human types" (1934a: 64). More profoundly, "abnormal" is a relative judgment, since it depends on a standard of normality, which "within a very wide range, is culturally defined" (1934b: 276). "Normal," she also realized, is a moral concept:

> It is that which society has approved. A normal action is one which falls well within the limits of expected behavior for a particular society. Its variability among different peoples is essentially a function of the variability of the behavior patterns that different societies have created for themselves, and can never be wholly divorced from a consideration of culturally institutionalized types of behavior.
>
> (276–277)

This is the most fundamental but also most subversive contribution that anthropology has made to the study of mental illness. If physical health and illness are substantially culturally constructed, mental illness is more greatly so. First, as with the Cashinahua above, not all societies have a concept of "mental illness" at all; indeed, not all have a concept of "mental" or "mind" as distinct from the body. On the other hand, many if not all societies have their own cultural conceptions of mind and mental illness, that is, **ethnopsychology**, including causes, symptoms, and therapies. While Western psychology and psychiatry purport to be scientific, it can be rightly asserted that, just as biomedicine is Western ethnomedicine, so scientific psychology and psychiatry is Western ethnopsychology. Indeed, insider critics of Western psychology and psychiatry, like R. D. Laing (1967) and Thomas Szasz (1961), have stressed the cultural and political nature of the science, premised on the power of some people or institutions to categorize certain conduct as "deviant."

The crux is that "mental illness" deals with non-normal ideas, experiences, and behaviors that are less concrete than non-normal organic conditions (and, as we have seen, even the latter are significantly culturally constructed). This provides wide latitude for cultural classification and elaboration of "mental illness." One sign of this relative freedom is the existence of so-called

Benedict, Ruth. 1934a. "Anthropology and the Abnormal." *Journal of General Psychology* 10 (2): 59–82.

See Chapter 5

ethnopsychology
the psychological "theory" or understanding used by any particularly society, including its ideas about and uses of emotions, dreams, mental illness, and personhood most generally

IMAGE 16.4 Cultures differ in their notions of, and treatment of, mental illness.

Culture-bound syndrome sometimes also called folk illness, a pattern of abnormal behavior or ideation recognized by one particular culture, which has no exact equivalent in Western psychiatry

"cultural-bound syndromes." Even Western bio-medicine recognizes a **culture-bound syndrome**, sometimes also called folk illness, as a culture-specific pattern of abnormal behavior or ideation, which may have no exact equivalent in Western psychiatry. In *The Culture-Bound Syndromes: Folk Illnesses of Psychiatric and Anthropological Interest*, Ronald Simons and Charles Hughes (1985) listed two hundred such ailments, including *amok* (Malaysia), *windigo* (Native America), and Arctic hysteria and *wiitiko* psychosis. In contemporary China, *koro* is a pathological fear that the penis will shrink or retract into the body; a similar anxiety has

been noted in West Africa. (See www.medscape.com/features/slideshow/culture-synd for a slideshow of culture-bound conditions.)

Robert Edgerton compared psychosis in four African societies, finding differences in notions of etiology, presentation, and prognosis. Among the Sebei, "madness" presented as public nakedness, "shouting and screaming, talking nonsense, wandering, eating dirt and collecting trash"; violence was also associated with insanity (1966: 413). The Kamba emphasized assault and murder, while the Hehe stressed fear and "retreat from people to a solitary life in the bush" (413). Interestingly, no group mentioned hallucinations, the hallmark of psychosis in the West. The Kamba and the Hehe believed that madness could be cured, but the Sebei and Pokot doubted it. The Sebei and Pokot had no indigenous explanation for insanity, but the Kamba and Hehe attributed it to magic, witchcraft, or ancestor spirits. The Kamba and Hehe combined magical rituals with native drugs, but the Sebei lacked a specialist to handle mental illnesses, and Pokot had little confidence in their medical experts or interventions.

Anthropologists have documented local conceptions and treatments of depression in India (Lang and Jansen, 2013) and Uganda (Okello and Ekblad, 2006), multiple personality disorder in Brazil (Krippner, 1987), and alcoholism among Australian Aboriginals (Chenhall, 2008), as well as eating disorders as mentioned above. Lyren Chiu et al. (2005) asked how Asian women living in Canada make decisions about mental health care, which are obviously affected by language barriers, transportation issues, and financial limitations, but also by cultural considerations such as the stigma of mental illness and beliefs about the spiritual causes

and cures of illness. Most women, they found, combined biomedicine with alternative therapies including diets, herbs, chi gong, acupuncture, massage, astrology, meditation, and prayer.

Most consequentially for Western psychiatry, Marjolein van Duijl, Etzel Cardena, and Joop de Jong actually tested the validity of Western categories as enshrined in the *Diagnostic and Statistical Manual* (DSM-IV) for Africa. Selecting so-called dissociative disorders such as amnesia, identity disorder, trance, and fugue, they determined that local laymen and specialists did not make quite the same distinctions or diagnoses as Western psychiatrists and certainly did not identify the same causes. In short, they found

only partial validity in Uganda for the DSM-IV classification of dissociative disorders, and varying conceptualizations of etiology and treatment. It cannot be assumed that the DSM-IV nosology is translatable wholesale to other cultures unless previous research shows its validity and reliability in that particular context.

(2005: 236–237)

MADNESS, MEDICINE, AND ISLAM IN BANGLADESH

BOX 16.3   AMONG THE SCHIZOPHRENICS IN JAPAN

"Mental illness is a disease of modernity," writes Karen Nakamura (2013: 35), both in the sense that it is a modern concept and that modernity seems to breed it. Thus, notions and practices of mental illness flow with modernization, as in Japan where "Japanese psychiatrists now use either the American DSM system of diagnosing and classifying mental illnesses or the more prevalent International Classification of Diseases (ICS) published by the World Health Organization" (37). As Japan embarked on its modernization phase after 1868, it incorporated German models of mental health; however, the mentally ill were legally confined to their homes until the Mental Hospital Law of 1919, which opened the era of public mental hospitals. Subsequently, the 1950 Mental Hygiene Law expanded facilities for "people with psychiatric disabilities" (46) who were interned there and subjected to the standard practices of the time—mind-numbing drugs, brain operations, and general warehousing. Interestingly, Japanese psychiatry came to differ from the Western variety in several ways: The vast majority of psychiatric hospitals are private rather than public, hospital stays are much longer (in 2007 averaging 318 days compared to seven days in the U.S.), patients are given multiple drugs together, and psychoanalytic-style "talk therapy" is almost unknown. When Dr. Toshiaki Kawamura settled at the Urakawa Red Cross Hospital in northern Japan in 1988, he brought a different philosophy—to shorten hospital stays and to empower patients to live independently. Central to this vision is Bethel House, a set of group homes and workplaces associated with the hospital, whose residents are mostly schizophrenics. Founded in 1984 in a church building, Bethel expanded to three group homes, three shared living facilities, and several other properties, where Nakamura did her fieldwork. What she finds is essentially a community of self-sufficient schizophrenics serving themselves with individual therapy, group therapy sessions, "social skills training" to help them function in the outside world, and "self-directed research" encouraging self-awareness through "concrete ways that you can help yourself or protect yourself and scenarios where you can practice them" (174). The expectation is not to be "cured," but to be functional; the hospital is open for return stays, but Bethel "provides a sense of community, belonging, and sanctuary for its members" (213). "Almost every aspect of Bethel focuses on the social—indeed, far from shying away from the problems of sociality, it welcomes them as a fundamental part of being humans in society" (210), and community members know that they are not alone, that "when the end comes . . . they will die among friends" (214).

MEDICAL PLURALISM AND THE GLOBALIZATION OF HEALTH CARE

A recurring theme in this chapter that deserves explicit attention is the co-existence of multiple medical models or traditions in a single society, known as **medical pluralism**. Just as the assumption that individuals belong to one religion is proven ethnographically false, the assumption that individuals solicit and trust only one kind of medical assistance is also untrue.

Kleinman's notion of explanatory models and medical arenas or sectors helps to make the fact of medical pluralism sensible. Rather than possessing one exclusive medical system, we can and should think of a society as a *field* of multiple—sometimes competing, sometimes cooperating, sometimes syncretizing—medical discourses, practices, and practitioners. We have seen numerous examples in the cases above. Even in "traditional" societies, options exist, as in the choice between Yoruba herbalists, priests, and *babalawo* diviners, who represent quite different perspectives and offer quite different treatments. Asian women in Canada take advantage of Western and non-Western healing options, as their finances and cultural beliefs permit.

A particularly strong case of medical pluralism emerges from Csordas' Navajo Healing Project, mentioned already. The Navajo, Csordas insisted, "orient themselves medically in a field of vital interaction among four modes of healing: conventional biomedicine, traditional Navajo healing, Native American Church (NAC) healing, and Navajo Christian faith healing" (2000: 463).

Traditional healing is that of the *hataalii,* who performs intricate chants and sandpaintings, and of the diagnostician who works by methods such as hand-trembling, crystal-gazing, or coal-gazing. NAC healing is that of the road man, who prays at his earthen altar or fireplace and administers sacramental peyote. Christian faith healing is that of the independent Navajo Pentecostal preacher, with his revival meetings and laying on of hands, and of the Catholic Charismatic prayer group, with its communal integration of Navajo and Roman Catholic practices. All of these forms are available on the Navajo reservation, and it is worth emphasizing that Navajos typically distinguish among them as representing three identifiably distinct religious traditions.

(464)

"Taken together, the four modes of healing," including biomedicine, "are the principal components of the 'health care systems'" (464).

Instances of medical pluralism abound and are the rule more than the exception. In northern Lebanon, patients get their oral health care from two different experts—scientifically trained biomedical dentists and informal traveling traditional Dom dentists, who are much cheaper (Bochi, 2014). Joan McFarlane and Michael Alpers report that the Nasioi people of Papua New Guinea "subscribe to both traditional and western medical paradigms. Western medical concepts have been assimilated but have not displaced traditional understanding of illness" (2009: 147).

Actual responses to illness and expressed attitudes showed that Nasioi respondents value both western and traditional treatment modalities. For the Nasioi it is not an "either/or" choice—respondents saw a role for and wanted

Medical pluralism

the co-existence of multiple medical systems or discourses in one society, and the tendency of individuals to avail themselves of multiple medical specialists and treatments simultaneously both western and traditional health care services. At present the formal health system offers only western medical services. Although traditional health care is a popular and much-used treatment option, it is only available through the informal sector.

(165)

Nor is medical pluralism a phenomenon only of non-Western and "traditional" societies. Many Americans and Europeans solicit biomedicine and other healing practices, including ones diffused from Eastern or indigenous societies. And many Westerners mix scientific and spiritual or magical treatment. Maria Coma gives an account of Spanish charismatic Catholics who believe in the healing powers of religion and "associate healing with salvation" (2015: 159), performing healing prayers and laying on of hands in their services. Yet these believers do not dismiss biomedicine and certainly "do not refrain from seeking medical attention when they are sick. The relationship between biomedicine and religion is not seen as contradictory, and combining prayers with pills causes no conflict at all" (167). Indeed, they subsume biomedicine within religion, as part of God's gift to humanity and as "a divine instrument for accomplishing His healing action" (167).

Although these cases suggest a distinction between formal and informal medicine, such a dichotomy does not map perfectly onto Western/biomedical versus non-Western/ethnomedical and is not entirely sustainable either. Studies of modern hospitals and medical schools have shown that much of biomedical knowledge and practice is informal too, and non-Western or "traditional" ethnomedicine can be formal, as in the apprenticeships and even texts of those systems. Colonialism and globalization has further spurred the formalization and modernization of pre-modern medical traditions. Lang and Jansen describe how Indian Ayurveda has been "biomedicalized" during contact with scientific medicine, transforming *bhūt vidyā* into "Ayurvedic psychiatry." Terms and understandings from Western psychiatry, like depression as a neurochemical imbalance, were found to correlate "with Ayurvedic notions of a fluent body and mind" (2013: 25), while indigenous ideas "are often hybridized with biopsychiatric notions to which they are linked" (26).

The overall aim of contemporary Ayurvedic psychiatry is to purify Ayurvedic psychiatry from its nonscientific and superstitious connotations and institutionalize it as a scientific approach to psychiatric disorders. *Bhūt vidyā* and *dosa* [body humor]-based concepts of mental illness are therefore revitalized and translated by adopting biopsychiatric categories, giving them a claim to modernity and contemporaneity.

(34)

Of course, as biomedicine is globalized, tensions and conflicts arise. Stacy Leigh Pigg and Vincanne Adams expose a number of such clashes in the realm of biomedical sexual health, which is particularly vexed by moral meanings. "Sexual health"—in terms of reproductive health and rights, contraception, sexually transmitted diseases, etc.—is not a morally neutral issue even in the U.S. or Europe, and the globalization of biomedical sexual knowledge and practices draws attention "to the hidden moral trajectory of these rationalizing projects and explore[s] the specific moral eddies created in their wake" (2005: 2). The case studies in their edited volume address anxieties about and resistances to the imposition of Western norms and values in countries from Russia and Greece to Uganda, Tibet, and India, where sexual health is intimately tied to gender concepts, the family, religion, and national identity and the very survival of the nation.

Nor does medical knowledge and practice flow in only one direction in the globalized world, that is, from West to the rest. Americans and Europeans, as mentioned already, embrace a variety of non-Western, "traditional," and indigenous preventative and curative practices, from meditation to acupuncture. Religious studies scholar Andrea Jain (2014) chronicles how Hindu yoga became a health and fitness behavior in the United States, overcoming initial opposition as a threat to Christianity and decency (with its "suggestive" postures and all), shedding most of its religious and philosophical content, and evolving into distinct styles, schools, or "brands" of Western yoga.

Perhaps less common but more consequential is the existence of **medical tourism**, defined on the Medanth website as "the practice of traveling to a different place to receive treatment for a disease,

Medical tourism
the practice of traveling to a different place often internationally to receive medical treatment based on cost, quality, or availability of care

IMAGE 16.5 A yoga class geared toward cancer patients in the United States.

ailment, or condition" (medanth.wikispaces.com/ Medical+Tourism). It further informs that medical tourists "are often seeking lower cost of care, higher quality of care, better access to care, or different care than they could receive at home." Those who travel, especially internationally, may be uninsured in their own lands, or procedures may be prohibitively expensive, or they may be chasing alternative treatments unavailable (or illegal) in their country. Of course, humans have been traveling to places of healing power, from spas and hot springs to sites imbued with spiritual energy, for centuries or millennia. Today's medical tourism highlights the global flow of bodies, knowledge, technology, and capital; many of the treatments sought in locations like Thailand, India, Mexico, and Malaysia are definitely biomedical, offered at private hospitals or hospital chains with highly qualified (even Western-trained) doctors within a market-driven neoliberal paradigm. (See www.cnbc.com/id/101487998 for a list of the top ten medical tourism destinations.) At the same time, many countries promote medical tourism as a strategic component of their overall economic development plan.

BOX 16.4 CONTEMPORARY CULTURAL CONTROVERSIES: OBAMACARE

Affordable Care Act
also known as "Obamacare," the 2010 American law meant to reform the health care system and extend medical insurance coverage to more Americans

One of the most contentious issues in contemporary America, health-related or otherwise, is the **Affordable Care Act** of 2010, commonly (and derisively) known as "Obamacare." Whatever one thinks of the law, it is a fit subject for anthropological examination, which can demythologize much of the debate. Sarah Horton, Cesar Abadía, Jessica Mulligan, and Jennifer Jo Thompson maintain that "anthropologists may use critiques of the ACA as a platform from which to denaturalize assumptions of 'cost' and 'profit' that underpin the global spread of market-based medicine more broadly" (2014: 1). For one thing, anthropology can inquire into how "the right to health has been reconfigured as a right to consumer choice" in a neoliberal manner and elucidate how "the U.S. employer-based insurance system is so entrenched because it serves particular class and industry interests" (3). We can also shed light on the texture of the political debate, pondering "the discursive work that has gone into transforming the individual mandate from a Republican solution to 'free-riders'"—which it originally was, as enacted by Mitt Romney while governor of Massachusetts—"into a 'socialist ploy' to revoke individual liberty" (11). What do you think?

SUMMARY

Health and illness are universal human experiences and concerns, where culture, body, knowledge, and practice intersect. In response, medical anthropology has emerged as a major subdiscipline examining cultural diversity in health-related concepts, roles, and behaviors and the cultural construction of health care and of the very notion of health and the human body.

Medical anthropology compares health concepts and practices, most fundamentally biomedicine and ethnomedicine. However, any medical system may have a professional, popular, and folk domain or sector, and a society may contain multiple diverse, even contradictory medical specialists and treatments. Ethnomedical explanations and cures are not necessarily "spiritual" or magical and often combine practical solutions like plant-based substances and massage. Anthropology also illustrates that the human body itself is culturally conceived and constructed, not always recognizing a dualism of body and mind or of individual body and social and natural environment.

Medical anthropologists have conducted research in multiple sites where medicine is learned and practiced, such as the medical school and the hospital. Both are social institutions unique in society and yet thoroughly tied to the wider society. Anthropologists have also been interested in policy and delivery of public health and have frequently applied their concepts and methods to the improvement of public health.

Psychology and psychiatry have long been allied disciplines of anthropology, and the anthropology of mental health and illness reveals the cultural classification of mental states and the cultural specificity of Western scientific psychiatric categories and practices. However, in both physical and mental health and illness, multiple medical discourses can and do share the same social field, and individuals frequently indulge in medical pluralism. As medical concepts and practices flow across boundaries through globalization, "traditional" ethnomedical systems may become modernized and biomedicalized, as Westerners adopt elements of those same systems in their own health regimens.

Q

MCQS

Q

FILL IN THE BLANKS

WWW

Key Terms

Affordable Care Act

biomedicine

culture-bound syndrome

ethnobotany

ethnomedicine

ethnopsychology

hidden curriculum

medical anthropology

medical pluralism

medical tourism

worthy patient

Seeing culture as a whole #3

Possessed by dispossession—the spirits of postsocialist society in Mongolia

During his fieldwork in northern Mongolia, Morten Pedersen noticed an epidemic of *agsan*, a kind of "drunken rage" in which a person "loses control over himself . . . and screams, cries, and aims punches in all directions" (2011: 1). The most obvious reason for these attacks was the political and economic trauma experienced by the end of communism and the chaos and poverty generated by entry into an era of less state regulation, higher unemployment, and generally more uncertainty. However, this is not how the local Darhad people understood the problem: For them, there were too many spirits afoot and too few people who were able to control them. Thus, many people were exposed to and troubled by spirits—they were like shamans—but were not sufficiently shaman-like to manage the situation.

Darhad country has a complex social history. The environment is some of the harshest in central Asia, with frigid winters and short, hot summers. In the past, Darhad people were pastoralists, but they shared the area with other groups such as Tuvinians, Hahls, Kazaks, and Chinese; Pedersen claims that Darhad society is actually "a heterogenous mix of cultural, linguistic, and political groups" (14), Mongolian and non-Mongolian. The region

has also been a site of political confrontation, invaded by Genghis Khan, then ruled by imperial China, and finally influenced by the Soviet Union, which helped make Mongolia the world's second communist state in 1925. In a word, "the ethnic group known as 'the Darhad people'" was "shaped by complex political processes on the fringes of the Qing [Chinese] Empire from the late seventeenth to the early twentieth century" (13).

The Darhad remember the socialist decades as a time of hard work but relative stability, even oppressive sameness. Oppression was especially cruel to religion: Buddhism was essentially wiped out, and shamanism was suppressed. The end of communism around 1990 ushered in a new era, one of "freedom" but also of "a growing sense of confusion and uncertainty" (21) resulting in a "seemingly irreversible slide toward poverty" (23), as the government provided fewer services while no longer guaranteeing jobs. As a result, many Darhad reverted to older pastoral forms—and the old spirits also reappeared. The problem for contemporary Darhad, though, was that those specialists who knew how to handle the spirits had been eliminated, and much of the knowledge and paraphernalia of shamanism had been lost.

All around the world, societies faced with the hardship and insecurity of modernization have experienced religious revivals—of spirit possession, of witchcraft, of fundamentalism. Many anthropologists have interpreted these religious expressions as symbolic attempts to grapple with unfamiliar social forces or to blame someone or something for the negative effects of those forces. Pedersen argues instead that there is nothing symbolic about the restless spirits in Mongolia; the end of communism really had unleashed the spirits, which were responsible for all sorts of misfortune and confusion.

We could say that the Darhad were understanding the postsocialist transition through the lens of traditional shamanism, but Pedersen makes a much stronger and more intriguing claim: Modern global society and the postsocialist state are more similar to shamanism than we ordinarily appreciate. The central experience of the modern age seems to be uncertainty: Social conditions change so rapidly, and the state provides so much less stability, and the world's societies are becoming so much more interdependent, that people are not sure what is happening and must continuously adjust to new (and often unpleasant) circumstances. Jobs are less stable, and the government feels like it is everywhere and yet nowhere; social life has a ghostly quality, with forces materializing in surprising ways out of what seems like thin air.

But Pedersen claims that this is precisely the shamanic reality. Shamanism is not exactly a religion in the sense of a belief system; rather, it is a worldview or ontology based on *transition*. The power of the shaman, at least in Darhad society but possibly across cultures, is to adopt and move between perspectives—worldly and spiritual—that is, to inhabit "fluid and multiple" positions (67), to perform transformations. The shamanic ontology is "perpetual metamorphosis, malleability, and fluidity expressed in the unpredictable movements of wild animals and the inchoate trajectories of the shamanic spirits" (164). Indeed, Pedersen suggests that we think of shamanic spirits less as beings and more as pure movement or transition—processes more than persons. The shaman, then, is the human who is most like the spirits, able to change and transform; s/he is also "the knot of knots in the community" (165), able to integrate in his/her person the multiple and shifting processes of spiritual and social life.

The key is that globalized society is like shamanism: "the spirits and the market were both variations on one immanent state of transition" (65). Unseen and incomprehensible forces seem to reach out from the void to affect the individual, the family, and the society. The "market" and the "state" have no face yet many faces, and they are as unpredictable as any spirit. Especially compared to the almost suffocating stability of communism, capitalism and democracy exhibit a "lability and capriciousness of forms" that resemble shamanistic reality. For the Darhad exposed to the modern global system, "the restless spirits simply *were* uncertainty as such; they were materializations, actualizations, instantiations, and condensations of the all-pervasive state of cosmological turmoil variously called 'democracy,' 'transition,' or 'the age of the market'" (39).

Again, this would all be potentially manageable if there were competent shamans among the people, able to absorb, embody, and control the agitated spirits. In their absence, instead the Darhad have individuals who are surrounded by and invaded by spirits—individuals who are *like* shamans in that they encounter spirits, but insufficiently like shamans in that they cannot handle the encounter. They are "not quite shamans" in a world defined by invisible and unstable supra-individual movement.

Glossary

Absolute poverty a level of income below what is required to have a decent standard of living, sometimes measured at less than $US 1 per day

Acheulian the stone tool technology associated with Homo erectus, which involves a more complex flaking of bifacial implements

Acculturation the process of acquiring a "second culture," usually as an effect of sustained and imbalanced contact between two societies. Members of the "weaker" society are compelled to adopt aspects of the dominant society

Accumulation by dispossession according to David Harvey, the extraction of wealth from society and its citizens that occurs under neoliberalism, through privatization of public assets, expulsion of people from their land, national debt, slavery and forced labor, and other such tactics

Adaptation changes in a system, including a species, in response to changes in its context or environment so as to make that system or species more fit to survive in the context or environment

Affordable Care Act also known as "Obamacare," the 2010 American law meant to reform the health care system and extend medical insurance coverage to more Americans

Age grade system a non-kinship-based corporate system in which members, usually of one sex, are organized into groups or "grades" according to age and assigned roles and values as a group

Age set a division or subset of a society based on shared age characteristics, as determined by the age grade system of that society

Agents of social control individuals, groups, or institutions that play a part in instilling social norms in members and protecting and perpetuating those norms through the use of their powers and sanctions

Ambilineal descent a descent system in which individuals trace their membership through both "sides" or "lines" of the family, or optionally through one or the other

Ambilocal a residence practice in which individuals may live after marriage with both "sides" of the family (perhaps alternating between them), or optionally with one or the other

Ancestor spirits the spirits of dead family members who are believed to continue to reside near and interact with their living kin

Animatism a type of religious belief in which impersonal spiritual forces exist in the world and affect human life and behavior

Animism a type of religious belief in which natural objects (animals, plants, hills, lakes, the moon, etc.) and forces (wind, rain, etc.) have spiritual components that interact socially with humans

Anthropological perspective the unique "angle" or point of view of anthropology, consisting of cross-cultural or comparative study, holism, and cultural relativism

Anthropometry the measurement of human bodies to determine individual and group ("racial") physical characteristics

Anti-language a speech style used by individuals or groups in the performance of roles opposing or inverting the society outside of their group

Apartheid in twentieth century South Africa, the official policy of separating the races within their society legally and socially

Archaeology the study of the diversity of human behavior in the past, based on the traces left behind by past humans or societies

Arranged marriage a practice in which family members (often parents) choose the partner for marriageable youths, sometimes with little or no input from or option for the partners themselves

Artifacts physical objects created by humans, often specifically the "portable" objects like tools, pottery, jewelry, etc. (as opposed to the non-portable ones like buildings and roads, etc.)

Assimilation the social process by which individuals and groups are absorbed into another, usually dominant, cultural group

Audit culture a system of power between scrutinizer and observed which depends on cultural concepts and norms an audit "repertoire" including "public inspection," "submission to scrutiny," "rendering visible," and "measures of performance"

Australopithecus a genus of the category Hominid, closely related to and earlier than genus Homo

Authority legitimate power or power that an individual, group, or institution is felt to rightly possess and exercise on the grounds of age, knowledge, office, and such

Avunculocal a residence practice in which a married couple lives with or near an uncle, often a mother's brother

Band a political system or "level of political integration" where small, autonomous, and typically leaderless groups constitute local segments of a decentralized society

Basic personality the psychological traits common to most or all of the members of a society

Berdache a "third gender" found in many Native American societies, in which biological men adopt some of the norms usually associated with women

Bilateral descent relating to both "sides," as in a kinship system, in which individuals regard kin related to the mother and to the father as socially equivalent

Biocultural the mutual interaction between physical/biological and behavioral/cultural factors, in which physical traits make certain behaviors possible, and behavior feeds back to influence physical traits

Biomedicine roughly synonymous with modern scientific Western medicine, the model that sees illness as the effect of physical and chemical causes in the individual body

Bipedalism the ability and tendency to walk on two feet

Blackbirding the colonial practice of abducting the populations of areas, often islands, and resettling them as a labor force in some other part of the world

Bound morpheme a morpheme that has meaning but only when used in conjunction with a word (such as the suffix -s to indicate plural)

Bride service the marriage wealth-exchange practice in which a man must labor for his wife's kin for some period of time before he may assume rights over his wife

Bridewealth/bride price the marriage wealth-exchange practice in which a man or his family must pay an amount of property to his wife's kin before he may assume rights over his wife

Cargo cult a form of revitalization movement, most associated with early-twentieth century Pacific island societies, in which indigenous peoples adopted aspects of Western cultures and modified or abandoned aspects of pre-contact culture on the expectation of receiving shipments of wealth or "cargo," often from the dead ancestors

Caste a closed socio-economic status, often ascribed by birth

Cephalic index a measurement of the skull/brain volume and shape, based on a ratio of the width of the head from ear to ear relative to the depth of the head from front to back

Chiefdom a political system or "level of integration" in which a central office, often hereditary, possesses formal political power and social prestige through some degree of redistributive control over surplus and the ability to organize and manage labor

Civil war a violent conflict within a particular state or between corporate or identity groups within the state

Civilization a form of society based on cities as the centers of administration and the focus of social life, usually dependent on intensive agriculture in the surrounding countryside

Clan a kinship group, sometimes an assortment of lineages, that can trace its descent back to a common ancestor

Clash of civilizations Huntington's notion that the key forces in the future will not be societies or states but regional cultural entities (like "Western civilization" or "Islam"); within a civilization a variety of cultural attitudes are shared, but between civilizations differences of attitude and interest will breed conflict

Class an (at least ideally) open socio-economic status, which members can change through their own achievements

Coercion power based on the threat or use of force

Colonialism the more or less organized system of occupation and exploitation of foreign territories through settlement and conquest, especially as practiced by Western states since 1492

Colonies of exploitation colonies to which few foreigners immigrate but the territory is still used for its resources, wealth, labor, markets, and/or strategic location

Colonies of settlement colonies to which many foreigners immigrate, sometimes such that they and their descendants become the majority population of the territory

Colony a segment of a population (not exclusively a human population) that moves into and occupies territory not previously occupied by the population, often displacing or subduing the previous occupants

Competence in language, the mastery of the elements (sounds, semantics, and grammar) of a language to be able to make intelligible utterances

Contagious magic the belief and practice that objects that come in contact with each other have some supernatural connection with each other

Core in dependency/world system theory, the states that make up the power-center of the world system, essentially the rich industrial states and former colonialists

Corporate group a social group that shares some degree of practical interest, identity, residence, and destiny

Corvée a colonial practice in which local people were required to provide a period of labor to the administration as a sort of "tax"

Counterculture a group or subset within a society that more or less intentionally adopts behaviors, beliefs, or practices that are at odds with or opposed to the mainstream of society

Country commonly used as a synonym for "nation" or "state," more properly refers to the territory that a society or polity inhabits

Creole a pidgin language that has become elaborated into a multi-functional language and distributed into a first language of the community

Cross-cultural study the examination of a wide variety of societies when considering any particular cultural question, for purposes of comparison

Cultural anthropology the study of the diversity of human behavior in the present

Cultural assimilation a type of assimilation which refers specifically to the loss of distinctive cultural traits, such as language or religion

Cultural competence the skills necessary in the workplace and in life to recognize and value diversity, see one's own cultural influences, understand the dynamics and challenges of intercultural interaction, institutionalize cultural knowledge, and develop practices and policies for delivering culturally appropriate services

Cultural evolutionism the early ethnological or anthropological position or theory that Culture started at some moment in the past and evolved from its "primitive" beginnings through a series of stages to achieve its "higher" or more modern form

Cultural loss the process by which elements of a culture disappear over time, through natural or environmental changes, social pressures, or individual choices

Cultural materialism the theory that practical, material, or economic factors can explain some or all cultural phenomena

Cultural ontology a society's system of notions about what kind of things (including kinds of people) exist in the world and their characteristics and social value. A socially specific way of categorizing and valuing the physical and social world

Cultural relativism the reaction to the fact of cultural diversity in which one attempts to understand and judge the behavior of another culture in terms of its standards of good, normal, moral, legal, etc. rather than one's own

Cultural tourism the practice of "consuming" culture as a form of entertainment and education. Traveling to foreign societies to observe their ways of life (not always "traditional" but sometimes designed for the tourist) in an informal manner

Culture-bound syndrome sometimes also called folk illness, a pattern of abnormal behavior or ideation recognized by one particular culture, which has no exact equivalent in Western psychiatry

Culture shock the surprise, confusion, and pain we feel when we encounter a way of life that is very foreign to our own

Decentered the absence or denial of a particular society's or culture's perspective from which to view the world, usually associated with moving away from a Western- or Euro-centric perspective. Could potentially imply the absence of any central perspective

Deculturation see *cultural loss*

Deism the form of theism or belief in god(s) that posits a creator god that does not take an active role or moral interest in human affairs

Dependency theory the theory of "Third World" underdevelopment that attributes the poverty and weakness of certain states to their ongoing unfavorable relationship to richer and more powerful states. Poor or weak states continue to be dependent on rich or powerful (mostly Western) states for capital, manufactured goods, and other key economic resources

Dependent accumulation according to Andre Gunder Frank, the colonial process by which colonies became poorer as colonizers became richer, since colonizers expropriated and accumulated the wealth of colonies for themselves

Descent the kinship principle of tracing membership in a kin-based corporate group through a sequence of ancestors

Development a form of directed change in which a state tries to change its internal economy and society, and/or foreign states and institutions try to change it, to promote economic growth, industrialize and urbanize, and ideally achieve a higher standard of living for its inhabitants

Development policy the general priorities and decisions set by a state or by development agencies to achieve economic, political, and social goals

Development project a specific activity or task settled upon to achieve the economic, political, and social goals of a development policy. Such projects often include transportation, energy (especially hydro-electric), agricultural, and resettlement schemes

Diaspora the dispersion of a social group from its historical homeland (often applied specifically to the Jewish community)

Diffusion the spread of a cultural trait (object, idea, practice, institution) from one society to another

Diffusionism the early ethnological or anthropological position or theory that Culture, or specific cultural practices, objects, or institutions, had appeared once or at most a few times and spread out from their original center

Diglossia the use of two varieties of a language by members of a society for distinct functions or by distinct groups or classes of people

Directed change a cultural process in which internal or external agents make more or less intentional, coordinated, and sustained modifications or reforms to a society and culture

Diseases of development   the lifestyle-related diseases that are common in developed industrial societies and increasingly common in developing societies, such as high-blood pressure, heart disease, diabetes, tooth decay, and obesity

Displacement   the linguistic feature that allows for communication about things that are "not here" in the sense of absent or out of view, past or future, conceptual or even imaginary

Diviner   a religious specialist who uses one of many techniques to "read" information from the supernatural world

Division of labor   the differentiation of the economy into a set of distinct production tasks, which are assigned to different individuals, groups, or classes, usually creating economic and political inequalities

Doctrine of discovery   the European colonial principle that the state that "discovered" or arrived first in a new territory had the right to occupy and administer it without interference from other states

Domestication   the process of modification of plants or animals to establish human control over them, leading to agriculture and pastoralism

Dominance   the social relationship in which certain individuals have higher prestige or power in the group, allowing them to enjoy more or better resources as well as the deference of lower-ranked members

Double descent   the kinship practice of reckoning one's membership in kinship-based corporate groups through two lines of descent, ordinarily the mother's and the father's

Dowry   the marriage wealth-exchange practice in which the woman's family is required to provide the husband with property (money, land, household goods, etc.) in order to make the marriage

Ecofacts   the environmental remains from past human social contexts, including wood, seeds, pollen, animal bones, shells, etc.

Ecotourism   a form of cultural and environmental tourism ostensibly characterized by responsible travel to natural areas that conserves the environment, sustains the well-being of the local people, and involves interpretation and education

Encomienda   in Latin American colonial history, a grant of land to a conqueror and explorer, much like medieval estates, which gave the grant-holder control over the land and inhabitants

Enculturation   the process by which a person learns or acquires his/her culture, usually as a child. Also known as *socialization*

Endogamy   the marriage principle in which an individual marries someone who is in the same cultural category as him/herself (e.g. marrying someone in your own race or religion)

Erectness   the tendency to have an upright posture based on a spine that is vertical rather than parallel to the ground

Ethnic group   a corporate group based on some shared cultural traits—language, religion, history, etc.—and finds itself in competition with other groups for wealth, power, opportunity, and recognition. An ethnic group shares an identity and a destiny and therefore competes as a group

Ethnicity   the phenomenon of organizing around some aspect of shared culture to integrate an identity group, differentiate it from other groups, and compete in a multi-ethnic context for resources

Ethnobotany   cultural knowledge and uses of plants, especially but not exclusively for medical purposes

Ethnocentrism   the attitude or belief that one's own culture is the best or only one, and that one can understand or judge another culture in terms of one's own

Ethnocide   the destruction of a group's culture, without necessarily killing any of the members of the culture

Ethnogenesis   the process by which ethnic groups come into being and attain their cultural characteristics

Ethnography   a written account or description of a particular culture, usually including its environment, economic system, kinship arrangements, political systems, and religious beliefs, and often including some discussion of culture change

Ethnomedicine   healing knowledge and practices that are specific and related to particular cultures, usually construed as non-Western, "pre-modern," or "traditional" cultures;

some analysts argue that modern scientific biomedicine is Western ethnomedicine

Ethnopsychology the psychological "theory" or understanding used by any particularly society, including its ideas about and uses of emotions, dreams, mental illness, and personhood most generally

Ethnoscience the anthropological theory or approach that investigates the native classification systems of societies to discover the concepts, terms, and categories by which they understand their world

Eugenics the scientific practice of "improving" a population or species by selective breeding or genetic engineering, to breed out "bad" traits and breed in "good" ones

Eunuch a gender category involving non-sexual individuals (usually men), who may be castrated or merely celibate, sterile, or lacking sexual desire

Exogamy the marriage principle in which an individual marries someone who is not in the same cultural category as him/herself (e.g. marrying someone of a different sex or gender)

Externalized control the source of social control that lies outside of the individual, in the form of individuals, groups, and institutions with the power to sanction behavior, such as parents, teachers, police, governments, etc.

Facial angle a concept in anthropometry that measures the shape of the face from the forehead to the bridge of the nose, on the assumption that sharper angles indicate "more primitive" kinds of humans

Features in archaeology, the large and non-portable objects or structures created and left by humans, including walls, buildings, roads, canals, and so on

Female circumcision also known as female genital mutilation; the practice of cutting off some or all of a female's external genitalia, for purposes of "beauty" or the regulation of sexual sensations

Feminist anthropology the anthropological theory or approach that focuses on how gender relations are constructed in society and how those relations subsequently shape the society. Also examines how gender concepts have affected the science of anthropology itself the questions it asks and the issues it emphasizes

Fieldwork the anthropological method of traveling to the society one wants to study and living there for a prolonged period of time to collect data first-hand

First World a term not commonly used anymore for the rich, powerful states in the world that dominate the international political and economic arena and consist basically of the former colonial powers

Folklore the "traditional," usually oral, literature of a society, consisting of various genres such as myth, legend, folk tale, song, proverb, and many others

Foraging Also known as hunting and gathering, the production of food by collecting wild (undomesticated) animals and plants

Formal sanction a method of social control employing rewards and punishments that are explicit and well-known, often written down, and administered by special agents of control who possess the authority to administer them (such as police or courts)

Fourth World a collective term for the "traditional," often small-scale and indigenous non-state societies that live inside states (frequently created by colonialism) that they do not control and in which they are the minority and typically the poorest group

Free morpheme a morpheme that has meaning in its own right, that can stand alone as a meaningful sound (for the most part, a word)

Functionalism the method, and eventually the theory, that a cultural trait can be investigated for the contribution it makes to the survival of individual humans, the operation of other cultural items, or the culture as a whole

Fundamentalism a type of cultural or revitalization movement in which members attempt to address perceived social problems or disadvantages by restoring the perceived "fundamentals" or oldest, most important, and most "genuine" elements of culture

Garbology the study of contemporary trash to examine how humans make, consume, and discard material objects in the present

Gender the cultural categories and concepts relating to sexually distinct bodies, sexual preference, sexual identity, and sexual norms

Genealogy kinship or "blood" and "marriage" information about a society

Genocide the destruction of a group or society by harming, killing, or preventing the birth of its members

Geopolitics the use of geographical territory for purposes of maintenance and projection of power; the control of strategic locations in the pursuit of political goals

Ghost a religious or spiritual being, generally regarded to be the disembodied spiritual part of a deceased human

Global apartheid the de facto division of the world's states into rich, powerful, majority-white states and poor, weak and dependent majority-non-white states

Glocalization a combination of the words "globalization" and "local," suggests the unique local and situated forms and effects of wide-spread and even global processes

Governmentality as formulated by Michel Foucault, the assorted practices, institutions, instruments, and discourses of power by means of which a "government" (state) or any other political entity can manage a population—and manage to get that population to manage itself

Grammar see *syntax*

Gross national product (GNP) the total value of goods and services produced by a society or state

Gross national product per capita the GNP of a state divided by its population

Guided reinvention of culture the process by which individuals, ordinarily children, acquire ideas, concepts, and skills actively by observing the behavior of others, extracting meanings and rules, and testing those meanings and rules in social situations; fully competent members "guide" the learning by providing models of behavior and correction for inappropriate behaviors

Hacienda the Spanish colonial practice in which land was granted as private property and in which these estates were run both for subsistence production and for the production of cash and export crops

Hidden curriculum the unofficial or implicit messages that are embedded in teaching practices and institutions, ones that may even contradict the official or manifest curriculum

Hierarchy see *dominance*

Hijra a "third gender" in India, in which biological men renounce their sexuality (and often their sexual organs) and become socially neither male or female

Holism the part of the "anthropological perspective" that involves consideration of every part of a culture in relation to every other part and to the whole

Hominid the category of primates that includes only modern humans and extinct human-like species that fall within the genera of Homo and Australopithecus (although other and even more ancient genera have been proposed)

Homo the genus that contains the modern human species (Homo sapiens) as well as several other extinct human species

Homo erectus an extinct human species that lived from approximately 1.8 million years ago until a few hundred thousand years ago or perhaps even more recently

Homo habilis an extinct human species that lived from over two million years ago until less than two million years ago. They are also known as the first stone tool makers.

Homo sapiens the species name for modern humans

Honorifics specialized forms of speech (terms, titles, tones, grammar, etc.) that convey respect or deference

Horticulture a production system based on low-technology farming or gardening, without the use of plows, draft animals, irrigation, or fertilizers

Household all of the people who live in the same house or compound of houses and act for some or all purposes as a corporate group

Hypergamy the marriage practice of marrying "up" with a spouse in a higher status, class, or caste than oneself

Identity politics the organization and mobilization of groups and parties on the basis of shared cultural characteristics, such that these groups and parties are seen to share an "identity" and to pursue economic, political, and cultural goals for and in the name of those who share that identity

Imperialism the pursuit of territorial and political domination of foreign lands and peoples (building an "empire"), known since ancient history but reaching its greatest extent in the late phase of European colonialism

Import substitution a development policy aimed at producing domestically what the state or society currently imports from other states, i.e. substituting its own local products for imported products

Incest taboo the nearly universal rule against marrying or having sex with kin

Industrialism an economic and social system based on the production of large quantities of inexpensive manufactured goods and the concentration of employment in urban factories

Informal economy according to Keith Hart, the marginal, unofficial, even illicit zone of the economy, consisting mainly of work that is impermanent, irregular (not full-time), and not guaranteeing a fixed wage

Informal sanction a "reward" or "punishment" that is widely understood in a society but not precisely defined, usually not written down, and for which no specialized role exists to administer the sanction

Innovation the invention or discovery of a new cultural concept, idea, behavior, or object

Intensive agriculture high-input, high-yield farming on permanent farmlands through the use of technologies like irrigation, fertilizer, pesticide, and the plow

Internal colonialism the practice in which a society (usually a state) penetrates and occupies territory within its jurisdiction (normally inside its borders) but that contains peoples who do not identify as and with the occupying society. In some usages, it can also refer to the condition in which colonized peoples internalize (in their minds and personalities) the institutions and values of colonialism

Internalized control a form or source of social control in which individuals make themselves conform to social expectations through the internalization of rules and norms; by enculturation, social rules and norms become part of the personalities of members

Irredentism a revitalization movement to reclaim a lost homeland

Jihad versus McWorld Benjamin Barber's notion that two opposing but related forces operate in the modern world, one to integrate the world into a single market dominated by a few multinational corporations, and the other to disintegrate the world into exclusivist and often hostile cultural or national groups

Kindred an ego-centered (that is, reckoned from the perspective of some particular individual) category of persons related by kinship, especially in bilateral societies, including members from "both sides" of the family in older and younger generations

Kinesics the study of how body movements are used to communicate social information, sometimes referred to as "body language"

Level of political integration the extent to which political institutions unite a group of people into a single political entity, as measured by the size of the society, the complexity of the society, the formality and centralization of political rules and roles, and the amount of coercive force available to political leaders

Leveling mechanism a practice to establish or re-establish social equality or parity, usually by "bringing down" individuals or groups that threaten to get "above" or "better than" others

Levirate a marriage practice in which the brother of a deceased man is expected to marry his brother's widow

Liminality the condition of being "in between" or "on the margins" of social roles, in particular of being in transition (as during ritual) between one social role and another

Lineage a kinship-based corporate group composed of members related by descent from a known ancestor

Linguistic anthropology the study of the diversity of human language in the past and present, and its relationship to social groups, practices, and values

Linguistic relativity hypothesis the claim that language is not only a medium for communication about experience but actually a more or less powerful constituent of that experience; language consists of concepts, relations, and values, and speakers of different languages approach and interpret reality through different sets of concepts, relations, and values (also known as the Sapir-Whorf hypothesis)

Market exchange a form of distribution based on the use of a specialized location (the "market place") and relatively impersonal principles of supply and demand and the pursuit of profit

Market-dominant minority "ethnic minorities who, for widely varying reasons, tend under market conditions to dominate economically, often to a startling extent, the 'indigenous' majorities around them" (Chua, 2003: 6)

Marriage a socially recognized relationship between two (or more) people that establishes a kin-based group and that provides norms and roles for residence, property ownership and inheritance, labor, sexual relations, and childrearing

Marxist/critical anthropology the theory, based on the work of Karl Marx, that emphasizes the material and economic forces that underlie society, relying on notions of power and inequality, modes of production, and class relations and conflicts

Matrilineal descent a descent system in which lineage relations are traced through a line of related females. Children belong to their mother's corporate group

Matrilocal the residence practice of living with or near the wife's family after marriage

Means of production the activities and tools that a society employs to satisfy its material needs; the form of "work" or "labor" that is performed in a society

Medical anthropology the branch of anthropology investigating the factors that influence health and well-being, the experience and distribution of illness, the prevention and treatment of sickness, healing processes, the social relations of therapy management, and the cultural importance and utilization of pluralistic medical systems

Medical pluralism the co-existence of multiple medical systems or discourses in one society, and the tendency of individuals to avail themselves of multiple medical specialists and treatments simultaneously

Medical tourism the practice of traveling to a different place often internationally to receive medical treatment based on cost, quality, or availability of care

Mercantilism an early modern European economic and political system in which wealth and power were determined by possession of gold and a favorable balance of trade with each other

Microfinance an idea first promoted in the 1970s, to provide very small loans directly to poor individuals or families, for the purpose of starting or growing a small business

Millenarianism a type of revitalization movement aimed at preparing for and perhaps bringing about the end of the "present era," however that era is understood, and replacing it with a new and better existence

Miscegenation a term for the undesirable effects of the mixing of different genetic types or populations, especially race groups. Often refers to the very notion of mixing the races

Modal personality according to Du Bois, the statistically most common personality traits in a society

Mode of production in Marxist theory, the combination of the productive forces and the relations of production that defines the economy and society at a particular place in and time in history

Modernism a type of revitalization movement intended to adopt the characteristics of a foreign and "modern" society, in the process abandoning some or all of the "traditional" characteristics of the society undergoing the movement. Also termed *vitalism*

Modernization theory the theory that the improvement of economic and social conditions in poor states entails the creation of "modern" (generally understood as Western-like) institutions, values, and habits; also, the specific processes or policies by which this form of social change can occur; W. W. Rostow offers one of the most complete and well-known modernization theories

Moiety one of the "halves" of a society, when kin groups are combined in such a way as to create a binary division within society

Monoculture the specialization of production of only one crop or product for which a territory is particularly suited. This can involve food crops like corn or rice, or raw materials like lumber, coffee, rubber, tea, and so on

Monogamy the marriage rule in which an individual may have only one spouse

Monotheism the form of theism that includes belief in only one god or goddess

Morpheme the smallest bit of meaningful sound in a language, usually a word but also a prefix or suffix or other meaning-conveying sound that can be used in conjunction with a word

Morphology the area of language dealing with how meaningful bits (usually but not exclusively words) are created and manipulated by the combination of language sounds

Mousterian the stone tool technology associated with Neandertals, first appearing less than 130,000 years ago

Multilateral development institutions organizations like the World Bank (officially the International Bank for Reconstruction and Development) and the International Monetary Fund that were established and are funded and operated by more than government for the purpose of disbursing money, advice, and technology in the pursuit of development

Multinational state a state that contains some or all of two or more distinct nations or cultural groups

Multiple modernities the perspective that "modernity" as known in the Western tradition is not the only possible form of modern society, and that other societies can and will devise their own particular experience of and response to modern and global forces

Multi-state nation a nation or cultural group that is divided across two or more state borders

Myth a narrative, usually of the activities of supernatural beings, often telling of how some or all of the natural or social world was established. In addition to an explanation of origins, it also provides a "charter" or model for how humans should live today

Nation a corporate group that shares an identity based on such traits as history, culture, territory, etc. and that recognizes a shared political destiny. A group that is politically mobilized to achieve certain goals, usually including political recognition, rights, and sometimes an independent state

Nation-state in modern political thought, the ideal form of state in which the state contains only and all of one nation, or in which a nation has its own territorial state

National character the purported personality traits shared by an entire society or country; the term was usually applied to modern societies and countries like the United States, China, Japan, or the Soviet Union

Nationalism a social movement to achieve recognition, rights, and sometimes an independent state for a nation

Nativism a type of revitalization movement aimed at perpetuating, restoring, or reviving "traditional" cultural practices or characteristics, which are thought to be the source of the group's strength and to be threatened or lost

Neandertal the species or subspecies of Homo that first appeared around 130,000 years ago and is associated with the cold climate of Europe. They became extinct in the last 35–40,000 years and are generally not regarded as direct human ancestors, although this interpretation is still somewhat controversial

Neocolonialism the reconstitution of dependent relationships between states in the post-colonial era, with poor states providing land, labor, and resources to richer industrial states; although invasion and military occupation may not be involved, the inequality of the relationship can lead to exploitation reminiscent of formal colonialism

Neo-evolutionism the mid-twentieth century revival of focus on the historical development of cultures and societies, as in the work of Leslie White and Julian Steward, which generally sought to repair the failings of nineteenth-century evolutionism by proposing specific processes and a "multi-linear" path of change

Neoliberalism according to David Harvey, a theory of political economic practices that proposes that human well-being can best be advanced by liberating individual entrepreneurial freedoms and skills within an institutional framework characterized by strong private property rights, free markets, and free trade

Neolithic the "New Stone" age, beginning around ten thousand to twelve thousand years ago with the first animal and plant domestication

Neolocal the residence practice in which married people start their own household apart from their parents' or families' households

Noble savage the notion, often associated with Rousseau, that non-Western or "primitive" people are actually happier and more virtuous than Westerners; based on the idea that humans are free and equal in "a state of nature" but that social institutions deprive them of that freedom and equality

Non-governmental organization (NGO) any non-profit, voluntary citizens' group organized on a local, national, or international level. Task-oriented and driven by people with a common interest, NGOs perform a variety of service and humanitarian functions, bring citizen concerns to governments, advocate and monitor policies, and encourage political participation through provision of information.

Office a more or less formal social position with specific rights and responsibilities; one source of "political" authority and social control

Oldowan the earliest known stone tool technology, associated with Homo habilis and named for the location of its discovery, Olduvai Gorge in East Africa

One-world culture the idea that all of the peoples and cultures of the world are becoming (or should become) more similar, to the point at which all humans share a single culture. Often attributed to globalization and the universal access to technology and cultural images (like American movies), it assumes that disparate groups will continue to become more similar until all groups share the same basic values, tastes, and media

Oracle a religious specialist (or any religious object or process) with the power to forecast the future or answer questions through communication with or manipulation of supernatural forces

Overurbanization the growth of large cities without the infrastructure to handle the urban populations, especially when a disproportionate amount of the state's population lives in one or a few such cities

Paralanguage the qualities that speakers can add to language to modify the factual or social meaning of speech, such as tone of voice, volume, pitch, speed and cadence, and "non-linguistic" sounds like grunts and snickers

Participant observation the anthropological field method in which we travel to the society we want to study and spend long periods of time there, not only watching, but joining in their culture as much as possible

Pastoralism a productive system based on domesticated animals as the main source of food

Patrilineal descent a descent system in which lineage relations are traced through a line of related males. Children belong to their father's corporate group

Patrilocal the residence practice of living with or near the husband's family after marriage

Peasant an out of favor term for rural and agricultural peoples who live in but are peripheral to a centralized and often urbanized society. The peasants provide the food for the society but generally have the least power and wealth in the society

Performatives linguistics utterances that do not merely describe but actually accomplish a transformation in the social world

Periphery in dependency or world system theory, the societies and states that have the least wealth and power and the least influence on the practices and policies in the global economy

Personality the distinctive ways of thinking, feeling, perceiving, and behaving of an individual, shaped by enculturation as individuals internalize aspects of their society's culture

Persuasion a source of social and political power, based on the ability to move people to agree with or obey the persuader. Often exercised through linguistic skill (e.g. the ability to give a good speech) and the manipulation of resources and social relationships

Phoneme the smallest bit of contrastive sound in a language, that is, the minimal sound unit that serves to distinguish between word meanings in a language

Phonology the study of how sounds are used in a language (specifically which sounds occur and the practices for how they combine and interact)

Phratry a kinship-based corporate group composed of two or more clans that recognize common ancestry

Physical anthropology the study of the diversity of human bodies in the past and present, including physical adaptation, group or "race" characteristics, and human evolution

Pidgin   a simplified version of a language that is usually used for limited purposes, such as trade and economic interactions, by non-native speakers of the language (as in Melanesian pidgin versions of English); usually an incomplete language that is not the "first" language of any group

Plural society   a society that contains various cultural groups; such groups often occupy "niches" in the broader social system, such that the groups do not interact with each other except in limited and often mutually exploitative ways

Pluralism   the co-existence of multiple social and cultural groups in the same society or state

Polyandry   the marriage rule in which a woman can or should marry two or more men

Polygyny   the marriage rule in which a man can or should marry two or more women

Polytheism   the religious belief in two or more gods

Popular culture   often contrasted with "high" or "official" culture, the cultural practices and creations of "the people"; often used as a pejorative term to indicate the poor quality and low intelligence of such culture, in the contemporary world it has also become an important and vibrant form of culture, although one that is not entirely "of the people," in the sense that large corporations often create and disseminate it

Post-modernism   a form of life or way of thinking, and the theory of these, of the mid- to late-twentieth century, in which earlier notions of unity, progress, reason, and the increasing integration of peoples and societies breaks down and is replaced by pluralism, "irrationality" or emotion or tradition, de-centering, and cultural disintegration

Pragmatics   the rules or practices regarding how language is used in particular social situations to convey particular social information, such as the relative status or power of the speakers

Prayer   a form of linguistic religious ritual in which humans are believed to speak and interact with supernatural beings

Precarity   the condition of vulnerability and insecurity associated with neoliberalism, as employers provide less in benefits, wages, and regular full-time work while states abandon many of their functions for regulating the economy and guaranteeing services and standards of living

Priest   a religious specialist, often full-time, who is trained in a religious tradition and acts as a functionary of a religious institution to lead ritual and perpetuate the religious institution

Primary innovation   the invention or discovery of a totally original cultural item, as opposed to *secondary innovation*

Primary production   the production of raw materials, in the form of farming, mining, foresting, etc.

Primate   the term for the classification of mammals, including prosimians, monkeys, apes, and humans, that share a collection of physical characteristics including a distinct tooth pattern, five-fingered hands, a tendency toward erectness of the spine, large eyes and good vision, and a relatively large brain in relation to body weight, among others

Primatology   the study of the physical and behavioral characteristics of the category of species called primates

Primitive accumulation   according to Marx, the process by which precapitalist modes of production such as feudalism and slavery were transformed into the capitalist mode of production, by forcibly, even brutally, separating people from common resources like land and converting those resources into private property owned by the few

Primitive mentality   according to Lévy-Bruhl, a way of thinking characteristic of "primitive societies" in which individuals cannot understand cause and effect and do not distinguish one object from another (e.g. they believe that an animal can be a person)

Productivity   the capacity of language to combine meaningless sounds to create new words or to combine words to create new utterances

Prophet   a human who speaks for or receives messages from spirits

Prosimian   the category with the classification Primate that includes the least derived or "most primitive" species, such as lemurs, lorises, bush babies, galagas, and so on. Most have long tails and protruding snouts, but they exhibit other basic features of primates

Proxemics   the study of how cultures use personal space (or "proximity")

Psychic unity of humanity   the position that all humans share a single set of mental processes, even if they think or believe different things; rejects the notion of primitive mentality

Psychological anthropology   the specialty within anthropology that examines the relationship between culture and the individual, that is, the mutual interactions of cultural processes and mental and psychological processes and the cultural variability of psychological experiences such as dreams, emotions, and mental illness

Racial assimilation   a form of assimilation in which the physical traits of a group are lost through intermarriage

Reciprocity   a form of exchange that involves giving and receiving between relative equals and as part of a larger ongoing social relationship

Redistribution   a form of exchange that involves collection of surplus or wealth by a "central" individual, group, or institution that controls how the wealth is redistributed and used

Relations of production   in Marxist theory, the social roles and relationships that are generated by the mode of production, including such things as class, ownership, "management," and in some lines of thinking, "family"

Relative poverty   the possession of less money than others in the same society, or the inability to afford the standard of living of more comfortable individuals or that is believed to be possible or appropriate

Residence   the kinship principle concerning where people live, especially after marriage, and therefore what kinds of residential and corporate groups are found in the society and what tasks and values they are assigned

Revitalization movement   according to Anthony Wallace (1956), the deliberate, organized, and self-conscious effort of a society to create a more satisfying culture

Revolution   a more or less sudden, complete, and often violent movement to change a political or social system

Rite of intensification   a form of ritual in which members of the society are brought into greater communion, in which social bonds are intensified

Rite of passage   a form of ritual intended to accompany or accomplish a change of status or role of the participants, such as initiation (change from youth to adult) or marriage

Ritual   any type of formal, repetitive behavior that is felt to have significance beyond the actions themselves; in particular, religious ritual is often composed of symbols, re-enacts supernatural or mythical events, and is believed to have efficacy if performed correctly

Sanction   any type of social pressure in the form of "reward" or "punishment" that can be imposed on people to influence and control their behavior

Secession   the act of separating from a state or such structured political entity to exercise self-rule

Secondary innovation   an invention or discovery that uses or combines existing ideas, objects, or techniques in novel arrangements

Self   the more or less enduring, bounded, and discrete part of an individual's identity or personality, and the reflexive awareness of this aspect of oneself

Self-determination   the concept that groups with a distinct culture and identity have a right to choose their own political arrangements and their own collective destiny

Semantic range   the set of meanings conveyed by a particular word, that is, the "range" of its referents or the variety of phenomena or conceptions that it names

Semantics   the study of meaning in language. See *morphology*

Semi-periphery   in Wallerstein's world system theory, the states "in the middle" of the core and the periphery or "in transition" from the periphery due to their successful development and industrialization

Separatist movement   a social movement that has as its goal the cultural or political disengagement of two groups or societies, often struggling to detach its territory from a multicultural or plural state and establish its own state

Serial monogamy   the marriage practice of having only one spouse at a time but perhaps having more than one spouse, at different times, during one's life

Sexual dimorphism   the occurrence of two physically distinct forms of a species, based on sexual characteristics as well as non-sexual ones such as body size

Shaman   a religious specialist, often part-time, who has personal power, based on unique life experiences or apprenticeship to a senior shaman, to communicate, interact, and sometimes struggle with supernatural beings or forces. Often a healer

Slash-and-burn   a horticultural practice in which trees and underbrush are cut, left to dry, and then burned as preparation for planting a garden. Also known as *swidden*

Social or structural assimilation   a form of assimilation in which groups are integrated into the society (for instance, sharing the same jobs or the same neighborhoods), whether or not they share the same culture

Social control   the political and general social function of getting members of a group to conform to expectations and rules and to obey authorities. Includes inculcating of social values as well as punishment of deviance from expectations

Social impact analysis   a fieldwork study of the consequences that a development project or other social-change policies have on the affected peoples

Social reproduction   the maintenance and perpetuation of society beyond mere childbearing, including enculturation and teaching of members to take their place in society and day-to-day activities to allow members of society to perform their specified tasks (including what is sometimes called "housework")

Socialization   from an anthropological point of view, a synonym for *enculturation*

Society   a group of humans who live in relative proximity to each other, tend to marry each other more than people outside the group, and share a set of beliefs and behaviors

Sociocultural appraisal   a study examining the *appropriateness* of a development or other social-change project, its likely *impact* on the various groups affected by it, and the distribution of the benefits that accrue from it

Sociolinguistics   see *pragmatics*

Sorcerer   a religious specialist who uses techniques, including spells and potions, to achieve supernatural effects

Sororal polygyny   the marriage practice in which a man marries two or more sisters

Sororate   a marriage practice in which a woman is expected to marry the husband of her sister in the event of the married sister's death

Soul   a religious concept of a non-material component or components of a living human; it is widely believed that a soul survives the death of the body, at least temporarily, and continues in another form of existence

Sphere of influence   in European colonial practice, an area of foreign territory where the power and authority of one European state was recognized

State   a political system or level of integration in which a formal centralized government has power over a delimited territory to make and enforce laws, to establish currency and collect taxes, and to maintain an army and declare war

State terrorism   the use of force and terror by a state government against its own people either a particular group or minority within the state or the entire population

Structural adjustment   a set of policies designed to reduce government control over development specifically and economic activity more generally, including "opening" or "freeing" local markets to foreign goods, eliminating economic protections like tariffs and subsidies, reducing taxes, deregulating industry, cutting government spending, and allowing the value of local currencies to "float" on international currency exchanges

Structural functionalism   the theory that the function of a cultural trait, particularly an institution, is the creation and preservation of social order and social integration

Structuralism   the theory (associated most closely with Claude Lévi-Strauss) that the significance of an item (word, role, practice, belief) is not so much in the particular item but in its relationship to others; in other words, the "structure" of multiple items and the location of any one in relation to others is most important

Structured interview   a fieldwork method in which the anthropologist administers a prepared set of questions to an informant/consultant

Subculture a group or subset within a society that is distinguished by some unique aspects of its behavior (such as clothing styles, linguistic usages, or beliefs and values)

Swidden see *slash-and-burn*

Symbol an object, gesture, sound, or image that "stands for" some other idea or concept or object; something that has "meaning," particularly when the meaning is arbitrary and conventional and thus culturally relative

Symbolic anthropology the school of thought (often associated with Clifford Geertz and Victor Turner) that the main goal of anthropology is to elucidate the meanings within which humans live and behave; rather than focusing on institutions and rules, it focuses on symbols and how symbols shape our experience and are manipulated by people in social situations

Symbolic capital "resources" that humans can use to influence situations and affect other people's behavior that are not "material" or "economic"; these can include knowledge, social relationships or debts, prestige, and so on

Sympathetic magic the belief and practice that objects that have something in common with each other (e.g. same shape or texture) have some supernatural connection with each other

Syncretism a type of revitalization movement in which elements of two or more cultural sources are blended into a new and more satisfying cultural arrangement

Syntax the rules in a language for how words are combined to make intelligible utterances of speech acts (for example, sentences). Also known as *grammar*

Terra nullius the colonial doctrine of "empty land," that colonized land was empty of human inhabitants and therefore could be claimed and settled by colonists

Theism the religious belief in one or more gods

Third World a term sometimes used to refer to the economically poor, politically and militarily weak, relatively unstable, and dependent states of the world, most of which emerged from colonialism in fairly recent history

Totemism a religious conception that human individuals or groups have a symbolic or spiritual connection with particular natural species, objects, or phenomena

Tradition some practice or idea or object that is (at least believed to be) continuous or associated with "the past"; a tradition may be very ancient or very recent, but as an ideological element it is often assumed to be important, authentic, and even "superior" to non-traditional (especially foreign) practices, ideas, and objects

Traditionalism a form of revitalization movement intended to preserve or restore "tradition" as that tradition is remembered or imagined by members of the movement

Travesti an alternate gender role in Brazil in which males take on certain physical traits and sexual behaviors typically associated with females

Tribe a political system or level of integration in which multiple local communities may be organized into a single system but in which political power is still relatively informal and usually flows from institutions that are not specifically political (such as elders, lineages, age sets, religious specialists, and so on)

Unilineal descent a principle in which individuals trace their ancestry through a "line" of related kin (typically a male or a female line) such that some "blood" relatives are included in the descent group or lineage and other relatives are excluded from it

Unstructured interview a fieldwork method in which the anthropologist conducts a relatively free-flowing conversation with an informant/consultant, either without prepared questions or unconstrained by these questions

Vitalism see *modernism*

Vocalizations non-linguistic sounds that can accompany and affect the meaning of speech

Witch a religious specialist, often conceived as a human with a supernatural ability to harm others, sometimes through possession of an unnatural bodily organ or an unnatural personality; sometimes viewed as an anti-social and even anti-human type who causes misfortune out of excessive greed, anger, or jealousy

World anthropologies the perspective that anthropology as developed and practiced in the West is not the only form of anthropology, and that other societies may develop and practice other types of anthropology based on their specific experiences and interests

World system theory the theory that explains the ongoing poverty and low standard of living in Third World states as the effect of external arrangements and relationships, specifically the global economic and political practices and institutions set up by the "core" of rich, powerful, industrialized states that function to their own advantage but to the disadvantage of the poor, weak, "peripheral" states

Worthy patient sometimes also called "good patient," the patient who has the qualities desired and preferred by medical professionals, such as wealth, education, youth, cooperativeness, and a lack of bad or unhealthy habits

Bibliography

Abramowitz, Sharon Alane. 2014. *Searching for Normal in the Wake of the Liberian War*. Philadelphia: University of Pennsylvania Press.

Abu-Lughod, Lila. 1985. "Honor and Sentiments of Loss in a Bedouin Society." *American Ethnologist* 12 (2): 245–261.

———. 2002. "Do Muslim Women Really Need Saving? Anthropological Reflections on Cultural Relativism and Its Others." *American Anthropologist* 104 (3): 783–790.

Ackerknecht, Erwin H. 1942. "Primitive Medicine and Culture Pattern." *Bulletin of the History of Medicine* 12 (4): 545–574.

Allerton, Catherine. 2013. *Potent Landscapes: Place and Mobility in Eastern Indonesia*. Honolulu: University of Hawaii Press.

American Anthropological Association. 1939 [1938]. "Resolution of December 1938." *Science* 89 (2298): 30.

Andersen, Helle Max. 2004. "'Villagers': Differential Treatment in a Ghanaian Hospital." *Social Science & Medicine* 59 (10): 2003–2012.

Anderson, Benedict. 1983. *Imagined Communities: Reflections of the Origin and Spread of Nationalism*. London: Verso.

Anderson, Walter Truett. 1990. *Reality Isn't What It Used to Be: Theatrical Politics, Ready-to-Wear Religion, Global Myths, Primitive Chic, and Other Wonders of the Postmodern World*. San Francisco: Harper & Row.

Anonymous. 2012. "The Popular Discourses of Salafi Radicalism and Salafi Counter-radicalism in Nigeria: A Case Study of Boko Haram." *Journal of Religion in Africa* 42 (2): 118–144.

Appadurai, Arjun, Ed. 1986. *The Social Life of Things: Commodities in Cultural Perspective*. Cambridge and New York: Cambridge University Press.

Apter, David E. 1968. *Some Conceptual Approaches to the Study of Modernization*. Englewood Cliffs, NJ: Prentice-Hall.

Aran, Gideon. 1991. "Jewish Zionist Fundamentalism: The Bloc of the Faithful in Israel (Gush Emunim)." In Martin Marty and R. Scott Appleby, Eds. *Fundamentalisms Observed*. Chicago: The University of Chicago Press. 265–344.

Asad, Talal. 1979. "Anthropology and the Colonial Encounter." In Gerrit Huizer and Bruce Mannheim, Eds. *The Politics of Anthropology: From Colonialism and Sexism Toward a View from Below*. The Hague and Paris: Mouton Publishers. 85–94.

———. 2004. "Where are the Margins of the State?" In Veena Das and Deborah Poole, Eds. *Anthropology in the Margins of the State*. Sant Fe, MN: School for Advanced Research. 279–88.

Atkinson, Jane Monnig. 1984. "'Wrapped Words': Poetry and Politics among the Wana of Central Sulawesi, Indonesia." In Donald Brenneis and Fred R. Myers, Eds. *Dangerous Words: Language and Politics in the Pacific*. Prospect Heights, IL: Waveland Press. 33–68.

Atran, Scott. 2002. *In Gods We Trust: The Evolutionary Landscape of Religion*. Oxford: Oxford University Press.

Austin, J. L. 1962. *How To Do Things with Words*. Oxford: Clarendon.

Axtell, Roger E. 1991. *Gestures: The Do's and Taboos of Body Language Around the World*. New York: John Wiley & Sons.

Bach, Jonathan. 2010. "'They Come in Peasants and Leave Citizens': Urban Villages and the Making of Shenzen, China." *Cultural Anthropology* 25 (3): 421–458.

Balandier, Georges. 1970 [1967]. *Political Anthropology*. A. M. Sheridan Smith, trans. New York: Vintage Books.

Banton, Michael. 1987. *Racial Theories*. Cambridge: Cambridge University Press.

Barber, Benjamin. 1995. *Jihad versus McWorld*. New York: Times Books.

Barreiro, Jose. 1993. *The Indian Chronicles*. Houston, TX: Arte Publico Press.

Barth, Fredrik, Ed. 1969. *Ethnic Groups and Boundaries*. Boston: Little, Brown & Co.

Barthes, Roland. 1997. "Toward a Psychosociology of Contemporary Food Consumption." In Carole Counihan and Penny van Esterick, Eds. *Food and Culture: A Reader*. New York and London: Routledge. 20–27.

Basso, Keith H. 1970. *The Cibecue Apache*. New York: Holt, Rinehart, and Winston.

Bastien, Joseph W. 1985. "Qollahuaya-Andean Body Concepts: A Topographical-Hydraulic Model of Physiology." *American Anthropologist* 87 (3): 595–611.

Bauman, Richard. 2001. "Verbal Art in Performance." In Alessandro Duranti, Ed. *Linguistic Anthropology: A Reader*. Malden, MA and Oxford: Blackwell Publishing. 165–188.

Beals, Alan R. 1980. *Gopalpur: A South Indian Village*. New York: Holt, Rinehart, and Winston.

Beidelman, T. O. 1971. *The Kaguru: A Matrilineal People of East Africa*. New York: Holt, Rinehart, and Winston.

Bell, Diane. 1993. *Daughters of the Dreaming*, 2nd ed. Minneapolis: University of Minnesota Press.

Ben-Amos, Dan. 1984. "The Seven Strands of Tradition: Varieties in its Meaning in American Folklore Studies." *Journal of Folklore Research* 21 (2/3): 97–131.

Benedict, Ruth. 1934a. "Anthropology and the Abnormal." *Journal of General Psychology* 10 (2): 59–82.

——. 1934b. *Patterns of Culture*. New York: The New American Library.

——. 1946. *The Chrysanthemum and the Sword*. Boston: Houghton Mifflin.

Benet, Sula. 1974. *Abkhasians: The Long-Living People of the Caucasus*. New York: Holt, Rinehart, and Winston.

Berlin, Brent and Paul Kay. 1969. *Basic Color Terms: Their Universality and Evolution*. Berkeley: University of California Press.

Beuchat, P. D. 1957. "Riddles in Bantu." *African Studies* 16: 133–149.

Bhasin, Veena. 2007. "Medical Anthropology: A Review." *Ethno-Medicine* 1 (1): 1–20.

Bilu, Yoram. 2013. "Habad, Messianism, and the Phantom Charisma of Rabbi Menachem Mendel Schneerson." In Charles Lindholm, Ed. *The Anthropology of Religious Charisma*. New York: Palgrave Macmillan. 213–238.

Birth, Kevin K. 2008. *Bacchanalian Sentiments: Musical Experiences and Political Counterpoints in Trinidad*. Durham, NC and London: Duke University Press.

Bloch, Maurice. 1983. *Marxism and Anthropology: The History of a Relationship*. Oxford: Clarendon Press.

——. 1998. *How We Think They Think: Anthropological Approaches to Cognition, Memory, and Literacy*. Boulder, CO: Westview Press.

Boas, Franz. 1896. "The Limitations of the Comparative Method of Anthropology." *Science* 4 (103): 901–908.

——. 1928. *Anthropology and Modern Life*. New York: W. W. Norton & Company.

Boas, Franz and C. Kamba Simango. 1922. "Tales and Proverbs of the Vandau of Portuguese South Africa." *The Journal of American Folklore* 35 (136): 151–204.

Bochi, Giovanni. 2014. "Exploring Pluralism in Oral Health Care: Dom Informal Dentists in Northern Lebanon." *Medical Anthropology Quarterly* 29 (1): 80–96.

Boddy, Janice. 2011. "Colonialism: Bodies under Colonialism." In Frances E. Mascia-Lees, Ed. *A Companion to the Anthropology of the Body and Embodiment*. Chichester, UK and Malden, MA: Blackwell Publishing. 119–136.

Bodley, John. 1975. *Victims of Progress*. Menlo Park, CA: Cummings.

——. 1985. *Anthropology and Contemporary Human Problems*, 2nd ed. Palo Alto, CA and London: Mayfield Publishing Company.

Boellstorff, Tom. 2008. *Coming of Age in Second Life: An Anthropologist Explores the Virtually Human*. Princeton, NJ: Princeton University Press.

Bogardus, Emory. 1933. "A Social Distance Scale." *Sociology and Social Research* 17: 65–71.

Boites, Salvadore Z., Pamela Geller, and Thomas C. Patterson. N.d. "The Growth and Changing Composition of Anthropology 1966–2002." www.aaanet.org/ar/changing_composition.pdf, accessed 21 November 2005.

Booth, Margaret Zoller. 2003. "'You Learn and Learn and Learn. . . . And Then You are an Adult': Parental Perceptions of Adolescence in Contemporary Swaziland." *Adolescence* 38 (150): 221–237.

Bourdieu, Pierre. 1977. *Outline of a Theory of Practice*. Cambridge: Cambridge University Press.

Bowen, John R. 2010. *Can Islam Be French? Pluralism and Pragmatism in a Secularist State*. Princeton, NJ and Oxford: Princeton University Press.

Bowman, Glenn. 2010. "Orthodox-Muslim Interactions at 'Mixed Shrines' in Macedonia." In Chris Hann and Hermann Goltz, Eds. *Eastern Christians in Anthropological Perspective*. Berkeley: University of California Press. 195–219.

Bowman, Marion and Úlo Valk. 2012. "Introduction: Vernacular Religion, Generic Expressions and the Dynamics of Belief." In Marion Bowman and Úlo Valk, Eds. *Vernacular Religion in Everyday Life: Expressions of Belief*. Sheffield, UK and Bristol, CT: Equinox. 1–19.

Boyer, Pascal. 2001. *Religion Explained: The Evolutionary Origins of Religious Thought*. New York: Basic Books.

Brauning, Fanny. 2009. *No More Smoke Signals*. New York: Filmakers Library.

Bregman, Peter. 2012. "Diversity Training Doesn't Work." *Harvard Business Review* (March 12). https://hbr.org/2012/03/diversity-training-doesnt-work, accessed 21 August 2015.

Brenneis, Donald. 1984. "Straight Talk and Sweet Talk: Political Discourse in an Occasionally Egalitarian Community." In Donald Brenneis and Fred R. Myers,

Eds. *Dangerous Words: Language and Politics in the Pacific*. Prospect Heights, IL: Waveland Press. 69–84.

Breusers, Mark. 2014. "Friendship and Spiritual Parenthood among the Moose and the Fulbe in Burkina Faso." In Martine Guichard, Tilo Gratz, and Youssouf Diallo, Eds. *Friendship, Descent, and Alliance in Africa: Anthropological Perspectives*. New York and Oxford: Berghahn. 74–96.

Briggs, Jean. 1970. *Never in Anger: Portrait of an Eskimo Family*. Cambridge, MA: Harvard University Press.

Brown, John Seely. 1991. "Research that Reinvents the Corporation." *Harvard Business Review* January–February: 102–111.

Brown, Judith K. 1975. "Iroquois Women: An Ethnohistoric Note." In Rayna R. Reiter, Ed. *Toward an Anthropology of Women*. New York: Monthly Review Press. 235–251.

Brown, Katherine Tandy. 2000. "Cultural or Heritage—This Tourism is Hot!" http://www,grouptraveler.com/roundups/6-00.html, accessed 26 July 2005.

Brueggemann, Walter. 2003. *An Introduction to the Old Testament: The Canon and Christian Imagination*. Louisville, KY: Westminster John Knox Press.

Burgess, M. Elaine. 1978. "The Resurgence of Ethnicity: Myth or Reality?" *Ethnic and Racial Studies* 1: 265–285.

Carod-Artal, Francisco Javier and Carolina Vázquez-Cabrera. 2007. "An Anthropological Study about Headache and Migraine in Native Cultures from Central and South America." *Headache* 47 (6): 834–841.

Carrier, James G. 2005. "Introduction." In James G. Carrier, Ed. *A Handbook of Economic Anthropology*. Cheltenham, UK and Northampton, MA: Edward Elgar Publishing. 1–9.

Carrithers, Michael. 2000. "On Polytropy: Or the Natural Condition of Spiritual Cosmopolitanism in India: The Digambar Jain Case." *Modern Asian Studies* 34 (4): 831–861.

Cassirer, Ernst. 1954. *An Essay on Man: An Introduction to a Philosophy of Human Culture*. Garden City, NY: Doubleday & Company.

Cattelino, Jessica R. 2011. "'One Hamburger at a Time': Revisiting the State-Society Divide with the Seminole Tribe of Florida and Hard Rock International." *Current Anthropology* 52 (S3): S137–S149.

Chagnon, Napoleon. 1992. *Yanomamo*, 4th ed. Fort Worth, TX: Harcourt Brace College Publishers.

Chang, Kyusik. 2014. "Christianity and Civil Society in Colonial Korea: The Civil Society Movement of Cho Man-sik and the P'yŏngyang YMCA against Japanese Colonialism." In Albert L. Park and David K. Yoo, Eds. *Encountering Modernity: Christianity in East Asia and Asian America*. Honolulu: University of Hawaii Press. 119–139.

Chang, Wen-Chin. 2014. *Beyond Borders: Stories of Yunnanese Chinese Migrants of Burma*. Ithaca, NY and London: Cornell University Press.

Chatters, James. 2002. *Ancient Encounters: Kennewick Man and the First Americans*. New York: Touchstone.

Chau, Adam Yuet. 2012. "Efficacy, Not Confessionality: On Ritual Polytropy in China." In Glenn Bowman, Ed. *Sharing the Sacra: The Politics and Pragmatics of Intercommunal Relations around Holy Places*. New York and Oxford: Berghahn. 79–96.

Chenhall, Richard. 2008. "What's in a Rehab? Ethnographic Evaluation Research in Indigenous Australian Residential Alcohol and Drug Rehabilitation Centres." *Anthropology & Medicine* 15 (2): 105–116.

Chidester, David. 2013. *Empire of Religion: Imperialism and Comparative Religion*. Chicago and London: The University of Chicago Press.

Chin, Elizabeth. 1999. "Ethnically Correct Dolls: Toying with the Race Industry." *American Anthropologist* 101 (2): 305–321.

Chiu, Lyren, Soma Ganesan, Nancy Clark, and Marina Morrow. 2005. "Spirituality and Treatment Choices by South and East Asian Women with Serious Mental Illness." *Transcultural Psychiatry* 42 (4): 630–656.

Cho, Mun Young. 2012. "'Dividing the Poor': State Governance of Differential Impoverishment in Northeast China." *American Ethnologist* 39 (1): 187–200.

Chua, Amy. 2003. *World on Fire: How Exporting Free Market Democracy Breeds Ethnic Hatred and Global Instability*. New York: Anchor Books.

Claxton, Nicholas. 1989. *The Price of Progress*. Oley, PA: Bullfrog Films.

Clifford, James. 1994. "Diasporas." *Cultural Anthropology* 9 (3): 302–338.

———. 1997. *Routes. Travel and Translation in the Late Twentieth Century*. Cambridge, MA: Harvard University Press.

Clifford, James and George Marcus, Eds. 1986. *Writing Culture: The Poetics and Politics of Ethnography*. Berkeley: University of California Press.

Clough, Paul. 2014. *Morality and Economic Growth in Rural West Africa: Indigenous Accumulation in Hausaland*. New York and Oxford: Berghahn Books.

Coco, Linda. 2014. "On Debt: Tracking the Shifting Role of the Debtor in U.S. Bankruptcy Legal Practice." In Rachael Stryker and Roberto J. González, Eds. *Up, Down, and Sideways: Anthropologists Trace the Pathways of Power*. New York and Oxford: Berghahn. 27–43.

Cohen, Lawrence. 2005. "The Kothi Wars: AIDS and Cosmopolitanism and the Morality of Classification." In Vincanne Adams and Stacy Leigh Pigg, Eds. *Sex in Development: Science, Sexuality, and Morality in Global Perspective*. Durham, NC and London: Duke University Press. 269–303.

Cohen, Robin. 1997. *Global Diasporas: An Introduction*. Seattle: University of Washington Press.

Collins, Francis S. 2004. "What We Do and Don't Know about 'Race,' 'Ethnicity,' Genetics, and Health at the Dawn of the Genome Era." *Nature Genetics Supplement* 36 (11): S 13–15.

Colson, Elizabeth. 2003. "Forced Migration and the Anthropological Response." *Journal of Refugee Studies* 16 (1): 1–18.

Coma, Maria. 2015. "Science in Action, Religion in Thought: Catholic Charismatics' Notions about Illness." In Carles Salazar and Joan Bestard, Eds. *Religion and Science as Forms of Life: Anthropological Insights into Reason and Unreason*. New York and Oxford: Berghahn. 153–170.

Comaroff, Jean.1985. *Body of Power, Spirit of Resistance: The Culture and History of a South Africa People*. Chicago and London: The University of Chicago Press.

Comaroff, John L. and Jean Comaroff. 1991. *Of Revelation and Revolution: The Dialectics of Modernity on a South African Frontier*, v.2. Chicago and London: The University of Chicago Press.

Condon, Richard G. 1990. "The Rise of Adolescence: Social Change and Life Stage Dilemmas in the Central Canadian Arctic." *Human Organization* 49 (3): 266–279.

Conklin, Alice. 2013. *In the Museum of Man: Race, Anthropology, and Empire in France, 1850–1950*. Ithaca, NY and London: Cornell University Press.

Cook, Susan E. 2011. "The Business of Being Bafokeng: The Corporatization of a Tribal Authority in South Africa." *Current Anthropology* 52 (S3): S151–S159.

Coser, Rose Laub. 1962. *Life in the Ward*. East Lansing: Michigan State University Press.

Costa, Albert, Alice Foucart, Sayuri Hayakawa, Melina Aparici, Jose Apesteguia, Joy Heafner, and Boaz Keysar. 2014. "Your Morals Depend on Language." *PLOS One* 9 (4): 1–7.

Counihan, Carole and Penny Van Esterick, Eds. 2007. *Food and Culture: A Reader*, 2nd ed. New York and London: Routledge.

Coupland, Nikolas. 2007. *Style: Language Variation and Identity*. Cambridge: Cambridge University Press.

Crăciun, Magdalena. 2014. *Material Culture and Authenticity: Fake Branded Fashion in Europe*. London and New York: Bloomsbury.

Crapanzano, Vincent. 1992. *Hermes' Dilemma and Hamlet's Desire: On the Epistemology of Interpretation*. Cambridge, MA: Harvard University Press.

Crystal, David. 1987. *The Cambridge Encyclopedia of Language*. Cambridge and New York: Cambridge University Press.

Csordas, Thomas J. 2000. "The Navajo Healing Project." *Medical Anthropology Quarterly* 14 (4): 463–475.

Cultural Survival. 2001. "Indigenous Sovereignty: An Ecuadorian Perspective." *Cultural Survival* (Summer 2001). http://www.culturalsurvival.org/ourpublications/csq/article/indigenous-sovereignty-ecuadorian-perspective, accessed 7 May 2015.

Dahlberg, Frances, Ed. 1981. *Woman the Gatherer*. New Haven, CT: Yale University Press.

Dallos, Csilla. 2011. *From Equality to Inequality: Social Change among Newly Sedentary Lanoh Hunter-Gatherer Traders of Peninsular Malaysia*. Montreal: University of Toronto Press.

Dalton, George. 1965. "Primitive Money." *American Anthropologist* 67 (1): 44–65.

Davies, Anna, Devin Fidler, and Marina Gorbis. 2011. "Future Work Skills 2020." Palo Alto, CA: Institute for the Future for the University of Phoenix Research Institute.

De Caro, F. A. 1986. "Riddles and Proverbs." In Elliott Oring, Ed. *Folk Groups and Folklore Genres: An Introduction*. Logan: Utah State University Press. 175–197.

Deger, Jennifer. 2006. *Shimmering Screens: Making Media in an Aboriginal Community*. Minneapolis: University of Minnesota Press.

Deng, Francis Mading. 1972. *The Dinka of the Sudan*. New York: Holt, Rinehart, and Winston.

Dentan, Robert Knox. 1968. *The Semai: A Non-violent People of Malaya*. New York: Holt, Rinehart, and Winston.

———. 2008. *Overwhelming Terror: Love, Fear, Peace, and Violence Among Semai of Malaysia*. Lanham, MD: Rowman & Littlefield.

DeVos, George. 1975. "Ethnic Pluralism: Conflict and Accommodation." In George DeVos and Lola Romanucci-Ross, Eds. *Ethnic Identity: Cultural Continuities and Change*. Palo Alto: Mayfield Publishing Company. 5–41.

Dharmadasa, K.N.O. 1992. *Language, Religion, and Ethnic Assertiveness: The Growth of Sinhalese Nationalism in Sri Lanka*. Ann Arbor: University of Michigan Press.

Diamond, Stanley. 1972 [1969]. "Anthropology in Question." In Dell Hymes, Ed. *Reinventing Anthropology*. New York: Random House. 401–429.

Dimova, Rozita. 2013. *Ethno-Baroque: Materiality, Aesthetics, and Conflict in Modern Day Macedonia*. New York and Oxford: Berghahn.

Dirlik Arif. 2012. "*Zhongguohua*: Worlding China—The Case of Sociology and Anthropology in 20th-Century China." In Arif Dirlik, Guannan Li, and Hsiao-Pei Yen, Eds. *Sociology and Anthropology in Twentieth-Century China: Between Universalism and Indigenism*. Hong Kong: Chinese University Press and New York: Columbia University Press. 1–39.

Douglas, Mary. 1966. *Purity and Danger: An Analysis of the Concepts of Pollution and Taboo*. London: Routledge & Kegan Paul.

———. 1972. "Deciphering a Meal." *Daedalus* 101 (1): 61–81.

———. 1975. *Implicit Meanings: Essays in Anthropology*. London and Boston: Routledge & Kegan Paul.

Dowell, Kristin L. 2013. *Sovereign Screens: Aboriginal Media on the Canadian West Coast*. Lincoln and London: University of Nebraska Press.

Downs, James F. 1972. *The Navajo*. New York: Holt, Rinehart, and Winston.

Dreazen, Yochi. 2013. "The New Terrorist Training Ground." *The Atlantic* (October): 61–70.

Driberg, J. H. 1936. "The Secular Aspect of Ancestor-Worship in Africa." *Journal of the Royal African Society* 35 (138): 1–21.

Du Bois, Cora. 1960 [1944]. *The People of Alor: A Social-Psychological Study of an East Indian Island*. Cambridge, MA: Harvard University Press.

Dundes, Alan. 1965. "What is Folklore?" In Alan Dundes, Ed. *The Study of Folklore*. Englewood Cliffs, NJ: Prentice-Hall. 1–3.

Durkheim, Émile. 1965 [1915]. *The Elementary Forms of the Religious Life*. New York: The Free Press.

Durrenberger, E. Paul and Gísli Pálsson, Eds. 2015. *Gambling Debt: Iceland's Rise and Fall in the Global Economy*. Boulder: University Press of Colorado.

Dussart, Francoise. 2000. *The Politics of Ritual in an Aboriginal Settlement: Kinship, Gender, and the Currency of Knowledge*. Washington, DC and London: Smithsonian Institution Press.

Edgerton, Robert B. 1966. "Conceptions of Psychosis in Four East African Societies." *American Anthropologist* 68 (2): 408–425.

Eisenstadt, S. N. 1999. "Multiple Modernities in an Age of Globalization." *Canadian Journal of Sociology* 24 (2): 283–295.

——. 2000. "Multiple Modernities." *Daedalus* 129 (1): 1–29.

Eissenstat, Howard. 2005. "Metaphors of Race and Discourse of Nation: Racial Theory and State Nationalism in the First Decades of the Turkish Republic." In Paul Spickard, Ed. *Race and Nation: Ethnic Systems in the Modern World*. New York and London: Routledge. 239–256.

El-Zein, Amira. 2009. *Islam, Arabs, and the Intelligent World of the Jinn*. Syracuse, NY: Syracuse University Press.

Eller, Jack David. 1999. *From Culture to Ethnicity to Conflict: An Anthropological Perspective on International Ethnic Conflict*. Ann Arbor, MI: University of Michigan Press.

——. 2005. *Violence and Culture: A Cross-Cultural and Interdisciplinary Approach*. Belmont, CA: Wadsworth.

Elliston, Deborah. 2014. "Queer History and Its Discontents at Tahiti: The Contested Politics of Modernity and Sexual Subjectivity." In Niko Besnier and Kalissa Alexeyff, Eds. *Gender on the Edge: Transgender, Gay, and Other Pacific Islanders*. Honolulu: University of Hawaii Press. 33–55.

Epple, Carolyn. 1998. "Coming to Terms with Navajo 'Nádleehí': A Critique of 'Berdache,' 'Gay,' 'Alternate Gender,' and 'Two-Spirit.'" *American Ethnologist* 25 (2): 267–290.

Eriksen, Thomas Hylland. 2002 [1993]. *Ethnicity and Nationalism: Anthropological Perspectives*. London: Pluto Press.

——. 2014. *Globalization*, 2nd ed. London and New York: Bloomsbury Academic.

Eriksen, Thomas Hylland, Christina Garsten, and Shalini Randeria, Eds. 2015. *Anthropology Now and Next: Essays in Honor of Ulf Hannerz*. New York and Oxford: Berghahn.

Ervin, Alexander M. 2000. *Applied Anthropology: Tools and Perspectives for Contemporary Practice*. Boston: Allyn and Bacon.

Estioko-Griffin, Agnes and P. Bion Griffin. 2002. "Woman the Hunter: The Agta." In Caroline Brettell and Carolyn Sargent, Eds. *Gender in Cross-Cultural Perspective*. Englewood Cliffs, NJ: Prentice-Hall. 206–215.

Evans-Pritchard, E. E. 1933. "Zande Blood-Brotherhood." *Africa: Journal of the International African Institute* 6 (4): 369–401.

——. 1937. *Witchcraft, Oracles, and Magic Among the Azande*. New York: Oxford University Press.

——. 1951. *Kinship and Marriage among the Nuer*. New York: Oxford University Press.

——. 1956. *Nuer Religion*. Oxford: Oxford University Press.

——. 1962. *Social Anthropology and Other Essays*. New York: The Free Press.

Fabrega, Horacio, Jr. 1971. "Medical Anthropology." *Biennial Review of Anthropology* 7: 167–229.

Fanon, Frantz. 1963. *The Wretched of the Earth*. Constance Farrington, trans. New York: Grove Press.

Ferguson, James. 2005. "Seeing Like an Oil Company: Space, Security, and Global Capital in Neoliberal Africa." *American Anthropologist* 107 (3): 377–382.

Ferguson, James and Akhil Gupta. 2002. "Spatializing States: Toward an Ethnography of Neoliberal Governmentality." *American Ethnologist* 29 (4): 981–1002.

Finke, Kaja, Cynthia Hunter, and Rick Iedema. 2008. "What is Going On? Ethnography in Hospital Spaces." *Journal of Contemporary Ethnography* 37 (2): 246–250.

Finke, Peter. 2014. *Variations on Uzbek Identity: Strategic Choices, Cognitive Schemas, and Political Constraints in Identification Processes*. New York and Oxford: Berghahn Books.

Finkelstein, Marni. 2005. *With No Direction Home: Homeless Youth on the Road and in the Streets*. Belmont, CA: Wadsworth Publishing.

Finnegan, Ruth. 1969. "How To Do Things with Words: Performative Utterances Among the Limba of Sierra Leone." *Man* (new series) 4 (4): 537–552.

——. 1991. "Tradition, But What Tradition and For Whom?" *Oral Tradition* 6 (1): 104–124.

Firth, Raymond. 2004 [1967]. "Themes in Economic Anthropology: A General Comment." In Raymond Firth, Ed. *Themes in Economic Anthropology*. London: Routledge. 1–28.

Fisher, Melissa. 2012. *Wall Street Women*. Durham, NC: Duke University Press.

Fiske, Shirley J. 2008. "Working for the Federal Government: Anthropology Careers." *NAPA Bulletin* 29 (1): 110–130.

Fletcher, Robert. 2014. *Romancing the Wild: Cultural Dimensions of Ecotourism*. Durham, NC and London: Duke University Press.

Foley, William A. 1997. *Anthropological Linguistics: An Introduction*. London: Blackwell Publishers.

Fortes, Meyer and E. E. Evans-Pritchard, Eds. 1940. *African Political Systems*. London: Oxford University Press.

Frake, Charles. 1962. *The Ethnographic Study of Cognitive Systems. Anthropology and Human Behavior*. Washington, DC: Society of Washington.

Frank, André Gunder. 1966. "The Development of Underdevelopment." *Monthly Review* 18: 17–31.

——. 1979. *Dependent Accumulation and Underdevelopment*. New York and London: Monthly Review Press.

Frazer, James George. 1958 [1922]. *The Golden Bough: A Study in Magic and Religion*. Abridged ed. New York: Macmillan.

Freeman, Derek. 1983. *Margaret Mead and Samoa: The Making and Unmaking of an Anthropological Myth*. Cambridge, MA: Harvard University Press.

Freudenthal, Hans. 1973. *Mathematics as an Educational Task*. Dordrecht: Reidel.

Fried, Morton H. 1967. *The Evolution of Political Society: An Essay in Political Anthropology*. New York: Random House.

Friedl, Ernestine. 1975. *Women and Men*. New York: Holt, Rinehart, and Winston.

——. 1978. "Society and Sex Roles." *Human Nature* 1 (6): 68–75.

Friedman, Thomas. 2005. *The World is Flat: A Brief History of the Twenty-First Century*. New York: Farrar, Straus, & Giroux.

Fujii, Lee Ann. 2009. *Killing Neighbors: Webs of Violence in Rwanda*. Ithaca, NY: Cornell University Press.

Fukuyama, Francis. 1992. *The End of History and the Last Man*. New York: The Free Press.

Furnivall, J. S. 1956. *Colonial Policy and Practice: A Comparative Study of Burma and Netherlands India*. New York: New York University Press.

Galemba, Rebecca B. 2013. "Illegality and Invisibility at Margins and Borders." *PoLAR: Political and Legal Anthropology Review* 36 (2): 274–285.

Gallup, Jr., Gordon G. 1970. "Chimpanzee Self-Recognition." *Science* 167: 86–87.

Garcia, Justin R., Chris Reiber, Sean G. Massey, and Ann M. Merriwether. 2012. "Sexual Hookup Culture: A Review." *Review of General Psychology* 16 (2): 161–176.

Garfinkel, Harold. 1967. *Studies in Ethnomethodology*. Englewood Cliffs, NJ: Prentice-Hall.

Garson, John George and Charles Hercules Read, Eds. 1899. *Notes and Queries on Anthropology, or A Guide to Anthropological Research for the Use of Travellers and Others*, 3rd ed. London: The Anthropological Institute.

Geertz, Clifford, Ed. 1963. *Old Societies and New States: The Quest for Modernity in Asia and Africa*. New York: The Free Press.

——. 1973. *The Interpretation of Cultures*. New York: Basic Books.

——. 1974. "'From the Native's Point of View': On the Nature of Anthropological Understanding." *Bulletin of the American Academy of Arts and Sciences* 28 (1): 26–45.

——. 1980. *Negara: The Theatre State in Nineteenth-Century Bali*. Princeton, NJ: Princeton University Press.

Gell, Alfred. 1998. *Art and Agency: An Anthropological Theory*. Oxford: Clarendon Press.

Gellner, David N. 1992. *Monk, Householder, and Tantric Priest: Newar Buddhism and its Hierarchy of Ritual*. Cambridge: Cambridge University Press.

——. 2013. "Northern South Asia's Diverse Borders, from Kachh to Mizoram." In David N. Gellner, Ed.

Borderland Lives in Northern South Asia. Durham, NC and London: Duke University Press. 1–23.

Gellner, Ernest. 1988. *Plough, Sword, and Book: The Structure of Human History*. Chicago: The University of Chicago Press.

Gershoy, Leo. 1957. *The Era of the French Revolution 1789–1799*. Princeton, NJ: D. Van Nostrand Company.

Gill, Sam D. 1981. *Sacred Words: A Study of Navajo Religion and Prayer*. Westport, CT: Greenwood Press.

Gilmore, David. 1990. *Manhood in the Making: Cultural Concepts of Masculinity*. New Haven, CT: Yale University Press.

Giovannini, Maureen J. 1978. "A Structural Analysis of Proverbs in a Sicilian Village." *American Ethnologist* 5 (2): 322–333.

Givens, David B., Patsy Evans, and Timothy Jablonski. 2000. "1997 American Anthropological Association Summary of Anthropology Ph.D.s." www.aaanet. org/surveys/97survey.htm, accessed 21 November 2005.

Glazer, Mark et al. 2004. "Susto and Soul Loss in Mexicans and Mexican Americans." *Cross-Cultural Research* 38 (3): 270–288.

Godelier, Maurice. 1978. *Perspectives in Marxist Anthropology*. Cambridge: Cambridge University Press.

Goodall, Jane. 1986. *The Chimpanzees of Gombe: Patterns of Behavior*. Cambridge, MA: Harvard University Press.

Goodenough, Ward H. 1956. "Componential Analysis and The Study of Meaning." *Language* 32: 195–216.

Gorer, Geoffrey and John Rickman. 1950. *The People of Great Russia: A Psychological Study*. New York: Chanticleer Press.

Gould, Drusilla and Christopher Loether. 2002. *An Introduction to the Shoshoni Language*. Salt Lake City: The University of Utah Press.

Gluckman, Max. 1956. *Custom and Conflict in Africa*. Oxford: Basil Blackwell.

Graeber, David. 2011. *Debt: The First 5,000 Years*. Brooklyn, NY: Melville House Publishing.

Gramsci, Antonio. 1971. *Selections from the Prison Notebooks of Antonio Gramsci*. Quintin Hoare and Geoffrey Nowell Smith, Ed. and trans. London: Lawrence and Wishart.

Grant, Madison. 1916. *The Passing of the Great Race; or the Racial Basis of European History*. New York: Charles Scribner's Sons.

Gray, John. 1992. *Men are from Mars, Women are from Venus: A Practical Guide for Improving Communication and Getting What You Want in Your Relationships*. New York: HarperCollins Publishers.

Grayzel, John. 1986. "Libido and Development: The Importance of Emotions in Development Work." In Michael M. Horowitz and Thomas M. Painter, Eds. *Anthropology and Rural Development in West Africa*. Boulder, CO: Westview Press. 147–165.

Greeley, Andrew. 1971. *Why Can't They Be Like Us?: America's White Ethnic Groups*. New York: E.P. Dutton & Co.

Green, John C. 1959. *The Death of Adam: Evolution and its Impact on Western Thought*. Ames: The Iowa State University Press.

Greenfield, Sidney M. 2008. *Spirits with Scalpels: The Culturalbiology of Religious Healing in Brazil*. Walnut Creek, CA: Left Coast Press.

Gregor, Thomas. 1981. "'Far, Far Away My Shadow Wandered. . .': The Dream Symbolism and Dream Theories of the Mehinaku Indians of Brazil." *American Ethnologist* 8 (4): 709–720.

Gregory, C. A. 1982. *Gifts and Commodities*. London: Academic Press.

Gremaux, René. 1994. "Woman Becomes Man in the Balkans." In Gilbert Herdt, Ed. *Third Sex, Third Gender: Beyond Sexual Dimorphism in Culture and History*. New York: Zone Books. 241–281.

Griaule, Marcel. 1965. *Conversations with Ogotemelli: An Introduction to Dogon Religious Ideas*. London: Oxford University Press.

Guest, Kenneth J. 2003. *God in Chinatown: Religion and Survival in New York's Evolving Immigrant Community*. New York and London: New York University Press.

Guichard, Martine. 2014. "Where are Other People's Friends Hiding? Reflections on Anthropological Studies of Friendship." In Martine Guichard, Tilo Gratz, and Youssouf Diallo, Eds. *Friendship, Descent, and Alliance in Africa: Anthropological Perspectives*. New York and Oxford: Berghahn. 19–41.

Guldbrandsen, Thaddeus Countway and Dorothy C. Holland. 2001. "Encounters with the Super-Citizen: Neoliberalism, Environmental Activism, and the American Heritage Rivers Initiative." *Anthropological Quarterly* 74 (3): 124–134.

Guneratne, Arjun, Ed. 2010. *Culture and the Environment in the Himalaya*. Abingdon, UK and New York: Routledge.

Gupta, Akhil and Aradhana Sharma. 2006. "Globalization and Postcolonial States." *Current Anthropology* 47 (2): 277–307.

Gurr, Ted Robert and Barbara Harff. 1994. *Ethnic Conflict in World Politics*. Boulder, CO: Westview Press.

Gutschow, Niels and Axel Michaels. 2005. *Handling Death: The Dynamics of Death and Ancestor Rituals among the Newars of Bhaktapur, Nepal*. Weisbaden, Germany: Harrassowitz Verlag.

Gutschow, Niels, Axel Michaels, and Christian Bau. 2008. *Growing Up: Hindu and Buddhist Initiation Ritual among Newar Children in Bhaktapur, Nepal*. Weisbaden, Germany: Harrassowitz Verlag.

Haeri, Niloofar. 2000. "Form and Ideology: Arabic Sociolingustics and Beyond." *Annual Review of Anthropology* 29: 61–87.

Haeri, Shahla. 2014. *Law of Desire: Temporary Marriage in Shi'i Iran*. Syracuse, NY: Syracuse University Press.

Hafez, Sherine. 2011. *An Islam of Her Own: Reconsidering Religion and Secularism in Women's Islamic Movements*. New York and London: New York University Press.

Hahn, Robert A. and Arthur Kleinman. 1983. "Biomedical Practice and Anthropological Theory: Frameworks and Directions." *Annual Review of Anthropology* 12: 305–333.

Haller, John S., Jr. 1971. *Outcasts from Evolution: Scientific Attitudes of Racial Inferiority, 1859–1900*. Carbondale and Edwardsville: Southern Illinois University Press.

Halliday, M. A. K. 1976. "Anti-Languages." *American Anthropologist* 78 (3): 570–584.

Hallowell, A. Irving. 1955. *Culture and Experience*. Philadelphia: University of Pennsylvania Press.

———. 1976. "Ojibwa Ontology, Behavior, and World View." In Paul Radin, Ed. *Contributions to Anthropology: Selected Papers of A. Irving Hallowell*. Chicago: The University of Chicago Press. 357–390.

Hann, Chris and Keith Hart. 2011. *Economic Anthropology: History, Ethnography, Critique*. Cambridge, UK and Malden, MA: Polity Press.

Hannerz, Ulf. 1980. *Exploring the City: Inquiries Toward an Urban Anthropology*. New York: Columbia University Press.

———. 2002. "Among the Foreign Correspondents: Reflections on Anthropological Styles and Audiences." *Ethnos* 67 (1): 57–74.

Hansen, Karen Tranberg. 2004. "The World in Dress: Anthropological Perspectives on Clothing, Fashion, and Culture." *Annual Review of Anthropology* 33: 369–392.

Harding, Susan F. 1987. "Convicted by the Holy Spirit: The Rhetoric of Fundamental Baptist Conversion." *American Ethnologist* 14 (1): 167–181.

Harlow, Harry. 1959. "Love in Infant Monkeys." *Scientific American* 200 (6): 68–74.

Harrell-Bond, Barbara E. 1986. *Imposing Aid: Emergency Assistance to Refugees*. Oxford: Oxford University Press.

Harrell-Bond, Barbara E. and E. Voutira. 1992. "Anthropology and the Study of Refugees." *Anthropology Today* 8 (4): 6–10.

Harris, Marvin. 1968. *The Rise of Anthropological Theory*. New York: Thomas Y. Crowell.

———. 1974. *Cows, Pigs, Wars, and Witches: The Riddles of Culture*. New York: Random House.

———. 1979. *Cultural Materialism: The Struggle for a Science of Culture*. New York: Random House.

Harrison, Faye. V. 2008. *Outsider Within: Reworking Anthropology in the Global Age*. Urbana: University of Illinois Press.

Hart, C. W. M. and Arnold R. Pilling. 1960. *The Tiwi of North Australia*. New York: Holt, Rinehart, and Winston.

Hart, Keith. 1973. "Informal Income Opportunities and Urban Employment in Ghana." *The Journal of Modern African Studies* 11 (1): 61–89.

Hart, Keith, Jean-Louis Laville, and Antonio David Cattani. 2010. "Building the Human Economy Together." In Keith Hart, Jean-Louis Laville, and Antonio David Cattani, Eds. *The Human Economy*. Cambridge, MA: Polity Press. 1–17.

Hart, Keith and Horacio Ortiz. 2014. "The Anthropology of Money and Finance: Between Ethnography and World History." *Annual Review of Anthropology* 43: 465–482.

Harvey, David. 2005. *A Brief History of Neoliberalism*. Oxford: Oxford University Press.

Hausner, Sondra L. and Jeevan R. Sharma. 2013. "On the Way to India: Nepali Rituals of Border Crossing." In David N. Gellner, Ed. *Borderland Lives in Northern South Asia*. Durham, NC and London: Duke University Press. 94–116.

Heath, Deana. 2010. *Purifying Empire: Obscenity and the Politics of Moral Regulation in Britain, India and Australia*. Cambridge and New York: Cambridge University Press.

Hedges, Chris. 2002. *War is a Force that Gives Us Meaning*. New York: Public Affairs.

Hefner, Robert W. 1998. "Multiple Modernities: Christianity, Islam, and Hinduism in a Globalizing Age." *Annual Review of Anthropology* 27: 83–104.

Heider, Karl. 1979. *Grand Valley Dani: Peaceful Warriors*. New York: Holt, Rinehart, and Winston.

Heitzenrater, Richard P. 2002. "Tradition and History." *Church History* 71 (3): 621–638.

Helman, Cecil 2007. *Culture, Health and Illness: An Introduction for Health Professionals*, 5th Ed. London: Hodder Arnold.

Herdt, Gilbert. 1987 [1981]. *Guardians of the Flutes: Idioms of Masculinity*. New York: Columbia University Press.

——. 1994. "Introduction: Third Sexes and Third Genders." In Gilbert Herdt, Ed. *Third Sex, Third Gender: Beyond Sexual Dimorphism in Culture and History*. New York: Zone Books, 21–81.

Herodotus. 1942. *The Persian Wars*. Trans. George Rawlinson. New York: Modern Library.

Herskovits, Melville J. 1958 [1941]. *The Myth of the Negro Past*. Boston: Beacon Press.

——. 1952. *Economic Anthropology: A Study of Comparative Economics*. New York: Alfred A. Knopf. Originally published as *The Economic Life of Primitive Peoples*, 1940.

Higashi, Robin T., Allison Tillack, Michael A. Steinman, C. Bree Johnston, and G. Michael Harper. 2013. "The 'Worthy' Patient: Rethinking the 'Hidden Curriculum' in Medical Education." *Anthropology & Medicine* 20 (1): 13–23.

Himpele, Jeff D. 2008. *Circuits of Culture: Media, Politics, and Indigenous Identity in the Andes*. Minneapolis: University of Minnesota Press.

Hine, Thomas. 2003. *I Want That!: How We All Became Shoppers*. New York: Perennial.

Hinton, Alexander Laban. 2010. "Introduction: Toward an Anthropology of Transitional Justice." In Alexander Laban Hinton, Ed. *Transitional Justice: Global Mechanisms and Local Realities after Genocide and Mass Violence*. New Brunswick, NJ and London: Rutgers University Press. 1–22.

Hoben, Allan. 1986. "Assessing the Social Feasibility of a Settlement Project in North Cameroon." In Michael M. Horowitz and Thomas M. Painter, Eds. *Anthropology and Rural Development in West Africa*. Boulder, CO: Westview Press. 169–194.

Hobsbawm, Eric and Terence Ranger, Eds. 1983. *The Invention of Tradition*. Cambridge: Cambridge University Press.

Hocart, A. M. 1936. "Spirits of Power." *Anthropos* 31 (3/4): 580–582.

Hockett, Charles F. 1958. *A Course in Modern Linguistics*. New York: Macmillan.

——. 1977. *The View from Language: Selected Essays, 1948–1974*. Athens: University of Georgia Press.

Hoebel, E. Adamson. 1960. *The Cheyennes: Indians of the Great Plains*. New York: Holt, Rinehart, and Winston.

Hoffman, Lisa, Monica DeHart, and Stephen J. Collier. 2006. "Notes on the Anthropology of Neoliberalism." *Anthropology News* (September): 9–10.

Hoffman, Susanna M. and Anthony Oliver-Smith, Eds. 2002. *Catastrophe and Culture: The Anthropology of Disaster*. Santa Fe: School of American Research Press.

Holy, Ladislav. 1991. *Religion and Custom in a Muslim Society: The Berti of Sudan*. Cambridge: Cambridge University Press.

Hook, Stephen. 1996. "Introduction: Foreign Aid in a Transformed World." In Stephen Hook, Ed. *Foreign Aid Toward the Millennium*. Boulder, CO: Lynne Rienner. 1–16.

Horowitz, David. 1985. *Ethnic Groups in Conflict*. Berkeley: University of California Press.

Horton, Robin. 1960. "A Definition of Religion, and its Uses." *The Journal of the Royal Anthropological Institute of Great Britain and Ireland*, 90 (2): 201–226.

Horton, Sarah, Cesar Abadía, Jessica Mulligan, and Jennifer Jo Thompson. 2014. "Critical Anthropology of Global Health 'Takes a Stand' Statement: A Critical Medical Anthropological Approach to the U.S.'s Affordable Care Act." *Medical Anthropology Quarterly* 28 (1): 1–22.

Horvath, Ronald J. 1972. "A Definition of Colonialism." *Current Anthropology* 13 (1): 45–57.

Howes, David, Ed. 1996. *Cross-Cultural Consumption: Global Markets, Local Realities*. London and New York: Routledge.

Hua Cai. 2001 [1997]. *A Society without Fathers or Husbands: The Na of China*. Asti Hustvedt, trans. New York: Zone Books.

Huntington, Samuel. 1996. *The Clash of Civilizations and the Remaking of World Order*. New York: Simon & Schuster.

Huxley, Julian and A. C. Haddon. 1935. *We Europeans: A Survey of "Racial" Problems*. London: Jonathan Cape.

Hviding, Edvard and Cato Berg. 2014. "Introduction: The Ethnographic Experiment in Island Melanesia." In Edvard Hviding and Cato Berg, Eds. *The Ethnographic Experiment: A. M. Hocart and W. H. R. Rivers in Island Melanesia, 1908*. New York and Oxford: Berghahn. 1–43.

Hymes, Dell, Ed. 1972 [1969]. *Reinventing Anthropology*. New York: Random House, Inc.

Igoe, Jim. 2004. *Conservation and Globalization: A Study of National Parks and Indigenous Communities from East*

Africa to South Dakota. Belmont, CA: Wadsworth Publishing.

Ingold, Tim. 1999. "Introduction to Culture." In Tim Ingold, Ed. *Companion Encyclopedia of Anthropology*. London and New York: Routledge.

———. 2008. "Anthropology is *Not* Ethnography." *Proceedings of the British Academy* 154: 69–92.

Jacques, Martin. 2009. *When China Rules the World: The Rise of the Middle Kingdom and the End of the Western World*. London and New York: Penguin.

Jain, Andrea R. 2014. *Selling Yoga: From Counterculture to Pop Culture*. Oxford and New York: Oxford University Press.

Jordan, Ann T. 2003. *Business Anthropology*. Long Grove, IL: Waveland Press.

Jusionyte, Ieva. 2014. "For Social Emergencies 'We are 9-1-1': How Journalists Perform the State in an Argentine Border Town." *Anthropological Quarterly* 87 (1): 151–181.

Kardam, Nuket. 1993. "Development Approaches and the Role of Policy Advocacy: The Case of the World Bank." *World Development* 21 (11): 1773–1786.

Kardiner, Abram. 1939. *The Individual and His Society: The Psychodynamics of Primitive Social Organization*. New York: Columbia University Press.

———. 1945. *The Psychological Frontiers of Society*. New York: Columbia University Press.

Kasmir, Sharryn. 2014. "The Saturn Automobile Plant and the Long Dispossession of US Autoworkers." In Sharryn Kasmir and August Carbonella, Eds. *Blood and Fire: Toward a Global Anthropology of Labor*. New York and London: Berghahn. 203–249.

Kaspin, Deborah. 1996. "A Chewa Cosmology of the Body." *American Ethnologist* 23 (3): 561–578.

Katz, Pearl. 1999. *The Scalpel's Edge: The Culture of Surgeons*. Needham Heights, MA: Allyn and Bacon.

Katz, Richard. 1982. *Boiling Energy: Community Healing Among the Kalahari Kung*. Cambridge and London: Harvard University Press.

Kauffman, L. A. 1990. "The Anti-Politics of Identity." *Socialist Review* 90 (1): 67–80.

Kawai, Masao. 1965. "Newly-acquired Pre-Cultural Behavior of the Natural Troops of Japanese Monkeys on Koshima Islet." *Primates* 6: 1–30.

Kearney, M. 1995. "The Local and the Global: The Anthropology of Globalization and Transnationalism." *Annual Review of Anthropology* 24: 547–565.

Keeler, Ward. 1983. "Shame and Stage Fright in Java." *Ethos* 11 (3): 152–165.

Keen, Ian. 1994. *Knowledge and Secrecy in an Aboriginal Religion*. Melbourne and Oxford: Oxford University Press.

Kelly, Raymond. 1977. *Etoro Social Structure*. Ann Arbor: University of Michigan Press.

Kendall, Laurel. 2014. "'China to the Anthropologist': Franz Boas, Berthold Laufer, and a Road Not Taken in Early American Anthropology." In Regna Darnell and Frederic W. Gleach, Eds. *Anthropologists and Their*

Traditions across National Borders. Lincoln, NE and London: University of Nebraska Press. 1–39.

Kern, Karen M. 2011. *Imperial Citizen: Marriage and Citizenship in the Ottoman Frontier Province of Iraq*. Syracuse, NY: Syracuse University Press.

Kertzer, David I. 1987. "Childhood and Industrialization in Italy." *Anthropological Quarterly* 60 (4): 152–159.

Kiefer, Thomas M. 1972. *The Tausug: Violence and Law in a Philippine Moslem Society*. New York: Holt, Rinehart, and Winston.

Kingfisher, Catherine. 2013. *A Policy Travelogue: Tracing Welfare Reform in Aotearoa/New Zealand and Canada*. New York and Oxford: Berghahn.

Klass, Morton. 1978. *From Field to Factory: Community Structure and Industrialization in West Bengal*. Philadelphia, PA: Institute for the Study of Human Issues.

Kleinman, Arthur. 1978. "Concepts and a Model for the Comparison of Medical Systems as Cultural Systems." *Social Science & Medicine* 12: 85–93.

———. 1980. *Patients and Healers in the Context of Culture: An Exploration of the Borderland between Anthropology, Medicine, and Psychiatry*. Berkeley and London: University of California Press.

Klima, George J. 1970. *The Barabaig: East Africa Cattle-Herders*. New York: Holt, Rinehart, and Winston.

Knörr, Jacqueline. 2014. *Creole Identity in Postcolonial Indonesia*. New York and Oxford: Berghahn.

Kopp, Kristin. 2011. "Arguing the Case for a Colonial Poland." In Volker Langbehn and Mohammad Salama, Eds. *German Colonialism: Race, the Holocaust, and Postwar Germany*. New York: Columbia University Press. 146–163.

Krige, Detlev. 2015. "'Letting Money Work for Us': Self-Organization and Financialization from Below in an All-Male Savings Club in Soweto." In Keith Hart and John Sharp, Eds. *People, Money, and Power in the Economic Crisis: Perspectives from the Global South*. New York and Oxford: Berghahn. 61–81.

Krippner, Stanley. 1987. "Cross-Cultural Approaches to Multiple Personality Disorder: Practices in Brazilian Spiritism." *Ethos* 15 (3): 273–295.

Kroeber, Alfred L. 1919. "On the Principle of Order in Civilization as Exemplified by Changes of Fashion." *American Anthropologist* 21 (3): 235–263.

Kulick, Don. 1997. "The Gender of Brazilian Transgendered Prostitutes." *American Anthropologist* 95: 574–585.

Kummer, Hans. 1995. *In Quest of the Sacred Baboon*. Princeton, NJ: Princeton University Press.

Kuper, Adam. 1983. *Anthropology and Anthropologists: The Modern British School*, revised ed. London and New York: Routledge.

———. 1988. *The Invention of Primitive Society: Transformations of an Illusion*. London: Routledge.

Laing, R. D. 1967. *The Politics of Experience*. New York: Ballantine Books.

Lakoff, Robin. 1975. *Language and Woman's Place*. New York: Harper.

Lambek, Michael. 1981. *Human Spirits: A Cultural Account of Trance in Mayotte*. Cambridge: Cambridge University Press.

Landmann, Michael. 1974. *Philosophical Anthropology*. David J. Parent, trans. Philadelphia, PA: The Westminster Press.

Lane, Harlan. 1977. *The Wild Boy of Aveyron*. New York: Bantam Books.

Lane, Harlan, Robert Hoffmeister, and Ben Bahan. 1996. *A Journey into Deaf-World*. San Diego, CA: Dawn Sign Press.

Lang, Claudia and Eva Jansen. 2013. "Appropriating Depression: Biomedicalizing Ayurvedic Psychiatry in Kerala, India." *Medical Anthropology* 32 (1): 25–45.

Lange, Matthew, James Mahoney, and Matthias vom Hau. 2006. "Colonialism and Development: A Comparative Analysis of Spanish and British Colonies." *American Journal of Sociology* 111 (5): 1412–1462.

Langer, Susanne K. 1942. *Philosophy in a New Key: A Study in the Symbolism of Reason, Rite, and Art*. New York: Mentor Books.

Laqueur, Thomas. 1990. *Making Sex: Body and Gender from the Greeks to Freud*. Cambridge, MA: Harvard University Press.

Lawrence, Peter. 1964. *Road Belong Cargo*. Manchester: Manchester University Press.

Leach, Edmund R. 1949. "Primitive Magic and Modern Medicine." *Health Education Journal* 7 (4): 162–170.

——. 1954. *Political Systems of Highland Burma*. Boston: Beacon Press.

Leakey, Louis S. B. 1930. "Some Notes on the Masai of Kenya Colony." *Royal Anthropological Institute of Great Britain and Ireland* 60: 185–209.

Lee, Dorothy. 1959. *Freedom and Culture*. Englewood Cliffs, NJ: Prentice-Hall.

Lee, Richard. 1984. *The Dobe !Kung*. New York: Holt, Rinehart, and Winston.

Lee, Richard and Irven DeVore, Eds. 1968. *Man the Hunter*. Chicago: Aldine Publishing Company.

Lehmann, Angela. 2013. *Transnational Lives in China: Expatriates in a Globalizing City*. New York: Palgrave Macmillan.

Lemke, Thomas. 2007. "An Indigestible Meal? Foucault, Governmentality, and State Theory." *Distinktion: Scandinavian Journal of Social Theory* 8 (2): 43–64.

Lenski, Gerhard and Jean Lenski. 1982. *Human Societies: An Introduction to Macrosociology*, 4th ed. New York: McGraw-Hill.

Lessa, William A. 1966. *Ulithi: A Micronesian Design for Living*. New York: Holt, Rinehart, and Winston.

Lester, Rebecca. 2014. "Health as Moral Failing: Medication Restriction Among Women with Eating Disorders." *Anthropology & Medicine* 21 (2): 241–250.

Levy, André. 2000. "Diasporas through Anthropological Lenses: Contexts of Postmodernity." *Diaspora* 9 (1): 137–157.

Lewellen, Ted C. 2002. *The Anthropology of Globalization: Cultural Anthropology Enters the 21st Century*. Westport, CT: Bergin & Garvey.

Lewis, Oscar. 1941. "Manly-Hearted Women among the North Piegan." *American Anthropologist* 42 (2, part 1): 173–187.

Lewontin, Richard C. 1972. "The Apportionment of Human Diversity." *Evolutionary Biology* 6: 381–398.

Li, Tania Murray. 2007. *The Will to Improve: Governmentality, Development, and the Practice of Politics*. Durham, NC and London: Duke University Press.

Linton, Ralph. 1936. *The Study of Man*. New York: Appleton-Century.

Linton, Ralph, Ed. 1945. *The Science of Man in the World Crisis*. New York: Columbia University Press.

Liu, Mingxin. 2003. "A Historical Overview on Anthropology in China." *Anthropologist* 5 (4): 217–223.

Livingstone, Frank B. 1962. "On the Non-Existence of Human Races." *Current Anthropology* 3 (3): 279–281.

Londono Sulkin, Carlos David. 2012. *People of Substance: An Ethnography of Morality in the Colombian Amazon*. Toronto: University of Toronto Press.

Lonetree, Amy. 2012. *Decolonizing Museums: Representing Native America in National and Tribal Museums*. Chapel Hill: The University of North Carolina Press.

Long, Debbi, Cynthia Hunter, and Sjaak van der Geest. 2008. "When the Field is a Ward or a Clinic: Hospital Ethnography." *Anthropology & Medicine* 15 (2): 71–78.

Lora-Wainwright, Anna. 2012. "Rural China in Ruins: The Rush to Urbanize China's Countryside is Opening a Moral Battleground." *Anthropology Today* 28 (4): 8–13.

Lorenz, Konrad. 1963. *On Aggression*. Marjorie Kerr Wilson, trans. New York: Bantam Books.

Ludden, David. 1992. "India's Development Regime." In N. B. Dirks, Ed. *Colonialism and Culture*. Ann Arbor: University of Michigan Press. 247–288.

Lutz, Catherine A. 1998. *Unnatural Emotions: Everyday Sentiments on a Micronesian Atoll and Their Challenge to Western Theory*. Chicago and London: The University of Chicago Press.

Luyendijk, Joris. 2011. "Bankers: An Anthropological Study." http://www.theguardian.com/commentisfree/2011/sep/14/bankers-anthropological-study-joris-luyendijk, accessed 23 February 2015.

Lynch, Owen M. 1990. "The Social Construction of Emotion in India." In Owen M. Lynch, Ed. *Divine Passions: The Social Construction of Emotion in India*. Berkeley: University of California Press. 3–34.

Lyon, Sarah. 2011. *Coffee and Community: Maya Farmers and Fair-Trade Markets*. Boulder, CO: University Press of Colorado.

Maggi, Wynne. 2006. "'Heart-Struck': Love Marriage as a Marker of Ethnic Identity among the Kalasha of Northwest Pakistan." In Jennifer Hirsch and Holly Wardlow, Eds. *Modern Loves: The Anthropology of Romantic Courtship and Companionate Marriage*. Ann Arbor: University of Michigan Press. 78–91.

Maia, Suzana. 2012. *Transnational Desires: Brazilian Erotic Dancers in New York*. Nashville, TN: Vanderbilt University Press.

Malefyt, Timothy de Waal and Robert J. Morais. 2012. *Advertising and Anthropology: Ethnographic Practice and Cultural Perspectives*. London: Berg.

Malinowski, Bronislaw. 1927. *Sex and Repression in Savage Society*. Chicago: The University of Chicago Press.

——. 1948. *Magic, Science, and Religion and Other Essays*. Garden City, NY: Doubleday Anchor Books.

——. 1961 [1945]. *The Dynamics of Culture Change: An Inquiry into Race Relations in Africa*. New Haven, CT and London: Yale University Press.

——. 1964. "An Anthropological Analysis of War." In L. Bramson and G. Goethals, Eds. *War: Studies from Psychology, Sociology, Anthropology*. New York: Basic Books. 245–268.

——. 1984 [1922]. *Argonauts of the Western Pacific*. Long Grove, IL: Waveland Press.

Malkki, Liisa. 1995. *Purity and Exile: Violence, Memory, and National Cosmology among Hutu Refugees in Tanzania*. Chicago and London: The University of Chicago Press.

Maltz, Daniel N. and Ruth A. Borker. 1996. "A Cultural Approach to Male-Female Miscommunication." In Donald Brenneis and Ronald K. S. Macaulay, Eds. *The Matrix of Language: Contemporary Linguistic Anthropology*. Boulder, CO: Westview Press. 81–98.

Maquet, Jacques. 1961. *The Premise of Inequality in Rwanda: A Study of Political Relations in a Central African Kingdom*. London: Oxford University Press.

Marak, Queenbala. 2014. *Food Politics: Studying Food, Identity, and Difference among the Garos*. Newcastle on Tyne: Cambridge Scholars Publishing.

Marcus, George E. 1995. "Ethnography In/Of the World: The Emergence of Multi-Sited Ethnography." *Annual Review of Anthropology* 24: 95–117.

Marcus, George E. and Michael M. J. Fischer. 1986. *Anthropology as Cultural Critique: An Experimental Moment in the Human Sciences*. Chicago: The University of Chicago Press.

Marett, R. R. 1909. *The Threshold of Religion*. London: Methuen & Co.

Mazurek, Brett. 2009. *Diamonds in the Rough: A Ugandan Hip Hop Revolution*. New York: Third World Newsreel.

McCabe, Maryann and Timothy de Waal Malefyt. 2010. "Brands, Interactivity, and Contested Fields: Exploring Production and Consumption in Cadillac and Infiniti Automobile Advertising Campaigns." *Human Organization* 69 (3): 252–262.

McCallum, Cecilia. 1996. "The Body that Knows: From Cashinahua Epistemology to a Medical Anthropology of Lowland South America." *Medical Anthropology Quarterly* 10 (3): 347–372.

McDougall, Debra. 2009. "Becoming Sinless: Converting to Islam in the Christian Solomon Islands." *American Anthropologist* 111 (4): 480–491.

McFarlane, Joan Elizabeth and Michael P. Alpers. 2009. "Treatment-Seeking Behaviour among the Nasioi People of Bougainville: Choosing Between Traditional and Western Medicine." *Ethnicity & Health* 14 (2): 147–168.

McKenna, Brian. 2013. "Dow Chemical's Knowledge Factories: Action Anthropology against Michigan's Company Town Culture." In Sam Beck and Carl A. Maida, Eds. *Toward Engaged Anthropology*. New York and Oxford: Berghahn Books. 55–74.

Mead, Margaret. 1928. *Coming of Age in Samoa: A Psychological Study of Primitive Youth for Western Civilization*. New York: W. W. Morrow.

Meigs, Anna S. 1984. *Food, Sex, and Pollution: A New Guinea Religion*. New Brunswick, NJ: Rutgers University Press.

Meneley, Anne. 2014. "The Qualities of Palestinian Olive Oil." In Christopher E. Forth and Alison Leitch, Eds. *Fat: Culture and Materiality*. London and New York: Bloomsbury Academic. 17–31.

Messenger, Jr., John C. 1965. "The Role of Proverbs in a Nigerian Judicial System." In Alan Dundes, Ed. *The Study of Folklore*. Englewood Cliffs, NJ: Prentice-Hall. 299–307.

Michaels, Eric. 1986. *The Aboriginal Invention of Television in Central Australia, 1982–1986*. Canberra: Australian Institute of Aboriginal Studies.

Mikkelsen, Caecille. 2014. *The Indigenous World 2014*. Copenhagen: International Work Group for Indigenous Affairs.

Miles, William F. S. 2014. *Scars of Partition: Postcolonial Legacies in French and British Borderlands*. Lincoln and London: University of Nebraska Press.

Miller, Daniel. 1998. *A Theory of Shopping*. Ithaca, NY: Cornell University Press.

Miller, Daniel and Sophie Woodward. 2007. "Manifesto for a Study of Denim." *Social Anthropology* 15 (3): 335–351.

Miller, Daniel and Sophie Woodward, Eds. 2011. *Global Denim*. Oxford and New York: Berg.

Mills, C. Wright. 1959. *The Sociological Imagination*. New York: Oxford University Press.

Moeran, Brian. 1996. *A Japanese Advertising Agency: Anthropology of Media and Markets*. Honolulu: University of Hawaii Press.

Monroe, Kristin V. 2014. "Labor and the Urban Landscape: Mobility, Risk, and Possibility among Syrian Delivery Workers in Beirut." *Anthropology of Work Review* 35 (2): 84–94.

Montagu, M. F. Ashley. 1945. *Man's Most Dangerous Myth: The Fallacy of Race*, 2nd ed. New York: Columbia University Press.

Moodie, T. Dunbar. 2005. "Race and Ethnicity in South Africa." In Paul Spickard, Ed. *Race and Nation: Ethnic Systems in the Modern World*. New York and London: Routledge. 319–335.

Moore, Wilbert E. 1963. *Social Change*. Englewood Cliffs, NJ: Prentice-Hall.

Morauta, Louise. 1972. "The Politics of Cargo Cults in the Madang Area." *Man* (n.s.) 7 (3): 430–447.

Morgan, Lewis Henry. 1877. *Ancient Society, or Researches in the Lines of Human Progress from Savagery, through Barbarism to Civilization*. New York: Henry Holt and Company.

Morphy, Howard. 1991. *Ancestral Connections: Art and an Aboriginal System of Knowledge*. Chicago: The University of Chicago Press.

Morren, George E. B., Jr. 1984. "Warfare on the Highland Fringe of New Guinea: The Case of the Mountain Ok." In R. Brian Ferguson, Ed. *Warfare, Culture, and Environment*. Orlando, FL: Academic Press. 169–207.

Mpofu, Busani. 2015. "After the Big Clean-Up: Street Vendors, the Informal Economy and Employment Policy in Zimbabwe." In Keith Hart and John Sharp, Eds. *People, Money, and Power in the Economic Crisis: Perspectives from the Global South*. New York and Oxford: Berghahn. 19–40.

Mühlfried, Florian. 2014. *Being a State and States of Being in Highland Georgia*. New York and Oxford: Berghahn.

Müller-Wille, Ludger. 2014. *The Franz Boas Enigma*. Montreal: Baraka Books.

Mumford, Lewis. 1962 [1922]. *The Story of Utopias*. New York: The Viking Press.

Murphy, Yolanda and Robert Murphy. 1974. *Women of the Forest*. New York: Columbia University Press.

Mustapha, Abdul Raufu. 2014. "Understanding *Boko Haram*." In Abdul Raufu Mustapha, Ed. *Sects & Social Disorder: Muslim Identities & Conflict in Northern Nigeria*. Suffolk, UK and Rochester, NY: James Currey. 147–198.

Mutsaers, Paul. 2014. "'All of Me': Psychologizing Turkish-Dutch Police Officers in the Netherlands." *Anthropology of Work Review* 35 (2): 72–83.

Myerhoff, Barbara. 1974. *Peyote Hunt: The Sacred Journey of the Huichol Indians*. Ithaca, NY: Cornell University Press.

———. 1978. *Number Our Days*. New York: Touchstone/Simon & Schuster.

Myrdal, Gunnar. 1968. *Asian Drama: An Inquiry into the Poverty of Nations*. New York: Pantheon.

Nader, Laura. 1972. "Up the Anthropologist—Perspectives Gained from Studying Up." In Dell Hymes, Ed. *Reinventing Anthropology*. New York: Pantheon Books. 285–311.

Nagengast, Carole. 1994. "Violence, Terror, and the Crisis of the State." *Annual Review of Anthropology* 23: 109–136.

Nakamura. Karen. 2013. *A Disability of the Soul: An Ethnography of Schizophrenia and Mental Illness in Contemporary Japan*. Ithaca, NY and London: Cornell University Press.

Nanda, Serena. 1999. *Neither Man nor Woman: The Hijras of India*, 2nd ed. Belmont, CA: Wadsworth Publishing Company.

Nash, June. 1979. "The Anthropology of the Multinational Corporation." In Gerrit Huizer and Bruce Mannheim, Eds. *The Politics of Anthropology: From Colonialism and Sexism Toward a View from Below*. The Hague: Mouton. 421–446.

Nash, Manning. 1962. "Race and the Ideology of Race." *Current Anthropology* 3 (3): 285–288.

———. 1989. *The Cauldron of Ethnicity in the Modern World*. Chicago: The University of Chicago Press.

Needham, Rodney. 1972. *Belief, Language, and Experience*. Chicago: The University of Chicago Press.

Neihardt, John G. 1961. *Black Elk Speaks: Being the Life Story of a Holy Man of the Oglala Sioux*. Lincoln: University of Nebraska Press.

Nelson, Cynthia. 1974. "Public and Private Politics: Women in the Middle Eastern World." *American Ethnologist* 1: 551–563.

Nelson, John K. 2013. *Experimental Buddhism: Innovation and Activism in Contemporary Japan*. Honolulu: University of Hawaii Press.

Nguyen, Nguyen, Edward F. Foulks, and Kathleen Carlin. 1991. "Proverbs as Psychological Interpretations Among Vietnamese." *Asian Folklore Studies* 50 (2): 311–308.

Nguyen, Vinh-Kim. 2005. "Uses and Pleasures: Sexual Modernity, HIV/AIDS, and Confessional Technologies in a West African Metropolis." In Vincanne Adams and Stacy Leigh Pigg, Eds. *Sex in Development: Science, Sexuality, and Morality in Global Perspective*. Durham, NC and London: Duke University Press. 245–268.

Nolan, Riall. 2002. *Development Anthropology: Encounters in the Real World*. Boulder, CO: Westview Press.

Oakdale, Suzanne and Magnus Course, Eds. 2014. *Fluent Selves: Autobiography, Person, and History in Lowland South America*. Lincoln, NE and London: University of Nebraska Press.

Ochs, Elinor Keenan. 1996. "Norm-Makers, Norm-Breakers: Uses of Speech in Men and Women in a Malagasy Community." In Donald Brenneis and Ronald K. S. Macaulay, Eds. *The Matrix of Language: Contemporary Linguistic Anthropology*. Boulder, CO: Westview Press. 99–115.

O'Connor, Kaori. 2011. *Lycra: How A Fiber Shaped America*. New York: Routledge.

Odebiyi, A. I. and Funmi Togonu-Bickersteth. 1987. "Concepts and Management of Deafness in the Yoruba Medical System: A Case Study of Traditional Healers in Ile-Ife, Nigeria." *Social Science & Medicine* 24 (8): 645–649.

Ohnuki-Tierney, Emiko. 1974. *The Ainu of the Northwest Coast of Southern Sakhalin*. New York: Holt, Rinehart, and Winston.

Okello, Elialilia and Solvig Ekblad. 2006. "Lay Concepts of Depression among the Baganda of Uganda: A Pilot Study." *Transcultural Psychiatry* 43 (2): 287–313.

Olson, Benjamin Hedge. 2013. "Voice of Our Blood: National Socialist Discourse in Black Metal." In Titus Hjeml, Keith Kahn-Harris, and Mark LeVine, Eds. *Heavy Metal: Controversies and Countercultures*. Sheffield, UK and Bristol, CT: Equinox. 136–151.

Ong, Aihwa. 1988. "The Production of Possession: Spirits and the Multinational Corporation in Malaysia." *American Ethnologist* 15 (1): 28–42.

Ortega Y Gasset, José. 1932. *The Revolt of the Masses*. New York: W. W. Norton and Company.

Ortner, Sherry. 1973. "On Key Symbols." *American Anthropologist* 75 (5): 1338–1346.

———. 1974. "Is Female to Male as Nature is to Culture?" In Michelle Rosaldo and Louise Lamphere, Eds. *Woman, Culture, and Society*. Stanford: Stanford University Press. 68–87.

O'Shannessy, Carmel. 2005. "Light Warlpiri: A New Language." *Australian Journal of Linguistics* 25 (1): 31–57.

Padden, Carol A. and Tom L. Humphries. 2005. *Inside Deaf Culture*. Cambridge, MA and London: Harvard University Press.

Pálsson, Gísli. 1994. "Enskilment at Sea." *Man*, n.s. 29 (4): 901–927.

Park, Yunjae. 2014. "Between Mission and Medicine: The Early History of Severance Hospital." In Albert L. Park and David K. Yoo, Eds. *Encountering Modernity: Christianity in East Asia and Asian America*. Honolulu: University of Hawaii Press. 140–161.

Parker, Melissa and Ian Harper. 2006. "The Anthropology of Public Health." *Journal of Biosocial Science* 38 (1): 1–5.

Parker, Richard B. 1958. "Lebanese Proverbs." *The Journal of American Folklore* 71 (280): 104–14.

Parsons, Talcott. 1951. *The Social System*. Glencoe, IL: The Free Press of Glencoe.

Patterson, Orlando. 1975. "Context and Choice in Ethnic Allegiance: A Theoretical Framework and Caribbean Case Study." In *Ethnicity: Theory and Experience*, Nathan Glazer and Daniel Patrick Moynihan, Eds. Cambridge, MA: Harvard University Press. 305–349.

Paul, Benjamin D. 1955. *Health, Culture and Community: Case Studies of Public Reactions to Health Programs*. New York: Russell Sage Foundation.

Paxson, Heather. 2013. *The Life of Cheese: Crafting Food and Value in America*. Berkeley: University of California Press.

Pedersen, Morten Axel. 2011. *Not Quite Shamans: Spirit Worlds and Political Lives in Northern Mongolia*. Ithaca, NY and London: Cornell University Press.

Pels, Peter. 1997. "The Anthropology of Colonialism: Culture, History, and the Emergence of Western Governmentality." *Annual Review of Anthropology* 26: 163–183.

Pena, Sergio D. J. and Telma de Souza Birchal. 2005–2006. "The Biological Non-existence versus the Social Existence of Human Races: Can Science Instruct the Social Ethos?" http://www.fhi.ox.ac.uk/teaching%20and%20posters/TT08/Birchal_paper_29_04.pdf, accessed 29 October 2008.

Philippine Center for Language Study. 1965. *Beginning Tagalog: A Course for Speakers of English*. Berkeley: University of California Press.

Pigg, Stacy Leigh and Vincanne Adams. 2005. "Introduction: The Moral Object of Sex." In Vincanne Adams and Stacy Leigh Pigg, Eds. *Sex in Development: Science, Sexuality, and Morality in Global Perspective*. Durham, NC and London: Duke University Press. 1–38.

Pinney, Christopher. 2011. *Photography and Anthropology*. London: Reaktion Books.

Pogge von Strandmann, Hartmut. 2011. "The Purpose of German Colonialism, or the Long Shadow of Bismarck's Colonial Policy." In Volker Langbehn and Mohammad Salama, Eds. *German Colonialism: Race, the Holocaust, and Postwar Germany*. New York: Columbia University Press. 193–214.

Polanyi, Karl. 1957. "The Economy as Instituted Process." In Karl Polanyi, Conrad M. Arenberg, and Harry W. Pearson, Eds. *Trade and Market in the Early Empires: Economies in History and Theory*. New York and London: The Free Press and Collier-Macmillan Limited. 243–270.

Pope, Catherine. 2005. "Conducting Ethnography in Medical Settings." *Medical Education* 39 (12): 1180–1187.

Power, Ben. 2013. "The Artisanal Instrument Maker in the Moment of Performance: Motivation and Meaning in the Scottish Smallpipes Revival." In Peter Harrop and Dunja Njaradi, Eds. *Performance and Ethnography: Dance, Drama, Music*. Newcastle upon Tyne: Cambridge Scholars Publishing. 67–85.

Prentice, Rachel. 2013. *Bodies in Formation: An Ethnography of Anatomy and Surgery Education*. Durham, NC and London: Duke University Press.

Prunier, Gerard. 1995. *The Rwandan Crisis: History of a Genocide*. New York: Columbia University Press.

Puzzo, Dante. 1964. "Racism and the Western Tradition." *Journal of the History of Ideas*. 25 (4): 579–586.

Pye, Michael. 2015. *Japanese Buddhist Pilgrimage*. Sheffield, UK and Bristol, CT: Equinox.

Pype, Katrien. 2012. *The Making of the Pentecostal Melodrama: Religion, Media, and Gender in Kinshasa*. New York and Oxford: Berghahn.

Qureshi, Sadiah. 2011. *Peoples on Parade: Exhibitions, Empire, and Anthropology in Nineteenth-Century Britain*. Chicago and London: The University of Chicago Press.

Radcliffe-Brown, A. R. 1941. "The Study of Kinship Systems." *The Journal of the Royal Anthropological Institute of Great Britain and Ireland* 71 (1/2): 1–18.

———. 1965 [1952]. *Structure and Function in Primitive Society*. New York: The Free Press.

Ram, Kalpana. 2013. *Fertile Disorder: Spirit Possession and its Provocation of the Modern*. Honolulu: University of Hawaii Press.

Ramirez-Esparza, Nairan, Samuel D. Gosling, Veronica Benet-Martinez, Jeffrey P. Potter, and James W. Pennebaker. 2006. "Do Bilinguals have Two Personalities? A Special Case of Cultural Frame Switching." *Journal of Research in Personality* 40: 99–120.

Rao, Anupama and Steven Pierce. 2006. "Discipline and the Other Body: Humanitarianism, Violence, and the Colonial Exception." In Steven Pierce and Anupama Rao, Eds. *Discipline and the Other Body: Correction, Corporeality, Colonialism*. Durham, NC: Duke University Press. 1–35.

Reed, A.W., Ed. 1969. *Captain Cook in Australia: Extracts from the Journals of Captain James Cook*. Wellington, New Zealand: A.H. & A.W. Reed.

Reeves, Scott, Jennifer Peller, Joanne Goldman, and Simon Kitto. 2013. "Ethnography in Qualitative Educational Research: AMME Guide No. 80." *Medical Teacher* 35 (8): e1365–1379.

Reiter, Rayna. 1975a. "Men and Women in the South of France: Public and Private Domains." In Rayna Reiter, Ed. *Toward an Anthropology of Women*. New York: Monthly Review Press. 252–282.

Reiter, Rayna, Ed. 1975b. *Toward an Anthropology of Women*. New York: Monthly Review Press.

Rey, Séverine. 2012. "The Ordinary Within the Extraordinary: Sainthood-Making and Everyday Religious Practice in Lesvos, Greece." In Samuli Schielke and Liza Debevec, Eds. *Ordinary Lives and Grand Schemes: An Anthropology of Everyday Religion*. New York and Oxford: Berghahn. 82–97.

Ribeiro, Gustavo Lins and Arturo Escobar. 2006. "World Anthropologies: Disciplinary Transformations with Systems of Power." In Gustavo Lins Ribeiro and Arturo Escobar, Eds. *World Anthropologies: Disciplinary Transformations within Systems of Power*. Oxford and New York: Berg. 1–25.

Riggs, Christina. 2014. *Unwrapping Ancient Egypt*. London and New York: Bloomsbury Academic.

Ringrose, Kathryn M. 1994. "Living in the Shadows: Eunuchs and Gender in Byzantium." In Gilbert Herdt, Ed. *Third Sex, Third Gender: Beyond Sexual Dimorphism in Culture and History*. New York: Zone Books. 85–109.

Rivers, W. H. R. 1920. "The Dying Out of Native Races." *The Lancet* 195: 42–44, 109–111.

——. 1996 [1924]. *Social Organization: A History of Civilization*. London and New York: Routledge.

——. 1999 [1926]. *Psychology and Ethnology*. London: Routledge.

Roca, Beltrán and Lluis Rodriguez. 2014. "Unionism and Employer Power Strategies in Spain: Ethnography of a Labor Struggle in an Iron and Steel Firm." *Anthropology of Work Review* 35 (2): 60–71.

Roche, Sophie. 2014. *Domesticating Youth: Youth Bulges and their Socio-Political Implications in Tajikistan*. New York and Oxford: Berghahn.

Rodhe, Joy. 2013. *Armed with Expertise: The Militarization of American Social Research during the Cold War*. Ithaca, NY: Cornell University Press.

Róheim, Géza. 1974. *The Children of the Desert: The Western Tribes of Central Australia*. New York: Basic Books.

Rosaldo, Michelle. 1974. "Woman, Culture, and Society: A Theoretical Overview." In Michelle Rosaldo and Louise Lamphere, Eds. 1974. *Woman, Culture, and Society*. Stanford: Stanford University Press. 17–42.

——. 1984. "Words that are Moving: The Social Meanings of Ilongot Verbal Art." In Donald Brenneis and Fred R. Myers, Eds. *Dangerous Words: Language and Politics in the Pacific*. Prospect Heights, IL: Waveland Press. 131–160.

Rosaldo, Michelle and Louise Lamphere, Eds. 1974. *Woman, Culture, and Society*. Stanford: Stanford University Press.

Rosin, Hanna. 2012. "Boys on the Side." *The Atlantic* (September): 55–59.

Roscoe, Will. 1994. "How to Become a Berdache: Toward a Unified Analysis of Gender Diversity." In Gilbert Herdt, Ed. *Third Sex, Third Gender: Beyond Sexual Dimorphism in Culture and History*. New York: Zone Books. 329–372.

——. 1998. *Changing Ones: Third and Fourth Genders in Native North America*. New York: St. Martin's.

Rosenberg, Bernard. 1957. "Mass Culture in America." In Bernard Rosenberg and David Manning White, Eds. *Mass Culture: The Popular Arts in America*. New York: The Free Press. 3–12.

Ross, Michael, W. Q. Elaine Xun, and Anne E. Wilson. 2002. "Language and the Bicultural Self." *Personality and Social Psychology Bulletin* 28: 1040–1050.

Rostow, W. W. 1965. *The Stages of Economic Growth: A Non-Communist Manifesto*. New York: Cambridge University Press.

Rubin, Julius H. 2013. *Tears of Repentance: Christian Indian Identity and Community in Colonial Southern New England*. Lincoln and London: University of Nebraska Press.

Sandall, Roger. 2001. *The Culture Cult: Designer Tribalism and Other Essays*. Boulder, CO: Westview Press.

Sanford, Victoria and Martha Lincoln. 2010. "Body of Evidence: Feminicide, Local Justice, and Rule of Law in 'Peacetime' Guatemala." In Alexander Laban Hinton, Ed. *Transitional Justice: Global Mechanisms and Local Realities after Genocide and Mass Violence*. New Brunswick, NJ and London: Rutgers University Press. 67–91.

Sapir, Edward. 1932. "Cultural Anthropology and Psychiatry." *The Journal of Abnormal and Social Psychology* 27 (3): 229–242.

——. 1949. *Selected Writings*. Berkeley: University of California Press.

——. 2001 [1938]. "Why Cultural Anthropology Needs the Psychiatrist." *Psychiatry* 64 (1): 2–10.

Scales, Christopher A. 2012. *Recording Culture: Powwow Music and the Aboriginal Recording Industry on the Northern Plains*. Durham, NC and London: Duke University Press.

Schäuble, Michaela. 2014. *Narrating Victimhood: Gender, Religion, and the Making of Place in Post-War Croatia*. New York and London: Berghahn.

——. 1995. "The Primacy of the Ethical: Propositions for a Militant Anthropology." *Current Anthropology* 36 (3): 409–440.

Scheper-Hughes, Nancy and Philippe Bourgois, Eds. 2004. *Violence in War and Peace: An Anthology*. London: Blackwell Publishing.

Scheper-Hughes, Nancy and Margaret M. Lock. 1987. "The Mindful Body: A Prolegomenon to Future Work in Medical Anthropology." *Medical Anthropology Quarterly* 1 (1): 6–41.

Schieffelin, Bambi B. 2008. "Speaking Only Your Own Mind: Reflections on Talk, Gossip, and Intentionality in Bosavi (PNG)." *Anthropological Quarterly* 81 (2): 431–441.

Schieffelin, Edward L. 1983. "Anger and Shame in the Tropical Forest: On Affect as a Cultural System in Papua New Guinea." *Ethos* 11 (3): 181–191.

Schielke, Samuli. 2010. "Second Thoughts about the Anthropology of Islam, or How to Make Sense of Grand Schemes in Everyday Life." Working Papers No. 2, Zentrum Moderner Orient.

Schrift, Melissa. 2013. *Becoming Melungeon: Making an Ethnic Identity in the Appalachian South*. Lincoln and London: University of Nebraska Press.

Schuller, Mark. 2012. *Killing with Kindness: Haiti, International Aid, and NGOs.* New Brunswick, NJ: Rutgers University Press.

Schwimmer, Eric. 1984. "Male Couples in New Guinea." In Gilbert Herdt, Ed. *Ritualized Homosexuality in Melanesia.* Berkeley: University of California Press.

Scott, David. 1995. "Colonial Governmentality." *Social Text* 43 (Autumn) L 191–220.

Scott, James C. 1990. *Domination and the Arts of Resistance: Hidden Transcripts.* New Haven, CT: Yale University Press.

——. 1998. *Seeing Like a State: How Certain Schemes to Improve the Human Condition have Failed.* New Haven, CT: Yale University Press.

——. 2009. *The Art of Not Being Governed: An Anarchist History of Upland Southeast Asia.* New Haven, CT: Yale University Press.

Sen, Mala. 2002. *Death by Fire: Sati, Dowry Death, and Female Infanticide in Modern India.* New Brunswick, NJ: Rutgers University Press.

Service, Elman R. 1962. *Primitive Social Organization: An Evolutionary Perspective.* New York: Random House.

Shakur, Sanyika (Kody Scott). 1993. *Monster: The Autobiography of an L.A. Gang Member.* New York: Penguin Books.

Sharabi, Asaf. 2014. "Deep Healing: Ritual Healing in the Teshuvah Movement." *Anthropology & Medicine* 21 (3): 277–289.

Sharp, Lauriston. 1952. "Steel Axes for Stone-Age Australians." *Human Organization* (summer): 17–22.

Sherzer, Joel. 1983. *Kuna Ways of Speaking.* Austin: University of Texas Press.

Shnirelman, Victor A. 2013. "Russian Neopaganism: From Ethnic Religion to Racial Violence." In Kaarina Aitamurto and Scott Simpson, Eds. *Modern Pagan and Native Faith Movements in Central and Eastern Europe.* Durham, UK and Bristol, CT: Acumen. 62–76.

Shore, Cris and Susan Wright. 2000. "Coercive Accountability: The Rise of Audit Culture in Higher Education." In Marilyn Strathern, Ed. *Audit Cultures: Anthropological Studies in Accountability, Ethics, and the Academy.* London and New York: Routledge. 57–89.

Shorter, Aylward. 1988. *Toward a Theology of Inculturation.* Maryknoll, NY: Orbis Books.

Shostak, Marjorie. 1983 [1981]. *Nisa: The Life and Words of a !Kung Woman.* New York: Vintage Books.

Sillitoe, Paul. 1998. *An Introduction to the Anthropology of Melanesia: Culture and Tradition.* Cambridge: Cambridge University Press.

Simmons, Leo W., Ed. 1942. *Sun Chief: The Autobiography of a Hopi Indian.* New Haven and London: Yale University Press.

Simons, Ronald C. and Charles C. Hughes, Eds. 1985. *The Culture-Bound Syndromes: Folk Illnesses of Psychiatric and Anthropological Interest.* Dordrecht: D. Reidel.

Simpson, George E. and J. Milton Yinger. 1972. *Racial and Cultural Minorities.* 4th ed. New York: Harper & Row.

Sinclair, Simon. 1997. *Making Doctors: An Institutional Apprenticeship.* Oxford and New York: Berg.

Skorupski, John. 1976. *Symbol and Theory: A Philosophical Study of Theories of Religion in Social Anthropology.* Cambridge: Cambridge University Press.

Slocum, Sally. 1975. "Woman the Gatherer: Male Bias in Anthropology." In Rayna R. Reiter, Ed. *Toward an Anthropology of Women.* New York: Monthly Review Press. 36–50.

Slotkin, J. S., Ed. 1965. *Readings in Early Anthropology.* London: Methuen & Co. Ltd.

Smart, Alan. 1999. "Expressions of Interest: Friendship and *Guanxi* in Chinese Societies." In Bell, Sandra and Coleman, Simon, Eds. *The Anthropology of Friendship.* Oxford: Berg. 119–136.

Smart, Alan and Josephine Smart. 2003. "Urbanization and the Global Perspective." *Annual Review of Anthropology* 32: 263–285.

Smedley, Audrey. 1999. *Race in North America: Origin and Evolution of a Worldview,* 2nd ed. Boulder CO: Westview Press.

Smith, Linda Tuhiwai. 1999. *Decolonizing Methodologies: Research and Indigenous Peoples.* London and New York: Zed Books.

Smith, Mike. 2014. *Boko Haram: Inside Nigeria's Unholy War.* London and New York: I. B. Tauris.

Sorenson, John and Atsuko Matsuoka. 2001. "Abyssinian Fundamentalism and Catastrophe in Eritrea." *Dialectical Anthropology* 26 (1): 37–63.

Sorge, Antonio. 2009. "Hospitality, Friendship, and the Outside in Highland Sardinia." *Journal of the Society for the Anthropology of Europe* 9 (1): 4–12.

Spencer, Baldwin and F. J. Gillen. 1968 [1899]. *The Native Tribes of Central Australia.* New York: Dover Publications.

Spindler, George and Louise Spindler. 1971. *Dreamers without Power: The Menomini Indians.* New York: Holt, Rinehart, and Winston.

Spiro, Melford. 1978 [1967]. *Burmese Supernaturalism,* expanded ed. Philadelphia: Institute for the Study of Human Issues.

St. John, Graham. 2010. *The Local Scenes and Global Culture of Psytrance.* Abingdon, UK and New York: Routledge.

Steiner, Martin. 2007. *The Refugee Show: The Plight of the Padaung Long-Necked People.* Princeton, NJ: Films for the Humanities and Sciences.

Steward, Julian. 1950. *Area Research: Theory and Practice.* New York: Social Science Research Council, Bulletin 63.

——. 1953. "Evolution and Process." In Alfred Kroeber, Ed. *Anthropology Today.* Chicago: The University of Chicago Press. 313–326.

Stocking, George W., Jr. 1974. *A Franz Boas Reader: The Shaping of American Anthropology, 1883–1911.* New York: Basic Books.

Storm, Hiroko. 1992. "Women in Japanese Proverbs." *Asian Folklore Studies* 51 (2): 167–182.

Strathern, Marilyn, Ed. 2000. *Audit Cultures: Anthropological Studies in Accountability, Ethics, and the Academy.* London and New York: Routledge.

Street, Alice. 2010. "Belief as Relational Action: Christianity and Cultural Change in Papua New

Guinea." *Journal of the Royal Anthropological Institute* 16 (2): 260–278.

Stryker, Rachael and Roberto J. González, Eds. 2014. *Up, Down, and Sideways: Anthropologists Trace the Pathways of Power*. New York and Oxford: Berghahn.

Suarez-Orozco, Marcelo. 1992. "A Grammar of Terror: Psychocultural Responses to State Terrorism in Dirty War and Post-Dirty War Argentina." In Carolyn Nordstrom and JoAnn Martin, Eds. *The Paths to Domination, Resistance, and Terror*. Berkeley: University of California Press. 219–259.

Subtirelu, Nicholas Close. 2013. "'English. . . It's Part of our Blood': Ideologies of Language and Nation in United States Congressional Discourse." *Journal of Sociolinguistics* 17 (1): 37–65.

Swancutt, Katherine. 2012. *Fortune and the Cursed: The Sliding Scale of Time in Mongolian Divination*. New York and Oxford: Berghahn.

Swider, Sarah. 2015. "Building China: Precarious Employment among Migrant Construction Workers." *Work, Employment and Society* 29 (1): 41–59.

Szasz, Thomas S. 1961. *The Myth of Mental Illness: Foundations of a Theory of Personal Conduct*. New York: Dell.

Tamari, Tal. 1991. "The Development of Caste Systems in West Africa." *The Journal of African History* 32 (2): 221–250.

Tambiah, Stanley J. 1970. *Buddhism and the Spirit Cults in North-East Thailand*. London: Cambridge University Press.

Tejirian, Eleanor H. and Reeva Spector Simon. 2012. *Conflict, Conquest, and Conversion: Two Thousand Years of Christian Missions in the Middle East*. New York: Columbia University Press.

Thompson, E. P. 1967. "Time, Work-Discipline, and Industrial Capitalism." *Past & Present* 38: 56–97.

Tinker, George E. 1993. *Missionary Conquest: The Gospel and Native American Cultural Genocide*. Minneapolis: Fortress Press.

Topinard, Paul.1890 [1876]. *Anthropology*, new ed. London: Chapman and Hall.

Trotter, Robert T. II, Richard H. Needle, Eric Goosby, Christopher Bates, and Merrill Singer. 2001. "A Methodological Model for Rapid Assessment, Response, and Evaluation: The RARE Program in Public Health." *Field Methods* 13 (2): 137–159.

Trouillot, Michel-Rolph. 1991. "Anthropology and the Savage Slot: The Poetics and Politics of Otherness." In R. Fox, Ed. *Recapturing Anthropology: Working in the Present*. Santa Fe, NM: School of American Research Press. 18–44.

Tsui, Bonnie. 2011. "The End of Chinatown." *The Atlantic* (December): 17–18.

Turnbull, Colin. 1962. *The Forest People*. New York: Simon & Schuster.

Turner, Victor W. 1967. *The Forest of Symbols: Aspects of Ndembu Ritual*. Ithaca, NY and London: Cornell University Press.

——. 1969. *The Ritual Process: Structure and Anti-Structure*. Chicago: Aldine Publishing.

——. 1981 [1968]. *The Drums of Affliction: A Study of Religious Processes Among the Ndembu of Zambia*. London: Hutchinson University Library for Africa.

Turney-High, Harry H. 1971. *Primitive War: Its Practice and Concepts*. Columbia: University of South Carolina Press.

Tyler, Stephen A., Ed. 1969. *Cognitive Anthropology*. New York: Holt, Rinehart, and Winston.

Tylor, E. B. 1958 [1871]. *Primitive Culture*. New York: Harper Torchbooks.

United Nations. 2008. *The United Nations Declaration on the Rights of Indigenous Peoples*. New York: United Nations.

United Nations High Commissioner for Refugees. 2007a. "2006 Statistical Yearbook." Geneva: United Nations High Commissioner for Refugees.

——. 2007b. "Convention and Protocol Relating to the Status of Refugees." Geneva: United Nations High Commissioner for Refugees.

USAID. 2012. "Youth in Development Policy: Realizing the Demographic Opportunity." Washington, DC: United States Agency for International Development.

U.S. Department of Defense. 2008. "The Human Terrain Team Handbook." Fort Leavenworth, KS: U.S. Department of Defense.

Valentine, Lisa Philips. 1995. *Making It Their Own: Severn Ojibwe Communicative Practices*. Toronto: University of Toronto Press.

van den Berghe, Pierre L. 1987 [1981]. *The Ethnic Phenomenon*. New York: Praeger.

van der Dennen, Johan M. G. 2002. "Nonhuman Intergroup Agonistic Behavior and 'Warfare.'" http://rint.rechten.rug.nl/rth/dennen/animwar.htm, accessed 29 May 2002.

van Duijl, Marjolein, Etzel Cardena, and Joop T. V. M. de Jong. 2005. "The Validity of DSM-IV Dissociative Disorders Categories in South-West Uganda." *Transcultural Psychiatry* 42 (2): 219–241.

Van Schendel, Willem. 2013. "Making the Most of 'Sensitive' Borders." In David N. Gellner, Ed. *Borderland Lives in Northern South Asia*. Durham, NC and London: Duke University Press. 266–271.

Veblen, Thorstein. 1934 [1899]. *Theory of the Leisure Class: An Economic Study of Institutions*. New York: Modern Library.

Velayutham, Selvaraj, Ed. 2008. *Tamil Cinema: The Cultural Politics of India's Other Film Industry*. London and New York: Routledge.

Vermeulen, Eric. 2004. "Dealing with Doubt: Making Decisions in a Neonatal Ward in the Netherlands." *Social Science & Medicine* 59 (10): 2071–2085.

Verrengia, Joseph B. 1993. "Vanishing Tribes." *Rocky Mountain News*, December 12, 1993.

Voll, John O. 1991. "Fundamentalism in the Sunni Arab World: Egypt and the Sudan." In Martin Marty and R. Scott Appleby, Eds. *Fundamentalisms Observed*. Chicago: The University of Chicago Press. 345–402.

Von Fuerer-Haimendorf, Christoph. 1969. *The Konyak Nagas: An Indian Frontier Tribe*. New York: Holt, Rinehart, and Winston.

von Hellerman, Pauline. 2013. *Things Fall Apart? The Political Ecology of Forest Governance in Southern Nigeria.* New York and London: Berghahn.

de Waal, Frans. 1998 [1982]. *Chimpanzee Politics: Power and Sex among Apes*, revised ed. Baltimore: Johns Hopkins University Press.

Wagner, Roy. 1975. *The Invention of Culture.* Englewood Cliffs, NJ: Prentice-Hall.

Waitz, Theodore. 1863. *Introduction to Anthropology.* London: Longman, Green, Longman, and Roberts.

Wallace, Anthony F. C. 1956. "Revitalization Movements." *American Anthropologist* 58 (2): 264–281.

——. 1966. *Religion: An Anthropological View.* New York: Random House.

Wallerstein, Immanuel. 1974. *The Modern World-System: Capitalist Agriculture and the Origins of the European World-Economy in the Sixteenth Century.* New York: Academic Press.

Washburn, Sherwood. 1963. "The Study of Race." *American Anthropologist* 65 (3): 521–531.

Webber. Michael. 2008. "Primitive Accumulation in Modern China." *Dialectical Anthropology* 32 (4): 299–320.

Weber, Max. 1968. *Economy and Society*, Vol. 1. Guenther Roth and Claus Wittich, Eds. New York: Bedminster Press.

Weiner, Annette B. 1983. *Women of Value, Men of Renown: New Perspectives in Trobriand Exchange.* Austin: University of Texas Press.

Wheelwright, Philip, Ed. 1966. *The Presocratics.* New York: The Odyssey Press.

White, Bob W. 2008. *Rumba Rules: The Politics of Dance Music in Mobutu's Zaire.* Durham, NC: Duke University Press.

White, Leslie. 1940. "The Symbol: The Origin and Basis of Human Behavior." *Philosophy of Science* 7 (4): 451–463.

——. 1949. *The Science of Culture.* New York: Grove Press.

——. 1959a. "The Concept of Evolution in Cultural Anthropology." In Betty Meggers, Ed. *Evolution and Anthropology: A Centennial Appraisal.* Washington DC: The Anthropological Society of Washington. 106–125.

——. 1959b. *The Evolution of Culture.* New York: McGraw-Hill.

White, Tim et al. 2009. "*Ardipithecus ramidus* and the Paleobiology of Early Hominids." *Science* 326 (October 2): 64–86.

Whitehead, Amy. 2013. *Religious Statues and Personhood: Testing the Role of Materiality.* London: Bloomsbury.

Whiting, Beatrice, Ed. 1963. *Six Cultures: Studies of Child Rearing.* New York: John Wiley and Sons.

Whorf, Benjamin Lee. 1940. "Science and Linguistics." *Technology Review* 43: 229–231, 247–248.

——. 1956. *Language, Thought, and Reality: Selected Writings of Benjamin Lee Whorf.* Cambridge, MA: The Massachusetts Institute of Technology Press.

Wiedman, Dennis. 2012. "Native American Embodiment of the Chronicities of Modernity: Reservation Food, Diabetes, and the Metabolic Syndrome among the Kiowa, Comanche, and Apache." *Medical Anthropological Quarterly* 26 (4): 595–612.

Williams, Thomas Rhys. 1965. *The Dusun: A North Borneo Society.* NewYork: Holt, Rinehart, and Winston.

Willis, Jr., William S. 1974 [1969]. "Skeletons in the Anthropological Closet." In Dell Hymes, Ed. *Reinventing Anthropology.* New York: Vintage Books. 121–152.

Wilson, Tamar Diana. 2012. *Economic Life of Mexican Beach Vendors: Acapulco, Puerto Vallarta, and Cabo San Lucas.* Lanham, MD: Lexington Books.

Wolf, Eric. 1982. *Europe and the People without History.* Berkeley: University of California Press.

——. 1994. "Perilous Ideas: Race, Culture, People." *Current Anthropology* 35 (1): 1–12.

Woodburn, James. 1968. "Stability and Flexibility in Hadza Residential Groups." In Richard Lee and Irven DeVore, Eds. *Man the Hunter.* Chicago: Aldine. 103–111.

World Bank. 2001. *World Development Report 2000/2001: Attacking Poverty.* Oxford: Oxford University Press.

——. 2015. *Global Monitoring Report 2014/2015: Ending Poverty and Sharing Prosperity.* Washington, DC: World Bank.

Worsley, Peter. 1968. *The Trumpet Shall Sound: A Study of "Cargo Cults" in Melanesia.* New York: Shocken Books.

Wrangham, Richard and Dale Peterson. 1996. *Demonic Males: Apes and the Origins of Human Violence.* Boston: Houghton Mifflin Company.

Wrigley, Owen. 1996. *The Politics of Deafness.* Washington, DC: Gallaudet University Press.

Wu, David Y. H. 2015. "Cultural Nostalgia and Global Imagination: Japanese Cuisine in Taiwan." In Kwang Ok Kim, Ed. *Re-Orienting Cuisine: East Asian Foodways in the Twenty-First Century.* New York and London: Berghahn. 108–128.

Yan, Hairong. 2003. "Neoliberal Governmentality and Neohumanism: Organizing Suzhi/Value Flow through Labor Recruitment Networks." *Cultural Anthropology* 18 (4): 493–523.

Yang, Jie. 2013. "'Fake Happiness': Counseling, Potentiality, and Psycho-Politics in China." *Ethos* 41 (3): 292–312.

Zaman, Shahaduz. 2004. "Poverty and Violence, Frustration and Inventiveness: Hospital Ward Life in Bangladesh." *Social Science & Medicine* 59 (10): 2025–2036.

——. 2005. *Broken Limbs, Broken Lives: Ethnography of a Hospital Ward in Bangladesh.* Amsterdam: Het Spinhuis.

Zamorska, Julia. 1998. "Modernity in a Different Way: Cargo Cults in Melanesia as Creative Response to Modernisation." http://www.geocities.com/southbeach/lagoon/3638/ anthro2.html, accessed 3 March 2004.

Zhao, Jianhua. 2013. *The Chinese Fashion Industry: An Ethnographic Approach.* London and New York: Bloomsbury Academic.

Zheng, Tiantian. 2009. *Red Lights: The Lives of Sex Workers in Postsocialist China.* Minneapolis and London: University of Minneapolis Press.

Zimbalist, Jeff and Matt Mochary. 2007. *Favela Rising.* New York: Third World Newsreel.

Index